Audrey
OF THE
MOUNTAINS

Other books by Dorothy Audrey Simpson

Beimer, Dorothy Simpson. *Hovels, Haciendas, and House Calls: The Life of Carl H.Gellenthien, M.D.* Santa Fe: Sunstone Press, 1986, 309 pages. ISBN# 0-86534-074-9.

Beimer, Dorothy Simpson. *Speaking for Life: A Speech Communication Guide for Adults,* Edina, Minnesota: Burgess International, 1990, 188 pages. ISBN# 0-8087-7357-7.

Croxton, Dorothy Simpson *Wreck of the Destiny Train.* Salt Lake City, Utah: Northwest Publishing, Inc., 1993, 158 pages. ISBN# 1-56901-127-3.

Simpson, D. A. as told by Stanley A. Hardin. *From Pajarito to Lungchow: Memoirs of Photographic Reconnaissance Pilot Stanley A. Hardin As told to D. A. Simpson.* Bowie, Maryland: Eagle Editions, An Imprint of Heritage Books, Inc., 2003. ISBN# 0-7884-2455-6.

Audrey of the Mountains
The Story of a Twentieth Century Pioneer Woman

Dorothy Audrey Simpson

SANTA FE

© 2008 by Dorothy Audrey Simpson. All Rights Reserved.

No part of this book may be reproduced in any form or by any electronic or mechanical means including information storage and retrieval systems without permission in writing from the publisher, except by a reviewer who may quote brief passages in a review.

Sunstone books may be purchased for educational, business, or sales promotional use. For information please write: Special Markets Department, Sunstone Press, P.O. Box 2321, Santa Fe, New Mexico 87504-2321.

Book design ◊ Vicki Ahl
Body typeface ◊ Granjon LT Std ◊ ◊ Display typeface ◊ Ex Ponto
Printed on acid free paper

Library of Congress Cataloging-in-Publication Data

Simpson, Dorothy Audrey, 1944-
  Audrey of the mountains : the story of a twentieth century pioneer woman / by Dorothy Audrey Simpson.
    p. cm.
  Includes bibliographical references.
  ISBN 978-0-86534-688-8 (softcover : alk. paper)
 1. Simpson, Audrey, 1912-1997. 2. Journalists--United States--Biography. 3. Women journalists--United States--Biography. I. Title.
  PN4874.S5167S56 2008
  070.92--dc22
  [B]
                    2008041435

WWW.SUNSTONEPRESS.COM
SUNSTONE PRESS / POST OFFICE BOX 2321 / SANTA FE, NM 87504-2321 /USA
(505) 988-4418 / ORDERS ONLY (800) 243-5644 / FAX (505) 988-1025

To my sisters,
Holly Alice Simpson and Crystal Simpson Lovett,
and to my brother-in-law, Wesley Lovett

CONTENTS

PREFACE / 9
ACKNOWLEDGMENTS / 13

Part 1
Mountain Girl / 15

1 Crossing the Devil's Backbone: From Lincoln to Avis _____ 17
2 Bronc Riding Dog _____ 25
3 One Bad *Hombre*: From Avis to Weed _____ 27
4 Cutting Teeth: From Weed to Lincoln _____ 32
5 Riding Her First Bronc: Lincoln to Shelton _____ 43
6 Santa Claus in Taos _____ 47
7 Mama's "Dairy" Cow: Taos to Black Lake _____ 56
8 Ma "Brought Home" the Bacon _____ 61
9 Stranger at the Door: Black Lake to Taos _____ 65
10 End of the War to End All Wars: Taos to Lincoln _____ 69
11 No More Shetlands! Lincoln to Bradshaw and Back to Lincoln _____ 75
12 Gambling in the First Las Vegas: Lincoln to Las Vegas _____ 79
13 Daddy Goes to Jail: MacInerney Ranch, Las Dispensas _____ 90
14 Cake in a Suitcase: Dimmick Ranch _____ 98
15 The Teacher Goes to School: Las Vegas _____ 102
16 Chapelle _____ 110
17 Summer, 1922: Peña Ranch then Las Vegas _____ 118
18 Babysitting: Las Vegas to Lagunita _____ 124
19 The Taste of Vinegar: Las Vegas to Chapelle—Again _____ 127
20 Bernal: A New Beginning _____ 137
21 Violence in the Village _____ 147
22 Salute Gregorio: First Love _____ 152
23 Riches Found and Lost _____ 158
24 Survivors: Bernal to Santa Rosa _____ 165
25 House Fire: Santa Rosa to Cuervo _____ 178
26 Daddy to the Rescue: Cuervo to Mosquero _____ 181
27 The Old Homestead Ranch _____ 187
28 Long Road to School _____ 197
29 Hunger Stalks Garcia Mill: From the Ranch to Garcia's _____ 212
30 Cold December: From Garcia Mill to Chaperito _____ 222
31 Budding Romance: From Chaperito to Reid Ranch, Taming Wild Horses _____ 228
32 Audrey's Song _____ 239
33 Reids' Ranch: Nebraska and Back _____ 244
34 Thirty-six Cents and a Letter of Hope: Reid's to San Geronimo _____ 250
35 Wedding Vows _____ 253
36 First Business Enterprise: Pecos, New Mexico _____ 265
37 Crystal: Brilliant, Beautiful, Blessed _____ 269

38 Forest Fire!	276
39 The Ten Dollar House	282
40 Forest Springs Ranch	301
41 The Fifteen Dollar House	318
42 Victory Garden *Par Excellence*	328

Part 11
Cabin for Three / 335

1 Dorothy: Gift of God	337
2 Their Sons' Brave Hearts	345
3 Troubles	357
4 An Empty Saddle	381
5 Thanksgiving under the Pines	388
6 Christmas at Forest Springs	394
7 Cabin for Three	398
8 Reading and Writing Lessons—and Another Fire	404
9 Stranger by the Roadside	412
10 Little Joys	415
11 No Rain and No Rain!	423
12 Crystal's Courage	433
13 The Barbed Wire Phone Line	436
14 Phone Call from Santa Claus	442
15 Thirty-two Below in Sunny New Mexico	446
16 Valiant Bonnie	452
17 Mountain Top Farewell	460

Part 111
Back to Her Mountains / 467

1 A Bride Again!	469
2 The Church, The House, The Home	493
3 A Notebook in Her Hand: Newspaper Reporter, Journalist, Author	502
4 A Pencil Over Her Ear: Writer, Editor, Career Woman	507
5 Holly: Heavenly Blessing	513
6 Fire at the Office	533
7 The House on Seventh Street	536
8 Building the Dream Home	549
9 The Day after Easter	555
10 Free-Lance	567
11 All Day the Ashes Fell: Most Destructive Forest Fire	585
12 By Your Boot Straps	595
13 Another Wedding!	612
14 Generations	620
15 Leaving a Legacy	635

NOTES / 641
REFERENCES / 671

PREFACE

"I don't know what it all means. These years I have fooled around on this whirling earth. I have appreciated it and sometimes wondered which one was actually whirling the hardest." So wrote Audrey Simpson, free-lace writer, journalist, wife, and mother, as she began to write her autobiography. It was never finished, but this book tells her story.

Part I is called "Mountain Girl" and tells of Audrey's experiences growing up in New Mexico. The name *Audrey* means *mountain girl*. Audrey Clements was rightly named. All her life she loved the mountains—so much so that she sacrificed material wealth to enjoy the riches of nature in the mountains she loved. Her story tells of a girl born in Lincoln, Nebraska in 1912 who learned to adapt in many different circumstances. Her father, L. C. Clements, moved the family from Nebraska when Audrey was a baby because he wanted to be a rancher in New Mexico—the "last of the wild frontier." Her mother, Mabel Waddell Clements, a prim and proper school teacher from Lincoln, was as comfortable riding horseback as she was in the classroom.

Audrey helped care for the younger children: Opal, Edward, Betty, Milly, Jessica, and Frank. She grew up observing the customs and culture of little villages in New Mexico. Audrey was invited to live with her affluent grandmother in Portland, Oregon and could have had a good education and a life of considerable wealth. But she would not leave her mother with a new baby coming—and Audrey would not leave "her" mountains. Determined to finish high school, she and her sister Opal walked from their mountain ranch into Las Vegas and found places to work for room and board. After Audrey's marriage to Clyde Simpson, the couple bought part of the Old Homestead Ranch in the Sangre de Cristo Mountains. They built a cabin there. They had two daughters, Crystal and Dorothy. Then during a separation Audrey cared for her two children under difficult conditions. Later Audrey and Clyde re-married and had another child, Holly, again under adverse circumstances. Audrey was a woman determined to survive in spite of great odds, to be cheerful even when the situation was dire, to provide for and nurture her family—a woman often alone but cheered by the ever present, sun-topped mountains of New Mexico.

As an author, I try to write objectively. However, I realize that in writing about Audrey my perspective cannot escape the view point of a daughter. (Hence, in Part II, I relate events in the first person rather than the third person.) As an adult, I realize that my mother fulfilled many roles in addition to that of a mother. She was a wife, an author, an editor, a journalist, a house builder and home maker, a colleague, a friend, a leader among women—in short, she wore many hats. Many women today are accustomed to that. But Audrey was a pioneer in that respect.

Part II is called "Cabin for Three" and tells of experiences my mother Audrey, my sister Crystal and I had when we lived in the isolated mountains while Clyde and Audrey were separated. Readers may find some nostalgic memories in the mention of old radio programs and comic books. The post-War years ushered in an era of interesting contrasts when the United States was a strong nation with a solid economy, but there was little awareness of environmental issues, as evidenced by the use of DDT and Compound 1080. The possibility of "flying saucers" and space exploration was a growing concept.

Audrey was a journalist, a newspaper editor, and a free-lance writer when a woman was expected to stay home, scrub floors, iron clothes, rock babies, and have meals on time for her husband. All those honorable and necessary activities my mother accomplished—but she went beyond them. Knowing there is no greater job in the world than that of "mother," Audrey accomplished that role and many more. Audrey was at home in a one-room log cabin cooking on a wood stove or in a large home in the city preparing meals with gas heat. Like her mother, she was as comfortable on a horse as she was in her living room rocking chair. She could ride, shoot, repair fences and build houses. Or she could attend social events—write up a wedding story for the Society Page—sitting as comfortably behind her typewriter as she had behind the wheel of her four-wheel drive truck. As a journalist, Audrey interviewed many well-known people such as actor Rex Allen. She also became personal friends with individuals she would not have met except through her writing, people such as artist/writer Clare Turley Newberry and writers S. Omar Barker and Elsa Barker.

Part III, "Back to Her Mountains," describes Audrey's work as a journalist and free lance writer. It was the time of the McCarthy era investigations, Operation Christmas, and the news of a cure for polio. After Audrey and Clyde bought a home in Las Vegas, their third daughter was born. Audrey nearly died of an illness prior to the birth Holly, a child with cerebral palsy. The family was happy in their house in town, but Audrey and Clyde began building their dream home in the mountains for their retirement. After Clyde's sudden death, Audrey resigned from her job at the Las Vegas Daily Optic where she had worked over fourteen years and began free-lance writing. Then a forest fire destroyed her new ranch house. After years of re-building, Audrey married Bill Reid and hoped to re-build her life as well. But Bill died after a short time and Audrey was alone again. She battled grief, illness, devastation from a fire, and the inevitable aging that brought a halt to her plans to complete an autobiography filled with history, humor, and inspiration. In her autobiography, Audrey planned to tell of her childhood where she was often "mother" to her six younger siblings; of her marriages; of her house building; of her writing career; and of the hardships and disasters she had survived.

Sometime after her eightieth birthday, Audrey wrote,"I birthed 3 girls after I cried when the doc told me I would never have any children. I helped build 13 houses—and buried 2 husbands, spent 14 years meeting newspaper deadlines to put my kids through school, lost everything to fire. But there's life in the old gal yet!" Audrey might have added a few more items to her summary of accomplishments. She fought to keep the U.S. Government from confiscating her mountain to use as a military camp, using the power of the pen. She used her persuasive writing to convince the public that Fort Union should not be lost, and it was subsequently made into a national monument. She wrote editorials and letters to protest incompetence in the government and to deplore the rising costs of goods and services. Her writing and petitions helped get the San Geronimo-Mineral Hill road improved and partially paved. Her writing supported American freedom, such as the right to bear arms, and decried policies she thought morally wrong. She was a journalist, always looking for news, hoping to preserve history, wanting to write to inform, to encourage, or to entertain.

As far as possible, I have verified my information with more than one source. The facts are related accurately insofar as I was able to verify them. However, not all information was available or verifiable. In such cases, my mother's notes or recorded tapes have been the only source. Although I tried to verify my sources, some names may be misspelled or omitted.

Names have not been changed except where, for obvious reasons, protection of the person's privacy should be maintained.

For clarity, I should explain that some of the women in the family married more than once; hence, the use of different names. Audrey Clements married Clyde Simpson. After his death, she married Bill Reid. Some of her work is written under "Clements," some under "Simpson" and some under "Reid." (Audrey also used a least one pen name—Shirley.) Audrey's mother Mabel Waddell married twice, first to Laverne Clifford Clements and then to Charles Vivian Shearer, so after her marriage, Mabel Waddell is referred to either as Mabel Clements or Mabel Shearer. Also, Mabel's first husband, L.C. Clements, married a second time as well. He married another woman named Mable—Mable Day. (So there are two women named Mable Clements in the story; but note the difference in the spelling of the names: *Mabel* Waddell Clements and *Mable* Day Clements.)

Photographs and references used in this book are in the Simpson Archives at Forest Springs Ranch. Audrey's son-in-law, Wesley L. Lovett, was instrumental in preserving and enhancing many of the old photographs and, as a photographer, took many of the newer ones.

Audrey always tried to entertain, to inform, and to inspire her readers. It is hoped that readers of Audrey's story will find those attributes and more in *Audrey of the Mountains*.

ACKNOWLEDGEMENTS

I wish to extend appreciation and thanks to all the friends and relatives whose contributions helped me with this book and to acknowledge the memory of those who thought this history was important enough to preserve. The names are too many to list here, but I am grateful for each one. I especially appreciate the contributions of Jessica Shearer Braziel, Shirley Clements Giles, Sam Dixon, Crystal Simpson Lovett, Wesley L. Lovett, Arthur B. Trujillo, Millicent Shearer Wickman, and, of course, Audrey Clements Simpson, whose extensive notes and files made this book possible. Special thanks is extended to Tom McDonald, Editor and Publisher of the Las Vegas Optic. Of Audrey's story, Milly Wickman said, "Audrey, I think this history is so precious. Somebody needs to remember these things." Because of the many individuals who helped to preserve information and photographs, the historical and biographical information in *Audrey of the Mountains* can now be shared.

Part 1
Mountain Girl

1

Crossing The Devil's Backbone: From Lincoln to Avis

It was the worst night Mabel Clements could remember. The wind blew sand in biting, horizontal currents across the desert floor. The young mother lay on a blanket under the wagon, her four-month-old baby Audrey held close in her protective arms.

Mabel had always loved fresh air and had slept with the windows open in Lincoln, Nebraska—except during the coldest winter nights. Home—until she had married Vern Clements—had been at her mother's place in Lincoln. Now it was with her husband Vern, wherever he wanted to hang his hat.

The first child of Edward and Alice Waddell, Mabel was born on October 26, 1890 near Cedar City, Nebraska. Mabel's mother, Alice, had left Mabel's father, Edward Albert Waddell, when Mabel was a little girl. Alice had remarried and had a comfortable home in Lincoln with her second husband, Tom Shirley. Mabel Edna Waddell had been a happy school girl who became a teacher as soon as she earned her license. The young school teacher with blue eyes and golden red hair liked teaching and her pupils liked her.

Mabel Waddell went to the Methodist Church every Sunday, and it was there that she met Lavern "Vern" Clifford Clements. Vern's parents, Emma and William Harper Clements, were also Methodists. Vern and Mabel were married on September 23, 1911. Vern had been assisting his mother, as she and Vern's father were separated at the time. (They had divorced and re-married three times. This time it seemed they would remain apart.) Vern was restless and wanted to move.

Here, traveling over a ridge called the "The Devil's Backbone" Mabel cringed as she pulled the blanket more tightly around her head to keep the sand from blowing in their faces. Beneath the blanket, Mabel could not muffle the sound of the blowing sand blasting her ears, whipping against the all-too-meager covering she had wrapped around herself and Audrey.

Lying next to Mabel and her infant was Mabel's mother-in-law, Emma Clements. Her daughter May Hammond Munson and husband Cecil had lured Emma and Vern to New Mexico with the promise of a better life. May had promised her mother a good horse if she'd move to New Mexico with Vern and

Mabel. Emma decided to travel south and see if the new state was all that May had promised. Now she lay next to her daughter-in-law wondering, too, when the wind would stop. Vern had said it was more sheltered under the wagon than in it, as there was no top or cover; so the women and baby were secluded beneath the wagon for the night.

While Vern lay in the uncovered wagon, wrapped up in wool blankets against the blasting wind, he, too, had trouble sleeping. Aunt May had sent her oldest boy George to meet them, so he also slept in the uncovered wagon and was, like Vern, restless. George wondered if Vern would turn back—return to Nebraska after experiencing New Mexico's wind. But Vern had no greater desire than to live in the land which he considered the last of the great, wild frontier—New Mexico. It was sparsely populated, had acres of cattle country, deep blue skies, and everything from hot desert-like terrain to cold, high timber country in the mountains. Vern wanted to ride horseback, herd cattle, own a ranch himself someday.

Yes, this was a "heck of a place," Vern said to himself, this "Devil's Backbone." But they were only passing through. They'd soon be living on a good ranch in a comfortable home. He had no thoughts of turning back. He went to sleep dreaming of the cattle ranch he'd own some day.

As Mabel wondered why she'd ever agreed to travel south with Vern, she realized that she couldn't deny the man she loved a chance at his dream. Vern had always wanted to leave the "civilized society" of Lincoln, Nebraska for the "wild" west.

Mabel recalled the day the letter had arrived from Vern's half-sister May. Vern and Mabel were invited, along with Vern's mother, to move to the ranch near Avis and help raise angora goats on the shares. May and Cecil had visited them in Lincoln and knew of Vern's dream of working on a ranch and even owning a spread himself some day. Vern's mother could hardly wait to see the horse May had promised her.

Years later, Audrey wrote: "By March, 1913, Grandma [Clements] and Daddy had decided that Avis, in Southern New Mexico, sounded like it beat Nebraska's snow and cold."[1]

Avis was seven miles southeast of Weed, a very small town located twenty-seven miles southeast of Alamogordo on the eastern slope of the Sacramento Mountains. May Munson was the postmistress at Avis, and her husband was a full time rancher. Angora goats were valuable because of the special angora hair that could be sold for a considerable amount. Vern needed to make more money, especially now that he was a father. Later Audrey wrote, "They boarded a train in Nebraska and got as close to the Sacramentos as the rails went. Then one of the Munson boys brought a team and wagon down to the low country and loaded us up."²

Mabel described that night. Based on her mother's description, Audrey wrote:

> The wind was blowing a gale—throwing sand in our faces as we crawled under a tarp placed over our makeshift bed under the wagon. Mother hated to cover up her head and was afraid that I would smother, but there was so much blowing sand there on the Devil's Backbone she thought we would smother if we didn't have our heads covered up."³

As Mabel lay there that night, she thought about the day Audrey had been born. Audrey later wrote:

> Daddy was only 19 when he persuaded mother to elope with him to Marysville, Kansas. She was teaching. It was September, 1911 and she wanted to finish out her school year. A teacher couldn't be married then. So she lost her job as soon as they found out she was married. Mother was a year older and always resented the fact Daddy lied about his age for she thought him older and had the idea that the man should be older than the woman. It was a bad start for their marriage. When my mother left Creighton to go back to 26th Street in Lincoln, so I could be born in a "civilized" home, Grandma [Emma Maria] Clements and Uncle Ed had a falling out and each lived in one room with my daddy carrying wood and water and messages to each room. The night I was born Daddy's dog, the big, beautiful collie, howled all night. The next day they got word I was born in Lincoln.⁴

Vern—born December 29, 1891 in Lincoln—was only a year younger than Mabel. Knowing Mabel wouldn't give him a second look if she knew his actual birth date, Vern lied in order to have a chance to win the beautiful young school teacher. Vern later pointed out that he'd only lied because he'd loved her so deeply and wanted to marry her.

Although Mabel was content with the school room, Vern knew the names of the wild plants, knew the ways of wildlife and birds. He loved horses and would enjoy riding through the sage brush, cedar, piñon, juniper and pine of New Mexico. Mabel often thought of the poem "Lasca" by Frank Desprez, a ballad about a beautiful girl of Mexican descent and her cowboy sweetheart—tragically caught in a cattle stampede.⁵ Mabel knew that Vern, like the cowboy in the poem, yearned to go to the great frontier west where the wide open spaces held adventure for him. Like the cowboy in the poem, Vern wanted free life and fresh air, the horses' canter after the cattle, the blue skies, the green grass, and the dash, danger, life and love of the west.

Lying under the wagon, Mabel shuddered. The romance of "Lasca" was just not like the reality of lying on the cold, hard ground with the sand-laden wind biting and ripping at the blankets. Mabel had heard there were scorpions crawling among the cacti and sage brush. There was little protection from them or from other "critters" under the wagon.

During that sleepless night, Mabel remembered discussing a name for their child with Vern weeks before Audrey was born. They discussed boys' names along with some girls' names.

"If our baby is a girl, we could name her after my mother, Alice," Mabel suggested.

"Alice is a nice name, but I like 'Audrey' better," Vern declared.

"Audrey? Isn't that the name of one of your old girl friends?" Mabel asked suspiciously. She had a jealous nature.

"It's just a name I like," Vern replied, avoiding the question about the old girl friend. Vern had lots of old girl friends. He liked to flirt with the ladies.

"Audrey means 'mountain girl.' I looked it up in a book of names," Mabel told Vern. "There are no mountains around here," Mabel said, looking out the window of her Nebraska home.

"But I intend to raise our child in the mountains," Vern said. "Someday I'll take you and our baby to the most beautiful wilderness country you've ever seen—with clear, fast flowing streams, snow capped mountains, and lush grass for our cattle. We'll own a cattle ranch," Vern dreamed. "It'll be a beautiful spread with a cozy ranch house—every luxury I can afford for you and our child."

So when the baby girl arrived, they named her Audrey, "mountain girl." Audrey Shirley Clements, born some time after midnight on November 11, 1912, was a strong, healthy baby. Years later Audrey wrote in some notes, "The Night I Was Born:"

> Old Shep howled from dark to daylight the night I was born. The 11th day of the 11th month. Daddy was with Shep and Uncle Ed Harris at his farm in eastern Nebraska at Creighton. Mama was at her mother's home in Lincoln, Nebraska. My grandmother, Alice Henrietta Applegarth Waddell Shirley, lived there with her husband, Tom Shirley, a construction worker (brick layer) and their two children, Thelma, about 8 or 10 then, and Bruce, two years younger. So I was born at the Shirley home, 26th

Street, Lincoln, Nebraska. Mama had to quit school in the 7th or 8th grade to stay home and take care of her mother while she had the young ones and later to help out. However, she managed to go through high school, graduating only a little older than her contemporaries.[6]

Mabel Clements with daughter Audrey, early 1913; this photo is currently used in a billboard/sign at New Mexico Primary Care & Midwifery Services, Inc., 1841-B, Old Hwy 66, Edgewood, New Mexico, the clinic of Karen Lovett, CNM, CFNP, Audrey's granddaughter. *Source*: Simpson Archives

Years later, Audrey recalled in her notes, "My Early Days:"

> I discovered there was a hard life when in the dim lamp-lit room the doctor held me by my feet, slapped me on my back, and I caught my breath. Then I heard him tell my mother and grandmother, "It's a girl."[7]

Audrey surmised that "Audrey" had been the name of "one of the girls chasing Daddy when he caught Mama." Audrey wrote:

> I always suspected there was controversy at my birth but couldn't prove it

until in my 50's when I sent to Lincoln, Nebraska for my birth certificate. The name on it was *Marjorie*. It was crossed out and *Audrey* inserted. I knew Mother never liked my name very well and several times noted that Audrey was the name of one of Daddy's old girl friends. In those strict western Nebraska school districts they didn't go for young married women as teachers. So she and Daddy and his mother, Emma Maria Roney, moved in with Grandma's brother, Uncle Ed Harris, at Creighton, Nebraska. Daddy helped him farm. Mother must have been a stabilizing factor before she left for 26th Street to have me at her mother's home. Anyway, when she returned to Creighton, Grandma and Uncle Ed were not speaking and he was doing his own cooking in his bedroom while Grandma and Daddy survived in the other two rooms of the house.

I wasn't doing much then to earn my way. Of course I soon learned to smile to please people. And I grew as fast as I could. By March, 1913, when I was 4 months old, Grandma's daughter, May Munson, postmistress down in Avis, New Mexico, wrote inviting us all to come live there. She promised Grandma a horse and Daddy and Mama a house to live in and a deal to look after her angora goats on the shares.

We rode the trains from Nebraska to Roswell. There Aunty May's big boy George met us with a team and lumber wagon. They loaded Mama's big trunk with all our household goods in it and the suitcases and we headed for Avis. It took about 3 days' horse and wagon travel time. Later Mama remembered thinking we would smother. When we camped at night on top of the Devil's Backbone, the wind was blowing a gale. George and Daddy spread out a bed room on a big tarp. The canvas was then pulled completely up over the bed to keep the blowing sand out of the bed. Mother never liked to cover up her head so she would gently lift the edge of the canvas to get a breath of air.[8]

"Instead," Mabel told Audrey later, "I would get a face full of sand." Somehow they weathered the sand storm and got to Avis.

Audrey became accustomed to hardships at a very young age. She wrote in her notes, "My First Days:"

When I was about three months old, Mother was driving a buggy and went around a corner fast. The buggy tipped up and I was thrown out and the back wheel ran over me. I was wrapped in blankets and apparently not badly hurt.[9]

Years later, Millicent L. Gensemer, a newspaper reporter, wrote a feature story about Audrey for *The Las Vegas Daily Optic* entitled, "Audrey Simpson: A Mother, Woman's Editor and Adventurer." The article, written in about 1957, stated that Audrey first arrived in New Mexico at the age of four months. "The New Mexico winds greeted the new ranchers with all their dust-filled fury and the mother had to risk smothering her baby under a blanket as opposed to having her choke to death from the dust."[10]

Once the little family arrived at the ranch, life did seem better at first. Before they realized that the goat business would be a financial disaster, Mabel and Vern were ready to settle in and work hard on the ranch. The young couple found time to enjoy life. They liked the warm climate and the abundance of sunshine. They made friends and went to social events.

Audrey wrote in notes years later: "Once there, [Avis] they went to a dance; going home in pitch black, Daddy fell with me, stretched out his arm and landed on his elbows. I didn't wake up!"[11]

Lavern Clifford Clements with daughter Audrey and dog Teddy, 1913. *Source*: Simpson Archives

Before long, Mabel and Vern realized that all was not as they thought it would be. The living conditions were very poor and the income was almost nil.

Audrey wrote that none of Aunt May's promises materialized, not even the horse she had promised her mother Emma. "Mother started teaching at Weed [about eight miles from Avis] in order for us to eat."[12]

When it appeared that raising goats was not going to be profitable, Mabel suggested that Vern look for other work. But it was not easy for Vern to find a job. Vern was not as well educated as his wife. Audrey explained in "Some Early Childhood Memories:"

> My father, an 8th grade student, dropped out—by way of a stairway window when the principal was going to punish him with a rubber hose filled with sand. He never went back. After he jumped out the window, Vern ran home; he never attended school again, quitting in the middle of the year.[13]

Vern's mother didn't want the school authorities to pick her son up as a truant, so she took the fourteen-year-old Vern to Colorado where one of her grown children, Clarence Hammond, lived. They moved to Weld County in the Greeley area and Emma Clements homesteaded there. Vern's half-brother Clarence owned a newspaper, so Vern worked for him, setting type.

Emma had a little one-room shack built. She and Vern were quite comfortable until the cold weather came. That bitter cold winter they brought their horses into the house with them because there was no barn, and they were afraid the animals would get away in the blizzard and freeze to death. Unwilling to face another such severe winter, Vern and his mother decided not to remain in Colorado.

Vern had to make his living using the skills he had obtained by various odd jobs. Later he became a painter by trade; but most of his life, he simply wanted to "cowboy." When the Avis venture proved to be a disappointment, Mabel suggested returning to Lincoln. She would have been content to stay in Nebraska and teach school for the rest of her life. She had enjoyed seeing her students learn.

In 1911 when Mabel had taught at Pine Top School in Sioux County, near Crawford, Nebraska, she had given each of her students a little souvenir card to take home at the end of the school year. She wrote across the card: "Not for School but for Life We Learn." Mabel liked to write poetry or verse. Inside the card she had the following poem she had written:

My pupils dear, this souvenir small
>   To you I dedicate,
In mem'ry of you one and all,
>   I tried to educate.
In mem'ry too, of pleasant days
>   We in the school room spent;
Our study hours, our sports and plays,
>   Which sweet enjoyment lent.[14]

In spite of Mabel's complaints, Vern's dream of working on a ranch could not be stifled. Audrey was on her way to becoming a citizen of New Mexico, to becoming the mountain girl her daddy had predicted.

2

Bronc Riding Dog

Audrey and the State of New Mexico were born in 1912. In that year the Territory of New Mexico changed its status to State. Previously, the land had been ruled by two governments. First, the land known as "New Spain" was under Spanish rule. When the King of Spain relinquished that rule, the area then fell under Mexican domain. After the United States fought the War with Mexico, the land was then acquired by the United States of America. In 1946, General Stephen Watts Kearney and his troops came to New Mexico and declared that New Mexico was now a part of the United States of America. The land became a Territory of the United States in 1850. Then, after over fifty years, New Mexico Territory became a State of the Union in 1912, the year Audrey came into the world.

Years later Audrey wrote: "New Mexico—the only place I have felt at home and the only place I hope to stay—" was her early home because "my father, with perpetually itching feet, left the ice covered prairies of Nebraska to test the New Mexico mountains."[1] At Avis, four-month-old Audrey was just younger than her two cousins, Claudia and Daisy. "I grew and cut my teeth on red squirrel, gravy and biscuits."[2]

"Vern, this place is not for us," Mabel declared, with marked disappointment. "May and Cecil gave us a false picture of it. There's no way we can live here and raise our daughter. They are barely eking out a living. If May weren't postmistress, they'd be starving to death. Those goats are not going to make them rich, much less them and us too! Let's go back to Nebraska!"

"I want to stick it out," Vern insisted. "We came all this way. We might as well stay and see if the goats bring any money when they're sold." Vern supplemented the family's table by bringing in any game he could find. But there was little game in that desolate country. Sometimes he'd bring in a jack rabbit or enough squirrels for a meal. But gophers, prairie dogs, and rattlesnakes were not on the family menu and little else could be found. They somehow managed to keep enough food on the table to survive.

Vern had a dog named Teddy, so named because his spirit reminded Vern of "fightin'" Teddy Roosevelt. The collie was Vern's constant companion and was Audrey's baby sitter except when the dog was helping out with ranch work or went along on pack trips. Audrey wrote in 1957, "Dog Was Horse Rider," *Las Vegas Daily Optic, Rodeo Edition:*

> From the age of two weeks, when a car got his mother, Teddy was a member of the L.C. Clements family. Clements participated in the Reunion rodeos in the early '20's when he ranched near Las Vegas. Teddy always went on pack trips, so when Clements saddled Nita and put a bedroll-pack on the half-bronc Dixie, both quarter horses, it meant a long trip across sharp flint rocks of desert and mountains.[3]

To help Teddy withstand the sharp flint rocks of the desert and mountain country, Vern made Teddy some soft, leather shoes cut to fit the collie, made out of tough leather strips and cut with a shoemaker's awl and hand sewn. When Vern put those shoes on Teddy, the collie would wag his tail joyfully because he knew it meant he was going on a long trip with Vern.

One of those trips was from Avis to Artesia, New Mexico—seventy miles as the crow flies. Years later, after having heard her father talk about that trip many times, Audrey wrote and published an article in *Dog Fancy* entitled, "Bronco-Bustin' Dog." Audrey stated:

> By the time they got out of the timbered mountains into the lower desert country, the leather soles wore thin on the dog's shoes. Teddy's foot pads wore thin with them. Finally, Teddy could not take another step. He lay down in the scorching sand and whined for Dad to notice him.[4]

Vern boosted Teddy onto the saddle in front of him and they rode together for a mile or two. But the saddle horn hurt Teddy and he squirmed until he nearly fell off. Vern held him as well as he could, but the sixty-pound collie was too heavy. So Vern put Teddy back on the ground. The dog refused to move a step. He sat and howled. Vern decided Teddy would have to ride the skittish pack horse, though Dixie was hardly even accustomed to the pack she was carrying on her back. Audrey's story "Dog was Horse Rider," published in the *Las Vegas Daily Optic*, described the events as her father had related them:

> With the pack carefully arranged so Teddy would have a comfortable bed, Clements slowly lifted Teddy onto the pack. He jumped right down, frightening the bronc. When he lifted Teddy up onto the pack again, the nervous bronc promptly started to pitch. Teddy fell off.[5]

Every time Teddy was gently placed on top of the pack, the bronc broke in two. Teddy would ride a few jumps and hit the dust by his own choice. After nine tries, Dixie let the bronc busting Teddy ride on top of the pack. He lay and licked his sore feet the 40 miles home. He never wore out another pair of shoes for he always rode the pack on Dixie. And although Dixie often "bucked her best when a man tried to ride her, she never again tried to buck with Teddy."[6]

Teddy lived to be an old dog, and when he died, Vern found another collie. He named him "Teddy the Second" and called him Teddy. But Vern never had another dog that rode broncs like that first Teddy did.

One Bad *Hombre*: From Avis to Weed

If crossing the Devil's Backbone and living a hand to mouth existence were not enough to discourage the school teacher from Nebraska, her ordeal when Vern was gone one day was enough to send her to the nearest train depot for a ticket home.

As a teacher, Mabel was naturally curious and adapted to new situations well. She wanted to learn everything she could about her new home, New

Mexico, which had just become a state. She learned it had an area of over 121,000 square miles. The states of Connecticut, Delaware, Rhode Island, Vermont, New Hampshire, New Jersey, Maryland, Massachusetts and New York could be tucked away in New Mexico with room left over. Mabel wanted to be a good housewife and mother in this new environment, and she spent much time in the kitchen cooking and making the best meals her meager budget could afford.

Mabel was home caring for Audrey, doing her household chores one morning. Vern was gone for the day. Grandma Clements was away visiting a neighbor. Audrey was a year old. She was a beautiful, dark-haired girl. She had her mother's blue eyes. Audrey's brown hair and dark eyebrows were like Vern's. Vern was black Irish, had brown eyes, and had the near-olive complexion and dark hair of his ancestors. Vern had a "tinkle" in his eyes when he was amused. Audrey inherited that expression, sometimes referred to as "smiling Irish eyes."

Mabel was of British descent and had very fair, porcelain skin and long, golden red hair to complement her blue eyes. She had a trim figure.

While Mabel was washing dishes in the kitchen, with Audrey asleep nearby, there was a knock at the door. A man Mabel recognized as a part-time ranch hand was standing on the doorstep.

"Is your husband home?" the cowboy asked.

"No," Mabel replied.

Then the man suddenly burst through the door. He was reeking of liquor. "Well, that's good," he said.

Before Mabel had time to react to the unexpected intruder, he had grabbed her and pushed her up against a wall.

"There's nobody around," the intruder said almost to himself, a crooked, drunken grin spreading across his face.

Mabel, taken by surprise, was momentarily stunned.

"Get out of here," she commanded when she had recovered her voice. "How dare you push you way into my home!"

The man laughed at her demand. He began to tear at her blouse. His intentions now were undoubtedly clear.

"You'll be sorry if you tangle with me," Mabel snarled. "I'm a school teacher and no one pushes me around!" She swallowed her fear. Anger rose in her throat as she tried to push him away. She looked around for a weapon.

"You've got spirit! I like that!" The man pushed his body against hers, crushing Mabel up against the wall. "You're a little spit fire—but you can't resist me!"

Mabel looked for a knife, but there was nothing handy—except a skillet on the nearby stove. But she couldn't reach it. With no weapons, Mabel began to fight back like an animal, clawing, scratching, biting, hitting. But the brute was strong and determined.

Fighting like a wildcat, Mabel grabbed at anything she could to thwart her would-be rapist. She reached for the broom and was thrown off balance. They were on the floor now—twisting, tossing and turning like a couple of amateur wrestlers until Mabel was nearly out of strength.

"My husband will kill you for this!" Mabel yelled.

The brute hesitated at that. Vern's quick temper was well known.

"I thought you wanted me," the cowboy said, still pinning Mabel to the floor. "You mean to say you'll tell your husband? You mean you weren't making eyes at me when I saw you before?"

"No! I never did!" Mabel replied. She told him in no uncertain terms that she certainly would tell her husband and that she had never "wanted" the stranger or "made eyes at him."

The drunken cowhand got up then and stumbled out the door, nursing the wounds Mabel had managed to inflict. She had succeeded in making his nose bleed while defending her virtue and had given his face some good sized scratches. Audrey recalled the story her mother told her after many years:

> I was about a year old taking a nap when one of the macho men came to the cabin and asked if Daddy was there. Mama said, "No." He said he would wait and pushed his way in. He attacked Mama and she fought and fought, rolling around on the floor and trying not to wake me up.
>
> Finally Macho Man gave up and breathing heavily said, "I thought you wanted me to—"
>
> "No!" Ma half-yelled. "I never did!"
>
> So he sneaked away.
>
> I had been peeking over the edge of the bed and saw the attack so 50 years later when she told me about it I realized that was why I was always afraid of men attacking me.
>
> Daddy was furious. Mama and Grandma left Avis and went to Weed where she taught school long enough to get money to go back to Nebraska on the train.[1]

Mabel had never been so frightened in her life. She had been afraid the man would rape her, kill her, and then kill Audrey. Mabel trembled, thinking of the incident, even later after Vern had returned. She didn't give him many details. She just said there had been an incident with an intruder and she had decided to go back to Lincoln, with or without him.

"I won't bring Audrey up in a savage place like this," Mabel declared.

Mabel described the man as she told Vern how he'd burst into the kitchen.

Vern tried to piece together what had happened.

"Did he *attack* you?" Vern asked. He did not want to use the word "rape." It was too reprehensible for him to think of.

"Yes, he attacked me," Mabel said, thinking Vern meant "attack" in the sense of grabbing her and struggling to have his way—even though he was not successful; and she had inflicted enough pain to make him flee.

Vern was furious. He used the word "attack" to mean "rape." He'd always had what Mabel called "a healthy Irish temper" and when he was angry, no one wanted to be in his way.

"I'll find that S. O. B. and kill him!" Vern declared. "I'll leave right now and track him down! I'd heard of some bad *hombres* around here, and I'm not going to have one of them coming anywhere near my house! I'll find that bastard and knock his head off!"

"Vern! Your language! Audrey's awake! Watch your words! Calm down! That man probably had a gun and wouldn't think twice about using it on you!" Mabel said.

"I'm not afraid of the likes of him!" Vern fumed. "I've got my gun too, and I know how to use it!"

Vern did know how to use a gun. He had fed his family on squirrels he'd shot as they scurried from tree to tree, shot his running target in the head, leaving the meat intact.

Mabel convinced Vern to sit down and cool off, have a meal, and discuss what could be done. She had already made up her mind. She was going back to Nebraska.

"With you or without you, I want to take the train out of here," Mabel said. "It was a mistake to come to this savage, uncivilized country."

"I'll find that vermin and stomp him into the ground," Vern vowed. "He's a bad *hombre*, but he's just *one* bad fellow—and I'll put a stop to him."

"There are more like him," Mabel said. "You can't get rid of them all."

Vern sympathized, but he didn't want to leave. He assured Mabel he would never let such a thing happen again, that he would protect her. He wanted a chance to prove that the ranch venture could be successful. Years later, Audrey wrote:

She [Mabel] was attacked but yelled and wiggled and fought. The man gave up. But when Daddy asked her if she had been attacked, she said *Yes*. Obviously she understood "attack" as an attempt [at rape] and Daddy evidently thought it was the completed act. They had "trouble" and Mother and I went back to Nebraska.[2]

Mabel knew there was no money to go back to Nebraska immediately. But her anger was slow and smoldering. She didn't flare up the way Vern did. But she didn't forget. She had a determined tenacity, the quiet temper that could not be appeased with the passing of time. She had made up her mind. She knew it was useless to argue with Vern. She had told him what she was going to do. Determined to move back to Nebraska, Mabel applied for a job at Weed and taught long enough to make money to move back to Nebraska. Audrey wrote in her "Early Days" manuscript:

> Years later Mama asked me to tell my father (who lived in Albuquerque) that what happened in the cabin at Avis was not what he thought. It was a matter of semantics. When Daddy came home he could tell something bad had happened.
> "Did he attack you?"
> "Yes," Mama said, not realizing that "attack" and "rape" were two different words and actions. She wanted me to tell Daddy [nearly 50 years later] it was only an attack—attempted rape that did not succeed. I never got to tell him, for he was dying when I saw him alone again.[3]

Apparently Mabel finally realized that all those years Vern had thought that she had actually been raped when she had only been the victim of attempted rape. She wanted Vern to know, even fifty years later, that she had successfully fought the man off.

Once Mabel was over her initial shock from the attack, she made plans to return to Nebraska. While she taught school at Weed, Grandma Clements took care of Audrey. True to her word, as soon as she could save up the fare, Mabel took Audrey, boarded a train for Lincoln, and headed back to "civilized" country.

Cutting Teeth: From Weed to Lincoln

When Mabel took a job at Weed, Vern continued to work at Avis on the ranch. He thought Mabel would forget her anger and go on with life as usual. But Mabel, her anger simmering within, saved up enough money for a train ticket, then packed a few things and took Audrey to the train station. She knew Vern would try to persuade her to stay and that he would not go with her, so she kept her plans to herself.

Mabel didn't want Vern to try to stop her. She was leaving the state she considered "uncivilized." She assumed her husband would be wise enough to make the same choice once she had left. Mabel undoubtedly left Vern a note of explanation that she was taking Audrey and going back to her mother's place in Lincoln as she had said she would. When Vern realized Mabel had been serious about moving back to Nebraska, he determined to go after her and convince her to come back. But Mabel had not left him any money for a train ticket. It was some time before Vern could earn enough money for the train fare.

Once safe in Nebraska at the home of her mother, Alice Shirley, Mabel wrote to Vern, urging him to come to Nebraska as soon as he could. She knew he had to get some money together, but she was impatient.

Vern had to admit there was no future in goat ranching at Avis. He had made no money in over a year. He worked hard to get the necessary money to move. His mother was content living with her daughter May at Avis, so she had no plans to return to Nebraska.

At her grandmother's home in Lincoln, Audrey began to try to talk. She pointed to her grandmother.

"That's *Grandmother*," Mabel said.

"Dam (grand) mother (muzzy)," Audrey repeated. "Dam-muzzy."

Audrey insisted on calling her grandmother *Dammuzzy*. So from then on Alice became *Dammuzzy* to her grandchildren.

Audrey had been a little over a month old when she had her first Christmas at her grandmother's house in December of 1912. Mabel took a photograph of the Christmas tree with a box camera she had bought when she started teaching school in 1910 in Crawford, Nebraska. Although Audrey did not remember the

1912 tree, she remembered the 1918 Christmas tree at her grandmother's home a few years later:

> My first Christmas [was] December, 1912, at the home of my grandmother, Mrs. Tom Shirley, 1916 (?) on 26th Street in Lincoln, Nebraska. I remember the 1918 tree as touching the ceiling. Among the trimmings were strings of pop corn and small candles held in metal holders that opened and shut like a clothes pin, so that they could be snapped onto the ends of the tree branches. Each had to be placed where its open flame could not set another branch a fire. The music on the piano included *Pony Boy* and *Put on Your Old Grey Bonnet*, songs I remember mother singing for years. The stove with isinglass front [kept the room warm.] The years have galloped away but the memories keep returning of pleasant, happy times at Grandmother's house. That was in nice, civilized Nebraska, before we came to wild and wooly New Mexico. Seldom have any of the 60 Christmas trees since then delighted me as did the ones at my grandmother's on 26th Street in Lincoln, Nebraska.[1]

Mabel was hoping that for Audrey's third Christmas, Vern would be working in Nebraska and would forget his ideas of ranching in New Mexico—a place that so far held only bad memories for her. Mabel had arranged to stay at her father's farm after a visit with her mother. Audrey wrote: "By the time I was 16 months old, Mother and I were at her father's near Shelton. He raised hogs and cattle."[2] Audrey's grandfather, Edward Waddell, had two farms, the Gibbon farm and the Shelton farm.

Audrey found a letter in her father's personal effects after he died in 1960. Audrey said her mother's letter "was a pitiful (to me) little girl letter begging Daddy to join us there."[3]

Audrey wrote: "Mama wrote little girl letters to Daddy still in Avis—saying I missed him and since Mama was Grandpa's only heir she would get the farm someday and tried to entice him to go up there to the farms."[4]

As soon as he could, "Daddy did come up [to Nebraska from New Mexico].[5]

In the *Las Vegas Daily Optic* article cited earlier, Millicent L. Gensemer wrote: "Deciding against their projected plans of raising angora goats, the family returned to Nebraska where they lived on one of her (Audrey's) grandfather's farms near Shelton."[6]

Apparently Vern's mother returned to Nebraska with him.

Mabel was delighted when Vern arrived. She figured Vern had his yearning for life in the "wild west" out of his system, and they could now settle down in a more refined life style.

"Well, Vern, you gave it your best try," Mabel consoled him. "If you hadn't tried, you'd have always regretted not going to New Mexico."

"We'll go back," Vern said stubbornly.

"What? Are you out of your mind?" Mabel responded.

"I don't mean to May and Cecil's place. I mean to a better part of New Mexico—a place with mountains and trees and streams. I'll find a nice ranch to work on and finally I'll buy a place of our own."

"It sounds good, Vern, but Avis sounded good; and it was horrible," Mabel reminded him.

"I know. But next time we'll find a nice place and I'll make money. I promise you," he vowed.

Mabel sighed. "Well, right now let's just enjoy being back in civilization. Audrey is growing fast. She needs a good home."

"She'll have one," Vern promised. "My mountain girl will have a good mountain home."

Vern and Edward Waddell didn't get along so the Clements family left the farm and went back to Lincoln. Vern's sister Belle lived next door to a store on 16th Street where she worked. She was married to Sam Zipp. He and his mother ran the store. Audrey wrote:

> I don't know how long we stayed there but when it was time for Opal to be born in October, 1914, we were back in Lincoln. Aunty Belle Clements Zipp [Vern's sister] and her husband and his mother had a store. Opal was born at their house, not a happy place apparently. Grandma Clements was living there too or close by. Daddy left for his half-sister's home in Missouri to find work.[Nettie Hammond's home] Mama stayed with me and Opal at Aunty Belle's. The old Mrs. Zipp made her pay for a bar of soap to wash Opal's clothes. At Nettie's in Missouri, Daddy got a job cutting hardwood with an axe for $1.00 a cord. Before long he had enough money to send for Mama and me and the baby. Grandpa Clements [William Harper Clements] was there, too. Once there, Mama was very jealous of Daddy's cousin who threw herself at him, enticing him in every way she could. As soon as they could get enough money for train fare, they went back to Lincoln. Daddy was an interior and exterior house painter by trade and was very good at it, but got lead poisoning from the paints used then, so couldn't work at it very long. He would work long enough for train fare some place, load up the big old trunk

with all their belongings, and they were gone again.[7]

Vern didn't get along very well with Tom Shirley, Mabel's step-father, so they never stayed very long at the home of Mabel's mother.

Mabel was fond of her half-sister Thelma and her half-brother Bruce. Her own full brother, Oliver—called Ollie—died when he was still a baby. Mabel had no other full brothers or sisters. Now that she was married and had a child, she didn't especially want to stay at her mother's home for very long. So Mabel and Vern moved in with Vern's sister, Belle. In "My First Days" Audrey wrote:

> Being just a teenager, [Vern was 19 when he married Mabel] Daddy had little opportunity for good, steady jobs. So he odd-jobbed it. Mother was expecting Opal so we went to stay with his sister, Aunty Belle Clements Zipp. She had two boys, Alvern and Harold. Opal was born there in a dark room off the side of their store. Grandma Clements was going to take care of her but when Opal was hardly a week old, Grandma's first husband, Mr. Hammond, died. So she went to his funeral. She had left him because he threatened to kill her—would not let her visit neighbors or do anything except work on his farm. She left him although her six children were standing at the gate crying and begging her, "Don't leave us Mama. Please don't leave us." It must have broken her heart to leave them but she did and later married my grandfather William Harper Clements. He had a number of children and the youngest lived with them. They [Emma Maria and William Harper Clements] had Aunty Belle [Belle Clements] and, eight years later, my father. [Lavern Clifford Clements] Sometime they had another baby, Caley, that died. Grandma had a total of 9 children that lived.[8]

William Harper Clements, Emma's second husband, had been born at Melford, Nebraska. Sometime after their son Caley died at five months of age, William and Emma separated. Vern was very close to his sister Belle and his half sisters May and Netti.

When Opal Emma Clements was born on October 25, 1914 at Aunt Belle's home, Audrey was just short of two years of age. On the dark, gloomy night when Opal was born, just a little lamp light brightened the scene when Audrey's sister came into the world. Audrey waited eagerly in her bedroom for news of the new arrival. But she was not allowed to see her little sister until a couple of days after the baby's arrival. Audrey was thrilled when she finally got to hold her little sister. For a long time, Audrey called Opal "Little Sister."

Audrey wanted to help take care of "Little Sister." They were living a meager existence at the Zipps. At two years of age, Audrey worried that Opal might not have enough to eat. Mabel later said that Audrey and Opal cut their teeth on squirrel meat. Mabel began to realize that even here in "civilized" Lincoln, it was not easy to feed a family when Vern was making such a meager living.

Soon after Opal was born, Vern went away to work on a job and promised to return with more money. He gave Mabel a nickel to live on while he was gone. But Mrs. Zipp expected Mabel to pay for everything. She kept an account of how much was owed and demanded every penny from Vern when he returned. Mabel did not even have money to buy a postage stamp to write to Vern to tell him how much she needed money.[9]

After some years, Belle divorced Sam Zipp and later married Fred Gushard. They had two children, Juanita and Kenneth Gushard.

Vern and Mabel finally managed to get away from Sam and his mother. They went to Missouri. Audrey wrote:

> After Opal was born Daddy's half sister Nettie lived in Missouri. So we went there to nearly starve. Daddy cut wood for $1.00 per cord into stove lengths with an ax and saw. That was hardwood, must have been mighty hard. He could cut one cord a day, four feet high, four feet wide, and eight feet long in the pile.[10]

Audrey remembered, "Vern got a job cutting cord wood—hardwood such as oak. It was a lot of work in one day for a dollar!"[11]

Mabel wrote home to her mother. Vern was working himself to death for such a small wage, she wrote. Alice urged Mabel to convince Vern to return to Lincoln. Vern's mother, too, wrote and said Vern could get work there. After inquiring several places, Vern decided to take a job that was offered in Shelton, Nebraska. There they stayed with Mabel's father for about a year. Mabel appreciated her father, for she had missed out on several years of knowing him when she was a child. Now she tried to make up for lost time.

Mabel had always had what her mother called "gumption." Mabel showed her mettle when she was about to graduate from high school.

Mabel knew all about her father and had heard her mother's side of their conflicts. Edward Albert Waddell and Henrietta Alice Applegarth married on March 15, 1888 in Nebraska. They had two children, Oliver William Waddell, and Mabel Edna Waddell. Oliver, known as "Ollie," was born December 23, 1888. He was just about three years old when he became very ill in March of 1891. A terrible Nebraska blizzard raged outside, and Edward didn't think he could make it through the storm to get a doctor. Apparently he did go for the doctor but it was too late. Ollie grew worse and died on March 12, 1891. Mabel, born October 26, 1890, was too small to remember her older brother.

Alice blamed her husband for their son's death. She never got over it. Finally she took Mabel and left. Mabel was about seven years old at the time. Alice did not want Edward to find her, so she used the name Reed or Read.

Alice had learned well from her mother, Eleanor Chase Applegarth, daughter of Levi Chase of Madison, Wisconsin, a banker. Eleanor Chase married William Henry Applegarth on March 15, 1888, and the couple had three children: Homer, Charlie and Alice. William Applegarth had enlisted as a Private for the Union on August 12, 1864 at the age of 23. He mustered out June, 1865 at St. Paul, Minnesota. As a veteran of the Civil War, he had learned that life is not easy, but he wanted to be a good father.

Alice Applegarth was born on April 13, 1870 at Atwater, Minnesota. When Alice was four or five years old, her mother Eleanor left her husband William, taking the children home to her father in Wisconsin. But Alice's father went after his wife and got the children. He was determined to rear his children, even though his wife had left him. After he took the children away from Eleanor, he brought them back to Nebraska and ran a store there.

Eleanor Chase re-married after the divorce and had a family in Colorado. William Applegarth also remarried, so Alice had a step-mother, a woman she considered very mean. The woman was a seamstress, a perfectionist who insisted that Alice learn to sew perfectly. On one occasion she did not allow Alice to attend a birthday party of a friend because she had not completed a sewing job to perfection.

Now that Alice was grown and had also left her husband, she would not make the mistake her mother had made. She would not let her husband know where she was. Then he could not find her to take Mabel away from her, as she had been taken away from her own mother by her father.

Alice earned her living as a seamstress. Mabel Waddell was known at school as Mabel Reed for several years. Alice wanted Mabel to sew as well as she did so she could also make her living as a seamstress when she grew up. Alice was strict with Mabel, insisting on perfection—but she was not mean, as her stepmother had been.

Mabel Clements wrote a poem entitled, "My Fingers are So Small." It was about a memory of her learning experiences:

> My fingers are so small
> Mama says you will be surprised

That I can sew at all.
Don't say my stitches are crooked
Where they should be in a row.
At least don't let me know it
Or I would cry, you know.

I stuck my fingers 40 times
But I just smiled, you know
Because 'twas for Aunt Ida
And I'm learning how to sew.

Don't say my stitches are crooked
Where they should be in a row
Each crooked stitch
Is a crooked kiss
But you like that kind I know.

I stuck my fingers 40 times
But I will learn, you know.
I laughed and didn't care at all
Because I love you so.

Each stitch is a kiss for you Auntie
Tho' crooked—there are many—
Each crooked stitch is a crooked kiss
But you like that kind, I know.[12]

    Then it was nearly time for Mabel's high school graduation. Mabel remembered her father; she had wondered about him all those years. He was not a bad man. She wanted him to know she was graduating from high school. She was no longer a child and did not have to follow her mother's every whim. So she found her father's address and boldly sent her father a graduation announcement and an invitation.

    "My mother will have a fit if she finds out what I did," Mabel confided to one of her friends.

    "What did you do, Mabel?"

    "I sent my father an invitation to my graduation ceremony," she whispered.

    "What if he shows up?" the girl asked.

"I doubt if he will," Mabel replied.

"He just might," her friend said.

"Well, I wish he would. Mother would never let me hear the end of it if he did show up; but I'm going to be on my own now. I'm grown up. I can do what I want. And my father has a right to come to my graduation!"

"But aren't you scared, Mabel?" her friend persisted. "What if he does show up?" the girl repeated.

"What if he doesn't?" Mabel said. She'd feel bad then, too. "Besides, what can he do? He can't take me away from Mother now that I'm grown. That's what Mother always feared."

"But if he does come to the ceremony, your mother will be furious with you, Mabel," the friend declared.

"I know. But I'll deal with it," Mabel said firmly.

"I'd never be brave enough to do what you did, Mabel," the friend declared. "You've got a lot of courage, sending him an invitation!"

"If something's right, then you ought to do it," Mabel stated.

As she sat with her class that evening, Mabel wondered if her father had received the invitation to attend her graduation ceremony. She didn't expect him to attend, but she hoped to receive a letter from him. Sometimes she dared to hope he would show up. As she looked out at the audience, she saw her mother and other friends and relatives, watched them as they came in and took seats prior to the ceremony.

And then she saw him—the man she hadn't seen in years! Her father! He had received the invitation! He had traveled to the event!

Mabel's heart was in her throat. She saw him take a seat. Then her eyes met his and he smiled at her! He recognized her after all those years! There were tears in her eyes. When Mabel walked across the stage to receive her diploma, it was the height of joy. She didn't care what her mother said. Her father had come to see her graduate!

Mabel's surprise and delight couldn't be diminished by her mother's displeasure at Mr. Waddell's showing up for the ceremony. Mabel got the tongue lashing from her mother that she expected. But she stood by her convictions. He had a right to be there. Surprisingly enough, as the years passed, Alice and Edward were on speaking terms again—thanks to Mabel's opening the door to that possibility. As for Mabel and her father, they became very close. Years later, Audrey wrote:

> At her graduation she [Mabel Waddell] saw her father Edward Albert Waddell for the first time in more than 10 years. Her mother had taken

her and run away from Edward Albert and his farm near Ord, Nebraska because she said he threatened to kill her, and she thought he meant it. However, Mother [Mabel Waddell] bravely sent him a graduation announcement and he came to Lincoln for the event. Mama [Mabel] went to the Nebraska State Normal school and acquired a teaching certificate and taught that winter in the Sand Hills of Western Nebraska.[13]

Mabel was glad she had found the courage to contact her father and that they had an opportunity to get to know one another. A few years later when Mabel, Vern, and their two daughters Audrey and Opal needed a place to stay, they were welcomed at Edward Waddell's home. In fact, they stayed with him several times. But he and Vern did not get along very well, so they never stayed long. Still, Audrey had a chance to get to know her Grandpa Waddell.

Audrey learned in later years, reading an old family Bible, that her grandfather, Edward Albert Waddell, was born June 2, 1861, in Columbus, Illinois, the son of James Oliver Waddell and Lucinda Ogle. After his wife Alice left him, Edward married two more times. He had two sisters: Laura Corrilla Waddell and Mary Young Waddell Powell. Upon inquiring about the family history, Audrey discovered that Laura Waddell, known as "Aunt Laura," had kept a detailed family history. Audrey learned from her mother that Laura had written the entries in the old Bible, such as the following: Edward's father, James Oliver Waddell, had a farm in Gilmer Township near Columbus, Illinois. He was born November 8, 1822 and lived until March 18, 1894. He was the son of Obadiah Waddell and Milla (or Milly) Thomson. James Oliver Waddell married Lucinda Ogle at Paloma, Illinois on November 4, 1851. He was active in the Methodist Episcopal Church at Columbus, Illinois. In 1866 he helped build a Methodist Episcopal church which was about a mile west of their home. Then he was superintendent of the Sunday School at Mt. Pleasant, Illinois. When his wife's sister died, he was appointed guardian of her five children, as their father had died several years before. Audrey wrote years later:

> With a good trotting team and light top buggy it still took more than an hour and a half to travel the 6 miles to the Mt. Pleasant Sunday School from the James Oliver Waddell farm about 17 miles from Quincy, Illinois. As the family increased and the buggy seemed to become smaller, [the] family faithfully traveled to Sunday School and church every Sunday unless it rained heavily.[14]

James and Lucinda settled on the home place which his father, Obadiah

Waddell, and mother, Milla or Milly Thomson, had acquired as compensation from the U.S. government for his efforts in fighting in the War of 1812. The old Bible showed that Obadiah Waddell was the son of Jesse Waddell and Elizabeth Griffin and that Milla Waddell was the daughter of William Thomson and Milly or Milla. "Jesse Waddell had a brother, David, who was scalped by Indians while at a sugar camp in Kentucky. He survived, married, and had a large family. He wore a skull cap the rest of his life to cover the damaged skin."[15]

Laura Corrilla Waddell, daughter of James Oliver Waddell and Lucinda Ogle Waddell, was born May 4, 1853 near Columbus, Illinois. Since Laura was a very bright girl, her father decided to take her to hear a political debate. They went to hear the Lincoln-Douglas debate prior to Abraham Lincoln's election as President. Laura often told the family about the debate and how it had impressed her.

As secretary of Mt. Pleasant Sunday School, Laura kept neat records in a 40 cent bound notebook. The faded ink records those elected in the 1875 Sunday School Election. Laura married Thomas Polk Pierce January 27, 1876 and had two children, Lucinda Pierce Ketchum and Grace Nettie Pierce. Grace had a daughter, Rose Henrietta Walker and a boy named Roy. Her brother was Edward Albert Waddell, the father of Mabel Edna Waddell. Hence, Mabel always called her "Aunt Laura." Laura lived to be over ninety years old and continued to keep excellent family records until her death.

Laura had several brothers, including Edward Albert Waddell (Mabel's father) and Charles E. Waddell who had two children, Elliot Waddell and Beulah Waddell—Laura's nephew and niece. Beulah had tuberculosis. She moved to live with Laura at Canon City, Colorado hoping the climate would help her. She died in her early 20's. It was for her that the wonderful piano (known as "Uncle Frank's piano) inherited by Mabel Waddell was purchased so that Beulah could learn to play for entertainment since she was a frail invalid most of her life. That piano took quite a journey in its 150 years, as the later story will describe.

Audrey was quick to learn the values of honesty and reverence that her parents modeled. She wrote:

> I don't remember whether it was Mother or my grandmother that taught me "Now I lay me down to sleep, I pray the Lord my soul to keep, Bless Papa and Mama and Little Sister and make me a good girl, Amen." All of my grandparents were God-fearing and, when possible, church-going people. Mama and Daddy went to the same Methodist Church and Sunday School in Lincoln, Nebraska when they were kids. In fact, that is where they met. Mother's grandfather Waddell had built

a church and kept it going near Quincy, Illinois where they settled, and my grandfather Clements, born in 1839, in Illinois or Iowa, recalled his father being unhappy with a ram that hit him when he was leaning over, knocked him down on a Sunday. It being against Biblical custom to do any unnecessary thing on Sunday, he waited until Monday. Then he went out and beat the ram on the horns for knocking him down the day before. My 6-year-old mind wondered if it did any good so long after the fact. But I suppose it did great-grandfather some good. He didn't desecrate the Sabbath.[16]

Audrey's Grandpa Waddell gave her a beautifully illustrated *Story of the Bible* by Rev. Jesse Lyman Hurlbut. When the family moved to Las Vegas, New Mexico, they went to the Methodist Church, a frame building where the big brick building stands now. Whenever the family was in town, Mabel sent the children to church. Audrey wrote:

> I think the reason she [Mable] didn't go was a lack of what she thought was a respectable hat and clothing. When we were little, mother's mother, Grandma Alice Shirley, kept us in [good] clothes as she was a marvelous seamstress. But Mother seldom had the right clothes and shoes all at the same time to go to church.[17]

The family often sang hymns. Mabel and Vern liked to sing together. Mabel played the piano. Audrey wrote: "Daddy—Laverne Clifford Clements—had a beautiful tenor voice and he could whistle beautifully and play the mandolin, musical saw, violin, and jew's harp and mouth harp."[18]

Audrey concluded in later years that her parents had both been true Christian believers—Methodists. Vern's second wife Mable Day was also a Methodist. Audrey wrote:

> She [Mabel Clements Shearer] always said she was a Methodist; and before Daddy died in 1960 he started to tell me about when he was saved in a cornfield. But Mable [Mable Day Clements] came in and kept him from it. He did join the church [Methodist] before he died.[19]

Audrey enjoyed living on her grandfather's farm and she was delighted when they stayed with her grandmother Alice, "Dammuzzzy." She especially liked her grandmother's ponies. Alice and Tom Shirley owned and trained Shetlands. Audrey could ride almost before she could walk.

5

Riding Her First Bronc: Lincoln to Shelton

As soon as Vern had earned a little money, he announced, "I'm going to buy my Audrey a little pony!"

"Pony! Pony!" Audrey clapped her hands and laughed with anticipation.

Audrey loved to ride the Shetland ponies that belonged to her grandmother. But this new pony was different than those she had ridden. He was larger than her grandma's ponies. Audrey wrote years later:

> I was about two when I rode my first bronc at the farm of my grandfather, E. A. Waddell near Shelton, Nebraska. Daddy bought me a cute little Shetland Pony, "gentle and well broke" the neighbor told him.
>
> So Daddy carried me piggy back, pretending to shy here and there so I would get a tighter hold of his shirt collar or sometimes an ear if he caught me off guard. Then he would yell and I would shriek with laughter. And the neighbors half a mile away would ring the party line and ask, "What are those crazies from New Mexico up to now?"
>
> I remember Daddy placing me on the back of the pony. I grabbed a handful of mane and remember him leading the pony along the road beside a fence covered with vines. "We will call him Prince," Daddy said. He was leading him by a hackamore rope.
>
> Suddenly the newly named Prince gave a little jump and grabbed Daddy by the shoulder with his teeth, shaking him (and me). I held on for dear life. Daddy said later he had a hard time knocking those teeth loose by turning around and hitting the pony on the nose with his other hand. When Prince let go Daddy's shoulder, he gave three or four jumps before Daddy could get hold of me. He always said, in telling the story, that I was holding on with might and main (mane). Daddy tied Prince to the fence and took me home, then turned right around and took Prince back to the neighbor.[1]

Audrey often told the story of how she had held two good hands full of mane when suddenly the pony reared up, stood straight up on his hind legs. Vern was not holding the lead rope very tightly. Years later, she wrote:

> Daddy had contracted to buy me a pony—a little Shetland stallion. He took me to the neighbors with him and sat me on it to ride home. En route, it grabbed him by the shoulder and shook him and began to buck. I held on to its mane with both hands and stuck like a bur. When Daddy controlled him he took me off and turned around and took the gentle pony back—rode my first horse before I was two.[2]

When they got home, Vern took off his shirt.
"Vern, this is a very bad bite," Mabel exclaimed.
"Oh, it's nothing," Vern protested bravely, although his pain was obvious.
Mabel proceeded to "doctor" the shoulder as Audrey looked on. Audrey was proud she had not fallen off.
In Millicent L. Gensemer's *Las Vegas Optic* story, cited earlier, she wrote:

> It was there (at the farm near Shelton, Nebraska) that Audrey rode her first bronc while not yet three years old. Her father had bought her a Shetland stallion and had just placed her on the pony's back to lead her around when the pony reared up on his hind legs, bit and pawed his way loose from Mr. Clements.[3]

Vern and Mabel enjoyed playing with their baby daughter. Mabel wrote a poem she titled, "Better'n' Walkin':"

> I read your poem, Mary,
> And I can't agree with you.
> For without my man and baby,
> I would be most dreadful blue.
>
> I may have to wash some dishes
> But that doesn't take all day.
> And there's time for lots of loving
> In the good old fashioned way.
>
> You may think your love adventure
> Will be filled with thrills galore

But a rosebud, cuddly baby
Brings you countless millions more.
Just to hear her lisping, "Daddy"
To the daddy you both love
Makes you feel God's right within you
Not in some abode above.

Just to feel her lips against you
Brings a thrill no man can give,
Compensates for every misery
That it cost to make her live.

When you've grown a little older
And your Romeo has flown
To a younger, fresher lassie
And you think and think alone—

Don't you think it sounds more comfy
Bright eyed youngsters—rosy pink
Romping with their grand old daddy
While you smile (and wash the sink.)[4]

Audrey's experience of riding her first "bronc" left her only slightly shaken. Her next experience left a much bigger "mark."

> Things were bad for them there [at Aunt Nettie's in Missouri] so about that time we went back to Grandpa Waddell's farm in Nebraska. I suppose I was nearly four. Mother sold eggs in Shelton from Grandpa's chickens and I think he gave her half of what she got. I was sitting on the egg cart at Mother's feet and Mother was carrying Opal in her arms. The little mule team was trotting along the peaceful country road under the full moon. Suddenly a monster—one of those new-fangled automobiles—came along beside us. The mules had no blinders but the faint lights of the horseless carriage and its ungodly "honk honk ooo-uuu—go—ooo-uuugh" scared them. Daddy pulled them over and the car went on by with the occupants yelling and laughing. The little mules took off. They had hard mouths, and Daddy was using all his strength trying to pull them down. Mother clutched Opal tightly and hung on to the top buggy seat. I had been dozing on the egg case but the noise jerked

me awake. I couldn't see over the front panel of the buggy but Daddy had his feet braced against the dash board, yanking on the line and yelling "Whoa! Whoa!" Suddenly one line broke, pulling the mules into a circle. As they circled the buggy tipped up and mother jumped out with Opal. I was thrown to the ground beneath the buggy and flying hooves. Daddy had jumped out by this time and tried to scoop me up out of the road. He couldn't do it with the mules and buggy circling over me. So he let go of the good line and yelled at the mules so they would quit trampling me. The mules headed off through a fence and a corn field.

"Are you all right, Audrey?" Daddy asked.

"Yes," I answered in a state of shock. He wiped the road dirt off my face and carried me over to the side of the road. There Mother and Opal and I sat in the bright moonlight. There was a big, dark house not far from the road, surrounded by huge trees. I remember the long shadows those trees cast—clear across the road. We had to sit there until Daddy went to the nearest house and called Grandpa on the phone (he was modern! had the first auto in that area.) As Daddy called every phone on the party line came to life and in a few minutes we were surrounded by neighbors who came to "help out." After we got safely in Grandpa's car Daddy went to find the mules. The buggy was badly damaged and the harness torn up. The corn field also suffered.[5]

The next day I remember mother lifting up my dress to show a neighbor lady the wheel marks of the buggy across my stomach and a mule hoof print on my back. Mother explained. "She must have fallen on her face and the mule stepped on her. Then she rolled over so the buggy wheels went across her. I saw them go over her two or three times before Vern let go of the lines."

"Are you going to take her to the doctor?" the neighbor asked.

"No," Mother answered. "She will be all right." In those days no one went to a doctor unless they had something he could do something about, like maybe a broken leg (and maybe not then!)[6]

That is probably why I have had so much stomach trouble through the years. A stomach exam showed me full of adhesions years later.

"Have you ever had surgery?" the doctor asked.

I said no, but knew that probably the spill on a Nebraska farm road with two mules and buggy running in a circle over me did it.[7]

Audrey wrote: "In later years, I had lots of stomach pain and Dr. Mortimer, after X-rays, once asked if I had had surgery. I never had but the adhesions were probably caused by 'a hard life.'"⁸

Audrey knew her parents were relieved and thankful that their daughter was not seriously harmed. Audrey knew her parents loved her, but she realized it even more when they had an opportunity to give her away. Grandpa Waddell had married again. He had not been married to his second wife very long. Mabel took Audrey to visit her. Audrey wrote:

> She [Mabel] went to her father's, E. A. Waddell. He had two farms in the area, the Gibbon farm and the Shelton farm. Grandpa apparently had a wife (second wife) and Mother told me she said if mother would give me to her she would stay with Grandpa. Mama wouldn't agree to that, so she left. It was whispered that she ran off with a neighboring farmer.⁹

Grandpa Edward A. Waddell married three times but apparently never had a happy marriage. As he grew older, he seemed to grow insecure and fearful. He was consoled that his daughter Mabel cared for him. He spent many happy days enjoying his grandchildren, always seemed cheered when his grandchildren were around.

Vern realized he wasn't making a good living for his family in Nebraska. He still had his dream of living in New Mexico and becoming wealthy on a ranch. He convinced Mabel to go back to New Mexico, using every argument he could think of. He could find the kind of work he liked in New Mexico. Staying with relatives in Nebraska was not a good option. Vern continued to persuade Mabel. And when Vern turned on his charm, he was hard to resist. So Mabel agreed to try living in New Mexico again.

6

Santa Claus in Taos: From Shelton to Taos

he life and love of the west still beckoned Vern. Someone told him Taos, New Mexico was the place to go.

"This time we'll live in a town with lots of people around so you won't be isolated," Vern promised his wife. "And there won't be sand storms because it's not in the desert. There will be mountains! We'll be surrounded by beauty everywhere we look!" Vern made it sound so good Mabel was willing to go.

Audrey wrote, "Mama's egg money proved to be enough for train tickets back to New Mexico. Daddy and Grandpa didn't jibe very well, and Daddy hated to be bossed, so there was no staying on the farm."[1]

There were no relatives in Taos. But Aunt Laura was living in Canon City, Colorado where she'd moved from Quincy, Illinois. Mabel's Uncle Frank and her father wanted to visit Laura Waddell Pierce. So the Clements family rode with Grandpa Waddell and Uncle Frank to Canon City to visit Aunt Laura.

At Canon City Edward and Frank bought a beautiful glass with a stem—a kind of glass goblet—for Audrey. They gave Opal a creamer and sugar set, green on the outside and gold on the inside. They let Opal pick what she wanted first, so she chose what appeared to be the prettiest. Audrey was jealous. The two sisters loved each other but there was at times some sibling rivalry.[2]

After they left Edward and Frank Waddell, the Clements family took the D & RG (Denver and Rio Grande) narrow gauge train straight down to Taos Junction. The well-known Long John Dunn ran a shuttle between Taos Junction and the D & RG depot and Taos. Dunn took the family up out of the gorge and straight on up to Taos. Dunn sped down the long, winding "shelf road." Audrey wrote:

> This trip to New Mexico was on the narrow gage to Taos. We rode with Uncle Frank Waddell in his car to Pueblo, Colorado or maybe it was to Canyon City where we took the narrow gage to Taos Junction. From Taos Junction, Long John Dunn met the train and in his big, long, open-topped touring car took us into Taos. Daddy had caught a freight wagon and gone ahead so we rode with Long John Dunn alone. Mama was scared to death, going along mountain cliffs and around mountain curves at ten miles an hour. I remember standing beside the train engine against a background of tall evergreen trees. Once in Taos, Daddy met us and took us to a house near the church. They were building a new church nearby and Opal and I enjoyed playing in the sand piled up near the new church site. We lived in a two room mud house, called "adobe" by the Taos natives and "mud" by Mama.
>
> Somehow we lived through the winter. Daddy driving a 4-horse team from Taos Junction and Mama tatting and selling her work door to door. She knew how to make marshmallows and Daddy whipped them with an egg beater for 30 minutes at a time. Then they sold them

and got money enough to make more. But it was a little town and there wasn't much demand for luxuries such as handmade tatting lace or marshmallows. I remember our breakfasts were oatmeal with bacon grease and sugar on it. Daddy would get up at 3 a.m. to freight to and from Taos Junction. Daddy made friends with the Indians and traded with them.[3]

Audrey gave a more detailed account:

> I can remember riding from Taos Junction to Taos in a big old "touring" car with the top down along a narrow road on the side of a high cliff. I wouldn't look over the edge of the car. Opal 2 and me, 4, and Mother had come in on the train (the little narrow gage from some place in Colorado where Uncle Frank had taken us from Grandpa Waddell's farm in Nebraska.) Grandpa Applegarth died in October or November, 1916 when we were in Taos. Opal and I were nonchalant when it came to riding in automobiles. After all, we had ridden from Grandpa Waddell's farm to Shelton often to Gibbon. On the narrow gage track the black monster was huffing and puffing around the curves into the Junction and made Mama so sick she embarrassed herself by vomiting into the handy spittoon. Of course being pregnant at that time, that bumpy train ride didn't improve matters. I remember a small railroad station and Opal and I playing there under the trees while waiting for John Dunn and his mighty mobile.[4]

Audrey remembered how happy Vern was when he got a job freighting for the railroad, taking a team of two or four horses to pull the wagon load of freight to and from Taos Junction out of Taos. Vern was a natural horse trader, and the Pueblo Indians liked him. He could speak some Spanish, as they could, and he was good at communicating with them.

Opal and Audrey Clements in Taos, 1916
Source: **Simpson Archives**

Mabel was surprised when several Pueblo Indians showed up one day asking for "Vern."

"He's not home. He's working," she told them.

She didn't know if they understood her or not. But instead of leaving, they sat down on the floor of the kitchen.

"Wait," one of them said.

On more than one occasion, they would come in to "wait" for Vern. Then they'd watch Mabel work—washing, ironing, washing dishes and cooking meals. Hours would sometimes pass before Vern came in from his work. But the Native Americans were patient. They didn't mind waiting—especially when Mabel fed them some of her homemade bread or cinnamon rolls.

One of the Native Americans who came into Mabel's kitchen to sit and wait was "Gold Tooth John." He had gone to Dr. F. E. Olney in Las Vegas and insisted that he wanted the dentist to pull all his teeth and put in gold ones. The dentist refused to pull all his teeth. He told him his teeth were just fine. The Indian talked him into pulling one front tooth and putting in a gold one. From then on he was known as "Gold Tooth John."

Years later when Audrey was a journalist and reporter, she wrote a good description of the man as she remembered him. This newspaper story in the Simpson Archives was marked as written by Audrey, although no bi-line was given. In "Gold Tooth John Colorful Early Day Character," *Las Vegas Daily Optic, Rodeo Edition*, Las Vegas, New Mexico, July 31, 1952, Audrey wrote:

> The old timer says, "I first knew Gold Tooth John in Taos. He was a Taos Pueblo Indian. I used to trade horses with John who got his name from a gold front tooth.
>
> "Then I trailed over the pass and hit Vegas. Gold Tooth John has said he got his tooth in Vegas. I didn't expect to meet up with the dentist who gave it to him but I did.
>
> "I got the tooth ache and hunted up Dr. Frederick E. Olney, D. D. S. He had been mayor of Las Vegas and owned a lot of property around the city.
>
> "It was said that one of his ancestors, Thomas Olney, came to America in 1632 with Roger Williams who founded Rhode Island. Dr. Olney himself was said to have been born in West Jefferson, Ohio, in 1845 and in 1886 tried the mountain air of Las Vegas for the sake of his health.
>
> "Las Vegas climate agreed with him. He began to practice here. When I came along with the toothache he was a fine looking, distinguished gentleman. And a good dentist that cured my toothache in short order.

"I talked to him a number of times after that. And I asked him about Gold Tooth John. He laughed and said he remembered him well. He said the Indian had come to him wanting a gold tooth.

"Dr. Olney refused to pull a perfectly good tooth and replace it with a gold tooth. Indian John kept coming back to the office begging for a gold tooth. The doctor tried to explain why he couldn't see his way clear to pull a good tooth and substitute a gold one. He finally got it across that if the front tooth was no good he could pull it and substitute a gold tooth.

"John went back to Taos, the Doctor told me. But he came back to Las Vegas in a few months. When he went back to the doctor's office he claimed his tooth hurt terribly. So Dr. Olney pulled it and fitted him with the new tooth. He was one of the happiest men that ever went out of the doctor's office, the doctor told me," the old timer said.[5]

The Clements family had known poverty before, but there had always been relatives around to help—at least to offer a meal. In Taos they had no relatives, and they became well acquainted with stark poverty. Mabel sold her beautiful crochet work and fancy tatting. None of the women around there could tat; most had never heard of tatting. Mabel sold it by the yard or by the piece. Vern's work was probably intermittent, so the income needed to be supplemented. Not only did Mabel and Vern have a recipe for marshmallows—something no one else in Taos seemed to have—but they also made taffy and sold some of it. Still, poverty stalked the family.

Christmas was coming and the Clements family in Taos was bitterly poor. One day Mabel took Audrey aside and told her not to say anything about Christmas to Little Sister because they wouldn't have any gifts this year.

Audrey opened her eyes on Christmas morning and wondered if Santa had found them. Or was her mother right? Santa couldn't come this year. There was no Santa in a home where there was no money. Could it be true? Audrey didn't want to get up. Opal was still asleep. Audrey didn't want to wake her little sister if there were no Christmas presents.

Suddenly, there was a knock at the door. It was the postmaster.

Mabel was surprised to see him.

"You should get the day off!" Mabel declared.

"I've got the day off, and I'm going home right now to celebrate Christmas with my family," he said. "But it occurred to me that there are some little kids in this house who need to have this package." It was an enormous box from Nebraska.

Mabel's eyes stung with tears. Her mother had sent Christmas gifts. There would be Christmas in the Clements home this year after all.

"Thank you for bringing this package to us," Mabel said. "You didn't have to deliver it today. But it will make all the difference in the world to my children. You saved Christmas for us."

"Happy to help, Ma'am," he said, tipped his hat, and left.

The box was filled with many gifts and good things to eat.

Audrey and Opal, like all children on Christmas morning, were excited and happy when they got up. Audrey received a big, tall doll—almost as big as herself. It had a beautiful porcelain face with blond hair and blue eyes. She named it Dorothy. Little did she know then that someday she would have a baby girl and name that daughter Dorothy.

As the girls enjoyed their toys, tried on their new clothes, and ate too many "sweets," Mabel fed the stove more wood and baked some bread to go with their pinto beans. Vern went out and came back in with a beautiful fir tree.

"We can't have Christmas without a tree," he said.

The children made some simple decorations to put on the tree. The scent of the fir gave the house the fragrance of Christmas, the way Dammuzzy's house had smelled in the room with the big Christmas tree.

Even though the family had a Christmas celebration with gifts after all, Audrey marked that Christmas as the year she had to "grow up" and realize that in a home with no money, life can be difficult. Yet, it was the kindness of caring people that kept the Christmas spirit alive.

The postmaster was the nicest man in Taos, Audrey thought. He went out of his way to do a small favor, but it was a deed of kindness that the Clements children never forgot. Years later whenever she could do a kindness for someone, Audrey never hesitated. The postmaster had taught her how much a small kindness can mean. In 1988, Audrey recorded on cassette tape:

> On Christmas morning we got up and had absolutely nothing that looked like Christmas! Suddenly the Postmaster came with a great big package from Dammuzzy. It was clear full of all sorts of goodies and gifts, and that's the year, I think, that I got that big doll—the "Dorothy" doll. If Mama had just held off, my heart wouldn't have been broken. Santa Claus did get there—late—but he got there.[6]

Audrey did not know the postmaster's name. Research shows that there was a man named Rhode Matthews who was a postmaster in Taos about that time. He and his wife, Henrietta Young Matthews, had two children, a girl and a boy. It is said that he had a warm personality and a friendly disposition which gave him a wide and close acquaintance with the Indians, Spanish and Anglo Americans in Taos. He died on November 7, 1918. He would have been about 33 years of age.[7] Possibly he died of influenza, as so many died of the epidemic that year. Whether Rhode Matthews was the postmaster who went beyond the call of duty to make two children very happy on Christmas morning is not known. Audrey remembered a man only as "the Postmaster." Whoever the postmaster was, he kept alive the Spirit of Christmas just as surely as if he had been Santa Claus himself.

Audrey Simpson submitted an item to the *Albuquerque Journal* in 1987. It is unknown whether the item was published:

> Christmas in Taos, in 1916, when I was four years old, left a lasting impression. My parents moved us to Taos that year from Lincoln, Nebraska. It was then that I really learned about Santa Claus.
>
> Riding the narrow gage railroad into Taos Junction, me and Pa Ohed and Ahed over the scenery. Those exclamations couldn't compare to what they sounded like as we rode with Long John Dunn in his big touring car from the Junction along the abrupt mountainside from the Junction into Taos.
>
> "He went five miles an hour and more," Ma wailed. "I'll never go over that road again," she vowed.
>
> They made a meager living with Pa freighting with four horse teams from the railroad and Ma tatting lacy edging for fancy handkerchiefs or pillow cases. Crocheting was common in Taos, but tatting was not. So she sold it door to door, sometimes trading it for something we could eat.
>
> Before Christmas the snow was too deep for freight wagons. Then Ma and Pa spent hours beating a sugar and gelatin concoction into marshmallows, a new taste for Taos palates. They could sell all they could make but it took hours to beat up a batch with a hand beater. Little Sis [Opal] and I got the lick the spoons.
>
> The day before Christmas, while little Sis napped, Ma whispered to me, "Don't mention Santa Claus or Christmas to Little Sis. We can't have any Christmas this year." Ma's voice sounded funny.
>
> "But Santa Claus—" I began.
>
> "There isn't any Santa Claus," she said bluntly.
>
> I ran out the door. I sat on the cold steps, looking through tears over at the sand pile where they were building a new Catholic church.

There Little Sis and I often played.

"No Santa Claus!" Back in Nebraska there was one. I had seen him myself when he came to Grandma's house. "No Santa Claus!" I sobbed over and over—but softly so Ma wouldn't hear me and say, "You're a big girl and big girls don't cry."

Christmas morning Ma cooked oatmeal as usual. We had no milk but we did have sugar to put on it. While Ma did the dishes Pa worked on a horsehair bridle he was braiding.

When there was a knock at the door Pa opened it hoping it was a call to work.

"Merry Christmas!" was the cheery greeting from the Postmaster, standing there with a huge package. "This finally got here and I figured you folks would like it today."

"Blessed Postmaster! Blessed Christmas!"

What excitement! The package from Nebraska contained everything! Dolls, toys, candy, nuts, clothing for little girls and Ma and Pa and some of Grandma's special fruitcakes.

I learned then and there that everything will turn out all right if you wait long enough and, in spite of everything, there is a Santa Claus.[8]

Audrey made up her mind that no matter how poor she was, she would always have a Christmas tree if she possibly could. Christmas was about celebrating with joy, regardless of how many gifts are—or are not—under the tree. It was the birthday of the King—Jesus Christ, the Lord. And no one would ever make her believe that Christmas could not be celebrated, even if there was no money for gifts. Audrey wrote a rough draft for a poem:

> It had been a hard year
> That week before Christmas
> In New Mexico Taos town.
> When Mother whispered, "Sit down.
> Don't mention Santa to little Sis.
> This is the year he will not come
> Because there is no Santa Claus."
> I nodded dumbly with never a sigh.
> I couldn't let mother see Miss 4-year-old cry.
> There was a blanketed Indian on a kitchen chair
> Waiting until my father got there.
> He would trade for some spuds

My folks had grown
In the Black Lake country's mountain loam.
There would be enough for a meager meal.
But no oranges or toys were a part of the deal.
We had come from Nebraska to Taos town,
Then lived on a ranch until we starved out.
Daddy "freighted" from Taos Junction.
But his 4 horse team barely fed themselves and him, two kids and wife.
Living in Taos was no easy life.
Back in Nebraska Santa always came.
My grandparents used Santa for a middle name
Always at their house was a wonderful tree
With gifts and toys for Sister and me.
Now mother had destroyed all Christmas hope
"No Santa Claus? How could that be?"
I had seen him once under Grandma's tree.
But Mother had said, "No Santa Claus"
And Mother was always right.
I crawled into bed and cried the whole night.
Why did she tell me then?
I'd never love Christmas again.
There was no tree the next morning.
It was just a day
Until the Postmaster came walking down our way.
He carried a huge box
and smiled as he said, "This just came in and I thought that you
Would need it before Christmas was through."
Oh, what a change!
Mother was laughing and Daddy near cried,
And I was so happy I could have died.
The box it was filled with candy and nuts
and even some oranges for each of us.
There were warm winter clothes for two little girls
And toys and a doll with necklace of pearls.
No matter what Mother had said
I knew there was Santa Claus
And since then my faith in Christmas
Has never been dead.[9]

On December 25, 1916 in Taos, New Mexico, the postmaster, whose name Audrey did not know—a postal employee who didn't mind working on his day off—brought the Christmas spirit into the home of a needy family and brought a lesson in love along with that package. The postmaster of Taos would always be remembered by the Clements family as the best helper Santa had ever had.

7

Mama's "Dairy" Cow: Taos to Black Lake

The doctor had been in the bedroom a long time. Audrey and Opal knew something exciting was happening. Opal was nearly three and Audrey was almost five when their little brother, Edward Laverne Clements, was born on March 5, 1917 at their home in Taos.

"You have a little brother!" the doctor said when he came out of the bedroom at last.

Then he opened up his little black bag—and there was Edward without a stitch of clothing on! Audrey knew then that doctors brought babies in their little black bags! She was almost ten when she told her friend Sophia Rael in Chapelle that babies came in doctors' little black bags. Sophie laughed and tried to tell her where babies "really" came from, but Audrey didn't understand or believe her. She had seen herself how Edward came into the family—in the doctor's black medical bag!

When Edward was six weeks old, the Clements family got up at three o'clock Good Friday morning and traveled past one of the *moradas* or small chapels where the Penitentes held their religious ceremonies all night on Holy Thursday. The family noticed fires, lights, and people all around as they traveled past the *morada*. In those days no one spoke of the Penitentes, as they were questionable in the eyes of the Roman Catholic Church. It was a secret society with the ritual of self-flagellation, done as penitence for sins, on Holy Thursday night and into the early morning hours of Good Friday. Since it was a brotherhood, women were excluded from the ceremonies. They did not participate in the whippings, but they often went on a kind of pilgrimage on their knees, sometimes up to the top of a large hill or mountain where the Penitentes often went for their ceremonies.

Mabel and Vern explained to the children that this was a sacred ceremony and the participants deserved their privacy.

The little family quietly proceeded on their way. Vern and Mabel had decided to go to Black Lake, a distance of about thirty miles from Taos. It was a long trip by team and wagon, and Mabel was badly sunburned by the time they arrived late in the day. (Black Lake is east of Angel Fire. Today it is about an hour's drive from Taos.)

The family spent the summer in the Black Lake area share cropping potatoes and other vegetables. They had a big adobe house that was fairly comfortable. It had one corner, however, where most of the adobe had fallen out and there was just a thin covering over the wall. Mabel worried that some animal might make its way into the house though that weak spot.

It was very hot when Mabel and Vern planted potatoes in the field. They put Edward under a tree nearby and Audrey was supposed to watch him and Opal.

"We have to watch out for wolves," Audrey's daddy said.

"And watch for eagles," Mama added. "An eagle could fly down and get Edward." Mabel recalled hearing that a woman had lost her baby to an eagle somewhere in that vicinity. Audrey didn't know what she could do except yell if either a wolf or an eagle came around. In any case, Audrey had been Opal's protector since she was born. Now she was Edward's protector too. She determined that no eagle would fly away with her little brother if she could help it.

Early one morning Vern called Audrey to look out the door.

"Audrey, come here!" He whispered. "See that lobo wolf?"

Audrey saw him some distance below the house. Audrey had heard the wolves howl, but the wolf she saw wasn't howling. He was just standing quietly under a tree, right where the folks always left the children when they were working in the field.

Audrey shivered. "Will he hurt us, Daddy?"

"No. If we had sheep or goats, we'd have to worry maybe. But we're just growing crops. He won't hang around the fields long unless he can hunt something. He won't be hunting us." Audrey hoped her daddy was right.

Vern and Mabel kept several firearms for protection. They had both learned to shoot early in life. They had been taught how to handle firearms safely. They would teach their children the same. Audrey learned how to shoot and knew the safety rules as soon as she was old enough to hold a gun properly.

It was that summer that Audrey and Opal acquired two pet lambs. Then Audrey did worry about the wolves. They might kill the sheep. But a wolf never came close to the house. Audrey wrote in later years:

Daddy brought home two lambs from a nearby sheep camp, one black and one white. We named them Snowball and Sammy. During the summer, the lambs grew faster than we did.

They knew Daddy was not to be trifled with. However, becoming good sized, if they saw Opal or me out in the yard they would run and butt us down. After being knocked over several times, Opal and I learned to quietly sit down on the ground in a sitting position. If we were still, the silly sheep, thinking they had already knocked us down, would wander away. Because of their rambunctious attitudes, Daddy soon sold them to a Taos Pueblo Indian.

Vern would go to Taos once in a while. It would usually take him three days by wagon—one day to go, one day to stay and do business, and one day to come home.[1]

It was thirty miles to Taos, a day's drive for a team and wagon. Doing business with the Native Americans was slow, so Vern wouldn't start back until the third day. Mabel was alone with the children for at least two nights. In these isolated mountains, she didn't have to worry about drifters dropping by like the one in Avis. But she did have to worry about wolves, snakes, and other wild creatures. Mabel would put the ax, the pitchfork, the shovel and the gun at the head of her bed every night because she was afraid a bear, wolf, or cougar would dig through the weak back corner of the big adobe house. With all her equipment handy, she was prepared. One night a pack rat ran across the floor. At first Mabel thought it was a coyote, as she was not fully awake. When she saw it was only a rat, she was relieved. Mabel didn't like rats and did what she could to get rid of them. But wolves and bears were her biggest worry. When Vern's tall, reassuring presence was not in the house, the sound of the lobo wolf howling at night sent chills down Mabel's spine.[2]

Vern and Mabel eked out a meager existence raising potatoes and meadow hay in the isolated, heavily timbered valley between high peaks in northern New Mexico. Vern always said Mabel, the red-haired school teacher from a big city, took to ranch ways "right pert." In later years, he would recall, "In those days it was 'root hog or die,' and that redheaded dynamite wasn't about to knuckle under to nothing'!"[3]

Vern was often away freighting with a four horse team and would be gone several days at a time. The wild range "milk cow," Wildee, would come to her corralled calf. Then Mom would "do the honors" to keep the milk pans in the spring house replenished. That milk was an important part of the diet that kept Audrey, Opal, and baby Edward healthy. Years later Audrey recalled her mother, a 120-pound woman, roping the wild cow, snubbing her to a tree, tying the hind legs to another tree and then squeezing spurts of milk into a big tin lard bucket.

In 1967 Audrey wrote a story about her mother's experiences milking the "wild" cow so her children would have milk. It was entitled, "Mom's Squeeze Play" and was published in *The Denver Post Empire Magazine* on May 28, 1976. Audrey described the entire milking situation very well.

> When Wildee came in toward evening, four-year-old Audrey would be the decoy at one end of the corral fence, trying to draw the cow's attention so Mabel could sneak up on her. Audrey would step out from the corner and move a little to make Wildee keep her eye on Audrey. If Wildee decided to charge, Audrey flipped under the logs into the corral. Usually she just stared at Audrey. Mabel would slowly slip around the corral fence, rope in hand; Wildee would be pressing her red and white spotted flank against the logs, trying to give the calf inside a chance to reach between the poles for a quick snack. If Mabel stepped on a stick or accidentally kicked a stone, the cow was gone in a swirl of pine needles and dust and it might be thirty minutes before the bawling calf lured her back to the fence. Then Mabel would try again.[4]

Audrey's article described her mother's roping abilities. She wrote that when Mabel got close enough she would shoot a quick loop from the hip—no whirling the rope around her head as they do on the wide open prairies, nor swinging it in an up and down motion by her side, as they do in heavy brush country. "Mom held the rope open in a big loop. At the right moment, she gave it one quick swish forward. If she was lucky, it snaked out and settled over Wildee's head," Audrey wrote.[5]

Next Mabel would run around a handy tree to hold the "dairy" cow. As the startled Wildee hit the end of the rope and then turned angrily back towards the woman, Mabel then would run the other way, taking up slack in the rope until she could run around another pine tree where she would tie the end of the rope securely.

"The 'heeling' deal was easy," Audrey wrote in her article. Mabel would move around behind the cow and throw a rope around those jumping, kicking hind feet. These she tied tightly together and anchored the second rope to another tree. Sometimes the moon would be easing over the purple shadows of the Sangre de Cristo Mountains before Mabel had the cow tied down enough to milk her.

Then Mabel would rope the calf and take it to the cow, letting it suck enough so that Wildee would let down her milk. After a minute or so Mable would jerk the calf away and with a swish of her long skirt, kneel down and ping thin streams of snowy milk into the lard pail. When she finished, she would hand the pail of milk to Audrey to take into the house.

One day Audrey looked at the half-empty, gold-colored pail with the big red letters. She remembered that her daddy got it full, with foam standing up on the top.

Audrey asked, "Why don't you get the pail clear full like Daddy does?"

Mabel straightened up to her full five-feet three inches and sternly answered, "I don't believe in starving a helpless little calf."[6]

Audrey didn't question her mother about that again. And she was always careful not to spill the milk, for she figured her mom didn't believe in starving helpless little children, either. Audrey would carefully set the pail of milk on the rough pine table where it would wait until Mabel came in and strained it through cheesecloth into the milk pan. Later, Audrey would help Mabel turn Wildee loose.[7]

Mabel always followed the old cowboy adage, "Don't never throw your loop on nothin' you can't turn loose." But sometimes she had to have a little help with Wildee, so Audrey was the helper.

Mabel would drag the bawling red calf back into the corral and tie its rope to the snubbing post. Then she would go to the tree where the end of the head rope was tied, while Audrey stood behind the other tree holding the end of the heel rope. When Mabel yelled, "Now!" they would both jerk the knots loose and let the cow tear into the corral to the bawling calf, dragging the ropes behind her. Usually she kicked the rope off her hind legs before she reached the calf. Mabel would swing the big corral gate shut and sneak in to remove the rope from Wildee's neck.

Sometimes Wildee was so busy placating her calf that she stood still until Mabel could get hold of the rope and pull it free. When the cow moved around too much, Mabel's trick was to use a long stiff wire with a hook on the end. She became quite expert in getting close enough to snag the hook through the rope, give a quick twist and jerk the loop loose enough for Wildee to throw it off her head. Sometimes Mabel would simply walk around front and, as the cow backed away, hold the rope with the wire until it came off.

Often the moon would be quite high, the great horned owls sobbing, "Who-who-whooo," or a timber wolf up on the ridge with his throaty song to the moon would curl Audrey's hair and send shivers down her spine before Mabel finished the milking chore. Then they hurried into the house where Mabel would drop the big bar, the only lock, across the rough slab door.

When Vern returned, he would always ask Mabel, "Have any trouble milking Wildee?"

Mabel's standard answer was, "It was just the usual milk situation."[8]

In the same *Denver Post* story about her mother's experiences milking the "wild" cow to provide her children with milk, Audrey wrote:

> Equality for women in those days in our mountains was ability to sling a man-size rope as well as flip a flapjack. My Mom was expert in both fields. But that range cow, Wildee, didn't believe in equality for women and never would knuckle under to Mom like she did to Dad. But then Mom didn't have dad's Irish temper and vocabulary. I don't think dad ever did know what that "usual milk situation" was. If he had found out, I am sure we would have had beef-steak instead of milk for breakfast."[9]

Most mothers today reach for a carton of milk in the dairy case of the supermarket, little guessing what some of their great grandmothers had to go through to provide milk for their children.

8

Ma "Brought Home" the Bacon

hile they were living on the isolated mountain ranch in the Black Lake area near the Sangre de Cristo mountain range, Vern bought a pig, not destined for pork, but to grow up and have lots of little pigs.

"Each of you kids can have a start in the pig business," Vern promised.

The pig lived in a log corral, built around a big pine tree, so she would have plenty of shade all summer. Vern hollowed out a trough from a pine log. As the early sun tinted evergreens on the surrounding peaks, Mabel would take a couple of buckets to Coyote Creek. She would dip them into the sparkling, icy water and carry them to the pen. While pouring water into the trough, Mabel would talk to the pig. "Here's your nice fresh water," she'd say.

Vern and Mabel taught their children to take care of their animals. Vern never came in to eat a meal until the animals had been cared for first. Mabel agreed. "Helpless animals are our responsibility."

Years later, Audrey recalled that summer at Black Lake when they cared for their pig and other animals and grew peas, potatoes, and various vegetables. In an article, "Mom Saved the Bacon," published in *Real West*, Audrey wrote a description of life at Black Lake:

> When the full moon brought howling timber wolves nearby, Dad would get up and lift the bar from the rough slab door. Picking his rifle off the wooden pegs beside the door, he would step outside and give a bloodcurdling Irish yell.
>
> "Git out a here you double eyed wolf devils! You ain't gonna git our Piggy." He never wasted valuable ammunition shooting when shouting worked just as well.
>
> Little sis and I would snuggle down under the covers, rattling the corn shucks in the old ticking that made up the mattress we slept on. We always felt safer when dad was home to scare the wolves away from our Piggy.
>
> When he was away on a freighting trip for several days at a time, Mom had a different method. A red-headed former school teacher from the east, she slept with the axe, pitchfork and rifle beside the head of the bed. And nothing would make her unbar the door after dark. When the wolves howled too close she would get up and build a fire in the kitchen.
>
> "That fire keeps the wolf from coming down the chimney," I would whisper to little sis. But mom said it was to let the big grey prowlers know that someone was up in the old adobe house.[1]

Audrey recalled that the mail was the big event of the week. The mail route passed about half a mile below the house. If they watched carefully from the top of a big boulder, Audrey and Opal could glimpse the spring wagon through the trees where the road dipped down into Coyote Creek. When the girls spotted the mail man, they would yell, "Mail! Mail!" Mabel would hurry across the fields to meet the mail carrier. There were usually letters from her mother and a weekly newspaper her folks sent. Sometimes Mabel took baby Edward and the girls to have a picnic in the deep meadow grass while waiting for the mail.

One day when Vern was away for a two or three days, Mabel swept the rough board floor, washed the dishes, bathed the baby, and then they were ready to go out and pick peas. Edward was placed on a blanket under a tree at the edge of the field. Before too long they had a wash tub full of fresh green peas. After eating some corn meal mush and milk, the family became to shell the peas.

"Now girls, don't eat more than you shell," Mabel admonished. Audrey and Opal loved peas. They dropped the peas into a gold lard bucket with big red letters.

According to a story Audrey wrote years later for the *Las Vegas Daily Optic*, the next morning Mabel took Piggy her fresh water and then dumped the tub of green pea pods into the trough. Sometime later, the pig began squealing loudly. Mabel ran out with the rifle, thinking something was attacking the pig. But the pig was sick. "The hog, weighing around 250 pounds, was acting like a mad thing. And bloating."[2]

Mabel told the kids to watch for the mail carrier so she could ask him what to do.

While Audrey and Opal watched from the big boulder, they held their hands over their ears to shut out the terrible squeals coming from the pig pen. As soon as they saw the mail carrier, they yelled, "Mail!" Mabel took off in a "high lope," holding her skirts up so she could run faster. She knew the mail carrier would know what to do for the pig.

The girls ran to the pig pen. The pig was twice as fat as she had been that morning. She ran here and there, jumping wildly and squealing shrilly. After every few jumps she would fall to the ground. The girls couldn't stand the squeals from the pig pen, so they ran into the house.

When Mabel came back, tears were streaming down her cheeks. She grabbed the rifle and a butcher knife.

"Whatcha gonna do? Whatcha gonna do?" the girls chorused.

"What I *have* to do," Mabel snapped. "Stay in the house!" Mabel slammed the door behind her.

"Mama's gonna shoot Piggy," Audrey said to Opal.

"She wouldn't hurt poor Piggy," Opal replied.

"Maybe that's all there is to do," Audrey said.

The squeals continued. Then there was the sharp sound of the rifle followed by complete silence.

Mabel was still crying when she came in and hung the rifle on its pegs.

"Why?" Audrey asked.

"The mail carrier said the pea pods bloated her. She would die a long, terrible, painful death. Shooting her was the merciful thing to do. He said I should butcher her to save the meat. He would have come to help us, but he has to get the mail through on time."

Mabel asked the girls to get a lot of wood and put it in the pig pen. While they carried wood and threw it into the pen, Mabel got the soot-blackened wash boiler. Setting it on rocks in the pig pen, she built a fire under it to heat water. While it was heating, she somehow "dressed out" the hog, using the axe, butcher knife and hoe.

When the water was boiling over the bonfire, Mabel poured the scalding water over the carcass and scraped off the hair, a foot or so at a time. Audrey thought her mother must have carried a hundred buckets of water from Coyote Creek before she finished.

Late in the afternoon, Mabel went to the pasture for Big Black, the horse. She rode him bareback up to the house and saddled him. When she led him to the pig pen, he snorted and was reluctant to get so close to the smell of death, but Mabel forced him in closer.

Mabel tied one end of the saddle rope to the hog's heels. The other end she threw over a high limb of the tree in the pen. Then she stretched the rope to the saddle horn. With the rope tied tightly to the saddle horn, Mabel moved Big Black away from the pen. The rope was then stretched taunt and pulled the hog's carcass high into the tree.

Mable then led Big Black around a little pine tree to keep the rope from slipping back and letting the heavy weight down; then she uncinched the saddle. She slapped Big Black out of the way. She swung the saddle around the tree again and fastened the cinch to hold the saddle in position so that the rope could not slip.

"Why did you cinch the saddle to the tree?" Audrey asked. "Dad never leaves it outside."

"I haven't got enough hands to hold the rope and take it off the saddle horn at the same time," Mabel replied. "The saddle will have to stay out tonight."

With the meat out of reach of wild animals, Mabel began the evening chores, finishing just as the timber wolves began a wild song at the far edge of the field.

When Vern returned the next day he was nearly speechless, marveling at the work Mabel had done.

"How did you ever do it?" he asked.

"She did it *crying*," Audrey answered.

"I'm sorry I didn't know better than to feed Piggy all those pea pods," Mabel sighed. "I didn't know she would bloat. But since it was done, I couldn't let the meat go to waste."

"That hog weighed twice as much as you. I don't see how you did it," Vern declared in his astonishment.

"It is sinful to waste good food," Mom said grimly. "So I did what had to be done to save the meat."

Mabel Clements, school teacher from Nebraska, little realized when she moved with her "cow-punching" husband to New Mexico how difficult it would be to "bring home" the bacon!

9

Stranger at the Door: Black Lake to Taos

At the end of the summer, the Clements family dug the potatoes they had struggled so hard to raise. Then they loaded the wagon and moved back to Taos with the crop. They rented a two-room apartment.

Vern began trying to sell the potatoes. Audrey never forgot an old man who came to look at the potatoes. He kept saying what sounded like, "See Fro." He was saying that the potatoes were frozen. Perhaps he was using part Spanish and part English, as was common with many native New Mexicans. He may have been saying, "Sí, fro." ("Yes, frozen.") Vern kept saying, "No, *no 'see fro.'*" The old man would pick up a potato and hold it in his hand and squeeze it and say the same thing over again. Audrey knew that the potatoes couldn't be frozen. They were in a room in the house, protected. But the old man was trying to get the potatoes for nothing. Even at her young age, Audrey knew her daddy desperately needed to sell the potatoes for a fair price.[1]

Vern traded with the Pueblo Indians, and one of them came to buy the pet sheep, Snowball and Sammy. Opal and Audrey cried. Years later, Audrey recalled in a taped interview:

> Opal and I were crying because he was taking our pets away and the Indian was being very sympathetic and telling us that he would be very good to them. He was petting them, talking real nice. I can't remember what he said now but for years Opal and I would repeat what he had said—under any similar circumstances when it was appropriate. He was trying to comfort us and assure us that nothing bad was going to happen to those lambs. He was going to take good care of them and they'd be just fine. He was very nice and caring![2]

When Vern wasn't freighting, he worked as a cowboy on various ranches. Vern enjoyed the children's delighted faces when he would come home with a surprise for them. His favorite surprise was a bag of peanuts. He would hold them behind his back and say, "Guess what I have."

Opal, already learning the native Spanish of the area, would reply, "*Cacahuetes*—peanuts."

If a lemon had been purchased and Mabel had made a lemon pie, Vern would hold the pie behind his back and ask the girls to guess what their mama had made for them.

There was a diphtheria epidemic in Taos. The little Martinez girl next door, Opal's best friend, was stricken. The doctor quarantined the house and did what he could. But the little girl died. Mabel gave her sympathy to the neighbors, but there was nothing anyone could do. The child was gone. Mabel began to worry about her own children.

"Opal was playing with the little girl next door just before that child got diphtheria," Mabel fretted.

"There's nothing we can do," Vern replied, clearly worried. As Mabel and Vern worried, they watched the children carefully and prayed for their protection. Edward was just about eight months old when the epidemic hit. Opal was just barely three years old. Audrey was five and very protective of her younger sister and brother. But she could not protect them from disease.

Their worst fears were realized when Opal developed the frightening symptoms of diphtheria. The Taos doctor was summoned. He came to the house and examined Opal. He would not give her the diphtheria antitoxin, either because he didn't have any or he did not think Opal needed it. Vern went to the local pharmacist and bought a throat spray that was supposed to help.

"Little Sister" continued to get worse, and the doctor still would not give her antitoxin. Audrey heard him mutter to himself as he left the house, "Well, it is best if they die while they're babies, anyway." Audrey was furious that the doctor didn't seem to care if Opal died.

Vern and Mabel were not going to give up on their little girl. Since there was only one doctor in Taos, and he would not give Opal the antitoxin she needed, Vern decided to take Opal to Dr. Martin in Mora—about 35 miles away. Vern borrowed a car—probably a Model T Ford—to take Opal to Mora. The family got into the car, hoping that Opal would soon get the help she needed. But the car would not make it up to the top of the very long, steep Holman Hill. They had to turn around and go back to Taos.

Mabel and Vern were desperate to save their child. Vern went back to the druggist. The pharmacist explained that Opal's severe diphtheria symptoms had developed because she had not been given the antitoxin. He feared she would not live long without medical help. "Get her out of this town and to a hospital," he suggested. Vern nodded and wondered where he would find the money for a trip out of town.

Vern and Mabel were terrified that their child would die. They were in such torment, having exhausted their resources, they felt helpless and fell into one another's arms. Weeping together, Mabel and Vern gave vent to their frustration and fear.

"What can we do, Vern?" Mabel sobbed. "If we could only get Opal to a good doctor!" Tears flowed down Mabel's cheeks. "She's getting worse by the minute!"

"I know," Vern said, choking back his own tears as he held his wife in his arms. "Maybe I can borrow a better car from another friend and we can try to get to Mora again."

"We must try something! We can't just do nothing and watch her die!" Mabel said, her shoulders shaking with sobs.

"No. We won't let her die," Vern agreed, his own arms trembling as he held his sobbing wife. He felt more helpless than he had ever felt in his life. "I'll borrow another car."

Audrey watched her parents as they stood in the living room, sobbing in despair after their futile attempt to get to Mora. They had all been praying for a miracle. Audrey knew that was the only thing that would save Opal.

Suddenly, Audrey heard someone knocking at the front door. Her parents didn't hear the knocking as they held one another, weeping. Audrey tugged on her mother's skirt.

"Someone's knocking at the door," Audrey said, getting Mabel's attention with a strong tug.

While her parents composed themselves, Audrey peeped out the window pane and saw a man standing there.

"There's a man at the door. I don't know who he is," Audrey declared.

After Mabel dried her eyes and Vern was composed, Mabel opened the door and admitted the man. Audrey wondered who he was. He might have been Vern's employer. He might have been the kind postmaster who had delivered their package on Christmas day. He might have been one of Vern's friends.

"What's wrong?" the man asked, seeing remnants of Mabel's tears and Vern's downcast eyes. He wondered if they had been fighting.

"Sit down," Mabel invited, "and we'll tell you."

She and Vern briefly described what they had been through and how sick Opal was. Vern explained that their situation was critical, that they were desperate.

"She needs a good doctor. The one here would not give her the antitoxin," Mabel explained. They had already described their frustration at failing to get Opal to the doctor in Mora.

"Well, the doctor in Mora may not have antitoxin to give her if there's so much of this thing around. Or he may be out, tending patients elsewhere. It might be a wasted trip," the visitor mused. "Besides, you need a doctor who is up to date on these things, a specialist. There is a train leaving here in an hour," the man said. "Where would you like to take Opal if you had the money?"

"Home to Lincoln where there are good doctors who can be trusted," Mabel replied. "And my mother is there to help nurse Opal back to health."

Years later, Audrey recalled:

Poor Opal! She couldn't hold her head up and she was cross-eyed and that scared Daddy and Mama to death. They were both crying and the Postmaster, or somebody, came along and looked through the front door window and saw them and thought they had been fighting. They hadn't been. So whoever it was, asked what was wrong and they told him about Opal, and he said they had better take her someplace to a good doctor right away.[3]

Mabel, Audrey, Opal and baby Edward were on that train headed toward Lincoln when it pulled out later that day. Vern came as soon as he could raise the money and dispose of whatever property wasn't needed. He left a lot of things, but every time the family moved some things were always left behind.

Mabel immediately found help for Opal. Later, after Opal had begun to recover, Mabel found an orthopedic specialist to examine Opal. The doctor said he would have to put braces on Opal's legs and provide a brace to hold her head up. Audrey recalled later that he had a modern, new car and made house calls.

Mabel's mother Alice had been going to a chiropractor and persuaded Mabel to take Opal to see him. He used an electric vibrator, among other things, and within six weeks Opal was well.

Several weeks later the orthopedic specialist came in his big fancy car and brought all the braces he had made for Opal. He walked up to the house and knocked on the door. Mabel told him Opal was already well. Audrey was sitting on the front porch swing. The doctor asked, "Is that the child?"

Mabel said, "No," and indicated Opal who was playing in the yard.[4]

The doctor was very surprised to see that Opal was well and then he left. Audrey listened to her mother and grandmother discussing Opal's full recovery, saying how grateful they were for the good help they had received.

Audrey never forgot the man who had come to the door in Taos that day when Opal's life was hanging in the balance, when her parents were gripped in the paroxysm of fear for their child's life. Whether he was an employer who gave Vern an advance on a salary or a friend willing to loan the money or some benefactor with a gift remains unknown. But he arrived just in time. Audrey knew the strange man at the door was responsible for saving Opal's life. To the Clements family, he was a hero. He would remain a mystery. When he gave or loaned the money for the trip to see a physician in Lincoln, he was an answer to prayer. Audrey thanked God for all the helpers who saved Opal's life.

Years later, after Vern had passed on, Audrey asked her mother if she remembered the name of the man whose timing was so apropos when Opal was critically ill. Mabel said that he was a complete stranger to her, although Vern seemed to know him.

"Angels don't always come to us with wings. Sometimes they come in the form of an ordinary looking man at the door," Mabel replied.

Audrey only knew that a stranger knocked at the door at a crucial time. And "Little Sister" did not die.

10

End of the War to End all Wars: Taos to Lincoln

Mabel was glad to be back in Nebraska, away from the diphtheria epidemic and the poverty they had known in Taos, New Mexico. They had been poor in Nebraska, too, but there were relatives there to help. They lived in a house close to Audrey's Auntie Belle and Sam Zipp and were not far from Alice and Tom Shirley's home. Vern found work at a dairy. Audrey had begun kindergarten before they went to Taos, so when they returned to Lincoln, she was able to return to school. In some notes, "Some Early Childhood Memories," Audrey wrote:

> I started to kindergarten before we went to Taos at Clinton School in Lincoln, Nebraska—the same school where my father, an 8th grade student, dropped out. I enjoyed kindergarten. There was a boy my age [Carl] with curly dark brown hair and most beautiful brown

eyes. I loved him and made up day dreams about him. There was much hullabloo about smallpox vaccinations. I hadn't been vaccinated, and my grandmother Alice Shirley (Mrs. Tom) was afraid for me to have one. She recalled first one neighbor and then another that lost an arm due to the scratching needle—and even one child that died. I went happily to school, unvaccinated. There we drew around bright colored fall leaves and learned ABC's. And I watched Carl when the teacher wasn't looking. I day dreamed that he was a doctor and gave me my vaccination—sticking me with a needle and I would retaliate by giving him one. Now I wonder how that came into my 6 year old mind. Was it in my genes to hurt the one you love? In later years I remembered other savage type thoughts and developed the theory that every human being goes through every state of development from primitive savagery and cruelty [until] gradually the phase passes with more civilized thoughts and actions.

There was a little blond boy, Joe, that was our contemporary. He used to walk home with me as he lived beyond 26th street where my grandmother lived. He was from a poor family and looked it. My grandmother was a seamstress so I had nice clothes. Carl was a rich boy and his white shirt and neat dark pants showed it. As Joe and I walked along the sidewalk, Carl would be on the other side of the street hurling insults at us. Then he took to throwing rocks. It broke my heart—the one I adored throwing rocks at me! Now with a few psychology classes and years of observation I know that was his way of showing that he liked me and was jealous of Joe. If I had mentioned my heartache to Mama or Daddy, they might have set me straight; but I didn't. After dodging Carl's poorly aimed rocks, Joe and I would go sit in an old piano case in Grandma's back yard discussing and pondering why Carl threw rocks at us. Joe's astute observation: "Carl isn't as nice as his clothes."[1]

Audrey was in first grade in Lincoln when the teacher asked the children to save all the cherry pits they could and bring them to school. World War I was going on, and somehow cherry pits were used to make gas masks. Audrey had saved a whole bag of them and had them in her desk. But she was too shy to tell the teacher she had them. One day they were gone. She wondered if the teacher had found them or if the janitor had thrown them out.

Diphtheria had been defeated in the Clements family, and they thanked God for sparing Opal and that the rest of the family was spared. But there were other deadly diseases in those days, the days before antibiotics when the average life expectancy for white men in the United States in 1900 was only 48.2 years and for white women was only 51.1 years. (For nonwhites it was 32.5 years for men and 35 years for women.) The Clements family was to confront the enemy of disease more than once.

> Daddy was coming home one evening and I was going to go meet him. He saw a mad dog coming toward me and he hollered at me to get back in the yard. I minded. I didn't stop and stand there and ask why—like half of our kids do now! I turned and ran. Daddy always said I got through such a tiny hole in that fence—even a rabbit couldn't have gone through it but I did! My Guardian Angel shoved me through I know because the dog couldn't get through! Mad dogs were very common in those days. If you saw one you did your best to avoid it.[2]

The year 1918 brings up images of thousands of people dying of the deadly influenza sometimes called the "Spanish flu." It hit the United States in two waves, in the spring of 1918 and in the fall of 1918. Vern was working at the dairy when he came down with influenza. He developed double pneumonia along with it. Since he couldn't work, the family ran out of money. All the children had "La Grippe" as well. Audrey's Uncle Bruce, who was about thirteen or fourteen, came to the house as soon as Audrey recovered and carried her over to Dammuzzy's house. Each child was taken there as soon as recovery was evident, to be cared for while the others recovered. Finally after the rest of the family was well, Mabel caught the "flu." By that time Vern was recovering. Apparently Dammuzzy and Bruce did not get sick.

Some families, however, were decimated; and few escaped without losing someone. Years later, Dr. Gordon E. Wickman (husband of Audrey's half-sister, Millicent Shearer Wickman) spoke of that time when he was a child in Wisconsin. He was just Audrey's age and remembered his family's being sick during that pandemic, although he was spared. He recalled that when he was just five years old, his entire family was bed-ridden with the flu. He said he never understood why he didn't get it. But since he was the only member of the family able to be up, he had to do everything necessary to keep the household going. He recalled having to get the stove going to provide heat. He had to carry food and water to those who were ill. He didn't know anything about preparing meals, but his mother would tell him what to do, and he would follow her directions. He recalled:

> One morning I went in to take some breakfast I'd prepared to my uncle who was in bed in one of the spare bedrooms. He was asleep and I couldn't

wake him up. He was very cold and very white. I told my mother that Uncle wouldn't wake up. She began to cry. She knew he was dead. I realized it then. It was the first time I had ever known anyone to die. Gradually my family recovered, but I never forgot that time when I was the only one not sick and how I felt when my uncle died.[3]

In those days there was no "sick leave" from work. If a man didn't work, he didn't get paid. Mabel was down to her last dollar at that time. For many years thereafter Mabel kept that dollar in her purse—a grim reminder.

Audrey learned in later years that the "Spanish flu" of 1918 took more lives than The Great War—World War I. About 43,000 servicemen mobilized for the war died of the "flu." The disease spread easily in the close quarters of the soldiers. Of the U.S. soldiers who died in Europe, half of them died of influenza. Influenza killed 25 million people in a single year. About 675,000 Americans, or 28 percent of all Americans, died of influenza.[4] A popular children's jump rope ditty of the time recalled the terrible disease:

I had a little bird,
Its name was Enza.
I opened the window,
And in-flu-enza.[5]

Audrey went to Clinton School for a little while when they were living in Lincoln. She was in kindergarten before they moved to Taos. When they moved back to Nebraska because Opal was sick, Audrey began first grade. Both Vern and Mabel had gone to Clinton School, a big, two-story brick building.

Audrey's Aunt Thelma Shirley and Uncle Bruce Shirley both attended Clinton School. Thelma and Bruce were in a school play there. Audrey wanted to go to the play but it was a nickel for a child's ticket. The day of the play Audrey begged her mother for a nickel, but Mabel said she had nothing to give her.

Audrey walked away from the house and went back to school after lunch that day feeling very disappointed. The play was in the afternoon. Audrey found a quiet corner and began to cry. She didn't want anyone to see her crying. She thought to herself, "I'm a big girl. I'm supposed to be grown up, and big girls don't cry."

All the children, including Audrey, who didn't have nickels to go to the play collected in one room upstairs. There were six or eight of them. They looked out the windows and down into a kind of walkway. The school building must have been in an "L" shape. The children got to see some of the actors dressed up as they went along the outside of the building and into the back or side door.

Audrey's heart was broken as she realized that she couldn't go to the play for the lack of a nickel! She sympathized with the other children in the room with her, those unable to attend because they were too poor.

"How come you're not goin' to the play?" one of the boys asked Audrey.

"Same reason as you—I don't have a nickel," Audrey replied.

"Well ain't your grandma got two kids in the play? She's gonna go see them. Why didn't she take you?"

"Yes, Thelma and Bruce Shirley are in the play," Audrey affirmed. She knew Dammuzzy would be going to the play to see them. She had been working with them on it for months!

"I guess she's been too busy helping them get ready to think about me," Audrey said. "She probably thought my mama would take me, but my mama doesn't have any money. Anyway, we can see the people going in. Let's watch!"

Audrey was too small to understand how many nickels it took to feed a family. She was also too young to understand much about the war. World War I had begun in 1914 when she was just two years old. She heard the adults talking about it, but she didn't pay much attention to talk about "The Great War." Mabel didn't speak of it to her because she didn't think children should worry about such things. However, Mabel kept a journal. She wrote:

> When we think of war we think in terms of human lives, the lives of our children. Now he (a child) is a potential sacrifice. There is something wrong when one man or any small group of men can declare a war and force youth to fight it.[6]

Mabel, along with other Americans, prayed for an end to war. She was a mother. She wanted her children to grow up in a peaceful world.

There was a bright spot in 1918 in spite of the illness and the poverty. It was the morning of Audrey's sixth birthday, November 11, 1918. It was Armistice Day—the 11th hour of the 11th day of the 11th month. President Woodrow Wilson called the Great War (World War I) the "War to End all Wars."

"Wake up, Audrey! Wake up!" Mabel shook Audrey gently.

Audrey was in a deep sleep.

"What time is it?" Audrey asked. "Is it morning already?"

"It's only two a.m.," her mother explained. "But listen! I wanted you to hear the bells!"

Audrey listened and heard all the bells ringing and whistles blowing. For a moment she thought it was a New Year's celebration, but she knew it wasn't New Year's Day.

"What is it, Mama?" Audrey asked.

"The war is over! It's over! Now all our boys can come home!" Mabel spoke in an excited voice.

Audrey got up, wondering what it all meant. She had never heard such noises at that time of the night. It took a few moments for the words to register: The War is over! Audrey recalled in later years:

> I remember the morning of my sixth birthday, November 11, 1918. Mama got up and got me up at two a.m. to listen to all the bells ringing and whistles blowing! World War I was over! Fireworks went off and the town was alive with sounds of jubilation! People were whooping and hollering and dancing in the streets. They were using anything they could find to make noise to celebrate! Some way the town fathers got a parade put together with floats by the afternoon in downtown Lincoln! They even had a float that had the Kaiser hanging in effigy. His head was hanging down with an old German hat on with a "spear-like" emblem pointing up out of the top! Everyone was ecstatic! After all it was the end of the War! The WAR TO END ALL WARS! It called for a truly great celebration![7]

The Clements family had Christmas at Dammuzzy's house that year—quite a contrast from the Christmas they'd spent in Taos. Audrey's grandmother always went all out for Christmas. Uncle Bruce dressed up like Santa Claus. The big tree was elaborately trimmed; the star on top reached the ceiling. Everything had to be fancy—and just right—when Dammuzzy was in charge.

Audrey managed to save one keepsake from those wonderful Christmas days spent at her grandmother's house in Nebraska—a candle from the tree. It is a two-inch high yellow candle, about a fourth of an inch in diameter. It sits in a little candle holder attached to a "clip" to put on the tree. The clip appears to be made of thin tin with a little copper wire spring. The top, where the candle sits, has red paint over it.

The year 1918 ended with a very grateful family. None had died from the "flu" as so many around the country had. The Clements family had good reason to thank God they had all pulled through. Mabel and Vern sang again, with Mabel playing the piano or Vern playing the violin.

Although it had been a difficult year, with disappointments, sickness, and war, Audrey's sixth birthday was ushered in with the biggest celebration she'd ever seen, the joy of the end of the war. The Great War, like the "flu," had devastated many families. It is estimated that between 112,000 and 116,600 American lives were lost in World War I, and many returned home wounded and maimed. As the year came to a close, it brought gratitude for the end of the Great War.

Audrey recalled that her mother had said, "This was a terrible war. When you grow up, remember how we celebrated when it ended. There can never be another war. From now on, this country will live in peace. Never again will we send our young men overseas to die in war." Vern nodded in agreement. War was too terrible. Too many had died. Nothing so terrible could ever happen again. The children believed it.

11

No More Shetlands! Lincoln to Bradshaw and Back to Lincoln

Every generation as far back as Audrey's history can be traced has been devastated by fire. In the early 1800's, Audrey's great, great grandparents, the affluent O'Roneys, boarded a ship in Ireland for a new home in America, bringing all their wealth with them. In the midst of the journey, their ship caught fire. Everyone scrambled for the life boats. No lives were lost, but the ship burned and its remnants sank. Money, jewels, clothes—everything was gone. The O'Roney's arrived in America with nothing except what they had managed to carry onto the life boat. They never fully regained their wealth.

The family apparently dropped the "O" and changed the name to Roney for a better "American" name. Lavern Clifford Clements was the son of Emma Maria Roney, the child of those immigrants. Her middle name "Maria" was pronounced with a long "i" sound in the second syllable—rather than an "e" sound for the letter "i."

Audrey's mother's side of the family, too, had experienced loss from fire. Mabel Edna Waddell, born in 1890 on a farm near Ord, Nebraska, was about two years old when her mother awoke in the middle of the night to find the house in flames. Since Alice Waddell's husband was away at the time, Alice could only rush outside with her daughter Mabel in her arms. Mabel always remembered watching the house burn from a safe distance away. The Waddells had nothing left but the clothes they wore.

Although the Waddell family tree had been traced back to Abraham Young with earliest records to 1767, Mabel always claimed that her father's roots could be traced back to William the Conqueror through the Ogle side of the family. A great aunt had completed a genealogy which took the family tree back from James Oliver Waddell and Lucille Ogle, Mabel's grandparents, through the Ogle family to various ancestors, including Edward I, Henry III, Henry II, Henry I, and to William the Conqueror. Mabel believed her father was a direct descendant of the famous Norman who overthrew the Saxons and became king in 1066 following the Battle of Hastings. In the Bayeux tapestry there is an appealing bit of work that pictures a burning house with a woman and a little child making an escape on the fatal day of William's siege in Britain. When Audrey saw a picture of the tapestry, she sympathized with those suffering loss to fire.

When Audrey was just a child fire struck the family again. Alice's second husband, Tom F. Shirley, was a brick layer and worked in construction. Tom and Alice had been married about 1901. They trained Shetland ponies. They had about fifty ponies. One large pony was named Julius Caesar, purchased in about 1917. The pony's mother had been hit by a car and the unborn colt had been delivered by Caesarian section—hence his name. The pony was trained to do tricks on stage. Tom had shows in theatres all over the area. Audrey got to see his show when Tom was performing with the pony in a theatre in Lincoln. The pony counted how old he was with his hooves and followed many other commands. For the last act of the show, the horse would lie down on a regular size bed, lean over, and pull the United States flag up over himself with his teeth. Although Audrey only saw him one time at the theatre, she sometimes had a chance to watch Tom teaching the pony at home.

Tom's business card read: "T. F. Shirley, Wood, Wire and Metal Lathing: Work Done When **You** Want it Done. Lincoln, Nebr., Phone B1262, 1903 North 26th St." On the other side, the card said, "T.F. Shirley, Shetland Ponies," with the same telephone number and address.[1]

Audrey's grandmother Alice Shirley had fancy pony teams that pulled a little light buggy. Audrey said in later years:

> Dammuzzy had real fancy pony teams that pulled a little light buggy and she'd drive. Her ponies were only about a yard high—they were special. I think they were thirty-two inches high. They were real small. She wanted them to be little and fancy. They were trained to act real fancy when she drove them. Dammuzzy was a show person. She would drive those ponies and look after them and train them. She displayed them. She'd

drive one or two ponies at a time. She hitched them to a buggy, and she was dressed up real fancy and would go around the track at the County Fair or go around the race track and show them off, but, incidentally, showing herself off too! She was very good at showmanship and she was very proud and looked it when she was driving those ponies.[2]

Then the tragedy of fire struck suddenly. Alice happened to look out the window one night and saw flames coming from the barn.

Alice shouted, "The barn's on fire! Quick, Tom! We've got to get the ponies out!"

Alice raced toward the barn. She could hear the terrified animals. Tom's swift legs carried him ahead of Alice and he reached the barn first. He went into the inferno and brought out one or two of the ponies. Alice, too, went in to save them. But the roof collapsed just as they had begun to rescue the ponies. Fortunately, neither of them was hurt. But it was too late for most of the ponies.

Neighbors came to help put out the flames before they spread to the house. Alice made her way back to the house and collapsed in her grief. The fire had been too rapid and left very little time to save the Shetlands. Only a few of the Shetlands were saved. Alice was broken-hearted. She and Tom gave up on raising ponies after that. For Alice and her family, there would be no more Shetlands.

There were more devastating fires in the family. Audrey's young life had only begun to see the tragedy of fire, as later chapters will describe.

Soon after the fire, Vern got a job working for a farmer at Bradshaw, Nebraska, a very small community. So the family moved again. Auntie Belle was helping load the wagon to help them move.

> The wagon was pretty full—pretty well loaded. They were putting everything in as fast as they could and the last thing to go in was the food. The last of the food to go in was the bread, so Auntie Belle wrapped all the bread up and there was no place to put it so she had some newspapers she wrapped it in and stuck it down inside the slop jar. Of course it was well protected—wrapped. Mama was just horrified! She never could believe that anybody would do that, but poor dear Auntie Belle did. I guess it rode just fine to Bradshaw![3]

The winter of 1917-1918 at Bradshaw had so much snow that there were deep drifts higher than the big granary. Audrey wrote years later, "A fox walked into the top of the barn and along the rafters and had rooster for dinner."[4] Audrey recalled how difficult the winters were in Nebraska. The snow would pile up and would not melt until the next snow storm came along to pile up more snow on top.

> The snow was piled very high up against it (the granary) and a rooster flew up and roosted on the cross beams in the top and thought he was safe there. A fox came up on top of the snow and went in and got the rooster—poor rooster! He wasn't safe after all! Just goes to show you—safe isn't always safe! You do your best to protect yourself but it doesn't always work! Somebody else or something else is going to do you in if they can![5]

When Edward was about two years of age, he would go into the barn and hit the huge horses on their noses with a long stick and say, "Whoa up Susie, Whoa up Major." Susie and Major were the big team Vern used in his work. Vern could never tolerate anyone being unkind to animals, so when he caught Edward hitting the horses, the boy was given a proper lecture.[6]

Vern only worked until summer. When Vern's job was finished, the family loaded the wagon to move back to Lincoln to stay with Dammuzzy once again. Vern had left to start his new job, so Mabel had to move by herself. As the family prepared to leave, they missed Edward. They looked in the storm cellar, in the barn, and every place, even down the well. They finally found him rolled up in a rug where he had crawled in and gone to sleep.[7]

When it was time to move, Mabel had no way of hauling all the furniture. Audrey wrote:

> Mabel had contacted a second hand man and told him we had bedsteads, tables and chairs, a kitchen stove, and other household goods—and the rug that Edward had been hidden in. He said he would give her $25 but when he came and it was time for us to leave, he only paid $5.00, and that's all.[8]

Mabel always said she was cheated, but she had no choice. So the family moved back to "Dammuzzy's" place and Audrey went back to school. Audrey always loved school but seldom got to stay in one school for a full year. Mabel's other children were no exception. Vern had what Audrey called "itchy feet." Soon he wanted to go back to New Mexico! This time Vern chose Las Vegas. Audrey wrote:

Before the leaves had all turned [fall of 1919] my folks decided to go back to New Mexico, [to Las Vegas] widely known for the Cowboys' reunion and Teddy Roosevelt's Rough Riders. "It is good cattle country," Daddy said. "Lots of big ranches. I can get a job with no trouble."

Daddy had survived a bout with the 1918 flu and double pneumonia and was not looking forward to another Nebraska winter. They had gone to Avis, New Mexico when I was four months old and later to Taos when I was four [years old] and the warm sunshine drew him back.[9]

The tragic fire that had put an end to the Shetland Pony business affected Tom Shirley, as well as Alice, very deeply. Before very long, Alice and Tom Shirley separated.

Alice later met and married her third husband, James B. Caldwell, and moved to Portland, Oregon. Alice's third husband was a veteran of the Spanish-American War. He composed a piece of music entitled, "Officer of the Guard March."[10] The front of the 3-page composition featured his picture with the caption, "Lt. J. B. Caldwell, 1st Wash. U.S.V." Mabel wrote on the sheet music, "My stepfather who was in the Philippine War, 1898."[11]

Alice continued to stay in close touch with Mabel and vowed to visit the grandchildren as often as possible. She hoped Mabel and her family had the fortitude to survive in that "wilderness" country of New Mexico.

12

Gambling in the First Las Vegas: Lincoln to Las Vegas

Las Vegas, New Mexico, the original Las Vegas, existed long before the Nevada city known for its gambling took on the name. Unlike the Nevada city, the Las Vegas of the Territory of New Mexico prided itself on its small town atmosphere—where gambling was illegal—although there were plenty of illegal activities going on. Around 1900, Las Vegas was the largest city in New Mexico. When the Americans began trading, bringing their goods over the Santa Fe Trail, the little Spanish settlement of Las Vegas began to grow and soon became the biggest town in that part of the west.

Las Vegas lies at the foot of the Sangre de Cristo Mountain range in the north central part of New Mexico. It was first established in 1835 under the Spanish Crown. Francisco Vásquez de Coronado, one of the first Europeans to explore the Southwest, passed through during his search in 1540 for the Seven Cities of Cibola. Three hundred years later covered wagons followed the Santa Fe Trail west through the area. The area became part of Mexican Territory (from 1821 to 1846) and then was acquired by the United States of America. In 1821, William Bucknell opened the Santa Fe Trail between Missouri and New Mexico. Located on the Gallinas River, Las Vegas was a main stopping place on the Santa Fe Trail. The area that is now Las Vegas was settled by Spanish colonists, many of whom had come over with priests to convert Native Americans.

Las Vegas, or "the meadows," located on the eastern slope of the Sangre de Cristo range on a Pecos River tributary known as the Gallinas River, was a quiet little town until the coming of the railroad in 1879. At that time Las Vegas became a boom town with many businesses, saloons, a trolley car system, and an opera house. Beautiful Victorian houses were built. The largest supply depot in the Southwest from 1851 to 1981 was at Fort Union, twenty-eight miles to the north of Las Vegas. The area was known for its wonderful climate, so in 1880 the Montezuma Hot Springs Hotel was built near the famous hot springs by the railroad people at the mouth of the Gallinas canyon. The growing Las Vegas got the first telephone line in the Territory. A line ran from Las Vegas to the Montezuma Hotel in 1880.

In 1893 the Territorial Normal School was established at Las Vegas—now New Mexico Highlands University. About the same time the Insane Asylum or the State Hospital was established. Founded by the legislature of 1889, it was opened for service in 1893. (Today the state psychiatric hospital is called New Mexico Behavioral Health Institute.) In 1879, a daily newspaper, the *Las Vegas Daily Optic,* was established. Additionally, a tuberculosis hospital, a Presbyterian Mission School, a Brothers School, the Las Vegas Academy, and the Academy of the Immaculate Conception were established in the late nineteenth century. It was not until 1941 that KFUN radio station was established, situated on a hill above Las Vegas.

Audrey was always interested in history. When she was a reporter in the 1950s, she wrote an article for the *Las Vegas Daily Optic,* "High-Wheelers of Santa Fe Trail May be Recalled:"

> Dusty, high wheeled, high walled wagons rocked slowly behind creeping oxen over the Santa Fe Trail to Las Vegas, nearly 125 years ago.

Lighter wagons, and buggies, drawn by mules and horses would pull out of the ruts that were growing deeper each year. They could swing around the slow oxen, and pull away from the heavy wagons at a steady walk.

Men on horseback could ride swiftly over the trail, covering 40 or 50 miles in a day. But the plodding oxen, yoked to the canvas covered freight wagons, did well if they put 10 miles behind them in a day. It would take a day of ox travel time to cover the distance from Upper town [Las Vegas] to Romeroville.

When the tired oxen ground down the hills into the valley of the meadows they watered at the rolling river.

If the wagons rolled in from the east they followed the trail along what is now University Ave. After the Plaza was established, wagons camped there, where mountain wine was plentiful.

While the freighters camped at night in the Gallinas valley, coyotes prowled just outside the circle of campfire light. Or howled at the moon from the meadows.

Today, not a half mile outside of the circle of light cast by the night lights at Perkins stadium, [on the campus of New Mexico Highlands University] residents of 8th St. have heard descendants of those early coyotes singing to the same moon.[1]

In another article for the *Las Vegas Daily Optic* in July of 1952, Audrey wrote:

The yellowed pages of an early New Mexico history printed more than 50 years ago says that until 1824 all goods brought into New Mexico territory were packed in on horses and mules.

In 1824 heavy freight wagons were introduced to the trail. The trip with wagons was longer and harder. For the heavy wagons had to detour around each boulder and gulley while pack animals could travel through narrow places the wagons could not go.

The old history says, "The first caravan of wheeled vehicles to cross the plains (from Missouri) was brought to Taos in 1924 by Colonel Marmaduke, of Missouri, and consisted of eighty men, twenty-five wagons and teams, and $30,000 in merchandise, besides a number of pack animals."

Legal Santa Fe trade began in 1924. Before that Mexican Law had prohibited the trade. It took from 45 to 60 days to cross the long miles from Missouri to Santa Fe. In 1830 the first oxen were used by the freighters on the Santa Fe Trail, according to old records.²

Audrey interviewed Milton W. Callon, author of *Las Vegas, New Mexico . . . The Town that Wouldn't Gamble*.³ He said that the first village in the area was San Miguel del Vado (Saint Michael's Ford) which is twenty-two miles southwest of Vegas—a settlement that had its origin years before that when a group of Indians who had been cast out of their tribe as a result of their conversion to Christianity settled there.⁴

Audrey knew Milt Callon when he ran the Texaco Station on North Grand Avenue in Las Vegas and worked on his book in his spare time. He and Audrey were acquainted, as she often took her car to his service station. There at times they compared notes about historical events. He liked to review the early history of Las Vegas and tell about the early explorers. In 1835 Las Vegas, the last Spanish colony established in North America, had its beginnings. It was named *Nuestra Señora de los Dolores de Las Vegas* (Our Lady of Sorrows of the Meadows.)

From the time of its founding, Las Vegas was the hub of trade. After 1843 trade boomed to an even greater extent. The caravans stopping at the Plaza provided merchandise for stores and created even greater employment. The freighting business was boosted.

In 1846 the U.S. declared war on Mexico. General Stephen Kearney captured Santa Fe and built Fort Marcy. Charles Bent was named governor. General Kearney declared that New Mexico was now a part of the United States of America. (Mexico had ceded New Mexico over to the U.S. under the Treaty of Guadalupe Hidalgo.) In 1850 the land of New Mexico became a U.S. Territory with Santa Fe as its capital. The population was 61,547 at that time.

When the railroad came through Las Vegas in 1879, the town grew. It became a town of saloons, gambling halls, and brothels. In the 1880s, the vigilantes sometimes conducted hangings. By 1885, Las Vegas was the commercial center of the Southwest. It had gas and water works, a telephone system, street cars, and a foundry. The large wholesale houses were outfitting centers for lumbering camps, mining camps, ranches, and even the military. Hay, lumber, wool, cattle, and ice became big business.

Well known people, including outlaws, came to Las Vegas, some just passing through, others to stay. Doc Holladay, Bat Masterson, and Wyatt Earp were among the famous men who walked the streets of Las Vegas in the 1880s.

Tom Mix films and other silent films were made in Las Vegas—and later the movie industry used Las Vegas as its setting more than once. Well-known movies filmed in or around Las Vegas include "The Evil" (filmed at the

Montezuma "castle") and "Red Dawn." More recently, "No Country for Old Men" was partially filmed in Las Vegas, with the Plaza Hotel featured in several scenes. Various business and industries have come and gone, but the population has stayed at about 15,000 for years.

Las Vegas became the ice kingdom of New Mexico. Ice from the big ponds in the Gallinas Canyon was shipped to El Paso, Texas and to railroad storage plants. A railroad track was laid up the canyon to remove ice by the carload from the great ice house at Montezuma where the famous Hot Springs were located—and where the beautiful Montezuma Hotel was located. (Today it is the site of the Armand Hammer United World College of the American West.) Audrey recalled that the big work horses wore cleats on their shoes so they would not slip on the ice as they walked across the ponds.

It is no wonder Vern was attracted to a place with such exciting opportunities. Even in 1915 Las Vegas was still the hub of activity in the State. Mabel and Vern both thought the climate in New Mexico was wonderful. Having lived through the cold Nebraska winters, even the northern mountains of New Mexico seemed mild to them. Although the growing season was short, Mabel could still plant a vegetable garden and a flower garden every spring, and she soon learned what plants would grow best in the northern New Mexican climate.

Mabel and Vern were told that in the Las Vegas area, summer day time temperatures seldom rise much above ninety degrees Fahrenheit, and it is usually fifty to sixty degrees at night. Winters seldom get below zero and highs on winter days are generally about fifty degrees. The annual average precipitation is about eighteen inches, very little humidity. There are only a few times when the sun doesn't shine sometime during the day. Compared to the Nebraska climate, New Mexico looked very promising.

In January of 1912 New Mexico became the 47th state of the Union. The population of the Territory in 1910 was 327,301. Las Vegas, New Mexico would later become known as the home of Teddy Roosevelt's Rough Riders when, after the famous Battle of San Juan Hill and the end of the Spanish-American War, the men met in Las Vegas for a reunion and later vowed to meet there every year "to the last man." That was the beginning of the famous annual Teddy Roosevelt's Rough Riders' Reunion and Rodeo that was held in Las Vegas as long as Rough Riders could attend. With the death of "the last man," the days of the Reunion were over, although the rodeo and the annual fiesta continued. Years later Audrey wrote in her "Cowboy's Reunion Notes:"

> The Cowboys' Reunion was going strong back then [1919].

Established in 1915, it commemorated the Rough Riders Reunion held in 1899 in Las Vegas with Teddy and the boys planning to return to Vegas for further get-togethers. However, the ramrodders decided since so many Rough Riders and their relatives were cowboys, this should be the "Cowboys' Reunion." It was widely publized and by the early 1920's the thing to do was "Git fer Vegas" for the annual big 4th of July Parade and several days of rodeoing at the Rodeo grounds. The street car went around and you could walk from there. All of the ranchers entered wagons and riders in the parade. The McNearney [or MacInerney] Brothers entered the Cowboys' Chuck Wagon. Daddy was an expert with horses and teams, as well as a pretty good bronco buster, as I remember it. Women contestants pretended to be camping. At a signal they jumped out of bed rolls, pulled on boots, grabbed the horses, and hitched them to the wagon. The wagon to arrive home first won. Daddy and his partner didn't win and as I remember he took part in the bronc riding. I remember him calming down some bronc while it was saddled; at that time much of the action took place in front of the stands. The Cowboys' Reunion continued for years, interrupted briefly by Depression and War. Years later, in the late 1950s and 1960s, it was killed off by forgetting to designate it as the Cowboys' Reunion. They headlined it as plain old rodeo. Every jerk water in the state had a rodeo, but only Vegas had a real Cowboys' Reunion. The death knell was sounded when a young green ramrod took over. They took over plans for the big event. Then to modernize the event they numbered all of the seats and sold tickets for certain seats in each section of the stands. I warned that sort of seating would kill the Cowboys' Reunion, and it did. I explained that the Cowboys' Reunion was just that—a reunion of home town and county friends and relatives. People would pop in from all sorts of places planning on a good time visiting with homefolks in the stands while watching the bronc busting or expert ropers. When each person was assigned to a certain numbered seat they couldn't meet and sit by all their friends and relatives close by. Under the old system if you had a big group you just arrived earlier so all of you could sit together. Now if Uncle Ed and his family showed up they had to sit widely separated. What was the fun of yelling for Pete or Joe out there in the arena if there wasn't a friendly ear close by to hear you? For your folks would "Git fer Vegas" and last minute visitors all found places by their pals, but with numbered seats everyone was stuck miles apart. Also the long time, hard working Optic Editor, Walter Vivian—mainstay in keeping the Reunion before the public, pushing and promoting it for months each year—the hard working editor displeased the new out of staters that had purchased the paper and they put him on the shelf. These new young green horns that came into Vegas, one after the other, did not know that the Cowboys' Reunion was a long time tradition in Las Vegas. They just designated it as a rodeo, *come to the rodeo*—so the Cowboys' Reunion died, killed [by] intending to modernize a tradition and killing it in the process. The lovely big grandstands, built by hundreds of hours of volunteer work by leading Las Vegans, were torn down and the land sold. [A super-center store is located there now.] Since then, the Jaycees have attempted to re-establish an annual rodeo and have built a small arena and stands. But the thrilling old Cowboys' Reunion was killed by attempts to modernization. As Society Editor of the *Optic*, I knew why people gathered in Vegas in early August. They came for a cowboys' or family or friends' reunion. The dumb promoters thought it was only for the rodeo so they promoted that and lost the show.[5]

While working for the *Las Vegas Daily Optic*, Audrey wrote a story entitled "Visit Of Teddy Roosevelt Is Recalled By Vegas Pioneer:"

> When Teddy Roosevelt and his Rough Riders held their first Reunion in Las Vegas in 1899, the future President of the United States slept in the southwest bedroom of the J. C. Schlott home on the corner of what is now Columbia and Ninth, after the wild echoes of celebrating cowboys died down and gave Las Vegans a chance to sleep.[6]

Audrey's work as a journalist gave her an opportunity to interview many interesting people, including some of the Rough Riders themselves. She interviewed Dee Bibb, world famous rodeo prize-winner; S. Omar Barker, well-known western writer; and some of the "old-timers" around the town such as Tom McGrath. He was the last child to be born at Fort Union before it closed. Audrey described him as "a colorful character." He wore a green chile on his shirt on St. Patrick's Day to show his heritage. "I'm half Irish and half Spanish-American," he said.

Audrey also interviewed Mrs. J. C. Schlott and wrote up the memories of the early Las Vegan.[7]

It was to the exciting, early Las Vegas that the Clements family moved in October of 1919. Vern Clements was not a gambling man and Las Vegas, New Mexico was not a place of legal gambling. But Vern did gamble there. He gambled that his family would be provided for in a place where they would be strangers. They knew no one, had no place to stay, no jobs, and very little money. Vern gambled that his family would be happy and prosperous there. Audrey wrote:

> Mama packed their big tin and wooden trunk with the leather handle and new lock with all of our belongings. That was bedding, including that [which] served as mattress when filled with straw. The dishes and a frying pan and a soup ladle and all our clothing and my school book—primer—hardly filled it. My grandmother [Alice] took us to the depot in her big buggy where my other grandmother Emma Maria Clements was waiting to "go to New Mexico with Vern!"[8]

Grandma Clements (Emma Maria) had gone with Vern and Mabel to New Mexico before. When she heard they were moving back, she asked to go along. She wasn't rich but she had a little pension from her husband, William Harper Clements who had served in the Civil War with the U.S. Volunteer Infantry. His folks lived in Illinois. He and Emma lived at 29th and Potter in Lincoln, Nebraska.

Emma Maria O'Roney had an interesting life. As mentioned before, at one time Grandma Clements' people had been very rich. Emma's great grandmother was called "Little Grandma." The family had come over from Ireland, but as stated before, the ship sank. They got into a life boat and managed to save some of their valuables, jewelry and money. With that money they bought a plantation in Kentucky. After the Civil War they lost it all. Their slaves left and the plantation owners didn't know how to do anything. Mabel was told that "Little Grandma" Clements didn't even know how to wash a pocket handkerchief.

Emma Clements had nine children, six Hammond children including Nettie, May and Clarence, and three Clements children: Lavern Clifford, Belle (who married Sam Zipp and later Fred Gushard) and Caley, the boy who died as an infant. After Emma left Mr. Hammond, she married William Harper Clements. Lavern's sister Belle was eight years older than Vern. Vern was born when Emma was over forty. He was frail and wasn't expected to live. But he became a strong young man who could tame a wild bronc, herd cattle, mend fences, and still have energy to go to a dance and flirt with the ladies in the evening. He wore cowboy boots that came high up on his legs and a "ten gallon" cowboy hat that made his six foot height look much taller.

The family had lived in Avis, Black Lake, and Taos. New Mexico was a state and should be a safe place, Vern told Mabel. It was becoming "civilized." And although Mabel didn't share his dream—she would have liked to stay to teach school in the more "civilized" Nebraska—she loved Vern enough to move. And she grew to love the climate in New Mexico. Audrey wrote:

I don't remember the train trip but I do remember arriving in Las Vegas and sitting in the train and looking out at a neatly kept bright green lawn by the Castaneda Hotel. [at the old Harvey House] Then Mama and Daddy helped us off and took us into the depot, Las Vegas depot. They told us to wait there for them. Mama was going out to find a place to live and Daddy was going to look for a job. The street car came close to the depot, so Mama took it and went house hunting while Daddy walked.[9]

The original Las Vegas which had been established by the first settlers in 1825 by the Don Louis C de Baca family had grown to the biggest town in that part of the country. In 1919 it was part of the new, thriving State, and the Clements family was excited about moving there.

Grandma Clements helped unload the family's baggage. They had a trunk and a bag or two—all of the belongings they had left after Mabel had moved the last time and sold the furniture. The children sat in the train and looked out the window while the adults gathered up their belongings. The lawn at the Casteneda Hotel was still green and perfectly groomed. The trees were still filled with green leaves. Audrey thought she had never seen such a pretty place as the Castaneda—the Harvey House. The Clements family arrived on the Santa Fe Railroad passenger train in Las Vegas, New Mexico on Opal's fifth birthday, October 25, 1919. Years later, Audrey wrote: "I was 6 going on 7 the day we landed in Las Vegas, New Mexico. I remember looking out the train window to a golden October day."[10]

Grandma stayed with them in the depot which was divided at that time—the men's waiting room and a lady's waiting room. Vern walked around town looking for a job and Mabel went to look for a place to stay. After taking the streetcar that ran from the depot in East Las Vegas over to the Plaza in West Las Vegas, Mabel found a three-room apartment at Mrs. Rainey's place, around the corner from the Plaza on West National. Then she went back to the depot to get Vern, the three children, Emma, and the luggage, and she took everyone to the Plaza on the streetcar to the apartment. To move to a new town with all their possessions in a trunk and to settle in, all in one day, was quite a feat. Audrey wrote:

> Mama found a small apartment on National Avenue just off the Plaza. It was behind Ike Davis' Meat Market and Grocery. A Mrs. Rainey rented it to her. Then she came back and got us and Daddy and the trunk from the baggage depot and [went] to old town and the Rainey apartment. It was Opal's 5th birthday. We got settled inside and Mama went around

the corner to Ike Davis' store and bought flour, etc. and came back and made a cake for the birthday girl.[11]

On October 25, 1919 Opal and Audrey sat on the high cement curb in front of the apartment and swung their feet against it while their mama baked the cake for the birthday celebration. Undoubtedly Mabel thought of the last time they'd been in New Mexico and how Opal had almost died of diphtheria. Opal's fifth birthday, now that they were back in New Mexico, was indeed something to celebrate! Audrey wrote in 1979 in unpublished notes:

> We are home, Ma said, with frying potatoes and onions and bacon perfuming the air. Through the good and the bad years—60 now—Las Vegas has been home base. We had a birthday cake for Opal. A two-room apartment—and we were at home in Las Vegas, New Mexico; and for the next 60 years Opal and I have wandered in and out of Las Vegas. But since that first birthday cake in Las Vegas, it has been home headquarters for us and still is.
> It hasn't all been cake and happiness—these 60 years since then—but it has been kind to us, and we still think it a fine place to call home. The Court House is newer since the 1930s. Our Lady of Sorrows Church has been renovated and changed. Cristo is still above the door and the devout, afoot or in high-powered cars, bow their heads and cross themselves today as then.[12]

In 1989, a newspaper article in the *Vegas Victorian Gazette* featured a picture of the children, Audrey and Opal Clements—a snapshot Mabel had taken when they had moved into the apartment. The girls were standing in front of it. The article was entitled, "Sisters Celebrate 70th," and told about the Clements girls. The story relates how they arrived by train in Las Vegas with their parents, Mr. and Mrs. L. C. Clements, brother Edward, and grandmother, Mrs. W. H. Clements. Their mother rode a street car to the Plaza, looking for an apartment. The article explains that street cars used to run up Sixth Street to St. Anthony's Hospital, to the depot, the Plaza, and the New Mexico State Hospital. The article said that Clements went to work for the MacInerney brothers on the Peña Ranch below Las Dispensas. It goes on to tell about the sisters graduating from Las Vegas High School (now Robertson High School) in 1934. In the 1930's they married brothers, Clyde and Robert Simpson. Opal, who married Robert, was a bookkeeper and employed at Hilton Motors for quite a while. Audrey, who married Clyde, was a free lance writer and employed by the Las Vegas Daily

Optic for fourteen years as Society Editor, Church Page Editor and a general reporter. The article explained that they often stayed at the Plaza Hotel in the early 1920's when their mother was teaching school at Chapelle, so to celebrate the anniversary of their arrival in Las Vegas, they stayed at the Plaza Hotel, noting changes in the Plaza park since 1919. They also went out to Bernal and Chapelle to see if they could find the old school house their mother taught in. The stone walls were still there, but the windows and roof were gone. According to the article, both women enjoyed remembering the good times they'd had as children in and around Las Vegas.[13]

In 1919 Las Vegas was not as "wild" as it had been in the 1880s when it was the largest community in the Territory. But it was still not immune to crime. Store owner Ike Davis was murdered and the crime remained an unsolved mystery. After New Mexico Territory became the State of New Mexico, people were supposed to be civilized. The legislators went to work. They thought of every detail. They even chose a State Song, ("Oh, Fair New Mexico") and a State flower—the yucca—as well as a State bird, the Road Runner. Years later, Audrey wrote an item about the State bird which appeared in the *Las Vegas Daily Optic:*

> New Mexico's State bird, the road runner or Chaparral, is found in the lower country around Las Vegas. A Road Runner when full grown is about two feet long from beak to the end of his very long tail. His short wings are not made for flying. But he sometimes uses them wide spread when running. The bird has a black crest on his head. His body is white and brown and black. And when he runs he makes a black and white streak through the sand among the cedars. Native New Mexicans say the Chaparral Bird can kill rattlesnakes. If any bird can do it, it is the Road Runner, which is said to be faster than a race horse.[14]

Fascinated with the history, culture, and climate of New Mexico, the Clements family settled into their new home. Sometime after their arrival and move into the first apartment, the family moved to a big square, adobe house on West National. It was on a big lot on the south side of the street. There were only two houses on that entire block, although there were no "blocks" there at the time. The house had a nice yard with a fence around it. Audrey went to North Public School and was in the first grade. Mary Graubarth (later Mary Solomon) was her teacher. Audrey recalled:

> We moved from the Rainey apartment up West National to the only house on the south side of that block. Before long Daddy got a job as ramroder

with the MacInerney [MacInerney Brothers Cattle Co.] on the Peña Ranch property near Las Dispensas north of Las Vegas. Hermit's Peak loomed behind the village, reflected in the clear water of the pond near the long adobe ranch house. There were a number of doors. We had rooms nearest the creek while hired men occupied some of the other rooms. With Harry Ackerman, 15 or 16 came to work, along with Bill Bragg.[15]

The family had only remained in Las Vegas in the fall of 1919 until Vern found a job as a foreman at the MacInerney Ranch. (Various spellings of the name were used, but Audrey most often used "MacInerney.") Audrey recalled in a taped interview:

I think Daddy picked Las Vegas because it was cow country and the Annual Rough Riders Cowboys' Reunion was widely advertised, and he came here (Las Vegas) wanting to be a cowboy. He always wanted to be a rancher and a cowboy. That's all he ever wanted[16]

Later, on the same tape, Audrey commented, "When we came to Las Vegas, it took! We stayed!"

13

Daddy Goes to Jail: MacInerney Ranch, Las Dispensas

"This is it!" Vern exclaimed when he brought his family to the place where he'd found his "ideal job." The MacInerney place, just eight miles northwest of Las Vegas, certainly appeared to have everything a ranch family would want. Vern was delighted with his new job. And Mabel had to admit the scenery was marvelous.

The MacInerney family was well known in the area. Some of the MacInerneys lived in Las Vegas at Eighth and Jackson, facing Lincoln Park in a big two-story house. One of them taught school in Las Vegas. The MacInerney brothers had leased the old Peña Ranch. Tom MacInerney and his brother were running cattle there. The Peñas had built a great, long adobe building on the ranch. There was an outside stairway in the back that went up onto a porch with living quarters on the second floor for the hired help. Just down from the house there was a pond and a little dam. From there one could see the MacInerney Headquarters. It had a beautiful view with mountains in the background, along with the buildings in Las Dispensas. The family now lived right at the foot of majestic Hermit's Peak! Las Dispensas had been an Army post where there had been a dispensary. Only about half a dozen men had been stationed there at the foot of Hermit's Peak. It may have served Fort Union, too.

Audrey, Opal, and Edward Clements, Christmas, 1920. *Source*: Simpson Archives

The first year, 1919 to 1920, the weather was beautiful. Vern and Mabel marveled at the sunny skies and warm weather on Christmas day. Nights were cold, but usually the sun came out at least part of each day. Audrey wrote:

> I remember Mama marveling at Christmas that we could have the door open and Opal and I could play out in the yard. We stayed there all winter and mother gave me a new 1st grade reader for Christmas! The pages smelled like ink and I read the words I knew and asked Mother what the other ones were. It had some pictures that I studied until all were memorized.[1]

Right after Christmas, Mabel Clements wrote a letter to a friend. It said, in part:

> I'm feeling like a million dollars this heavenly morning. Isn't this the finest climate you just ever saw? I've lived in a lot of different climates, but never, never have I found one so satisfying for all-year-round comfortable

living. Sometimes I get almost mad at the folks back East who haven't been here—when they talk about how desolate it must be out here in the wide open spaces. Golly, I've got to have wide open spaces to breathe. I never could stand the mobs and gas fumes and smoke and noise of big cities, and thank goodness I've never had to stay long in such spots. But just as soon as people come here and smell our good air and visit our lovely mountains and other swell vacation spots they change their tune and wonder why more people don't live here. Well, maybe it's a good thing they can't all come here or there wouldn't be any nice wide spaces left. We took out the Christmas tree today—kinda makes you sad—to part with the happy thoughts that go along with Christmas. But it's time now to get going on another important project, for here comes spring! I just got my first seed catalogue this year and spent all last evening reveling in carrots and chrysanthemums and lettuce and larkspur and beans and bachelor buttons and peas and pansies and radishes and roses. Oh! The roses! I'm going to have more new roses this year or know the reason why. (Hope I won't have to know the reason why.)[2]

Vern seemed to like this job and planned to keep it. He liked the MacInerney brothers and the huge spread. He had never met any of the Peñas, but he had heard of the well known José Teodoro Peña, known as Teodoro Pena. (He was the great-grandfather of the present-day writer, Juan José Peña.) The Peñas were a prominent family, descendants of Don Juan de la Peña who came to what is now New Mexico with Don Francisco Vásquez de Coronado in 1540 and Don Baltazar Francisco de la Peña, who came with a later group of soldiers brought by Don Diego de Vargas to Santa Fe in 1693 and settled in New Mexico.[3]

Not every December was as mild as their first one there. Apparently the previous winter had been cold, with an abundance of snow, as described by Audrey:

Devastation from heavy snows the winter of 1918-19 showed in mashed down roofs and flood ravished canyons. Grandma went down to Avis to visit her daughter May Munson, Postmistress there. While she was gone Grandpa Clements [William Harper Clements] came to visit us. He was a tall, gaunt man with snow white hair and a hate for rattlesnakes. If he saw one, quick as a flash he would grind its head under his boot.[4]

For an 80-year-old man, Grandpa Clements was very quick to be able to kill a rattlesnake with his boot heel. Born in 1893, he was, like his wife Emma, of

Irish descent. After Belle was born, they separated, but then married again about seven years later. Then Laverne and Caley were born.

After Grandma Clements had stayed a while with Audrey's family, her grandson, George Munson, came and took her to Aunt May and Uncle Cecil Munson's place at Avis. She and Grandpa Clements would live together for a while and then would "agree to disagree" and she'd go away to visit some of her kids.

The family stayed at MacInerney's through the spring of 1920. It was at Las Dispensas that Audrey learned not to rope anything she couldn't hold. Millicent Gensemer in her *Optic* story wrote:

> When her father became foreman at a ranch near Las Dispensas she (Audrey) was an apt pupil in the art of roping. At the same time the lesson was brought violently home to her that one should never rope anything from which he can't remove the rope. A fat sow became her target one day, a target that pulled her through the creek bottom, over stones and through the thorns and bulrushes, back again and up into the yard where the young roper snubbed the rope around a post until her screams brought adult help.[5]

The children didn't go to school that spring. They helped their parents. Audrey learned that her mother was not one to shirk work, and she didn't want the children to neglect their chores.

Mabel had several statements written down in a journal. She wrote: "Work, like cold water, isn't half bad after you once dive in." Another one said, "The proper thing to put off 'till tomorrow is worry." Sometimes she would admonish the children with words of wisdom, such as, "Even a prairie dog knows you have to dig in before you can come out on top." Mabel had many common expressions that she repeated to her children, such as, "Pretty is as pretty does," "You can't tell a book by its cover," "If it's worth doing, it's worth doing right," or "Think before you speak."[6]

Vern should have followed his wife's advice when he lost his temper once again—this time when he was working, for he did not think before he spoke. He was building a new corral when a man he hadn't seen before rode up. Vern sized him up and thought he looked like one of the typical local fellows.

"I don't want that corral there," the dark-haired man said in somewhat broken English.

"Well, I'm in charge and I'm putting it here!" Vern retorted. He resented some stranger riding up and telling him what to do.

"I say *no*. Take it down. I want it over there," the man pointed. His brown eyes seemed to take command over Vern, like a man who was accustomed to getting his way. His voice demanded obedience.

"To hell with what you want! Git outta here before I bust yore jaw open!" Vern threatened.

"You dare to threaten *me*?" the man shot back.

"You bet I do! It's none of your business to tell me how to run a cattle ranch! Now git your sorry —- outta here, you—— ——- ——-!" Vern began to curse at the man, calling him vile names.

The man got off his horse and approached Vern. Vern was ready for a fist fight.

"Do you know who I am? Take back what you said!" the stranger yelled.

"I know who you are, all right! You're a ——- ——- comin' in here and tryin' to tell me what to do!" Vern yelled back. "I'll take back what I said when hell freezes over!"

The man whistled and beckoned to some of the ranch hands. They immediately ran up and asked the visitor what he needed.

"I am going to have this man arrested," the stranger said.

"Did he hit you?" one of the men asked.

"No, but he called me names. That's verbal assault. I will have him in jail for that! Get the sheriff to come out here and arrest this *gringo*!"

"Yes, Mr. Peña," one of them said as he rode off.

"*Mr. Peña?*" Vern said to himself. "*I just insulted the owner of this place! I didn't know he was the boss, the Mr. Peña who owns this ranch land! I never met him!*"

Vern knew he'd made a fool of himself this time with his hot temper. He asked permission to go into his house for a few minutes before the sheriff came. It was granted and he went to find Audrey.

Vern didn't use bad language around women and children, but when he was angry with another man he could "out-cuss" anyone! Mr. Peña took great offense at the vile names he'd been called and determined to file charges against Vern Clements for his vociferous outburst.

Vern found Audrey and quietly took her aside.

"I have to go take care of some business in Las Vegas," he said. "I've got a little trouble I have to clear up. I don't want your mother or anyone else to know. But someone needs to know in case I don't come back," he said. "I'll be riding off with some men in a little while. I don't want you to worry but I may not be home for a few days."

"Is it dangerous, Daddy?" Audrey asked.

"In a way, yes," Vern replied. "I told a guy off and I have to go to jail. I don't think I'll have to stay long"

"Only bad people go to jail! You're not bad, Daddy!" Audrey whispered, tears filling her eyes.

"No, but I guess the guy thinks I am. I called him some bad names and said some things I shouldn't have said. I'll get it straightened out," Vern assured her. "It turned out the guy I was cussing out was the owner of this ranch, Mr. Peña. I didn't know he was the boss. I'd never seen him before. He's really mad about it."

"When will you be back?" Audrey questioned.

"In a day or two, I hope. But if I'm not back in a week, tell your mother—because that would mean something bad happened," Vern said. "I don't want anyone to know about this, especially Mama, so don't say anything unless a week goes by and I don't show up."

"All right," Audrey agreed, holding back her tears.

"Promise me, Sweetheart," her daddy said, putting his arm around her to give her a hug.

"I promise, Daddy," Audrey said.

Audrey had heard of the vigilante committees hanging criminals on the bridge between West and East Las Vegas, just beyond Bridge Street. She was scared. What would happen to her daddy in jail?

Vern was only in jail half a day until the ranch manager, Tom MacInerney, bailed him out. Vern's temper was always getting him into trouble, leading to fist fights as well as verbal fights. But he'd never had to go to jail before. He learned that calling people names can have unpleasant repercussions—especially when that person is the boss! Fortunately, he did not lose his job over the incident. Although Mr. Peña was not actually Vern's boss, he was the land-owner who leased the place to the MacInerneys. So Vern thought of him as "the boss."

Audrey was relieved to see her daddy come home so soon. She had not said a word to anyone, although she had been sick with worry. She had imagined many terrible things that could happen to her father.

The next day everything seemed back to normal. Vern winked at Audrey to let her know he appreciated her keeping his secret. Audrey never told her mother that Vern had gone to jail. In later years Audrey said in a taped interview:

> One day Mr. Peña came up to the ranch where the men were working and, maybe giving orders or making suggestions about "running a ranch." Daddy didn't know who he was and he began cussing and calling him

names and telling him it was none of his business telling them how to run a cattle ranch! Daddy didn't know he "owned" the ranch! Mr. Peña put Daddy in jail for that outburst! He [Vern] made me promise not to tell Mama that he had to go to jail! He was in jail a half a day until the ranch boss (Tom MacInerney, I think) bailed him out. He had a bad temper, but he learned he could go to jail for verbal assault! In later years Mama bragged that no one in the family had ever been in jail—Daddy had, but she never knew it![7]

Mabel had learned to ride when she was a young girl. But she'd never ridden horses like they had at the Peña ranch. Audrey said:

> I remember Mama rode a horse to take some water over to the men that were working there. Something scared the horse and it ran away with her. I was up on the hill when I saw her come riding by on that horse and her hair had fallen down so it was long, red-gold flowing out behind, and that horse was running like the wind and she still had the water bucket in her hand![8]

Mabel delivered the water as soon as she calmed the horse down—and only a little of it had spilled out! In some notes, Audrey wrote about the same incident:

> Mama took water to Daddy supervising cattle roundups. She rode a big dapple gray and carried water in a syrup bucket. I was out on the path to the east pasture when . . . made me jump out of the trail. Here came Dapple in a dead run, Mama astride bareback with reins in one hand and the water bucket in the other. The horse thundered past me with Mama riding for her life. Her yard-long red hair had lost all of its pins and was flying in the back wash behind her. I turned and ran after her and saw her control the animal and drop off unperturbed in the yard, tie the horse, and begin to wrap her hair in a big bow she wore at the back of her neck.[9]

Audrey discovered that even children can be helpful on a ranch, especially if they are observant of the livestock. One noon that spring Audrey watched forty or fifty goats as they were eating at the base of a big haystack. They ate away under it on each side. All the ranch hands were eating lunch in the house, and Audrey was playing outside. Suddenly the haystack collapsed and fell on the goats. Audrey ran as fast she could to tell the men.

"The haystack fell on the goats!" Audrey yelled through the door.

"Quick! Grab all the pitchforks!" one of the men said as they jumped up from the table.

As the men moved the hay, sometimes they'd stick a goat and it would make a crying noise. They tried their best to get all the goats out from under the heavy hay. Although a few goats were crippled, most of them were saved and were just fine.

"If it hadn't been for you, Audrey, all the goats would have died," one of the men said.

Later Mr. MacInerney also praised Audrey. "You deserve a reward!" he said. "I'm going to give you a goat of your very own!"

Audrey picked out her favorite kid. The animal followed Audrey everywhere so she named him "Shadow." Audrey gave Shadow special treats when she could.

"It [Shadow] grew to be a nice big gentle goat. Daddy made a cart with shafts and a harness for the goat. I harnessed it and went riding or took Opal and Edward for rides."[10]

Just when Mabel thought they were settled into a nice house for a long time, Vern told her that they would have to move again. The MacInerney brothers went broke! Almost all the cattle ranchers went broke along about that time. Before World War I there were lots of big ranches and big herds of cattle. After the war and the heavy winter snows in 1918, circumstances merged to create financial problems for many of the ranchers. Mabel, Vern and the children had been so happy at Las Dispensas, and except for Vern's unfortunate "run-in" with the law, their happy home at been unclouded. All that country in that area belonged to the Peña's. As long as there were ranches, there were cattle. And as long as there were cattle, there was a need for cowboys. So Vern easily found another job. Audrey's notes state:

> Then Daddy got more pay from Frank? Dimmick over in the Sapello and we moved over there in a wagon. The house at Dimmicks was real nice—even had a bathroom [indoor bathroom] which we couldn't use. [Plumbing was not hooked up.] There were rabbit cages and sheds near the little house—not so little—it had a stairway from the kitchen to two rooms with gable end windows upstairs. The Dimmicks had built a big adobe house across the road and up on the hillside. There was a big red hay barn down close to the Sapello River bank. I took care of the rabbits—before and after school. The school house sat at the end of the hill about 1/2 mile from our house. Opal and I were thrilled to be so close to school. Now

we could go to school! I don't remember Mama taking us the first day, but later I remember trucking along that dusty road.[11]

Mabel always loved learning. Vern liked to read, too, but his life had led him down a path of learning from nature and the great outdoors. He knew how to communicate with animals and how to get them to obey his commands. He knew how to spin a rope, delighting the children with his rope tricks. His practical knowledge, along with Mabel's "book learning," gave the children a basic foundation for an education—and a love for learning.

14

Cake in a Suitcase: Dimmick Ranch

Mr. and Mrs. Dimmick from Florida had bought a place below the Mosimann's Place. They had a big adobe house—almost finished—up on the hill. It was at the Dimmick place on the Sapello River that Vern found a job in the late summer of 1920. There was also a nice little cottage below the road and the Clements family moved into it. It had three rooms and an upstairs. A ladder with a narrow set of steps led to the upstairs where there was a front window with a wonderful view. The three Clements children enjoyed playing upstairs. Mabel enjoyed the view and the cozy house. A poem entitled "Autumn Storm" was found in her journal:

> A wind whirls 'round my cabin,
> A cabin of rough hewn pine,
> Snugly hugging the mountain side
> Unafraid of winter's sign.
>
> A wind whirls 'round my cabin,
> And with it comes blustering snow,
> Beating in gusts and drifting
> To the valleys down below.

A wind whirls 'round my cabin,
But I am safe and warm
By my crackling, cheery fire-place,
Ne'er minding the ringing storm.

A wind whirls 'round my cabin,
But I, with a thrilling book,
Curl up in undisturbed content
In my comfy, fireside nook.[1]

It was from that cabin window that Audrey and her family watched the Penitentes up on top of the hill above the house in the spring of 1921. The men had a big cross used in their ceremonies every year. Audrey could hear the men wailing and see them jumping all around in front of the big cross in the early light of Good Friday morning.

The Dimmicks told Audrey that if she'd take care of their rabbits, she could have some of them. It was a tough job. She had to go out in the bitter winter to feed and water them. It was so cold that some of the rabbits froze to death. Audrey cared for them as best she could, and she was given a few of her own.

Sometimes Mabel would ride horseback into town. Vern would be working at the barn. He couldn't hear the children yell for him because he was about a quarter of a mile away. He told the kids that if they needed him, they could hang something on the clothes line and he would come to the house.

One day when the children were left alone, Audrey told the other children that it was their mother's birthday.

"Mama always makes a cake for each of us on our birthdays! Nobody ever makes a cake for her! Let's surprise her!" Audrey suggested.

"That's a good idea!" Opal agreed.

"Cake! Cake!" Edward chanted happily.

"When Mama gets home, won't she be surprised!" Opal exclaimed.

Audrey remembered seeing her mama mix up a cake. Audrey didn't have a recipe but she knew what ingredients her mother used.

"I know how to do it," Audrey declared.

"We want Daddy to be surprised, too!" Opal said. "What will we do if he comes home before we're ready?"

"We'll hide everything in the attic," Audrey suggested.

The children sat on the steep steps and stirred the cake so if their daddy came in early they could run up to the attic and hide the evidence of their surprise.

They kept the cook stove hot and then baked the cake. It looked perfect when it was turned out on a big plate.

"Where can we hide the cake until it's time to bring it out?" Audrey asked. She and Opal discussed it and then came up with a perfect idea. They would put it in a suitcase!

After the cake had cooled and was frosted, Audrey found a suitcase, gently put the cake in it, and slipped it under the bed.

Mabel returned, prepared supper, Vern came in, and the family sat down to eat.

After supper, Audrey announced, "We have a surprise for your birthday, Mama."

"Oh?" Mabel wondered what it could be.

Audrey pulled the suit case out from under the bed, opened it, and there was the master piece! Mabel was totally surprised and delighted.

"How did you manage all this?" Vern asked, amazed.

"Cake! Gimme!" Edward pleaded.

The family devoured the cake enthusiastically.

In 1920 and 1921 Audrey and Opal went to school at a small village just above Sapello—Las Tusas—a place four miles west of Sapello and fifteen miles northwest of Las Vegas. The Clements family lived just about half a mile from the school house. The girls were dismayed because they could not understand the teacher. A native of New Mexico, the teacher was of Spanish descent. He spoke very broken English because English was his second language. The kids from Nebraska were not accustomed to the "strange" pronunciation. The girls complained to their mother, so Mabel went to visit the school, a one-room school house.

Audrey recalled:

> When she got to the door the teacher yelled, "Git in." He had beginners up to big boys in seventh grade. He had a seventh grader, an older boy, he was teaching, and they kept talking about the *gormant* and Mama couldn't figure out what the *gormant* was!
>
> She was so shocked. She couldn't figure out what the heck he was talking about. It finally dawned on her—the *government*!
>
> The teacher kept an axe handle on his desk to use on the big boys to keep order in the school. No axe—just the axe handle. Opal and I were scared to death of him, and us poor little ignorant kids from Nebraska couldn't understand a word he said. He was nice but we were awfully scared of him![2]

Audrey wrote years later in her notes, "Some Early Childhood Memories:"

> The teacher was a Spanish American man. Opal and I could not understand his Spanish American accent. Almost every day we would go home crying because we couldn't understand what he told us to do. He was inclined to shout . . . to make [us] understand him. She [Mabel] looked around the room with an iron box heater, desks, and his desk with the proverbial axe handle lying at ready.[3]

After visiting the school, Mabel understood why her girls were so frustrated. The next week Mabel rode horseback to Las Vegas to see the County School Superintendent, Mrs. Green. She wanted to teach the children at home.

"No," Mrs. Green said. "You can't keep your children out of school and teach them at home when you live so close to the school."

"Even though I was a teacher in Nebraska and down at Weed, New Mexico?" Mabel asked. "My children can't understand the teacher; his English is so broken."

"It can't be helped," Mrs. Green said. "There are not enough highly qualified people applying for the jobs. We take what we can get. Since you were a teacher in Nebraska, why don't you go to the Normal University in Las Vegas and take New Mexico History and Civics and then apply for a teaching position?"

Mable came home elated. She would go back to teaching. Audrey wrote years later:

> Since Mother had taught in Nebraska, Mrs. Green urged Mother to become a teacher here. [New Mexico]
>
> "These people are Americans and the official language is English so we need good teachers to teach the children to read and speak English. Otherwise the native population will never made any progress," she predicted. "If you will attend the Normal University this summer, taking New Mexico History and Civics, I will see that you get a school this fall," Mrs. Green assured her.
>
> Mother came home very excited about returning to teaching since New Mexico did not have a rule against married women as teachers.
>
> Mama went to town on horseback several times, looking for a place to rent for the summer. She found a good house at the corner of 8th and Columbia.[4]

When the superintendent advised Mabel to go to the Normal school (New Mexico Normal Teachers College in Las Vegas) to take two classes, Mabel knew she would then get a teaching certificate for New Mexico and felt that the family would be better off financially.

By the time New Mexico Normal University's 1921 summer session started, Mabel had rented the house on Eighth Street. The Las Vegas schools were not out yet when they moved in from the Dimmick Place, so Mabel took Opal and Audrey to Douglas School and entered Opal in Mrs. Cone's first grade room and Audrey in Second grade taught by Miss Mary Hanson.

It has been said that a teacher's influence never ends. Mabel later taught a fifth grade class at Chapelle, New Mexico. One of her students, Sophia Rael, became a fifth grade teacher. One of Sophia's fifth grade students was Cipriano Aguilar. He also had a long career as a fifth grade teacher. Undoubtedly, one of his many students has become a fifth grade teacher. Mabel's love of learning has been passed down through the generations. Mabel did not know any Spanish, but she was willing to learn. And she would teach the students who spoke English as a second language to the very best of her ability, with patience and understanding. Audrey said in later years: "She did a fine job in both languages! The students loved her and she loved the students."[5]

Whether she was in the country or the city, Mabel could make a home cozy as she continued to teach her children and to learn herself:

> But I, with a thrilling book,
> Curl up in undisturbed content
> In my comfy, fireside nook.[6]

15

The Teacher Goes to School: Las Vegas

abel planned to move to Las Vegas from the Dimmick Ranch on the Sapello before school was out in 1921. Vern continued working at the Dimmicks but he was ready to quit once Mabel moved to Las Vegas. According to Audrey:

Once mother was going to move to town, Daddy became more and more dissatisfied working for the Dimmicks. He "hated" to be bossed by a woman, especially a "greenhorn uppity up" so he gave her "come upance" and up and quit, just in time to move us all to town. He borrowed a team and wagon and loaded up the new kitchen range they had bought when we moved there, as well as the table, chairs, the big bed and the couch—a metal affair one side of which would lift up and the other side down, making a couch during the day. Then at night flattened out. We three kids slept on it. The other stuff, dishes, clothes and bedding went into mother's big trunk.

I remember the first night in town sitting there looking north up 8th across the street to the Jewish temple and watching the street lights come on that night. We were still using the coal oil lamps but mother had the electricity turned on next day by Las Vegas Light and Power Company. I felt shivery sitting there watching the lights come on. I remember I kept wondering what it would be like to live in a town again. I was thrilled by the sight of the street lights.[1]

Mabel rented a large frame house at the corner of Columbia and Eighth Street, facing Columbia. She rented out a room or two in order to get enough money to pay the rent and to go to the Normal school. One of the teachers who rented an upstairs room was named Bess. Audrey recalled:

I remember Bess got sick and Daddy hung over her and rubbed her arms and made Mama jealous. Daddy quit Dimmicks and moved to town with us but soon rented part of Peña's place and ran cattle there for someone on the shares. We kids were at loose ends. Mama gone to school some hours of the day. I was to look after Opal and Edward since I was going on 8, a big girl.[2]

There was a large house next door where a little boy named Arthur lived. He often came over to play with the Clements children. Audrey enjoyed having a close neighbor. She recalled:

I wondered what living in town would be like and marveled at all the lit up houses. Within a day or two I was enrolled in North Public School. Mrs. Mary Graubarth (later Mrs. Harry Solomon) was my first grade teacher. The children were mostly Spanish American. New Mexico had only been a state for 6 years and no one spoke [English] without a marked

Spanish accent. But I had played with such children in Taos and Opal's best friend, her age, died with diphtheria.[3]

One day there was a wedding at the Jewish Temple across the street on the northwest corner of Columbia and Eighth. Mary Graubarth, Audrey's First Grade Teacher at North Public School, was getting married. Her folks had the Hoffman and Graubarth store at 514 Douglas Avenue in Las Vegas. Miss Mary Graubarth was marrying Mr. Harry Soloman. Audrey was able to see the people in all their finery through the window. Then Audrey saw the bride get out of the car and go into the Temple. She had on an absolutely beautiful wedding dress. Audrey thought she looked like a queen, the most beautiful bride!

Since they had moved to Las Vegas two weeks before school was out, the three Clements children had to get their smallpox vaccinations. They had to go to the old stone court house, a huge place. Audrey was afraid and she felt sick. Audrey said years later:

> We had to go upstairs to the doctor's office and get our "scratches!" Well, the doctor was an old guy and he put us in line. I was the oldest—stair steps—so the oldest had to go first to show the others how to do it. He was scratching my arm and I fell over in a faint. I heard him say, "I hate it when the first one faints because it scares all the rest." I hated it too because I bumped my head.[4]

Audrey had never had any kind of inoculation before. Recollections of her grandmother's dire warnings about getting vaccinated were probably responsible for some of Audrey's fear which caused her to suddenly blackout—the first time she'd ever fainted. She decided she would stay away from doctors as much as she could in the future. She determined never to go to a doctor unless she had to. Most of the time, doctors were not readily available, nor were school nurses, even when children were injured on the playground. Audrey wrote:

> I remember Opal swinging on the giant slides; someone pushed her high and her fat little arms gave out. I came around the school in time to see her lose her grip on the metal bar and fall flat on her stomach.
>
> The kids teased us some, but Opal and I still made friends and enjoyed school. When school was out and we were waiting for report cards all the kids repeatedly told us that we would not pass because we hadn't gone to school long enough. In those days it was not the custom to pass one to the next grade unless they had completed required work.

Opal and I both passed. We were elated and delighted to find out that the town kids weren't as smart as they thought they were.

The end of grade school and the start of New Mexico Normal University began an entirely new phase in our lives. Mother rented 2 bedrooms to some teachers attending Normal University.[5]

When Mabel was going to the Normal school that summer, 1921, there was a school picnic at the ponds at Montezuma. All the students were invited to ride the train and take their families to the picnic, so Mabel took her three children. It was a great thrill for them. They marveled at the big ice ponds where ice was put up every winter and shipped out on the train.[6]

Mabel thought Audrey, age eight, and Opal, age six, should take piano lessons. After they got out of school at Douglas, they went down to the alley between a bank building and a store and up the side stairs to someone who gave piano lessons. After they took three lessons, Mabel realized that the girls weren't practicing enough, didn't really seem interested, so they were allowed to quit.

Audrey was in charge of three-year-old Edward when their mama was at school. Edward thought it was funny to run across the street whenever he saw a car coming to show that he could beat the car. Audrey tried to make him stop but she couldn't control him. He insisted on playing "chicken" with the automobiles. One day someone came along in an old Model T with no top on it. It had a kind of a truck in the back end for hauling things. After Edward pulled his usual stunt, the man stopped, got out, took hold of Edward, and set him on the edge of the sidewalk. He gave him quite a lecture. "Don't you ever do that again!" He scared Edward, so after that the boy stopped running in front of cars.[7]

In later years, Audrey wrote a commentary in verse about why children don't behave. She might have thought, for instance, if Vern had been more willing to talk about his quick temper and the trouble it got him into, maybe Edward would have been inclined to mind better. As it was, Edward often got into trouble, sometimes fighting with other kids, sometimes not obeying his mother. Audrey wrote in later years in "Pride Does It":

> The young never believe a word we say,
> Though we harp on "what happens" every day.
> As we won't show them our ghastly mistakes,
> We make them suffer the same fierce aches.
> For we hide them carefully as we grow old,
> Yes, our ugly mistakes we guard like gold![8]

While they were still living at the house in Las Vegas, Grandpa Waddell came to visit. They called him "Grandpa Bug" because he called the kids "the little bugs." Grandpa Bug stayed for quite a while that summer. Audrey was glad to have an adult around because she couldn't always make Opal and Edward behave—especially Edward—while their mother was in class. Years later, Audrey wrote in her notes, "Close Escapes:"

> I must have been 7 and Sissie [Opal] 5 and Edward 3. Grandpa saved Bubby [Edward] from no telling what. I heard him yelling. A quick look in the backyard showed him hanging by both hands from a limb of the big tree. He was at least 10 feet above the ground, his golden blond curls jiggled as he screamed for dear life. Grandpa rushed out and climbed up the tree enough to reach Edward and get him down.[9]

Every morning Grandpa would get up early and take a walk up Eighth Street, past the Comstock Dairy. Audrey liked to go with him. "I would get up and go along, up beautiful 8th street with its lovely trees and dairy cows on the west side of the street. We sometimes went over to 8th in front of St. Anthony's Hospital to walk home down 7th. Not many houses [were] there then."[10]

Audrey had noticed in Nebraska that Grandpa Waddell was very cautious and frequently seemed scared. He always pulled all the shades before he lit the lamps in the evenings because he was apparently afraid someone would be looking in from outside. Whatever he was afraid of, Grandpa Waddell advised the family that you should never say anything into the telephone that you didn't want anybody to hear, other than the person you were speaking to, because someone might have the receiver up and be listening to you. And in New Mexico he was just as cautious as he had been in Nebraska. There were some dangers, however, that could strike in a second. One of them was lightning. Audrey wrote:

> Another close escape was when Sissie [Opal] and Bubby [Edward] decided to go around the block. I was sitting inside on the floor under the electric light cutting out new paper to made paper clothing. As I sat there a bolt of lightning popped down, striking the house across the street. Fire ran along the scissors in my hand. The clap of thunder made me jump. Sissie and Bubby, around the block, thought the good Lord was reminding them that they were disobeying so they made it home in breathless double time.[11]

When they told Mabel what had happened, she was thankful that the children had not been hurt. Audrey's hands were fine in spite of the close lightning encounter.

That summer the children played "Run Sheep Run," "Hide and Seek," and "Statue." Audrey recalled: "I had the Indian suit that had been Uncle Bruce's before he outgrew it. I wore it proudly and wondered why I was never picked as the most beautiful statue."[12]

Audrey recalled how some of the older children tried to explain the "facts of life" to her that summer, although they were not very knowledgeable themselves. Audrey realized she was quite ignorant even after learning some of the "facts" from neighborhood children. She wrote in her notes, "Some Early Childhood Memories:"

> The next year out at Chapelle, I learned a little more. Sophia Rael, age 10, enlightened me when she said her mother was going to have a baby.
> I asked, "How do you know?"
> "Look at her. See how fat she is getting." I had noted that and supposed it was the result of *mucha frijoles y pan* [many beans and bread] and butter.
> "Babies come out of the doctor's bag," I protested. "When my little brother was born, the doctor at Taos opened his black bag and showed us the little naked baby in it, then took him out and wrapped him in a blanket and gave him to my mother. So I know babies come in the doctor's bag."
> How Sophia laughed and laughed. "What a dumb *Gringa!*"
> "Well I saw it myself and so did my little sister. I can prove it by her."
> Sophia just kept laughing and I think I accepted Sophia's theory that babies grew inside mothers [so] that I didn't ask questions and remained naive or as it was called "protected and innocent."[13]

Audrey emphasized that in those days children were not told much about "the facts of life."

> Then I was 13 and mother thought I should be told something. It was obviously beyond her, the teacher with mouthfuls of words. She was trying to tell me something about menstruation, as I had just started, when the neighbor's dog came running down the street, pursued and caught by the other neighbor's big male; right there in front of us the big dog caught her and they were one. Mother went out and threw rocks at them; and with the female yipping unhappily they ran off together.
> "What were they doing?" I asked my blushing and flustered mother.

"Making babies. Now go peel potatoes for supper." She dismissed me. Later that mother dog came around followed by a bunch of pups—but I was still in the dark about it.

I still didn't understand or know a thing about the birds and the bees as it was called when I grew up. The next year at the school at Bernal the kids played tag and running games all over the big yard. There was one older boy—already man-size—in the 6th grade that over took me one day. I had on my long winter coat so couldn't run very fast. He grabbed me from behind and held me tight against his body. I struggled and kicked and yelled so soon got away just as Miss Gerk rang the bell calling us in from recess.

For the next several months I worried, "Was I going to have a baby because he grabbed and held me?" Finally when I didn't get fat I knew I had escaped.[14]

Audrey learned some that summer—and more the next year at Chapelle. She discovered that reading, as well as observing, could help her learn about life. If no one would talk to her about "adult things," she would read and find out for herself.

By the end of summer school, Mabel got her teaching certificate. The Superintendent of Schools gave her the school at Chapelle for the 1921-1922 school year. In the meantime, Vern left the Dimmicks' place shortly after Mabel left. Audrey commented:

Daddy didn't stay at Dimmicks' very long after Mama left! Somebody should have kicked my father on the shin! He couldn't stand to be bossed by a woman so he quit and then somehow he rented some part of the Peña place away from where the MacInerney's Headquarters were and was going to run cattle on the shares. It was the other side of where Storrie Lake is now.

There was no dam at that time. Sometimes they would go by in the wagon and see the men working, getting the area ready to build Storrie Dam.[15]

Vern moved the children back out to the country.

Grandpa [Waddell] left so Daddy took us back up to Peña Ranch (east end no doubt) to a big long adobe house with an upstairs with windows in the ends. He would put us on an old black horse and we would ride around the house while he worked.[16]

Audrey wrote that her experiences of staying alone in charge of the younger children left her with some anxieties, especially when she was teased by some of the neighborhood children, such as the boy next door who kept insulting her.

> That was a hectic summer—but looking back I can't remember any that [Vern and Mabel] weren't looking for a job or good "deal." Once when he [Vern] was home he heard the boy next door [teasing.] He told me how to turn the tables and in the last line say, "Just like you!" I was so grateful to be able to turn the tables on a sophisticated city dude.[17]

With her secured teaching certificate and new job, Mabel was glad when she and Vern moved their little family out of Las Vegas and to the village of Chapelle, about seventeen miles south of Las Vegas. That school year, 1921-1922, Vern leased a part of the Peña Ranch, the part the MacInerney Brothers had leased before they went broke and lost it. So while Mabel taught at Chapelle, Vern worked at the Peña ranch. In spite of hardships, Mabel was never too tired to write poetry:

> Down beside the river
> Where pussy willows sway
> Pale pink roses nod their heads
> Inviting you to stay.
>
> Columbines are waving
> Huge Tiger Lilies glow
> Ferns display their graceful hands
> We thrill and watch them grow.
>
> Oh, heartless city cousins
> Why can't you love my flowers
> Why pull them up and spoil them
> In one or two short hours.
>
> You prove you do not love them
> You let them wilt and die
> Why can't you love—and let them
> Thrill other passers-by.[18]

16

Chapelle

Vern took the house hold goods by wagon to Chapelle. Audrey wrote that Mabel and the children "went by the train that stopped along the track to pick up and let off passengers."[1]

Chapelle, in San Miguel County, was a trading point twenty-five miles south of Las Vegas. It was established as a switch on the AT & SF Railroad.

> Chapelle had a depot, a section house were the track foreman and family lived, a big water tank where steam engines took on water, a new two-room stone school house, and a scattering of houses up and down the hillside behind the village. On the right below the school house was Solano's Store which was seldom opened, 'tho it seemed to do some business. Mother rented an L-shaped house up against the hill behind the school house. Everyone carried water in buckets from either the depot or section house faucets that were connected to the water tank.[2]

In "Remembering Chapelle," Audrey wrote:

> Superintendent Green told Mother, "We need someone to teach these people English. They are trying to speak a combination of Texas cowboy lingo, AT & SF Railroad workers' words and something of broken book English learned in two schools."[3]

Audrey later described her first impressions of Chapelle:

> The AT & SF local puffed into Chapelle and stopped in front of the depot. Mother and Edward, 3 1/2, and Opal, going on 6, and me, going on 8, stepped down out onto the Chapelle cinder. They [cinders] covered the railroad right of way area along the tracks to the big modern platform that surrounded the two-story depot with its big bay window staring out at the tracks.[4]

Then Mabel went to find out where she was supposed to live. Audrey wrote that her mother wasted no time.

> "I'm the school teacher," Mama said, with her three tag-along kids trying to shrink behind her as the huge station agent approached. I wondered why she didn't say "new" teacher because at 28 she didn't feel very new. But boy! Did she look spiffy in her shiny gray silk dress and matching wide brimmed "merry widow" hat combination with bright red gold hair and her creamy pink and white complexion! She was gorgeous. The station agent, no slouch for looks himself, stuttered a "pleased to meet cha.'"
>
> "Could you direct me to the house my husband rented for us?"
>
> Suddenly the agent found his voice. "It's that L shaped adobe with the tin roof about 200 yards up back of the school house. The school house is that big rock building over there."
>
> The agent pointed towards the middle of the village. There were two or three dozen houses with the depot at the east end of town and the other end somewhere out of sight in a depression beyond the big black water tank and the section house.
>
> The agent pointed out the house and mother and her three tag-a-longs—looking like ornery little whelps—started up through the Chapelle sand. We were all wearing sandals and the sand soon worked into them until it felt like we were walking on sand. When Daddy came along with our wagon load of furniture from the Dimmick place up on the Sapello mother soon had things underway.[5]

At Chapelle Audrey started in the third grade and Opal started in the second grade, just before their next birthdays in the fall. Audrey recalled:

> Mama had to cope with teaching English to Spanish speaking children and she didn't know a word of Spanish. So she developed visual aids long before that form of teaching was initiated in public schools. I remember: Amelia Maestas; Emelia Castellano, Esquepulito Montoya and his sister Maria; Benjamin, a big boy who knew a little English; Lola Espinoza; José Solano; Jacobo Solano; José Zamora; Librideta Zamora; Zacarias and Sophia Rael; and Juan Rael.[6]

The family lived in a house behind the school house. The school house had two big rooms with a hall in between them. There were big windows all along the front of the school but they were too high to see out of when the children were sitting at their desks. The school faced the railroad tracks.

Left to right: Opal, Edward, Audrey and Mabel Clements at Chapelle, 1921. *Source*: Simpson Archives

Mabel was a very good disciplinarian. The tone of her voice usually made most of the kids behave. However, some of the bigger boys were sometimes a problem. Audrey recalled an incident that hurt her feelings. "Mother spanked me as an example to the others to scare them into minding—and I had not done anything. The parents told her if the kids didn't mind to spank them and then they would get more at home. So she proved she could—on me."[7]

Mabel was making about eighty dollars a month. In order to get about twenty dollars more, she taught home economics in the evening for the village women. She taught them how to make different breads, pies, or cakes. Quite a number of women were enrolled in her class.

Mabel had a beautiful black velvet dress with fringe on the bottom. It set off her lovely complexion. She hung the dress out on the clothes line one day, and a little dog came along and began jumping at it. He got all tangled up in the fringe. The station agent, a young fellow named F. E. Klein, was at the depot. He saw the dog and came to help Mabel get the animal untangled. Mabel's dress was ruined. The dog soon met his demise, as the men of that time thought any animal mean enough to destroy a ladies' dress should not be allowed to continue his naughty ways. At the same time a man named Charles Vivian Shearer was working for the Santa Fe Railroad there.[8]

Soon the family moved from that first house behind the school. Perhaps Mabel did not want to pay rent on the house any more. They moved into the big room off of the school house, the one on the other side of the hall that wasn't being used for classes. Mabel put wires up around the room and hung sheets on them to divide the room into bedrooms and living area so they could have some privacy. At times she would push the sheets back to the edges of the room, and they would have just the one big room.

The custom was to hold dances at the school house on weekends or holidays. The desks would be moved out of the way and the schoolroom became a wonderful hardwood dance floor. Mabel was glad she didn't have to clean up afterwards. The next morning the classroom had been cleaned and was ready for school again. However, one morning the iron stove lid was broken. It had been broken it over someone's head! The next day they saw a fellow going around with his head all bandaged up. Audrey described a typical "dance" evening years later.

> One night there was a very bad fight in the hall. All the people were trying to get out the front door of the school house and the hall was full of pushing and shoving. Lola Espinosa jerked the door open and began to holler, "Clemente, Clemente," her father. He was Clemente Espinosa. She was trying to get him to get in our room and Mama had pushed the door shut! She wouldn't let anybody push into our room like they would have with Lola standing there hollering for her father and holding the door open. Some of the women went out the windows. They jumped out to get away. It was a real bad fight in the school room! You could hear women screaming and yelling for their husbands and some of the men hollering for their wives, trying to find them. They eventually all left. The next morning the school room was all cleaned up and ready for school![9]

Whenever Mabel went into Las Vegas to get her paycheck or conduct business, she would ride the train in and come back the next day. She hired a couple of big girls, Lola Espinosa or Libby Zamora, to stay with the children. Libby was about eighteen or nineteen and Lola was about seventeen. Mabel's experiences as a school teacher were many and varied:

When Mama first started teaching at Chapelle she saw something crawling down a young student's forehead—Amalita Maestas—when all the kids were lined up to go into school. She asked a big boy (Benjamin) what that was. He said, "Oh, that's a little animal." Mama didn't know anything about *piojos* (head lice.) She was horrified when she found head lice on us kids! The boy called the *piojos* [in English] "little animals"[10]

For Thanksgiving, Mabel planned to take the children to stay at the Plaza Hotel in Las Vegas for a big Thanksgiving dinner. She thought it would be a great treat for the children and herself to get out of the village for a day or two. They were ready to go when Mabel, checking the grooming and appearance of each child, noticed they all had the dreaded "head lice." Mabel was mortified.

Audrey said she had seen some of the kids pulling lice off of their heads and dropping them on somebody else's head, the person seated in front. Mabel was disgusted. Audrey wrote:

> So just when we were going to town she discovered we had lice. Horrified, she wouldn't let us go to town for fear someone would discover we were lousy. She got some kind of stuff from Murphey's Drug Store and a fine tooth comb and de-loused us daily. There was not a nit left. From then on she went over our hair daily to keep from getting another start. She was always chagrined that we got lice but how could we help it if they were dropped in our hair?[11]

Mabel Clements' class at the school in Chapelle, 1921. *Source*: Simpson Archives

Mabel was fond of drama. She had always participated in school plays, and as a teacher in Nebraska she had helped her students prepare several plays. She thought a play would be good for the students at Chapelle, as well as for the community. So at Christmas, 1921, Mabel and her class prepared a play.

Mabel re-wrote "A Christmas Carol" so that Charles Dickens' story would be more relevant to New Mexicans. Mabel abbreviated it and picked out parts of it that could be used. Scrooge and the Ghosts of Christmas Past and Future were in it. Many community people took part in it. Some of the older men and boys took part, having a great time rattling their chains. The whole town came to see the play. Mabel even had a "chorus line" of dancing girls, and Audrey was one of them. It was quite a feat for a teacher from Nebraska to put together a play written by an Englishman, directed by a mid-Western American, and adapted by New Mexican Americans with their own unique Spanish-American flare. Audrey wrote:

> At Christmas she put on a play. She adapted Charles Dickens' Christmas Carol to primitive school room with some townspeople taking part. The ghost with rattling chains was a big [success]. Most of the people could not understand English but they got the idea from their kids and others. Mother hung sheets across the front of the room on a clothesline wire and kids pulled them back and forth by hand. Opal and I and other little girls were in a dance she made up—1, 2, 3, 4—kick left leg in front of the right and then repeat with the other leg. There was a Christmas tree and [there was] candy for everyone. It was a fine success. Mother conducted cooking classes for women in the evening and was paid $20 extra for that but when we moved from the house at the foot of the hill into the spare school room that was discontinued. Daddy didn't get along with the land lady—used a box or a board of hers for something and made her mad.[12]

In Nebraska school plays were so popular that there was one for almost every occasion. As long as Mabel taught, she used drama to make the work more exciting. Even in later years when she no longer taught, she wrote many skits for her own children to act out.

Vern was still working at Peña Ranch, taking care of all the cattle. One day Vern roped a calf and its neck was broken. He had to shoot it and then butchered it so the meat would not be wasted. He put it on a pack horse and brought it to Chapelle so Mabel could cook it. They cut it all up and Mabel began frying meat. She didn't have a canner or a cooker so the only way she knew to preserve the meat was to fry it and pack it in her big stone jar. She put a layer of grease in there and a layer of fried meat, then another layer of grease and another layer of meat, and so on until she got all the meat friend and preserved in the grease. She saved the meat![13]

Laverne and Mabel Clements at Chapelle, 1921. *Source*: **Simpson Archives**

Aunt Belle and Uncle Fred Gushard wanted to come to Chapelle. They were in Avis at Aunt May's. Vern rode horseback all the way down to Avis with an extra horse. Juanita Gushard was a baby, so Aunt Belle took the train to Las Vegas from Alamogordo. It took three days. Fred and Vern, riding horseback, took only three days to ride from Avis to Chapelle, a distance of approximately 190 miles. They beat Auntie Belle home—she on the train and they on horses.[14] She probably had a layover somewhere.

Vern and Fred camped along the way. In those days, riders would sometimes stop at a ranch and ask if they could stay all night. They stopped at a ranch and asked if they could sleep in the barn. The owner said, "Yes, if you'll take off your guns and leave them with me."

"Fred, do you want to give up your gun?" Vern asked.

"Heck no," Fred replied. "I wear this gun for a reason. I'd feel naked without it!"

"Well, I'd feel pretty defenseless, too," Vern agreed. "I can't see surrendering my weapon just for a barn to sleep in. Let's go find another place."

And that's what they did rather than give up their guns.

Auntie Belle and Uncle Fred got a little two room house at Chapelle. The station agent at Chapelle was Charles Vivian Shearer. Aunt Belle made lunch for him every day. She mixed up a concoction of mashed beans. There was no place in Chapelle to buy anything such as groceries or meat, even for those with money. Belle mashed up beans until they were like butter and then made a sandwich with them, adding a lot of pepper and other spices. Audrey was given a taste once and thought it was the best thing she'd ever had—except for Grandmother Dammuzzy's creamed cabbage.

After Belle and Fred lived in Chapelle, they ran the dairy at the old Romero house at Romeroville, helping Elmira and Fred Lewis. They milked the cows and cared for the milk, made butter, cottage cheese, and other such things. Mabel was appalled at the flies around the place.

After a time, Belle and Fred moved above what is now Storrie Lake on the road to Mora and later moved to the Gerk's place where they worked for someone. That place didn't have so many flies, but it had rattlesnakes!

Soon it was time to move again. Audrey wrote:

> When school was out Daddy came down from Peña Ranch where he was running cattle on the shares and loaded all our stuff into a lumber wagon and we three kids on top and we started for the ranch. We got a few miles out of Chapelle and the wagon tire rim came loose. We stopped at a creek. [near Bernal] Daddy fixed the wheel—soaked it in water and we came on with the load. He camped for the night at the old Gross Kelly wagon yard and Mama took us to the Plaza for the night. The next day we finished the trip to the Peña Ranch. It was not the MacInerney area but farther east than their headquarters. It was a big long adobe house with a log cabin at one end and a board lean-to at the other. We may have slept at Aunty Belle's—later Gerk Place—en route to the ranch.[15]

Audrey was used to moving by now. It seemed they never stayed in one place more than a year. She thought to herself that she'd like to be able to go to school in the same place for at least a full year, and, better yet, for several years. But it was not to happen.

17

Summer, 1922: Peña Ranch then Las Vegas

"Watch out for rattlesnakes!" Mabel warned the children. She explained that rattlesnakes can thrive at the high elevation of 6,000 feet and even to the top of a mountain range of 9,000 feet. It is often thought that they live only at lower elevations, but they can also survive in the mountains. Vern knew they were entering "rattlesnake territory" when they moved to Peña Ranch at the end of the school year in the spring of 1922.

Vern had brought a lumber wagon from Peña Ranch to move the family. As mentioned before, a wagon wheel came off and had to be repaired before they could continue. In the meantime, Mabel took the train to Las Vegas so she could pick up her last check for the school year. Then Vern picked her up and they continued the trip, past the present day Storrie Lake, to Aunt Belle and Uncle Fred's place. The rattlesnakes were all over the place, even in the chicken's nests. Belle had to be careful when she went to gather the eggs.

The floor of the house had big knot holes all over it, and the kids—Audrey, Opal and Edward—had to sleep on the floor that night. People sometimes used green lumber when building houses and floors. When it dried, it would shrink, so the knots would fall out. Hence the walls and floors were full of cracks and knot holes!

Audrey was afraid rattlesnakes would come up through the knot holes in the floor. It was one of the most miserable nights she ever spent. She was afraid to go to sleep; she was so scared of the snakes.

Audrey recalled:

Somehow Vern got the other side of the place at the other end of the ranch. It was thousands of acres, and he leased the other side of the ranch with a long, old adobe house on it that had a little lean-to log cabin as well. That's where Mabel put her new baby chickens. Mother bought 1000 baby chicks and with a wood stove in the log cabin part started to raise chickens. When she let them out crows and magpies dived down in every direction, snatching up chickens and carrying them off. I would stand out there and shoot my cap pistol and yell and bang things to try to keep the big birds away. As they grew bigger, they ran all around the place. We had an old sow with a batch of little pigs in a pen west of the house. The chickens would come and climb or fly into the pen and the old sow would give one gobble and they were gone. I filled all the cracks with sticks and rocks to keep them out. I remember crying and trying to keep those dumb chickens out of that pen. Daddy came in on horseback and saw me and knew what was happening before he got to the house. He helped tighten the pen and shoo the chickens back where they belonged.[1]

Although Vern sometimes came down off the mountain where he was herding cows, he was gone much of the time. Mable sometimes went to town, at times seeing a doctor in Las Vegas. Audrey was in charge when her parents were gone. She was nine, Opal was seven, and Edward was four. As ranch children, they observed animals. They knew the difference between male and female livestock. Sometimes bulls were called "gentleman cows." Audrey wrote:

Like lots of other ranch kids in those days, Big Sis [Audrey] going on 8, looked after the other two. Little Sis [Opal] was going on 6 and Edward was a handful, already 4. When Daddy was out checking cattle and fences, we kids under strict orders, stayed in the house. When the cattle would come to the salt lick below the old adobe we would climb the ladder to the attic and watch them through the small window in the gable end of the house.

Often his bulls would bellow, paw the ground, and threaten each other or actually wham each other with the crack of horns resounding around the meadow. At such times we kids clung together in the attic. The bawling cattle and roar of the bulls scared us. We would recall the story "Lasca" that mother often sang concerning stampeding cattle. We had never seen a stampede but well knew the damage such an event could cause. We would cower in the attic and wait for the cattle to leave or for Daddy to come home. What a relief when we would hear his whistle or his charming tenor voice as he rode up to the house. We kids would drop quickly back downstairs. We didn't want anyone to know we were "scardy cats." If the tear stains were visible I would give each face a swipe with the wash cloth that hung on a nail by the wash pan, not forgetting to give my own a quick once over. To this day I never let on how that milling, bawling, fighting wild cattle terrified us. If the cattle hadn't kept us stymied in the attic I would have 6 or 7 potatoes peeled ready for daddy to fry as soon as he could build a fire in the big old cook stove. When Daddy was working around the place, he would saddle a big black mare, Old Bess, place the three of us on her and we would ride up and down in front and around the house for hours. If we were lucky Daddy would let us ride her down the canyon for several hundred yards before he called us back. Sometimes we got a milk pen calf into a corral chute and would try to climb on it to play "cowboy."[2]

One day Opal decided to ride a calf. Vern said he'd help. Audrey recalled years later:

> Daddy was holding her (Opal) on the calf and the calf was jumping. She was riding with a circingle or belly girth around it, and Daddy was holding it but the calf got away from him and Opal slipped around underneath and fell off.
> When he picked her up and asked if she was hurt, Opal said, "Well, he stepped on my ear." That's all she hurt! I remember Daddy telling that story. I guess he thought it was funny!
> Well, it was funny—but it was tragic and scary too. Heck we played with those animals that Daddy would bring in. We would get the little calves into the chutes and play cowboy. Mama wasn't around all the time. She was someplace else a lot of the time and that's where I was so scared so much of the time![3]

Although the children feared the cattle might break into the house, they felt safe upstairs. And they knew their parents would be home before long, sometimes with a surprise. Once Mabel rode to get the mail and came back with only one stocking on. She'd had two on when she left. She reached into her pocket, pulled out the stocking, and showed the children several little baby rabbits. So once again, Audrey had rabbits to take care of.

Mabel wanted to move back to Las Vegas in late summer of 1922. She was expecting another baby. Audrey wrote:

> The chickens were a disaster. We had about 500 when we moved to town to the old Papen House at the end of Friedman and 11th street on Mora Avenue next to Rogers place. It is in what is now the north part of Highlands University Athletic field.[4]

They put the few chickens they had left in the chicken house. They also kept the rabbits there. The chickens were about ten weeks old—the five hundred chicks left out of the thousand—by the end of the summer. They sold a few of them. More were lost. They all piled up and smothered each other at night, standing on one another. And then they all got the croup. Audrey didn't have any help and she didn't know what to do.

> From the Papen House I started to school in the 4th grade at Douglas School. Daddy got a job as a painter of Locomotive Engines at the AT & FS Round House at the other end of town. My hands got so bad from cold that they were splitting across the knuckles. Daddy discovered them and got pure glycerin at Murphey's Drug Store. The glycerin fixed them up fine. I was trying to help mother who was very miserable—and look after Opal and Edward—and take care of the many chickens at night. I would go out and put them on roosts but they would stack up and smother.[5]

Audrey and Opal again enrolled at Douglas School, Audrey, in the fourth grade and Opal in the third. They walked together across all the vacant space over to Eighth Street on their way to school. There were hardly any houses in that area then, except for two houses to the east. A lot of people had milk cows and let them graze out in that area during the day. Audrey recalled years later in unpublished notes, "Betty:"

> Mother cried a lot when pregnant with Betty. She didn't really want more than the three [children] she already had, and it forced her to miss teaching school.
> We moved to Las Vegas in late summer and the folks rented the old Papen house which had an old chicken house for the remainder of our chickens. Mother rented out the upstairs rooms. Daddy went to work for the Santa Fe [Railroad] as a painter, painting engines—fastest painter they ever had, according to Chance Honest when [he] came to see me when I was in the Presbyterian hospital in 1968 for surgery and skin graft [for leg ulcer.][6]

The family had settled into their new place and seemed comparatively happy. Mabel was feeling better. Then one day a letter arrived—a letter edged in black. It was for Vern. Mabel's heart sank as she gave it to her husband. It was from his sister May in Avis. It was the custom in those days to cover the edges of an envelope with black ink to warn the receiver that there was bad news inside.

When Vern saw it, he said, "Oh, no! Oh, no!" Vern knew even before he opened the letter that it probably meant that his mother had died.

Vern's mother, Emma Maria Roney Hammond Clements, died on September 1, 1922. She had gone to visit Aunt May at Avis. Audrey wrote that she "died a while before Betty was born. Daddy got a letter edged in black—from Aunt May. He sat on the edge of Mother's bed and cried. He was very close to his mother."[7] It was one of the few times Audrey saw her daddy cry.

Audrey had only known her paternal grandmother for ten years, but she was greatly influenced by her. She taught her many things, including some of the superstitions that undoubtedly originated in Ireland. Grandma Clements believed in the "little people," such as leprechauns and fairies. She taught Audrey that just because we can't see something doesn't mean it doesn't exist.

> Daddy's mother, Emma Maria Clements, died down at Avis just a little while before Betty was born—I remember when the letter, carefully edged in black with a pen, came from Aunty May Munson, and Daddy and Mama sitting on the edge of the bed as he read it and he cried and cried and Mama tried to comfort him.
>
> Then Betty was born there in that house in that bed. I can't remember who took care of Mother. Later I know my grandmother, Dammuzzy, came. We moved from the Papen house to 101 Tenth Street to be closer to Daddy's work. Mother had phlebitis after the birth. Betty was tiny and frail and she cried a lot. Mother stayed in bed with her foot up. I went to Douglas School, 4th grade.[8]

Vern apparently liked his job at the Round House for the Santa Fe Railroad where he painted engines. It was a long walk for Vern from the Papen house to work at the Round house, and it was quite a distance for Opal and Audrey to walk to Douglas School. So Dammuzzy found a house on Tenth Street, a much more convenient location for Vern's work and the children's school. It had a bathroom in the back. It had a built-on back porch like the one they'd had at the house at Eighth and Columbia in 1921.

After Elizabeth Hope "Betty" Clements was born at the Papen house in Las Vegas, Dammuzzy came from Lincoln, Nebraska to stay until Mabel was on her feet again. Audrey wrote:

> Mother's mother came either just before or after Betty was born October 24, 1922. Mother had phlebitis. They called it milk leg then; she had to stay in bed. [*Milk leg* has been defined as thrombosis of the iliac or

femoral vein followed by swelling of the leg.] I remember when she came she cooked "Ladies Cabbage," and how good it tasted. I don't know what we had been eating—but not much but potatoes and gravy. Dammuzzy cleaned us up and insisted we move before Christmas to a house closer to Daddy's work.[9]

Audrey in later years recalled that before her grandmother arrived, "I was in the Fourth grade and looking like a little waif—and feeling like it."[10]

Audrey checked on the chickens every night, trying to keep them from smothering each other. But every morning she'd find more dead chickens. She cared for the rabbits and chickens all that winter. It was very cold to go out and feed them, but she did it faithfully. Since they were her rabbits, she sold them to John Nelson and he took the rest of the chickens off her hands, too. He said, "I'll pay you a fair price. I don't believe in cheating the kids out of their money."[11] He gave Mabel fifty dollars for Audrey, and Mabel put it away to save for her.

Audrey was delighted that Dammuzzy was there for Christmas. The house had a beautiful bay window on the south, facing Prince Street. She put up a gorgeous Christmas tree in the big bay window. They had a wonderful Christmas that year, due largely to Dammuzzy's efforts. Audrey was grateful for her grandmother's help. She began to feel less neglected. Audrey elaborated in a taped interview:

> My hair had been a mess for a long time. It was stringing down in every direction. Dammuzzy cut it and my fourth grade teacher at Douglas stopped by my desk and said that my hair looked very nice! That really made my day!"[12]

When Mabel had phlebitis and her legs would swell terribly, she couldn't get up to take care of Betty or the older kids. Even with her mother's help, Mabel knew that the older children were sometimes not supervised very well. At the house on the corner of Tenth and Independence there were big trees across the street. Audrey climbed trees around the house on Tenth Street. Nothing was built there then as it was all undeveloped land. The kids would wade in the Gallinas River after a rain, not realizing that they could have been swept away by rushing water after those heavy rains. Audrey recalled that later someone built a trailer court in that place and ran a little store there.

In January, 1923 Mabel was well enough to get up, so Dammuzzy went home. Audrey was very attached to her grandmother and knew she would miss her terribly.

Babysitting: Las Vegas to Lagunita

Mabel had planned to return to Chapelle to teach another year. Due to Betty's birth and Mabel's subsequent illness, Mabel was unable to return so her position was taken by another teacher. However, in January, 1923, Mabel was given the school at Lagunita where another teacher had quit. Lagunita was about three miles beyond Chapelle and about fifteen miles south of Las Vegas.

Mabel found a house close to the school, the only house available in the entire village, a block or less from the cemetery. Apparently Vern continued living in Las Vegas, working at the Round House. Audrey wrote:

> Daddy was at 101 Tenth Street. Sometimes he would drive out and he and Mother would have heavy, angry, arguing discussions.
>
> One of the Chapelle girls I remember wanted to borrow Mother's pretty brown coat. Mother lent it to her and saw her take off down the country and by the canyon edge meet a young man. Mother was horrified for fear someone thought she [Mabel] was in her widely known coat meeting Juan at the canyon. Mother never lent her coat again.[1]

Mabel was nursing the baby, so she had to hurry over from school at noon and also be home by four o'clock in the afternoon, as Betty was on a four-hour schedule. Mabel couldn't find anyone who would stay at the house. All the women Mabel asked to babysit offered to keep Betty at their homes, but their homes were too far away from the school house for Mabel to keep up with the exact feeding schedule. So Audrey, who had just turned ten in November, was the only person to care for Betty. Audrey wrote:

> Mother rented a house across the road from the school house and next to the cemetery. She got a girl from the village to stay with Betty. I went to school and remember looking the kids over to see who could be my best friend and boy friend. There wasn't much choice and I didn't have to worry about it really because the village women were afraid to stay so close to the cemetery. She [Mabel] hired a girl or two but they would stay

1/2 day and quit. So I had to stay home and look after Betty. I spent the day caring for her, and as soon as she was big enough she had a jumper type swing that she spent a lot of time in and I read. I read my school books and did lessons for Mother at night. I read all of James Oliver Curwood books. Vivian Shearer, still the agent at Chapelle railroad station, rode his horse Old Jug over once in a while and brought *The Denver Post* and other books.²

Whenever Mabel would go to Las Vegas on the train to get her check, she would return on the train the next day. Once Mabel brought a book back and she hid it. Audrey heard her mother talking about the brand new book called *The Sheik*. Rudolph Valentino played the part in the movie that was made from it. It was supposedly very risqué. Naturally, Audrey was curious, so she discovered its hiding place and read it. She wrote years later: "Mother bought a new book on the train riding from Vegas to Chapelle, a daring sexy book, *The Shiek*—which I also read and didn't understand half of it but I thought it a fine book. I was ten."³

Audrey recalled:

> One night we were gathered around the bed where mother lay reading to us by the dim lamp light. Suddenly we heard a scratch, scratch on the building paper nailed to the door we didn't use. The bed was across the door. Mother decided it was a bug and began pounding the spot with her shoe. The thing gradually went down to the bottom of the door. We pulled out the bed and there on the floor was a 14 inch centipede smashed flat by mother's shoe. She lifted it up and put it in the back of the wood range. I never would lift up that back lid for fear it might still be alive and crawl out.
>
> Vivian [Charles Vivian Shearer] used to ride horseback from Chapelle—in the snowy weather. He would bring the *Sunday Denver Post* and I "devoured" the Sunday sections, crying over the sad stories. I remember reading dire predictions that the U.S.A. birth rate would be on a decline by the 1970's (and it is.)
>
> Betty was a frail little baby—skinny. After school was out Mother didn't move back to town. She rented a house up back of the depot at Chapelle, close enough to carry water from the depot faucet by the station platform. She was to teach at Chapelle that next winter. We kids rode the train back and forth some.⁴

Charles Vivian Shearer, the station agent at Chapelle, continued to come over on Sundays and bring books or magazines. Mabel called him "Vivian." That was his middle name and was apparently what his mother called him. Audrey read everything Vivian brought to the house. She liked the newspapers that had stories in them—serials. Audrey only attended school two or three days that year. Audrey loved her baby sister Betty and didn't mind staying home to care for her. But sometimes she missed school and friends her own age. She missed the fun of taking part in the play they were preparing.

When Mabel put on a play at the end of the year, Audrey's part was very small. Mabel put a picture frame up and hung a sheet all around it and then let some of the kids pose in front of that frame for a picture. Then Audrey would pull the curtain down. So that was Audrey's "part" in that play. Audrey wrote:

> Mother put on a program for the end of school. She had children [recite] verses, etc. and fixed a picture frame to let kids look through as a portrait when a sheet was pulled back. I was in that. The poor little boy that was supposed to say a verse—probably no word in it was one he understood but with prompting he was able to show off his learning by reciting: "I see the moon; the moon sees me; God loves the moon and God loves me." Nobody in those days objected because God was mentioned inside a school house.[5]

There was a little lake at Lagunita behind the house. Audrey saw one lone little duck that swam around and around on it in only about a foot of space. When the water froze up, the little duck stayed in the middle of the ice. Before long the duck was gone. That duck had been there ever since they moved there in January. Audrey asked her mother about it.

"That duck must have been sick or injured or it would have left with the other ducks," Mabel observed. "It's gone now," Mabel replied.

"Poor little duck. All the others flew away to the warmer weather together. It was here alone in the cold. Do you think there's a chance it might be alive?" Audrey asked.

"Oh, we might be surprised. It might have survived. Maybe we'll see it when the warm weather comes again," her mother replied.

As Audrey watched the other children getting ready for school or various social events, she knew how that little duck must have felt—left behind and alone. She realized that being cold and hungry and alone was very difficult. But if you were tough, you'd survive.

19

Taste of Vinegar: Las Vegas to Chapelle—Again

When school was out, Mabel moved the family back to 101 Tenth Street in Las Vegas so she could go to summer school again. The previous summer she had taken the classes she needed to obtain her New Mexico teaching certificate, but she had to take another class or two.

Mabel's teaching certificate was issued September 27, 1921 and was in Home Economics Education. (State Vocational Certificate, 1921) Then she was issued a State Elementary Certificate on September 1, 1922, as follows:

> This is to certify, that Mrs. Mabel Clements, having furnished satisfactory evidence of moral character, academic scholarship and knowledge of the theory and art of teaching, as required by law and by the rules of the State Board of Education, is hereby granted this First Grade Elementary Certificate which authorizes her, if otherwise qualified by law, to teach in the Public Schools of the State of New Mexico during a period of two years from date, without further examination, unless this certificate is revoked for cause.[1]

Standings secured included: Reading; Penmanship; Orthography; Grammar and Composition; Geography; Arithmetic; Physiology; U.S. History; Civil Government; N.M. History and Civics; Pedagogy and School Management; and Psychology.[2] The Certificate was signed by the State Superintendent of Public Instruction and Secretary State Board of Education.

Vern was working at the Round House while Mabel went to the Normal University. The kids were on their own again, with Audrey in charge.

Sometimes when Edward would misbehave, Mabel would send him to bed without any supper—her favorite punishment. But Audrey knew what it was like to be hungry. She'd feel sorry for Edward and get a plate of food, quietly go outside to his window, tap on the pane, and give him the food when he opened the window. Sometimes they had difficulty getting the window opened. Audrey later wrote: "In trying to get it open Daddy heard me and came and helped.[3]

Another time Edward was being punished when their daddy was home. To Audrey's surprise, when she went around to give Edward some food through the window, Vern was there doing the same thing! Audrey and her daddy looked at one another a little sheepishly.

Then Vern said, "Well, your mother's a little hard on Edward. I thought he ought to have a little something for supper."

"Me, too," Audrey said.

So that time Edward got two plates of food!

After Betty was born, Mabel thought the kids should be in church so Mabel found out where the Methodist Church was. Then the children starting going to the Southern Methodist Church in Las Vegas. It was in a house almost straight across from Springer Hall on the University campus, a big two-story house with a porch on it. That's where the preacher and his family lived. They had Sunday School in some of the downstairs rooms. Audrey later wrote:

> I ran wild climbing the trees across the street and playing with little Mary Suiler that lived across from us facing Prince Street. I wanted Mama to meet her folks but I don't think they ever met. I also played with Helen Maria Nolan—Pat Nolan's granddaughter. Opal and I played with her a lot.[4]

One afternoon one of the neighbors had a birthday party at the stone house next door to where the Clements lived on Tenth Street. Audrey was outside playing in the yard and watching the kids next door—especially the little girls in their beautiful dresses—playing games in the yard. The Clements children had been playing with those neighbors the entire time they had lived there, so they were good friends. But the Clements kids had not been invited to the party. The little Woods boy who lived next door also saw the party children and wanted to go but had not been invited. Then a mother or grandmother suddenly realized there were some kids who were always around but hadn't been invited to the party. The woman called them to come on over to the party and have ice cream and cake.

The little Woods boy went right over. But Audrey said, "No, thank you," and went into the house. She was insulted. She felt that if they were going to ask her to the party, they should have asked her and the other Clements kids beforehand so they could get dressed up and be ready. She knew they had only asked her and the Woods boy to come over because they'd seen them watching the party and didn't want to be rude. She wasn't going to go when she had only been asked at the last minute out of an impulse to be polite—not because she'd been on the original guest list. Furthermore, Audrey refused to go over there in her old clothes, even though she had nothing as fancy to dress up in as the little girls she'd seen.

Audrey went into the bedroom and sobbed. Mabel came in just then and asked Audrey why she was crying, but she couldn't tell her. She didn't want to mention the fact that she had been left off the party invitation list or that she had no pretty clothes to wear to a party, even if she had been invited. All the girls over there wore pretty summer dresses, looking like little angels. Audrey was in her overalls. It was a sad time for a ten year old girl. Audrey described that incident later:

> Then she [the neighbor girl] had a birthday party with all the "in" kids—big shot friends of her folks. They were all dressed so beautifully and I was in dirty overalls and an old shirt. The little boy next door was playing with Opal and Edward and me in our yard [just across] from the fancy party. The mother or grandmother saw us and called and invited us over to the party. The little boy and Opal and Edward went for ice cream and cake. I wouldn't go. I went inside and cried. When Mama got home from school she asked why I was crying. I couldn't tell her but it was because I was good enough to play with but not good enough to be invited except as an after-thought. I don't know who looked after Betty that summer. I must have when Mama was gone.[5]

Mabel was in a play that summer. Audrey remembered the play she had wanted to see so badly when they were in Nebraska and wasn't given a nickel to go. But his time she did get to see the play. Audrey recalled:

> Mama went back to school at the Normal University, now Highlands University. She was in a play with long green underpants so when she sat in a chair and it tipped over backwards she fell back with legs straight up. The big green bloomers showed and brought down the house.[6]

The family moved back to Chapelle in the fall of 1923. The post office at Chapelle was across the railroad tracks and down the road toward Lagunita, about a mile or a mile and a half away. Audrey walked there a time or two with her friends, the Raels. They had to walk through corn fields and open country. Mr. and Mrs. Rael and their daughter Sophia liked to pick some of the corn. It was corn on the stock; each of them had an ear to chew on as they went. The people who ran the Chapelle Post Office were the Salazars. [Albino Salazar]

Their ranch was about a mile and a half below Chapelle. The Salazars didn't live in Chapelle—they lived on their ranch and had to go and bring the mail and take the mail, back and forth, to the train depot in Chapelle every day.

One day Audrey didn't have to walk to get the mail because Charles Vivian Shearer drove down and picked up Mabel and Audrey to go to the post office. Audrey was grateful to get to ride in a car and not have to walk to the distant post office. She noticed that Mr. Shearer was showing up quite often to help out.

The Clements family lived on the other side of the school house. The community still held dances at the school. Mabel sponsored a dance or two to try to raise money for the school. When Mabel put on a school-sponsored dance, all the big, rough men, including one they called "Gooberlip," would keep "peace" at her dances. Gooberlip had huge hands and was the biggest person Audrey had ever seen. There were no fights if it was a school sponsored dance. The older people held down the trouble. Audrey thought maybe the fact that Gooberlip was there helped.

Mabel and Vern found the New Mexico culture—like the weather—varied and unique. The native New Mexican food was unique. The music was unique. And some of the customs were, as well. Mabel thought some of the Christmas customs were absolutely wonderful. At the same time, some of the customs—some originating in Spain, some in Mexico—were unique enough to be difficult to understand. One such custom was what was called a "rooster pull." Audrey wrote about it years later for the *Las Vegas Daily Optic, Rodeo Edition*, "Rooster Pull Is Big Event Held by Top Horseman:"

> Each village around Las Vegas has at least one "corrida del gallo" or rooster pull every year.
>
> The younger men and boys gather in the village plaza with their horses. Good horses, mustangs, broomtails, any kind of horseflesh that can carry a young caballero is ridden in from the surrounding ranches to take part in the event.
>
> The combined horse race and display of acrobatic skill brings out every girl in the village dressed in her best. Many a young man has won his wife at a rooster pull.
>
> The rooster is buried in the sand or adobe with only his head and neck exposed. Those taking part in the event race full tilt across the plaza. Swinging down from the saddle the contestant must avoid the flying hooves of his horse as he tries to snatch the moving head of the live rooster.

The rooster may be quick and jerk its head from the fingers of the racing man. If his *latigos* are not cinched tight to the running horse he may suddenly find his saddle slips and he is swung under the flying horse.

The man who has a fast horse and quick fingers may be able to pull the head from the rooster in the split second of contact. Then the fun begins.

The man with the prize must defend it from all comers. As soon as a sharp eye spots the fact that the rooster has lost his head a howling mob on horseback starts after the lucky rider. He has to avoid all of the men who will try to take the trophy away from him.

If his horse is fleet he may out distance the mob. But they will circle back and try to way lay him as he attempts to take his prize back to the official starting point. This last requirement prolongs the horseplay.

The men ride madly through the cedar and piñon trees and over the rocky trails, or in the higher villages the race will be through the pine and fir timber. The rider may be able to hide in a canyon while the mob thunders past. But usually it is a violent race lasting for several hours.

In the *corrida de gallo* even the losers have fun. And they can always dream that maybe next year their horse will be faster and the rooster less quick and tough.[7]

Today the game may be considered cruel; but it was commonplace when Audrey was growing up in the little villages of northern New Mexico.

While the Clements children learned and grew in the refreshing, crisp air of northern New Mexico, under its circular blue skies and surrounding cobalt colored mountains, all was not as peaceful as it might have appeared. Vern and Mabel were having marital problems. So they decided to separate. They were, in fact, already separated, as Vern was still living in Las Vegas and Mabel was back in Chapelle. Vern took the kids on several picnics. He would come by in his little old car, pick them up, and take them over to the Pecos or some other nice place. One time Audrey was holding Betty and there was a big bump. (There were no seat belts in those days.) Betty hit her face on the car door and ran her two front teeth through her lower lip. She always had a little scar underneath her lower lip where her two front teeth went through it.[8]

Petra Trogsted and a lady named Beth were teaching at San José. Sometimes Vern would stop there and visit with them. Once Audrey noticed Vern spent at least half an hour trying to get Beth or Petra to kiss him goodbye. It was cold in the car and the kids were freezing, but Vern sat there with his head out the car window, ignoring the kids while he flirted with the ladies.[9]

Vern continued to stay at the house on Tenth Street, working with the railroad. A man named Joe Honest worked with Vern on the Santa Fe. The Honests later lived at Doretta, which is on the road to Santa Fe—eighteen miles southwest of Las Vegas. They had a store there. Joe said that one day a bunch of the men came to ask Vern if he could paint one of those great big train engines in just one day. Vern said he could, and they didn't believe it, so they began laying bets on it. Vern was true to his word. He painted the engine in one day. He was known as a very fast, efficient painter. However, before long Vern suffered from lead poisoning so he had to quit.

That school year, 1923-24, Mabel and Vern decided to get a divorce. Mabel didn't rent the big school house room to live in as before; she rented a little house surrounded by piñon trees behind the depot. Like most rural homes, there was no indoor plumbing. There was an outdoor toilet in the back. Water for the house had to be carried from the depot or the section house which was up at the other end of town from the depot. The Santa Fe had a water tank where water was provided for the town. The kids carried it in buckets from the depot or the section house for home use and for the school. The railroad had water piped to the section house which was at the other end of town from the school house to the right of the school. The depot was off to the left and about the same distance from the school. The Clements kids carried water for their mother and all the children helped carry the water for the school. There was a dipper in the school pail for everyone to drink out of. Mabel didn't approve of that. She wouldn't let the kids drink out of that bucket with a common dipper. Each had to have his or her cup. In those days people shared drinking utensils, but Mabel knew that diseases could be spread that way and discouraged it.[10] However, disease was only one of many dangers school children faced. They also had to contend with other youngsters.

One day Audrey was standing at the blackboard in the front of the room when a boy named Abel came in the door at the back of the school and yelled at her. She turned around to look. He said, "Hold still." Then he threw a knife over the length of the room. It hit the blackboard right beside her. It barely missed her and stuck in the blackboard.

At Thanksgiving, 1923, Mabel decided to go to Las Vegas and stay at the Plaza Hotel for Thanksgiving dinner—as they had planned once before and then discovered the head lice. This time they went, but, unknown to them at the time, they were all exposed to the measles before they returned home to Chapelle. When the incubation period went by—from the time they'd been to Las Vegas—they all got sick, so they knew they'd caught the disease in Las

Vegas. Unknowingly, they exposed some of the villagers. The measles hit the native Hispanic kids very hard, a lot harder than the blond "Anglo" kids. One little baby died, and Mabel felt very bad. She thought if she hadn't taken her kids to Las Vegas, they wouldn't have caught the measles and brought the illness back to Chapelle. But there was no way she could have known.

The villagers decided to put on a Christmas play, *Los Pastores*. Three men went around the village in a wagon. One man stood up in the back of the wagon, playing a guitar and singing to get everyone's attention, advertising the fact that there was going to be a play at the school house—a Spanish production. The school was the only place big enough to hold all the people. The Board of Directors let them use the school house. The room was packed!

Basilio Griego, the postmaster, played the devil with a big forked tail. He hopped around rattling his chains and threatening everyone, making them scream. He was grabbing at everyone and scaring them. All the bigger boys, at least ten of them, were shepherds. Their staffs were decorated with tinsel or crepe paper. They wore costumes which Mabel assisted in making in spite of having very little to work with. There weren't many decorations because everyone was poor, but in spite of that it was a very good production.

Audrey sat in the window during the play with a little boy, José Solano. In later years, Audrey recalled, "He was a skinny little woebegone waif and we held hands."[11] The kids sat in the windows, as all the seats were taken. There were big windows all across the front of the classroom facing the railroad tracks. Kerosene lamps where placed around the room and in some windows to light the room.[12]

There was a sweet little girl playing the part of Mary. She was a frail girl, about seven years of age. She sat next to the manger in the middle of the room on the floor, holding a small doll, the Infant. Everybody was supposed to take money and drop it in a bowl beside her for a donation. Everyone got in line and dropped to their knees and went by her, dropping pennies and other change into the bowl. Audrey gave her nickel to José. He went to Mary on his knees and dropped it in the bowl. The donation went to the Church.[13]

Audrey wrote: "[I] Sat in a school window and held hands with José Solano while *Los Pastores* was presented with Griego as the devil, eliciting wild screams from various ones as he tried to claim them."[14]

Christmas was a wonderful time, even though the ones in Nebraska had always been the best. Mabel spent a great deal of time writing to each member of the family and sending a little gift. One time Audrey saw a note that her mother had written to her Aunt Laura Waddell. Mabel's note was as follows:

> Aunt L.:
> If the love that we are sending were measured by size and weight
> The US mail couldn't carry it;
> 'T would have to go by freight.
> Worlds of love from Mabel and all.[15]

It was heart breaking for Audrey to see her parents arguing and finally separating. Vern would come out to visit the kids every so often. Audrey never forgot the day her father took her aside and told her that he and Mabel were going to get a divorce.

"Who do you want to stay with—me or your mama?" He asked. Vern didn't realize what an unfair position that question puts a child in. Audrey felt a sinking feeling in her heart. She loved her daddy and her mama. She didn't want to have to choose between them.

"I want to stay with both of you!" Audrey declared. She tried to explain that she could not choose between them. For many years the memory of that moment pierced her heart with sadness. Vern came to visit the kids once every two or three weeks but it was not the same as before. Years later, Audrey wrote:

> Sometimes Daddy came and took us kids on picnics to Pecos and San José—where a teacher was—Bess—who wanted to marry him. I saw her 25 years later at Mrs. Richard's Beauty Shop in Las Vegas, and she asked about Daddy. I think she still loved him. She lived in California somewhere then. (Who was it that kissed his corpse at his funeral? A tall dark woman!)[16]

It wasn't very far from Las Vegas to Chapelle but the trip of about twelve miles probably took about two hours. Audrey recalled in a taped interview years later:

> Mama and Daddy were divorced but Daddy would come out to visit us every once in a while. Once time he came out he had a banged up face and a black eye. Daddy liked to "play" across the bridge. He'd go over there to dances. There weren't any dances in East Las Vegas that I knew about. Anyway, Daddy had been walking home from a dance in Old Town (West Las Vegas) when he heard something, or someone, behind him. He turned his head and someone hit him, but it was a glancing blow because he had turned his head to see who was following him. He was on the East side of the bridge in front of Mrs. Bosh's little store on the South side of the street (National after it crossed the bridge) across the

street from Monsimer's Bakery. When he got right in front of her store, under the "over hang"—she had a porch up over her store—somebody said something and then hit him. He looked a "sight"![17]

According to Vern, before he proceeded down the street, the other guy looked worse!

Vern looked worse when he came to visit one day and his face was burned black and starting to peel. Vern had gone to Maloof's Garage, next to the Optic, on his way to work at the Round House one day. Someone always started a fire in the big heater in the morning to warm the place up. When Vern got there that morning, some fellow had prepared the stove to light. So Vern took a match out of his pocket and scratched it on the back hip of his pants and flipped it into the stove. That's what he always did, but the guy that had laid the fire had put a lot of oil or something in the stove so it would be easier to light. It flared up and followed Vern's arm to his face. It just exploded when the match hit him. He suffered a lot until his face all peeled off and the new skin healed up.[18]

It was bad enough that her daddy had moved out and her parents were divorced. But Audrey was old enough to understand something about finances. She knew her mother and father had only been able to eke out a living with both of them working. She knew that Mabel would depend on Vern for child support if she were to continue providing for the children as the two of them had. But Vern was angry and bitter.

Vern said to Audrey, "I will never pay her [Mabel] one dime of child support. I will go to Mexico if I have to. But I won't pay!"

Even then Audrey was old enough to realize that it was the children who would suffer. She and the other children were the ones who would be deprived if Vern didn't help. But he didn't see that. He simply said, "I will never give Mabel one cent of child support!"[19]

True to his word, Vern never paid a penny of child support. Sometimes he bought the children clothes or other gifts. After he re-married he did invite the children to visit from time to time. In fact, the younger children, Edward and Betty, often stayed with him and his new wife Mable Day Clements. Mable Day had been a school teacher and had never been married.

In later years Vern told Audrey, "If I had it to do over again, I'd do things differently." Audrey knew it was her father's way of saying he realized he should have paid child support.

Life went on, even under the hardships imposed by the divorce. After school one day Sophia Rael and her two brothers, Zacarías and Juan, began throwing rocks at Audrey. Audrey's family lived in a little house directly behind the depot. Her classmates had thrown rocks before, and she had usually run home as fast as she could. But this time she got angry and decided to throw a few rocks herself. Audrey's rock hit Sophia in the head and she began to bleed. Blood was running down her face, but she continued to throw rocks at Audrey. Then Sophia's brothers began running after Audrey, shouting that they were going to kill her. She believed them. Audrey reached the outdoor toilet and locked the door. They pounded on it and banged on the door until Mabel came home from school to get something and the boys ran home. Audrey later told her mother what had happened. Audrey and Opal walked over to Raels' house and asked Mrs. Rael if Sophia was all right.

"Oh, yes, she's fine," Mrs. Rael said.[20]

Apparently Sophia did not tell her mother what had happened. She was probably ashamed because she had started the rock fight. Audrey was relieved. She resolved never to throw rocks again. Her aim was too good. She might kill someone next time!

Audrey recalled that on her eleventh birthday, "It was a nice warm day."

I tried to fix myself a birthday party. I had water seasoned with vinegar and sugar for lemonade. I think I must have tried to make myself a cake but I don't remember. I set a wooden box of some kind out for a table in the yard. I don't remember if anybody was around except us kids—Opal, Edward, Betty and me. We had a party of some sort![21]

It is unknown whether Audrey's mother baked her a birthday cake later that evening. In any case, that day Audrey felt as if she was going to have to give herself a party if she was going to have one at all. It has been said that if someone gives you a lemon, make lemonade. But if you don't even have a lemon, what can you do? Find some vinegar and sugar and make the best of what you've got! Audrey was learning that life is not always sweet. Sometimes the bitter or sour side of life provides the most poignant, the most valuable lessons. It had been a difficult year for Audrey. She'd had to take care of Betty much of the time and missed school. (Her mother had promised to pay her, and that promise would be kept. In the meantime, Audrey had to wait.) She'd made friends in Las Vegas but had been rejected when she wasn't invited to their birthday party. Her parents separated and divorced. She'd lost her temper and hurt her classmate. And for her eleventh birthday she had to make her own birthday cake—or wait until her mother found time to do it. She wondered if her parents would ever get back together again. And if they did, would they all be happy? She drank her vinegar "lemonade" and wondered.

20

Bernal: A New Beginning

It was exciting! Vivian talked of sure wealth. He was going to find oil. Mabel supported him in his new enterprise.

Charles Vivian Shearer quit his job as Station Agent on the Santa Fe Railroad in Chapelle and moved to Bernal to start his own business—the Meadows Oil Company. Vivian sold shares of stock to raise the money to drill. He and his father, Richard Arthur Shearer, got a well drilling outfit. As soon as school was out, Mabel moved the family to Bernal. Audrey later wrote:

> Mother divorced Daddy—said he was running around. I know he had danced and went to dances and had a good time. He was a lady's man, but I never thought of him as a "rounder." I suppose "swinger" is the word in use now. Mother started going with Vivian [Shearer] and took Betty along. Betty was there when they got married in Santa Rosa in June, 1924. After [that] Vivian quit the Railroad and moved to Serafina to be a wildcat oil promoter. When school was out at Chapelle we moved to Serafina and lived in a house on the Plaza in front of the old church. Mother boarded (fed) all the oil well workers. Opal and I helped and did dishes.[1]

Undoubtedly, with stacks of dishes to wash, Audrey and Opal played the game they had made up. It was called "Five Ahead and Catch Up." If the dishwasher could get five dishes ahead of the dish dryer, then the dryer had to finish the dishes. If the dish dryer caught up and had no dishes to dry, then the dish washer had to do the rest of the dishes by herself—drying with the dish towel as well as washing. So the dish dryer hurried in order to try to get ahead. Of course, the dish-washer would hurry so that she would not have to dry the dishes.[2]

Vivian could speak Spanish and he knew all the people there. After he leased much of the land around Bernal and Chapelle, he got a good crew together. They began drilling for oil. Mabel provided meals for the crew, about five or six of them.

Mabel and the children lived on one side of the Plaza. Vivian and his crew rented a house across on the other side the Plaza. Audrey recalled that Edward slept behind the kitchen range, covered by a blanket or two, perhaps because it was warmer there or maybe because there was no place else to sleep.[3]

Years later Audrey wrote about Bernal for the *Rodeo Edition* of the *Las Vegas Daily Optic:*

> Bernal, N.M. is located a few hundred yards to the left of the new highway 85 [now I-25] about 14 miles south of Las Vegas, as you travel to Santa Fe.
>
> Formerly called Bernal Springs, the post office is Serafina, named for the adopted daughter of Basilio Griego in the 1920's. Once it was a good day's trek with plodding ox teams from Tecolote to Bernal springs where the heavy wagons would camp before pulling on over the rolling piñon covered hills to San Miguel.
>
> This was Indian country. The ruins of many small pueblos dot the broken canyon and mesa land. Rising abruptly behind Bernal is the storied Starvation peak where legend says more than 100 Spanish settlers were driven by raiding Indians and starved to death.
>
> The original settlement was built in a tight square around a small plaza. The thick walled adobe houses had no windows on the outside. That is they had windows facing into the plaza but none looking out into the country side. The narrow alley way or street between the long row of houses could easily be barricaded at the lower end. At the upper end there were a few more feet between the houses on each side of the plaza. And at the upper end of the tiny plaza was the church. A few feet which could easily be barricaded separated it from the closest house.
>
> Thirty years ago the church had lost its roof and was grown with weeds where once the devout knelt. But the steeple was intact. The graveyard at that time was filled with fancy stones where souls could rest in peace under dates of born 1850—died 1870. And even older.
>
> Today the old church is melting back into the church yard. And the new church, built closer to the highway, is beginning to be considered as an old church.
>
> Sometimes the wind howls and throws gravel until the villagers cannot face it. And sometimes when the heavy rains come the two dry arroyos whirl with red water ten feet deep as they race to join at their junction at Bernal. And the walls of the old church melt down a little more into the land.[4]

Audrey remembered the old church that was falling down. It wasn't used any more, as there was a new church. The old church had a kind of open space in front, half-circling it, with houses built around the semi-circle facing the Plaza and the church. Settlers built their communities like that in the early days for protection from marauding Native Americans. Mabel's bedroom was on the side facing the front opening of the old church where a door had once been. Audrey noticed she could see inside the old church from her mama's bedroom window. One snowy morning Audrey and Opal were looking out the widow where they could see the old church very clearly. In later years, Audrey recalled in a taped interview:

> I don't know what Opal and I were doing on Mama's bed, but we were there, looking out that window on a very snowy day—probably in early spring—and here came two fellows with a little tiny box about the size of a shoe box and they went into the church through a side door. We could see them very plainly inside there—there was a sheer curtain over our window so they couldn't see us watching them. I think that church had been deserted for at least fifty years! The men dug a hole in the floor of the church and buried that tiny box. I knew who they were. One of the fellows had been married in the last six months or so and obviously his wife had a baby and it died. Of course they couldn't have a priest bury it because it died before it ever got "sprinkled." They buried it themselves to give it the best chance they could to get into heaven.[5]

Audrey surmised that since there was no priest at this burial "ceremony" and probably the baby had never been baptized, the men wanted to bury the baby themselves in the old church because it was still sacred ground. She later wrote in her notes, "These Things Happened:"

> By that time we were living at Bernal, in what had been a plaza, in front of the old church—built in 1870 or 1880. No double doors barred the church entrance to sand and tumble weeds. Part of one wall was caved in and the roof was gone. The bell tower stood straight and lonesome above the wide doorway.
>
> From our window a couple of hundred feet directly across from that gaping door we once watched a funeral. One of the girls I had gone to school with had married. Now, months later, she had birthed a premature child that did not live.

It was a cold, cloudy day with a light drizzle falling, when I happened to look out of the window. I saw the girl's father and brother enter the ruined building through the side where the wall had fallen out. They carried a little box about the size of a shoe box, and a shovel. I softly called mother and the other kids. We watched while they dug a deep hole. Then with heads bared to the chill rain, they placed the box in the hole and covered it over. Mother explained that since the baby had not been baptized, it could not be buried in the cemetery that was in the church yard at the side of the church. Therefore, they buried it in the most holy place they could think of—the floor of the deserted church building. Now, more than 55 years later, I can still see them in their rough winter coats and dark caps. They knelt there to place that tiny box in sacred earth. And I still want to weep for their sorrow and the tiny baby that never got a breath of Bernal cedar smoke or heard the train's whistle as they passed the Starvation Peak crossing.[6]

The house Charles Vivian was living in was also very old. One day when the crew was working at the oil rig there was a loud crash and dust blew out everywhere. The roof and back wall of the adobe house fell in. A huge cross beam or *viga* from the roof fell right in the middle of a bed, a bed where a great big fellow slept. Fortunately, he was at work when it happened. If it had happened at night when he was in bed, he would have been crushed.[7]

The first oil well rig was sitting right at the foot of Starvation Peak. Audrey had some pictures taken of her there with some of the village girls. The family hoped it would be their way to more prosperous life.

Although Mabel and Charles Vivian Shearer were married that summer—on June 27, 1924—they didn't tell the kids for a while. Audrey wrote:

> I was about ten when my mother and father were divorced. We were living at Chapelle, about 14 miles southwest of Las Vegas on the Santa Fe railroad. When I saw mother sitting on the station agent's lap, I wrote a letter to my father in Vegas. When I tried to mail the letter, mother got it and read it. She cried and I cried, down there by the old Salazar house in Ojo de Chapelle, where we got the mail.
>
> So they [Mabel and Vern] were divorced and when mother asked if I minded if she and the station agent married, I said "No." I remember her asking as we walked in bright moonlight from Chapelle to Bernal one spring evening. It was warm and when we got to Bernal, the teacher [that] mother wanted to see was in her home playing a piano. A group

of young men were standing under the huge cottonwoods in the yard, listening. I stood out by the gate while mother went inside and enjoyed the music too. In those days you took your music wherever it floated on the breezes, for there was no radio or TV. Mother did buy an Edison phonograph and we were lucky to have music at the two room Chapelle school house where we lived in one room.[8]

Vivian had previously been married to Edith Martin. They had a daughter, Ellen Grace—usually called Grace. When the little girl was two or three years old, Vivian was working as a forest ranger some distance away. He came home one night to find a man's rig parked at the house, his horses tied there. Vivian entered the house, went to the bedroom, and was stunned to find his wife and her lover there. He claimed they were in bed together. He was furious.[9]

Vivian sued for divorce and tried to prove that Edith was an unfit mother. He tried to get custody of Grace. But the judge gave Grace to her mother. Later Edith married Fred Shutt and Grace stayed with them.[10]

The day Mabel announced her marriage to Vivian, they took the children to go swimming in the Pecos River near San Juan. There was a good swimming hole there and the river was quite deep along the edge by the bank. Mabel thought she would teach Edward how to swim by the "sink or swim" method. She threw Edward into the water. Edward was terrified; he sputtered and went under. Vivian jumped in and got him out. "He never got over his fear of water and never learned to swim. He had on faded brown overalls and she picked him up by them and threw him in the river. I can still see the scene."[11]

Mabel's old-fashioned method of teaching failed that time! Audrey learned a lesson: Never throw someone into deep water to teach them to swim. They'll just drown! The old "swim or sink" theory would not work! In any case, Mabel's dress got wet. She may have been embarrassed that Vivian had to save Edward. In any case, Mabel then told the children she and Vivian had been married in the Santa Rosa Methodist church.[12]

Just before that July Fourth, Vivian went to town and bought fireworks! He spent five dollars to entertain the kids with a real Fourth of July fireworks display. Audrey thought maybe he was celebrating his marriage, too!

Mabel was a good student and she was a good teacher. But being a mother alone was difficult. Going through separation and divorce called for her courage. She was tired of moving, tired of being poor, tired of struggling to make ends meet. She had not grown up in wealth, but she had never suffered extreme poverty as she did from time to time after she and Vern were married. She wrote a poem entitled, "Oh, God Give me Courage:"

> Oh God—give me courage
> To face each new day
> My love's love is dead
> My heart's torn away;
> But I'll dance and sing,
> Pretend to be gay
> 'Till something new turns up.
> Now! What do you say![13]

Did Mabel refer to her love for Vern as "dead" and was she hoping for a new love? Did she find it in Charles Vivian?

The Clements children liked their step-father and were glad to have a man at home again. Mabel wrote a poem which was much more cheerful than the previous one entitled "Cramming."

> 'Twas the nite before finals
> And all thru the room
> Not a thing had been touched
> Not even the broom.
> The dishes were stacked in the sink thru the day
> In hope that tomorrow my grades would be "A."
> Tests and measures, statistics—
> My head was in whirls—
> My mind wandered off.
> Should I do up my curls?
> Then out at the curb
> There arose such a clatter
> I ran to the door
> To see what was the matter.
>
> As usual, 'twas Charles.
> "Come on, Kid, let's go.
> I hear there's a peach of a film at the show."
> I cried, "Not tonight
> I simply must cram
> For tomorrow's the day
> Of our final exam."
> Charles was disgusted:

"Gee, whiz, what a bore,
Why didn't ya study
A little before?"
"Goodnight, then," I said.
"See you some other day.
I must cram tonight
For I must have an A."

Well, I crammed and I crammed
'Till my eyes and my head
Just simply quit working.
I crawled into bed.
Next day I felt rotten. I'd slept 3 hours in all.
Statistics! Statistics! I couldn't recall.
How I wished I had studied
My lesson each day.
But there always was Charles,
There was always a play.
Dr. Wells wrote the questions.
Then I took a fall.
The things I had studied on
Were not asked, at all.
Isn't that a fair test? I had to agree.
'T was such a shame
He gave me a B![14]

One of Vivian's friends, Ambrosio Solano, had owned a store. He and his family had managed a big business. The store had a big glass front but was no longer open for business because Ambrosio was about eighty years of age. He enjoyed telling Vivian stories of his youth.

Ambrosio told Vivian a story about when he was a little boy living in the Bernal area. He followed a Native American who went into some rocks where there was a room full of gold. He said he waited until the Native American came out. The old man went on his way and disappeared. So the kid decided to see what was behind the rocks. He pushed on the same rock and it opened up like a door into a cave. The room was full of gold! He dug some out and put it in his pockets. But later he told a different version of the story. He told about hitting the opening with a rock and accidentally breaking it so it would not open again.[15]

Ambrosio was going to take Vivian and show him where the cave was, but he was very old and Vivian was very busy. Maybe Vivian didn't believe the story. Somehow he never got around to locating the hidden room. So he never knew where the gold was supposedly hidden—or if it even existed. He was too busy getting his own "black gold" out of the ground!

Years later Audrey wrote about the story in one of her "history" items in the *Cowboy Reunion and Rodeo Edition* of the *Las Vegas Daily Optic*. The story was entitled, "Old-Timers Hand Down Chapelle Treasure Story:"

Nearly every village and town in New Mexico has a story of buried treasure somewhere close by. Chapelle, about 13 miles south of Las Vegas, has one of a different type.

Chapelle is on the main line of the AT & SF Railway and about a mile to the left of highway 85 as you travel from Las Vegas to Santa Fe.

The following story was told years ago by a very old man who had been born in the cedar country at the foot of Starvation Peak.

"When I was a little boy," the old man said, "I took the goats from the corrals to eat the grass, every day. I would wander among the piñon trees while the goats hunted the grass.

"One day when I put the goats in the corral for the night there was a black and white one missing. It had been with the others when I began to drive them home. So I went back to look in the canyon for it.

"There were many big rocks. As big as my house, some of them were.

"Suddenly I saw a shadow move through the rocks. I became still where I was, hidden by some rocks.

"The movement was caused by an Indian. A very old Indian. I watched him move about the rocks, find the one he was looking for and grasp a strange lump on the side of the rock. He pulled on the lump. The rock opened like a door and he went in.

"I crept silently to where I could see into the open hole in the rock. The last rays of the sun were dipping into the opening. It was lined with stacks of gold.

"The Indian was filling a sack he carried with some of the gold. He was pulling the top of the little sack shut with a string when he turned and saw me.

"He ran out of the gold filled room and slammed the door of rock behind him. He started after me. I swung my sling around my head and let fly a big stone in his direction. The stone hit the lump of door which he had used to open the door to the gold filled room.

"The Indian heard the crash of the stone and looked around. He rushed back to see the lump of rock shattered. He tried to open the door again but could not. I watched only a minute or two before running home.

"I ran home like the wind. The Indian might be after me. I did not tell my family for many years about the Indian and the gold. Often as I grew older I have hunted for the rock which must have sent the stone against stone. I have never been able to find it."[16]

Vivian's parents—Mr. and Mrs. R. A. Shearer—had homesteaded a place southwest of Las Vegas in the mountains. They called it "The Old Homestead Ranch." For their honeymoon, Vivian and Mabel decided to go over to the Falls Creek that ran through the ranch. The kids went too. Vivian wanted to survey the additional forty acres his parents had bought next to the homestead, so Audrey carried the chain and helped him. They put up a camp there on the Shearer property that they always called "The Forty."

Audrey had never seen anything so beautiful. The scent of pines, the cold water splashing over the rocks, the wildflowers dotting the grass with a rainbow of colors, the high clouds over the blue mountain peaks: she tried to take it all in. She had never known a place so beautiful, so serene.

I'd like to have a little cabin here someday, Audrey thought. *I'd like to have a loving husband, ten children, and a garden. I'd write a book. I'd be happy here in these mountains.*

The well-known rancher and world champion bulldogger, Dee Bibb, rode up on horseback and greeted the family. He told them they were welcome there and could stay as long as they wanted to. Mabel didn't tell him they were camped on their own property! She thought he'd realize it eventually!

In the fall of 1924, the Clements kids went to school in Bernal. Miss Leona Gerk was the teacher. It was her first school, and she was twenty. Her brother, Fred Gerk, came and stayed with her. He was just younger than Audrey.

It was election time that fall—the first of November. One of the civic-minded citizens spoke to Miss Gerk. "Are you going to vote?" he asked. She explained that she was not yet twenty-one, although she would be in a few days.

"You're going to be twenty-one in a few days so you might as well vote," was the reply.

Miss Gerk was very strict with her discipline. If anyone turned around to see who was coming into the room from the door at the back of the school, she would take three points off that pupil's deportment grade. Talking without permission meant ten points off. Edward soon had a zero for his deportment and

Opal was almost as low. Audrey didn't like the rules although she could obey them. So at age twelve, Audrey decided to teach the teacher a lesson. She turned and looked back at the door when someone came in—on purpose. She also talked in class twice on purpose. The rule was: twice of talking without permission or turning around to look at the door three times meant one had to go up front and sit with one's feet upon a chalk box.

"Audrey, come here. You know the rules. Sit on the floor and put your feet on the box," Miss Gerk ordered.

"No, it's too dirty," Audrey said, surprising the teacher with her defiance.

"Fred! Go and get a broom and sweep this floor!" the teacher commanded her brother.

Then Audrey sat down on the chalk box instead of on the floor. Audrey saw the fury in Miss Gerk's face. Just as Miss Gerk was going to make her move, Audrey got up and walked out and went down to the creek. She hid in the bushes and then went on home and told her mother what she'd done. She went upstairs into the attic to hide because she expected Miss Gerk would come to the house. She did, and she was crying.

"I don't know what to do," she sobbed, seeking sympathy from Mabel.

Mabel, a more experienced teacher, was glad to advise her. She told her she was spending too much time marking zeros down for everybody and making them sit on the floor. She needed that time to teach. She suggested she change her ways of doing things.

Miss Gerk changed her methods and began to do more teaching and less "marking off points."

Audrey noticed during her school years that some of the children had difficulty learning English. Audrey recalled in an item submitted to *Grit*, February 12, 1986:

> Dear Editor:
>
> Back in the 1920's I was a fifth grade student at Bernal Springs School in Serafina, N.M. The one room of adobe was some distance from the main part of town.
>
> It had a nice board floor that had been laid green. As the lumber dried and shrunk, large cracks appeared between each board and knots fell out, leaving holes. When the teacher swept the floor she seldom needed a dust pan, for dirt and paper scraps all fell through the cracks.
>
> One day a 10-year-old boy from a near-by ranch came to school. Not being used to the school routine, he had time on his hands, I noticed.

> Suddenly I saw him light a match. When he realized that I saw him, he dropped it. It fell straight down through a crack in the floor.
>
> Within a few minutes smoke was pouring up from the floor, followed by flames. Ordered out, I grabbed my books and ran out with the 15 other students.
>
> "Empty your lunch pails and bring water from the creek," the teacher ordered. She was busy with the tin dipper and the water bucket pouring water down the knot holes and cracks surrounding the culprit's desk.
>
> Water from various lunch pails refilled the water bucket several times. Teacher kept dipping water and pouring it in a wide area around the fire area until the smoke stopped. Then we resumed school as though nothing had happened.
>
> The match lighter received the school teacher's usual punishment. He had to sit on the floor in the front corner of the room, with his back to the class the rest of the month[17]

Audrey doubted that her classmate learned much that year. She hoped he learned not to play with matches.

21

Violence in the Village

One day Mabel and Vivian had business in Las Vegas. They all went into town in Vivian's old car. Little did they know that some of the school children would go through a very difficult time that day.

A boy named Elfego, a very rough character, had been sent to reform school. His little brother Victoriano lived with their mother and an alcoholic father, referred to here as Pablo. Pablo had gone home early from his job that afternoon and was very drunk. He threatened his wife. Pablo's wife ran to her father at the post office. Her father, the postmaster, was quite upset to see the condition of Pablo. Audrey wrote years later:

> After running his wife out of the house with a butcher knife, he

and knife visited the school to take Victoriano home. Frightened by the mad drunk in the door, Ticher [teacher] and all of the children made a quick escape through the windows. Once in the open, everyone scattered and hid in the arroyos and scrub cedar. Mr. Butcher Knife staggered down the hill to the store and post office. There the storekeeper and postmaster, who had a gun, might have shot him. Instead, when attacked, the storekeeper hit him over the head with the gun barrel.

Stunned, and bleeding profusely, the drunk staggered to our house and spilled blood all over our doorstep. Then he staggered around behind our house and fell in our neighbor's courtyard. In the evening when we got home and heard him moaning, I ran up to the Attic. I looked out of the window. There in the grey mist I could see the bare headed man in a thin blue shirt, fallen in the mud. Once in a while he would scream for help."[1]

There was a long string of houses in a semi-circle facing the Plaza and the church. Pablo lived back on the main street in a group of houses that were behind the Shearer house. Pablo had fallen down in a yard and was lying there crying when Vivian saw him and tried to get help, tried to get some of the men to help him move Pablo off the cold ground and into some shelter. Vivian knew he couldn't move Pablo by himself, especially if the man was still combative as he had been. Vivian reasoned that it would take two men to manage the injured man without causing him more harm. Not only did the village men refuse to help, but they warned Vivian to stay away from Pablo.

It was too muddy for Vivian to drive his car over to Chapelle, so he walked over in the very cold sleet. He tried unsuccessfully to find someone there to help the poor drunken man. Everyone was afraid of Pablo. Since Vivian couldn't find anyone to help get Pablo in out of the weather, he called the sheriff in Las Vegas. The sheriff told Vivian that he would come right over to see about Pablo.[2]

True to his word the sheriff showed up—in the morning. By then, Pablo was dead. Vivian was angry that the sheriff had not come right over as he had promised. He regretted that he had believed the sheriff would come right out and help; otherwise, he might have tried to move the man himself since none of the village men would help. Audrey recalled:

My folks tried to get some help for him. [Pablo] The villagers were crazed with fear of the madman with the knife. No one would go near him. The sheriff, 16 miles away, did not come. All that dark night the injured man lay in the thin rain with his cries of "*¡Aye! Mamá!*" and "*¡Por Dios!*"

growing steadily weaker.

In my warm bed I heard the lost child wail for *mamá* in the suffering man's voice. As I shivered, I felt guilty because there was no man nor woman to take him in out of the rain. In the morning he was dead—from loss of blood and exposure. The storekeeper was tried and judged innocent. The guilty villagers that let fear cause his death went untried.[3]

It was the tragic death of his father that brought the 16-year-old Elfego home.

In later years when Audrey was an editor at the *Las Vegas Daily Optic* she often wrote historical events for the Rough Rider's Reunion edition, often referred to as the *Rodeo Edition* of the *Las Vegas Daily Optic*. She wrote the following in 1952 with no bi-line, although she indicated with a mark on a paper that she had written this story. The story, "Bernal Historic Village 14 Miles South of Vegas," read as follows:

Bernal, peaceful today in the warm New Mexico sun, has seen primitive fright and blood on every door step.

In the 1920's one of the citizens drank too much *vino*. The wine combined with moonshine whisky, put the man in an angry mood. He threatened his wife. She took her babies and ran to the combination store and post office, seeking protection from her husband who was armed with a knife.

He followed her down the rocky path to the store and entered against the protests of the storekeeper-Postmaster. When his wife refused to see him or to return home the man became violent.

The Postmaster, to protect his own family, took his revolver and hit the intruder on the head, opening a wide gash.

The man staggered from the store and back up the hill towards his home. On the way he had to pass the school house. His small son was in there in the first grade. He would make him go home.

He flung open the door of the one room school and stood covered with blood, angry, and demanding his son.

The teacher, Miss Leona Gerk, now a teacher in Las Vegas City schools, tried to argue with the threatening man as he dripped blood on the school house floor.

Realizing he was dangerous and could not be pacified, she ordered the children out the windows. While he barred the door and yelled at them the children climbed from the windows with Miss Gerk following.

They scattered into the cedar and piñon like frightened quail. Some of them hid until it became dark, afraid to go home with death loose in the village.

The man, perhaps no longer dangerous, but looking for help, wandered about the plaza, dripping blood on every doorstep. Every door was barred to him. The people were afraid.

A light rain began to fall. He staggered and fell in a doorway. There he lay yelling and wailing, "Aye! Mamma!"

Some residents of the village who had been in Las Vegas all day returned in the late afternoon. There was not a movement of life in the entire place. And not a sound but dripping rain and the agonized cry of the wounded man.

The new comers, with blood on their doorstep too, tried to get some help for the man. They were ordered to leave him alone. No one there could help him. The man of this family tramped through the rain to the nearest telephone and telegraph office at Chapelle. He called the sheriff in Las Vegas, explaining that the injured man was lying outside in the rain. The sheriff, expected to go to Bernal at once, did not go until the next morning.

The frightened children crept from their hiding places in the dripping canyons and scrub timber and went home. Some of them could look down from attic windows and see the man lying sprawled on the ground with the rain washing the blood from his face and head.

And all could hear the cry of "Aye! Aye Mamma!" which grew fainter as the hours passed. Night covered the pinion (*piñon*) country but it could not shut out the dying man's cry.

In the morning, the man was dead. The Postmaster was tried in the San Miguel court. He was acquitted.[4]

Audrey was inspired to write an article: "Fear—Our Deadly Enemy," published by *The Joy Bearer* in 1951:

Fear is crouching in every corner of the world, waiting to destroy mankind. Formidable fears are frightening individuals and nations. Yet, those who master fear can accomplish untold good. Remember that the Bible tells us to conquer fear.

Why are we afraid? It must be that we are afraid because we do not fully grasp the many verses [in the Bible] where we are told countless times, from the book of Genesis to the book of Revelation—"Fear not, for I am with thee, and will bless thee"—(Gen. 26:24) "Fear thou not; for I am with thee: —I will strengthen thee; yea I will help thee" (Isaiah 41:10).

Then too, time and again, people in positions where they might well find themselves full of fear, were told to fear not. We find in Matthew 28:5 the angel telling the good women to fear not.

Therefore, because they could conquer fear, those faithful women [at the empty tomb of Christ] were able to carry the angels' message to His disciples. If they had been fear stricken as the guards had been, they would've been unable to carry the vital message that Christ had risen.

Those who are obeying God's commands should never fear. To allow yourself to be fear ridden is to doubt the very goodness of God. Those who do right have no reason to fear. We should never so far forget His words as to let desperate fear come upon us.

Today, many of our world leaders seem fear driven. Yet now, as never before, when the bombs could reduce the earth to atoms, we need leaders who have cast out fear. We need leaders unafraid of themselves, and unafraid of others. Fear that prevents them from standing and working for the basic rights of all men, as laid down by the Bible, is a fear that can undermine our very civilization, and perhaps destroy it and us.

If we follow God's principles with confidence, we will soon find our fear disappearing. And as each personal fear vanishes we will come a step closer to world peace. So try the **fear not** remedy! It is the road to peace.[5]

As she grew and matured, Audrey developed a deep faith in God. When she made a formal commitment to Christ, she realized that He is truly the Prince of Peace. She thought about how the children in the villages like Bernal or Chapelle threw rocks at one another, how the men fought at the dances, how there always seemed to be jealously and strife. She wondered why people couldn't be kind and live in peace. She realized that the entire world was something like those little villages in northern New Mexico. The same kind of violence went on all over the world, and in some places it was much worse. She wondered if people would ever change.

Salute Gregorio: First Love

Audrey was not immune to the violence of her classmates at Chapelle. At age twelve she and a friend, Gregorio, stood up to some of the rough boys in the school. In an unpublished story entitled, "Salute Gregorio," Audrey wrote a description of Gregorio:

> My family was the only *Gringo* ("Anglo") family in a large group of Spanish-Americans the March we moved into the tiny New Mexico piñon country village. My mother had taught school in the vicinity. However, she never taught in Gregorio's village.
> At twelve I was a skinny, serious, blue-eyed, ash blond. Gregorio, the same age, was rail thin and frail looking. His perfect teeth were snow white against a very dark brown skin. He was even darker than most of the Spanish-Americans in this village. Perhaps a good bit of Apache accounted for this, as well as his high cheek bones in the delicate face below the huge, luminous brown eyes. We were the same height. But Gregorio was scare-crow thin, while I was merely skinny.[1]

The other girls of Audrey's age were interested in getting married. Traditionally, the villagers married young. The girls went for older men who could work to support them and the babies they hoped to have. It was not unusual for a twelve-year-old to marry a man in his twenties.[2]

> I remember standing aside with Gregorio to let a wagon drawn by sleepy horses pass. Following it were three *musicos* lustily playing two guitars and a fiddle. Seated regally on a brightly draped kitchen chair behind the wagon seat, was the bride. She wore a white satin gown, with a high built up head dress and yards and yards of veil. She seemed no more mature to me than she had two weeks before when she quit school at fourteen to marry. And the groom, standing behind her, holding to the back of the chair, was Filimon. He used to lean lazily against the adobe store front and flirt with every girl that passed.
> Nevertheless, they were now important people. This was their

day. There was a huge wedding feast in their honor. Tonight there would be a wild wedding dance. Probably there would be several fights, with woman and children jumping out windows. Maybe there would be another stove lid broken over another head as happened at the last dance.[3]

Audrey was not interested in marriage at the age of twelve. However, some of the boys were interested in her. Audrey's turquoise blue eyes, her fair complexion, and her winning smile could not go unnoticed.

>At this age my Anglo ancestry gave me a different heritage of thought than that of the Latin girls who were my contemporary playmates. At that time the ambition uppermost in my being was to out play the native boys of my own age at marbles. Or out run them in foot races, and out bat, out catch, and out play them when we played a perverted form of baseball called "*Iglesia.*"
>
>Those dark-eyed senõritas of twelve were shocked by my antics. Already they were boldly casting shy glances toward the older boys and grown men. Most of them were pretty, and very, very clever about holding hands behind the schoolhouse. I was completely untouched by the wild longing for a man that seemed to drive every other twelve year old village girl to any length to fulfill nature's plan. There was slender María, an inch taller than I and completely mature at twelve. She was led to the altar by an *old man* in his twenties. Later when dark tales of how he beat María slid through the village, delicious horror kept the girls whispering for hours in the comparative privacy of the outhouses.
>
>Here, fourteen was the ripe age, and an unmarried twenty was a hopeless old maid. The grooms always seemed too old to me. They were all five to ten years older than the girl brides. Their contemporaries, a thirteen to sixteen year old boy, couldn't build an adobe house and get a job on the section gang or elsewhere to support a wife as the older men did. So the younger boys watched their recent playmates marry the *men*, while they must wait until the first graders reached the fourth or fifth or sixth grade. That depended on their ability with the English language and books.[4]

Audrey enjoyed playing marbles.

>I remember kneeling in the dusty road, knuckling down at the edge

of the magic circle, with a marble in my grimy fist. Gregorio, kneeling opposite me with a sharp eagle look in his ordinarily soft brown eyes, was ready to holler "No Fudge" if I did not shoot right.[5]

Audrey described the rains that came that summer, "with the arroyos running six feet deep with roaring red water when a cloud burst from the rolling mass hanging over the summer mountains."[6] The *piñons* (pine nuts) ripened. The children went hunting for the *piñons* they liked so well. They cracked them with their teeth and ate them in school. They drove the teacher crazy with *piñon* shells dropped on the floor where they crunched under busy feet and sometimes left grease spots.

Audrey and Gregorio followed the same path home from school. When the wind blew, "his patched clothes flapped furiously about his pitiful cold body. I was always warmly wrapped in a heavy tan wool cape with a bright tam-o-shanter [hat] swinging on one side of my short braids."[7]

Heavy snow fell that winter. One day Audrey was walking home from school across a field when Gregorio's big fifteen-year-old cousin (referred to here as Roberto) pelted Audrey and Gregorio with snow balls. Roberto had put rocks inside of each icy white ball. Gregorio kept his frail body between Audrey and the pursuer until he was hit squarely between the shoulder blades and fell full length in the snow. Audrey wrote:

> The big boy advanced menacingly between the scattered cedars. I knelt beside Gregorio and lifted his head out of the snow. He was gasping and tears stood on those half inch lashes.
>
> "Run! Run fast!" he whispered.
>
> "No!" I said and jumped up to face the boy with more snowballs.
>
> "You leave us alone!" I screamed. "Go home! You hurt Gregorio bad!"
>
> His only answer was a grin—and a fast one to my middle. I leaped swiftly aside and tried to hurl sense into him with words. I caught a hard one on my shoulder for my trouble. It hurt. Suddenly I realized how helpless I was there in the snow covered pasture. Running was my only hope. Then I remembered that I had seen the big boy beat a little dog tied with a short rope to a wagon wheel. He had used a stick longer than the rope. He had laughed at the poor dog's painful howling. I couldn't leave Gregorio lying there helpless when his cousin was in that black mood. Every drop of my Irish blood boiled with fury. He met me head on and

blinded me with soft snow. Then he slapped me hard, and with a wild satisfied yell, ran around Gregorio and on home.[8]

The story went on to describe how Audrey used her cape to brush the snow off her face and then brushed snow off Gregorio's thin, torn coat and helped him up. His brown skin seemed several shades lighter. He leaned heavily on her arm, staggered a little now and then, but told Audrey he could make it home by himself. Audrey ran inside the old house and climbed the ladder into the attic. She hurried to the broken paneless window in the gable and looked out over the nearby roof tops. She could see Gregorio slowly climbing out of the snow filled arroyo and start up to the hill to his house a half mile away. She knew he had saved her from that rock-snowball that Roberto had meant for her. Audrey wrote:

> Worshipful gratefulness filled my whole being. Gregorio was sick at home for a week after that. I wondered if he was lying on a dirty sheep skin in a dark corner, such as my mother had described seeing in some of the homes when she was visiting the sick. I didn't tell on Gregorio's cousin. But I didn't take the short cut anymore.[9]

Audrey recalled years later that the family lived right behind the school house. She recalled an incident with an older boy, Elfego, who had been to the boys' reform school at Springer, New Mexico. When he came back, everyone was scared of him. He was a big boy and harassed the other kids. One noon Miss Gerk had left the kids and gone home. She lived near the post office at Bernal. It was called the Serafina Post Office because there was another Bernal in New Mexico, so they had to change the name. Basilio Griego, the postmaster, named it Serafina, his daughter's name. So the town was known both as Bernal and Serafina.[10]

Miss Gerk had gone to the post office at lunch time but didn't return. She sent a message that she had become ill and would not come back after lunch and that school was dismissed for the day. Before getting the message, the pupils sat around talking, waiting for the teacher to return. Audrey had a cape made out of an army blanket. Mabel had put a cape-like collar and two big buttons on it so Audrey would have a coat. While the kids were alone, they decided to play hobo. Audrey had her cape on. Elfego was flirting with the girls. "Elfego had a sophistication acquired 'outside' that turned the heads of all the school girls except mine. His strong heavy body was that of a man's, with a man's ideas."[11]

For the "hobo" game, Gregorio was appointed a part. But when the message arrived that school was dismissed, Audrey started to leave. Elfego saw her move toward the door as he was teasing some of the other girls. Audrey recalled:

> "Watch this," he [Elfego] muttered to them in Spanish and made for me. He was between me and the door hollering, "One kess! Gimme some keeses!"
>
> I knew he meant to take those kisses in front of all the giggling school children who retreated around me. In a moment I had my back to the wall. Elfego grabbed me by my swinging cape. I fought like a wildcat, hitting and scratching even as I was twisting away. With a quick jerk I pulled my head inside of my heavy cape and jumped out of it, leaving it dangling in his empty hands.
>
> With a blistering curse he dropped the cape and sprang after me. He would lose face if he didn't reach his goal. I raced between the long line of desks toward the door. Gregorio, his face full of lightning and thunder, was in the next aisle. As I dashed passed with Elfego's fingers almost touching me, Gregorio dropped like a flash into the seat and stuck out his foot. Elfego hit the floor with a heavy thud. I heard him curse and snarl like a wild animal as I leaped from the door ready to streak for home. As I jumped out into the bright sunshine, I suddenly realized that where I would have only been kissed, Gregorio might be killed. I wheeled back into the room. Gregorio's thin arms and legs were flailing fast. But he was no match for the huge Elfego, who had him down choking him and pounding his head violently against the floor.
>
> "Elfego!" I screamed in the sudden silence that was taut with the mind of each child expecting murder to be done. I grabbed a book and bounced it off Elfego's head. At my scream, and the thud of the book, Gregorio's brother jumped on Elfego's back. He grabbed Elfego's black curls with both hands and yanked with all his might. At the same time Gregorio's cousin—the one of the snow ball fight—jumped in to help lick Elfego.
>
> Outnumbered, Elfego let go of Gregorio, who was very purple in the face. For a minute Elfego fought on. Then he gave up and slammed out of the door, muttering threats. With a collective sob of relief, the children began to go home.
>
> I picked up my cape and looked down at Gregorio sitting weakly on the floor.

"That *Loco*! He might have killed you! Are you all right?" I asked.

"*Si*—yes," Gregorio answered. He pulled himself to his feet by holding to the side of a desk. In his eyes there was no regret. They were full of triumph at being able to save me once more.[12]

One day in the spring Gregorio grinned at Audrey and asked, "Pretty soon you will git pretty white dress and marry?"

"No." Audrey replied. She explained that she had no time to think of marriage yet. She wanted to finish school. She wondered if Gregorio was proposing:

Gregorio kicked a pebble in the red dust and said knowingly, "I will buy my *novia* (fiancée) TWO trunks full of pretty, pretty clothes."

At that time one trunk was the customary gift of the groom to the bride. I believed that Gregorio really would buy two trunks of finery. For a moment I wondered which of the little girls he might marry.[13]

Audrey knew he had eyes for her. She liked him, too. She liked him more than she liked any boy. But she had no intention of getting married at the age of twelve. She and Gregorio remained friends and in time went their separate ways.

Years later, in 1944, Audrey picked up the county paper. She saw that Gregorio was listed in the death notices. He was still a bachelor at thirty-two. He had died of tuberculosis. He had probably had it for years.

I thought of the dead past and wondered. Why had Gregorio never married? Gregorio with that beautiful bright grin, and the pure Prince Charming manner. Perhaps the answer might be found back there when we were twelve . . . . Salute! Gregorio! I know you make a delightful addition to heaven![14]

23

Riches Found and Lost

Early in the summer of 1925, Vivian's oil company seemed close to success. He had a business card: "Meadows Oil Company—No Stockholder's Liability; Incorporated under the Laws of New Mexico; Chas. V. Shearer, President, Serafina, New Mexico."

Mabel was hopeful that finally her family would have a substantial amount of income once the oil started coming up. They were sure it was there.

Mabel was pregnant. She and the children—Audrey, Opal, Edward and Betty—moved into Las Vegas to a place on South Pacific, across the street from Herman's Grocery Store, now Ludi's Grocery Store. It was on the corner of the street that crossed South Pacific going west to east. The Ludis lived in a house right next door. It had a large porch with big open arches around it. The Ludi kids would come over and play. One of the neighborhood boys was about Audrey's age and was very good looking.

He asked Audrey, "If you were the queen, could I be the king?"

Audrey only grinned, embarrassed.

Audrey was trying to learn to ride the bicycle that her daddy had given the kids for Christmas. The hill from the house on South Pacific slanted down towards the Gallinas River. As she rode the bike, it was wobbling along down the hill. There was an outhouse building down there, and she hit it. After a few bruises, she learned to ride.

One Sunday in late August Vern came to take the kids on a picnic to Pecos in an old topless car—maybe a Model T. It was quite a contrast to the horse-drawn buggies they usually travelled in, although Mabel and Vivian had a Chevy without a top on it. Vern's was a one seat car. But all three kids could sit in the front seat if one of them held Betty.

Betty ran out to meet her daddy. He picked her up and started to carry her to the car, just as Mabel hurried out the door.

"You can't take Betty. She's too little," Mabel shouted angrily.

Vern kept on walking toward the car and shouted back over his shoulder, "She's my kid and I'm going to take her."

Audrey thought her parents were going to get into a knock down drag out fight right there.

Just at that moment Vivian drove up in his 1922 car and parked on the street in front of the Ludis' home, as close as he could get to their house.

"What's going on here?" Vivian yelled, walking toward the house as fast as he could.

"I'm taking the kids on a picnic—Betty too!" Vern shouted back.

At some point Betty was transferred from Vern's arms to Mabel's arms. Then Vern took Betty away from Mabel and put her in the car.

Mabel began crying and sobbing, "My baby! My baby!"

Vivian wondered if Mabel was referring to her unborn child. Perhaps she was going into premature labor, he thought. He asked, "Is the baby all right?"

"Yes," Mabel answered.

"I don't see what's wrong," Vivian said. He urged Mabel to let Betty go.

"No! I refuse!" Mabel insisted. "I said *no*, and Vern has to honor my wishes!"[1]

Audrey later wrote, "Vivian helped Mother, crying, into the house to lie down and we got into the little old Model T Ford and drove off. We stopped some place on Bridge Street for Daddy to buy some lunch stuff."[2]

Vern had stopped in front of Mrs. Bosh's store on the east side of the bridge on National Avenue to buy some things for the picnic. In her notes, "Betty," Audrey wrote her memory of the incident:

> I remember holding Betty and wondering if I should jump from the car and run with her back to Mama. Then I thought Daddy would only come after us and he and Vivian had been so mad at each other that someone might get killed. So I held Betty close and sang to her and was so scared inside. I knew Daddy didn't *really* want us all the time, so he would take us back that night. I didn't have a good time that day, worrying about Mother. Milly was born soon after and we moved back to Bernal.[3]

Vern gave each child a turn to drive. They'd get under the wheel and their daddy would help them steer. When it was Opal's turn to steer, they were near the village of San José when a chicken ran across the road. Opal hit it.

"Daddy, I hit that chicken!" Opal exclaimed.

"That's all right. Sometimes you can't help hitting something like that. It's better to go ahead and hit it than to try to avoid it and cause a wreck." Then Vern took the wheel and Opal sat back in her seat, shaken.

"But the poor chicken!" Opal cried, tears streaming down her face.

"It didn't suffer. It happened to quick," Vern assured her.

"I didn't mean to hit it!" Opal said.

"Everyone knows that," Vern said.

Edward added, "Stop bawling, Opal!"

Audrey tried to comfort Opal.

They went on to Pecos, had a picnic, and then went back to Las Vegas. There were other picnics after that and Betty always went without another outburst from Mabel.

Mabel had given birth to her other children at home. But in 1925 she went to the hospital, as more women were having babies in hospitals. She was in the first or second door on the north side of the old two story adobe building on the corner of Eleven Street and Mora Avenue. (Arrott House, part of the Highlands University student housing, is there now.) There were big double doors on the front, and they opened in to a big, wide hallway. Dr. Roberts, a professor at the Normal University, later bought the building and turned it into the El Moro Apartments.[4]

Millicent Laura Shearer was born on September 3, 1925. Mabel stayed in bed for over two weeks. Audrey would walk over every day from South Pacific and take fresh diapers, baby clothes, and clean night gowns for Mabel, taking all the dirty clothes back to wash and bring back the next day.

Lucy Sanchez from Bernal came and took care of the kids while Mabel was in the hospital. Vivian came in every day or two to see Mabel and Milly and to check on the older kids. As soon as Mabel was able, they all went back to the house in Bernal where they had been living. With the exception of the newest addition to the family—Milly—the children went to school in Bernal the fall of 1925. Miss Gerk was still teaching there.

Ellen Grace, Vivian's daughter by his first wife, was close to Opal's age. She wanted to visit and get acquainted soon after Mabel and Vivian had married. Grace and Audrey slept in one of the rooms in Vivian's house. The oil drillers had been let go, so they were gone but Vivian kept the house where he had all his things. If he had wanted to move in with Mabel and the kids, there was no room. Their house was very small, a long adobe house with tiny rooms, maybe 10 by 12 in size, and it had an attic. The house where Vivian lived was a long, low adobe with a stone step out front, with larger rooms than those in the house Mabel was living in.

Vivian thought he was close to hitting oil. Then another wildcat driller moved in just a short distance away from the Meadows Oil Company well. The two were competing, trying to strike oil first. Vivian didn't have anyone guarding the oil well at night. One night someone threw a bunch of iron—some old well drilling bits or a bunch of irons—down the Meadows Oil Company well. The men couldn't get the drilling bits to go through all that mess of iron and there was no way to get it out. Vivian suspected the deed was done by the other wildcat drillers who were located nearby and were competing with them. In any case, they had to abandon that well.⁵

There was nothing to do but move to a new location and start over. They moved the drilling rig across the highway and about a mile north of the original well. Audrey wrote:

> A rival oil driller supposedly cut Vivian's tools loose and lost them down Well #1 and they couldn't get them out. So they [Vivian's company] moved the rig across the highway and farther north to the one by Starvation Peak. We kids were set on guard duty at the well and sometimes took Betty with us.
>
> Vivian had the Meadows Oil Company money in one of the banks in Las Vegas. He had sold a lot of shares of stock to fund the operation. Then the bank went broke. Vivian and his father, Richard Arthur Shearer, had no more money to pay the crew, so they had to let them go. They tried to keep it running by themselves. They used a steam engine to run the drilling rig which meant they had to haul a lot of wood to fire the boiler and water for the steam. Opal, Edward and I would watch the gauge on the steam boiler for them. If the steam started to get too high, we would yell at Vivian and tell him. Or if it started to come down, then we'd let him know and he had to come fire the boiler with more wood to keep the steam up.⁶

Vivian's father had a little cash that hadn't been in the bank, so they lived on that until it was gone.

One day Vivian shouted, "Oil!"

"We've finally struck oil! Look at that!" Someone else yelled.

All the kids gathered around to see it, with excited exclamations about how they would be rich now. Years later, Audrey recalled, as recorded on tape:

> It was getting along towards November, 1925, when I remember the last time Grandfather and Vivian lowered the bailer and then brought it up. It had a real thick gooey black stuff on it! *Oil* they said. I saw it myself! We all saw it and we were all so excited and thrilled! We were going to be rich! There was the oil they had been drilling for! We could all see it! They kept trying to work a little bit longer but we were hungry—we had nothing to eat! They were flat broke and we were starving to death! Vivian and Grandfather had no money left to buy necessary supplies—food and gas to haul water and wood.⁷

With no money, they could not continue. Audrey wrote later, "Oil came up dripping on the boiler but they couldn't get enough—no money to buy groceries for the family. Grandfather had used all he had, too."[8]

Vivian had quit his job as station agent on the Santa Fe Railroad without much notice when he started the Meadows Oil Company, so they weren't happy with him. It had been a gamble to get rich, and he had lost. But he knew he could get on with the Rock Island or Southern Pacific, which ran through Santa Rosa. The Rock Island Line ran down from French, New Mexico, near Raton; and it joined the two routes—the Santa Fe and the Southern Pacific. It came down through Mosquero to the Southern Pacific line. The station agent at Santa Rosa had taken leave for a year, so Vivian got his job—from January, 1926 to January, 1927. It meant another move. Vivian went to Santa Rosa as soon as he could. Mabel and the children were alone for a while until Mabel decided to join Vivian. In one letter Mabel wrote:

> Now, dear, don't say you know we are having a hard time. We are not, in the sense you mean. We get along all right, have plenty , etc. But the only thing I *crave*, and haven't,—is you. Yes, I'm glad "it's a long road that has no turning"— all will be lovely soon, I know. As soon as we have enough cash to be together.[9]

Mabel and Vivian were separated at Christmas time. But right after Christmas Mabel went to Santa Rosa, leaving Audrey, Opal and Edward until she could get settled. Mabel wrote to Vivian:

> A lonesome Xmas, dear—and may it never occur again. We are going to hang up Millicent's stocking tonight—and Betty will hang up hers. The other kids are quite grown-up about Xmas this year and don't expect anything—'tho I have a little surprise for each. We all know better times are coming.[10]

In another letter, she wrote:

> I sent Aunt Laura a hdk. [handkerchief] too—and Papa's wife—and Papa a tie—we sent for it—to Wards. [I don't] see much change in baby. She is still bald. Some babies are for 6 mo. Audrey was.
> Now I believe in the fish-wife tale that, "All hair and no brains—no hair and all brains!"
> I do so much want Millicent to be my masterpiece.[11]

Mabel wrote to Vivian that the children were going to enjoy Christmas. In another letter she wrote details:

> We have almost enough stuff in the house—or will have when Watts brings the meat over—to do a month now.
> I'd like to come up there to be with you Xmas but will see what you say about it.
> The kids trimmed their tree last night. They got a dandy piñon—and they will have Xmas all week.
> I only got them 8 pounds of candy—and strung thru a week may not make them sick. Got 3 pounds of nuts and a doz. oranges and popcorn to pop and they are having a good time.
> Got squash and sweet potatoes and will try to get a chicken. So we will have a good dinner. If I come up there Xmas we will have dinner here the night before I go. I hate to spend the car fare and father will think it the height of folly to spend it that way when it might pay taxes. But heigh ho! They'll get paid—and "it will all come out in the wash."[12]

On Christmas day, 1925, Mabel wrote to Vivian:

> Dearest,
> Just got yours of 23rd and am too lonesome for you to write anything pleasant, dear. The kids are having a happy day—ours will come. No news at all. I appreciate your nice long letters. I can't write 'em. Too lonesome and feel too cryey—but of course I don't do that.
> Your loving
> Wife[13]

After the children had a visit from Vern, Mabel wrote:

> Vern came out Sun. and brought the kids a bunch of stuff and as they had the tree decorated it was like Xmas to them. (I didn't see him—I *never* do.) We are stringing it along all week—having Xmas every night. They enjoy it more this way and it is much safer—none of them have been a bit sick yet—and won't be.[14]

Just after Christmas, Mabel wrote:

> Just got yours of 26th and I've decided to come and leave the kids here until the 15th. I believe it will be best—and then they will come wherever we are. I've decided it will be better and maybe cheaper. I'm black in the face from planning—so am going to quit and come and stay with you. Father [Vivian's father] says he and the kids will be fine here. He thinks we better leave them here till the 15th anyway—so I guess we will—the kids are willing to manage this way.[15]

After Christmas Mabel wrote to Vivian:

> I am planning to go tomorrow unless the weather gets so bad I can't get to the depot. It is pleasant but cold today. I will bring Betty [and Milly] and leave the [other] kids here till we get settled. They will be O.K. and Father [Vivian's father] is willing to look after them so I think it's the best I can do.
>
> All this unless I get a letter from you by tomorrow a.m. telling me to do something else. I don't think you will.[16]

In later years, Audrey wrote, "Grandfather Shearer stayed with us. I had to keep house. We went to school every day. After school Opal would run down to the corner to play marbles with Edward and the boys."[17]

Audrey was disappointed that she could not do the same. She had to "keep house" and fix meals.

Mabel was used to moving from place to place. Vern had never stayed in one place more than two years, and Mabel wondered if Vivian was going to do the same thing. She was getting very tired of moving. But it was move or starve, so they moved. Audrey, Opal and Edward may have felt abandoned until they were able to follow the family to Santa Rosa, but Grandfather Shearer was with them at least some of the time.

In later years, Mabel and Vivian lamented the fact that they had not been able to continue with the oil business. Vivian said, "Just a few more weeks of work, and we could have made it. I've always had bad luck. I was always close, very close, to success and wealth when something would happen and it would slip away."[18]

Audrey recalled that Vivian and another fellow had invented what Vivian called a "governor" for a car. Vivian liked tinkering with cars and was a fairly good auto mechanic. A patent for the "governor" was obtained. Vivian and his partner tried to sell the idea to a major auto company, but they said they weren't interested. "Who would want it?" they asked in a reply letter. Yet as soon as the patent was up, cars started coming out with it. Today it is a common feature on most cars. It is known as "cruise control."

Vivian and his partner never got a penny for it. Nor did Vivian get any money from the oil well he found.[19]

By January of 1926, Vivian had capped the well, given up the lease on the land, and walked away from his dream of riches. Audrey and the other children realized they were not going to be rich, at least not for a long time.

24

Survivors: Bernal to Santa Rosa

Mabel had been tired of Vern's restless moving from job to job. Now her second husband had been employed in three jobs in the short time they had been married. Mabel thought they would be in Bernal a long time, but when the oil business went broke, it was time to move again. While Vivian and Mabel moved to Santa Rosa, taking Betty and Milly—the two youngest children—Audrey, Opal and Edward stayed in Bernal until the folks could get a house and get settled. They probably needed to get a paycheck or two before they could rent a house big enough for all of them.

When Vivian moved to Santa Rosa, Audrey was thirteen, trying to study for school and to keep Opal and Edward fed, dressed, clean and in school. She was expected to cook meals for them and care for the house after Mabel left to join Vivian. Audrey had been "mother" to her younger sisters and brother before, but this time it was a full time job!

Opal and Edward would play while Audrey did the cooking and housework. Then when she would call them to supper, they wouldn't come! Audrey was not a happy homemaker. In later years, Audrey wrote:

> I thought I was doing the right thing helping Mama look after the kids. I was taking on adult responsibilities from the time Sissy (Opal) was born when I was 2. I wouldn't eat my breakfast until Sissy had hers. Mama [Mabel] and Daddy [Vern] and any visitors that came

by thought I was cute. "So serious! So grown up!" they would say. That seemed to please Mama and Daddy so I kept it up. Taking on more and more responsibility. Then came along Bubby [Edward] and Betty.

"She'll be a wonderful mother someday," Daddy said, not knowing that all the responsibility of all work and no play . . . it would be a wonder if I ever had any children to mother.

Mother was a school teacher and not too strong, a baby every 2 or 3 years and substitute teaching in between pregnancies kept her busy. Daddy had a full time job with good pay but Mother liked fancy things—like a piano and clothes and a nice house, which I had to help her keep clean. She called me "Mother's little helper." Which I was and I never minded, for she and Daddy praised me for all the good work I did.

When I was 9 (going on 19) and little Betty was born [October 24, 1922] Sissy [Opal] and I were doing all the dishes, keeping our room clean and neat and since I was "bigger" I took over a lot of Betty's care. Edward and Opal managed to get out of the house to play marbles down at the corner with the neighbor kids and "tom boy" Sissy would finish her chores and run to play with the boys. I as Mother's helper was above play. I stayed inside and if there was no work to do, I read fairy tales.[1]

Vivian's father, always referred to as "Grandfather Shearer," or more often just as "Grandfather," came over every once in a while from the Old Homestead Ranch to check on the kids. Then Grandpa Clements (Vern's dad) came to visit the kids while they were alone there. It was a big relief for Audrey. Years later, Audrey remembered her Grandpa Clements. She recalled that William Clements, who was over six feet tall, had excellent hearing and was very vivacious. He suffered sunstroke in 1910 and palsy afterwards. But when he was in Bernal, he was in good health and entertained the children.

William Harper Clements had been born on February 15, 1839 in Kentucky. Both he and his wife, Emma Maria Roney, had been married before and both had children from their first marriages. (Grandpa's first children were: Cora, H. J., and Bert Clements.) Grandpa had lots of interesting stories. Like his wife Emma, he was of Irish descent. When he was twelve, his parents moved from Kentucky to Illinois and then to Iowa, then to Nebraska. The folks were strict Methodists who did not work on Sunday. Once the children, including William, were gathering hickory nuts in their yard and their father made them drop them back on the ground because it was Sunday and no work could be done on the Sabbath Day according to the Scriptures, as it was the day of rest.

One of Audrey's favorite stories told by her Grandpa Clements was about one of his uncles who had raised two oxen—Big Boy and Blue. The uncle had a brother who was going to Oregon with his family. The two oxen were given to them for the trip over the Oregon Trail with a wagon train. There were many disasters along the way. They had to fight savage natives who attacked the wagon train. There were various diseases that decimated the pioneers. The weather was bad. The few survivors ended up leaving most of their possessions behind along the trail to try to get to Oregon before winter. Finally, they had to leave their wagons and travel with their remaining live stock. Other travelers went another way or died. At last, of the group that had left Missouri together, only Mr. Clements, his wife, and their two children were left. They, too, had found it necessary to leave their wagon behind on the trail. Blue had died, but Big Boy was still strong enough to walk. They had almost reached civilization when Mr. Clements collapsed. Mrs. Clements and the children were riding Big Boy when they finally stumbled into a town. Mr. Clements, too weak and exhausted to walk, had thrown himself up over the horns of the ox and was clinging there when they came to the town.

"They were the only survivors," Audrey said in a taped interview. "And they survived with the help of Big Boy. He just kept going. 'He was the strongest animal my uncle ever raised,'" Grandpa Clements said. "And that Clements family stayed in Oregon, but they sure had a trial getting there."[2]

Audrey's grandfather frequently repeated the story about that family's journey over the Oregon Trail, the only survivors of a wagon train. He embellished it a bit with his descriptions of battles with hostile Native Americans, snow storms, and so on. But Audrey was always proud that some of her ancestors had not only gone over the Oregon Trail, but had been survivors in spite of all the odds. When her daddy told the story and described how Big Boy had carried the family into Oregon, Audrey would often weep at the thought of the hardships the family had gone through. Even years later whenever she told the story of the sole survivors, she fought to hold back her tears.

Another of Audrey's favorite stories was told by Mabel about her great uncle, David Waddell, the brother of James Oliver Waddell, Mabel's grandfather. He had been scalped by hostile Native Americans and lived! Mabel remembered seeing him when she was a little girl. He always wore a skull cap on his head because the tissue that grew back over his skull was very delicate. Audrey thought he was a good example of a tough ancestor!

After a visit, Grandpa Clements went back to Nebraska and lived in the Old Soldiers Home in Milford, Nebraska. William H. Clements died January 10, 1927. He fell out of his bed there and broke his hip. He didn't live long after that.

He was buried at Milford.³

Vivian, who was to work for a year as station agent for the Union Pacific Railroad, had rented a small house. Soon they rented a bigger house, the Casaus house which was right across the street from the back of the Catholic Church and just up the street from the school. It was the bigger house that made it possible for Audrey, Opal and Edward to move from Bernal to join the family. It must have seemed a long time to Audrey as she was in charge of the two younger children, Opal and Edward. Grandfather Shearer moved everything to the ranch that wasn't needed. He also somehow moved the steam boiler and the smoke stack from the oil rig to the ranch. After a pay day, Mabel wrote and asked Grandfather to bring the kids to Santa Rosa. They went on a cold day in January, 1926 in his open Model T, which went about twelve to fifteen miles an hour.⁴

Grandfather Shearer had taken everything off of the car that was originally on it so that it wouldn't be so heavy. Fortunately, he left the windshield wipers on. The car had one front seat, but he had built a little box-type seat on the back. They started from Bernal early in the morning and drove to Romeroville and took the Coronado Trail road to Santa Rosa. Audrey always remembered that miserable trip:

> We nearly froze to death! We had a blanket or two and tried to cover ourselves up completely with them. Grandfather had his gloves on, his ear flaps down, and his sheepskin lined coat on with the collar turned up. We kids were all squeezed in. Edward rode on the box behind the seat. When we got past Delia, to the Pecos River bridge, Grandfather turned off the road and went down under the bridge. It was about noon. The road was just a rough country road, not a paved highway. We were protected a little under the bridge. Grandfather built a fire and heated water and made some tea and fixed something hot for lunch before we went on to Santa Rosa. The trip took all day to travel about 70 miles. The winter winds blew ice cold all day.⁵

When they got to Santa Rosa, a "long-necked, tall girl" was standing with some other kids on the street corner. She pointed at them and yelled, "Look at the hobos!" Opal was embarrassed and insulted. She met the girl later. Opal never forgot how she felt at being called "hobo." Audrey wasn't upset. She was too cold to think about it. She was just glad to get there and get out of the cold.⁶

Grandfather Shearer stayed that night and then went back the next morning. He moved all of their things from Bernal to the ranch, both Mabel and

Vivian's household goods, probably using a team and wagon. He didn't bring any of it to Santa Rosa, however, as it would have been a long trip. Since the folks had no furniture with them, they rented a furnished house. The Casaus house had a huge, old fashioned radio console in it. That was the first radio they had ever seen or heard. Vivian kept turning the dial to see how many stations he could get. He was excited because he could get a Las Cruces station, among others. He didn't listen to any of them after he heard their call letters and found where they were. But the radio only stayed there two or three days until Mr. Casaus got someone to help him move it to his place.

Milly was only a few months old. The other children started school in the middle of the school year, 1925-1926. Audrey was supposed to be in the sixth grade. But Miss Gerk had put Audrey back in the fifth grade because Fred, Miss Gerk's little brother, was in the fifth grade and she didn't want to teach two different grades with only one student in each! So at Santa Rosa, Audrey was put in the seventh grade where she belonged. However, she had missed a lot of things she should have learned in the sixth grade, due to Miss Gerk's decision, so Audrey was behind.[7]

Audrey wrote: "I went into 7th grade—Roy Wiley, teacher—so I skipped most of the 6th and half of 7th."[8] Although Audrey had missed the first half of the seventh grade, she made good grades. Once Mr. Wiley was out a day or two and his wife was the substitute. She gave a graphic description of having tonsils out, which she had just had done. For the second time in her life, Audrey fainted. She fell over and the kid behind her, Abel, caught her and kept her from falling out of her seat. Audrey wasn't used to hearing about such "gory" things. But she finished the seventh grade there with good grades. Audrey wrote:

> In the 8th grade, with Mr. Wiley as the teacher, I loved school. Mother took care of the little kids. I learned to make Prune Whip in Home Ec. and proudly made it at home. Betty must have been sort of lonesome at home with only baby Milly to play with when we were in school. When Milly was learning to walk, we all went to the ranch and Grandfather, watching her, announced she had a congenital dislocated hip. Mother took her to El Paso to find out for sure.[9]

Milly did have a hip problem, and Mabel soon found a good doctor to correct it.

Audrey had a school record book with verses and blank spaces for autographs, entries for special activities, and so on. She used it when she was in school at Santa Rosa and when she was in school at the Normal Training

School in Las Vegas, so the dates of entries are varied. She had written the dates 1926-27 and 1929-30. In it, several friends had written. One page has a note written in black ink:

> Santa Rosa, NM
> March 2, 1927
> Dear Audrey:
>
> I think it is very sweet of you to ask me to write in your book. Although I am not much on such things I will do my best.
>
> I haven't know [sic] you very long but as long as I have, I have found you to be a very sweet girl—also I have heard many good remarks about you and I am sure I can second every one of them. I have also found you to be a very studious and smart classmate. I hope to always be counted as one of your friends.
> Your classmate and friend,
> Ethel Mae Miracle[10]

In addition to the note by Ethel Miracle, there was another letter found inside the book listed under "Miscellaneous" and dated March 2, 1927, written by her friend Opal Luna:

> At Home
> 3-2-1927
> My Dear Friend Audrey,
>
> I thank you very much for giving me the pleasure of writing in your little book. I'm not much on writing in memories books but will do my best. We have had many good times together while staying at Mrs. Miracle's. I think you are a very nice girl and you have great dreams which I hope will come true and that someday you will have your beautiful home in the mountains where you can draw pictures and be a great "left handed" artist. I had better lay my pen aside now but here's wishing success and much happiness in your future life.
> A friend,
> Opal Luna[11]

Under "My Studies" Audrey listed History, New Mexico History and Civics, Arithmetic, Reading, Geography, Domestic Science, English, Spelling, Civics and Writing.[12]

Audrey recalled an incident at Park Lake:

We all went over to Stink Lake—later Park Lake. There was a raft on the lake under the big trees. We kids stood on the bank and watched Mother and Vivian get on the raft. He pulled it out a few dozen feet from shore. Mother leaned over to put her fingers in the pretty water. The raft jumped out from under them. Mother couldn't swim. She screamed as she went under. Betty stood on the bank and screamed and screamed and screamed.[13]

Vivian rescued Mabel and pulled her to shore. He swam with one arm, the other holding Mabel's head above the water. The kids stood there horrified, holding their breaths, waiting to see if Vivian could manage to bring their mother to shore. At first she had gone under, as people do when they don't know how to swim. Everyone was scared, thinking Mabel might drown right there in front of them.

Virginia Wood was a good friend of Opal's. She lived straight across the street from the Shearers. They went to Park Lake (they called it Stink lake then) and went wading, spent most of the day there. Audrey enjoyed wading, but she wanted to learn to swim. Mabel bought Audrey a bathing suit from Moises Department Store. It was about fifteen dollars, which they thought was a terribly high price. Twin Lakes was close to Santa Rosa, down the road past the Electric Company water ditch that furnished the electric power for Santa Rosa. A lady with two little daughters would often ask Audrey and Opal if they wanted to go swimming with her. They always did. Audrey had to look after her kids, but she got to go swimming, too.

Audrey and Opal started to learn to swim there—just to dog paddle—but they could keep themselves up and they learned how to float, too. Audrey could float pretty well. That summer was so hot in Santa Rosa that they welcomed the chance to go swimming every afternoon.

Lisa Smith was a good friend in the same class with Audrey. Her parents ran the electric light plant at Santa Rosa. Years later, Audrey recalled a frightening incident:

> There was a ditch of water that came down through the country across the Smiths' place and then fell down through all the grates and stuff to turn the wheels to make electricity and then it dropped off suddenly from the ditch to the grates that were over the water where it ran through the grates and fell down into and onto the wheel. Several of us got in the water and were playing in our swim suits and we were swimming in the

ditch. Well, I got too close to the grates and I got caught in the force of the water and it just threw me against the grate. The force of the water was too great and I was just stuck there against the iron bars and I couldn't get off. I looked up and yelled and Woodrow Smith, Lisa's brother, was up there on the top of the bank. He was a big boy. I don't think he was in my grade. But he jumped into the water and, with brute force, pulled me away from the grate so I could get out of there. If he hadn't, I guess I'd be there yet![14]

Audrey was always grateful for her rescuer! The Smiths were good neighbors the entire time they were in Santa Rosa. Once they had a watermelon bust, a Halloween party. They had a field as far as one could see, an acre or two of nothing but watermelons. Lisa remained Audrey's friend all the time she was in Santa Rosa.[15]

The summer of 1926, Audrey was fourteen. She helped care for all the younger children, including Milly who was nearly a year old. Since school was out, things were easier for Audrey. She had time to dream about herself and her future. She became aware of her appearance. She tried to look nice, keeping her hair clean and well groomed and her clothes as nice as possible. She never went anywhere without putting on a clean dress.

One day Audrey noticed that her mother was in her bedroom. She had not come out since lunch time. Mabel never took a nap or rested unless she was sick. But Vivian was in the bedroom with her, so Audrey didn't worry too much. She was reading a book.

Vivian suddenly opened the bedroom door, saw Audrey, and cried out, "Run get the doctor—hurry!"

"All right. I'll just change into a clean dress and I'll hurry," Audrey replied.

"You haven't got time to change your clothes!" Vivian exclaimed. "Your mother's going to bleed to death! Now run! Run get the doctor!"

Audrey didn't even stop to reply. She just took off running and forgot she was wearing old clothes. Dr. Sanford lived just down the street about a block and a half from them.

Years later, Audrey spoke of the incident. "I had been taught to change before we went anywhere, but I got over that in a hurry! Clothes didn't seem to make much difference to me after that. I just went in whatever I had on—which probably left me pretty sloppy some of the time."[16] Audrey didn't find out what had been wrong with her mother. She wrote, "That summer Mother evidently had a miscarriage or [spontaneous] abortion—and was hemorrhaging."[17]

Vivian apparently taught Mabel about hypnotism.

> He [Vivian] began educating mother in the occult. Mother tried to pass on the explanations to us. And she tried out some of the things on us kids. Among the unusually unexplained things was hypnotism which was often scoffed at in those days.[18]

Audrey recalled that her mother tried to hypnotize her in a semi-dark room. But Audrey looked out of the window and thought of the baby in the box she'd seen buried, thought of its heartbroken mother. "It didn't take with me."[19]

Then Mabel tried to hypnotize eight-year-old Edward. He wouldn't stand still or pay attention. But Opal made the perfect subject.

> Mother somehow got her [Opal] under a "spell." Then she told her to put her right arm straight up over her head and hold it there. I remember watching her sort of unseeing eyes and her Dutch bob around her little full face that hadn't lost its baby fat yet.
>
> When mother tried to pull the plump little stationary arm down it stayed fast in the air. Mother could not budge it. Then she snapped her fingers and Sissy came out of it and could not remember holding her arm up with "super-human" strength as Mother called it. Forever after we all knew that hypnotism was not fiction.[20]

Later Audrey read about hypnotism. She concluded that hypnotism should never be used as a game, and that it should only be used in the hands of trained professionals; even then, it should be used cautiously.

Audrey recalled that when they moved to The Old Homestead Ranch in 1927, they acquired a Ouija board. They used it a great deal. Mabel and Opal were the best combination in working it. Each would put a finger very lightly on the Ouija board and someone would ask a question. There was a YES word and a NO word at the top of the board and all the letters of the alphabet were there. When the little triangular spaced wooden piece on little legs was held lightly with the finger tips of two people, one on each side of the wooden piece, it would move to answer a question, pointing to either YES or NO   or would spell out a word by pointing to the letters of the word, one at a time.

> They [Mabel and Opal] got so good that the little three legged Ouija would run so fast to the *yes* or *no* that it sometimes flipped off the board. If there was just conversation between us and "it" I would write down

the letters it pointed out. Many verses were written on it, some good enough to print and some were sold as they came off the board. There were several different personages that spoke through the board. "Evelyn" was one that was there most often and wrote the best poetry.[21]

Vivian gave the children several lectures on the "danger of letting an unknown force or entity take hold of our bodies and working through our arms and fingers, move the Ouija." He said, "They will do you damage, and if they get a chance they will turn on you and inflict you with more trouble than you can ever guess."[22] Audrey believed him. She wrote, "Gradually some of the conversation used 'kill' more and more—kill this or that person—kill your kids."

But Mabel did not believe there was any danger. Audrey wrote:

> Mother continued to try to explain the phenomenon as some type of electrical currents in our bodies that moved the Ouija. She also thought that it could not answer questions that someone around the room did not have knowledge of. Since some of us were widely read and there were books on everything under the sun in the house, almost any information was available there if one knew where to find it. We could never prove or disprove her theory.
>
> However, I believed CV [Charles Vivian] and swore off playing with Ouija after it gave so many orders to "kill, kill." Besides, in March, 1931 we moved to Garcia Mill and left the board at the ranch.[23]

When Audrey was older she studied the Bible and went to church. She also learned more about the occult. As a Christian, she concluded that much, if not all, of the occult was outside the will of God. Audrey studied various religions and discussed religion with many people of different religions, including some with no religion. She chose Jesus Christ. "He is the One people should trust and follow," she said. "I made up my mind that was what I was going to do." Audrey wrote:

> I went to church and decided that since this is a Christian era only asking for things in the name of Jesus Christ was safe. Praying to God in other words for what I wanted and asking it in Jesus name.[24]

The Clements children were adjusting to the changes in their lives. They welcomed the opportunity to spend time with their father. Vern came to take the kids to Roswell to visit him and his new wife, Mable Day Clements. He had married a school teacher in Albuquerque on June 12, 1926. She was originally from Fulton, Missouri. Her folks were farmers there. It is ironic that Vern married twice, both times to a woman with the same first name (although Mable Day spelled her name differently from Mabel Waddell.) Both women were school teachers. Also, both of them were born in October—Mabel Clements on October 26 and Mable Day on October 27. It was ironic, too, that Mabel Waddell married both times to men who had names that could be either masculine or feminine. (Lavern and Vivian.) Also, both men's names started with the letter V—Vern and Vivian. Both men moved around a lot from job to job. The kids, of course, had to adjust. Mabel called her husband "Jack" rather than "Vern." Audrey wrote:

> Daddy married Mabel Day—a teacher in Albuquerque. They moved to Roswell and Daddy came to Santa Rosa to get us kids. I expect Mother let us go because she wasn't too well. He came in a Dodge coupe. We left Santa Rosa in the late afternoon and headed for Vaughn. After dark the miles went slowly by with the dim lights of the old type car flickering up and down on the bumpy dirt road. When we got down on the flats of the rolling hill country between Vaughn and Roswell a violent storm came up. Edward had been riding in the turtle back of the coupe but when it started to rain Daddy got him up front. It was crowded. I guess Opal held Betty, and Ed sat on my lap—or Daddy's—not much room in those old narrow seats. Lightning flashed and thunder crashed and rain came pouring down. In the flashes of light it seemed that the whole earth was a sheet of water. A great flash came and the car stopped, probably flooded out. Daddy opened the door to get out and see if he could start it again. I guess it took a hand crank at the front end under the radiator to start it. Anyway, when he opened the door I heard him whisper, "God in Heaven!" Daddy never swore in front of us kids. The worst I ever heard him say was a "damit to hell" in a case of dire stress. But this was a sort of prayer. He shut the door and we waited for morning. Later he said the ground was covered with water and in the flash he thought water was up to the running board. After that he strained to see with each flash whether or not we were in a low place—or a dry arroyo. We dozed and Betty slept some. When daylight finally came we found we were on a slight rise with the flooded land awash in every direction. Daddy waded mud and got the car started. We went a few hundred yards farther and came to a deep arroyo. There had been a bridge there—it was washed out! If we had continued to travel in the stormy night we could have drowned, following the road. Flash floods swallow victims

every year in New Mexico, so the guardian angel that stopped the car on a high place was truly on the job. (Note: list all the times like this—jeep in cemetery—our car in Santillanes Canyon—Lord keep all my family in the hollow of Thy Hand). After an hour or so highway workers came along and several cars of people going south. Somehow they mended the bridge. It was a shaky situation. Daddy had us walk across and then he was the second one to drive across. [25]

Audrey began to think about the guardian angels her mother and grandmothers had always spoken about. Now she knew for sure that such angels were real.

Usually rain was welcomed in the dry country, and Audrey enjoyed it when it fell gently, unlike the torrent they went through with her father that day. It was a miserable night, but when morning came they thanked God for their safety.

Years later, Audrey Simpson wrote a poem, "Desert Rain," inspired by a rain storm she had seen in the flat lands or semi-desert country.

> Lightning rips like a giant cat's claw,
> Whipping angry red 'cross black ink sky.
> Yowling thunder drowns the wailing wind
> And life pours down as the wild clouds cry.[26]

When they arrived safely in Roswell, the four Clements' kids were excited to meet Mable.

> We got to Roswell and greeted Mable Day Clements—our new stepmother. She was a young and pretty bride. I am sure 4 kids dropping out of nowhere nearly floored her. I remember hearing her crying a few days later and Daddy trying to comfort her. I tried to look after Betty and help around the house. I wanted to go barefoot and did some on the grass although Daddy and Mabel thought I was too old to go barefoot—I was 13 going on 14. They cut my hair. I had always wanted long hair—braids. I had finally managed to let it grow enough to braid scrawny braids. Mother had let me let it grow when I was old enough to take care of it myself. Then they cut it off. I hated the short hair round my ears and the bristles on the back of my neck. The summer went fast. We drove out every evening around the lovely countryside through the fields and under the giant trees. On weekends we went to the bottomless lakes and

to a creek in the area where everyone went swimming. Betty had water wings and the rest of us [had] old inflated inner tubes. That swimming hole is where Opal dived from a little rock, hit on her stomach, and knocked the wind out of her and seemed to go unconscious. Someone grabbed her out of the water. I remember her staggering around later. One weekend we headed for the Sacramento Mountains and Avis where Aunty May was postmistress. The car broke down at Jerrigans ranch. We had to stay there all night and by the time Daddy got the car fixed it was time to head back to Roswell. So I never got to go back and see the place I had lived as a baby. We went back to Santa Rosa when it was time for school to start. I went into the 8th grade. Roy Wiley was teacher.[27]

Vern and his new wife Mable moved from Roswell. They lived in Las Vegas, in Albuquerque, in California, and Oregon and then came back to New Mexico. They lived on Carlisle in Albuquerque and then finally, in 1942, bought a place on South Broadway in Albuquerque. There was an acre or two of flat land, and Vern had a barn for a horse or two.

Audrey realized that people seem to have troubles much of the time. But there were also the rescuers—both human and angelic. There were many "close calls" when Audrey and her family were in dire jeopardy, such as when they traveled the flooded road to Roswell that night. Audrey was grateful for the persons such as the stranger in Taos who helped them get out of town to a doctor. She was grateful for both the angelic and the human "rescuers." We can all be rescuers from time to time. Yet there are times when we need to be rescued and there is no help available; then only the strongest survive.[28]

"My family has been tough," Audrey would often say. "If they hadn't been, they wouldn't have lived through. We're survivors."[29]

The Shearer family was just getting settled in firmly at Santa Rosa. Audrey liked school. That fall of 1926 Audrey was working hard to be Valedictorian. Juan Enojos and she were competing with one another for that honor. They were in school until January, 1927 when the station agent came back and Vivian no longer had his Santa Rosa job. He then got a job as station agent at Cuervo, eighteen miles north east of Santa Rosa. The Southern Pacific Railroad had been built through there in 1901 or 1902. Mabel just sighed heavily as she packed. It was no surprise: Another move!

25

House Fire: Santa Rosa to Cuervo

Mabel had always been afraid of fire, especially because of her mother's account of losing everything in a house fire when Mabel was just a baby. Then her mother and step-father had lost the barn and most of the Shetlands to fire. So when Mabel found a huge old hotel to rent at Cuervo for ten dollars a month, she checked all the exits in the house, as she always did.

Most of the places she had lived had been small. But this place was huge. There were numerous rooms upstairs. The place had a big, long dining room and kitchen combination on the ground floor with a big kitchen range at the back end of the dining room. It also had a little kitchen at the back. It the early days, it had been a beautiful hotel next to the railroad tracks. All the rooms had been refurbished. It had beautiful wash basins and pitchers in every room and all the lovely linens and furniture for each of the six or eight rooms upstairs. Downstairs there was the main room with a piano and a comfortable sitting room. In former days when people would come in to take the train, the country ranchers would stay at the hotel over night. The place had quite a good business once, but nobody had used it for years as a hotel. The owners wanted to keep it rented so they could keep their insurance.

The Shearer family moved to Cuervo and into the big house—except Audrey. She wanted to finish school in Santa Rosa and finish at the top of the class. Mabel agreed it was a good idea. Audrey stayed with Mrs. Miracle and her daughter, Ethel Mae—also in the eighth grade.

Audrey was studying hard and didn't get enough sleep. She rode the train to Cuervo on weekends because Vivian's family had passes on the Southern Pacific. One time the only train she could catch was a cattle train. It was loaded with cowboys and carrying a load of cattle to Kansas City. In later years, Audrey recalled in a taped interview:

> I was the only girl on the train and I was scared to death. Mama had always warned me about men and acted like they were dangerous. By the time I got off, I was a mess. I was really worried and had been under such a great deal of stress that I got sick. I should have known that if any of

the younger fellows had said anything to me the older ones would have knocked their block off.[1]

Audrey's health continued to deteriorate. Lack of sleep and poor nutrition might have contributed to what she called a "nervous breakdown." In March, she lost control of most of her muscles. She couldn't hit her mouth with the spoon when she was eating. She was diagnosed with Chorea or St. Vitus' Dance. She didn't go back to Santa Rosa, so that ended her school year and her dream of being Valedictorian. She still passed to the eighth grade because of her good grades.

The fact that fourteen-year-old Audrey didn't sleep well may have saved the lives of the family. One night Audrey smelled smoke and woke up her mother. Mabel rushed around and told everyone to get out. The old hotel was on fire! As Audrey was on her way out of her room, she looked out her bedroom window and saw Mabel, Opal, Betty and Edward walking out of the house. Mabel had jammed a straw hat down on Betty's head, a bonnet with red and navy blue ribbons hanging down from it. Mabel was carrying a China cup she had kept beside her bed for water. She also had a kerosene lamp. They walked out the side door to the sidewalk. Milly was a baby and was in a body cast she was wearing to correct a hip problem, so Vivian carried her out.

Audrey watched the whole back end of the hotel go up in flames. That old two-story lumber hotel burned like at tinder box. Audrey could see the family against the bright light of the fire. Mabel had said to hurry, so Audrey got a dress on—inside out and backwards—and got out quickly, bringing nothing with her.

Mabel had been making trips with Milly to Dr. Bull in San Francisco to correct the defective hip that Milly had been born with. Mabel had a trunk full of clothes she had made for the children for an upcoming trip to Oregon. After taking Milly back to the doctor in San Francisco to change the cast on her legs, they would all go to Portland to visit Dammuzzy who had moved there from Nebraska. Nobody thought about saving the trunk of clothes.

The neighbors rushed over to see if they could help save anything. The helpers thought the big player piano in the front office, as well as Mabel's new sewing machine, should be saved. Unfortunately, the helpers got the piano stuck in the door. Everyone inside had to climb out through the windows. Since the piano was in the door, nobody could get in and out to get anything else. It was too difficult to get in and out of the windows, and the smoke was too bad to go back in anyhow. The only thing they had left the next morning was the lamp and cup Mabel had carried out—and the clothes they wore.

Vivian told all the kids to get into the car, an old Chevy. Then he drove the vehicle out of the yard and over across the tracks, parking it against the corrals. Audrey held Milly. Opal and Edward and Betty stood outside part of the time and watched. The hotel burned to the ground.

Mabel frantically ran back and forth, hoping to get things out of the hotel; but she couldn't get anything except Milly's little cart which Vivian had made for Milly to ride in with her body cast, a sort of stroller. Someone had been able to get through a window and rescue it.

In later years, Audrey recalled that the men had just unloaded a whole load of stock that day or the day before.

> Also, there was a freight train standing there that had a load of California fruit. It was a refrigerator car and the ice began to melt so they had to move it. Well, when they moved it, they were told that they had a carload of explosives—dynamite—sitting right there between the hotel and the depot! The depot was right across the road that ran in front of the hotel and across the tracks. The boxcar began to smoke. Vivian tried to get the engineer to pull it out of the way but he wouldn't do it! He wouldn't hook on to it to pull it away. It may have been on a siding, I don't know, but it was right there and it was beginning to smoke. Anyway, Vivian hollered at all the men that had gathered around and got them all against that carload of dynamite and they pushed it by hand and they managed to push it out of the way of the heat and on down the tracks! If they hadn't moved it, it would have blown everything to kingdom come! I can still see, in my mind's eye, that car smoking and the men straining and groaning and pushing it out of the way.²

Often when someone is burned out, neighbors give them donations to help. The only thing the Shearer family received was an offer of credit from the Cuervo grocery store; the owners of the general store agreed to give the Shearers credit to buy a few necessities until Vivian's next pay check. Mabel just bought enough to eat and some plates, cups and utensils. She didn't buy anything else because it was too expensive and she did not want to owe a bill at the store.

The next day Mabel rented another old hotel down by the tracks. It wasn't nearly as nice as the one they had been living in. It had almost no furniture, but it was enough to get by with. Cuervo had originally had two hotels. It was a day's journey from Santa Rosa to Tucumcari, and they were both on the railroad. People would ride the trains and get off in Cuervo to catch their buckboards back out to their ranches or wherever they lived.

This hotel had one big, long room in the center with two or three bedrooms on both sides of it. It had a long table in the center of the room where meals had been served to guests. Audrey had her own bedroom on the right side of the building near the front door. Mabel and Vivian had a bedroom on the other side. As in the other old hotel, there was enough space for each child to have a bedroom.

Vern came from Albuquerque and took Edward, Opal and Betty home with him. But Audrey was sick and her coordination was not good, so she stayed with Mabel and Vivian. She was still barely able to feed herself.

Audrey and her family mourned the loss of their possessions but thanked God they all got out of the burning inferno unhurt. They hoped there would never be another house fire. It was Audrey's first experience with the terrible destruction of fire. It would not be her last.

26

Daddy to the Rescue: Cuervo to Mosquero

Before long, Vivian got "bumped" at Cuervo and was sent to Mosquero. It was on a spur line from the AT & SF—the Santa Fe Railroad—and the Southern Pacific. The summer of 1927 the family moved to Mosquero. There were no apartments or rooms for rent, so they had to stay at a hotel. The hotel was run by a lady with two daughters, one of them about Audrey's age. They became good friends. Audrey was slightly better but was still sick. The doctor who had diagnosed Saint Vitus' Dance prescribed arsenic, one drop the first hour in a glass of water and every hour after that increase the drops each hour until it got up to fifteen drops, then start over and go back to one drop the next hour. Whether she actually had that condition is uncertain and whether the "cure" was effective is also questionable.

Mabel had to take Milly back to San Francisco for her checkup. The child was still in a cast for her dislocated hip. Since her mother was going to leave, there was nothing for Audrey to do but go to Albuquerque and stay with Vern, Mable, and the other kids, Opal, Edward and Betty.

Audrey was put on the train in Mosquero to ride up to French, the junction between the AT & SF and the Southern Pacific. The train, a cattle and passenger train combined, consisted of several cattle cars, a mail car, a baggage car and one or two passenger cars. Audrey was very nervous. When they arrived at French everyone had to get off the train. Audrey had to wait at the depot until the Santa Fe line came by headed for Albuquerque. She had to stay outside because the station agent locked the depot when he went to supper. She wandered around outside by herself. She sat on the porch for a while. Then she got on the AT & SF train and had a long, lonesome ride through the night. The train didn't get to French until after dark, maybe nine o'clock. It was a three or four hour trip to Albuquerque. The train arrived at Albuquerque after midnight.

When the train pulled to a stop, Audrey got up and, somewhat unsteadily, made her way to the exit. She was relieved and overjoyed to see her daddy was at the station waiting to meet her.

"Daddy!" she exclaimed.

Vern gave her a big hug.

"How's my girl?" he asked. "Ready to go home with me?"

"Yes, Daddy," she said. "I'm so glad to be someplace where someone knows who I am! It was lonesome on the train. I'd look out the window, but it was too dark to see anything! Sometimes there would be a window with a light in it, but mostly it was pitch dark!"

"I'm sorry you had to travel alone," Vern said. "But you're my brave girl."

Brave? Audrey thought. She never thought of herself as brave. But life would prove her to be as brave as her pioneer parents—her schoolteacher mother from Nebraska and her cowboy daddy at home in the wide open spaces. Audrey thought her daddy was very brave. She wrote some notes stating that someone had said her father had lacked courage. Audrey wrote that it wasn't true. "Whoever said that just didn't know what Vern Clements was made of."[1]

> I knew dad. When he was the wildest, toughest cowpuncher north of the Rio Grande. He wasn't afraid of man or beast and proved it countless times. Oh, he was soft spoken—mild—around the house. But he never backed down from man or beast. I remember when he [faced] a blizzard and came in half frozen with medicine for the kids. Then there were the wild broncs he busted for $30 per month so he could feed his family. Or the time a wild boar was chasing little May. He ran it down and kicked it in the teeth so that it turned and attacked him so May could get away.[2]

Audrey's daddy was her "hero," and when he met her at the train station, she knew she would get well under his care.

Vern wondered if Mabel and Vivian had been taking proper care of Audrey. There was no reason she should be sick, he thought. "I wish your mother had let you come along when I picked up the other kids."

Vern and Mable lived on South Edith on a little side street, South Pacific, just off Edith. It ran between Edith and Walter. Vern's wife was greatly concerned about Audrey too. Although she had never had children of her own, Mable took to the role of mother very well. She had more time than Audrey's mother who was usually busy with her other children and her work. Audrey's step-mother Mable helped nurse Audrey back to health. Knowing her daddy was there with his love and support, as well as her step-mother, gave Audrey the boost she needed. She began to improve.

Vern and Mable immediately took Audrey to a chiropractor. In fact, there were two of them—a man his wife. Audrey was still very nervous. Her hands and feet would jerk almost continually. One of the first things the chiropractors suggested was to stop taking the arsenic drops the medical doctor had prescribed. Then they began daily treatments.

Audrey continued to see the chiropractor for quite some time and got better. Audrey remembered that a chiropractor in Nebraska had helped Opal recover from the ravages of diphtheria and saved her from having to wear that horrible cast the medical doctor had made for her. Audrey felt hope for the first time in a long time.

It was time for school, but Audrey was still too sick to go. Audrey's mother had her hands full with Milly—traveling to San Francisco to the doctor frequently. Opal, Edward and Betty started to school in Albuquerque. Opal joined the Campfire Girls which met once a week. Audrey was too sick to join. When Audrey had left Mosquero, her mother had given her five dollars. Audrey used it to go to the movies at the Kimo Theatre, a lovely new theatre. She had nothing else to do and she couldn't foresee an "emergency." Audrey would go about once a week to an afternoon matinee. She would walk down from South Edith to the downtown area, about eleven blocks.

The Campfire Girls were going to sell shamrocks on the street for St. Patrick's Day. Vern got a bunch of little silk shamrocks to sell. Audrey and Opal sold them all. Audrey was well enough by that time to join the Campfire girls. When officers were to be elected, Opal nominated Audrey to be the reporter. She was elected. That was the first experience she had as a reporter; she would have many more. Every week she wrote up a little item to take down to the *Albuquerque Tribune* or *Albuquerque Journal* and they would print it. She did that the rest of the year until school was out. In later years when Audrey was a full time reporter in Las Vegas, she saw one of the Camp Fire Girls' reports signed by

Audrey Clements in the "Twenty-Five-Years-Ago" column of the *Albuquerque Journal*. She realized that many times a little job given to a child provides a sense of responsibility, pride, and even the jumping point for a future career. She had enjoyed being the official reporter for the Campfire Girls' chapter to which she belonged. Little did she realize then that years later she would serve in the office of reporter for numerous clubs and would work as a professional newspaper reporter.

When school was out, Vivan's job took him back to Santa Rosa. Mabel and Vivian moved again and all the kids went back to live with them. All went to school there in the fall of 1928. Audrey took the New Mexico State Exam and passed it for her Eighth Grade Certificate. She was happy that she had overcome her illness and finished eighth grade. Her daddy had come to her rescue and she was back on her feet. He and Mable had seen how chiropractic treatments had helped many people. The fact that Audrey responded to them so well when the medical doctor failed to help her was something she remembered later in life. Her recovery from whatever ailed her impressed Audrey with the fact that the body can heal if given the proper care.

Audrey started in the ninth grade. She took Spanish. But after only a short time in school, Vivian was out of a job again in Santa Rosa. So the folks decided to move to the Old Homestead Ranch where Grandfather Shearer was living. He and Vivian thought they could make a living running a saw mill there.

Once again Mabel prepared to move all her belongings. Vivian and Mabel had two milk goats. They carried them on the running board of the car in some kind of cage that Vivian put together. If the girl who had called Grandfather's rag tag crew moving into Santa Rosa could see them now, she'd probably have more to say about "the hobos." Although Opal had been insulted, Audrey told her that it was just good old American ingenuity to make do when you didn't have the money for anything better.

Somehow they got all their things moved to the Old Homestead Ranch. This time, Mabel thought perhaps they could settle down for good. That Christmas Mabel felt isolated from her family. She would spend Christmas in New Mexico, enjoying better weather, perhaps, but missing the grand Christmas tree, her mother's company, and many of the familiar things of her mother's home.

Mabel prepared packages to send to her family. The little gifts showed thoughtfulness and love. Mabel had this list:

Papa—Towel
U.F. (Uncle Frank Waddell)—4 hdks (handkerchiefs)

> Mother—
> 2 pads (hot pads)
> Towel
> 2 doilies
> 2 hdks (handkerchiefs)
> A. I. (Aunt Ida)—
> 2 pads—B & M (Betty and Milly)
> 2 doilies— A & O (Audrey and Opal)
> 1 towel—M (Mabel)
> 1 hdk (handkerchief)—Ed (Edward)[3]

She had the gifts lined up to send to each person from each child and herself. Mabel wrote this note to her mother:

> Mother—
> A simple gift
> But we wish you bliss,
> And tons of love
> Are wrapped in this.
> M

On the next page, she continued:

> A tiny hanky for Grandma dear
> But wrapped in it is Christmas cheer.
> Betty sends her love
> Sewed up in this small pad.
> Don't burn your fingers on a pan
> If you should, she'd be sad.
>
> Betty made this pad for you:
> But her sewing looks quite sick.
> She doesn't practice very much
> Except arithmetic.

Then she wrote:

> A jolly Xmas I wish for you,
> May your days be gay and never blue.

> Xmas day brings love along
> Same as Me to Dammazy. [Dammuzzy]
> In each little loop
> On this wooly towel
> I'm sending a bunch of love.

To her uncle Frank, Mabel wrote:

> We wish you merry Christmas
> As gay as anything
> This simple gift
> Is poor makeshift
> For the love that we would bring.

Mabel was close to her Uncle Obadiah Franklin Waddell. She called him "Uncle Frank." He had married Ida Moellring on April 5, 1917. To her Aunt Ida, Mabel wrote:

> If fate had made us richer
> We'd "thank the stars above"
> And send you stacks of presents
> But we couldn't send more love.

She also wrote a note for her father:

> Audrey wishes you joy and cheer
> Today and many another year.
> Opal wishes you health and peace.
> For health and happiness we pray
>
> For our dear Grandpa every day
> Audrey wishes you health anew
> And love and peace
> Is her wish for you.

The verse to her father continued:

> Edward wishes for Grandpa dear
> A brimming measure of Christmas cheer,

Health and peace and prosperity
Is our constant loving
Prayer for thee.

It can't express my love to all.
May you have a jolly Xmas day—
Forget to work—just laugh and play.

Betty sends dear Grandpa
A great big hug and kiss
A million dollars at a store
Can't buy such gifts as this.

Me—
I wish you happy Christmas
As bright as the stars above.
In each little loop
On this wooly towel
I'm sending a bunch of love.
We wish you a merry Christmas.[4]

27

The Old Homestead Ranch

Vivian and Mabel moved to the Old Homestead Ranch in late 1927 or early 1928. They referred to it simply as "the ranch." Soon after they got settled, Audrey, Opal, Edward and Betty were taken out to the ranch. They went through the village of San Geronimo, past what his now the Gardner place, through Santillanes Canyon, then on about two more miles to the ranch.

Audrey noticed, as she had the very first time she'd been to those mountains, the wonderful, heavenly scent of the pine trees. At one point they could get a good view of Hermit's Peak. Then the beauty of Barillas peak as they neared the Shearer property was overwhelming. It was nothing like the flat lands of Nebraska, nor was it like southern New Mexico. At Avis and even Santa Rosa or Cuervo, predominately flat, dry, semi-desert type terrain could be seen from horizon to horizon. Taos had a good view of mountains. But this place was actually in the high timber in the heavily forested mountain range!

This was high country with snow-tipped mountains lording majestically over the deeply shadowed canyons and the brightly colored meadows edged with forests of dense pines. The little brooks babbled happily down from the mountain where they would eventually find their way to the Tecolote River. Audrey took in deep breaths of fresh air. She felt wholesome, well, and fully alive for the first time in a long time, felt she wanted to live in these beautiful mountains for the rest of her life. Audrey knew this was "home." She remembered that her name meant "Mountain Girl." She knew this was where she was meant to be.

Richard Arthur Shearer and his wife Ollie Atwell Shearer had moved to Las Vegas in about 1900. They had two children, Charles Vivian Shearer and Arolvi Shearer. Arolvi was born at Woods Cross, Utah where her father worked for the railroad. Charles Vivian was born September 19, 1890 at Elko, Nevada, the same year Mabel Waddell was born.

The Shearers owned the Savings Bank Store at 518 Sixth Street in Las Vegas. But they lost money because of all the shop lifting. The Shearers homesteaded property in the Mineral Hill Area in 1901. They moved all the store stock they'd had in their store in Las Vegas to the Mineral Hill Store, called the Ferndele Store, at the Old Homestead Ranch. They ran the Store and Post Office. People came from San Geronimo, from Mineral Hill and the entire surrounding area to get mail and supplies. But again, the shop lifting was heavy. When they had proven up on that homestead, which took five years, they got the deed from the U.S. Government. They moved over to the adjoining 160 acres and proved up on it. Later Richard Shearer and his wife separated. She owned a beauty shop in Las Vegas for a while. Grandfather Shearer built the rock house where the family lived off and on through the years. Vivian built the big adobe house just down the road from the rock house, and he built several one-room cabins. He and Mabel lived in the big adobe house during many of their retirement years.

The area was rich in history. Mineral City was just a few miles to the north, a thriving mine boom town in the 1880's in what is now known as the Mineral Hill district. Mineral City once published its own newspaper. An article in the *Las Vegas Daily Optic* stated:

> Tecolote Creek (or Right Hand creek as it is commonly called) rises some seven miles northwest of Mineral City, where it receives the Blue

canyon creek, which flows south of Mineral Mountain. Its waters flow continuously. Its bed is never dry, and it flows probably three times the volume of water as does your Gallinas at Las Vegas.[1]

The article stated that there were twenty-eight cabins and frame houses in the district, and there were twenty-five or thirty tents and brush houses. The Fairview Hotel was advertised as the "finest mountain resort hotel, with 20 rooms."[2] Silver was being mined and people were excited about it. However, it didn't last. "The Fairview hotel eventually burned down. And the miners wandered to other boom towns. Today the site of Mineral City, at the junction of the Blue Canyon and Tecolote, is lost in the timber."[3] Audrey wrote a poem, "Mineral Hill Miner" which appeared in the *Las Vegas Daily Optic*:

> His pard was black mountains.
> His master pure gold.
> His task to wrest nuggets
> From canyon stronghold.
>
> Roll out as dawn breaks
> For flapjack and lick
> And coffee as strong
> As Diablo mule's kick.
>
> Then into Blue Canyon
> With sharp kick and tin pan
> And prayers to the guardian
> Of gold crazy man.
>
> His pard was black mountains.
> His master pure gold.
> His task to wrest nuggets,
> From canyon stronghold.[4]

Besides all the mining in the Mineral City area and all the farming in the San Geronimo area, there were other activities such as sawmilling.

Falls Creek was a beautiful area; the children always liked to hike to "the Falls" to have a picnic.(Today, because the old access road has been closed to vehicle traffic, many people do not know the beautiful falls, which are on the Santa Fe National Forest, exist.) The Falls were just up the path from the Shearer property on what they called "the Forty," an additional forty-acre piece they owned.

Grandfather Shearer enjoyed the two bedroom rock house he had built. It had a large kitchen, big living room, and bedrooms on either end of the living room. When Vivian moved his family to the ranch, Grandfather had the bedroom on the north side and Mabel and Vivian had the one on the south side. Vivian put lumber across the two by four beams in the attic so the kids could put their pallets down and sleep up there. There was a ladder leading to the attic from the kitchen through a small hole in the ceiling. Grandfather Shearer was a self-educated man. He loved his library of books and he played an organ which was the pride of his living room.

Grandfather and Vivian began operating a saw mill at the ranch. Vivian was also working to establish a real estate business and was doing some writing. His real estate letterhead said, "Land Industries and Income Property and Business Opportunities." In the center it said, "Buyers and Sellers, Sales and Exchange Anywhere." It also had in big letters, "Charles V. Shearer, Specialist in Nationwide Selling, P.O. Box 336, Las Vegas, New Mexico."

Mabel's mother Dammuzzy came to the Old Homestead Ranch to live with Mabel and her family in late 1928. Mabel was glad to have her mother there. Dammuzzy started to build a house next to the path that went up from the creek to the ranch house. But it was never finished. She built a chicken house right below it near the creek and bought some chickens. Sometime after the saw mill was running, Vivian began building a large adobe house for the family. While it was being constructed, Vivian built three cabins east of the main house—a play house for Milly; a cabin for Opal and Audrey and Betty to share; and another one that Mabel and Vivian lived in later. Edward apparently stayed with Mabel and Vivian in Grandfather's house. Dammuzzy raised chickens and sold eggs to some of the stores in Las Vegas. Of course, someone had to help get her eggs to town. Dammuzzy was at the ranch a year or so before she decided to go back to Oregon.

Grandfather Shearer and Vivian bought two burros. Edward built a two-wheeled cart for the burros to pull so he could haul water up from the creek in ten gallon milk cans. That was easier than carrying water from the well two buckets at a time, especially on wash days and bath days. For drinking water, he had to go to the well in the garden. The well had a bucket on a rope, so he had to fill the big cans one bucket at a time.

The donkeys were very obstinate. They would stop in the middle of the creek. Audrey was taking Dammuzzy to the Tecolote River, riding the burros, to catch a ride to town with a man they called "Goat Roberts." It was March, freezing cold, early in the morning. That burro stopped right in the middle of the Tecolote. Audrey pulled and pushed and the burro pulled back. Audrey fell right into the middle of the creek. Her clothes froze solid on her. When she got Dammuzzy delivered to her ride, Audrey went back to Falls Creek and down to where Harold Saunders and his family were living. They weren't up yet, but they got up and built a fire so Audrey could warm up and thaw out. She was very grateful. Their quick action probably saved her life.

Audrey had one or two other painful incidents. She was standing near a horse named Molasses when the horse saw a bear, kicked Audrey in the abdomen, and took off running. Another time Audrey rode horseback, taking eggs across what became known as "Nelson's Prairie" where the old Nelson house sat. It was a two-story structure that had housed tuberculosis patients in the late 1800's. The flat field was also known as "Prairie Dog Town," several acres full of prairie dog holes. The horse ran away across Prairie Dog Town, missing the holes. Audrey arrived at her destination after getting her horse under control, and she boasted in later years that "not one single egg was broken."[5] In her notes "Everyone Has Choices," Audrey wrote:

> The summer of 1929 (?) came along. Mother was raising a bunch of hens. She got a start from someone in San Geronimo. When she brought them home she dipped each one in a bucket of Lysol water to get rid of any lice or mites. That was the spring she sent me on horseback six miles over to Mineral Hill Post Office to get a setting of eggs. I rode over on Gypsy, a skittish little mare. At the P.O. run by Mrs. Beisman and her daughters, Christine and Emma, I paid fifty cents for the setting eggs. Mrs. B. carefully wrapped each of the 15 fertile eggs in a couple of sheets of outdated Montgomery Ward Catalogue. [paper] Then she put a layer of wadded up paper in the bottom of an empty round oatmeal box, put in a layer of eggs, a layer of wadded Ward's pages, then another layer of eggs until a setting of eggs was in the box. I placed the oatmeal box full of eggs into a sack that formerly held 50 pounds of flour. I tied a good knot in it to keep it from slipping through my fingers. Christine came out front and waited while I climbed into Grandfather's huge old stock saddle with the stirrups shortened to my legs' length. Then to keep Gypsy from being frightened she carefully handed up the flour sack holding the eggs. I carried it in my left hand while the bridle reins were in my right hand. About an hour later and half way home, we came to the John Nelson Prairie Dog town. The 100 acres or so of cleared area in front of the old deserted house that was once built for a "lungers" rest home was

filled with Prairie dog holes. The out posts began to holler I was coming. Hundreds of the little animals were sitting on the raised edge of their homes ready to dive into their "cellar" doors. Gypsy was used to Prairie Dog town, for when she wasn't kept home for me to ride she had often been ridden by Opal or Edward to the Mineral Hill School house just up the hill across the Tecolote from the Gonzales Place. Opal graduated from the 8th grade there when Alta Jones, later Alta Beisman (Mrs. Henry Beisman) was teaching her first year of school. That one room school house with its small back room for supplies and dry wood was built about 1912. All of the Mineral Hill area residents got together and had a school house rising. It sat on donated land. It was made of adobes donated by some, with lumber roof covered with tin, also donated. All the county or state had to do was provide teachers.[6]

Students had to ride a slow school wagon, unlike Audrey's ride. She wrote:

> Gypsy was used to the shrill yips of the little mammals standing on the small "walls" around the countless holes which they dived into and disappeared as we approached. Perhaps my right arm, slightly bent at the elbow, tired from trying to hold the eggs so that my arm would give with Gypsy's rough trot or slow walk, I may have accidentally touched her shoulder with it or she may have caught a glimpse of it from the corner of her eye. Suddenly she shied, jumping sidewise. Somehow I kept my balance as she broke into a run. Still holding the eggs in my hand, I pulled on the reins, yelling, "Whoa! Whoa! Whoa, Gyp! Stop it, Whoa!" She didn't even slow down. The prairie dog holes stretched away for half a mile. I tried to guide her on the faint trail winding around the various holes. She wasn't about to neck rein. She decided the closest way over into the timber was a straight line and she took it. The prairie dogs dived into the holes and we raced toward them; as she jumped each hole as she came to it she jarred my eye teeth. All I could do was ride—the flour sack with its precious eggs swung from my hand. My arm and elbow absorbed most of the jolts. I tried frantically to calm Gypsy. "Whoa, Girl! Steady! Whoa!" I repeated over and over, although the wind and jarring from jumps over the holes nearly took my breath away. I continued to pull frantically on the reins. I knew if I didn't get that little mare slowed down and under control before we hit the timber she might try one of her well known tricks—going under a low limb to knock off a rider. I had her slowed down to a fast trot by the time we reached the first pine

timber. She dropped down to a slow walk with both of us huffing and puffing.

"Don't you ever do that again!" I scolded. "You could have busted Mama's eggs!" Oh, gosh! Mama's eggs! I was still carrying them carefully at nearly arm's length. I knew I had not jarred them enough to hurt them during that wild ride. However, I also knew that if I told Mama of that harrowing experience, she would not set those eggs, thinking they would be addled. I also considered the fifty cents that would be lost. "Gyp!" I said aloud. "If you promise never to do it again and don't say a word, I won't either."

"Were you careful with the eggs?" Mama asked as I thankfully let her take them from my aching hand before I dismounted.

"Of course!" I answered.

Mama carefully removed them from the oatmeal box and promptly put them under a nice big broody Rhode Island Red hen. Then came 21 days of holding my breath, not literally, but I was scared. What if none of them hatched? What if Mama found out about that wild ride through Prairie Dog town? She'd be so mad losing fifty cents and also the eggs which we could have eaten!

I was so full of fear and guilt and thankfulness that Gyp hadn't stepped in a hole and broken her neck, I could not even play.

"What's the matter with you, Audrey! You half asleep?" Somebody would ask and I would try to act more normal.

After three weeks of terror the eggs hatched. I went with Mama to the hen house. She carefully lifted Mama Hen off the nest to expose the chickens. Quickly I counted them aloud. "15." I exclaimed. "Wonderful!" Oh what a relief that count to 15 gave me. I never let on or told of that terrible ride until I was in my 30's. Then I wrote the episode up for *Capper's Weekly* in a brief unsigned article. Mother recognized it as mine. After so many years we could laugh about it. I still doubt that I would have told why they didn't hatch—if they hadn't. For if anyone [thought] that Gyp would run away again none of us could have ridden her. And when she wasn't kept home for me to ride, Ed would be riding her to the Mineral Hill School. Opal had graduated from there the year before when Alta Jones [later Alta Beisman] served her first year as a teacher. We got a number more clutches of eggs from Beismans to set that spring but none ever took such a wild ride and neither did they all hatch out as well as the ones I carried safely on a runaway horse across a live prairie dog town. The prairie dog town was in a cleared pasture of more than

100 across in front of the old Nelson house which served as headquarters for a TB "lungers" rest home run by Kate Nelson. The house had been turned over to the rats and rattlesnakes for years, gradually deteriorating until the 1970's when E. J. Gallegos bought it, remodeled and restored it. In the late 1930's John Nelson poisoned out the prairie dogs. So now the vast town is only a memory in the minds of the few old timers.[7]

Years later when Audrey was an Optic reporter and editor, she wrote a poem for the *Rodeo Edition* of the *Las Vegas Daily Optic,* perhaps remembering her wild ride. She was given a bi-line for "Day's Work:"

Get fer the corral
To rope a paint hoss,
Bowl out the frost kinks
Till he knows who is boss.

Stick to the saddle
Like a tick in an ear
And hunt through the brush
For that lost loco steer.

Run old Loco home
Through prairie dog town.
"Miss them holes Paint,
Or we both will go down."

"Don't break a leg
And don't throw a shoe.
Chousing that steer
Is now up to you!"

Old Loco's corraled,
A day's work is done
For cowboy and Paint
And the fast sinking sun.[8]

One day in the fall Audrey got ready to go to town with Dammuzzy in the wagon. They were taking in a case or two of her eggs to sell. Audrey noticed her mother as she and Dammuzzy were leaving the yard. Mabel was walking in front of the cabin. Audrey suddenly realized that Mabel must be expecting another baby. Nobody ever said anything about such things in those days. But Audrey knew where babies came from because Sophia Rael had told her when they were in Bernal.

Audrey and her grandmother went down on Railroad Avenue, got a room and stayed there all night. The next day Audrey's grandmother bought her a pair of beautiful shoes. They had a little heel on them and it was the first "high" heel Audrey had ever had.

As they were on their way home, Dammuzzy told Audrey she would be leaving soon to return to Oregon. She liked it in New Mexico's mountains, but she wanted to go back where she had been before.

"I've known you since the day you were born," Dammuzzy told Audrey. "I'd like you to come and stay with me in Portland, Oregon. I'd provide for you and you could go to school and get to meet lots of nice people," she said. "You're my oldest grandchild and you've always been very special to me."

Audrey was pleased that her grandmother wanted her to go and live with her. "You're special to me, Dammuzzy," Audrey replied.

"I'll start packing up tomorrow," Dammuzzy said. "So you need to decide soon if you want to live with me—or stay here. If you go with me, I will see that you get through high school and even go to college if you want to."

Audrey looked up and saw Barillas Peak and the other mountains in the Sangre de Cristo mountain range above their home. She had fallen in love with those mountains. Audrey wondered, *How can I leave these mountains?* She was hesitant to say anything. It was a difficult choice to make, but she knew she couldn't leave the mountains she had grown to love. It was a "cameo" moment, one of those moments that becomes etched in the memory for the entire life.

As if she could read Audrey's thoughts, Dammuzzy said, "There are mountains in Oregon, too, you know. Beautiful, high mountains!"

Audrey nodded. She imagined life with her grandmother where she would visit the mountains and the ocean often. She would have the good company of the grandmother she loved. She'd be able to go to school, a good school; and her grandmother would undoubtedly support her in good style. She might meet the love of her life there. It was a fork in the road, a turning point. Whatever she chose would affect the rest of her life. It was one of those decisions one can never forget.

Audrey decided to say YES. She would have a better life with her grandmother and she could get the education she so deeply desired. Just as Audrey was about to say she would go, she thought of her mother. She recalled Mabel as she'd seen her before they left for town—walking heavily in front of a cabin.

Her dress could no longer hide her pregnancy. Audrey realized that her mother would need her help more than ever with a new baby coming. Audrey loved her mother as well as her grandmother, and her heart went out to the mother whose life had been filled with poverty and disappointment. Now yet another child was on the way and Mabel would need all the help she could get. Audrey loved her mother too much to desert her and forsake the new baby when her help would be badly needed.

"Thank you for the kind offer, Dammuzzy," Audrey said affectionately. "But Mama needs me. She'll need my help now more than ever." She didn't explain why. She thought Dammuzzy knew another baby was on the way. But Dammuzzy said afterwards that if she'd known Mabel was pregnant she would not have left; she would have stayed to help her. Audrey thought Dammuzzy certainly should have known, but apparently she did not. And Mabel would not have mentioned it. Years later, Audrey recalled:

> How well I remember that day I looked up at the mountain peak and could not go away. Oh, I knew Oregon had mountains—more spectacular than these—and the ocean, one of seven seas. But today I could hear the same roar of that ocean when the wind swished in the pine trees. So I kissed my grandmother goodbye and stumbled back into the mountains to cry for her and for me and my untested future.[9]

Audrey missed her grandmother, but she was glad she had stayed behind at the ranch. Her mother needed her. And the Sangre de Cristo Mountains grew more and more dear to Audrey. She would listen to the wind rushing through the pine trees, look up at Barillas Peak and its neighbor, Fox Peak, and thank God for the beautiful mountains. "This is right next door to heaven," she'd sometimes say.

The day Audrey had to choose between going with her grandmother or staying with her mother was one of those crossroads in life we all have. Audrey chose to stay and help her family instead of going to live with her grandmother where she'd have a life of comparative luxury and an opportunity for an education. In later years, Audrey indicated that she did not regret her choice, that she was glad she had stayed to help her mother. Yet at times Audrey would sigh, "I wonder how my life would have turned out if I had gone to Oregon with Dammuzzy."[10] Audrey wrote in her notes, "Everyone Has Choices:"

> I often think of that time. I would have had a completely different life— no comparison with the one that I've had. I had a choice. People always

have a choice. Sometimes they don't have sense enough to pick the right one always or even know which one is the right choice.[11]

Audrey wrote years later about her choice:

> Well, it turned out to be one hell of a life: diet poor, hard and bitter, pulling myself up by my bootstraps, gritting my teeth, bowing my head and saying my prayers, struggling on and on and on here by my mountain.
>
> Now 50 years later I wonder. My grandmother was such a dear. She promised to help me get through high school and would have provided a beautiful, clean, warm home and probably I would have found a nice, loving, faithful, gentle husband instead of the type I got. Oh, Clyde was loving—but then I didn't understand loving. And Bill was wonderful but we never could do the things we wanted to do.
>
> Oh, Fate lifted me up, then knocked me down and kicked me around until I didn't know which way was up. Now somehow 50 years have passed since I was 17—a long time.[12]

Audrey had chosen to stay in her New Mexico mountains. She had regrets and cried over her broken dreams. But often when she would travel the road from Las Vegas to her mountain home, Audrey would say, "I could have gone to Oregon with Dammuzzy. But I just couldn't leave Mama when she needed me, when Jessica was about to be born. And, besides, I just couldn't leave these beautiful mountains that I love."

Long Road to School

Transportation in the 1920's in northern New Mexico was not "modern." Paved roads were not commonplace. Although motor cars existed, many people still relied on horse drawn modes of travel or rode horseback. Audrey had her first horseback ride when she was one or two years old, so travel by four-legged method was nothing new to her. Mabel's children went to the Mineral Hill School in the fall of 1929. They rode on the school wagon, a lumber wagon drawn by a team of horses. It came from Santillanes Canyon past the ranch and on up the Tecolote to the Trujillo's and then back down to the School, which was near the Tecolote crossing. Audrey had finished eighth grade and wanted to go to school in the spring of 1928, but there was no high school in the Mineral Hill area. Opal finished the eighth grade in the spring of 1929, with Alta Jones as her teacher. Alta taught there from 1928 to 1930, according to Audrey.[1] Opal and Edward rode burros sometimes and horses other times. Sometimes they walked the four miles to school and back.

One day Audrey was riding the biggest burro to get the mail, about three miles from the ranch. She rode past the place that was later Mr. and Mrs. Clark Raney's place. It was a shortcut to the mail box. She was riding through a little level place, a field close to the creek. She described the incident in later years:

> Harold Saunders came racing his horse behind me, whooping and hollering, and it scared the burro. Of course I was just riding it with maybe a string around its neck or something, but I didn't have a saddle or anything—just riding it bare-back. It promptly threw me and I looked up and there were all four feet coming down right in my middle and I rolled! Boy! That was split second timing! That was the fastest I ever moved! All four feet were off the ground above me so I got out of the way! Quick! Harold thought it was so funny. He just came tearing down behind me as fast as his horse could go! Of course, he was a smart alec kid. That was the horse that he eventually tied to a tree while he was cutting another tree and the other tree fell on his horse and killed it! People do the most stupid things! That's the first and only time that I was ever thrown from a four legged critter. I rode horses all the time but usually with a saddle and bridle. That time I was bareback and didn't have a bridle! I didn't expect him to "scare" so easily! I didn't expect him to "double up" and buck—jump up and down![2]

All the kids learned about guns at a very early age. They learned to shoot and to shoot well. They also learned about gun safety. The neighbor Harold Saunders and their good friend, Bill Reid, were visiting the Shearers at the ranch one afternoon. Audrey recalled later:

> We were all sitting around in a semi-circle by the large chrome trimmed heater in the living room. Bill was sitting in the old Morris chair by the

old pump organ when he decided to show off his 45 Cal. "thumb buster frontier model." Harold had a .32 Cal pistol he wanted to show off. He took the shells out and laid them on the table and passed the gun around for all of us to inspect. After all it was a nice gun! When the gun got to Opal—she was sitting directly across from Harold—she pointed it right at him and then she remembered that Mama and Vivian had preached to all of us that we never point a gun at anything we didn't intend to kill. That was an absolute rule in our home! She took her sight off Harold and pointed it at the ceiling and pulled the trigger at the same time. It scared us all to death! The gun fired! Harold was only a few feet away from her. Had she not remembered to point toward the ceiling she would have killed him! We were always taught that any gun we had was loaded and ready to fire! Nobody knew how that cartridge got into Harold's gun when it had been empty! Somebody stuck a bullet in it and nobody noticed! Nobody admitted it! Only Opal's early training kept her from killing Harold right there in front of all of us![3]

Later when they lived at García Mill, Mabel was testing the 22 caliber rifle and pulled the trigger to see if it was on safety. She pointed it toward the ceiling and it went off and went through the floor of the attic where Audrey was lying on the bed reading. She heard the shot but didn't know what her mother was doing.

In a few seconds, Audrey heard her mother's scared, questioning voice: "Audrey?" Audrey answered her mother immediately. "Yes, Mama?"

"Are you all right?" Mabel asked.

"Yes, Mama."

"Thank goodness!" Mabel exclaimed.

That shot went through the ceiling made with one inch boards but it didn't come very close to Audrey or she would have heard it whistle.[4]

Audrey learned a very good lesson. She said that everyone should always treat every gun as if it is loaded. It's always the "unloaded" gun that kills someone. Children should learn never to point a gun—not even a toy—at anyone for any reason so they will never get into the habit of doing so. They should never even pretend to shoot someone.

Mabel had received her new State Elementary Certificate. It was signed by A. Montoya, State Superintendent of Public Instruction. It authorized her to teach for a period of three years without further examination.[5]

Mabel was usually able to get a teaching job, but whenever she was pregnant she would usually quit as soon as she could. However, Mabel worked when she was pregnant this time because they needed the money so badly. Once, however, Mabel applied for a job and was told that someone else had applied for the job also and that the other candidate was "an unmarried woman so she will get the job instead." The superintendent explained to Mabel that an unmarried woman was always hired over a married woman because "You have a husband to support you." However, that school year of 1929-30, Mabel got the school near San Geronimo (about four miles from the Old Homestead Ranch.) She rode Old Jelly to school every day. The Great Depression had begun and anyone with a job felt lucky.

That fall of 1929, Audrey and Opal wanted to go to school. But there was no school in the area beyond the eighth grade. Graduating from high school was not easy in those days if one lived on a farm or a ranch. There were no school buses to take students to school when they lived in the remote mountains as Audrey and Opal did. The nearest high school was nearly twenty miles away in Las Vegas and the roads were little more than cow trails in places.

Vern and his wife Mable were living in Las Vegas in an upstairs apartment looking over the street. They had lived there at the place of a lady named Mrs. Organ for several months. Vern was working with Mr. Dalgard, painting. Audrey recalled in later years:

> Opal and I had gone to town several times and played bridge with Daddy and Mable. We stayed all night a time or two in a room across the hall. It was available by the night, week, or month. When it was time to go to school in the fall, we were considering renting it. Immediately, before we could move in, Daddy and Mable decided to move back to Albuquerque! Mama was teaching at San Geronimo the school year, 1929-1930. We wanted to go to town and go to school and thought Daddy and Mable would help. It is a terrible situation when nobody wants you! I think Daddy wanted to help us but she [Mable] wouldn't hear of it! We were too much trouble.[6]

Audrey and Opal were disappointed that their father and step-mother moved away. They didn't know anyone in Las Vegas they could stay with.

Vivian didn't think the girls needed to go to school any more. The girls discussed finishing high school at some length. They knew their mother believed in education for women; she made her living as a school teacher. But convincing their step-father to help was another matter. Audrey and Opal had been in and out of different schools, having moved "from pillar to post" all their lives. Audrey was sixteen, soon to be seventeen. Opal was fourteen, soon to be fifteen. They needed to be in school if they were ever to finish high school.

"Mama would be happy if we'd finish high school," Audrey asserted.

"I think Daddy would be pleased, too." Opal replied.

"Vivian doesn't think we need to go, so he won't help," Audrey continued. "He thinks education is only for boys who want a career—like a lawyer or doctor. He doesn't think girls need an education. They're just going to get married and then their husbands will support them."

"And if we sit up here at the ranch, how will we meet our future husbands?" Opal asked. "We'll end up being unmarried, doing ranch chores all our lives."

"Well, I want to learn. I need to know more. I want to be a writer," Audrey said.

"I do too," Opal said. "I want to write poetry."

"You write wonderful verses!" Audrey exclaimed. "You'll be a great poet!"

"You write good verse, too! Of course your penmanship needs work!" Opal teased. Audrey wrote with her left-hand most of the time but she was actually ambidextrous. She had never had "a beautiful hand" in writing as Mabel did and as Mabel desired for all of her children to have. Opal's handwriting was very much like Mabel's—beautiful smooth curves, easy to read, pleasant to look at. Audrey's was "scribble-like," she was told, and sometimes difficult to read.

Ignoring the comment, Audrey continued. "You are a better poet than I am. But we both would do better if we graduated from high school."

"Mama always says if someone wants something bad enough, they can find a way to get it," Opal said.

"Yes, that's right. But you have to be willing to pay the price," Audrey said. "Leaving here to go to school means getting into town, finding a place to stay, working to pay for that place, working for food and other things we need, and finding time to study. And we can't expect any help."

"We can do it," Opal said stubbornly. "Let's make up our minds to it."

"All right," Audrey said. "I'm willing. Let's tell Mama we've made up our minds to finish high school no matter what. She'll help us all she can."

"I'll go to school if I have to *walk* to town!" Opal exclaimed with determination. Little did she know that the day would come when that was just what the girls would have to do.

Audrey and Opal couldn't stay at Mrs. Organs because their daddy had left. So Mabel went to Las Vegas to see Mr. P. P. Mackel and rented an upstairs room for the girls. It had a tiny kitchenette. She was concerned about her daughters living in town by themselves, so she asked Mr. Mackel to take care of them. They had an upstairs room at the Southeast corner of the house.[7]

At that time students from out of the city went to the New Mexico Normal Training School. "Local area" kids not living in East Las Vegas ("New Town") were not allowed to go to the public city schools. Later, when Mr. W. J. Robertson became Superintendent of Schools, he changed that policy so that country kids could then go to the city school. (Las Vegas High School was later named Robertson High School.) The Training School at Normal was getting all of the "out of area" high school students. Even the people in "Old Town" (West Las Vegas) couldn't send their children over to the Las Vegas City Schools in East Las Vegas. And they had no high school in West Las Vegas, so they sent their students to the Normal Training School too. (The two towns, East Las Vegas and West Las Vegas, were not consolidated until the late 1960's.) When the Immaculate Conception High School was built on University and Sixth Street, students were accepted there from anywhere.

One day Audrey was in a Spanish Class. Suddenly she remembered that she'd failed to turn the fire off under beans she had put on to cook at the apartment. There was a three burner kerosene stove that she and Opal cooked on. Audrey asked permission to leave, explaining the situation to her teacher.

The teacher said, "Well, it's almost noon, so it if burned, it will already be burned up." She refused to give Audrey permission to leave the classroom.

Audrey rushed home at noon and turned the fire off under the charred, ruined beans. The whole apartment was solid soot. The coal oil made oily soot, and there were strings of it hanging down from all over the ceiling of the tiny kitchen. (The apartment had a kitchen, a bedroom, and a living area.) Audrey and Opal had to work furiously to clean the apartment.[8]

Opal gave Audrey a birthday party soon after the apartment was cleaned up. Mr. Mackel had one daughter, Vera. She was an only child and was going to Normal Training School, the same place Opal and Audrey attended. Opal invited her as well as another girl friend, Billie Maxey. Opal fixed a nice luncheon.

Audrey wrote a letter to one of her grandfathers on a single sheet of blue paper, written in dark blue ink. The letter said:

Box 339
Las Vegas, NM
December 19, 1929

Dear Grandpa and all:
    I hope you are well. We all are fine. We have been having fine weather lately.

Our school is out tomorrow. We will start in again Jan. 2. Mother's school is out about the same length of time. We will spend the whole vacation on the ranch. I will certainly enjoy being there again. I wish you all could be with us now.

I got A in English, A in Algebra and B+ in Home Arts. Opal got B in Algebra, B in English and B+ in Home Arts. Last month I was the only one on the Honor Roll in our grade. Edward is doing fine in the sixth and seventh grades. Betty can read and write very well now.

We have moved since Opal wrote to you. Our box number is 339. We received mother's package but we have not received anything else. I hope it has not been lost.

I am learning to skate. Our class enjoys skating parties quite often. We skate about six miles up the canyon from here.

The Normal University gave a Cantata the other night. Opal and I were both in it. It took many weeks of hard practicing. It was well received.

I am leaving now to yell for a basketball game as I am one of the "Purple Peppers," our—[9]

Apparently Audrey was interrupted, as the letter was not finished but was put away in her *My Golden School Days* book. Perhaps she wrote another letter later or perhaps she forgot and never mailed the letter.

Audrey and Opal stayed at Mackels until Christmas, then went home to the ranch. Mabel wanted some kinnikinnick berries and leaves for decorations. The perennial plant, sometimes called Bearberry, looks somewhat like Holly but without the prickly leaves. So Opal and Audrey walked over to "the Forty," (an adjoining piece of property on the road to the Falls.) They had half gallon tin syrup buckets with bail handles. There was a cabin on that property. They saw lion tracks in the snow outside the window where the cat had jumped in. There was no glass in the cabin window. They thought the mountain lion might still be in the cabin. There were no tracks showing the cat had jumped out of the window! The girls pushed the door a little. There was no lion in there. They decided he had jumped out the window and missed the snow bank that was up against it.

"Let's get back to the house," Opal suggested.

"That's a good idea," Audrey agreed.

"It feels funny—like something is behind us," Opal said after a few minutes.

"I feel it too," Audrey said. They quickened their pace.

"I hear something following us now," Opal said then.

"Let's bang our pails. That will scare the cougar off if it's stalking us," Audrey said. "I think the noise will keep it away."

The girls walked back to the ranch, banging their pails together. Just as they got to the upper gate on the ranch, a large mountain lion jumped the fence beside them and ran off toward the north in the brush. They were going south to the house. They had very little kinnikinnick in their pails when they arrived home.

After Christmas Audrey and Opal returned to town. They found an apartment upstairs on Eleventh Street that was cheaper than the Mackel's place. He lived in a nice home. The new place the girls had rented on Eleventh Street wasn't so nice but it was cheaper than the ten dollars a month Mabel had paid for Mr. Mackle's apartment. Ten dollars a month was about the going rate then, so they were glad to find a place for less. A friend's father had a truck and he helped them move. Mr. Mackel came to help. He wanted to know if the girls had done any damage, broke any dishes or anything. He didn't want them to move out. As the girls were trying to move out, he said, "Your mother told me to take care of you! I'm responsible for you!" They assured him they would be fine. They were enjoying their freedom and their school days.

Under "Miscellaneous" in Audrey's *My Golden School Days*, Opal wrote:

Dec. 8, 1929
822 - Eleventh St.
Dearest Sister,
    I have known u forever & have found u very sweet (at times.) Please forgive me for the times I called u "names." Don't forget also the good times we've had together & how we went riding with Paul and Eleck & all the rest. Hope to know u for many years to come.
Your sister,
Opal

At the top margin, Opal wrote: "Age 15. Pretty big girl now"[10] In the far left hand margin, someone (probably Audrey) wrote: "She is only 15 and knows no better place for living than this world." Written under that in a different handwriting (probably Opal's) was: "Please excuse me for living." Obviously, the girls had fun with this book. There were several entries from classmates.

Audrey and Opal had to quit school before very long, as Audrey recalled later:

> In January, 1930, we had to quit school. Mama was expecting a baby and she and Vivian were out of money again. They couldn't help us with rent and tuition so we could stay in school. Mama said there just wasn't enough money for us to continue to go to school. We weren't working for our board and room at that time. We weren't paying our way and there wasn't any more money. Vivian had been working for Crossmans, where Blue Haven (Camp) is now, doing carpentry work for them and I suppose that's where we got some money to go to school at that particular time. We had to leave at the end of the first semester. We had to go back to the ranch. I cried. I sat down in the Home Ec. Building and I remember the teacher patted me and tried to make me quit crying but I couldn't. I couldn't go to school any more. I was a freshman that year—1929-1930. I was heartbroken![11]

That summer of 1930 Audrey helped Mabel who was pregnant with Jessica. She said:

> Mama was pregnant that year and riding horseback on old Jellico, a white horse named for a World War I general, four miles down to San Geronimo to teach every day at the one room school. I knew she needed me. Grandmother hadn't noticed that Jessica was on the way, but I knew. That was why Opal and I had to quit school at New Mexico Normal Training School. It cost us $10.00 a month for rent and about the same for groceries. We took most of our food from home. I remember at the Home Economics class I cried. The dear, sweet teacher, Miss Alice Sundt, put her arms around me and tried to comfort me. I cried harder. Sympathy has always made me cry harder for I have had little of it. I wanted to go to school above all things, but Mama's husband said we had to stay home so Mama could save up the money we might have spent for having the baby. I think the total cost for her staying at Mrs. Persingers on Columbia Avenue where [a] Highlands University building now stands and for doctor William Howe was about $100. She was making $90 per month so somehow this figure didn't work out from January to May in my mind but I just decided I wasn't good at arithmetic and forgot it.[12]

That summer Audrey took care of her mother's chickens while Mabel was in at Mrs. Persingers in Las Vegas waiting to give birth. Audrey was in charge of everything. She raised about seventy-five baby chicks. The hens were laying very well, so she set the hens.

Groceries were scarce, especially meat. The family was hungry, so Grandfather decided to butcher the old cow. They had planted some vegetables, but early in the summer before the crops were grown, there was very little to eat. The cow was past calving and her milk was decreasing. Vivian would have hunted to bring in meat, but game was scarce; and there were hunting laws in place by that time. One could only hunt certain times of the year and had to obtain a license. Vivian wasn't a "poacher," and he never wanted to break the law.

Butchering day was a long, hard day for everyone. They had to cut up the meat and hang it in the cool, screened-in closet-like area built on the north side of the house in the shade. That evening it was almost dark before Audrey ran down to the chicken house to shut them up. As she walked back in near darkness, she felt as if she were being watched or followed. But the dogs weren't barking so she told herself nothing could be around. Still, the hair was raised on the back of her neck, which tingled as she walked back to the house.

In the morning, Vivian and Grandfather discovered the cow's head was missing. They saw where it had been dragged down toward the creek. Lion tracks were everywhere around. Vivian said the dogs had eaten so much the day before (of left-overs) that they were asleep and never heard the lion or barked. Vivian and Milly found the cow's head down by the creek about a half a mile from the house. It was covered in the oak brush and leaves. Audrey realized that the cougar had been watching her the night before when she felt so "spooky."

Audrey worked hard to raise chickens, hoping to sell the eggs or the chickens in town for money to go to school.

> We brought more eggs from Beismans and hatched little chickens into the summer. Mother went to town in June awaiting J's [Jessica's] arrival at Mrs. Persingers. I was left in charge of getting three meals a day for Grandfather Shearer, my step-father, C.V. Shearer, my brother Ed and sisters Opal and Betty Clements and Millicent Shearer. Milly was six and would not let me or anyone comb out her fine, golden hair. She would run and scream if I tried to so I ignored it. It took Mother hours to comb it after Jessica was born. The most I remember is the struggle I had trying to grind wheat in the small kitchen meat grinder to feed those little chickens. They could not eat whole wheat so I tried pounding it between stones which didn't really work. Finally I settled for the meat grinder, struggling with it at the kitchen table every day for weeks until all the chicks were big enough to eat whole wheat. At the same time, G [Grandfather] worked the garden. He was an expert gardener, raising

ten pound cabbages, corn and peas, and beans by the peck. Opal helped with the meals and dish washing. While 13 years old, Ed struggled to keep us in water. He had a team of burros and a cart and some ten gallon water cans. It would take more than an hour to go to the creek, get twenty gallons of water, and drive the balky burros home again. This was for dish washing and washing. We carried water in buckets for drinking water.

Somehow between the hens and me we raised 75 baby chickens. I planned to sell them or their eggs for money to go to school on. When they were good sized fryers, I took a few in a lumber wagon to town to a little grocery on 10th Street in Las Vegas. We had been in and out of there for years but when I was trying to sell something they were not friendly.

I screwed up my courage and with the young roosters went into the store, asking, "Would you like to buy a couple of fryers?"

The store keeper lifted one of the Rhode Island fryers out of the bag, felt its crop and said, "This chicken is full of feed."

"It can't be," I said. "I didn't feed or water them this a.m."

"I'll give you 15 cents for this bird," he said.

I shook my head, took the bird out of his hands and put it back in the sack. I decided I would let the family eat them for 15 cents each. That spring my grandmother sold her old hens for $1.00 each so I felt a young chicken was worth more than 15 cents.

"Their crops are full of feed," the man repeated. "I don't buy second hand feed," he said.

I know now he was being "funny" for the benefit of others in the store. But I was a scared kid needing money, so could only shrink into myself and run. I never tried to sell him any more chickens.[13]

Audrey wrote later:

School was out in May at San Geronimo. On July 8, 1930, Jessica Edna Shearer was born at the home of Mrs. Persinger, a nurse.

At that time the Forest Service had a telephone line that ran from Pecos up to the top of Barillas Peak to the "fire lookout tower" and then down to San Geronimo. It then ran along the mountains, past the Shearer place, where they had put a telephone in, and on over to the Gallinas Canyon and the Ranger Station there. From there it went to Las Vegas and also ran across the mountain to the Barker place above

Rociada where S. Omar Barker's family had a ranch.[14]

Audrey, recalling her disappointment following her attempt to sell the chickens, concluded: "Going to school was a struggle—Getting to town and having enough money to pay tuition and enough to live on! But by golly we made it!"[15]

Not only did Audrey and Opal find ways to continue in school, but they also met their family obligations. Audrey was at the ranch helping with the chores when Mrs. Persinger called the Las Vegas telephone operator and asked her to relay the message about Jessica's birth on the Forest Service line that went to the Shearer ranch. In Audrey's notes, "Jessica's Arrival," she wrote:

> The day Jessica was born someone called the ranger station up the Gallinas and reported to the ranger's wife, Mrs. Max Bruehl. Somehow there was a lack of proper communication. She called us on the long Forest Service line that ran from Barkers up the Sapello, past the Gallinas Ranger Station to Trujillos and then to us and then up to the lookout tower on Barillas Peak and then to Reid Ranch and to several other places on the other side of the mountain and into Pecos. When she called I answered the phone and thought she said mother had a boy. This I reported to Vivian. He promptly shut down the sawmill and set out for Vegas, thinking he had a son.[16]

Naturally, Vivian was surprised but delighted to learn that he had a daughter. The folks didn't have a name planned. Mabel had named Milly, so she wanted Vivian to have the privilege of naming the new daughter. He took a long time to decide but finally named her Jessica, adding a middle name, Edna, since that was Mabel's middle name. Audrey recalled one incident that her mother often talked about:

> One day a lawyer and his wife came by to buy some lumber. The woman looked around at all Mama's kids (there were six of us then) and said, "I don't know how you manage to keep shoes on all of these children!" Then she also said, "I had one once but I sent it back!" In other words, she had adopted one and sent it back, I guess. Mama always laughed about that. She hadn't sent any of us *back*! Anyway, the couple did not pay for their lumber for many, many moons.[17]

Sometime later, Mabel wrote about the incident in a letter to her half sister

Thelma. It seemed to have left quite an impression on her:

> Two years ago, a Las Vegas lawyer put up a place near us for a summer home. He and Mrs. — came to us and arranged for the lumber they needed. We were to deliver it also.
>
> While at the house, Mrs. — looked over the five children [and Jessica, the baby] and exclaimed: "How in the world do you manage to buy shoes for such a large family?"
>
> I explained that it was quite a job—but that people always managed somehow, when they had to.
>
> And after that, two years begging for our money! It was paid in very small amounts—at long intervals—and the last $5.00 only recently when my high school daughters had repeatedly asked for it, stressing the fact that they (Audrey and Opal) needed *shoes*! After many unsuccessful trips to Mr. —.'s office, my daughter finally saw his stenographer cash a check for him. She followed the lady up to his office and was on hand when he received the cash. He couldn't say, as usual, that he didn't have the money. She persuaded him to pay the last five, by stressing the fact that she needed shoes![18]

Whether that high school daughter was Opal or Audrey, she did not say; but either of them would have had the persistence to ask for the money that was owed, and both of them needed shoes.

In the late fall of 1930—after Jessica was born—Grandfather Shearer and his son Vivian had a major disagreement. They had been running the saw mill and selling lumber in Las Vegas to places like Gross Kelly Company. They were making enough for the family to live on, just barely. Apparently Grandfather Shearer had been afraid of losing the ranch at some point, probably after the bank went broke and he lost nearly all the money he had in the oil well investment. In any case, he had signed the ranch property over to his son Charles Vivian so that it would not be lost—since Vivian had a job at the time. But suddenly Grandfather asked Vivian to sign the ranch back over to him. He wanted to *give* the property away to a friend! Vivian would not hear of giving away the family homestead, especially since his family was eking out a living by staying there. Audrey heard angry words. Her step-father and his dad were having serious problems. Years later in taped interviews with Milly Wickman, Audrey said she had heard portions of the argument which went something like this:

"I've always respected your decisions but this is going too far!" Vivian exclaimed. "How can you even think about giving the ranch to a friend while your own family is living here? Where would we go? How would we make a living? We're in a Depression! We're lucky to have a place where we can eke out a living with the saw mill and grow a garden and have some livestock! Would you have your own family out on the street? And where would you live?"

"He'll let us stay here!" Grandfather declared. "I just want to sign the deed over to him."

"Once it's in his name he can do what he wants with it!" Vivian declared."We can't depend on a friend's charity to let us stay here!" Vivian retorted.

"It's my property and I trust my friend. I want you to sign it back over to me!" Grandfather insisted.

"Not if you are going to give the family property away!" Vivian snapped.

"You agreed when I signed it over to you to sign it back over to me whenever I wanted," Grandfather reminded his son.

"I did. But you're being unreasonable," Vivian retorted. "If it hadn't been for me, you would have lost the ranch!"

"If it hadn't been for *you*, I wouldn't have been in *danger* of losing the ranch! It's your fault I lost all my money, investing in your foolish oil well scheme!" the older man's voice persisted.

"I couldn't help it if the bank went broke!" Vivian yelled."I'd give anything if I could have anticipated that so we wouldn't have lost everything!"

"I gave you all my money and nearly lost the ranch! Now I want the property back in my name!" the older man insisted.

"Not so you can give it away to someone out of the family!" Vivian roared. "I'll take my family and leave, but I won't turn the deed back over to you!"

"Then go!" Grandfather shouted. "Get out!"

"I will! I don't want to see you until you come to your senses!" Vivian shouted back.

"Get out!" Grandfather roared. "Get off my property!"

"It's still legally *my* property," Vivian replied. "The deed's in my name. But we'll go! We'll be out of here tomorrow!" Vivian bellowed.

Vivian began to pack and made arrangements to work at García Mill, a saw mill a little further up the mountain. The next day, Vivian loaded up the wagon and the kids to move.

As they were ready to leave, Grandfather yelled: "Mabel! You forgot your broom!"

Mabel had left it sitting on the front step.

"I don't move brooms!" Mabel shouted back.[19]

Mabel had learned from her former mother-in-law that moving a broom is bad luck.

Vivian and his father had constantly disagreed on how to operate the mill at the ranch, were always bickering. Vivian's decision to move was final. Mabel didn't try to argue with him, although Jessica was just a tiny baby and they were in the heart of The Great Depression. Mabel kept her sense of humor. She wrote a letter to a "Mr. H." at the *The Denver Post*, as follows:

> We probably owe our lives to you—and the *Denver Post*. Many a time, during this depressing Depression, we would gladly have shuffled off— only had to wait and see the next Sun. *Post* to see if anybody's orneryness had hit a new low. And Mrs. Horton says it's lies! All I've got to say is that she has lived a very innocent and sheltered life. She ought to have to bump into a few that the rest of us have met![20]

Audrey and Opal wanted to finish school even though it meant they had to walk to town and knock on doors to find work. Audrey later commented that the Clements girls had their father's determination and their mother's persistence. Even little Betty could be a little spit-fire when her temper was roused, and she had the same perseverance that the other Clements kids had. Betty, in contrast to the other Clements kids with blue eyes, had brown eyes. They had all inherited some of their father's "black Irish" characteristics, but only Betty inherited the brown eyes. Brought up with tenacious parents, all of Mabel's children were determined to succeed in their endeavors. "We were stubborn! We had to be or we wouldn't have survived," Audrey said.

Audrey and Opal had made up their minds to go to school. Little did they know how very long the road would be.

29

Hunger Stalks García Mill: From the Ranch to García's

Mabel was not happy about another move, especially when it meant leaving the Old Homestead Ranch which she and the children had grown to love. The timing was bad, too. With the Great Depression upon the nation, there was very little money and very few jobs were to be found. Nevertheless, Vivian felt he could not get along with his father, so Mabel and the kids moved to a place up the mountain where Vivian could work. Vivian was able to lease the García Mill and property.

García Mill was about nine miles, by the road, northeast of the ranch, up the mountain range. It was about six miles beyond the Mineral Hill Post Office, which was only about three miles from the ranch—where Mrs. Beisman was the postmistress and was assisted by her two daughters, Emma and Christine.

Audrey, Opal and Edward helped run the García saw mill all spring and part of the summer of 1931. Later Audrey recalled:

> Opal, Edward and I helped run the García sawmill all spring and part of the summer. We were "sawmill savages!" We were helping to run the cut off saw and we stacked lumber; and Vivian paid us—more or less—the wages he would have to pay someone else.[1]

Some of the men from San Geronimo came up to haul lumber to town for him. They quit when he couldn't run the mill for long periods of time whenever the creek was dry. Then when it did rain the road got so muddy that the men couldn't get their horses and wagons over it. Then all he could do was stack the lumber. The mill operated with a steam engine so it had to have water. With no water, there was nothing to do but shut it down. It was a dry summer and the creek finally dried up completely. If Mabel thought things had been tough at the Old Homestead Ranch, she now realized the family hadn't even known what real poverty was! Now they were in dire need—malnourished and in danger of starvation.[2]

Mabel kept a list of what the kids had earned. She also kept a list of items needed and how much they would cost. For a long time, they had to go without, for there was very little money. What money there was went to purchase flour and beans to keep the family alive. In part, one of Mabel's lists from the fall of 1930 follows:

> Overalls (Ed.)—$1.10
> Shoes (Ed.)—$1.69
> Sox (socks) (Ed.)—.25
> Comb—.25
> Ink—.15
> Note book—.15
> Shoes (M)—$3.98
> Envelopes—.05
> Notebook—.45
> Red Leads—.15
> Hose and Sup.—$1.47
> Cream—.08
> Tuition —$19.00
> Rent—$3.00
> Stamps —.20
> Cups—.30
> Underwear (father)—.70

Mabel's list was undoubtedly longer, but these were probably the most necessary at the time.[3]

Sometime during that summer a couple of fellows came from Texas and bought a load of lumber. Audrey and Opal hadn't seen anyone outside of the family all summer. The visit made them realize that their life was devoid of any social life, of any chance to improve themselves in school, of any outside stimulation. That, coupled with extremely poor nutrition, made life almost intolerable at the isolated place. Audrey thought about how she had given up the chance to go to Oregon with her grandmother. She could be enjoying school, parties, meeting new people, preparing for a career. Whenever she got discouraged, she'd look up at the mountains she loved and smell the sweet scent of pines. She'd look at her sisters and brother in their "make-do" clothing, and she'd be glad she had stayed. She had stayed, in part, to help her mother with the new baby, Jessica. And she was glad.

That summer Audrey often took Jessica outside in the evening. She would show her the stars and the moon. One evening there was a full moon, and little Jessica pointed and shrieked with delight. She was about a year old at that time, able to enjoy the warm evening air as she looked up at the moon. It was in 1931 that Kate Smith's popular song, "When the Moon Comes Over the Mountain" was heard over the radio in homes all over the country. The song about the moon over the mountain became one of Audrey's favorites, for Audrey was truly a mountain girl. Whenever Audrey looked at the moon in the still mountain air, with the scent of pines carried along the gentle breezes, she thought of Kate Smith's song and how she, too, enjoyed strolling beneath the mountains. Audrey not only loved the mountains; she felt very possessive of them. They had become very much "hers." There was Hermit's Peak (sometimes called "Old Baldy") that could be seen along the road to the ranch. Approaching the ranch itself, which was nestled at the foot of the Sangre de Cristo range, one could see Elk Mountain, El Cielo, The Falls Peaks, Barillas Peak—the highest one—with its neighbor Fox Peak, the one with the sharp point. There was the small rounded hill or small mountain that Grandfather Shearer called "The Fumarole" with its "Bottomless Pit" at the top where warm air kept everything green around the mouth of the abyss even in the winter time. And there was Fisher Hill, a small mountain with a rather flat top. Fisher Hill was named for S. L. Fisher. The taller and lower mountains that made up the mountain range stretched all the way from the north to the west, where to the east they tapered off. From the highest mountain tops one could see the entire country, including the flat "meadows" of the Las Vegas area to the east.

A good friend, Bill Reid, would ride over to visit quite often, coming over the mountain at Reid Ranch in the Sebadilla Canyon. When Bill would come over, Edward, Opal and Audrey played poker with him at night after Vivian, Mabel, Betty, Milly and Jessica were all asleep. They played for pinto beans since no one had any money. Audrey wrote about ranch living and horseback riding in her notes, "Mountain Living:"

> The high mountains were tipped with pink, reflecting on the oblong tent where my sis and I slept. I didn't open my eyes at once for I wanted to concentrate first and see whether or not we would have company that day. This was a morning routine for me as we were so isolated that if company was coming I needed to go out and pick more lambs quarter for greens to go with cornbread, to make a double batch of cornbread, and cook an extra cup of beans. I received the answer in a split second. No visitors today. Then I opened my eyes. The inside of the old canvas was patterned with stains and dirt. I saw a big Granddaddy Long-legs [spider] on the little peeled log that was the ridge pole. I watched it reach out with two feelers as it tried to decide where to go

next. Usually I would jump up and throw it out of the tent. However, I was too comfortable to get up and get it so I watched it until it crawled out of sight over the ridge pole. Back of the house a coyote yipped. Old Tick, Vivian's blue tick hound, gave a couple of quick barks, ran frantically around the house. The coyote took off up the canyon. I knew the coyote was leading her away. I hoped she wouldn't go so far away that another of the pack that ran in the area could come over to the barn and steal one of the hens that were already up looking for the early worms. When we had old Blucher he would stay by the barn and if an unwary coyote thought he would have a fat hen for breakfast, Blucher would give him a run for his life. Vivian had Blucher taken out and shot because he got to running deer, and Vivian's forest ranger training wouldn't let him leave the big broad chested hound loose to run and kill deer. Once the dogs caught a fawn close to the house. I can still hear how it screamed as they tore it up.

Tick's barking must have awakened Mother and Vivian, for pitch pine smoke from the tin chimney of the cook stove began to scent the air. The Grand-daddy had crawled on top of the tent center pole. I crawled out of bed, stood up and pulled off the old dress I used for a nightgown. I glanced down and just to the right of my belly button a tick was swollen to the size of a cherry—on my blood. Horrified, I hit at it and it popped off my stomach and fell through an inch-wide crack between the boards of the tent floor. Hitting it that way I didn't get the head out. Now I knew it was too late to stick a match near the back end of the tick to make it withdraw its head. Thoughts of Rocky Mountain Spotted fever hit me hard. I untied the tent flap and pushed open the wooden gate with the leather hinges that served as a gate in the lower part of our bedroom.

"Oh, Mama!" I called as I ran to the house. "I had a tick."

"Don't make so much noise! You'll wake the baby." Then she added, "Get some coal oil and put on it so it will withdraw its head."

"I can't," I wailed. "I hit it and knocked it off and the head is still in there!"

Startled awake, the baby gave a yelp.

"You woke her up!" Mother snapped. "Put some Vaseline on it!"

I went to the kitchen wall and looked at the collection of bottles on the exposed 2 x 4. Iodine, ST-37, a jar of pale yellow Vaseline beside the Metholatum and the Musterrole. I reached for the Vaseline.

Then I took a peek at my sister Opal, cute, pretty, popular Opal.

She was the one all the boys fell for, passing up stuffy me. They were drawn to her like bees to a clover patch. I looked at her creamy profile. I had pimples. I looked at Opal and shivered. If it hadn't been for me she might have been sleeping peacefully, but not there beside me. She would have been dead, smashed by a two ton boulder.

The day before, a couple of fellows and a girl had come up to the Sebadilla and we had saddled some horses and ridden down to the Box Canyon. Since we didn't have enough regular saddles, I was stuck with an old army pack saddle. It sure was miserable to ride. It cut into me and pinched and hurt every inch of the miles down the canyon and back. I didn't know how badly until several years later in the hospital having my first baby the nurse shaving me in preparation for the birth asked what kind of surgery I had had. I said I had never had any. "I thought you had. You have so many old scars," she said. Then I remembered the pinching pack saddle and the blood on my panties when I got home that night.[4]

Audrey explained later that she realized that the cinch had not been tight enough. Hence, the saddle turned sideways so she was sitting on the cinch itself. When Audrey finally got off and turned the saddle, she tried to tighten the cinch in place. But her thin clothing had not protected her flesh from getting "chewed up" by the metal cinch and she was in pain until her delicate skin healed. In spite of her painful saddle, Audrey still enjoyed the beauty of the mountains. She wrote:

> We had stopped at an old dugout where one of the pioneer settlers had once lived. A door opened in the side of the hill and the dug out was well hidden. It would have been almost impossible to find if one didn't know it was there. The boys pushed the door open. A pack rat scurried over the dirt floor. Cobwebs festooned the vigas.
>
> "Not a single deserted bottle!" Bill said and pulled the door shut.
>
> "Let's go up on top of the rim of Box Canyon," Buddy [Edward] said.
>
> We followed a deer trail through scrub oak and finally came out on the canyon rim.
>
> The boys took the horses to tie them to trees back from the rim. Opal and [the other girl] and I angled off the top of the rim on a wild green covered ledge. Opal sat down and dangled her legs over the edge above the next ledge. The scenery was scary. Having aerophobia, I did not get close to the edge but kept my eyes on the top of the opposite rock wall—the other side of the box canyon.

I moved up towards the rim of the canyon to the back.

"Oh, look down there. The trees look like toys," Opal called.

"Be careful," I said. "Don't get too close to the edge."

She plopped down on the rocks, making a pretty picture against the abyss below—for the boys above.

I could hear them talking and laughing 15 or 20 yards above us.

I moved on down the canyon 100 yards or so to find a less abrupt spot to climb back on top. The canyon curved in there and looking back I could see the boys on top. They were pushing at a huge balancing rock. I had noticed the boulder and said, "That must weigh a ton. Sure funny how it balances there so pretty on the little end."

Now the boys were working with it, pushing and shoving as hard as they could.

Suddenly I saw the rock move. They boys had finally got it started.

"Opal!" I yelled. "Move! Come here quick!"

Obediently she jumped up and started towards me.

At the same instant the giant boulder toppled over the brink of the canyon wall, landed with a crash on the ledge exactly where Opal had been sitting and then bounced over the edge. In seconds we heard it smash into the timber below.

"Oh, Gee Whiz!" Opal said when she realized what a narrow escape she had. The boys looked over the edge laughing.

"Did we scare you?"

"That landed right where Opal was sitting!" I yelled. "She moved in the nick of time or she would have been squashed flat."

"Sorry. We didn't know she was there below us," Bill apologized.[5]

Bill became aware of the extreme poverty of the Shearer family. Since Vivian couldn't run the mill any more due to lack of water, Bill suggested taking "dudes" out on pack trips and Vivian agreed that it would be a way to make some money. Bill had good horses, so he and Vivian thought they could take people out on overnight or week camping pack trips. Vivian had good pack saddles, and he built some good pack boxes to carry camp outfit supplies on the pack horses. They had about a half dozen people or so on their first trip.

Vivian and Bill took the first group—including a couple of women—camping in several areas up in the high country, going to beautiful spots including Brazil Park on top of the main range where Vivian had built a cabin in his younger days when he'd kept cows there. Someone named "Brazil" had carved his name around on a lot of trees there, so it was known as Brazil Park. Vivian and Grandfather knew it was hard to find. It was well hidden until rancher Dee Bibb cut a trail up to it from the other side and fixed it so anyone could see it and get to it. It was still very isolated but not so well hidden after that.[6]

Then the riders went across to the top of the range to the big burn and along the Big Cross Trail and then dropped back down into the Tecolote area where they had started from, back to García Mill. The pack trip enterprise was very successful, a good camping trip for a week or ten days. Years later Audrey found out that they had only made one trip and never took anybody out again. They could have done it many times and made quite a bit of money. But when Mabel found out those same women wanted to go on another camping trip, she would not allow Vivian to continue the trips. She was too jealous. She didn't want any women going on the camping trips with Vivian. Audrey said in later years:

> She [Mabel] absolutely blew her top when they suggested that these two women wanted to go on another camping trip. She was extremely jealous and she wouldn't let Vivian go with two women along even though Bill [among others] was with them! They had even had letterheads printed. Bill had the horses and Vivian had the know-how, but they were finished as far as that business went due to Mabel's jealous temperament. That ended their Camp Trip business![7]

In desperate need of money, Mabel wrote a verse in her notebook: "Aunt L. used to hide her pin money in a sugar bowl. If we just have a little SUGAR to hide in ours, we think we're lucky!"[8]

Jessica cut her teeth on beans and gravy at García Mill. The diet consisted of flour, pinto beans, and lard. Mabel made bread without yeast—sour dough—and water gravy. Audrey hunted the hills for wild garlic or wild dill to season the beans. She looked for edible plants like wild Lambsquarter, known to natives as *Calites*, a spinach-like plant. She looked for a clover-like plant called Sheepsoil. It looked like clover but had a sour taste, something like lemon. In the spring, there were Dandelion plants that were edible. In the fall, Audrey looked in vain for wild berries. It was a dry year, and even the raspberry bushes were not producing that year. In the fall acorns came out on the oak brush, but they were not really edible. One might eat one or two, but Vivian said that the tannic acid in them made them toxic. Piñon nuts would have been wonderful, but there were no piñon bushes that high on the mountain—even if it had been a year for piñons.

If Audrey saw a rabbit, she'd tell Vivian where it was and he'd go see if he could shoot it to add to the meager diet of bread and beans. Audrey later said that they almost starved to death at García Mill.

When Edward was fourteen, he could not get along with his mother. She wanted to be obeyed without question. As a teacher and as a mother, Mabel expected children to measure up to her standards, using correct grammar at all times, having good table manners, and so on. Edward didn't want his mother "bossing him around." So they had one conflict after another. One morning he got so angry he decided to run away from home. He figured he was old enough to get a job and be on his own. Audrey saw Edward take off on his horse. He had a gun with him. Audrey didn't think he was old enough to leave home. She knew Edward didn't have any food with him. So when late afternoon arrived and Edward had not returned, Audrey walked along the ridge of a canyon where she thought Edward might be resting.

Audrey began to sing and to whistle, "When It's Springtime in the Rockies," one of their favorite songs. That particular song came out in 1929. More than once Edward had sung it to her. It promised that the singer would come back to the little blue-eyed sweetheart of the mountains when spring time came again.

Audrey sang out, knowing Edward was somewhere in the trees of the canyon.

Sure enough, as Audrey sang, Edward came up out of the canyon. Audrey told him she'd brought him some food. She begged him to return to the house and "try to get along with Mama." Audrey later said she had to "talk till I was blue in the face" to get Edward to go back. "You're too young to go out on your own," she argued.

"I can take care of myself!" he countered.

"Maybe, but you don't have any assurance of a job," Audrey argued. "You're going to get awfully hungry. I bet you're hungry now and you've only been gone today."

Audrey unwrapped a clean cloth and took out some pinto bean sandwiches she'd made.

"I don't need my big sister to tell me what's good for me," he snapped, but he took the sandwiches and quickly consumed them.

"We need you at home," Audrey said. "We can't get along without you."

Somehow Audrey persuaded Edward to return home—temporarily.

In the fall of 1931, Audrey and Opal wanted to go to school in Las Vegas again. (Audrey had been to thirteen schools before she started high school in Las Vegas.) But there was no money. Audrey and Opal discussed the possibility of going back to school at length.

"You said once you'd walk to town just to get to go to school," Audrey reminded Opal. "Do you still feel the same way?"

Opal said she did.

"I want an education so bad, I'm willing to walk to town," Audrey said. "But do you think we can make it that far?"

"Maybe we can catch a ride with someone," Opal suggested.

"Maybe," Audrey sighed. "But we can't count on it. And what about Mama? Can she get along without our help?"

"Jessica's getting bigger now," Opal said. "I think Mama can manage."

Again they discussed the idea with Mabel. She told them she could not help them financially as she had before, so they would be on their own. But she admired their courage and did not try to discourage them. She knew they both needed a good education. So Audrey and Opal walked over to the Gallinas, about three miles, hoping someone would offer them a ride. There was some traffic up and down the canyon in and out of Las Vegas. Audrey recalled later, "When we got to the Gallinas Creek we were so tired we just sat down and took off our shoes and soaked our feet in the cool water!"[9]

Then they walked to the top of the long hill and finally got picked up by the Adams girl. Miss Adams had a small Roadster loaded with people, but she picked them up anyway and took them down into town. Opal and Audrey each had to sit on another girl's lap. Audrey got sick going around all those narrow curves with the sheer cliffs and canyons on one side of the road.

When they got to town, they had no place to stay. They started walking on Bridge Street, and they stopped at a long, brick house where they knew a lady to ask if she could suggest anyone who would hire them. They explained that they wanted to find a place to stay and would work for their room and board. The woman didn't need help and couldn't think of anyone who did; so the girls continued to walk, knocking on many doors and asking everyone if they needed any help.

Finally they went to Trogsteds. Mrs. Trogsted lived on Railroad Avenue, and Julia Kenival, her daughter, lived next door. They both said they needed help. The Trogsteds had a little store on Railroad at the corner of Railroad and University. Audrey worked for Julia Trogsted Kenival for her room and board. Julia had six children. Her husband had a hauling and freight business. She had a back porch where Audrey could sleep. Opal got a job at Trogsteds next door. Mrs. Trogsted said she had no place for Opal to sleep. So if Audrey would look after Julia's six kids (one was a tiny baby in diapers) then Opal could sleep on the back screened-in porch with Audrey. It was extremely cold on that porch in the winter. But the girls had food and a roof over their heads. They were willing to work hard to go to school.

The sisters registered to go to the Normal Training School. Audrey discovered it was a lot of work taking care of the six kids and going to school. On Saturday there was washing to do in the morning. In addition to babysitting, Audrey had to prepare supper every day and had to keep the house clean to pay for her board and for sleeping quarters for Opal and herself. She had no time to study at Julia's, so she stayed a half hour every day after school was out to study. Julia got angry when she found out. She said Audrey should come right home and take care of the work. Audrey did after that although she feared her grades would suffer.

The Trogsted boy, Billy, came to the back door of Julia's one day. Audrey was carrying a cardboard box, holding it up in front of her. Billy, Julia's little brother, threw a knife and it went through the cardboard box up to the handle. If Audrey hadn't had the box to shield her body, she would have been hit. Shaken, Audrey realized that was the second time a boy had thrown a knife at her without fatal results.

Julia Trogsted Kenival, the oldest of the Trogsteds, had been a teacher. In those days a person could get a teacher's certificate after graduating from the eighth grade. Audrey would have applied for one when she graduated from the eighth grade, but she had been too ill. Julia had a younger sister and two younger brothers. The youngest brother was Bill. He later married a nurse and they were both in Bataan when the Japanese took over. Bill died in the Bataan death march and his wife, too, died before World War II was over.[10]

It wasn't long after Edward's first attempt to leave home that the same thing happened again; he and his mother had a huge fight. Audrey wasn't there to go after Edward. She was in school in Las Vegas. But this time Edward had thought about where he'd go to get a job. He would ask for work at a ranch across way. So when Edward took off on a horse, he didn't just hide out in the canyon. He rode as fast and long as he could. Later, Audrey learned that Edward had nearly ridden his horse to death. "When he got to his destination, the horse lay down and didn't get up for a couple of days!" Audrey said. Edward never lived at home full time again, although he did visit from time to time.[11]

Audrey and Opal struggled to "work their way through school." At one point, Mabel wrote in a letter to her Uncle Frank Waddell. It said, in part:

> Lately we seem to be getting closer to the "ragged edge" all the time—so now if you came you would have to "camp out" with us and live on imagination, mostly.
>
> But depressions have come before and always had an end—so we can only hope and pray that this won't last long, but it is certainly fearful while it lasts.

> I am enclosing an article from the *Las Vegas Optic* concerning Audrey and Opal. I wish you would return it as it is the only copy I have and I would like to keep it.
>
> I wish they hadn't had to miss so much school. And now I fear they may have to miss next winter, but we will hope. So many children have every advantage in the world and don't appreciate it—and mine are so eager to study and enjoy school so much and then have a hard time getting to go.[12]

It was discouraging for Mabel to think about how her girls struggled, especially during those dark Depression years, just to stay in high school and graduate. To make matters worse, Mabel missed Edward since he had left, taken a job at Reid Ranch, and considered himself "grown up and on his own." The girls had found jobs, so they could stay in school. Mabel was grateful for that. Unlike her husband, she believed everyone needed a good education—girls as well as boys. She was glad the girls had the "gumption," as she called it, to go out and find jobs to work their way through school.

It was not unusual for students to "work their way through college." But for young girls to "work their way through high school" was unusual even in the Depression years. Audrey and Opal worked very hard and lived on very little. They were grateful for their positions to earn their way. But little did the girls know how precarious those positions could be.

30

Cold December: From García Mill to Chaperito

Mabel and Vivian decided to move to Chaperito. From García's Mill it was up above the Pecos Canyon area. Mr. Elliott Barker's wife's family—the Arnolds—owned one or both ranches and they lived there. The Arnold girl was quite young when Mr. Barker met her up there. Walter Phillips was caretaker there, and he needed some help so Vivian worked for Walter. He lived at the Vivash—the headquarters of the ranches. Walter Phillips was about four miles away.

Bill Reid came to Las Vegas and took Opal and Audrey up to Chaparito at Christmas. Bill was very fond of Opal, as well as Audrey, and he spent as much time with the family as he could. He took them by the "Oldest Well" and they visited with his Uncle Tom and Aunt Stella Greer and their son. Then they went up to the Vivash over to Chaparito where the folks were, riding horseback. Horseback was the only way to get there.

Christmas, 1931 was spent in a big, two story house with a white picket fence around it. All the kids were home for Christmas and Bill Reid was there as well.

Betty Clements, Milly Shearer, Opal Clements, Audrey Clements holding baby Jessica Shearer; and Bill Reid and Edward Clements, Christmas at the Arnold Ranch in the upper Pecos country at the Vivash, 1931. *Source*: Simpson Archives

Milly Shearer, Betty Clements, baby Jessica Shearer on porch; Edward Clements; Audrey Clements, Bill Reid and Opal Clements on horseback, 1931. *Source*: Simpson Archives

Vern came to get Betty to visit at his place, but Vivian wouldn't let him take her. Milly Shearer Wickman recalled the incident years later. She said when they were living at the Vivash, Vern came up to get Betty and Edward, around Christmas time. Vern walked up and came up to the wooden fence.

Vivian saw Vern and grabbed his rifle. He came storming out of the house with his gun pointed at Vern and said, "Get out of here!"

Vern put his hands up in the air. He knew better than to argue with a furious man pointing a weapon, so he said, "I'll leave! I just came to ask if I could get my kids."

"No, you can't! Now git outta here before I shoot!" Vivian yelled.

Vern turned and walked away without an argument. He was unarmed and wasn't going to question a man with a loaded gun aimed at his heart.

Milly said it was one of the few times that she saw her father so angry.[1]

Audrey didn't understand the hostility that Vivian had toward her daddy. Audrey said in later years, "I never understood why all the animosity. Vivian lured Mama away from Vern, so why did he resent Vern?" Audrey speculated that maybe Vivian thought Vern had not provided well enough for his family. But Vivian, too, moved from job to job and the family often existed on very little, especially at García's Mill. And at San Geronimo Vivian had not had a job and was down to a few cents. But she added, kindly, "They both did the best they could, and that's all anyone can do."[2]

After Christmas, Bill Reid came and got Audrey and Opal. He took them back to Las Vegas, using the same mode of travel—horseback.

Edward was no longer angry at Mabel, but he still wanted his independence and was glad to be working on his own. Edward was very talented. He had learned to sing from both parents. He could sing beautifully and could play the guitar, the harmonica, and could whistle and yodel. In later years, he was given an opportunity to sing at the "Grand Old Opery" but did not go even though he was invited after he took second place in an audition and after the first place person had dropped out.

Edward was a good cowboy, too, as taught by his father. He had learned to use the rope well. Once he came upon a bear cub. The mother was nowhere in sight, so Edward decided to rope the cub and take it home, tame it, and have a pet. When he roped it, his well-trained horse did his duty, holding the rope taunt as Edward had taught him to do. But the bear, instead of pulling back and trying to get away by backing up, as a calf would have done, jumped forward in terror and climbed right up Edward's stirrup and leg, over his lap, and down the other leg. While Edward and the excellent cow pony did their best to hold the rope steady, the little bear proved to be stronger. Again, the cub climbed up Edward's other leg, scratched his way over Edward's lap, and down the other side. This happened several times. Edward struggled to cut the rope. Finally he succeeded and the cub took off into the woods, the rope still around his neck, trailing behind him. Edward was bleeding from all the deep cuts and scratches inflicted by the bear. He realized he had done a foolish thing and went back to the ranch. His clothes were literally in shreds, ripped in small pieces; and before he had ridden very far, his clothes were gone. He got off his horse with only his cowboy boots and his leather gun belt intact. He tried to get to the bunk house before anyone spotted him. He did not want to have to explain. He just wanted to get cleaned up and get some clothes on. But, unfortunately, he was seen before he made it inside. He was told he was lucky the mama bear hadn't shown up to defend her cub.

Edward's scratches healed. But he took a lot of kidding over that incident. Someone yelled: "Hey, Ed, remember when you rode into camp wearing nothin' but yore gun belt and yore cowboy boots? You gonna tangle with another bear?"

Edward never heard the last of his episode with the bear.[3]

Mabel was at Chaparito when she got a call on the Forest Service line that her father, Edward A. Waddell, had passed away in Quincy, Illinois on January 21, 1932. Mabel wrote in a letter in 1932 to her Uncle Frank:

> I am always filled with regret that I didn't write much oftener to poor, Dear Papa, when it would have helped him to pass away the tiresome days when he was so miserable.
>
> But I couldn't believe he would leave us so soon. I always felt he would surely get well. I couldn't help hoping and expecting that we would have many more happy years together. He might have had 30 years more.[4]

After some time passed, Mabel found out that her father's third wife, Minnie Waddell, had inherited everything, including the two farms in Nebraska. At first, however, Mabel thought she stood to inherit something, as she had received some letters stating that she would inherit some land.

In a later letter to her uncle Frank, Mabel expressed her disappointment that she received nothing in the way of an inheritance from her father. Apparently Minnie Waddell wrote to Mabel and told her that Mabel's father wanted Mabel to have one of those farms; Mabel said "so she said that she was turning over the Shelton farm to me." Later she said that she would "try to do it next Spring."[5]

Mabel realized later that the woman apparently wanted to keep everything for herself and was just stringing Mabel along. If Mabel's father did leave a will, it was nowhere to be found. Mabel wrote to her father's brother, Frank:

> No doubt you know how Papa felt about all these things and you know I want to uphold the good old Waddell tradition of being MORE THAN FAIR about everything.
>
> I think it is so queer that Papa did not make a will or express himself in some other definite way as to the exact disposal he wanted made of his estate, especially since he must certainly have known what my legal share would be—because you know I would only want what he wanted me to have. I do not know what the amount of his estate was, outside the two Nebraska farms.
>
> We have been having such a hard time lately moving about without a permanent home that we would like to move to Nebraska if we could see our way clear to get settled there. At least we can make a living farming there and the school advantages would be so much better for the children there.
>
> Poor Papa always valued your opinions and advice so highly and I know that for his sake you will advise me as best you can. It is about Papa's estate that I want your advice. I do not wish to express any dissatisfaction with any arrangements Papa had in mind and wish to be entirely agreeable all the way around and for this reason would not wish to accept any kind of a settlement, regardless of what it might be, without having your advice on it for you know more about it than anyone else and I have no one else in the world to go to for this advice.[6]

Apparently Frank did not know how to get Mabel's rightful portion of the estate. Mabel and Vivian made a trip to Nebraska and had a lawyer look into the matter. The lawyers bickered back and forth for years. Taxes accumulated. In the long run Mabel did not inherit one of the farms. She got nothing from her father's estate for some time, but she eventually received a little money—whatever was left after legal fees. Mabel was Edward Waddell's only child. She believed she should have had half of his estate. Life would have been so much better for her and her family. "Since no will was found, Mother did not inherit even one of the two farms as she thought she would," Audrey later said.

However, Uncle Frank Waddell did not forget her. He made sure that he wrote a will for himself. When he died in about 1940, he left Mabel a good part of his own estate. Mabel inherited six-hundred dollars, as well as furniture from Uncle Frank. He left her a dining room set and some family heirlooms, among other things. Mabel had most of the items, including an upright Tryber &

Sweetland piano made in Chicago, shipped on the train. There was also a child's spool rocking chair that had belonged to Laura Waddell when she was a child, probably purchased about 1860.

Mabel and Vivian were living at 409 Eleventh Street when the furniture came. They used the six-hundred dollars to finish the adobe house they had started building at the Old Homestead Ranch, just down the road from Grandfather Shearer's rock house. (By then Vivian and his father had patched up their differences.) With the little money from her father's estate and the six-hundred dollars from her Uncle Frank, Mabel was able to do a few things that would have otherwise been impossible. In a letter to Aunt Laura, Mabel expressed her gratitude.[7]

Audrey and Opal continued to struggle to finish school. Julia Kenival not only wanted Audrey to come right home after school to do her work, but she decided she wanted Audrey to leave school *two hours early* every day. Audrey had complied when she was asked to come home right after school, even though she had wanted to stay an hour after school to study. But leaving school two hours early did not seem reasonable to Audrey. It was all she could do to get up at six o'clock every morning and do the washing, get it on the line, prepare breakfast, and wash the dishes before school. She did as much after school when she cleaned house, helped prepare supper, did the dishes and cleaned up the kitchen. She also cared for the children, including the baby who was often sick. She thought she did plenty for her room and board and that she should have some time to study. But Julia wanted Audrey to put in more time. Audrey resisted the order to leave school early. One day Julia told Audrey she would have to make different arrangements for the next year. Audrey recalled in a taped interview in later years:

> In the meantime I got the flu and had a bad cold and cough. She [Julia] called Daddy and told him that I was sick and she couldn't keep me there while I was so sick. Daddy came up and took me to Albuquerque and let me have the flu down there![8]

Once again, Audrey's daddy rescued her. It took her several weeks to recover, but Vern and Mable took good care of her in Albuquerque. Audrey had been making good grades, but when she returned to school her Algebra grade had dropped. She had missed out on the things the others had learned while she was gone. After she was well, Audrey returned to work for Julia for the rest of the school year, knowing she'd have to find another place for the next year. When school was out, Opal still had her job at Trogsteds, although she would have to find another room in the fall since she had been staying in the room Audrey worked for at Julia's.

Audrey was hurt when she realized she had lost her place because she did not meet what she considered to be unreasonable demands. Yet she was determined to find a way to finish school. She suffered from fatigue and from sleeping in a cold, screened-in porch—the "room" she was working for, a room with no walls and no heat!

Audrey had known deprivation all her life and she knew she had to depend only on herself for success. She could not rely on anyone else. Sometimes people made promises that they did not keep. Sometimes expectations were not met. Some people could be thoughtless, even cruel. The old song, "April is in my Mistress' Face," reminded Audrey that there are those who may seem to be lovely outwardly but have cold December in their hearts. Yet Audrey would not be defeated in her quest for an education. She met one disappointment after another with her quiet determination. December might be cold, but she was used to cold.

31

Budding Romance: From Chaperito to Reid Ranch, Taming Wild Horses

"*No! I refuse! I'm tired of moving!*" Mabel thought about making that statement, considered putting her foot down when Vivian mentioned moving again. But she held her tongue. Bill Reid and his father had offered Vivian thirty dollars a month to work at their ranch. It was more than Vivian had been making. And in those Depression years, that was a good amount of money—especially when so many people had no jobs at all—although it hardly seemed enough to support a large family.

Moving again would be difficult. At the age of 42, Mabel was pregnant again.

Before school was out in the spring of 1932, Mabel and Vivian moved from Chaperito to the Reid Ranch. Audrey and Opal were in Las Vegas working and going to school that spring of 1932. When school was out, Opal and Audrey went to the Reids' for the summer.

According to Audrey's later recollections, the house they stayed in that summer of 1932 at Reids' ranch was so small that Vivian put three tents outside for the kids. Edward had a tent, Milly and Betty shared one, and Audrey and Opal had one.

Audrey and Opal took a pack horse one day and went down to Pecos to Harrison's Store to get groceries. It began to rain furiously—one of those hard, fast mountain showers that often appears with little warning. Audrey recalled in later years:

> It rained furiously and when we got to the store we were dripping wet—talk about drowned rats! We were! That hard mountain shower came up so fast and it really soaked us! The people at the store built a fire in their big heater that they used to heat the whole store in the winter! They got us warm and dried us out![1]

Usually Edward or Bill went to the store, but that day they went to try to catch a wild horse. It took the girls longer because they didn't know how to throw half-hitches to keep the pack steady. Their half-hitches wouldn't stay and hold. They had to stop every little while and re-tie the pack on the horse, but they didn't know how to do it right. So they were late getting home.[2]

There were herds of wild horses all around. In her "Notes on Wild Horses," Audrey wrote about how Edward would chase after the herds of wild horses:

> My brother was chasing the wild horses, a bunch of horses that was in Sebadilla Canyon and across from La Cuba meadow [or La Cueva]—a form of entertainment for mountain kids in the early 1930's. Edward, a lanky 15, rode down several of the ranch horses riding hell for leather trying to get close enough to rope one. We would see them by the old San Louise [or San Luis] Cemetery. There would be a flash of gold, legacy of some remote Palomino Stallion, grazing around the fallen down fences we'd forgotten. If we started up the winding road out of the Sebadilla to the top of the hill they would watch us a few seconds and then take off in a high run, manes and tails streaming in the breeze their running created. If it was storming they might be down along the creek in the willows or under the cottonwoods nibbling a blade of grass or stomping at the flies that also looked for cover in the trees.[3]

Sometimes Bill Reid and Edward, still working on Reid Ranch, rounded some of them up. If they could catch one and bring it in, they would tame it down enough to sell or would use it themselves. Years later, Audrey wrote "Wild Horse Herds Once Roamed Open Spots in Region," for the *Las Vegas Daily Optic*:

> The mountains, canyons, and mesas around Las Vegas supported a number of wild horse herds until recent years.
>
> Many a local cowboy has added to his wealth by catching wild horses.
>
> Wild and smart as they were, a man with patience could build a corral in some canyon and trap at least a few horses.
>
> Holding them and taming them after he caught them was hard work. Many wild horses could jump a corral fence like it wasn't there. Sure footed on a rocky mountainside, they could climb like a goat in making an escape.
>
> A Las Vegas ranch woman recalls the ease with which a wild horse can place his feet where he wants to, although on a dead run.
>
> Her garden sat on a mountain near a spring where the wild horses drank during the dry seasons. One morning while quietly working there she heard a wild horse herd. She dropped to the ground to sit still, hoping to see the wild beauty of some of them.
>
> A rider crossing above the spring frightened the herd. One skittish mustang ran straight for the garden fence, built 6 feet high to try to keep out the mountain deer. He cleared the fence easily.
>
> The center of the garden was lined with cabbage plants. Each of the several hundred plants had a glass jar turned over it, a common practice to protect the small plants from the cold nights.
>
> The wild horse cleared the fence at a hard run. He ran through the center of the garden, says the woman, and turned and ran back again through the glass jars. He cleared the fence once more with feet to spare and was gone down the canyon.
>
> In examining her cabbage plants the gardener was surprised to find that not one jar was broken, not a one was even tipped over. The horse's tracks were sunk inches deep in the soft garden soil, but he knew where he placed each foot. Used to running over rocky hills he knew how to avoid loose rock and sharp roots.
>
> Horses have played an important part in New Mexico since the first ones carried Coronado into the land of enchantment.
>
> The wild horse, thrilling everyone who was lucky enough to see him, may still be found in isolated sections. But he has bowed to progress

and although the cowboys miss him, they all hope he has found a range with deep grass, plenty of water, and no fences.[4]

Although the above story had no bi-line, it was Audrey's, as she was the woman in the story and had told it many times. She had marked "my story" on a copy of the newspaper.

One morning Bill came by the house and announced, "Ed and I are going to try to catch a wild horse or two today. Anyone want anything special?"

Betty figured if he was taking orders, she'd put one in.

"I want one! I want a little pony all my own! Get me a colt, please!" she begged.

"So you'd like to have a little colt all your own?" Bill responded.

"I sure would!" Betty's face beamed with anticipation. "I'd tame it and teach it everything, and I'd ride it when it was big enough. We'd race like the wind! I could ride all the way to Las Vegas and go shopping!"

"Well, don't count your chickens before they're hatched," Opal put in.

"What do you mean?" her sister asked.

"I mean they haven't even got a horse yet, and they may not be able to catch one!" Opal retorted.

"They'll catch one—a little colt, just for me!" Betty replied.

With that kind of confidence in them, Bill and Edward were determined not to disappoint the little girl. True to their word, they came back with a colt! Betty was ecstatic.

"Oh, you did it! Your brought me a colt!" Betty jumped up and down in her excitement when she saw they had succeeded in bringing in a very young horse. "He's so cute! I want to tame him right away!"

"Not so fast, Betty," Audrey said. "That colt could hurt you. He's scared and wild. You let someone bigger tame it down."

"Don't look at us," Bill said. "We've done our part. We've got other work to do now. Ain't got no time to break a wild colt."

"Will you do it?" Betty begged, looking to her oldest sister.

"All right, I'll try," Audrey agreed.

"I'm gonna name him Lightning!" Betty said.

Audrey stood in that old dirty barn for several hours with the colt and tamed him down so he would take milk out of a bottle. She had seen her father work with horses plenty of times. She knew patience and kindness would finally pay off. After the colt was somewhat tame, Audrey turned him over to Betty. Betty put a board across the top of the fence to protect the colt. But the board was loose; it was just propped up on top of the fence railings. That night the board somehow fell across the colt and broke his fragile little neck.[5]

Betty was heart-broken. They all blamed themselves and began to say that they should have done something differently. If only they had done this or that, or not done this or that, the colt would still be alive. Audrey and Betty cried.

Mabel finally intervened, "Don't cry over spilt milk." That was one of her favorite expressions. There was nothing to be done about it, so there was no use crying and prolonging their sorrow.

Audrey had been discharged at Julia Kenivals at the end of the school year, so she thought she wouldn't get to go to school that fall.

"You go on, Opal. You still have your job," Audrey said.

"But no place to sleep!" Opal protested. "You were providing that!"

"Ask Mrs. Trogsted to find you a place," Audrey suggested.

"Well, I hope I can find a better place than that cold screened-in porch that was called a 'room,'" Opal lamented.

"You'll work something out," Audrey assured her.

"But what about you, Audrey? You've got to finish school, too!" Opal declared.

"I don't know," Audrey shrugged. "It's very discouraging."

Billie Maxey was visiting the Shearers at Reid Ranch at the time, as she and Opal and Audrey were good friends. Brock Maxey, Billie Maxey's father, came to get Billie. Brock was appalled to learn that Audrey wasn't going to go to school.

"You can come on with us and I'll find a place for you to stay," Brock said. He took all three girls to town. By the time they got there, it was late, so they stayed at the Maxey's house that night. In the morning Brock Maxey took Opal to Trodsteds.

Brock took Audrey to the Keens' Apartments on Douglas. He was a good car salesman and he proceeded to "sell" Audrey to Mrs. Keen. He had a nice spiel about how much Audrey was needed because their baby was still little. He persuaded both Mr. and Mrs. Keen that they needed Audrey. He convinced Mrs. Keen that if she had some help, she could have some of the college students come for meals. So Audrey was given a room upstairs where she, as well as Opal, could stay. Audrey knew she would have to work extra hard for the room for both herself and Opal. It was what Audrey called "a dinky little room," just big enough to sleep in—a bed and dresser. But it was much warmer than the porch they'd had before! There was one problem, however. There were bed bugs! In those days it was very difficult to get rid of bed bugs. Audrey was afraid to mention it. She might be accused of bringing them in, even though she knew she had not. She and Opal did the best they could to deal with them.

It was about that time that Audrey and Opal attended church services at the little Nazarene Church. When the preacher gave the invitation for anyone to come forward and be saved, everyone was praying. Audrey knew they were praying for her and for Opal because they had never gone forward to accept an invitation. They had never had the gospel explained to them as this preacher did, although their parents certainly had been church-going believers. The preacher was saying that everyone who believed in Jesus should make a public profession of faith. Audrey believed in Jesus. So she went forward to say she was saved by her faith and to make a public proclamation of her salvation. Also, she wanted to be baptized. Everyone was very happy. Audrey wondered why Opal did not go forward. Years later, Audrey wrote in her notes, "Religious Experiences:"

> While going to high school in Las Vegas, Opal and I went to the Methodist Church and Sunday School, though as country kids in the height of the Depression, working for our board and room to get to go to school, we looked pretty crummy. I had high moral values and tried to be honest and trustworthy. I don't remember whether Opal and I went to Miss Keltnon's (or Kelton's) Nazarene church revival services before or after we met Clyde. I think before. The services were held at the small church building. across from 1st Baptist Church on a site later used by Safeway's back on University and Seventh Street. It was the second building from the corner. I heard some of the "old" women talking later. They thought I had prayed through and was saved and they weren't too sure about Opal but thought she had been [saved] also.[6]

It may have been about that time when Audrey wrote down a verse for a song:

> I'm going forward
> I'm going forward
> I'm going forward to Jesus.
>
> I'll never go away
> I'll never go away
> I'll never go away
> I'll never go away from Jesus.
>
> I'll always stay
> I'll always stay

I'll always stay
With Jesus.

I will stay there
I will stay there
I will stay there
I'll stay there all the day.[7]

Las Vegas had a new, modern hospital in the building that had been the YMCA. The Las Vegas Hospital was a big, two story brick building with clean, modern facilities and up-to-date nursing care.

Mabel came into town in late August or early September and rented a room at Mrs. Minter's house across the street from Keens' Apartments on Douglas. She had to be close to the hospital to wait for the new baby. Franklin Charles Shearer was born September 30, 1932 at the Las Vegas Hospital on Sixth Street, the old YMCA building next to the Las Vegas Fire Station. When Audrey and Opal walked from school, they would see their mother sitting up in her bed on the second floor, looking out the hospital window to wave at them.

Milly went to Douglas School during the time Mabel was in Las Vegas to give birth and recover. It was the first time Milly ever went to school. She started in the first grade, but the teacher realized she was too advanced for first grade. So Milly was sent to the second after lunch. The next day she found herself placed in third grade, as the teachers agreed she was ready for that level. She stayed in the third grade until her mother recovered.

Mabel had "milk leg" or phlebitis again, the same thing she'd had before. So Mabel stayed at Mrs. Minter's for a week or so after she got out of the hospital until her leg stopped swelling. Then they went back to Reid's Ranch. So Milly's school days at Douglas were limited.

Next to the beautiful Coronado Theatre on the northwest corner of Sixth and University, across from the old Police and Fire Station, was a skating rink. Gambles Store now occupies that half block on Sixth Street. The theatre and the skating rink next to it took up all the space from University Street to the alley. The skating rink, a big building with a good floor, had big posts to hold up the ceiling, so skaters had to maneuver around them.

While Mabel was in the hospital after Franklin Shearer was born, she could look across the street to see the building where the skating rink was located. Audrey would wave at her when she went to go skating. Although Opal and Audrey were both working after school, they sometimes stopped in briefly at the skating rink when school was out for the day. (Audrey's employer this time was not so strict about what time she returned from school in the afternoon.)

Opal had met Robert Simpson at school. His father, William Ernest Simpson, worked for the railroad. His mother was Addie Bain Simpson. They had seven children, including Robert who was called Bob. He and his older brother Clyde were working at the skating rink, helping to run the place, so they were allowed to skate without charge. Audrey had seen Clyde Simpson there but didn't know his name and didn't know he was Bob Simpson's brother. Bob would go to the skating rink as soon as he got out of school, and Clyde was usually hanging around, too. Audrey wrote:

> When I met Clyde in 1932—at the skating rink—his brother Bob (Robert) had been talking about him a lot. Bob and Opal and I were all in the same grade in high school. Bob and Clyde hung around the newly established skating rink on 6th street next to the Coronado Theatre and opposite the Las Vegas Hospital.[8]

One afternoon in early October, 1932, Opal and Audrey had time to go to the skating rink on their way home from school. Audrey was trying to learn to skate, struggling alone. A young man she had seen but not met came up to her.

Audrey was surprised when the handsome young man put his arm around her and said, "I'll show you how to skate."

Without missing a beat, he continued skating, helping Audrey glide along by his side. If she faltered, a strong arm was there to hold her.

"You're learning fast," he encouraged with a smile. They continued around the room.

"Thanks," Audrey said when they came to a stop in a corner of the room. The young man skated away, smiled, and waved.

Audrey didn't know his name. She asked someone who he was. "That's Clyde Simpson," she was told. They were never formally introduced. Later Opal told Audrey the young man who helped her skate was Bob Simpson's brother.

Clyde was about six feet tall, lanky, had dark brown hair and green eyes. He had slender hands with long, slim fingers—the strong hands that had helped her learn to skate. Audrey thought he was very handsome and hoped to see him again soon.

The cost to skate was ten cents. Anybody with a dime could skate but they had to rent the skates, too. Audrey and Opal couldn't afford to go often, but they did learn to skate. Sometimes Bob or Clyde paid for them. Audrey enjoyed skating—except for the one time when she got hurt.

Audrey was still learning to skate one afternoon when Bob Simpson came along with his friend Charley Geiss. Bob took hold of one of Audrey's arms and Charley took her other arm. Holding her up between them, they skated with her as fast as they could. There were posts on both sides of the room and down the middle. Bob went on one side of a post and Charley went on the other side—with Audrey in between them. She hit the post hard. It knocked her down and she couldn't breathe. She sat there for several minutes in pain, trying to get her breath, stunned. Then she felt a warm hand on her shoulder.

"Can you get up? I'll help you." It was the handsome young man, Clyde Simpson. Audrey remembered he had helped her skate before.

"I saw what happened from across the room," he said. "My brother should have been more careful."

"I'm all right now," Audrey said, taking a deep breath. "I can breathe again."

"Are you sure you're OK?" he asked. "No broken bones or anything like that?"

"No. I can walk."

"I'll help you off the floor," Clyde said. "I'm sorry that happened."

Audrey leaned on Clyde's strong arm and she was held firmly as he gently guided her off the floor.

"I should be leaving now," Audrey said. "But I'll be back again, maybe tomorrow."

"Next time *I'll* help you skate," Clyde said. "If you'll let me."

"Thank you," Audrey said, feeling a warm glow from the kindness that had been extended to her. "That will be nice."

After that Audrey looked for Clyde whenever she went skating.

Although Opal and Audrey were both working after school, they began stopping by the skating rink after school more often.

One time that winter Audrey and Opal went to the ice skating pond at Montezuma with Bob Simpson and someone else. Bob was holding Audrey up, trying to teach her to skate. She was trying to keep her feet under her when somehow Bob slammed her into a rock and she went down. "He got me over to the edge and then just pushed me down. I was going down anyway——my feet were going out from under me. So I had two bad experiences on skates," Audrey recalled.[9]

There was a taxi in Las Vegas owned by Charley Geiss. His father had a blacksmith shop on the northwest corner of Douglas and Railroad. His mother had died and left him an insurance policy that he was to inherit when he was eighteen. He bought a car and turned it into a taxi that was stationed at the Home Café on Grand Avenue.

Clyde Simpson was hired to drive the taxi for Charley much of the time. Clyde liked to be around the Home Café because of the taxi business and because they'd give him something to eat once in a while.

One morning in sub-zero temperatures, Audrey was walking to school when she heard a car pull over at the curb beside her. It was the taxi! Clyde Simpson rolled down the window.

"How about a ride? It's too cold to walk on a morning like this!" Clyde called out the window, his breath showing in front of his face.

"I know. I'm freezing! But I have no money to pay," Audrey replied.

"I'll take care of it," Clyde said.

So Audrey got in, grateful to get out of the cold. She was not adequately dressed to walk in such weather. After that, on cold mornings, Clyde would come by and pick Audrey up when he wasn't busy taking a passenger somewhere. The taxi business in Las Vegas was slow, so he was usually not overwhelmed with work. Audrey was grateful for the rides on those sub-zero mornings when Clyde picked her up and paid the fare out of his wages.

That school year of 1932-1933 Audrey and Opal did very well until almost Christmas. They felt their jobs were secure. Mr. Keen worked for the Public Service Company, known in those days as "Reddy Kilowatt." They had a boy called Sonny and a girl, Sandy. Mrs. Keen's sister lived in the apartment next door; she and her husband did not do so well. The sister's husband lost his job. About Christmas time of 1932 Mrs. Keen had her appendix removed. Audrey took care of her children and ran the household while she was in the hospital. Then Mrs. Keen told Audrey she had to help her sister financially and she couldn't afford to have Audrey there to help any more.

Once again, Audrey faced Christmas with the prospect of having to stay out of school in the spring. She had been blessed with a good school year so far. Audrey had enjoyed school, even though she had to work hard to earn her way. She had enjoyed the little free time she had skating, especially when Clyde was there to help her. Again, she wept silently at the prospect of being without a place to work and stay so she could finish school.

"Something will turn up," Opal encouraged. "It has before. It will work out."

Having no money and few job prospects made it difficult to be cheerful, especially at Christmas time. Still, she had met a nice young man. He had been kind to her. She liked him. She had always been attracted to Bill Reid, but Bill was more interested in Opal. While Bill had eyes only for Audrey's younger sister, Opal wasn't interested in Bill romantically. After Opal met Bob Simpson, she wasn't interested in anyone else.

Bill was good looking—about six feet fall with dark hair and blue eyes, slim and handsome, especially in his riding boots and cowboy hat. Yet Audrey had to admit that Bill had a wild side to him, seemed somewhat unsettled, while Clyde seemed like the gentle type of man who would like to settle down. He was the type to hold down a steady job, buy a house with a white picket fence around it, and raise a family. While Bill's adventurous spirit was exciting, there was great appeal in Clyde's more mature, serious outlook on life.

Audrey began to learn more about Clyde and his family. His father, William Ernest Simpson, was born September 10, 1875 to William Hawkins Simpson and Minerva Isadora Stephens. William Ernest married Addie Bain. She was born in Timble County near Bedford, Kentucky on November 7, 1882. William—usually called Ernest—filed on a place in Oklahoma in about 1898; and then he bought another one-hundred and sixty acres from his wife's brother, Landy Bain—land which another brother, Russell Bain, had orginally filed on. So Ernest had a total of three-hundred and twenty acres of land. Then the Simpson family moved to Clovis, New Mexico and opened the first general store there in about 1918. They bought one-hundred and sixty acres of land in Estancia valley. Ernest worked for the railroad and lived at San Marcial. In 1928 the Rio Grande flooded and washed the town away, so Ernest was transferrred to Las Vegas. Ernest and Addie had seven children. Clyde, born on June 7, 1911 in Mobeete, Texas, was just about a year older than Audrey.

Clyde talked about getting married. Audrey said she had to graduate from high school first; but he was on her mind all the time, even when she was trying to study.

In later years, Audrey wrote a poem, "Evening Rain," about the joy of lovers when they met.

> Long shadows dance about the street
> While rays from the street lamp
> And tears from the cloud camp
> Caressingly kiss as they meet.[10]

32

Audrey's Song

"I wish I was as skinny as you are," a girl from the east mesa area told Audrey one day. With her busy schedule, running back and forth to school and working the rest of the time, Audrey hardly had time to eat.

She and Opal walked several long blocks to school every morning, and at noon Audrey walked back to the Keens' place to eat a hasty lunch and wash all the dishes for the Keens and the college students who were eating at their house. Then she would dash back to school all within thirty minutes. She didn't have time to eat more than a bite or two.

After Mabel left the hospital with the new baby, Franklin "Frank" Charles Shearer, she stayed at Mrs. Mitners until her leg stopped swelling and then they returned to Reid's Ranch. Vivian had bought an old Whippet car. When Frank was just a few weeks old, Mabel and Vivian decided to move to Nebraska. The car had cardboard in three windows, so it was cold to ride in! Apparently Mabel wanted to investigate her father's estate, as he'd owned two farms, one near Shelton and the other near Gibbon. Mabel still had hopes that she might at least inherit the farm at Shelton. They moved there in the dead of winter and only stayed until May or June of 1933. Vivian did not like Nebraska and Mabel's inheritance did not materialize. Vivian was able to get his job back at the Reid ranch.

When she lost her job, Audrey felt desperate. It was nearly Christmas time, December of 1932. Her folks were in Nebraska with Milly, Jessica and Frank, so she had no place to go and nobody to help her. Vern and Mable were in Albuquerque and had their hands full. Betty was living with them and Edward stayed with them some of the time. Christmas looked bleak to Audrey, knowing she had no way to go to school after the holidays. Opal still had her position, but Audrey's future looked bleak; and since Audrey worked for Opal's place to sleep, Opal worried right along with Audrey.

Audrey walked to school nearly every day with a girl friend, Billie Harmon. She was older than Billie but they were good friends. One day when they were walking to school, an oil truck stopped and the driver said, "Get in."

Billie said, "Come on! Get in."

Audrey got in, but when they got to the school she asked, "Who is that man?"

Billie said, "I never saw him before in my life. Maybe he was just an oil man."

Audrey exploded: "I thought you knew him! Don't ever ride with anybody you don't know! Don't ever get into a truck with a stranger! That's very dangerous!"

Billie doubled up with laughter. "I was just kidding! That was my father!"

Billie was amused and told her mother about the incident and how Audrey had "bawled her out good" for riding with "a stranger."

Billie's mother agreed. "Audrey's advice was right. You should never get into a vehicle with a stranger." The mother was extremely pleased with Audrey for giving Billie good advice and for showing that she had a protective attitude toward the young girl.[1]

Audrey had told Billie she was out of a job. When Billie told her mother about Audrey's situation, Mrs. Harmon told Audrey that she wanted her to work for her. Mrs. Harmon told Audrey that she was impressed by her wisdom. So Audrey had another job. The Harmons lived in the same apartment house, down at the other end of the building from where the Keens lived, but they were moving up to the 1000 block on Seventh Street to a big, two-story house next to Mrs. D. U. Harris' home. Mrs. Harmon asked if Audrey could help her over there. She wanted her to start work immediately. Audrey told Mrs. Keen she was quitting right away. Mrs. Keen didn't think that Audrey would find another job so quickly. She expected her to stay a little longer.

"I meant for you to stay until Christmas," Mrs. Keen told her.

Audrey stayed until the end of the week. The Harmons didn't have a sleeping room for Audrey and Opal, so Audrey rented a room at Mrs. Minter's place across the street, a room facing the side porch with an outside entrance. It was the same room that Mabel had rented when Frank was born. It was about five dollars a month. Audrey had enough to pay a month's rent.

Audrey and Opal moved across the street into Mrs. Minter's apartment and Audrey worked for the Harmons, starting in December of 1932. She was sick for a while, but Mrs. Harmon "rescued" her. She stayed there the rest of the winter. She walked from Mrs. Minter's place up to the Harmon house every day, many long blocks, very early every morning. She helped clean house and wash clothes on Saturdays. She made biscuits for them for breakfast every morning. She had learned how to make them at Bernal when she was twelve. Mr. Giles, the geologist, came by one day when Audrey had made biscuits.

"They are wonderful. They'd make the angels sing! They're so nice and light," he said. Audrey was pleased that she knew how to make biscuits so well.[2]

About that time, Mabel wrote a letter to a friend:

> Are you getting the Xmas blues? Well, I thought so. I know why. You have a foolish habit of giving presents that take too big a bite out of your budget. Am I right—or am I a mind reader! That isn't the way to have a Merry Xmas—you are sure to have some back firing on Xmas.
>
> We have been raised in a family which believed in giving till it hurts—but after having it hurt for years and years I've found we can have a happy Xmas without bustin' the budget.
>
> Big business will murder me—but I feel like the lady who said—Go ahead—knock my eye out. I've seen it all.
>
> But of course we can assure "big biz" that all our money goes for something—so that will help business—whether we buy knickknacks for gifts for the things we have been needing—doing without ourselves.
>
> Do you know, I always buy for the other fellow something he wants, but chiefly because I want the same thing myself so badly. I gave a silver tray to a bride recently—I've always been dying for one (not dead yet, tho.) And when I need new linens I *give* linens. Crazy I guess! But I know how to do without things. Heigh - ho! I come from old pioneer stock and don't like the ads begging us to go in debt for Xmas gifts and pay next year.[3]

The Harmons were going to move back to Texas as soon as school was out. Mr. Harmon was employed by the Magnolia Oil Company. They liked Las Vegas, but the altitude was too high for Mr. Harmon. Mrs. Harmon told Audrey that she would see that she got a place to stay, and Audrey appreciated her thoughtfulness. Mrs. Harmon spoke to Mrs. John S. Jones across the street from her on Seventh Street. She made arrangements for Audrey to work with Mrs. Jones under the same conditions she'd had at Mrs. Harmon's house. Audrey would work for her board there and continue to walk back and forth from her room at Mrs. Minters. So Audrey had a job for the next school year, 1932-33.

Opal was still working for Trogsteds. But suddenly Opal received bad news. Mrs. Trogsted dropped dead one day in Funks Five and Dime store on Douglas. Opal was shocked and saddened. But even though Mrs. Trogsted was gone, Mr. Trogsted still needed Opal to continue to keep house for him and get his meals. So Opal continued to work for her meals. She still needed a place to sleep, so they kept the room at Mrs. Minter's place.

One day late in 1932, Bill Reid asked Audrey and another girl, one of Audrey's classmates, to go on a picnic to Terrero with him and a friend of his. However, the other guy, Bill's friend, didn't show up, so it was a "threesome" that went. They spent the day and half the night. Later Audrey described that trip in a taped conversation with Millicent Wickman:

> That was one of the worst days I ever spent in my life! It was the worst trip I ever made—Bill got us down off the hill from Terrero. (I could not have driven down that mountain) to the pavement in Pecos, and he said he was too sleepy to continue to drive, so he said, "Here Audrey, you drive from here on in." And he proceeded to go to sleep. I couldn't drive! I hadn't ever driven! I could steer the car down the road but I couldn't shift gears—I didn't know how to do anything! I was all right as long as I just needed to steer. I think I drove in low gear all the way to Vegas (about 46 miles). I was too tired and those darned cedar and piñon trees along the side of the highway seemed to be dancing around and seemed to be right in front of the car! They jumped around all night in front of me! I'd slow down because I thought a tree was right in front of me on the road! I knew where the brake pedal and the gas pedal was—heck yes, but I couldn't shift gears! It was tough! We got to Vegas and I let the other girl out near her home about two o'clock in the morning and I proceeded toward my "abode." I went down National—down that steep hill—and I put on the brakes and barely avoided the big brick building on Twelfth and National! I had a heck of a time! Anyway, I parked the car on Twelfth about at Douglas and got out and went up Douglas to Mrs. Minter's where Opal and I had a room. I couldn't get in because Opal had locked the door. I banged and hollered at Opal and I had to wake practically everybody up in the neighborhood before I could wake Opal up to let me in![4]

In spite of Audrey's unpleasant journey and her embarrassment at arriving home late, she was not angry with Bill.

Audrey had another unpleasant ride—a terrifying one—when Clyde took her on a motorcycle ride. She hadn't been seeing much of him, as he had been pressuring her to marry him and she had refused. They were still friends. In later years Audrey recalled:

> I took a motorcycle ride *once*. I had been going with Clyde and he promised to take me for a ride on Glen's big Harley-Davidson motorcycle.

About the same time I told him we had to break up. He was getting too "mushy" and I wasn't ready to get married—no profit in us continuing to see each other—so we had agreed to stop going together. I hadn't seen him for some time when he came around the corner at Penney's old store on the corner of Sixth and Grand and Lincoln. I said "Hello" and he said he had Glen's motorcycle and didn't I want to take that ride. For some reason I did—boredom maybe—curiosity? I don't know. Anyway we rode up Grand avenue at the top of the hill on the old dirt road; we were going really fast. As we topped the hill a car came fast on the wrong side of the road. Clyde had to hit the ditch. He did and really struggled to keep the bike right side up. It was sidewise at an angle, but we didn't wreck. I guess the scare gave us something in common again. He took me back to the Las Vegas Hotel where I lived with Opal.[5]

Audrey stated: "The near-accident should have been a warning to me: Don't travel with Clyde. But maybe I took it the other way subconsciously—that we were safe together. Anyway, we started going together again and eventually I married him."[6]

Audrey had seen a lot of heartache during those Depression years. She tried to encourage those who were downhearted. Sometimes one of her friends would be discouraged. She would always have a positive word of encouragement for everyone. She believed in looking at the bright side of things. "If I have a choice of looking at a garbage heap or looking at roses in bloom, I'm going to choose to look at the roses," she said. She believed one could "pull yourself up by your boot straps" and come out ahead of the game. Later she wrote a poem, "Maneuver for Victory," which was published on the front page of *The Friendly Journal*:

> Would you fling 'way a precious stone
> If you should find the setting cheap?
> I hear you sit and sign and moan—
> You think you fall in Life's trash heap.
>
> Now do stand up and smile again.
> Your life cannot be ruined yet.
> This life's just a shower like rain—
> And diamonds are not hurt by wet.
>
> Your life is like a treasured jewel

Which you are given just one time.
Turn it into a worthwhile tool!
Don't waste it like an unheard chime![7]

Audrey had learned that rain doesn't hurt diamonds. She'd suffered through the hard times, but she, like a gem, only shone brighter for it. It was good to get back to the mountains she loved when school was out. She spent summers with her mother, often gathering around the piano to sing with her family while Mabel played familiar old songs.

Whenever Audrey heard the old song, "When It's Springtime in the Rockies," she thought of those family times. Audrey once told Clyde about the family's singing and about her favorite song. Clyde told Audrey that it was *her* song because she was his little sweetheart of the mountains. Clyde had proposed many times. Audrey had refused. But if high school graduation ever became a reality, she would consider his proposal.

33

Reids' Ranch: Nebraska and Back

By the time school was out in May of 1933, the Shearers had moved back to Reids' Ranch after returning from Nebraska. Mabel was disappointed that her father's third wife got the farms and houses. She would eventually get a little money from his estate, but no land. Vivian realized he could make no money in Nebraska. He was not a farmer. So it was useless to stay.

Audrey returned to the mountains she loved at the Old Homestead Ranch each spring when school was out. As always, she helped her mother with the younger children and with the chores.

Clyde had proposed to Audrey; but she had refused to marry until she got her education. She wanted to go to college. Years later she wrote:

> I dreamed of a prince charming who would carry me off someday, not knowing that with the kind of life I was leading, I could hardly

recognize him when he came by and certainly wouldn't know how to entice him. I knew how to baby sit, change diapers, wash dishes, shine windows, and mop floors but from the fairy tales I read I never learned how to attract a man. They all told of beauty enticing a man who kissed them on their cheek and they lived happily ever after. That I thought was life.

In high school Sissy [Opal] had lots of boyfriends—she grew up playing with them and had an easy manner. But I, shut in my work and dream world, didn't know how to talk to a boy. "Be a nice girl, be a good girl, and your turn will come," Mama said as Sissy dashed off to a party and I stayed home to babysit while Mama and Daddy went to a meeting. Be a good girl? I didn't know how to be anything else![1]

Audrey recalled that she wasn't allowed to do anything except work or babysit most of her life. "I never learned how to play," she said more than once. She wrote: "Age 10—I wanted to go to the dance. I got ready. Mother and V [Vivian] wouldn't go—just sat and looked at me at Chapelle. I cried and was embarrassed and mad."[2]

Audrey wrote a verse:

> I hate being small
> Can't do anything at all
> These big people get to do it all.
> I eat my spinach and try to grow
> But I grow so slow, so slow.
> Why it's this way, I'll ever know!
> I hate being small.[3]

Audrey also remembered how hungry the family was during the Depression years and was grateful for everything she had. Audrey recalled that Vivian bought a radio and the family enjoyed it tremendously. Vivian's radio ran on one or two big car-size batteries. When he first brought it in, hooked up and got it working, the first words they heard were: "This is KOA Denver." Two-year-old Frank exclaimed, "Oh, yeah?" Mabel laughed about that for years. They listened to Jack Benny. They also liked Amos and Andy. They always listened to the news. However, they couldn't listen too long because it would drain the battery. Everyone listened an hour or so a day.

Mabel learned to make a cake called "War Cake" when there wasn't much money for ingredients. It had no sugar, no butter, no eggs, and no milk. But it was very good. Some people called it "Depression" cake. When items were rationed or unaffordable, the ingenuity of the American housewife allowed for good substitutes for the usual ingredients. Mabel wrote:

> Combine the following ingredients in a large saucepan:
> 1 cup raisins
> 1 cup water
> 1 cup molasses
> 1 teaspoon ground cinnamon
> ½ cup shortening
> ½ teaspoon ground ginger
> ½ teaspoon salt
> ¼ teaspoon ground cloves (optional).
> Boil together for 5 minutes. Then add:
> 1 teaspoon baking soda
> 2 cups flour (or enough to make a thick cake batter.)
> Bake at 325-350 degrees for about 1 hour in an 8-inch by 12-inch pan. Variations in the amount of flour and oven temperature will be influenced by altitude.[4]

Mabel always said, "Experiment and find what's right for you." When Mabel had more money after the Depression, she added walnuts to the recipe. It is a heavy, brown cake, something like a coffee cake with a distinctive molasses flavor. Frosting is optional.

While Audrey spent her summer vacation in the mountains, Opal decided to stay in town. She still had her job at Mr. Trogsteds but no room to live in, so she shared an apartment which was five dollars a month at the Las Vegas Hotel. With a roommate from Rowe Mesa to share expenses, Opal paid only half the amount. Mrs. Rainey owned it. She was the lady Mabel first rented from on National Avenue, the little apartment they lived in when they first arrived in Las Vegas. Opal's roommate stayed for a while and then went home, but Opal kept the room anyway. Audrey moved back to town when school started in the fall of 1933 and moved in with Opal. She walked several long blocks to Mrs. Jones' house every day from there.

When Audrey helped Mrs. Jones for her board—no room—she cleaned and did all the ironing once a week. Audrey was paid twenty five cents an hour to iron. She could usually get it all done in two hours. She had to clean and wash the beautiful white tile fireplace inside and out every morning. There was a furnace, so the fireplace was just for decoration. Mrs. Jones had been the Home Economics teacher at the high school when she was young, so she knew how to thoroughly clean house and expected Audrey to be the same perfectionist she was. "Mrs. Jones taught me to clean house to perfection," Audrey said.

As mentioned before, Bill Reid had always been attracted to Opal but Opal wasn't especially interested in him. Opal was interested in Robert "Bob" Simpson. In June of 1933, Opal and Bob Simpson were married in Mora when Opal had just finished her junior year of high school. Maybe that was the reason Opal stayed in town that summer instead of joining her family at the ranch; Bob had proposed and they planned to marry. But they kept the marriage a secret. Bob knew his parents would not approve of his marrying so young and would not support him anymore. Bob knew his mother would be very upset if she found out he had married.

Soon after Opal's secret marriage, Bill Reid asked Opal for a date, not knowing that she was married, of course. He did know that she had been going steady with Bob Simpson for a long time. Since Opal was married, she made it very clear to Bill that she was not at all interested. Soon after that, Bill married a thirteen-year-old girl named Helen. Someone signed a paper stating that Helen was fourteen and had permission to marry. When Bill took Helen to the Reid home, he went up to the door and told Mabel that he was married to the young girl. Mabel was so startled she didn't believe it at first. Bill loved practical jokes, so Mabel was suspicious when he told her he'd married Helen, who was little more than a child. Bill was about twenty-five years of age, and Mabel didn't believe he'd marry such a young girl. Mabel insisted on seeing their marriage license. Helen went to the car and got it. Mabel had to believe it then. Naturally, Bill wanted a nice place for his bride to live. They wanted to live at their ranch in the big ranch house. So Mabel and Vivian had to give up the house and leave Reid Ranch.

Mabel and Vivian had no place to go, so they went back to San Geronimo to live. They lived in the same house where they had lived for a while once before. This time when Mabel and Vivian moved to San Geronimo they had very little. Mabel had taught school before but had to quit when she was pregnant with Frank. They were nearly penniless, as there were few jobs to be found in those Depression days. Since they were jobless, they had no rent money but promised to pay the rent when they could.

Vern had brought Betty up to stay with Mabel and Vivian, so she started school in the fourth grade at San Geronimo. The teacher, Mr. Gallegos, was from a community south of Romeroville. He walked home weekends and then back to San Geronimo for school Monday, a trip of about twelve miles. Betty was about eleven years old then and enjoyed school. She and Milly liked the teacher. He would bring them gum or candy sometimes. The two girls got along very well. They had their chores to do, but afterwards they were allowed the freedom to play or do their homework together.

Audrey knew the folks were flat broke again and worried about them. There were still four children at home to feed. Sometimes they had mutton when Vivian and Mabel were able to trade with a sheep-herder. Mabel did ironing for one of the village women to try to earn a little money. Vivian would not "poach" game although he had guns and ammunition. He knew the country and the trails of the deer. But he would not break the law. At some point Edward came to visit and saw that there was not a morsel of food to eat in the house. So he went out and came back with some meat. Mabel never questioned where it came from, nor did anyone else.

Milly and Betty helped with the chores. Milly recalled how she and Betty would play together and observe the villagers in their various daily activities. She recalled that she and Betty sometimes watched funeral processions. In the early days the men carried the coffin up the hill from the village to the cemetery at the top of the hill. They would often place a cross at the spots where they stopped to rest. In later years, they used a horse-drawn wagon to take the coffin to the burial place.[5]

One day Milly and Betty watched the people gathered around the horse-drawn wagon. They knew the family whose daughter had died. The rumor was that the young woman had disgraced her family because she had become pregnant out of wedlock. It was said that she died in childbirth.

The two sisters were curious."Did the baby live?" Milly wondered.

"No one has said anything about it, just that she died having the baby," Betty replied.

"It probably didn't live," Milly speculated.

Suddenly Milly and Betty were shocked to hear muffled screams coming from inside the casket. The horses had started pulling the wagon up the hill. The two little girls heard screaming and hitting sounds from inside the wooden coffin. But no one stopped to open it! All the people seemed deaf to the noises.

Milly wondered if the family had mistakenly thought the young lady was dead and then didn't want to let her out of the casket because of fear. There were a lot of superstitions about death. Then Milly wondered whether they intentionally put the young woman in the casket alive because she had disgraced the family. In any case, the people ignored the screams and pounding from inside the wooden box. The men buried the coffin. Milly and Betty watched from their hiding place in the distance, too scared and horrified to tell anyone until much later.[6]

Audrey and Opal walked out to San Geronimo at Christmas to visit the folks. They were still living at the Las Vegas Hotel and Audrey was working for Mrs. Jones. She was happy to receive five dollars from Mrs. Jones as a Christmas gift. Money was scarce that Christmas of 1933. Neither Audrey nor Opal had any coats. They went to school for years in below zero weather with no coats. Audrey had a cotton sweater and Opal had a thin, leather-like jacket, an imitation rubber material. It was black and long, down past her waist but not warm. Audrey used her Christmas gift from Mrs. Jones to buy warm coat sweaters for herself and Opal. They were about a dollar and ninety-eight cents each. They were beautiful, the girls thought. So they wore them when they walked to San Geronimo for Christmas. Whenever Audrey had something extra, she would share it with someone else. She would manage to give some kind of gift for birthdays if she could, sometimes a greeting card with a quarter in it if she had it.

The walk from town was tiring, but the girls had a chance to really look at the scenery. They went through "Kearney's Gap" and talked about the history of the place. Later, Audrey wrote a story for the *Las Vegas Daily Optic* when she was a reporter there in 1957:

> One of the most important passes in the southwest in early New World History, was Kearney's Gap, just west off of Highway 85, [now I-25] south of Las Vegas, on the Mineral Hill Road. [State Road 283]
>
> Named for Gen. Stephen Watts Kearney, the pass was old when Kearney stopped in Las Vegas and proclaimed New Mexico a territory of the United States in 1946. Known history of the gap dates back 400 years to the time when the Indians from what is now the Pecos ruins, fortified the pass, to prevent the return of Coronado from his hunt to the east for the seven cities of gold.
>
> When the high wheeled wagons began swaying from the Missouri to Santa Fe, cutting the first ruts in 1824, in which became the Santa Fe Trail, the wagons rattled through the old gap and rocked on west toward Santa Fe.
>
> A Torreón [rock wall or fort] was erected on the ridge to the north to serve as a fortification for outposts of the village in the meadows. Bubbling springs and the stream at the gap, the last water for wagons from the west, before they reached Las Vegas, was used for "cleaning up," before arriving at the Plaza. The water was also used to douse away the final cobwebs of hangovers from mountain vino, the morning after, when leaving civilization in the meadows.
>
> After the railroad came and the Indian menace was gone, school

and church groups hiked to Kearney's Gap for picnics. A shallow cave in the side of the cliffs on the left side of the road as you look through the gap toward the Sangre de Cristo mountain range, has been explored repeatedly through the years by boys and girls who later became staid citizens of the world.[7]

The family didn't have much that Christmas of 1933. The country was still suffering from the Great Depression. But they had their family and their health. And they had the beauty of the mountains that towered over the San Geronimo area—Hermit's Peak, Barillas Peak, and all the others. Audrey took in deep breaths of the fresh mountain air and thanked God for her blessings. She began to sing "When the Moon Comes Over the Mountain." She never thought she had a good singing voice like the rest of the family, but when she was alone and happy she sang her favorite songs.

34

Thirty-Six Cents and A Letter of Hope: Reid's to San Geronimo

Thirty-six cents! In the winter of 1935, Charles V. Shearer had thirty-six cents to his name.

He had a wife and children at home in San Geronimo to support.

By 1935, the three oldest children were grown, but there were four remaining children at home to care for—Betty, Milly, Jessica and Frank. Mabel had quit teaching school in 1932 to have Frank and could not find a job after that. Audrey and Clyde were struggling to make ends meet. Clyde drove a taxi cab in Las Vegas, earning a dollar a day. Due to the Depression economy, the cab company's calls were few and far between.

Then, in January of 1935, Clyde and Audrey learned of the potential job for Vivian. Audrey wrote a letter home explaining that there was a job opening with the government—the agency known as the CCC (Civilian Conservation Corps). Audrey saw an item in the newspaper which mentioned that one of Vivian's friends, Frank Andrews, was in charge. Audrey suggested that since he knew the man in charge, he might want to apply for the job.[1]

Vivian contacted his friend and was told that he should come into the office for an interview. However, Vivian did not receive a letter advising him when he should come in for the job interview.

On February 14, 1935 Vivian typed a letter on the back of some old business stationery. He wrote to the Social Service Department, stating that he had not received a reply to follow up his request about the job application with an interview. In part, he wrote:

> Mr. Stern very kindly offers to give his personal assistance if I will come to town and let him know in advance when I will be there, and I most sincerely appreciate his interest and offer of personal assistance. However, I hope that I may be pardoned for calling attention to the fact that when one has reached the limit of their resources as I have, that coming to town constitutes a major effort, and the idea of planning such a trip several days in advance, must be predicated upon an adequate supply of provisions and general resources to make the element of time a secondary item.[2]

Vivian then went on to explain that he had no way of getting into Las Vegas except on the chance of catching a ride with someone or walking. He explained that getting a ride was uncertain and "my shoes are hardly equal to the strain of walking." He also explained that he would not have any food while making the trip to and from town, should he walk the round trip distance of forty miles over rough, unpaved roads.[3]

"I have a car," he explained in the letter, "but it has a weak battery on account of the generator not working, and about one gallon of gas in the tank."[4] He wrote that he thought it would make the trip one way, but he could not depend upon it both ways. He added that he would need to be assured that he would be able to make the necessary repairs and add the additional gasoline before taking the car in.

> I have cash on hand in the sum of thirty-six cents, which I am saving for postage stamps, in hopes that I can get some definite action on my request with that sum before our food supply is entirely exhausted.[5]

The letter went on to explain the Shearers' desperation—that the car had not been fully paid for or it would have "long since gone in trade for goods." He continued:

It is impossible for well-fed people to get away from thinking in terms of the leisurely development of affairs. It is quite impossible for them to come into full realization of the possibility of an emergency in which the element of time is the vital and consuming factor. There are cases when today is much more important and vital than tomorrow. In our case, if this thing must drag along, I might say that one more sack of flour will keep myself and wife and four children from actual hunger for another week.[6]

This was the letter of a desperate man, a man asking for a job interview that would accommodate his situation. At a cost of two cents to mail a letter, Vivian would be left with only thirty-four cents to his name after he mailed the crucial letter.

The request got immediate results. A letter by return mail, delivered the next day by the rural mail carrier, replied that certainly Vivian could come for an interview as soon as it was convenient for him. Vivian went for an interview and he got the job. He was sent to Socorro, New Mexico for a while. Then he was transferred to San Isidro.

After working for the CCC camps, Vivian then got a job with the Soil Conservation Service. He worked there twenty years until he retired. Sometimes Vivian was disgusted with his job, but he was grateful to have it. He once told Audrey it was "her fault" that he was "stuck" with a government job because she had given him the initial tip.[7]

Milly recalled that one of the first things her daddy did after he got the job in Socorro was to send a package to her. Milly recalled: "Some packages arrived in the mail—and there was one for me! It had my name on it!"

There was a little something for each child. But Milly was the most excited over her gift. She jumped up and down and said, "Daddy sent me a present!"

When she opened it she saw that it was an orange! She hadn't seen an orange in a very long time. She held it in her hand and felt the firm, cool roundness of it. She anticipated biting into the sweet, juicy fruit.

"I'll share it with everyone!" Milly said generously. "But we have to make it last a long time." She gave one section of orange to each of her siblings. "We will each have one section every day." And that's just what they did! But after a few days the orange began to spoil, so some of it was wasted. Milly cried about that, realizing they should have eaten more of it when it was fresh.[8]

The Shearers were never so deprived again. Prosperity had not yet come, but it was just around the corner for the nation and for families like the Shearers. Clyde and Audrey Simpson, along with the other members of the family, prospered after the dark years of the Depression were over.

"Happy Days are Here Again" was indeed a popular song! Vivian undoubtedly never forgot that day when he invested two of his thirty-six cents on a letter. He had sent it with fervent prayers and a heart filled with hope.

35

Wedding Vows

Audrey and Opal were in town rooming together, but they didn't have much money. During the Depression, being healthy and able to work was considered fortunate. A newspaper was about 2 cents. A pair of shoes was a dollar. The average wage was a dollar a day. "If you had a quarter you thought you were rich. You could go to a movie for a nickel."[1]

The girls were doing well until Opal got very sick. Audrey didn't know Opal was married. Bob came to visit Opal often. Opal was deathly sick but she refused to have a doctor. Audrey gave Opal the best nursing care she could.

Later Audrey was outside the room when she overheard Opal telling Bob that she'd had a miscarriage. Bob wanted to get a doctor. They argued. Opal said she didn't want anybody to know that she had been pregnant. The secret would come out, and they had agreed not to upset his parents, Opal reminded him.

Opal said, "If the doctor comes, everyone will know about it."[2]

It was heart rending to Audrey to be unable to get any help because of Opal's stubborn refusals. Audrey was very upset but Opal was adamant. Gradually Opal recovered.

Many years later when Audrey and Opal were able to talk about it openly, they agreed that things would have been better if Opal and Bob had told the truth about their marriage in the first place.[3]

In the spring of 1934, March or April, Mabel rented a house at 512 Tilden Street in Las Vegas. She and the kids moved to town in a wagon piled high and loaded to the hilt. She had to hold Frank on her lap to keep him from falling out of the wagon. Mabel thought it was one of the most miserable trips she had ever made, riding in a horse drawn wagon over such a rough road. The trip took nearly a day. Vivian was still working in Socorro, so there was no one to help her move. When she got to town, Audrey and Opal helped her move into the house and organize it. Then she asked them to move in with her and save money, so they moved from the Las Vegas Hotel to the Tilden house. No one knew Opal was already married, although everyone expected she and Bob would marry soon.

Audrey and Clyde saw each other often but Audrey was not ready to get married. However, they went to movies or to church or other places together. Audrey wrote:

> When Clyde began courting me we usually went to church. There were revivals in all sorts of places [including] the site where Wackers was fifty years later in 1980. [now the Salvation Army site] Mrs. Simpson and Clyde tried to start Church Services in Dr. Christee's building after Sister Kelton moved out and had services in her home, a small house on the corner of University and Eighth Street where the doctor's clinic is now and was built on that site when she moved out.[4]

Both Audrey and Opal liked to write. Opal wrote verse or poetry. Audrey did, too, but she also wrote prose. About that time *The Denver Post* paid Audrey five dollars for something she had submitted. With that money, Audrey took Opal and Betty to the J.C. Penney Store—at the corner of Sixth and Lincoln and Grand—and bought hats, one for each of them and for herself. In those days, if one went anywhere, including church, a restaurant or a movie, one was expected to wear a hat. But none of them had hats, so Audrey thought it was the best thing she could do with the five dollars she had received. Opal bought a Princess Eugenia—a little tight black cap with a very narrow brim that rolled up around the face. She wore it a long time. Betty picked out what she wanted. Audrey bought herself a wide brimmed summer hat. She still had some money left over after the hat purchases.[5]

In late May of 1934, Audrey and Opal graduated from Las Vegas High School. (Today it is known as Las Vegas Robertson High. The old high school burned in 1945; when it was rebuilt in the same place, it was renamed Robertson High School for Mr. W. J. Robertson, a school superintendent.) Vern bought both of the girls a dress to wear. But he didn't think about shoes. Neither of them had good shoes to wear. They were able to borrow from friends. Audrey's feet suffered that evening from shoes that didn't fit, but her spirits were high. All the hard work had paid off. She and Opal had reached their goal!

Audrey Clements, 1934. *Source*: Simpson Archives

After graduation day, Mabel rented a house at 1113 Eleventh Street. Audrey cleaned the house from top to bottom, washed the woodwork, windows, scrubbed the floors and cleaned everything as well as she knew how from working with Mrs. Jones. Audrey and Opal moved in with Mabel there too. Mabel rented out rooms to pay for the rent for the house.

After living in Las Vegas a while, it was time to move again! Vivian had returned from Socorro. His work from then on required some transfers. He and Mabel moved to the Watts Place two miles north of old Highway 85, now I-25. The turn off was just across the highway from San José, New Mexico.

One day Charley Geiss and a girl friend, Clara, invited Clyde and Audrey to go with them to the Santa Fe Fiesta. Charley let the two out at the Santa Fe Plaza and then he took the car and left with Clara. Clyde and Audrey took in all the sights. They went to the Catholic Church and were expected to give a donation. They hardly had any money, but they gave fifteen cents, which left Clyde with only a dime. Audrey had twenty-five cents, and that was a lot. Clyde had been asking around to find someone from Las Vegas to catch a ride home with because Charley and Clara had disappeared. But Clyde had no success, so they couldn't do anything except sit there in the Plaza and wait for their friends to return. Finally around two o'clock in the morning, the couple came back. Audrey made up her mind never to go with them again. However, while she had been waiting around, she wrote a poem, perhaps inspired by some of the fiesta activities. She knew she could write well enough to be published, so she later sent in the poem and it was published under the title of "Bonfire."

> The salamanders dance tonight—
> Wild fire spirits on glittering leaves
> Seething and whirling—leaping bright
> They tinsel stark and naked trees.
>
> With power of Jove—wild will of boy—
> Their southern king sends out flame hordes
> To blaze—devour—reduce—destroy—
> Those tongues of fire are bloody swords.
>
> In deep piled leaves long sere and dead
> Still twisting fierce—but held to plan
> These spirits writhe—wild flame outspread
> Under the rake of master man.[6]

Clyde again asked Audrey to marry him. Clyde had been asking Audrey to marry him for a couple of years. Audrey had refused, thinking she was not yet ready to marry, nor could they afford to get married. Audrey joked later, saying if she had known Opal and Bob were married, she might not have considered marrying Clyde, Bob's brother. "It was just too many Simpsons!" she quipped. Sisters marrying brothers meant each couple's children would have the same grandparents on each side; they'd be double cousins! Opal Clements became Opal Simpson and Audrey Clements became Audrey Simpson.

Clyde had dropped out of school after the tenth grade. He had driven a taxi part time, as mentioned before, but he had begun working more often at the Home Café in Las Vegas. He made one dollar a day at the Café and worked seven days a week. After President Franklin D. Roosevelt came into office, a new law prevented anybody from working seven days a week. Since Clyde could only work six days, he lost a dollar a week. However, he did have a day off. Audrey didn't know what Clyde was making and never thought to ask before they were married.

After Clyde finally convinced Audrey to marry him, he had to explain that he could not afford a big wedding. Audrey said she realized that. They decided to elope about a month after Audrey's high school graduation. Clyde borrowed a car from his oldest brother, Glen. Then Clyde took Audrey to Estancia where Clyde had a friend, Clarence Cochran. Clyde knew the Cochrans from having lived at Estancia as a boy. The wedding was held at the home of the Cochrans on July 16, 1934.

Clarence Cochran had been married not long before that. His wife met the couple at the door of their home and welcomed them.

The barber was the preacher. Clarence took Clyde to the barber shop to get the part-time minister. He came to Clarence Cochran's house and married Audrey and Clyde. Clyde had asked Clarence what he should pay the preacher. He asked Clarence if he thought five dollars would be enough. Clarence told him not to give him that much. Clarence said, "Just give him the change that you have in your pocket."

Clyde had about two dollars and eight-five cents in his pocket, so that's what the preacher got. It was the height of the Depression, and the preacher had no complaints.

Someone took a snapshot of Audrey and Clyde outside the home, so that was their wedding photograph. Audrey wore a white print dress with short sleeves and a short jacket. The dress came down almost to her ankles. She wore high heeled pumps with a strap across the front. Her dark brown hair was waved and pulled back behind her head in the popular style of the time. Clyde wore a white, long sleeved shirt with a tie which had a stripe across it. The wide tie came down to the middle of the shirt. He wore light colored pants with a leather belt. His shoes were leather street shoes that he probably wore to work as well. They were dressed in simple clothes, the best that could be managed during the Depression.

They were a good looking couple. Audrey stood at about five feet four inches, was slim and lithe. Her turquoise blue eyes were beautiful under her thick, dark eye brows and dark eye lashes. Clyde's taller form, about five feet, eleven inches, seemed to hover over his bride in a protective way. His fair complexion was highlighted by his dark hair. His green eyes smiled under black eye brows. His brilliant smile lit up his whole face and was contagious.

It was a short marriage ceremony. There was no one to play a traditional "wedding march" but there was a man who could play the violin, or so he said. He played the only tune on the fiddle that he knew how to play: "Pop Goes the Weasel." It may have seemed like a strange sort of wedding, but during Depression Years, any wedding ceremony at all was appreciated by a young bride and groom. Mrs. Cochran baked a cake and served lunch.

Clyde and Audrey left Estancia that evening and went to Santa Fe. They went to a Chinese Restaurant and had their wedding dinner—Chinese food. Audrey had never eaten Chinese food before. But Clyde that been to California and had experienced different kinds of food. He had been there twice to attend school. He was a member of the International Church of the Foursquare Gospel and attended L.I.F.E. Bible College—the Lighthouse of International Foursquare Evangelism. It was founded by Aimee Semple McPherson. "Sister Aimee" was very popular and was well known as a preacher and founder of the Church, known simply as the "Foursquare Gospel Church" or "Foursquare Church." She founded the well-known Angelus Temple in Los Angeles. Clyde did not complete his studies, however, because he ran out of money. Instead, he found another Bible college that had a shorter course of study, so he was ordained by that church.

The newlyweds came back to Las Vegas the next day. That evening Clyde went to an old motel on South Grand to rent a room, assuring the clerk at the desk that they were married. Audrey was standing outside, embarrassed, while Clyde rented a room. Clyde wanted to keep the marriage a secret. He was afraid his mother would be unhappy, as she didn't want any of her children to marry. But Audrey didn't want to keep it a secret, so in a couple of weeks she told her mother about the marriage. Mabel was happy for the young couple.

Since Clyde wanted to keep the marriage a secret from his family, he was careful to hide the evidence—the marriage certificate. After the certificate had been properly signed by the preacher and recorded, the couple waited for it to be taken care of properly, as there was no mailing address to send it to. The clerk at the court house in Estancia had handed Clyde the marriage certificate. Clyde had put it in his pocket. When he got home, Clyde hid it behind a picture in the Simpsons' living room. Bob found it! Even though Bob had succeeded in keeping his own marriage a secret, he didn't want his brother to succeed in the same endeavor. So Bob went to the Las Vegas Optic and put in an announcement of the marriage. Then Clyde went next door to another newspaper office—which published once or twice a week. Clyde put in an item denying that he and Audrey had been married and stating that it was, rather, Bob Simpson and Opal who had been married and that the Optic had mixed up the names by mistake.

Audrey was irate when she saw Clyde's denial announcement. It wasn't true, and she didn't like keeping her marriage a secret. So she promptly put an ad in the paper the next day, stating that Clyde's announcement had been a mistake, that the first announcement in the Optic had *not* been a mistake, and that they were, indeed, married! Audrey had the last word.

Audrey was annoyed about the false newspaper announcements, but she realized that Clyde and Bob were feuding; Clyde wanted to get back at Bob. Although Clyde didn't want his mother to know he had been married because it would upset her, he had nothing to lose. He had been supporting himself for quite a while and was not depending on his parents. On the other hand, Bob's parents were supporting him to go to school; and Bob knew that they would stop giving him money if they knew he was married. Hence, Bob wouldn't tell his parents that he was married because they had said they wouldn't send him through college if he got married; and he wanted to go to college. The Simpsons knew Bob and Opal were together all the time. Fearing that they were getting too serious, they sent Bob to Albuquerque to the University of New Mexico and forbade Opal to go to Albuquerque to see him. But they realized that Opal's father lived in Albuquerque, so they could not forbid Opal to go and visit her father when she wanted. So of course Opal went to Albuquerque whenever she wanted, and she continued to see Bob. Although Bob and Opal had been married for more than a year, they had kept the marriage from Bob's parents.

Addie Simpson didn't want any of her "kids" to get married, not even her daughter Rhea when she married Clint Oglesbee. Ouida married Thomas Sheffield. Glen married Clarabelle McDonald. Addie felt that she was losing her kids and she didn't want to lose them. Mary, another of Clyde's sisters, stayed home to take care of her mother all her life. If she married, she kept it a secret. At the time of Bob's marriage to Opal and Clyde's marriage to Audrey, Addie was still insisting that her boys must stay single a long time. Donald, the youngest, was engaged but not married.

After all the newspaper announcements, Mabel Shearer went to visit Addie Simpson. Clyde had admitted he and Audrey were married. The two had a nice visit.

Audrey realized that when she and Clyde got married, she should not have let him take the marriage certificate. She should have taken it and kept it in her purse; then perhaps all the trouble over it between Clyde and Bob would have been avoided. Audrey decided that a girl should always keep the marriage certificate to prove she is married, as Helen Reid did.

Mabel moved into a house at 1117 Eleventh Street. She rented out rooms to pay for the rent for the house. Mabel invited Audrey and Clyde to move into a room upstairs in the "sky light attic" room of the house she was renting. They had a problem that was common in those days—bed bugs. Mabel had been able to get rid of them in the downstairs part of the house, but she never got them out of the upstairs room. Audrey would wake up in the night and cry out, "There comes a bed bug down the wall!" It was too dark to see them, but her grandfather Clements who had excellent hearing always swore that he could hear them crawling along a wall and that he could hear them sing. Audrey must have heard them too. When the light was turned on, they would scatter. It was a miserable situation.

Audrey's grandmother, Dammuzzy, asked her what she wanted for a wedding present. Audrey told her grandmother she'd like a suitcase because she didn't have anything except a little wooden dynamite box to put her things in to preserve them. Dammuzzy sent her a good suitcase. Audrey used it all her life. She used it for keeping her photographs and special papers. Whenever there was danger of fire, Audrey knew she would grab that suitcase and save her photographs.

Vivian came home to 1117 Eleventh Street after he finished working in Socorro where he had been for several months working as Foreman of the CCC Camp there. Mabel enjoyed being able to shop in Las Vegas; and although they had more money than they had had for a while, she was still very careful with her budget. As mentioned before, hats were popular in those days, so Mabel decided to buy a hat.

It was about that time that Mabel wrote a poem which might be called "I Went to Buy a Hat Today." It was about shopping:

> I went to buy a hat today.
> I only had a five.
> The clerk said, "Say—
> Be on your way—
> My goodness sakes alive!
> Five dollars for a hat these days!
> You cannot find one, ever.
> Five dollars for a hat! Absurd!
> Them days is gone forever!"[7]

Vivian was looking for another job when they moved over to Pecos in 1934. He must have been doing something for the Forest Service because they lived in the Forest Ranger's house across the street from Miss Reuter's Hotel and Café for two or three months. Audrey and Clyde stayed at the house in the "sky light" until the folks moved.

Clyde's mother had moved back to Albuquerque. She would only stay in Las Vegas a short while each time she moved back. William Ernest Simpson was living alone at 1012 Tilden, so Clyde and Audrey were given permission to move in with him after Mabel and Vivian moved to Pecos. Clyde and Audrey paid the electric bill, which was about a dollar and twenty-five cents a month. That was the minimum, and they did not use more than the minimum. They didn't have to help with the cost of the heat because Ernest brought coal from the train station. Whenever the coal cars were unloaded at the train station, coal splattered all over the place; so the workers were allowed to shovel it up and take it home. Otherwise it would just go to waste. Bob and Opal lived there later and some of the other kids stayed there from time to time. Audrey and Clyde didn't stay with Ernest long, however. They did not want to impose. Ernest worked at night and slept in the day time, so the house had to be very quiet. Audrey read a lot. She couldn't have any company, so she borrowed a small phonograph and she had a few records. However, she was afraid to play it, as she didn't want to disturb her father-in-law. Much of the time Audrey was bored—but that was a good change from her hectic days of working her way through high school.

Ernest Simpson told stories about the Oklahoma Land Rush. He said all the folks were crowded together trying to grab land. They made a law that if anyone needed to relieve himself/herself, that person had to be fifty feet away from anybody else. It was a good way for people to "make believe" they had privacy in that flat land where there was little cover. The Simpsons were among the early settlers in Oklahoma.

In 1932 William Irby Carrington and his wife Ruth Desire Carrington moved to Las Vegas. Ruth and W. I. Carrington were married in 1921 in Lubbock, Texas and lived in Texas until 1929. Then they moved to Clovis, then to Raton, then to Las Vegas. William, who was always called "W.I." by Ruth, operated a Raleigh Products business. Ruth served the area as a practical nurse, assisting Dr. William Howe with countless births in Las Vegas.

The Carringtons bought the old Trambley property, a big, adobe building under huge cottonwoods where there had been a grist mill. (The land belongs to Highlands University today.) The Carringtons put in the first help-yourself laundry in Las Vegas and lived in a part of the building. Then Mr. Carrington got sick, and they sold that building to Dr. Roberts. It was made into the El Mora Apartments. Carringtons then bought the big two-and-a-half story red brick house at 921 Lincoln Avenue—on the corner of Tenth and Lincoln. They bought it for eighteen hundred dollars. W.I. Carrington got his five hundred dollar award from the U.S. Government for serving in the Armed Forces in World War I, so they had enough for the down payment on the house. The house had been known as the haunted house of the neighborhood. Windows were broken out, and it was in shambles. The people who had owned it lost it to a mortgage company. Their name was Wells. The woman's name was Lena. The Wells family had bought the house from Mr. A. H. Hamilton. He had built the house and lived in it for a time until the Wells bought it around 1900. Carringtons bought it in the early 1930's.

W. I. Carrington was an excellent carpenter, among other things, and he restored the house. The Carringtons were to become best friends with Audrey and Clyde and family, and the big brick house at 921 Lincoln became a very familiar place. The Carringtons made the upstairs rooms into apartments, as well as one of the rooms downstairs. They also acquired the house next door on Lincoln and rented it out, as well as a little house on the property which faced Tenth Street, 410 Tenth. There was also a tiny house in the back yard that was rented out.[8]

As Audrey got to know the Carringtons better, she realized what a strong woman Ruth was and learned something of her background. Ruth Desire Wilde was born September 27, 1898 to Mr. and Mrs. William Wilde in Salina, Kansas, one of six children. Her mother died when she was about ten. Ruth married when she was fairly young. She gave birth to a child alone because the drunken doctor did not arrive in time. The baby was dead before the intoxicated physician stumbled into the home. Later Ruth gave birth to a son, Jasper, called Jack. Soon after that her alcoholic husband left her, and she divorced him. Ruth served as a telegrapher for the Union Pacific Railroad prior to moving to Lubbock, Texas. There she met W. I. Carrington in 1920 and they were married in Lubbock. The Carringtons had one daughter, Lelama Carrington, born March 10, 1922 in Lubbock, Texas.[9]

Ruth assisted W. I. Carrington in establishing the original Church of Christ congregation in Las Vegas in 1933. In 1939 they opened a neighborhood grocery at 410 Tenth Street. The store burned in 1946. It was restored and rented out as an apartment house.

Ruth Carrington's son Jack married a woman named Marcreta—called Creta. They had two boys, Bryce Carrington and Jack Hulen Carrington. While the boys were very young, Jack Carrington was killed in Dallas, Texas in 1947.

After Lelama's first marriage to Herby Henry ended in 1948, she married E. E. "Pete" Gardner. They had four children: Bill, Jack, Ruth and Mike. The Simpson, Carringtons, and Gardners remained good friends throughout many years. The Gardner ranch was just down the canyon from the Simpson ranch. W. I. Carrington died in 1965. Ruth Carrington lived to be 86. The Carringtons operated an apartment house at 921 Lincoln from 1935 until the 1980s. After Ruth Carrington became ill the place was sold. It was at the Carrington apartments that Clyde and Audrey lived numerous times throughout the years.[10]

Soon after they were married, Clyde and Audrey wanted to have a place of their own, so they moved to Carringtons in the little house out back of the garage. It had one big room with a little partition that hid a kitchen sink and a wood cook stove. The house became very hot in the summer. Audrey fixed up the house as well as she could. She put curtains up and did all she could to make it comfortable. Mr. Carrington had used it for a work shop and then fixed it up for living quarters to rent. Mrs. Carrington had it cleaned, but it needed some "dressing" up. It had electricity and running water, luxuries Audrey had not always had. The flush toilet was outside in a separate room beside the coal shed.

Later Clyde and Audrey moved into the Carringtons' little two room house that faced Tenth Street. It was very comfortable and had a back porch. Audrey fixed it up until it was what she called "cute." Audrey was contended there. They used the same "bathroom" they'd had before, which was in a separate room outside. It wasn't a fancy, modern bathroom like the one at the Simpson home. But it was better than most of the facilities Audrey had known as a child. It was certainly better than an "outhouse."

Audrey liked to walk in the cool evenings. She liked to go down Lincoln to the depot and back. She would go and meet Clyde at two o'clock in the morning when he got off work at the Home Café. She never thought of any danger in walking at night alone on the streets of Las Vegas. Ruth Carrington warned her about walking at night, but Audrey paid no attention.

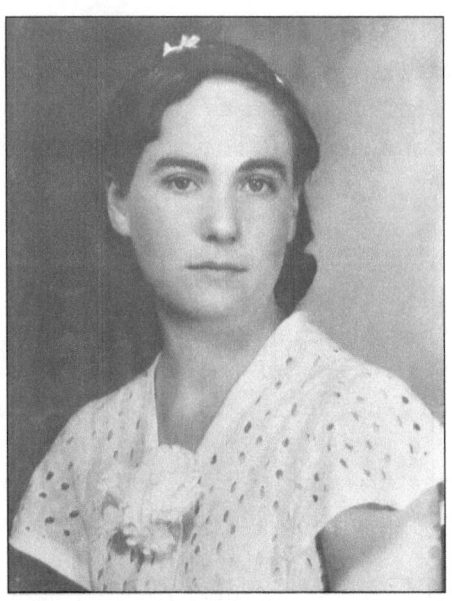

Audrey Simpson, 1930s. *Source:* **Simpson Archives**

One evening when the National Guard was in town on maneuvers—they came every summer—she was walking to the café when a couple of soldiers made some vulgar remarks. Also, there was a couple lying in the weeds in a vacant lot just off the sidewalk below the old Las Vegas Post Office. That was the last time Audrey walked to the depot or the café at night. She realized that Ruth Carrington was right. The town was changing; times were changing.

The Carringtons remained good friends and usually had a place to rent. Four years later when Audrey and Clyde were waiting for their first child to be born, they were once again living in the one-room house at the back of the Carrington property.

Clyde brought home a little black dog he'd bought for a quarter. He named the puppy Skip. Clyde got that twenty-five cent dog while they were living on Eleventh Street with the Shearers. Audrey thought a quarter was too much to pay for a dog when they were so pitifully poor. The pup was hardly old enough to be weaned. Clyde would bring steak trimmings and scraps from the Home Café every day, so it grew to be a very big dog. One day Skip left and they never knew what became of him. Years later, Audrey recalled, "After we were married one of the first things Clyde wanted was a dog! His folks would never let him or the other kids have a dog or any other animal. So we always had a dog."[11]

Bob and Opal had kept their marriage a secret for a long time, but finally the secret came out. Mrs. Simpson was still unhappy that any of her children had left home to get married, but she had accepted it. Once she had grandchildren, she was glad that the family had left the nest and grown. In later years, Audrey recalled:

> Sometime during that summer, after Mrs. [Addie] Simpson had moved to Albuquerque, we went down to see her. Daddy's wife Mable came over to see her and us. Mrs. Simpson made the remark that she wasn't sure Opal and Bob were married. She said, "I've never seen their marriage license so I don't know if they are married or not!" That really got under Mable's skin. In a polite, very nice tone of voice she said, "Well, Opal's father has seen their marriage license and they are married!" That put a stop to that speculation right then.[12]

Before long, Bob and Opal would have had to admit they were married anyway since a baby was on the way. Robert "Bobby" Russell Simpson was born November 8, 1935. Then on March 20, 1937, Jacqueline "Jackie" Jewel Simpson was born. Clyde thought his brother's son, Bobby Simpson, was so cute and handsome. He told Opal and Bob, "I want one just like that," pointing to Bobby. Audrey thought Jackie was "a little doll." Clyde and Audrey hoped to have children of their own someday.

The summer that Audrey and Clyde were married, Audrey went to Phoenix Lake by Watrous with Clyde's brother Glen. He took her there to get acquainted with his new sister-in-law. He was a swimmer and had won medals at the University of New Mexico. They went out in a boat to the middle of the lake where there was a marker sticking up that said "Fifteen Feet."

Glen said, "Let's get out of the boat and swim." They got out of the boat, but the boat had a mind of its own and took off. There was quite a wind, and the boat was swept across the lake and left them out in the middle. Glen took out after it. Audrey was left with nothing to hold on to except the little depth marker post sticking up out of the water. She paddled some and floated a bit, but she held on to the post all the time. She was not a swimmer. Glen finally caught the boat. He really had to swim "like the dickens" to get it, Audrey said later. It was an old thing and had a tin edge with nails sticking out. Audrey ran a nail across her leg and cut it badly. That was the last time she went swimming at the Phoenix Lake.[13]

Clyde was still working at the Home Café. Sometimes he would visit the Carringtons and carry on long theological discussions with them. They belonged to the Church of Christ and his leanings were toward the Pentecostal or "full gospel." They enjoyed their long talks. Clyde was a nervous person and his health was not always good. But he always kept his sense of humor. He talked to his dogs and even sang funny little songs to his pets. He gave funny little nick names to just about everyone, teasing them gently. He joked with his co-workers and family. As far as Audrey knew, he never had an enemy.

Clyde and Audrey wanted to have a child, but Audrey's doctor had told her she couldn't have children. Audrey cried tears of sorrow then. But in time she would be crying tears of joy.

36

First Business Enterprise: Pecos, New Mexico

abel had lost count of how many times she had moved. She and Vivian moved from Miss Reuter's in Pecos to the Elmer and Ann Watts' place up the river a mile or two, off the highway from San José. Audrey went to stay with the kids once when Mabel

and Vivian had to go some place. A few times she rode with Mr. W. I. Carrington. He sold Raleigh Products and traveled to the Pecos area—the Mill and Terrero mines—quite often. Audrey rode with him one morning to the Watts' turn off. When she was staying with Betty, Milly, Jessica and Frank, Audrey had quite an adventure. Betty ran to tell Audrey there was a snake on the path to the creek. Audrey got a hoe and shovel and killed a very big rattlesnake. The kids were impressed, but she'd seen her grandfather kill them with the heel of his shoe.

In 1936, eggs were ten cents a dozen. The Dow Jones Industrial Average stood at 149. Radio, known as "theatre of the mind," was popular. FDR's fireside chats were very well received. The nation was still in Depression, although the President was hopeful for better times.

Miss Emma Reuter ran a restaurant but was ill and needed help. She didn't want to close the café, so she asked Clyde and Audrey to run the place. She knew Clyde was an excellent cook. The couple decided to try this new enterprise and moved to Pecos in May of 1937. They worked very hard. Clyde did the cooking. Audrey did most of the baking and served as waitress and cashier. They both washed dishes and kept the place clean. They lived in the back room in the same building so they didn't have to pay rent.

Then Opal came with her two children, Bobby and Jacqueline, to help; and they stayed there a couple of months while Bob was gone. Bob and Clyde had tried several times to leave New Mexico and make money elsewhere. They once even went to the Simpson family farm in Oklahoma, near Elk City. But they nearly starved to death. They found out they didn't have the resources they needed to make a go of the farm.

One day a physician and his wife from Las Vegas stopped in at the Reuter's café and ordered hard boiled eggs "in the shell." Audrey thought she would "dress up" their plates and went ahead and shelled the eggs. The doctor was furious that she did not bring him the eggs as he had ordered them, "in the shell." She offered to go back and bring him more eggs, this time as ordered. But the couple said they would go ahead and eat the ones she had brought. Audrey was chagrined that she had not followed the customer's exact orders and had to take the brunt of his wrath.

However, humor as well as complaints, were a part of the daily life. One day some tourists stopped in. After they were seated by the window, the lady kept remarking about how lovely the mountains were.

"I've never seen anything like these mountains!" she exclaimed. "And those beautiful red and brown ridges that run horizontally across the mountains! They look so perfect, so unusual! Did the WPA put in those ridges?" she asked.

Audrey was aware of the many projects Franklin D. Roosevelt's Works

Progress Administration was accomplishing, but the ridges along the mountain cliffs were not among them. Audrey answered simply, "No the WPA did not build those. God did that."

The Terrero mines were going to close, and Clyde thought the business would drop off. For a while Terrero was a "fantastic boom town, born of the urge to tear cooper, gold, silver and zinc from the weather worn canyon walls of the upper Pecos." Terrero was named "due to the fact that animals came into that area to lick the earth for salt—a salt lick."The entire area was Terrero until the boom town grew around the first mine shaft, the old Katy-did mine which was later sold to the American Metals Company. But as the mining business slowed down, the restaurant suffered. They were barely making it as it was, and they needed the miners' business. Emma Reuter was amazed when Audrey told her they had made only eight dollars in profit in all the months they had been there. They paid Emma thirty dollars month, then bought groceries, paid electricity, and so on. It wasn't much money for the hours they spent working with the "wild" miners, preparing all the food. Emma Reuter was very disappointed, but they closed the café. Clyde and Audrey left in November of 1937. Their first business enterprise was hardly a success, but it was good experience.[1]

In her *Las Vegas Daily Optic* story, report Millicent L. Gensemer wrote: "In 1937, the Simpsons managed Miss Emma Reuter's Café in Pecos until the closing of the mine at Terrero slackened business and the couple returned to Las Vegas."[2]

Vivian was working with the Soil Conservation Service. They moved from Watts to San Ysidro, northwest of Albuquerque, on the Jemez River. They were there two or three months and then Vivian was transferred to Albuquerque in the summer of 1936, just before the beginning of the 1936-37 school year. That was the first year Milly ever went to school in the same place for a whole school year.

It was while the Shearers were living in Albuquerque that Frank had Scarlet Fever and was very sick. Milly recalled that Mabel found a centipede in Frank's bed and killed it. Frank, never one to lose his sense of humor, quipped, "What did you do that for? It was keepin' me warm." Mabel proceeded to put clean sheets on his bed.[3] When the café was closed, Clyde and Audrey went to visit Mabel and Vivian at 1115 South Walter in Albuquerque in the fall of 1937. Audrey said it was unbelievable that the folks had been in the same place for nearly two years! That had never happened before. Clyde and Audrey stayed a couple of weeks and slept on the front porch They considered moving to California, but instead, they put all their things in a two wheeled trailer and moved back to Las Vegas. Clyde decided he would get his old job back at the Home Café. Once again they asked Ernest Simpson if they could move in with him and he was agreeable to have them at his house on Tilden. Clyde had been working at the Home Café in Las Vegas for several years before they went to Pecos and rented Reuter's Café. When he got back from Albuquerque to apply for his old job, Self Counce, the owner, was glad to see Clyde back and immediately hired him again. Clyde went around the corner of the Simpson home to the grocery store and asked if he could get credit to buy some groceries. The owner asked him if he had a job and he explained that he was going to get one but had not started working yet. They would not give him credit. Even though they knew Ernest Simpson and had known the Simpsons for years, they still would not give Clyde even a nickel of credit. Clyde had a reputation for always paying his bills on time. He had never skipped out on paying. But in those days it was difficult to get credit. Audrey wrote in her notes, "The Grocery Store:"

> Three or four years later after Clyde and I were married he was temporarily out of a job. We were living at 1012 Tilden, down the alley from the store. Mr. Simpson brought stuff there. So Clyde asked for credit at the store. He was turned down and came back to the house looking like he had been whipped. They missed out on years of our grocery money. Clyde and I had a long list of promptly paid bills; no matter what else we did without we paid grocery and doctor bills first. Even when Clyde only made $7.00 a week. He was making $10 when C. C. [Crystal Clydine] was born.[4]

Clyde and Audrey moved out of Ernest Simpson's house as soon as they had rent money. Addie Simpson had decided to move back to Las Vegas from Albuquerque. She would come and go from Albuquerque to Las Vegas. She didn't like Las Vegas, but she came to stay with her husband Ernest periodically. When Addie moved back, Clyde and Audrey moved to the Carringtons where their little back house was again available to rent. Audrey recalled, "From 1012 Tilden we moved to the Carringtons. I had two 98 cent wrap-arounds that I had to wear for months. We went to every change of the movie."[5]

Life was good in those early married days. Audrey and Clyde hoped for a baby. They knew they would be good parents and able to support a child. But after three years, they still did not have a child. Audrey continued to hope.

37

Crystal: Brilliant, Beautiful, Blessed

Audrey had always wanted children. She had discussed her dreams when she was a girl, along with Opal and other friends such as Bill Reid. Bill always said he wanted two children. Audrey always said she wanted ten. Ironically, Bill ended up with ten children! Audrey had the two—and then much later one more to make three!

Audrey and Clyde had moved back into the little one room house that had been W.I. Carrington's shop. Audrey enjoyed her visits with the Carringtons. Clyde, too, enjoyed the Carringtons' company and they often had long conversations. Audrey told her of different places she had lived, including the Simpson home on Tilden. She said that Mr. Simpson told some of his relatives in Clovis that Clyde and Audrey were very considerate, that Clyde had always asked to move in and held up his end of the expenses. He told them that Clyde and Audrey were quiet so he could sleep during the day. He said other family members would just move in without asking. "I'm glad he feels like we are trustworthy and considerate. He mentioned that we helped pay the bills. I'm glad he appreciated our efforts."[1]

It was very hot that summer. Audrey fixed the room up again as well as she could. Sometimes she spent a few pennies to buy flowers to brighten up the room.

Clyde had kidney problems and went to a new doctor in town. The doctor was H. M. Mortimer. He arrived in Las Vegas in 1933 and opened up a private practice in the Crockett Building above Murphey's Drug Store. There were only a half dozen physicians in Las Vegas at the time: Dr. Crail, Dr. Muir, Dr. Fleming, Dr. Woodling, Dr. Howe and Dr. Kaser. In 1934 Dr. Mortimer moved his office to the second floor of the Masonic Temple Building. Clyde was one of his first patients when Dr. Mortimer opened his office in Las Vegas.[2]

Dr. Mortimer recalled in an interview in November of 1980: "I was charging two dollars for an office call. Clyde Simpson used to come in every week to pay on his bill. He never failed to come in and pay. When I found out later that Clyde was only making six dollars a week, I was appalled."[3]

After Dr. Mortimer found out how little Clyde was living on, the next time the patient came into the office to pay on his bill, the doctor told him the balance was only one dollar.[4]

Audrey went to Dr. Mortimer also. She was told she could never have children. She was very disappointed because she wanted children. But then she did get pregnant and she and Clyde were delighted.

> Before Crystal was born I was very ill. I remember going to church where Dr. Dillenger's office was later. A very nice old lady was the preacher. I remember once as I was leaving to go back down to Mrs. Carrington's little back house "home," that she said, "I hate for you to walk back down there alone so late and dark." I smiled and told her, "I never walk alone. The Lord is with me." "Bless you!" she said and a few other kind words for my attitude. I really felt that way. I couldn't have survived those bitter years without a deep feeling that the Lord was taking care of me.[5]

When Audrey was eight months pregnant, Dr. Mortimer said he would have to force the birth "or he might lose us both." Audrey later wrote:

> I went into the Las Vegas Hospital and took a lot of medicine to cause the baby to come. That perturbed me. Mrs. Simpson got a group of church ladies and prayed the baby wouldn't come until it was full term. There I lay for two days with birth pains every minute or two, and they were praying the baby wouldn't come. Daddy came up from Albuquerque and visited me there and Mother and family came from Capitan and then went on to the ranch. After two days of pounding pain Dr. Mortimer said I could go home but to stay in bed. Clyde took me home in the car. That night about three a.m. I began to have real pain and the water broke. So Clyde took me back to the hospital. I kept saying my prayers that I would have a good, live baby that I could help to grow up into a fine person.[6]

Clyde was delighted when his first daughter was born on July 30, 1938; but Audrey went through a very difficult time to bring her into the world. Years later, Audrey wrote in her notes, "Crystal:"

> I don't like to speak disparagingly of commercial establishments but hospitals and I have had a considerably disagreeable acquaintance. When little sis stepped on a rusty nail, Mama and Daddy plastered a bread and milk poultice on it and it got well. When one of my nine year old friends

went rabbit hunting and was accidentally shot in the stomach, he died in a hospital. Maybe that was when I got the idea that hospitals were a place to go to die. At the age of 12, I went through the door of the old Las Vegas Hospital at the junction of Mora Avenue and Seventh Street in Las Vegas, New Mexico. Mama had her first hospital-born baby, her fifth child. I was delegated to carry clean clothes to her and baby and take dirty diapers home to wash. It was a big, dark and gloomy adobe building, north doors opening off each side of a long entrance hall. Years later after the hospital moved to Sixth Street into the former Las Vegas YMCA building, the Mora Avenue building became an apartment house. Then Highlands University bought it and all the property along Ladies Home Avenue—and used the site for dorms like Arrott House. My next hospital experience was visiting mother and her 7th child at Las Vegas Hospital in 1932. It had a wide front door with a few steps up to the main floor. On the left, steps led to the upper floor. Mama's room was at the front and when I left I could look up and see her leaning on her elbow in bed, watching me go along the street. I remember being in that building when it was a YMCA. Then there was a sort of balcony along the south wall and we looked down on ball games or some other event. I never expected that six years later I would be in that same room expecting my first. I had continual trouble carrying CC [Crystal Clydine]. Maybe because when I was first married the doctor told me I probably would never conceive and if I did I couldn't carry a baby full time—as I was too small. Then three years later here comes Crystal. The doctor's office was on the 2nd floor of the Masonic building on Douglas Avenue. Just before the 8th month I could hardly make the stairs. I was so ill with uremic poisoning and high blood pressure and other complications that the doctor said he would have to force the birth or maybe lose us both. He also asked Clyde if it became necessary and he had to make a choice which should he save, mother or child. Of course Clyde said "Audrey." He knew me and a baby was an unknown quantity. I was put to bed and started on medication to induce labor. My father came up from Albuquerque to see me and Mother and family came from Capitan. The medication took effect and I had labor pains every two minutes for 24 hours. But no baby arrived. My mother in law and her church friends came and prayed for me, and prayed the baby wouldn't come until it was full time—with me lying there in agony as each pain hit. I was exhausted and wondering what the delay was doing to my baby. Finally the doctor gave up and sent me home, July 29th. Home was a tiny one room house back of 921 Lincoln.

About 3 a.m. July 30 I had to get up. When I did the water broke so it was back to the hospital for me. Clyde stayed with me all morning until time to go to work at the Home Café at 12 noon. He left just before they took me to the delivery room.

"Where is Clyde?" the doctor said.

"He had to go to work."

"Send for him," he said.

I was so weak and exhausted I could not give the final push. The doctor said, "I see its red hair," and told me to push but I did not have one ounce of strength left. I heard the noon whistle blow, 12 noon; he picked me up by the middle and somehow he squeezed and twisted me and the baby popped out. What a relief. No one can imagine how thankful I was and grateful to the doctor for his help. Clyde came and the doctor said he had a baby girl. I was taken back to my room and after a while the doctor asked if I could see him at the foot of the bed. I could in a hazy sort of way. My heartfelt thanks was still going out to him for helping me, for pulling me through. A young nurse brought my baby to me. I looked at her and the poor baby looked like a drowned rat. But she was mine! I had held her less than a minute when another nurse rushed in saying I wasn't to nurse her. My body was full of poison. That was the reason they forced the labor. I asked Dr. Mortimer to keep me in the hospital until I could take care of Crystal.[7]

Clyde was delighted to have a daughter. Crystal was born July 30, 1938. Clyde thought she was beautiful, but Audrey had seen newborns often enough before, and she knew Crystal was not a healthy, full term baby. She was skinny. The skin hung off her arms and legs and she was covered with fine hair. In those days there were no incubators, so the premature baby was just kept warm and fed often. Audrey kept a China tea cup in her hospital window to show how little Crystal was. The tea cup would sit right over her head and down over her tiny face! Later, Audrey wrote:

They said we had to name her right way. Clyde came up with "Crystal," the name of one of his cousins, then "Clydine" after him. The first afternoon a nurse was in my room when we heard a tiny meow. "How did a cat get in here?" she asked and went looking for it. After a while she came back and saw it was my baby. They didn't have an incubator then so kept her warm with hot water bottles. I stayed 12 days. The last day or two I got to feed her and bathe her.[8]

In those days there was no time off for sick leave or personal leave as most employers give now. When it was time to leave the hospital, Clyde took Audrey and Crystal home and then went to work. Audrey wrote:

> Self Counce gave him [Clyde] a note to pay whoever filled in for him [Clyde] while he went to the hospital when CC was born. I thought it was a gyp—just as it was a gyp when Glen gave Counce a $5 check that bounced, so he [Counce] took it out of Clyde's $6 per week wages. Glen was a school teacher at Kiowa (up near Raton) then.[9]

Audrey had no help taking care of the new baby, and she got very little sleep, as she had to feed Crystal often in order to get any nourishment down her. Later Audrey recalled:

> The day after I took her home I built a fire in the big old wood stove and got the already stifling house to about 100 degrees before I undressed her to bathe her. I had a little kitchen scale on the back of the stove. I laid her on it and she promptly kicked and slid off head first toward the floor. Like lightning I jumped and grabbed her by her ankles, saving her from a possibly fatal bump on the head as she hit the floor.[10]

Audrey struggled to do everything possible to help the new baby thrive. But as a new mother, she was exhausted and weak.

> After about a week of struggling to keep her alive, working an hour to force her to swallow one ounce of milk, I was out on my feet. One night about two a.m. I got up to feed her and was heating her bottle—no hot plate, no hot water. Build up the old wood range, get just enough fire to heat a tiny pan of water . . . for the little low ceiling room with one built in closet, a bed, baby basket, table, chair and built in cabinet. I was at the sink when I passed out and flopped onto the floor. I came to with Clyde pulling at me and in a scared voice crying, "Audrey !Audrey!" I recovered enough to continue spending one hour out of every two, day and night, working to help Crystal Clydine live through.[11]

Clyde and Audrey tried to get help but found that most people were not interested in staying with a mother and new baby. Audrey wrote:

When we got back to our house Clyde went and asked his sister to come to stay with me that afternoon as I was still very weak. He went to work at 12 noon and she came and sat a few minutes with her hat and summer jacket on. Finally she said she wanted to go to the show—so I said go on. So I staggered around looking after my dear little tiny one. I tried to feed her. They gave me a bottle of formula at the hospital to take home. I tried to get her to eat and she wouldn't, so I set the bottle back in the window—our only refrigerator. Later when I picked it up again I noticed it had curdled in that July heat. I didn't know what to do. I didn't have any canned Pet milk or Karo syrup to put in it. And wouldn't have until Clyde got home—unless Mary [Simpson] came back by after the show. She did, and I sent her for a can of Pet. [milk] But I still didn't have any syrup. I had to spend one hour out of two to get Crystal to take one ounce of milk. Trying to keep her awake and make her swallow. She just wanted to sleep because eight month babies aren't ready to wake up.[12]

Audrey did have several visitors after she got home from the hospital. Mrs. John Jones came to see her. Also, when Crystal was four months old, they went to Española to visit Glen Simpson and his wife Clarabelle and their daughter Marilyn. Several days after that three ladies came to visit to see the baby. In her manuscript, "Crystal," Audrey wrote:

I thought they were old maybe in late thirties or early forties. As they left, going across the yard I heard one say, "That baby won't live through." And the other agreed with her. I clasped Crystal to me and vowed, "By the grace of God she will live."[13]

Crystal did thrive. She began to improve and soon looked like a normal, healthy baby, although she was small. At her six week's check up, Crystal weighed six pounds.

When Crystal was about two or three months old, Clyde wanted to move to a place on Grand. It had a bay window on the front. Clyde rented an apartment in the back part of the house. Crystal was so tiny that Audrey could put her in a laundry sack and hang her on the cloths line in the backyard to take her picture. After living there a couple of months, Audrey and Clyde moved back to Carringtons. Ruth Carrington had been very disappointed when they moved, as she was so fond of Audrey and Clyde; so she was glad when they moved back—and they were too. This time the little two room house that faced Tenth Street was available, so they moved in there.

> We lived mostly at Mrs. Carringtons, one apartment or another. When we moved from the tiny one room house, we moved into the two room house, 410 Tenth Street. That was a nice, cute little house and we were happy there. Crystal rolled over the first time on that bed in the front room.[14]

Audrey was happy. She was comfortable in the two rooms and back porch—a great improvement over the one-room they'd rented before. However, the Carringtons wanted to make that little house on Tenth Street into a store, so the Simpson family had to move into another apartment. Audrey wanted to be the best mother and Christian she could.

> She [Crystal] was less than six months old when I decided to be baptized into the Church or Christ. The Church of Christ preacher came to see me there and talked to me about baptism. I knew very well about it from hearing Clyde lecture repeatedly. When I decided to be baptized, Mrs. S.[Addie Simpson, Clyde's mother] came to see me.
> "Why do you want to be baptized now and in that church?" she asked.
> "I believe in baptism, and want to be," I said.
> "Well you can be baptized any place, any time," she said.
> "Well, I haven't been and I want to be," I said.[15]

Apparently Mrs. Simpson would have preferred that Audrey be baptized in the church she was going to at the time; but Audrey was such a good friend of the Carringtons that she decided to be baptized in the church they attended.

> The little building on University near 7th street that belonged to Dr. Christie, a black osteopath in Las Vegas, was filled to capacity as it was revival time. I felt exalted and renewed when I came up out of the water. A couple of women hurried me into the dressing room cubby hole.[16]

Audrey was glad she was baptized. She had been saved in the Nazarene church while still in high school but had never had the opportunity to be baptized. She wrote: "When Crystal was about four months old, I had been going to the Church of Christ with Mrs. Carrington. I was baptized and I felt renewed and clean and holy."[17]

When Addie Simpson came to Las Vegas to visit, Audrey took Crystal to

275

their house. Addie wouldn't allow her husband Ernest to hold Crystal.

"He's too dirty," she would say. "He can't touch the baby."

"He'd been touching her all along!" Audrey exclaimed whenever she talked about those times. "Whenever he'd come to their house, he would sit down in the rocker and hold Crystal."

Audrey liked to let Crystal's Grandpa Simpson play with her. Just because he worked at the round house at the railroad depot and got dirty was no reason to keep him from the baby. Mr. Simpson would come home and wash his hands and play with Crystal when his wife wasn't around. As he rocked her, he called his granddaughter "my little humming bird."[18]

Audrey was happy as a mother and homemaker. She had always wanted a baby. She had admired the famous Dionne quintuplets, born in Ontario, Canada in May of 1934. They were the first known quintuplets to survive infancy. Audrey wished she could have at least half a dozen children. "I'd take the frailest ones," she said to herself, "and nurture them so they could have happy lives."[19]

Being premature, Crystal was certainly frail. But she began to blossom under her mother's constant care and her father's proud, doting, playful ways. She was becoming what Audrey would later call her: brilliant and bright as the name of Crystal implied, like a beautiful, clear crystal. She had been blessed with the ability to overcome adversity. The dire predictions of the early visitors—that Crystal would not survive—did not come to pass.

Crystal would shine as a star on a clear, brilliant night. Under her parents' love and care, she would be a precious gem, crystal clear as a diamond, growing to inspire the lives of many throughout the years. Audrey was thrilled to have her own baby to care for.

38

Forest Fire!

There were two words Audrey came to dread more than almost any others: forest fire. Audrey had seen fires before, but she had never been in a forest fire until the summer of 1939.

Audrey was living at the Old Homestead Ranch at the time. Vivian and his father had reconciled. Vivian kept the deed to the place and

Grandfather was agreeable. The family could move back to the Old Homestead Ranch. However, Vivian's job with the Soil Conservation Service kept them from moving back there for quite a while.

Audrey and Clyde asked if they could live at the Old Homestead Ranch and were given permission to move to there in late 1938 or early 1939. Clyde stayed with his father in Las Vegas during the week and came out to the mountains on his days off. Often he rode a bicycle to the ranch and back when no vehicle was available. They moved into the middle cabin that Vivian had built for Opal and Audrey. Vivian had built several little bedroom sized cabins for the kids and had one for himself for his office. There he could do his correspondence, writing, reading, and, in later years, would have his amateur radio equipment set up. However, at this time that cabin was empty.

Shortly after Audrey and Clyde moved to the ranch, Opal and Bob moved there too. Audrey and Clyde then moved into Vivian's little cabin and Bob and Opal moved into the middle cabin.

Crystal was eleven months old in June, 1939. Someone wanted to buy "The Forty" part of the Shearer property on Falls Creek. A forest fire broke out in the Falls Creek area. Audrey suspected the man who was looking at the property accidentally started it. A fire crew was over there working on that fire. At the same time, someone in a wagon was traveling around on the National Forest behind the main ranch, probably looking for fire wood to cut. Apparently someone lit a cigarette and threw the match out in the dry grass. Another forest fire started up the canyon right behind the ranch houses. That was on June 26, 1939.

Audrey could see the smoke and smell it, but she didn't know where the fire was. She walked across the canyon and up on the south hill with Crystal. From there she saw that the fire was right behind the ranch, not up on Barillas peak, but much closer.

Opal and Bob had gone to town that morning in Clyde's old Nash, so there was no transportation that day until they got back. Apparently they had taken Grandfather with them, as Audrey, Clyde and Crystal were alone at the ranch. Clyde walked to Santillanes Canyon to the U.S. Ranger Station to report the fire. But the station was locked and no one was around. He couldn't get in to use the telephone. Grandfather Shearer had been upset with the Forest Service and made them take the telephone out of his house, so there was no telephone there either.

After Audrey had observed the distance of the fire, she went back to the cabin and packed some things. Clyde had not returned yet. She knew he would walk for help if he couldn't get it at the Ranger Station, so she did not expect him.

She hurried to get away from the approaching fire. Crystal's little white shoe was lost on the other ridge. It was her first pair of white ankle high "tie" shoes. There was no time to go back and look for it. Later she did, but the fire went through there so it probably burned. When the day ended, Audrey had ruined her shoes, too. She had walked so much that the soles were nearly torn off and they were ragged. In later years, Audrey recalled in a taped interview:

> Bill Reid was up on the Lookout Tower on Barillas Peak and he called the Forest Service Headquarters and told them that they needed at least fifty men up on "our" fire—right now! The two fires were really taking off because it was June—the dry month—and it was really dry that year! He called on the "Lookout" telephone and spoke to Mrs. Bruehl. She said that her husband would take care of it. She didn't think Bill had any right giving orders to her husband. He was Forest Ranger in this area! That's probably the reason Mr. Bruehl and the Forest Service men did not get up to the ranch until almost dark! I don't know where he had been all day—maybe on the other fire in Falls Creek—but the fire over here at our place got a "head start" on them. Some of the men came up from San Geronimo earlier and began fighting it. It had gotten down by the fence right behind the houses.[1]

The men from San Geronimo, nine miles west of Las Vegas on the Tecolote River, were fighting the fire as hard as they could without sophisticated equipment. But the fire raged.

Audrey didn't know the fire had been reported by Bill. She didn't know whether there was a chance that it would be put out any time in the near future. She put Crystal, along with some clothes and necessities—and the suitcase of valuables—in the baby buggy and started walking up to the flat, open field they called "The Mesa." The fire was getting so close Audrey thought it would take the houses. By then it was burning down against the garden fence and the houses were only a short distance away. Audrey got up to The Mesa and then walked on down to the gate and the cattle guard going out of the "sheep fence." Suddenly a big tree right beside her seemed to explode and burst into flames. That fire had jumped a half mile—from the back fence down in the garden area up across the canyon—and started a fire right where Audrey was, beyond The Mesa, with Crystal. Audrey grabbed Crystal out of the buggy and began to run. She had always carried her keepsakes in that suitcase that Dammuzzy gave her as a wedding gift. But this was a matter of survival. She just took Crystal and ran, leaving the baby buggy and the suitcase behind.

When Audrey saw that the fire didn't seem to be jumping any more—it was just furiously burning the tree that exploded—she decided she could go back and get the baby buggy with the necessities and suitcase in it. She got back to it, put Crystal in it again, and pushed it all the way to the nearest village of San Geronimo, about four miles away. She had to get some place where she could get some food, water, and help. She was sure the fire was going to take the ranch houses. She got to the telephone in San Geronimo and called town, looking for Bob Simpson. She also called the Forest Service to report the fire.

Bob, Opal and Grandfather finally came home. Tthey evidently thought there wasn't any immediately danger from the fire. Clyde had returned by then and came down to San Geronimo in the old Nash. He picked up Audrey and Crystal and took them back to the ranch. As they went back, they saw the Forest Service people just coming in—just before dark. They were so late getting to the fire that Audrey suspected Mrs. Bruehl failed to give the message of Bill's call to Mr. Bruehl. If she had given him the message, he had delayed in taking action.

Mabel and Vivian were living in Capitan, New Mexico. They got word about the fire and drove to the ranch. By the time the folks arrived, the fire was contained. When it was totally out, the folks went back home to Capitan but they left Milly and Betty. Betty had been living with Vern and Mable in Albuquerque, but she was back; so now the two girls stayed with Audrey and Clyde for a few weeks. They slept in Milly's cabin, the one Vivian had built for her when she was about four years old. Audrey later recalled:

> Those two, Betty and Milly, put a little fun in our dull life once—maybe several times! The one that stands out in my mind was the time they almost set another forest fire! They went up to the "outhouse" (a two holer) and were experimenting with Clyde and/or Bob's cigarette papers and tobacco. They got their cigarettes rolled and when they lit them, one or both of them, threw the match down the hole. The hole was full of toilet paper. Anyway, the papers down below began to burn! The girls were scared to death! Betty ran down to the house yelling "Fire!" By the time Bob, Clyde, Opal and I got up there with buckets of water, we found Milly holding her head above the seat by holding herself up there with her arms extending, hanging on for dear life, and stomping the fire out with her feet! It could have been very serious and Milly knew it! The outhouse was surrounded by big trees. Milly knew that if the outhouse burned the whole forest would catch fire! She had to put it out! She was very thin and she could slip through the hole and avoid another forest fire! You wouldn't have expected her to jump in there with her feet in all

that mess to put out a fire! It really gave us all a very good laugh—many good laughs every time we'd think about it! I think that cured both of them of experimenting with cigarettes and matches![2]

Somehow the children escaped various dangerous situations. In the summer of 1941, when Crystal was three and Frank was about nine, Mabel and Vivian were watering and weeding the garden they had planted. Crystal was running ahead of Audrey as she was walking up out of the creek. Frank was playing on the old logs left from the saw mill days. Suddenly, one of the logs began to roll and Frank rode it for a little while. Then he disappeared down into the log pile. Audrey thought he would be killed. She ran up to where he'd been. He got up and walked out from between two of the logs. They had not crushed him! He wasn't even hurt even though he fallen between two logs. Audrey said he had a good guardian angel!

Living in the mountains gave the children a good education about such things as nature, gardening, and wildlife. Before they were grown, the children were very well aware of the importance of soil conservation, not only because Vivian worked for the Soil Conservation Service, but because both he and his father had always been aware of the need to conserve the natural resources of the country.

In July of 1943, Charles Vivian Shearer, Assistant Soil Conservationist, gave a lecture on "Soil and Moisture Conservation" at New Mexico Highlands University. Part of that lecture entitled, "Man's Stewardship of the Earth," follows:

> One-fourth of our crop land and one-fourth of all land gone is the record of our stewardship in this great country of ours. The rate of loss is alarming. In crop land alone, it represents a loss each year of about one million acres.
>
> We are told that three billion tons of soil are washed and blown from our lands each year. Now let us try to reduce this to some sort of a figure that will make it comprehensible. Suppose that we are loading dump trucks with it. The dump trucks, each carrying a big load of four tons, travel along spaced 52.8 feet apart, or one hundred to the mile. Therefore, to carry the total annual load of soil lost from our lands, our truck train would have to be 7,500,000 miles long. The mean distance to the moon is about 240,000 miles. Therefore our train of dump trucks would reach more than fifteen times around the route to the moon and back again, or 31 times one way.[3]

Vivian emphasized the importance of conserving the natural resources that were here when the European invaded this continent. "Self-preservation calls for action," he said.[4]

His father, R. A. Shearer, spent much time fighting soil erosion on the Old Homestead Ranch. On the "The Mesa" where Audrey and Opal grew corn one summer, he had built a rock wall, carrying and stacking rocks to fit together until he had a wall over six feet high.[5] He did not use any cement. A photograph of Grandfather Shearer standing against that wall was taken in about 1948. It was taller than he was. Today that wall stands only about two feet high. The soil has filled in that much. Had not the wall been there, it would have washed away down to Falls Creek, down to the Tecolote, down to the Rio Grande River, and out to the Gulf of Mexico.

Audrey always worked on erosion and taught her girls to "fill in ditches" whenever they could. If there was the beginning of an arroyo, they would fill it in as well as they could with rocks and sticks. "We don't want our soil to wash away," she'd say. "Let's retain our soil." Vivian had said in his lecture: "An adequate vegetative cover is the best erosion control means that can be found. It is Nature's own way of doing it."[6]

Mabel had always had a little vegetable garden and a flower garden whenever they stayed in one place long enough. After Vivian retired, Mabel always had a little garden. She had to have flowers. She loved her pink and her red hollyhocks. She also loved her many colored pansies. She accumulated a few house plants and was fond of her African violets and her Christmas cactus.

Like her mother, Audrey always planted flowers. She especially liked pansies, hollyhocks, sweet peas, lilacs, and roses, especially Spanish roses—yellow roses. She sometimes quoted the well known statement: "If I had but two loaves of bread, I would sell one and buy hyacinths, for they would feed my soul."

39

The Ten Dollar House

In the fall of 1939, Mabel came and got the kids from the ranch before school started. Vivian worked in Capitan and they lived there until the summer of 1940 when the family moved to Santa Fe. Bob and Opal and their two children, Bobby and Jackie, moved too. Clyde was working at the Home Café in Las Vegas and only came out to the ranch on his day off. Audrey stayed at the ranch with Crystal, living in Vivian's little cabin, until about December, 1939. She was doing her best to look after the place and Grandfather Shearer.

Audrey noticed that Grandfather Shearer seemed paranoid. He thought Bob Simpson was hiding out in the woods and feared him. He wouldn't open the door to Audrey, even when she brought him food. He put a logging chain around the engine of his Model T and put a big padlock on it so nobody would steal the motor! Grandfather made it obvious that he did not want anyone else around. He said he could take care of himself and made it clear that he wanted to be left alone. Clyde got Nash Romero who worked with him at the Café to bring him out. They packed all their things and moved back to town.

The Simpson family lived at the Carrington's place again. Since the little two-room house had been made into a store which Ruth Carrington owned and managed, it was no longer available to rent. But they moved into an apartment upstairs in the main, big brick house. The Carringtons lived downstairs. Their apartments were always full because their rent was reasonable and they kept everything in good repair.

About that time, Clyde bought a little puppy for two-year-old Crystal—a white collie. All the other puppies were brown and white, but this one was all white except for a little brown about her ears and face. They tied her to the clothesline in the back yard so she could run back and forth on the line. Unlike Skip, she appeared to be a stay-home dog. They named her Bonnie Snowwhite Lassie. For two-year-old Crystal, she was the perfect pet—loyal, intelligent, affectionate, gentle, and protective.

In the summer of 1941, Mabel and Vivian moved back to Las Vegas from Santa Fe. They found a house at 409 Eleventh Street, just a block from the Carrington house. It was there that Vivian became interested in amateur radio.

He put up a "ham" radio station in a big walk-in closet and passed the test to become an amateur operator.

Mabel and Vivian moved to the ranch every summer, then back to town every fall to keep the kids in school. Later, Vivian worked at the Federal Building, which is now the Rough Riders' Museum. The Shearers rented the house across the street at 728 Grand Avenue and kept that house until Jessica and Frank graduated from high school. It was not until 1946 that the big adobe house at the ranch was finished, with the help of a little money Mabel inherited. At that time Mabel began moving things into the adobe ranch house, both from town and from Grandfather Shearer's attic where things were stored.

In 1941, Clyde got sick. He had to quit working. They moved to the basement of the folks' house, the Loren Jones house. They stayed there for a while and then the folks gave them permission to move out to the ranch and build a house on the property where the original Shearer homestead house had been—on the one hundred and sixty acres that R. A. Shearer and his wife Ollie had first homesteaded.

Since Clyde was sick and couldn't work, they couldn't pay rent. He had kidney problems. He could work a while but would have to rest. Dr. Mortimer gave him various medicines. However, most of them had little effect. Later when sulfa medicines became available, Clyde quickly improved. The couple could have continued to live with the Shearers but Audrey didn't want to stay there very long, feeling it might be an imposition.

In later years, Audrey started writing an autobiography. Her rough draft was simply called "My Book." She wrote about the various aspects of house building as an important part of her life. In her notes, Audrey wrote:

> However, I knew that on the south east corner of my mother and stepfather's Old Homestead ranch, we could build a cabin and live for practically nothing. Earlier I had seen the handwriting in the European war news and had insisted we get new tires before rationing hit. Those new tires proved to be money in the bank, for to finance our house building venture, Clyde traded our new Model A tires with his boss, Self Counce. For each tire he got an old Counce tire and ten dollars to boot. That gave us $40 plus his final week's wages of $15. We used most of that $15 to pay our grocery bill and buy staples such as flour, sugar, salt, coffee, beans and potatoes.[1]

Consequently, Audrey and Clyde moved to the Old Homestead Ranch to build a little cabin. Audrey and Clyde had about twenty-five dollars and Clyde's last pay check. It wasn't much to last all summer until Clyde could get well enough to go back to work.

They loaded up the old Model A, got to the top of Shearer Creek hill, cut off down through the brush and went on down in the corner of the Shearer place, almost to the fence line. Audrey and Clyde then found a couple of trees where they could string a rope between them. Then they hung a piece of canvas to make a semblance of a tent. They carried the bed out on top of the car. They set up their bed under their imitation tent and slept there in the woods until they got a cabin built.

Audrey later published a story in *New Mexico Magazine* entitled, "Ten Dollar House." She described the trip to the property on May 7, 1941. They "built road" in spots. They also waded in swift, high water to remove boulders so that the fords would be passable. Audrey explained that after bumping over the last of those eighteen miles from Las Vegas, the car straddled oak brush, jumped a few gullies, and reached their Shangri-La. Audrey then wrote that the fantastically loaded jalopy "erupted four occupants." They were "Clyde, weak with a chronic illness; Crystal Clydine, proud of being almost four; Bonnie Snowwhite Lassie, indispensable Collie, and the one who used to be a mountain maid."[2]

Audrey was, of course, referring to herself—"the one who used to be a mountain maid." She was still a mountain girl, married with a child, but with a youthful spirit that welcomed the brisk, pine-scented breeze that caressed the snow-tipped peaks and rippled the water of the little stream that ran through the meadows and canyons. Though a wife and mother, she still had the pure heart and spirit of the carefree maiden she had been when she first roamed the mountains with her little sister Opal. She still loved those mountains and would grow to love them even more as the dream of living there began to grow more solid.

> On May 7, 1941, dead tired from fording high water in the mountain streams, fighting oak brush as we cut and pushed along an overgrown track, we arrived at our building site. Clyde stopped the Model A against a thick stand of pines.[3]

Audrey described in the article that she and Clyde wanted to build a cabin and that his health only permitted his working part time. They chose "unimproved timber land one mile north of the San Geronimo Ranger Station cabin."[4] The mountains seemed to them to be the only place where a couple of month's rest would restore health and strength. Audrey explained that they had put all their savings in War Bonds, so they had very little money to work with.

Each pay day the previous winter they had bought a necessary tool. When Clyde quit working, their fifty dollars in cash seemed to be enough for two month's groceries, cost of a cabin, and miscellaneous. They had very few tools, but they had pioneer spirit and "the urge to do as our forefathers did."[5] Audrey explained that although neither of them was a carpenter, they believed they could build a house, even though they had never before built as much as a dog-house. They had seen others build and they had read books on building. Hence, they had the confidence that they could put together something adequate enough to keep the rain and wind out.

> For house building we had gradually been collecting tools. We had a heavy double bit ax, a light axe, a hatchet, a hand saw, hammer, several pounds of spikes and shingle nails, a yard stick, a shovel, hoe, rake, a couple of 30 foot ropes, and a roll of heavy crochet thread for string. At the time we didn't know what we needed, so we didn't know what we lacked. If we had known, finances would have prevented its acquisition anyway. For later building we found a cross cut saw, a chain saw, a square, a lever and a carpenter's steel tape measure were almost indispensible items.[6]

The brisk mountain air and the fact that they were "on the most peaceful 160 acres this side of heaven" gave them a new lease on life.[7] In her article, "Ten Dollar House," Audrey described how at first they had unloaded their good double bed and child's bed from the top of the car, strung a piece of canvas over a pole between two trees, and the Simpsons "were at home under the stately old pines where we planned to build our cabin."[8]

> We jumped from the car and went from tree to tree looking for a likely spot to hang the raggedy piece of canvass that would be our shelter until we built a house. We fastened a rope between two trees and hung the canvas over it, making a sort of lean-to shelter. Then we set up our double bed and the baby bed and we were "home."[9]

Audrey continued her story by explaining that after they ate some sandwiches, they walked around looking for a building site to the west of where they had parked. The site was near the location of the old Shearer store and post office where there was a clearing under some huge old pine trees. Audrey wrote that the store "flourished while serving the many San Geronimo, Mineral Hill and other area residents."

Then World War I called the family away to the war effort. Now a little more than a quarter of a century later, nothing remained but a few scattered, rotting boards and the outline of the barn's foundation. When the Shearers returned in 1918, they moved their establishment over the hill into Hyde Canyon.[10]

Audrey and Clyde walked over the land where the post office and store had been. Audrey wrote:

> "We don't want to build so close to all those lost dreams," I said. So we turned east and went a few hundred yards in that direction. Under trees probably only 150 years old we found a fairly level spot.[11]

Audrey wrote that when they had selected a spot, they had to clear the oak brush from part of it. Clyde used the light ax and Audrey used the hatchet to cut the brush to clear a space for the cabin. "We had a spot approximately 14 x 14 feet cleared by the time the stars began to bloom in the evening sky. So we called it quits for the first day."[12]

They were up before the sun the next morning. Audrey built a fire in the center of the spot they had cleared for the house. Then she carried water from the spring in the canyon and boiled coffee in a tin bucket propped on two rocks at the center of the little fire.

> I also fried eggs in the Dutch over a friend, Kay, had given me when she moved to Socorro. These were probably the last eggs we would have all summer so we enjoyed them as the sun came over the east ridge.[13]

Audrey explained that there is scarcely a foot of land in that section of the Sangre de Cristo mountains that is completely flat, so they had to level an area for the floor. Clyde dug and shoveled. As he shoveled, he threw the dirt from the high side to the lower side so that the floor was comparatively level after a few hours of digging. Then they trampled the dirt down.

> While Clyde dug Crystal and I hauled rocks from the hillside in her little red wagon. This was the small child's wagon. In later years we bought a large 36-inch wagon. A wagon is an almost indispensable time and labor saving device—wheels are wonderful for moving everything from rocks to garden produce, such as corn and pumpkins.[14]

Clyde chopped down pine trees, trimmed off branches, measured the sixteen foot length they wanted, and chopped off the top. They cut the logs sixteen feet long in order to be sure to have a full twelve foot by twelve foot room. After the logs were laid up they found that they might have built a fourteen foot room instead. Crystal helped as they loaded and hauled rocks in her little red wagon for a foundation. In later years they acquired a wheelbarrow for carrying rocks and for use in mixing cement.

They dragged the cut logs to the cabin site. Some were pulled with a chain by hand and some were dragged behind the car. Finally enough logs were on site.

Audrey explained that she found four extra large rocks with at least one fairly flat surface. They would serve as cornerstones to hold the bulk of the weight of the logs where they joined at the corners.

> With the floor looking level we measured out a 12 foot square with the yard stick. At each corner of the square we placed one of the large stones. Clyde dug out a slight depression, three or four inches deep, to place them in so that they wouldn't slide around when the logs were set on them. As we placed the stones we realized that our 12 x 12 foot room would not be that large, unless we gave ourselves a little more space. The logs, centered on the stones, would round into the room. So we moved the stones out about 4 inches, so that we would have a 12 x 12 foot room. As it turned out, we still lacked an inch or two after the logs were up.[15]

Audrey explained that after they had measured, they took her white crochet thread and, using it as a chalk line, tried to get each stone in a straight line from its opposite corner.

Audrey described how they put up the walls, using timber from straight trees "about eight inches in diameter at the bottom and five or six inches in diameter towards the top. Tall perfectly straight trees we called lodge pole pines." She explained that since they wanted fourteen foot lengths, some of the logs made two house logs when cut in two lengths. They used forty-six logs in the walls. After Clyde cut the trees, Audrey measured them with a yard stick and Clyde cut each to the right length. Audrey used the light axe or hatchet to cut off the limbs. They did not peel the logs, as they were in a hurry to get a roof over their heads, although they knew peeled logs would last longer. Clyde's illness demanded that he rest often, sometimes taking a nap.[16]

Clyde moved the logs up to the cabin site and they used the larger logs for the bottom logs. Clyde cut a dent in the lower side of the log to fit over each corner stone so the log would stay in position. Clyde notched the lower side of a log in a U shape and placed it over the log below it. Then he made a shallow U notch in the top of the same log for the next log to fit into when it was put into position. However, they later discovered that moisture collected in the notches so in later cabins they did not cut a notch in the top of the log; they only cut the bottom of the top log, fitting it over the lower log. In that way moisture was prevented from collecting in the hollowed out area. In later cabins they also used a big spike to hold the corner logs in place and to make the interlocking area stronger.[17]

Within two days of their arrival at the building site, they had thirteen logs in place. Audrey cleared an area outside in a wide space, dug a hole and surrounded it with rocks for a camp fire. She kept a tin bucket for coffee sitting in or near the fire, "as Clyde was a slave to hot coffee, a habit he picked up as a café cook."[18]

Audrey enjoyed cooking over a campfire. She dug a hole in the middle of a large open space, built a fire in it, put her Dutch oven on the fire, and covered the hole with an old piece of tin. Then she covered the whole thing with earth, leaving only a tiny vent for air. Sometimes when the wind blew, sparks would be drawn out; Audrey watched her cooking area carefully. She didn't want to start a forest fire! Audrey's article in *New Mexico Magazine* stated:

> An important part in any building project is fuel to keep up the workers' strength. At the time we built the Ten Dollar House we were so poverty stricken that pancakes, potatoes and gravy and beans were our main diet. I fixed at least four meals a day and kept snacks on hand, even although the snack might only be a cold hot cake. You don't expect your car or other machinery to run without gas and oil, or fuel. So workers cannot be expected to work on empty calories—or little or no food. If you have oleo and syrup or honey to put on the cold hotcake, or biscuits, or bread, dotted with sugar, it is a quicker pick-me-up. Also a cold boiled potato with oleo and salt on it will put strength back into an exhausted ax man's arm. I baked biscuits over the camp fire in the Dutch oven but I never could get enough baked at once to have leftovers. They were always gobbled up hot. One of our favorite meals was potatoes, onions, and a couple of strips of bacon cut up fine and placed in a tin lard pail full of salted water. The lid of the pail had some nail holes in it so it wouldn't explode when left on the fire all morning. By noon it was cooked down to a heavy soup. Pinto beans were the hardest to cook. I would look them over in the evening and soak them all night in plenty of water. Early the next morning they were put in a lard bucket, or Dutch oven, whichever

I had empty, and placed over the fire. Sometimes I built a fire in a hole in the ground, until I had a deep bed of coals. Then I would place the beans in their container with lots of water on them and put them in the hole. Sometimes I cooked them overnight this way. It took seven or eight hours for them to reach the non-rattle stage. If they rattle around when stirred with a spoon they are not done. Now days we used pressure cookers and after soaking all night an hour under pressure cooks them well done. I also baked potatoes by rolling them in a layer of clay and placing them in the ashes under the fire. At times I just laid the potato in ashes or at the fire's edge. If one plans outdoor cooking for any length of time it would pay to build up a foundation of rocks to about waist level and build the fire in a depression on this rock pile. This is easier on the back and also prevents small children falling into the fire, or clothing catching. A log frame filled with dirt waist high with the fire in the center on the dirt is also a good idea. However, we did none of these as we did not expect to cook outside for any length of time. I just squatted beside the very small circle to cook. Never build a big fire—you can't get close enough to it to handle pots and pans unless it is a small fire. Besides, you might set the grass on fire and start a forest fire. Several rocks, placed solidly around the fire, help hold heat and they make a foundation for strips of iron if you can find some. These strips will hold pots up off the fire so that it can burn better. Rocks also make a prop to lean skewered hot dogs over—or kish-ka-bobs. With problems of survival, I was too busy to try anything fancy, so confined my out-door cooking to the Dutch oven, tin buckets and gallon tin cans.[19]

The family was in bed by seven p.m., listening to the sleepy turkey calls echoing across the canyon.[20] They planned their activities for the next day before falling asleep. They planned to use a hard packed adobe floor and put linoleum on top. So they brought out linoleum on the jalopy fenders.

After the logs were in place, Clyde went to town with a neighbor in a truck and brought out gallon tin cans they had collected and saved to use for the roof. The sides of the cans were opened with tin snips and flattened out, then put in place like shingles. While Clyde was gone, a wind storm came up. Audrey decided she and Crystal should sleep in the car.

Being out so many miles from somewhere, with mountain lions prowling around, bear cubs following hungry mamas, coyotes yelping, and great horned owls curdling my blood, I was really glad for an excuse to sleep with the car window between us and the elements.[21]

After Clyde returned, they finished putting up the log walls. As soon as a door was cut with the handsaw, they put a canvas over one corner for a roof and moved inside out of the wind. There, in spite of wind coming through the unchinked cracks between the logs, they could be comfortable. They dug a hole in the middle of the floor for the cooking fire. By covering it well, they were able to add more variety to their meals without endangering the forest, as they were protected somewhat from the wind. Audrey wrote:

> Clyde chopped the sides flat on the eight pieces of logs, each a yard long taken from the doorway so that they would fit together evenly. After they were more or less flat on two sides, he spiked four of them in the center of the front wall, one on top of the other. He also set four of them up one at a time on the back wall, spiking each to the one below. These would give some slant to our roof when it was finished. With these in position we were ready for the ridge pole, the main support for the center of the roof across the cabin from north to south. Because ours would be a different sort of roof we decided we would have to have two ridge poles. It was quite a struggle getting good sized logs in place on top of the four stacked and nailed logs. We used a rope and chain, pulling and hauling to raise them to the top of the wall and then to get them in position. After they were on top of the gable ends, Clyde then nailed them in place, side by side, so that they could not roll or move. After the center ridge poles were in place we cut small trees to use as rafters from the walls to the ridge poles. One ridge pole might have been enough but we were afraid that using the green trees might be too much weight for just one, so we settled on two for safety's sake. Besides, some winter there might be three or four feet of snow on the roof; it could cave it in if we did not make it extra strong.[22]

Most of the time the weather was good and the family enjoyed the fresh air and sunshine while making progress on the house. There was time to sit and enjoy the sunset or to listen to the birds in the trees or to enjoy the wild flowers along the path to the creek. Every day there was a different sunset behind the western purple mountains. "No artist can match those colors," Clyde observed.

Audrey had time to reflect. She wrote several articles of a philosophical nature. She had read a book called *The Enchanted Spring* and thought it was very thought provoking.[23] She wrote an article to submit for publication entitled,

"The Urge Behind the Ego." It is not known whether the item was published or not.

> Every human action may be traced to a hunger for Beauty. That which is sordid and ugly has been caused by . . . some misguided human being for loveliness. The answer to every action in all mankind's striving is a longing for beauty in its various forms.
>
> This hungering hunt for beauty is behind every act of mankind. We do not seek riches in order to gain horror and filth. We want money in order to acquire more beautiful things. It takes unhurried leisure to create and enjoy beauty. We hunt riches that we may acquire the time to enjoy to the utmost all beauty to our tastes—landscapes, art, jewels, or the written word.
>
> Those who have been most remembered are those who in some manner have helped increase the loveliness of the world. When we recognize the fact that the goal of every human is the same in different forms, then and only then can we begin to work together to really attain every man's desire, more and greater beauty.[24]

Audrey treasured that beauty so much that she was willing to give up the luxury of city living for the "rough" living on the county. But a roof over one's head is almost a necessity, so she and Clyde continued to build their little cabin. A neighbor gave Clyde a door and windows from an old building which had been torn down. They had little monetary value, but they served the needs of the little log cabin very well. Audrey wrote about how Clyde put in the door:

> As soon as we had the 46 logs up for the walls Clyde cut a door in the front of the cabin. He nailed an old 2 by 6 and some one inch boards rescued from the old barn area to each side of the place where the door would be. We chinked between the logs on each side of the door area—that is placed small logs in the spaces between the wall logs to hold them level and solid when the door was cut out. With the 2 x 6 on one side of the door area and a couple of flat one inch boards nailed on the inside of the wall to hold the logs in position while the door opening was being sawed out, and with nothing but the hand saw to work with, Clyde struggled to get the eight logs sawed in on each side of the 36 inch door space. As soon as he had the door opening cut he nailed a 2 x 6 on the bottom log, which was not cut. This he placed against the ends of the freshly cut logs in the door opening and put a spike through the 2 x 6 into

each log. The bottom log was not cut in order to make the walls stronger. This made the door casing and held the wall logs in position at the same time. By being nailed tightly they could not move in any direction. Once they were solid and the door casings in place, Clyde hung the door which a friend had given us when a building was torn down in town. It was a fancy door with two glass panels in the upper half, not exactly appropriate for a humble log cabin, but we were very glad to have it. In hanging the door, that is putting hinges on it and fastening them to the 2 x 6 so the door would swing in, Clyde put them on upside down; but we didn't know the difference until someone told us they were not on right. Anyway, they worked. Once the door was cut we hung our canvass over one corner of the house and set our beds and belongings under it. We felt safe and some warmer inside four walls—even though we could look out in any direction between the logs.[25]

Next Clyde chopped eight blocks—pieces of logs removed from the door—until they were flat on two sides. He spiked four of them, one piled on top of the next, to each end of the cabin with huge spikes. When the ridge pole was placed on these, the roof would have a proper slant. They had a struggle placing two good sized trees in place for the ridge pole. Those two were toe-nailed to the blocks. Small poles were laid like rafters from the center pole to the cabin wall. Then they were ready for the roof, a most unusual roof, as described by Audrey:

> We had been planning our cabin for some time so Clyde had saved gallon tin cans at the café. We had more than 200 of them for our roof. We had stored them in a friend's garage in Las Vegas and a neighbor with a truck had hauled them out for us. In the evenings, after it became too late to work on the cabin, we used hand type kitchen can openers to cut the bottoms out of the gallon fruit cans. Then we cut down the side of the cans to open them up flat to make into shingles for our house.[26]

But the cans would not lie flat. Clyde put them on anyhow and tried to smooth them out, but they bulged up so the roof wasn't tight. Audrey explained:

> We placed the poles (rafters) the distance apart that the gallon cans opened out. We were ready for the tin can shingles on May 15. [1941] We lapped the flattened out tin cans like shingles and after a few feet found they really wouldn't do. The tin tended to bend, trying to resume its tin can shape. This left small cracks at the lower side of the shingle

where it lapped over the can below it. We realized our tin can roof would shed rain in the summer but snow would blow through these cracks. We wanted a year around cabin so we had to improvise some more. If we had had a flat lumber surface—a board roof where we could nail the tin cans flat and tight to board, we could have made do with them. As it was impossible to do this with the poles 18 inches apart, we decided to buy heavy roofing to lay over them.[27]

Clyde went to town to buy the heavy roofing. Due to the war, he could only buy two rolls of the extra heavy roofing. So he also bought a light roll to use on the eaves. After Clyde and Audrey put a layer of roofing material over the tin, that roof had a lot of humps and cracks that let in the wind, rain, snow and cold, but it was a roof. At a cost of seven dollars, the roofing was the most expensive item of the whole cabin. Audrey figured that if the tin cans had been satisfactory as roofing alone, the cabin would have cost less than five dollars. Had they been forced to buy a door and a window, the cabin could have still been constructed for less than twenty dollars, but fortunately, the door and window had been given to them.[28]

Inside the walls, Audrey began to chink the cracks and mud them up while Clyde worked on the roof. Audrey had watched men mix adobe when she was a child. She had seen women mix mud and straw to plaster their houses. She found a patch of dirt, spaded up a yard or so, carried water from the creek, threw a few handfuls of dry pine needles into the dirt to take the place of straw, and began the very hard job of mixing the mud thoroughly with the garden hoe. For several days her arms and shoulders were sore from mudslinging. She found that the first layer of mud should be fairly stiff to fill in cracks and level up the rough logs. This was smoothed over and pressed down with the spatula. Then she threw on a smoother coat of mud "which was soupier and messier. It splattered badly."[29]

While Audrey was still mudding the walls, Clyde had the roof half finished. Then they moved in an old stove that a neighbor had given them. They set it up and put the chimney through the roof. Audrey wrote in her notes, "My Book:"

> We had the tin roof on the east side half of the cabin when the storm gods frowned on us. That was the day we acquired a kitchen range. It came from our neighbors and was considered junk—something they were glad to have used by someone rather than hauling it to the dump. The fire back was burned clear through to the oven and the entire

stove was thick with rust. However, we set it up on the west side of the cabin and stuck the chimney up through the area that would later be roof. Clyde held the chimney in place with flattened tin cans. No wood was anywhere near it. In New Mexico most house fires are caused by faulty chimneys so we always tried to see that extra large spaces were left between all chimneys and any wood of any kind. With the stove in position, Clyde went to help the neighbors—in exchange for the stove, although they had said it was free. C. C. [Crystal Clydine] and I went up on the hillside where I had discovered good red clay when we were gathering rocks. I filled a gallon tin can with the red dirt, took it to the creek and mixed it to a stiff consistency. When it was stiff enough to work and shape with my hands, such as might be done in making clay pots, I took it into the partially finished cabin and repaired the stove. I put a thick wad of clay against the burned out area and smoothed it out over the edge of the oven and along the fireback. I put several layers along the side of the fire box until it was a couple of inches thick, making the stove fireproof. The clay baked like iron and served satisfactorily for years.[30]

Audrey explained that while she was beginning to plan a "real" supper using the new kitchen range, the storm clouds whirled and swirled from the north over the mountains. At first she didn't notice them because she was so involved in getting supper on the new range.

It may be fun to cook over a camp fire for a day or so but as a regular diet it is a tiresome task. Therefore, I was delighted to have a stove. I thanked old almanac specialist Ben [Franklin] for inventing the first wood eating monsters, as I built a fire in my "new" stove for the first time. Pine needles in the bottom of the fire box, overlaid with a layer of chips from our building logs and a few broken branches on too, soon heated the oven to bake real biscuits. And what a relief to stand instead of squatting while stirring soup or bacon gravy![31]

Clyde had gone down the canyon a mile or so to help do some road work. The clouds were rolling and swirling around. One could see the hail back up across the hill toward the ranch. The forest grew strangely still as every living thing was hidden and quiet. Audrey knew the mountains well enough to know how rapidly a thunderstorm could develop in the summer time. Her father had also taught her to recognize clouds that held hail in them. Audrey knew what was coming.

Audrey had been starting the process of making "adobe" to put in the cracks between the logs. Even though it is good to have all pounding finished before mudding or cementing, they were in a hurry so Audrey and Clyde began to chink and mud up the walls with half of the roof on. If too much space remained between the logs of the wall, they cut small trees or limbs and filled in the wide cracks with them or with small rocks, anything to provide a background to keep the adobe mud from flying through the cracks between the logs.

> I suppose I had seen women in the village of Chapelle when I was a child mix adobe mud, for I knew how to do it. I know I had seen them plaster their homes when Mother taught school there in the early 1920's, and so I knew the procedure, even though I had no experience and had never been personally shown the process. Although the men would make the heavy adobe bricks and lay them up as walls, the women always did the finishing work, the plastering and smoothing the walls to a satin finish. I never accomplished that but did a fairly smooth job. In later years when I hired local men to plaster some of my cabins with adobe, they tried to put it in with trowels, avoiding getting their hands in the gooey stuff. I was not that squeamish, but I did not mix it with my feet as is said to be the most efficient way. We found likely looking dirt with a red adobe cast, spaded up approximately a square yard and threw a few hands full of dry pine needles into the dirt. The pine needles took the place of straw in the adobe. Dried grass will also serve as a binder for the mud, but the needles were the most plentiful so I used them. The main objection to dried pine needs is the fact that their sharp ends would often stick my hands when mudding.[32]

Audrey and Clyde mixed the dry dirt and needles with the garden hoe and then poured creek water over the dry dirt. Audrey thought that mixing the dirt into a thick mud with the garden hoe was the hardest job of the whole building process. "Sometimes I wondered if working it with bare feet might not be simpler, but I never tried it."[33]

> After the adobe mud was the consistency of thick bread dough, I began slinging mud. I stood away from the wall and wound up like a baseball player, before letting fly for some particular crack. I could soon score a bull's eye, high or low, sitting or standing, wherever I wanted the mud to stick. After throwing a foot or two of cracks full of mud, I took an extra heavy kitchen spatula for a trowel and smoothed up the layer of

mud over the crack. With the spatula "trowel" I pressed the mud flat in the cracks and against the rounded part of the log and smoothed it flat. I found that for a smoother outer coat the mud needed more water so that it was about the consistency of hotcake or regular cake batter. Both types of mud spattered, with the thinner mud proving really messy. The soupy stuff was soon splattered all over the unfinished room. We soon had flying mud or dried mud stuck to everything. I waded mud spilled on the dirt floor until I felt like a kid in a mud puddle bog hole.[34]

Due to the flying mud, Audrey and Clyde had moved nearly everything out of the room.

I had the side of the room under the finished roof muded when the afternoon storm gods frowned and decided to test out our "tin can roof." Clyde had gone with the neighbors to build road on the steep mountain side down towards Falls Creek. We had put everything outside the walls to avoid coating of mud. When I saw the high ink black clouds rolling along the Sangre de Cristos I rushed to get our belongings back inside before the storm broke loose.[35]

Audrey raced to get everything under the half roof before the clouds broke.

Thunder roared as the grey-green, swirling clouds were split by lightning bolts. Somehow I wrangled the heavy baby's bed and our bed, bedding, and springs and mattress, clothes, and food supply inside under the roofed portion of the room. As the thunder grumbled and the clouds sat down on the mountain, hiding Barillas Peak in a grey shroud, the nearer clouds began to swirl like dancing dervishes. These were hail clouds. One area would swoop upward and another flash downward. Then the roar of the hail beat out the circling and doodling of the erratic storm gods. All living wild things hid under trees, bushes or under rocks as the roar of the coming hail deafened the forest. Bonnie crawled under the bed I had just set up. Crystal Clydine continued to play in the yard, but nothing ever filled her with fear. I climbed upon the roof to nail our piece of canvas to the ridge pole. There it would hang down and help protect our roofed possessions. In trying to climb down on the logs extending from the corner, I sat off the house. The hard ground where we had been working felt as though it nearly pushed my hip bones through my shoulder blades. Mighty startled, I sat there trying to regain my breath and wits.[36]

Audrey gave a description in her *New Mexico Magazine* story:

> Before I could climb down the first hailstones hit. Somehow I sat off the house. The ground sprang to spank me. I was startled but unhurt. As I sat there gathering my breath and wits Crystal Clydine called:
> "What's Mommy doing?"
> "Falling off the house," I said.
> "Oh," she answered. I laughed at her nonchalance. Then we hurried in out of the stinging white.[37]

Audrey sighed with relief. She had managed to get their belongings in out of the weather and she, Crystal and Bonnie were safe. But she worried about Clyde. Surely he had found some kind of shelter out there where he was doing road work.

> Bedlam began as a million hail stones hammered our unfinished tin can roof. Bonnie whined and CC and I pulled a quilt over our heads and held our hands over our ears. The noise was unbelievable. The uncovered half of the floor became a sea of bouncing white marbles. Many bounced under the canvas to the dry side. After about two inches of hail fell, a hard rain poured down, floating the hail and then as it melted, turning our floor into a sea of mud.[38]

The hail storm put about six inches of water in the cabin. Crystal and Audrey stayed under that half roof where the bed was located until the storm was over.

> Clyde came in soaking wet. He had been sheltered from the hail by an overhanging rock down the canyon but as soon as the hail let up he had hurried on home. While he shoveled hail off of the floor I built a roaring fire in our "new" cook stove. What a godsend that heat was. He changed into dry clothing while I baked feathery biscuits, all the while thanking Ben Franklin for his marvelous invention—pieces if iron placed together into a stove![39]

Audrey was grateful that the men had found an overhanging cliff for shelter from the hail and that they were all safe. She worried about Clyde because of his kidney problems. He also had back problems from a fall when he was young. Someone had left the cellar door open at their Oklahoma home. Clyde, thinking it was closed, had run and fallen down into the hole, down the ladder, and hurt his back. Consequently, he had to work carefully and rest frequently. He didn't need to catch cold in a bad storm! Audrey thanked God for Clyde's safety.

Naturally one of the first things Clyde built was an outhouse for the necessary "bathroom" facility.

Audrey described how they improvised a "shower" to clean up after a long day of building.

> Another luxury was bathing after the sun went down. Before the advent of the stove we usually bathed at midday in the wash tub with a blanket hung between us and the raw May breezes. Now, with the stove, we could carry out our "cleanliness is next to godliness" penchant in real comfort.[40]

They could heat water carried from the creek and could bathe inside in their big tin tub. The cost of the cabin was less than ten dollars; hence, they always called it the "Ten Dollar Cabin." It took about three weeks to build. The cabin lasted over twenty-five years and then was destroyed in the 1971 forest fire. A few tin "shingles" still lie on the ground, a testimony to the rustic little cabin that once housed a man and his wife, their child, and her dog. Audrey itemized the cost of the cabin as follows:

Gas and oil used in car to haul logs $1.00
Nails $.60
Door Hinges $.47
Window Hinges $.35
Roofing $7.00
Total: $9.42.

For less than ten dollars, the little family had a place to stay in the mountains.[41]

Half the roof was put on with fifty small poles, well trimmed and placed side by side, covered with a thin layer of mud and covered with the roofing material. The other half was formed with the tin cans covered with roofing in the same manner. Clyde and Audrey filled in the gable ends of their cabin and made some shelves with scrap lumber lying near the cabin site. A house had been there years before. They also found some scrap lumber from a fallen gate that was no longer used. The neighbors were glad to get rid of it as it was an eyesore beside their new gate. Purchased new, the lumber might have been about two dollars. Even including the cost of lumber and new windows and a door, the total expenses would still have been less than twenty dollars had it been necessary to buy the things they had been given.

Within two weeks Clyde and Audrey "had built a snug log cabin without any help."[42] Audrey concluded her article: "Our experience proves that, even in these days, any inexperienced greenhorn with $10 and mighty few tools can still build a habitable house."[43]

Before the house was finished, Dammuzzy came to visit Mabel, so she decided to go to the ranch to see Audrey. Audrey was cooking outside over a hole in the ground with a piece of tin over it for the lid. The smoke could escape around the tin. It wasn't tight on the ground.

Dammuzzy wanted to know how Audrey had learned to build a fire in a hole and cook over it.

"I must have read it in a book sometime," Audrey replied.

"Well, if it was in a book, I'm sure you read it," her grandmother replied.

Everyone knew Audrey was an avid reader. Audrey liked to write, too, and that was to become her profession. She would be one of the first female journalists in the area. She had published in *The Denver Post* and other magazines when she was a teen-ager. With a family to care for, she had little time for free-lance writing, yet she was very prolific and published a large percentage of what she wrote. Audrey wrote in "My Book:"

> It is easy to build a house if you live in a forest and own an ax and a piece of string. Actually, you can get along without the string, but it can be of help in leveling walls and such. A willing worker on the end of the ax handle is the other necessity. We found this out 50 years before the "hippy back-to-the-land movement" began.
>
> Way back in 1941 my husband and I had found that we could build a primitive log cabin for ten dollars in less than two weeks. Today a good big completely modern log house might take about three months and $2,000. However, a quickie frame house can be put up in eight days for $400, as son-in-law Gary Beimer did, [in about 1975] working alone during his vacation.[44]

Audrey realized that things changed through the years, but she was convinced that anyone could build themselves a house. She wrote:

> Of course in 1941 there was no harassment by HUD, environmentalists, contractors or labor unions. Housing was a big problem, we thought. But freedom to do your own thing, build what you could and live in it was smiled upon and encouraged. The REA did

require a licensed electrician to install wiring in the 1950's, so when I wanted to modernize my second log cabin, the $15 dollar house, I had to pay $60 for installation of overhead lights and two outlets. However, in my big 22 x 50 ft. log cabin and the one where I now live, son-in-law Wesley [Lovett] passed the state home owners' electrical exams and for $20 we received a permit to install wiring in each house which was later inspected and passed by a state electrical inspector and green tagged before the REA would light it up.[45]

After the digression about rules and regulations, Audrey continued to write about building the Ten Dollar House:

When Clyde and I built our Ten Dollar House, as reported in *New Mexico Magazine* for May, 1943, we were complete greenhorns. Clyde had a very slight acquaintance with an ax and a hammer. However, being left handed I was never allowed to use either one, for fear I'd cut off a toe or smash my fingers. As we learned, our practice never made perfect but resulted in a snug cabin that stood sturdy and strong for nearly 30 years—until a forest fire destroyed it.[46]

Audrey, Clyde and Crystal lived in the Ten Dollar House off and on for several years, whenever Clyde needed rest from city life. Canned goods stored there in the winter did not freeze even at more than twenty degrees below zero, proving the worth of the thick adobe mud job on the walls. There was no modern insulation, but mud has long been the choice of native New Mexican home builders. Later Opal, Bob, Bobby and Jackie occupied the Ten Dollar House, while Audrey and Clyde had moved on to their Fifteen Dollar House, built soon after they had bought their own ranch property nearby. Finally, a couple from New York, the Hellers, rented the Ten Dollar House for fifteen dollars a month.

After finishing the cabin, Clyde and Audrey lived in that Ten Dollar House for about a year. They had very little, but they had a house built with their own hands. It keep the rain and wind out, it had a stove, beds, and simple necessities. Most of all, it held the love of a family. It was a snug and cozy log cabin.

It is no wonder that Clyde began to recover his health as he began breathing in the pine-scented air that blew down from the snow-tipped mountain canyons and drinking the water from a spring that came out of the hillside. He had a wife who would work at this side with shovel and hoe to build a house, plant a garden, cook for the family, and care for their child. Clyde thought, as he watched Audrey, Crystal and Bonnie walking down the path to the spring, that a man could hardly ask for more. Audrey had always known these mountains were "the best thing this side of heaven," and now Clyde knew it, too.

40

Forest Springs Ranch

Clyde, Audrey and Crystal had just settled into the Ten Dollar House when Grandfather Shearer became ill. Vivian took his father to the hospital in Las Vegas. Clyde and Audrey offered to take care of his place at the Old Homestead Ranch while he was in town since Mabel and Vivian were living in Santa Fe. There were chickens and other animals to care for.

Clyde and Audrey had to walk over to Grandfather's house, carrying two-and-a-half year old Crystal, about half a mile from where their cabin was; the snow was too deep to drive over. They went to his place every morning to feed the chickens, taking Bonnie with them. In the evenings, they would close the chicken house door, listening to the coyotes. Audrey wrote an article for *New Mexico Magazine*, published in February of 1946:

> Deep purple and white snow patches made the mountains mysterious. A coyote or two, sounding like ten, would chill my blood. One evening thin cloud streams across the top of the sky, deep haze far to the south, and the different note in the coyote chorus told us snow was coming.[1]

Clyde and Audrey had permission to move into one of the cabins Vivian had built at the Old Homestead Ranch so they could look after the place. They decided they should move over there until Grandfather returned from the hospital—for fear that deep snow would prevent even foot travel on the steep north slope between the two places.

One January night soft, heavy snow began to fall. Early the next morning the Simpsons moved a few necessary things over to the Shearer cabin. Snow continued, piling deeper throughout the day. Wildlife were silent and hidden. The chickens sat disconsolately on their roosts. Bonnie curled up to keep warm.

While Crystal, like an arctic cub, rolled and played in the soft white, Clyde and Audrey tramped through deep snow, collecting wood and settling themselves for the cold that would follow the storm. In the evening the mercury dropped fifteen degrees in half an hour. They knew it would be extremely cold in the morning. They kept a fire all night in the fat little wood stove. Still, the cold crept through the frame cabin where they slept. Crystal slept in Milly's little bed in the small alcove at the foot of her parents' bed. But it was so cold that Audrey put Crystal in bed with her and Clyde to keep the child warm. However, the few added pounds was too much. The old bed fell down. It was a rude awakening for Audrey and Clyde when the bed collapsed, to say the least. They laughed at their plight and decided to sleep with the springs resting on the floor the rest of the night. Crystal, tired from her day of play, didn't even wake up.

The next morning Audrey looked for a thermometer that was capable of registering more than ten below zero, but there was none. She wrote, "But since the mercury in those we found had slid to the bottom of the glass, and curled up tightly to keep warm, we judged it was at least fifteen degrees below zero."[2] Las Vegas recorded more than twenty below zero that night.

Audrey and Clyde discussed Grandfather and wondered if he would make a full recovery. Audrey worried because he was old and had lived a long, difficult life.

"He's tough. He'll be OK," Clyde replied.

Audrey recalled that she had learned that Richard A. Shearer had been born in 1860 to Richard Hooker Shearer and his wife. They had moved from Virginia to California to start a newspaper business in San Francisco. During the Civil War, the Union soldiers threw his printing press into the Bay and destroyed his office because of his editorials sympathizing with the Southern cause. When he was an old man, Richard Arthur Shearer told his family he remembered the end of the Civil War. He was five years old, sitting on a fence watching the soldiers march by, clapping his little hands because everyone was so happy. But he had a step-mother he didn't get along with, so when he was twelve years of age he left home to find a job. His younger brother wanted to go with him. They found a job in a saw mill. The little brother got his hand in the way of a saw. He bled to death in front of his older brother. Richard Arthur always blamed himself for his little brother's death. He married Ollie Atwell and they homesteaded the property in the Mineral Hill area. They established a store and ran a post office on the land that bordered what was the property Clyde and Audrey later bought.

Finally Grandfather Shearer was well enough to return home. Clyde and Audrey moved back to the Ten Dollar Cabin. Audrey was pleased that her thick mud job on the inside walls of the Ten Dollar House had proved its worth. Her jars of canned food had not frozen; nothing was broken.

When school was out, Mabel moved back to the ranch. In May, 1942, Clyde and Audrey moved back to Carringtons into the same little back house where they had lived when Crystal was born. Milly had just graduated from high school, and she stayed in town with the Jordans and worked that summer at the C. J. Penney Store. Mr. Jordan was manager there. When school started in the Fall of 1942, Mabel rented the house at 728 Grand Avenue so Milly moved in there. Vivian worked in an office across the street. The Depression was over, the jobs were good and the family, for a time, seemed settled and happy.

As mentioned before, the Old Homestead Ranch was in an area called the "Mineral Hill" area. Mineral City had been a hub of activity in the late 1800's. Audrey once wrote for the 1952 *Rodeo Edition* of the *Las Vegas Daily Optic:*

> Only a very small portion of the mineral belt running through this section of the country has been prospected to any extent. The Pecos River Forest Reserve, the Mora Land Grand and the Las Vegas Land Grant present a fine field for prospecting. The veins running through these tracts of land can be traced from the southern part of Colorado into New Mexico for a distance of about 150 miles, passing through various mining camps such as Elizabethtown, Guadalupita, Mora, Rociada, Mineral Hill and Tecolote.[3]

In the same *Rodeo Edition* of the *Optic* Audrey wrote:

> There are a number of outcrops of coal in the Las Vegas area. It is said that the Onava area is underlined with coal. Wells drilled in that area strike a coal bed between 100 and 200 feet.
>
> There was a coal mine in the Pecos Canyon where a good deal of coal was once mined. Another small mine was up the Tecolote on property now owned by Henry Beisman. The strip of coal, pressed between hard rocks in what geologists call the "fern age," is too thin to be profitable in the Tecolote canyon.
>
> Another coal mine in the area is above Montezuma. This mine, which once had a company organized around it, proved to have the coal at a 45 degree angle. This made it extremely difficult to mine, although the coal was said to have been of good quality.[4]

The Simpson family returned to their mountain cabin as often as they could. But the roads were little more than cow trails. In those days the cars did not always pull up hill or through mud as well as the vehicles of today, especially if the tires were poor. They didn't have four-wheel drive, either.

The road from Las Vegas to the Old Homestead Ranch was especially bad, filled with ruts and rocks. One had to be careful not to "high center" when the wheels went down into the deep ruts or when rocks stuck up in the creek crossings. Eventually the road became a San Miguel County road, but the County didn't put much money into it. Few people lived out that way. However, as the years went by and more people lived along the road, the complaints became more frequent. Nearly everyone got "stuck" more than once and had to dig out of the mud or have someone pull them out.

In later years Audrey wrote a verse, "The Mineral Hill-San Geronimo Road," that was published several times throughout the years in *The Optic*. It appeared in "Public Forum," *Las Vegas Daily Optic*, September 15, 1945, as follows:

Gentlemen:

The Mineral Hill-San Geronimo Road
It's rain washed rocks and gullies,
It's a cow trail with a name.
And the cows all lose red points
When they travel over same.

It's bog-holes and high centers,
It wrecks every car and truck.
We carry picks and shovels
To dig out with when we're stuck.

We fight it and we cuss it,
Till we'd like to move away.
But we all own our ranches
And THEY AIN'T HAY!

Sincerely,
Audrey Simpson
Forest Springs Ranch
Box 656
Las Vegas, New Mexico[5]

Audrey wrote another verse which she probably submitted to the *Las Vegas Daily Optic*. However, it is unknown whether it was published. Her original typewritten copy was found.

> This really is a "NO" road
> A gummy worn out trail
> Hear the people weep and wail.
>
> "Broken springs and busted tires
> Hub deep mud that clings and mires."
>
> We don't want an oil road
> We do ask for gravel!
> We desperately need
> A ROAD WE CAN TRAVEL![6]

In later years, Audrey attended many meetings to try to get the road improved, especially County Commission meetings. She also wrote many letters to editors, such as the following two letters which were published in the *Las Vegas Daily Optic*:

> Dear Sir:
> Several camps for young people in the Mineral Hill area had to reduce camping time for after a few years they found summer rains and no all-weather road ruined too many cars. So instead of 12 weeks of camping, it was reduced to six, losing money for Las Vegas merchants and healthful pleasure for young people.
> In the 1960's, I drove around this area and got 99 names of adult voters on a petition which a group of us took to the State Highway Commission in Santa Fe. We were given many promises which were never kept. We still do not have an all weather road.
> That bumpy often muddy track known as State Highway 283 still takes its daily toll of broken car parts or yells for help. "Bring a truck and chain! We're stuck again!"
> Losses to individuals, the county and the state, year after year, due to the deplorable conditions of Mineral Hill Road, are countless.
> When this State Highway 283, access to Mineral Hill and San Geronimo, is improved to an all weather road, Las Vegas and the area residents will all greatly benefit.[7]

Audrey wrote:

> With pros and cons of the Mineral Hill Road, State Highway 283, being discussed, may I present the viewpoint of one who has fought to travel that road, trying to get over it to town or home, for more than 50 years. I've been stuck in its mud, stuck in snow banks, and stopped by high water.
>
> Lack of an all weather road into the very scenic and fertile area southwest of Las Vegas, serviced by this road, has cost the county and state millions of dollars in tax revenue. Rancher after rancher has been stymied by the cow trail road until they were licked and forced to sell out to bigger investors who could afford to buy up their property and use it for subdivision or income tax losses (but not living there.)
>
> About 1900, San Geronimo was one of the most prosperous villages in the country with a milk cow herd of 200. A few years later an old Optic reported 50 wagon loads of flour and meal arrived that day from the Grist Mill at San Geronimo. Even if each of the wagons hauled less than a thousand pounds, the fertility of the area was proved.[8]

In her rough draft, not included in the above letter, Audrey wrote:

> My step-father's family, the R. A. Shearers, homesteaded up here in 1906-07 and had a store and post office, so they were well acquainted with the productivity of the area. The road was always a problem for when the mud was deep the teams could not haul out the area produce or haul in supplies. They had to wait until the road dried out.
>
> When my mother and C. V. Shearer were married more than 50 years ago, I met the road and have been battling it since then. He often had to turn his Model T Ford around and back up over the stair-step rocks on the Lischner place. Or we kids had to get out and push in deep mud to try to get un-stuck. That road gave us nightmares and still does.
>
> In those days part of the tax structure was "working on the road." Each family was required to do a certain amount of work, or hire it done for them. At that time the people knew where the worst spots were and usually repaired them first.
>
> Then it was a fairly decent wagon road, passable in dry weather. You could say the same for it now, PASSABLE IN DRY WEATHER.[9]

Methods of transportation changed from teams to gas buggies, but the road did not change. During the Great Depression many area residents lost their property to the State for taxes. Others had to curtail their herds due to the fencing of the Santa Fe National Forest and restrictions on land use. The Forest Service shot horses to eliminate the wild bunch that ranged around Barillas Peak. The road continued to defeat small ranchers.

Because the road was always in such bad condition, many people moved to town, letting fertile fields lie idle. WPA came along and the road was improved and re-aligned. However, it still was not an all weather road.

My grandmother, Alice Shirley, had a chicken ranch with contracts to furnish eggs to Las Vegas cafés, including a case a week to the Home Café. Too often she could not make it to town with a good team hitched to a two-wheeled cart. So after a couple of years she gave up.

The R. A. Shearer family, who homesteaded above San Geronimo about 1906, had a store and Post Office. When War I arrived they closed it to go contribute to the war effort. When they returned they found many area residents who had also gone afield, did not return. They tried sawmilling and found they could not get their lumber delivered on schedule. How the teams used to struggled in the mud of the road! Trucks just gave up and stayed stuck.

From 1946 to 1950, while Federic Roybal was a County Commissioner, the road during that time was worked more often and improved. A County Planning Commission was established. Time and again the Mineral Hill road was given priority for improvement and then forgotten. About 1960 during a meeting of this group in Las Vegas, a vote gave the Mineral Hill road third priority after Pecos and Villanueva. We beat out Rociada by the vote. But Rociada got their paved road. That year the State Highway Commission ceased to follow County recommendations. And as usual, the Mineral Hill road was lost in the shuffle.

After a very narrow bridge was built over the Tecolote between San Geronimo and Mineral Hill, access to Las Vegas was more nearly possible unless the Falls Creek water was too high to cross. Several years ago a safe crossing at San Geronimo was promised and large cement culverts were placed there beside the river, waiting to be put in place. The number is not the same as it was, but the rest are still waiting on the unfulfilled promises.

Salty Sparks ramrodded road improvement one year and a few of the worst spots were fixed by donations of money and trucks and labor by area residents. The last large agricultural activity up here was the Axtell Dairy just below San Geronimo. They struggled through mud and snow trying to get their milk out on time. Without an all weather road they finally gave up and moved out.

Almost any family with roots in the Mineral Hill-San Geronimo area has the same story—licked by the lack of a good road. Rancher after rancher gave up, unable to get their produce to town on time or cattle buyers unable to make it into the high country, were stopped by the road. In the 1960's, I drove around this area and got 99 names of adult voters on a petition which a group of us took to the State Highway Commission in Santa Fe. Once more we were graced with promises never kept.

Several camps for hundreds of young people are located in this area. After a few years they had to curtail the length of the camp time, due to summer rains and no all weather road. Countless parents got stuck in the mud, or worse, ruined their cars on the cow-trail Mineral Hill Road.

This road is a school bus route and just recently the bus had to be pulled out of the mud of the road. The Post Office has been unable to serve the Mineral Hill-San Geronimo area promptly since they are no longer required to deliver the mail by horseback as they once were. Last year they cut delivery from daily during summer months, to three times per week, due to the lack of a good road.[10]

Audrey included in her rough draft:

According to the Post Office there are at least 26 permanent families that get their mail on the route. And there are many, like the Robert Simpsons and me that get mail in town for if we travel 4 miles of nearly impassable county road to reach the state highway, mail route area, we might as well go on to Vegas, so we are not counted. My daughter and I were not counted in the last census either, although in 1950 Luis F. Armijo came up to count me and my two daughters [Mr. Armijo, the census taker, had to walk back to San Geronimo for help when he hit his car on a rock and damaged his oil pan].

The road leading into San Geronimo was an absolute disgrace when Mrs. Victoria Quintana died in November, 1974. A couple of hundred people eased over the boulders and washouts to attend the funeral at San Geronimo church. Someone attending must have had some influence, for the portion of the road on the hill was improved a great deal shortly afterwards.

Losses to the county, state and individual travelers due to the deplorable conditions of the Mineral Hill Road are unmistakable. If the road to Mineral Hill and San Geronimo is improved to an all weather road, area residents will breathe easier as they go to and from town, and the entire Las Vegas community will feel the impact in their cash registers.[11]

Whether the above letter was published is uncertain, but a similar letter was published in the *Las Vegas Daily Optic* some years later.

For about 70 years, five generations of my family have bumped over the Mineral Hill Road, State Highway 283. I have been stuck in the mud of this road, stuck in snow banks and stopped by high water. Since no longer required to deliver mail on horseback, the mail carrier sometimes cannot get over the road for two weeks at a time. The mail service was cut back to three times a week last summer, instead of daily, due to the bad road. The school bus often cannot get over the road in wet weather, and if it does may have to be pulled out of the mire along the way.[12]

Indeed, State Highway 283 was finally paved to the turn off on County Road A18A, due to the persistent efforts of Audrey and others. Then Audrey was left with only about four miles of travel on an unpaved road to her ranch on County Road A18A or what was known as "Falls Creek Road." In 1996, after the County did some major work on the County road, Audrey said the road was better than she'd ever seen it as she traveled from Forest Springs Ranch on the unpaved road to State Highway 283. Audrey was thrilled when the County road was improved, though not paved. Audrey was well past eighty years of age, but she took the effort to write a thank you letter to the San Miguel County Commissioners. In part, it said:

Thank you and the County Road Department for the fine work on County Road A18A. Last Fall for the first time in more than 60 years it was a GOOD Road, the first time I had ever gone over it when it was more than a cow trail.

We are proud of our County Road Department workers' prompt action in coming up A18A. Thank you all.[13]

Audrey wrote several thank you letters in 1996 when the County Road was improved more than it had ever been. Most of the credit went to Presillano, "Pres" Santillanes, the oldest son of Ramón Santillanes, an old family friend. "Pres" had been San Miguel County Sheriff several years and then became County Road Superintendent. He later said, "Before I retired I wanted to make sure that road was good so Audrey could get in and out."[14]

He did. Audrey said she had never seen the road as good as it was when "Pres" and his crew finished working on it. Presillano once said that Audrey had been like a mother to him, as his own mother had died soon after the birth of the youngest of Ramón's boys. "Pres" said he always liked to visit her home. She treated him as a son, and he never forgot that.[15]

The history of the Old Homestead Ranch and Forest Springs Ranch provides some interesting background. According to Audrey's handwritten notes, in the early 1890's the U.S. Government, having taken over New Mexico by Stephen Kearney's proclamation in 1846, recognized that the unpopulated land was not making the U.S. any tax money. So they opened up a vast area to be homesteaded. The old Santillanes family homesteaded the area northwest from the Las Vegas Land Grant to the abrupt rise of the Sangre de Cristo mountain range. Audrey wrote: "They had to have a real brave pioneer spirit to move so far up the mountains."[16]

The people then were noted for their urge to live in close built villages where there was safety from wild animals and hostile Native Americans. There was a saw mill in Falls Canyon just above the Falls Creek Crossing on County Road A18A. Some of the men sold trees for railroad ties in Las Vegas. About 1890 the Santillanes family built a big house and several smaller buildings just north of the big Spring in the main canyon bottom. The houses were built on what later became The Mesa of Forest Springs Ranch. There the women and children could carry water by the bucket up the hill for use in the house.

> The old people had several sons—Melequias, Higinio, and an adopted son Miguel. I think there was another boy and a girl or two—maybe Catalina was one. When they reached 21 they each took homesteads until the Santillaneses owned most of this section of the mountain. They were still living up here when the Shearers homesteaded their place joining Santillanes on the north side of Santillanes property. There were several families in the area then.[17]

In another set of handwritten notes Audrey wrote more detailed history:

> Forest Springs Ranch area was homesteaded by the Santillanes family

in the early 1890's. They built a house and several buildings on a hill [Mesa] above the conjunction of Roaring Canyon and Happy Creek—our names for the canyons—close to the bottom of the up thrust known as the Fumarole. The location was just above a good spring in Happy Canyon where they got drinking water. In 1895 Santillanes received a patent on his land from the U.S. Patent office. His sons also homesteaded or inherited the original homestead. The land passed to the young men after 1900. The original homestead was divided up and about in 1916—or earlier—Higinio sold his portion, 160 acres to C. V. Shearer. This included 160 acres joining the [then] recently established national forest. They had established a home close to the mountain where grass was plentiful for their cattle, horses and goats. With the establishment of the U.S. Forest Service their grazing land was cut off. They removed all usable parts of the buildings and they [what remained of the buildings] melted back into the earth. Some of them (maybe the old ones) established a house beside what is now the main county road—just north up out of Santillanes Creek. They lived there in 1927 or 1928 or 1929. The road went right by their yard. Later they or Miguel built a house right at the top of the hill climbing out of Santillanes Creek. Miguel and his family lived there in the 1920's and 1930's, moving to town after the girls grew up.[18]

Audrey gave a few more details in the other set of notes:

The old Santillaneses died and their property was divided among the kids. Higinio got 160 acres. He gave his daughter Rosita Santillanes Benavidez 80 acres to the south of the 160 acres. After Charles Vivian Shearer worked for the U.S. Forest Service, he bought the 160 from Higinio.[19]

In 1920 those acres which C.V. Shearer bought were deeded to his first wife, Edith Martin Shearer—later Edith Shutt.

They [Vivian and Edith] had a big fight when he came down off the mountain at a camp (Forest Service) and found a team there [outside his house] and —— in bed with his wife. He went to court and there was a nasty divorce case. He fought to keep Ellen Grace, born in April, 1914. He lost the case and Grace stayed with her mother. So to avoid paying alimony [or child support] he deeded the place over to her. She married Fred Shutt and had a daughter, Ruth Shutt, now married to

Billy Grounds. Mrs. Shutt tried to sell their place in the '30's depression—no takers—she tried to sell the mineral rights or lease them; and J.M.T. "Salty" Sparks said in the '30's he prospected up here and had a little cabin below the spring. [at Forest Springs Ranch] When we came up in the '40's there was still the outline of a tiny—maybe 8 by 10—remains of a cabin this side of the creek—on the back at the upper end of our first [old] garden. Must have been his—of course all log cabins that are left standing deserted are soon hauled off for wood.[20]

Audrey's notes continue to explain that in about 1915 or 1920, Charles Vivian Shearer and Edith Martin Shearer were divorced and Vivian gave Edith the hundred and sixty acres in lieu of alimony or child support:

C. V. (Vivian) Shearer always felt that his daughter Ellen Grace should have the property. Edith married Fred Shutt. Then during the depression they tried to sell the place—they had an ad on the window of their garage business at the corner of National and 12th Street. They lived upstairs. J.M.T. "Salty" Sparks and someone else came up here [to the ranch] to "mine." They built a tiny cabin at the top of the old garden on the east bank of the creek. The outline and remains of logs were still there when Clyde and I bought the place.[21]

Audrey had written to Edith soon after Crystal was born in 1938. Audrey knew that Edith did not intend to live on the property, so Audrey wrote to ask her for first chance to buy the place if she ever wanted to sell it. Audrey had one hundred and fifty dollrs in the postal savings that Mabel had paid her for work Audrey had done throughout the years. That included the months she had taken care of Betty in Lagunita, the sale of rabbits and chickens—including those sold to John Nelson—and help at García Mill, as well as other such "debts" that had been acquired through the years. Mabel had promised to pay Audrey eventually—and she did.

When Mabel gave Audrey the money, Mabel asked her what she would do with it. Audrey knew her heart's desire was to buy land in the mountains, but none was available at the time, so said she would buy War Bonds, and she did. But she also put some in Postal Savings.[22]

Audrey gave details about acquiring the land from Edith in her notes:

Edith Shutt's husband died and she was ill, wanting to sell this place to get money. Grace was already married. I wrote to her and said if she ever wanted to sell, give me first chance to buy it. Vivian wanted me to do this, thinking he might get it back, although he and mother had the Shearer ranch, homesteaded in 1906. He still resented giving it to Edith and sort of wanted it back.

Crystal was going to be 4 years old and had just had her tonsils out when Hugh Trainer came on Sunday from Albuquerque, where Edith was sick, and said he wanted to sell it for $250.00 for 160 acres. I told him my money was in the P. O. [post office] Savings, and I would have to get it out Monday. I had $150.00 which I had earned as a kid and mother paid me back when she got her money from her father's estate about 1939 and I put it in the Postal Savings or War Bonds. Early the next morning Clyde drove up here to Shearer's ranch and asked to borrow enough money [$100.00] to pay for the place with the stipulation that we would buy it and pay Vivian and Mother back for it. But if Ellen Grace wanted it she could have it if she would pay for it. So I turned the money over to [a] lawyer and he gave me the signed deed. Trainer had gone back to Albuquerque. The lawyer asked if I didn't want to quiet title to it then and there. I said No, it had only gone through 3 or 4 hands and I couldn't afford to do it. He said it would cost about $25. We were so poor $25 sounded like $500 now.

Vivian thought Grace should have the place, so she and her husband came and Vivian took them horseback all over the place. She decided it was not worth $250—or anything—in spite of heavy timber. So I got my money and paid the folks and then gave them as much a month [as possible] until it was paid off. We had to skimp to do it. Clyde was making about $14.00 a week then and we lived in the one room and kitchenette in the upstairs front of Mrs. Carrington's at 921 Lincoln. We already had our Ten Dollar House on the S.E. corner of Mothers [and Vivian's place] built in 1941. Clyde was sick at the time so it was skimping and do without all the time.[23]

On Monday morning Audrey went to Mr. Truder's office and turned over the two hundred and fifty dollars to get the deed signed by Edith Schutt. The deed was made out to Clyde alone and did not have Audrey's name on it! That was later changed, but at first it was a great disappointment to Audrey. It was just one of many situations where she would discover that women were often treated as second class citizens.

The one hundred and sixty acres that Audrey and Clyde bought for two hundred and fifty dollars in the Mineral Hill area southwest of Las Vegas is worth much more today. At the time the price was about one dollar and fifty-six cents an acre.

After a year or two, Clyde and Audrey paid off the balance they owed Vivian and Mabel. In a notebook, Audrey recorded in handwritten notes the deed history of the place she and Clyde bought and named Forest Springs Ranch. She wrote:

> Quit Claim
> Deed Number 101 or 30656
> From Edith Shutt to Clyde Joseph Simpson
> July 15, 1942 recorded
> Warranty Deed of
> Higinico [or Higinio] Santillanes to Rosita Santillanes de Benavidez,
> February 6, 1937—Jose —— [name cannot be read]
> #1266
> Juan J. Santillanes to Higinico [or Higinio] Santillanes,
> November 4, 1947, Libro 151—deed made out
> January 28, 1930
> Tax deed 1267—Rosita from State for
> Tax Sale 2533
> 8.88 Taxes paid on Tax deed 2869
> Rosita and Tomás Benavidez to Clyde [Simpson] 80 acres
> No. 268 - recorded Nov. 4, 1947
> Homestead Certificate #1958—application 2848
> Recorded Vol. 5, page 131, Santa Fe, February 1910.

Audrey noted that the document was signed on May 26, 1894 by President Grover Cleveland.[24]

In her notes Audrey explained that they were glad they had built the Ten Dollar House on the Shearer place. "We already had a foothold up here. The next time Clyde got too sick to work, we came up here and began to build the Fifteen Dollar House." The Simpson place was a mile long and a quarter of a mile wide.[25]

The trip from Las Vegas to the ranch home was scenic and beautiful even if the roads were bad. From certain parts of the road one could see the mountains clearly. Standing up alone in solitary dignity was Hermit's Peak (Old Baldy) to the north. The western mountain chain included Elk Mountain, the Falls Peaks, Barillas Peak—the highest point on that side—and next to it Fox Peak. Further to the south was Fisher Hill. Audrey wrote in notes: "S. L. Fisher—Vivian named Fisher hill for him, lion hunter."[26]

Clyde and Audrey traveled over the rough road, sometimes a very muddy road, and walked around the place, admiring every canyon, every wooded area, every open meadow. Their property was next to the Shearer property where the two places joined at what Vivian and Grandfather called "The Bottle Neck."

In February, 1943, Audrey and Clyde hiked up the canyon and looked for a suitable cabin site. They considered several spots where they would start building, probably in May. There was an old road across the creek and up a steep hill leading to what Audrey would call The Forest Springs Ranch Mesa—the mesa on the Simpson place as opposed to The Big Mesa on The Old Homestead Ranch. There had been a village in the late 1800's on that high, flat place. They considered building high on the hill (the Mesa) where the Santillanes houses once stood when the original homesteaders, Juan Ignacio Santillanes and his sons, lived there. However, it was a steep climb from the spring to the old house area on the mesa. Carrying water up a sixty degree incline was not a very good prospect. There were still rock foundations, a few old boards and nails, bits of broken glass, pieces of iron wagon parts, and so on lying around to show that a village had been there once. It was a beautiful spot where one could see Barillas Peak, Fox Peak, and all the surrounding areas, even into the east where Las Vegas lay. But it was too far from the creek and from the best road, so they decided against building at the top of The Forest Springs Ranch Mesa.

As Clyde and Audrey walked along, they came to a little clearing that seemed warm. It was high enough to be dry but it was not far from the creek. This spot was about half a mile up the creek from the Ten Dollar House, just below the old wagon road that came down from The Mesa. The spot they decided upon was in an open space under three hills at the forks of two canyons. The site was sheltered and warm when the sun touched it, in spite of two feet of snow clinging to the opposite, shady "north slope."

So Audrey and Clyde decided on a fairly flat spot at the foot of a hill above the junction of what they would name Happy Canyon and Roaring Canyon, where Happy Creek babbled cheerfully on one side and the deep canyon rocks made the creek on the other side roar, hence the name Roaring Creek. The land surrounding the cabin site was beautiful where it lay between the two tiny creeks in a valley that would grow clover six feet high. The surrounding hills and canyons were covered with pines, firs, quaking aspens, and was home to bands of wild turkeys, passing deer, wild cats, and bear.

"What shall we name the place?" Audrey asked as she and Clyde surveyed their property.

They played with several choices.

"There are lots of springs on this place," Clyde said. He took a dipper and filled a bucket of water from one of the springs. "This is the best water I've ever tasted," he declared with a satisfied sigh.

"That's because it comes straight from the snow on the mountain and it's in this beautiful forest. Smell the pine trees! And the fir! I've often said if you could bottle that scent, you'd be a millionaire," Audrey exclaimed.

"Water from the forest, springs from the woods, or springs from the forest!" Clyde mused, still thinking about names.

They played with words for a few minutes.

"Forest brooks," Audrey added. "Springs from the mountain forests!"

"Forest springs! That's it!" Clyde exclaimed.

"Forest springs! That has a nice sound to it," Audrey said.

"So Forest Springs it was—the 160 acres of property adjoining the Old Homestead Ranch. Later we bought an adjoining 80 acres from a neighbor, a total of 240 acres. We would build a bigger, more perfect cabin."[27] They planned to build the new cabin while living in the Ten Dollar House.

> However, with our usual "best laid plans," they changed. My sister, Opal and her two children wanted to come home to the mountains while her husband, Bob, went to Texas to work in the shipyards. She wanted to arrive March 15. The Ten Dollar House was big enough for the three of us—but three more? We would have to rush in constructing our new cabin.[28]

Since they had a name for the place, one of the first things Clyde and Audrey wanted to do was to make a sign for the property. A friend had given them a couple of signs that they painted over and then painted "Forest Springs Ranch" across each of the two signs.

While Clyde worked, Audrey peeled the bark from a pine tree to hang the sign on. Within the day they had a sign hanging at the north entrance to the place, nearest the Ten Dollar Cabin on the Shearers' place. Then they did the same thing and hung the other sign at the south entrance to their place, the route into Santillanes Canyon. The north entrance was near the Mineral Hill side. The south entrance road led directly to San Geronimo. It was the same distance to the ranch from town either way.

To secure the signs, Clyde dug two holes three feet deep with a shovel for each sign. He realized they needed a post-hole digger. So when Audrey's birthday came around he gave her a post-hole digger—not a very romantic gift—but one that would get a lot of use at the ranch. They laughed about it in future years.

"What do you want for your birthday?" Clyde asked a few years later.

"Anything but a post-hole digger," Audrey replied.

"What's wrong with a gift like that?" Clyde teased. "We needed it to build and improve our place."

"Well, you have a point," Audrey conceded. "So whatever you choose will be just right."

"Well, I'll try to choose something more personal this time," he said.

He bought her a new hoe to use in her gardening that year.

As Audrey and Clyde walked through what was left of the village on what they were to call the "The Mesa," they thought about the people who had lived there years ago.

The Santillanes family was well known in the area, having settled there as some of the earliest of the Spanish families. Ramón and Yvangelista Duran kept some of their land near San Geronimo, but Yvangelista died after the birth of her son Augustin.[29]

Presillano, the oldest, was born on June 25, 1933 in San Geronimo to Ramón Santillanes and Yvangelista Duran and died August 15, 1997. At the time of his death, the obituary listed that he was preceded in death by his parents and one sister, Nadine Archuleta and three brothers, Geronimo—known as Jerry—Manuel, and Augustine Santillanes. Presillano Santillanes served as San Miguel County Sheriff from 1977 to 1981 and worked at the San Miguel County Road Department as Foreman until he retired in May of 1996. He had previously served the City of Las Vegas as Police Officer from 1969 to 1976, according to the August 18, 1997 "Obituary," which appeared in the *Las Vegas Daily Optic*.[30]

The Santillaneses were good neighbors of Clyde and Audrey Simpson. Audrey sometimes hired Ramón and his boys to help with work that needed to be done, especially when Clyde was gone and Audrey was unable to chop wood or do other necessary chores alone. In later years, Presillano was very helpful. When he was a sheriff he worked with Audrey's son-in-law Gary Beimer, who was under-sheriff at the time. They made a good team and accomplished a great deal while "Pres" was in office.

If the Ten Dollar Cabin was an accomplishment, the Fifteen Dollar House was to be an even greater success. It would give the Simpson family a much better cabin, fourteen feet by sixteen feet in size, one with a cement floor. It would cost them only fifteen dollars and fifty cents because they did all the work themselves. Audrey wrote a great deal about her house building projects because she believed other people could also accomplish such things if they set out to do it. She was always an independent woman and believed that if someone could "do-it-yourself," great satisfaction, as well as monetary savings, would be the reward.

She believed her writing would inspire others to undertake such tasks, giving detail from her own experience, as well as encouragement. She hoped others would learn from her experiences, which is one of the reasons she loved being a writer.

Audrey was pleased with the Ten Dollar House and was even happier with the Fifteen Dollar House, the one that would become a real "home." However, Audrey did not pay to have quiet title on the place. Apparently, she did not think it was essential to do so and did not have the money. She lived to regret that decision years later when some new-comers to the country bought a piece of adjoining property and claimed a strip of Audrey's land (as well as land of other neighbors) due to a boundry line they disputed.

Audrey recalled that a poet had written that it takes a "heap of living" to make a house a home. As she and Clyde planned their new log cabin, they knew that this little house would become a true home.

41

The Fifteen Dollar House

Audrey always felt that her own mountain ranch came to her in a most unusual way. She had loved the mountains from the time she could remember seeing her first mountain in New Mexico. She especially loved the Sangre de Cristo mountain range where the Old Homestead Ranch was nestled.

As mentioned before, "Grandfather" Richard A. Shearer had deeded the first homestead to his son, Charles Vivian. Then when Vivian and Edith got a divorce, that property was deeded to Edith. In 1942, Audrey was surprised when Edith Shutt wanted to sell her ranch property. She was even more surprised to learn that Edith's daughter Grace did not want the property. Audrey and Clyde raised the money, assisted by Mabel and Vivian's loan, along with money Mabel had paid Audrey for her work as a youngster. Now Clyde and Audrey owned their own piece of the mountain. Audrey was ecstatic. She and Clyde determined to live there—to build a cozy cabin that would endure even the worst weather.

A warm February, with grass greening on the creek banks and tiny purple and yellow flowers blooming in the slush, found Clyde and Audrey racing with time to build another cabin. They were living in the Ten Dollar Cabin on the Shearer place, planning to build a cabin on their own property next door in May, when news from Opal changed their plans.

Bob was going to work in the Texas shipyards. Opal, still living in Santa Fe, wanted to move into the Ten Dollar House with her two children, Bobby and Jackie. Mabel and Vivian had assured Opal that she and her family were welcome to stay at the Old Homestead Ranch. Opal would plant a garden and raise hogs and chickens. Clyde and Audrey decided to accelerate their plans to build a cabin on their own place so they could turn the Ten Dollar House, which was on Vivian and Mabel's land, over to Opal and her family to live in. The Ten Dollar House was not made for housing three or four adults and three children, so Audrey and Clyde hurried to finish building the Fifteen Dollar House. The new cabin, Audrey recalled, "built by our more experienced hands, lacked some of the amateurish mistakes of the 10 dollar house. However, it would have still given a real carpenter nightmares."[1]

> They [Bob and Opal] planned to come out March 10 or March 15. We hurried but the Fifteen Dollar House wasn't done by that time, so they moved in with us—6 people in [the] Ten Dollar House and Opal helped on the plastering. I froze my hands mudding—using water out of the creek to make mud with pine needles for straw. Clyde set up a little two hole laundry stove and after that we heated the water. Clyde put in a window he brought out from town, and Bobby threw a rock through it so Clyde had to get a new glass. We got into the house about a week later than expected.[2]

Audrey remembered later:

> Sometime that spring or the next in April, I think, Nash Romero came by looking for Clyde. I didn't see him but Clyde met him on the road. He said Clyde could get a job at Camp Luna so he went in at once and applied for it and got a job at the Camp Luna Fire Department as a driver. He worked 24 hours and was off 24 hours. It was war time so we planted "Victory Gardens," more like fields. Opal and I and the kids walked over to the folks' mesa every day and planted corn. Opal planted garden below the 10 dollar house and I planted garden up above—below the [Forest Springs Ranch] spring. That was the year I had 50-some cabbage plants under glass jars. Some wild horses—scared by something—came

running over the mountain and jumped the fence into the garden and ran through the quart jars and didn't knock one over, jumped the north fence and were gone.[3]

Clyde thought that at least during the summer months he could commute the eighteen miles to work. Audrey and Crystal could continue to live at the ranch. When they learned Opal and family were coming to move into the Ten Dollar House, Clyde and Audrey had three weeks in which to build the cabin once they decided on a site. The weather was perverse. It snowed hard on the other side of the range in the Pecos country, and, Audrey wrote later, "Constant flurries flipped over the mountain top to whip us and urge us to quit."[4]

> At first the weather seemed to cooperate. But the usual false spring of February suddenly changed.
> Thin clouds streamed across the top of the sky. A deep haze far to the south and the different note in the coyote chorus, stationed on the high ridges, warmed of a coming storm. The snow came soft and deep. All wild life became silent, hiding and conserving their strength in order to combat the cold that would follow the storm.
> After the storm dumped nearly two feet of the heavy white blanket, the air cleared, and the thermometer mercury fell to the bottom of the tube and curled up there to try to get warm. It was 15 [degrees] below [zero] one morning, but our snug Ten Dollar House with its thick inner coat of adobe weathered the cold nicely. Only a little ice appeared in a few jars of my canned fruit.[5]

After the deep snow began to melt, storms on the other side of the Sangre de Cristo range kept riding the wind over the top of the mountains.

> The wind ridden snow whipped us as we walked the half mile from the Ten Dollar House to the new cabin site. The perverse weather seemed to try to force us to quit. When we gritted our teeth and kept on keeping on, the fates smiled and warmed us into spring again.[6]

Their tools were an axe, a hand saw, a big wood saw, a hammer, a spade, a garden hoe, a meat cleaver and a kitchen spatula. They had no square, no level and no draw knife, all of which would have made the work much easier. However, they knew nothing about carpentry work, (despite the success of the Ten Dollar Cabin) so they didn't know the difference.

Clyde and Audrey cleared the oak brush from the comparatively level spot. Then Clyde placed the four huge corner stones he had bought up from the creek bottom. Next Clyde peeled the first four logs. They put them across the stones. They sighted along them and moved them over an inch this way or that, until they had the foundation looking square and level. Audrey had read that a weight on the end of a string makes a level, but they depended on their eyes, for the most part. The finished cabin looked as though it was squared up and leveled in an orthodox manner. They discovered that "by sighting by a straight stick or carpenter level two people—one with a rod or 2 by 4—could get something level, not true level, but close."[7]

Crystal and Audrey used Crystal's red wagon for hauling small boulders from the canyon bed. They used those rocks to fill in under the foundation logs while Clyde cut more trees.

Clyde cut fifty-two logs and dragged them to the building site with a chain tied to the trailer hitch of their 1930 Ford. On March 1, 1943, all the logs were on the spot, waiting to be peeled. All the bark had to be removed from the trees to keep wood bugs from boring in under the bark and eating up the wall. Also, peeled logs do not gather moisture and rot as do those with the bark left on. "We found it very hard work 'scratching' bark from frozen logs. Again we found unthought-of muscles that took turns torturing us."[8]

Clyde soon became an expert with the ax, taking even strokes to remove long slices of bark without touching the creamy pine wood underneath. Audrey struggled with a light ax and finally tried to slice bark off with a meat cleaver. She wrote:

> All of the logs I peeled continued to look as though a tired mouse had chewed that bark off an inch at a time. A draw knife might have helped in the log peeling—but we didn't know such an implement existed.[9]

Each time they got four logs peeled, Audrey helped Clyde lay them up into the walls. After they were in position he notched them in the right place and set the notches together so that they would not slip apart. Once in a while Clyde was not satisfied with their solidarity. Then he drove a huge spite through them in the center of the notches to give them added strength.

> When Crystal and I caught cold and didn't dare face the icy string of whirling white that whipped over the mountains, Clyde peeled and laid up the logs alone. Sometimes the sun shone brightly, even as we were enveloped in wildly swirling snow. Altogether nearly a foot and a half of

snow fell while we built our cabin. Luckily at our building site most of it melted as it fell.[10]

Certainly they would have chosen a warmer time of year to build a cabin had they been given a choice, but the Ten Dollar House they had built was not on their land. It was on the Shearer place, part of the Old Homestead Ranch, so there was no guarantee they could stay there indefinitely. When Opal and Bob asked to move their family into the cabin Clyde and Audrey had built, Audrey and Clyde, feeling fortunate to have been able to purchase their own ranch land next door, were glad to be able to turn over the cabin to Mabel Shearer's second daughter and family to stay. Audrey and Opal were very close sisters, and Bob and Clyde were very close brothers. Their children were almost like siblings, being double cousins. So Audrey and Clyde built their new cabin as quickly as they could, despite the adverse weather.

The lower logs were fairly simple to place. But when the walls became five or six feet high, it was not easy for the couple to boost one end of a log to the top of the wall and then slide and push the other end up and around until it was even with the other logs in the wall.

On March 5, 1943, the newly peeled logs were all in place. Clyde nailed two-by-sixes against the walls where they wanted the door and two windows. With the two-by-sixes holding the logs securely, he cut the spaces for the door and windows. They had been given old windows and the two-by-sixes when a friend remodeled a house. This time they were not given a door, as they had been for the Ten Dollar House. But Clyde bought lumber and nailed together a rough door at a cost $1.35. "Later he covered it with part of the left over roofing, so then the wind couldn't flow through the cracks."[11]

The unfinished walls, looking like creamy open-work lace, gave some protection from the blowing snow. Inside of them, Audrey began to level off the sloping floor with the spade. Clyde hung the door and the two windows on hinges. All opened outward so that eventually screens would be placed on the inside.[12]

Clyde wanted to take the trailer to town to get lumber for the roof. But the combined snow storms and spring thaw left a sea of mud where the roads meandered through the canyon country. The deep mud holes did not freeze hard enough at night or stay frozen long enough the next day to go to town and back with a load of lumber. It was only ten days until March 15. "We had to have it finished in ten more days so that we could live in it, and we could not live in it without a roof."[13]

When they had built the Ten Dollar House, their money was very limited so they had used pine poles for a roof. Now they had enough money to buy material for a roof but couldn't get to town when they needed to due to the bad road. Audrey wrote in her published article *Next Door to Heaven:*

> Financial difficulty had caused us to roof our Ten Dollar House in an unusual manner. Now, deep mud prevented us from hauling lumber for our roof, so we peeled more than a hundred and fifty little trees, two to three inches in diameter, laid them side by side, tacked asphalt roofing over them as though they were smooth boards, and had a satisfactory roof.[14]

Audrey explained:

> We put up two ridge poles instead of one in order to have more room from the end of each little log to meet its counterpart from the other side. Because this would make an extra heavy roof, we placed a pine pillar in the center of the room under the two ridge poles. This lessened the risk of a caving roof during heavy snows.[15]

The small peeled trees were placed side by side and were nailed securely at each end on top of the wall and the ridge poles. These hundred and fifty trees did not make a completely solid surface. Nevertheless, Clyde and Audrey covered them with the heaviest type of asphalt roofing they could buy.

> They [the ridge poles] did not make a completely solid surface. However when we tacked asphalt roofing over them, one layer of thinner material and the top layer the heaviest type we could buy, it lasted 19 years, or until we had a bad hail storm. The roofing had been guaranteed for 17 years so we felt it proved to be a very satisfactory roof.[16]

For the chimney hole Clyde left a large space between the poles and placed a large roof jack between the logs.

> Because our mountain yellow pines are full of pitch, fire in a stove can make a chimney red hot, so we liked lots of space between the chimney and any wood. We also put a piece of asbestos along the logs.[17]

As soon as the roof was in place, Clyde and Audrey began the task of chinking the cracks between the logs. They cut small poles to fit and wedged or nailed them into the openings between the logs. Then they covered the whole inside wall with adobe mud plaster. The cabin had three or four of the little "port-holes" in addition to the two big side windows.

> As we chinked the cracks we took several pieces of glass and fastened them in large cracks between the logs, holding them in place with small sticks. These little port-holes gave a good deal of extra light and also a brief view of the various areas outside the cabin.[18]

Adobe plaster was very satisfactory, in spite of the back-breaking work involved in mixing it. Not far from the cabin was a suitable adobe earth which did not contain too much clay or too much humus. This type of adobe would stick tightly to the logs, so Clyde hollowed out a hole in the center of the loose dirt, poured in a bucket of partly frozen water from the creek, and mixed it with a garden hoe. Audrey added a few handfuls of dry pine needles from the heavily carpeted mountain side to act as "straw" to bind the mixture together.

> With it mixed, I began mudslinging and found that I hadn't lost the touch I acquired in plastering the Ten Dollar House. As the sun went down that first day of mudding, I found my hands were numb and clumsy in handling mud. I did not realize that I had "frozen" them with the icy adobe, until washing the mud off. Then I had to rub a million red hot needles out of my fingers with snow. The next day we heated the ice water from the creek before we mixed it into the adobe dirt and saved my hands from a second round of "frostbite."[19]

Rubbing snow on an over-exposed area of the body was a treatment Audrey had heard about and used. However, it should be noted here that such "treatment" *cannot be recommended* as a method of preventing or treating frostbite or over-exposure to cold.

Audrey explained that they set up a little "sheep-herders" two-hole cook stove to heat water and warm the cabin so that the mud would not freeze and crack at night. "By the Ides of March deadline our new home was complete except for a floor. The dirt was hard packed from our tramping on it so we laid a cheap linoleum on it and moved in."[20]

Later Audrey was able to sell several articles about her house building experiences. One was an article entitled "We Housed Ourselves for $15.50," in *Profitable Hobbies*," February, 1949. An example of Audrey's description follows:

While Clyde worked mixing fresh mud, I slung it onto the walls. This mudslinging would be good practice for a baseball pitcher. You take a handful of nice, gooey mud, aim at the crack you wish to fill and let fly. Put all of your swing into each mud ball. The mud hits the crack with a force that plasters it tightly into the cracks and to the logs. It is then easy to smooth up with a trowel—a kitchen spatula in our case. This work left new sets of muscles howling for relief.[21]

The March 15, 1943 deadline found their cabin nearly completed. Once spring came and the weather warmed up, they moved everything outside and laid a cement floor. They had seen cement laid but did not know how to do it. They finally decided upon one portion of sand from the creek bed mixed with an equal amount of cement. Later they realized it should have been one to four—one shovel of cement to four shovels of sand. "The mixture was too rich in cement but after it was mixed with water until it had the consistency of a gooey cow pie (according to Clyde) it made a floor."[22]

They also did not know that to make a glaze finish it is a must to work the cement with a trowel as it "cures." When it was smoothed into place with the heavy spatula, it made a satisfactory floor. There was some roughness but the floor was fairly level and the minor waves in the cement were not noticeable. Later they covered the cement floor with linoleum.

The Fifteen Dollar Cabin built by Audrey and Clyde Simpson, 1943
Source: Simpson Archives, photo by Audrey Simpson

In her "Next Door to Heaven" article, Audrey wrote:

> On March 15, we moved into our new $15 cabin, leaving our $10 house for my sister and Bobby and Jacqueline. Since we had not bowed and quit under their lashing, the mountain gods now smiled on us. They gave us mild, cloudless days with the blue curtain of heaven so bright we could scarcely look into the sky. And the nearly celestial music of the small birds was accentuated by the heavy voice of a turkey gobbler as they all enjoyed Spring.[23]

Audrey and Clyde had built a fourteen foot by sixteen foot cabin at the cost of $15.50. It was built much better than the Ten Dollar House, as they were now "experienced" builders. An itemized list of the cash cost of the cabin was as follows:

Nails $.75
Door (30 board feet of lumber) $1.35
Hinges, strap variety $1.10
Asphalt roofing, three rolls $9.30
Cement, three sacks $3.00
Total: $15.50

Audrey wrote:

> Altogether, 209 trees were cut. There were 4 logs for the foundation, 56 for the walls, 2 ridge poles, one large center pillar, plus 150 small trees for the roof poles. For less than sixteen dollars, the little family had a place to stay in the mountains. Afterwards, two more little cabins were built, 12' by 12' in size behind the bigger cabin. One would serve as an extra bedroom or storeroom and the other as a chicken house.[24]

So now the little family had a cabin on their own property "next door to heaven."

In April of 1943, Clyde asked a neighbor, a farmer at San Geronimo, to come and plow up a garden spot. But they failed to ask him to harrow it, so the rough sod was not ready to plant after he left. They knew he was busy with his own plowing three miles away, so they didn't want to ask him to make a return trip. Clyde pounded spikes left over from the building into a two-by-eight plank. He tied that to the Model A and bucked over the rough ground until they had a make-shift harrowing job completed. Then they planted until the first of June.

About the middle of April, Clyde was well enough to go back to work in Las Vegas. Audrey and Crystal set out a hundred wild plum trees. With a shovel and a water bucket they put them at random along the creek. Once they saw a bear track close to the cabin. Audrey wrote, "We heard bears grunting like a couple of pigs. I didn't want to scare a bear in that tangle of creek bottom brush, so we planted garden the rest of that day in a wide open space."[25]

On Holy Thursday Audrey would often hear the cries of the Penitentes. There was a morada in Santillanes canyon, just about a mile from her cabin at Forest Springs Ranch. But too many people were moving into the country and the Penitentes valued their privacy. They moved further up the mountain. However, Audrey could still hear their activities. They would come from their homes in San Geronimo and surrounding areas, go up to Santillanes Canyon, go up the road to the Santa Fe National Forest gate, past the U.S. Forest Service cabin, and up the Big Cross Trail, sometimes to the top, or nearly the top of the mountain, where a big wooden cross had been erected years ago.

Rocks at the foot of the the Big Cross show where each traveler at various times placed a rock in the pile in keeping with some tradition too old for its origin to be remembered. Audrey wrote a story published in *New Mexico Magazine* in March, 1951, "The Big Cross Trail." She described how to get to the trail from Las Vegas, the beautiful mountain scenery along the way, and the view from the top. A forest fire destroyed the cross and another one was put up in 1884 and was still standing in 1950 when Audrey, Crystal, and Pete Gardner walked up the Big Cross Trail.[26]

Audrey wrote a fictional story based on fact about Spanish-American villagers taking San Ysidro, the saint of the farmers, up the mountain to see the dry land whenever rain was needed. The story, "A Walk for Rain" described Barillas Peak and the Big Cross Trail. That trail was a place for various kinds of religious ceremonies in the early days, although it never gained the popularity of Hermit's Peak and the legend of the Hermit or Holy man. Audrey also wrote about that story in "Hermits Peak Legend" which was published in 1988 in *Old West*.[27]

Clyde came to the ranch on weekends. A bridge was needed to make the creek crossing easy. The cabin was built at the intersection of two canyons, situated between two creeks, Happy Creek and Roaring Creek. The one on the east was a deep gully. If they bridged it, they could have a shorter and better road. So when Clyde came out on a weekend, they worked at bridge building—something else they had never done. Clyde cut four huge trees close to the bridge site. He pulled them into position on the east bank with the Ford. Then he traveled around the long way to the west bank, hooked the Model A onto them with a heavy wire clothesline and several long strands of barbed wire, carefully stepped on the gas, and one at a time he eased them across the gully into position. "That excellent little fifteen-foot bridge, planned and built by no engineer, has saved much gas and wear on tires."[28]

The bridge, like the Fifteen Dollar Cabin and the Ten Dollar Cabin, was still solid and in use until it was destroyed in the 1971 forest fire.

In the summer of 1943, Opal and their two children were living in the Ten Dollar House. (Bob also stayed there when he wasn't away working.) Crystal enjoyed playing with her two cousins, Bobby and Jackie. Clyde's mother came up and visited them while they were there. She was amazed at how much work had been done. In addition to planting a garden, Clyde and Audrey had a few chickens. There was a bobcat that liked to watch them. He finally killed a rooster, so Audrey immediately had to cook the rooster to save the meat. She shot the bobcat just after he had killed the rooster. She then proceeded to drag the cat off down to the north gate where she hung him on the fence, perhaps as a warning to any other predators.

Millicent L. Gensemer's *Las Vegas Daily Optic* article summarized Audrey's abilities:

> While our society editor was on vacation we did a bit of delving into her past and jotted down some recollections from conversations to find that the Optic can boast not only a good reporter but a most versatile one. Audrey Simpson is equally skilled with a typewriter, a rifle, or an ax and can recount tales from her own experiences that rival a TV western.[29]

Audrey was at home with a hoe or a typewriter. She could shoot as well as any marksman in the country, stay on a bucking bronc, or tenderly rock a baby in her favorite rocking chair. She worked hard and she could match any farmer or rancher in putting in a full day's hard work, as her Victory Garden was to prove.

Victory Garden *Par Excellence*

After the Japanese bombed Pearl Harbor, Americans determined to stop Hitler and his allies. The fear was that the Japanese would invade the homeland. Americans are at their "toughest and best" when defending their homes. No sacrifice was too great. Ration stamps, the scarcity of certain commodities, the hardship of driving without good tires—patching, substituting, "making-do"—became the American way of life in those days. A Victory Garden was something anyone with a little land could contribute. Everyone was being urged to help the war effort by planting Victory Gardens, even folks with only a few yards of soil in their backyards.

Audrey wanted to plant a garden. Someone from San Geronimo was hired to plow the field. Audrey and Opal decided to plant the entire Old Homestead Ranch's "Mesa," an open field consisting of over an acre of land. They would plant corn. The Mesa was about a quarter of a mile below the big adobe house on the Shearer place and a little over half a mile from the Simpson cabin. That was the field which Grandfather Shearer had worked on years before, putting up a rock wall taller than his own height—about six feet—to conserve the rich soil.

That summer Audrey and Opal planted the biggest "Victory Garden" in the area. There was enough rain that summer so the corn grew and produced a good crop. They had so much that they canned it and gave it away. They proved that with work and enough rain that rich mountain soil could produce!

Ramón Santillanes, was one of the members of the old time Santillanes family. They had lived in the area for several generations. Ramón was willing to give advice based on his experience as a farmer. He said, "When the leaf on the oak brush is the size of a mouse's ear, then it is time to plant the corn—not before." That would be in late April or early May, Audrey figured. Audrey wrote in her article, "Next Door to Heaven:"

> Opal and I, with our children and two dogs [Crystal's Bonnie and Opal's Penny] a shovel, hoes, and ten pounds of golden Bantam seed corn, walked the three-quarters of a mile to the field every morning. There we dug holes, dropping in three or four grains of corn, covered it over, let the children dance a jig on it when they cared to (which wasn't often) and worked slowly across the field. The delightful odor of rich, warm, moist soil, combined with mountain pine, gave us strength to continue working when our muscles ached with a weariness that made us long to fall flat on the earth and soak up life and strength as the seed did.[1]

Opal and Audrey were proud of their work. At the end of the summer, Audrey said, "We mountain gals planted six thousand hills of sweet corn and two thousand hills of field corn. And then by hand, we fought the everlasting fight with the weeds, and waited for the rain."[2]

June was dry and the creeks began to dry up. Audrey and Opal hoed the corn. July's thunderheads blackened over the mountains but there was not as much rain as usual. Still, the corn grew tall. Ramón came by and admired their work.

"When do you think it will rain?" Opal asked. "We can't irrigate this mesa land. It's too far from the creek. And it's up hill from the creek."

"Do you think we'll get some rain soon?" Audrey asked the farmer.

"The old men say when the moon turns over and the points are down, the rain comes," Ramón replied.

Audrey and Opal watched the moon. One night they saw the moon with the "horns" pointed down. Sure enough, rain clouds stormed along the mountain. But the showers were light and scattered. The women worried about their crop. They hoed around the plants to give them a chance to "breathe" and hold in any moisture they got.

Every evening Audrey and Crystal would go up the hill to their own Forest Springs Ranch Mesa to look at the mountains surrounding the place and check for smoke. Audrey was now deathly afraid of forest fire, having barely escaped with Crystal in the baby buggy in the last fire. They would close the cabin door at night and feel secure behind the sturdy, home-made door Clyde had built. When he was there on weekends, they felt much safer.

One midnight, Audrey awoke to a strange, hideous howl. The dogs Bonny and Penny were barking furiously. Audrey looked out the window into the bright moonlight night. She wrote in her article for *New Mexico Magazine*:

> The black tree shadows, seen through a too thin screen wire (for my windows were open) did nothing to relieve the weirdness of the cry. I did not light the lamp for fear of interesting the banshee outside. I have heard coyotes in all circumstances. This was not a coyote. Once in the Black Lake country I heard a Lobo's deep-throated howl. I think that this was not a wolf. When truly frightened, my heels ache with a peculiar pain. I stood at the window with throbbing heels, gazing at the black pooled hillside, trying to see deep into the trees. I saw Penny run baying up the hill to the crest about a hundred feet from my window. His neck hair had been stiffly erect. In a moment that huge red hound came down the hill so fast he was almost rolling. Then a wail, with a satanic laugh sounded plainly through it, shattered my heels again. Very silently, I reached for the .30-.30. Such an animal might decide to investigate my cabin. [After I went to bed] I laid the gun at my head, covered my frightened heels, thoroughly, and heard the strange cry twice more as it traveled down the canyon. A few days later neighbors on Falls Creek reported the passage of a strange wailing animal, saying, "We never heard the likes of it before." I hunted for tracks but could find none. A mountain lion does not deliberately chase dogs. I am still wondering what type of animal would case the brave red hound, Penny.[3]

Years later, as Audrey described the animal, Bill Reid suggested that it probably was a cougar or mountain lion. "They can make a scream like a woman," he said. But Audrey never understood what that laughing noise had been or why the dogs had been so terrified.

Later that summer a rattlesnake struck Opal's dog Penny. Penny lay down under the bed in the Ten Dollar Cabin and did not move for a day or two. Opal gave him water but knew there was not much else to do. In a few days Penny recovered. Penny was not a young dog, but after his recovery he seemed just like a puppy. Somehow he was rejuvenated.[4]

In late August and early September, harvest time arrived. Audrey and Opal had anticipated losing some of the crop to birds, worms and insects so they had planted more than enough for themselves. They had a bumper crop. Soil Conservation officials brought farmers from across the country to inspect their remarkable crop. It was a very good crop for a dry year, they explained, proving the worth of terracing. Grandfather had saved the soil and the two young women had done the rest of the work in cooperation with Mother Nature.

Audrey thanked God for the crop which was remarkable for a dry year. She was grateful for the rich soil of the Mesa and the rock retaining wall that "Grandfather" Shearer had built to conserve the soil. She recalled years when she and Opal had not had enough to eat. Now they had more than enough corn. That summer of 1943 Opal and Audrey planted the grandmother all of Victory Gardens.

They began to can the corn, adding it to a large supply of home-canned beans and peas they had also grown. They canned several hundred jars, sent truckloads to town. They cooked it slightly, cut it from the cob, dried it on trays in the oven, and ate fresh corn, giving fresh corn to friends and neighbors. Several years later Audrey and Opal were still feeding their children canned corn from that crop. In notes she wrote years later, Audrey said:

> We raised truck loads of corn. Vivian came and hauled off several pick up loads and the SCS [Soil Conservation Service] marveled at our crop. Opal had chickens and a pig pen for a hog. The creek dried up and when Clyde came out, he would haul barrels of water for her pigs and chickens. Once a lynx cat snarled at Opal when she went out at dark to shut them [in].[5]

Audrey knew the summer was short, and she prepared for the next winter. Audrey wrote, "Up here next door to heaven we rejoiced in our victory garden. And blue smoke circled the mountains as their peace pipes blazed to herald a change. The reign of summer was ending. Winter would be the new king."[6]

In Audrey's article about building the Fifteen Dollar House, published in *Profitable Hobbies* in February, 1949, she finished the article with the statement:

> Each time we build we learn how to do a better job. So someday when we have time to build that large house on the hill we will really know how! That dream house there in the future will take much hard work and about $200 cash. For the present we are content to lick the housing shortage with our hand made cabins.[7]

Audrey wrote a poem, "Mountain Dusk," published in the August 1, 1957 *Las Vegas Daily Optic:*

> A night hawk soars upward
> Then dives with loud zoom!
> That echoes through canyons'
> Pine-scented night gloom.
>
> Horned owl gives a "Who,"
> To freeze warm mountain blood,
> And a coyote sings long
> By a stream's silver flood.
>
> Log cabin doors close
> And oil lamps wink bright
> While all of the forest
> Prepares for the night.[8]

Audrey felt safe and cozy in the little cabin, especially with Clyde by her side, Crystal safely tucked into her little bed, and Bonnie on guard at the door. She couldn't help thinking of the horrible war on the other side of the world. She prayed every night for the safety of the troops, as well as the protection of her family. She thought about how peaceful it was in the little log cabin, nestled in the beautiful forest at the foot of the majestic Barillas Peak. It seemed impossible that the world was engaged in the horrible battles of World War II and that the outcome of that war would affect their children. One night Audrey awoke in a sweat, terrified. She'd had a nightmare about a horrific battle going on, deep anguish and death all around.

"It was only a dream. My mountain girl is safe," Clyde assured her, taking her into the circle of his arms. "Surely the war will be over soon. We'll keep praying. God will see us all through this." He held her until she went back to sleep.

Although Clyde had returned to work when the cabin was finished, he and Audrey lived in the Fifteen Dollar Cabin for the rest of the summer. He drove a car or rode a bicycle from town on weekends. But as winter approached, they moved to town.

The fall of 1943 brought about several changes. Audrey wrote in her notes that sometime in the fall of 1943 Opal left and went to Beaumont, Texas where Bob had a job in the shipyards. Crystal and Audrey moved back to Las Vegas into one of the Carrington apartments where Clyde had already been staying during the work week. Audrey had canned hundreds of cans of corn, peas, etc. Opal had raised pinto beans, enough to have dried beans to last for years. Clyde fell into the routine of work. Audrey did the cooking, cleaning, and caring for Crystal.[9]

In spite of their busy lives in town, Audrey and Clyde dreamed of having time to build a large house to live in at Forest Springs Ranch. Audrey would always love her mountains and would long to live within their sheltering presence. Sometimes she remembered her nightmare about the war. She always prayed for world peace. She wished everyone could know the peace and solitude of her mountains. The summer of the Victory garden, in spite of all the hard work, was one of the best Audrey had ever known.

Part 11
Cabin for Three

1

Dorothy: Gift of God

Audrey chose a warm day at the end of September to tell Clyde the secret that lay under her heart. They sat under a big pine tree, surrounded by the yellow and purple wild flowers that spoke of the end of summer. The couple heard the sounds of blue jays in the tall oaks trees, watched their antics as they flitted from branch to branch. Audrey looked up at the endless blue sky, a bowl of deep turquoise turned upside down over the world. A few fluffy, white clouds drifted above in gentle, benevolent breezes. Those breezes carried the scent of fir and pine down the canyon from the high brown mesas, the red ridges, and the blue summits of the surrounding peaks—Barillas Peak, Fox Peak, and the twin peaks where the Falls Creek cascaded down in three tiers. The fragrance of the pines as one approached them was indescribable. The scent after a rain was even more wonderful.

Clyde remarked to Audrey, "I remember the first time I saw this place and told you I loved the smell of the pines. You told me 'If you could bottle that scent, you could make a fortune.'"

The sun was warm on the faces of the young couple. They watched their daughter Crystal playing near the babbling brook—"Happy Creek"—that carried its icy flow from the high mountains down to the Tecolote where it would find its way to the Rio Grande. The pine trees waved their branches gently as though in agreement with the words the young couple spoke.

"Your eyes are the same color as the sky," Clyde observed. "Robin's egg blue, the prettiest color of blue there is!"

Audrey smiled in reply. "Our prayers have been answered," Audrey said after a long silence. "I visited the doctor last week. We're going to have another baby."

Clyde broke into a grin, his green eyes shining with joy. "I thought the doctor said you couldn't have any more babies."

"I guess God didn't agree with him," Audrey replied. When she smiled, her blue eyes twinkled. "Maybe we'll have those ten kids after all!"

Clyde laughed and drew Audrey close.

"The doctor told me I'd never have *any* children, so how can he explain Crystal?" Audrey continued.

"Mama! Daddy! Look at the butterfly!" Crystal pointed and danced about in the grass, trying to catch the colorful creature. Bonnie ran about in the meadow, happy with her joyful charge. Crystal's light brown hair flew in all directions as she ran, first after the butterfly, then after the white collie.

Audrey and Clyde talked about how nice it would be if they could spend the coming cold nights under warm blankets in their little log cabin. They wished that somehow they could remain in this mountain paradise for the winter, but the necessity of earning a living and Crystal's schooling loomed before them.

"We'll live here full time as soon as we can," Clyde promised. "I'll build a big house—with a room for each child! You won't have to do anything but sit under a pine tree and hold our newest baby. Sometimes things take a while," Clyde admitted. "But it will happen. You're my little Sweetheart of the Mountains; you deserve the best."

Audrey smiled as Clyde mentioned a favorite song, "When It's Springtime in the Rockies." Crystal came running up with a bouquet of wild flowers she had picked. "For you, Mama," she said, her green eyes shining with happiness. "If I had a little sister I'd give some to her."

"Well, you may get a little sister—or brother—before too long," Audrey promised.

Crystal danced away, "I want a sister! My own little sister! We'll have fun chasing butterflies together!" she exclaimed.

Although Clyde and Audrey knew they would have to live in town to work and send the children to school, they never lost sight of their dream to build a big house at the ranch and retire there. When it was time for school to start, Crystal, eager to learn to read, was enrolled. Audrey looked forward to the new arrival. Audrey wrote a poem which was published in *The American Baby Magazine*:

> Will your hair be curly?
> Will your eyes be blue?
> Really we care not at all—
> They'll be part of you!
>
> We know you'll be beautiful—
> Hair as soft as down
> Oh, how very proud we'll be
> Strolling 'round the town.

> Now we feel close to heaven—
> Filled with love for you.
> We've not very long to wait
> Sweet, dear baby—(pink—or blue!)[1]

Audrey wrote:

> Dr. Mortimer had said I mustn't have any more children after Crystal. So I was scared to death when Dorothy came along. I was real sick at first until I put my thinking cap on and bawled myself out and said my prayers early and often. Then I had no more trouble and got through that pregnancy very well.[2]

Audrey, Clyde and Crystal once again were living in the little back house at Carringtons, the one-room apartment house that Mr. Carrington later used as a shop. Audrey had a neighbor who was also expecting a baby any day. In late February, the woman said, "I refuse to have my baby on Leap Year!"

Audrey thought, "The sooner the better," although she knew her baby was not due for two weeks. Both of them had labor pains on Leap Year, but the neighbor refused to go to the hospital. She didn't have her baby for another two weeks. Audrey went to the hospital and gave birth to a second daughter, Dorothy Audrey Simpson, about 1:20 p.m. on February 29, 1944.

Clyde was delighted to see such a "fat, healthy" baby, not frail as Crystal had been as a premature child. Crystal beamed with the joy of having the little sister she wanted. Audrey thanked God that her second baby was healthy.

The author of this book is that second child, hence the <u>switch to the use of the first person</u> in writing the remainder of my mother's story. At times I may refer to Audrey as "Mother" or "Mama" or "Mom," and may refer to other family members by my relationship to them, such as "Daddy" instead of Clyde.

My parents named me "Dorothy" which means "Gift of God." My middle name, Audrey, was for my mother. When I was born at the Las Vegas Hospital on Sixth Street in Las Vegas (the old Y.M.C.A. building) I weighed six pounds, four ounces, and I was nineteen inches in length. My grandmother, Mabel Shearer, wrote in a letter:

> Audrey had a new baby born this afternoon—1:20—at the Las Vegas Hospital—a fine girl. She [Audrey] has a girl 5 years old. She and her husband live here in town. He is a fireman at our army camp here. February 29. She won't have a birthday very often. Audrey and baby are fine.[3]

The entire family was growing. Opal and Bob, after having Bobby and Jacqueline, had a third child, Donna Dolores Simpson, born October 30, 1944. Opal had quite an ordeal when she was pregnant with Donna. The doctor told her she had a tumor which would have to be removed. During the surgery, the doctor discovered there was no tumor; there was a fetus. The doctor sewed Opal up and admitted he'd been wrong. He had told her she had a tumor, but she was pregnant. Opal had to go through pregnancy while healing from the incision. Fortunately, Donna was a healthy baby.

Edward had married Voline Loretta McCurdy. She had a boy, "Sonny," from a previous marriage. Edward adopted him—William Edward Clements—and called him "Bill." Edward and Voline then had two children, Shirley Ann Clements, born July 2, 1945 and Eddie Clements, born September 13, 1947.

Betty Clements, married to Stanley A. Hardin, had their first child, Tana Marie, born September 12, 1943 in Raton, New Mexico. Janie Lee Hardin was born July 26, 1946 in Davenport, Iowa, and several years later Twila Dee Hardin came on the scene on November 30, 1955 in Portales, New Mexico.

Through the years the family continued to grow. Milly married Morton Alpern and had Roger Lee. That marriage ended, and later Milly married Orval Dixon. Then Sam Dixon and later his sister Dianna Dixon were born.

Jessica and David "Red" Braziel had three boys—Dwight, Russell and Paul—and two girls, Yvonne and Yvette. Frank and Dorothy Shearer had Frankie and Carol Ann Shearer. After Dorothy's death, Frank re-married. He and Margaret Aaron Shearer then had Carl Shearer. As the family grew, Audrey's mother, Mabel Shearer, was a proud grandmother. She had brought up a family of seven children. Now they were having children and Mabel seemed to thrive as she spent time with each child.

Clyde's mother, too, was proud to be a grandmother. "Granny" Addie Simpson had high hopes for Clyde. She wanted him to make a career of the ministry.

In his personal Bible, Clyde had written: "I have this day, May 9, 1929 publicly accepted the Lord Jesus Christ as my Personal Savior, and by His Grace I hereby pledge my life to His service, and will follow Him all the way." Signed: Clyde J. Simpson. There was another note in his hand writing: "Baptized in water: December 4, 1930."

Clyde had been ordained after completing the course work at a Bible college in Los Angeles. He had left the L.I.F.E. (Lighthouse of the International Foursquare Gospel) college due to lack of funds, although he would have preferred to graduate from that college started by Aimee Semple McPherson. But he was able to get his ordination papers sooner at the other college. His certificate stated:

> CERTIFICATE OF ORDINATION
> The Church in the Name of Jesus Christ and of the First Born
> Evangelist NONA A. HOUSE, Pastor
> LOS ANGELES, CALIFORNIA
> Unto All Mankind Be It Known:
> That on this *22nd* day *May* month *1932* year, Before GOD and the HOSTS of HEAVEN, and WITNESSES on EARTH
> *Clyde Joseph Simpson*
> was examined, and acknowledged established in the FAITH, and therefore has been ORDAINED a MINISTER of the Full Gospel of the LORD JESUS CHRIST, to perform all the duties, and assist in all the Sacramental services according to the customs of the Church in The Name of Jesus Christ and of the First Born, and the Faith once delivered to the Saints.
> Witness *E. E. Allen, Evang.*
> Signed: *Nona A. House, Pastor*
> *O. A. Allen, Deacon*

Audrey knew Clyde wanted to preach:

> He [Clyde] was fresh out of Amiee Semple McPherson's Foursquare Gospel Church and Bible Institute in Los Angeles and was trying hard to preach. But was discouraged at every side. We often went to a revival at First Christian Church at the south west corner of University and Eighth, later torn down to make way for a Highlands University building.[4]

Clyde, with his mother's encouragement, opened a small church in Las Vegas. It was a full gospel church in a little building on University Avenue. His mother attended and persuaded a few of her friends to go with her. She tried very hard to help Clyde and Audrey "make a go" of the church and gave as much as she could financially. Audrey wrote:

> Clyde started a mission again in Dr. Christie's building which was empty. He got a deferment as a preacher. He had been ordained in Los Angeles in 1931 or 1932. [He had ordination papers and a diploma.] He rented a little building and started services. Very few came. If there were 6 or 7

there, including us, it was a big crowd. After a while he gave up.[5]

Then Clyde decided to open a church at San Geronimo, the old Spanish-American village which had one church, a Roman Catholic Church. As far as Clyde knew, there had never been a Protestant Church there before. He rented a little adobe building and put up a sign: "Full Gospel Mission, Services Sunday, 2:30 p.m." The hours would not conflict with those of the Catholic Church. However, very few people attended.

Audrey wrote later in "Religious Experiences:"

> Dorothy was still a baby—born in February—when we moved to the ranch in the summer. Clyde was working at Camp Luna and worked 24 hours and was off 24 hours. He started a mission at San Geronimo on the corner where the road behind the Catholic Church joins the east-west road from the mountains to San Pablo. It was a large hall—used for dances—etc. He had as many there as we ever had in Las Vegas. He painted a sign "Full Gospel Mission" and put it over the door. Some fellow preacher [who spoke Spanish] wanted to come over with us, and Clyde thought that he could get the idea across [in a sermon] more easily speaking Spanish. He came out a couple of times. The last time some of the village men decided to break up the meeting. They came across the plaza playing guitars and violins and singing and talking loudly. They had been drinking. They came up outside the open door. I went to the door and invited them in. They argued among themselves and finally, led by Juan [a pseudonym] whom I had known since I was 16—they came in and sat down. Some of them heckled the Spanish speaker. Finally the meeting was over and they all went away without a fight. Mr. Carrington reported Clyde came in very perturbed that evening. The girls and I were staying at the ranch. He [Clyde] talked and then paced the yard there at 921 Lincoln for hours. She [Mrs. Carrington] talked to him and I think helped him to make up his mind to close the mission. He knew we barely avoided a fight and couldn't have avoided it if I hadn't known Juan and invited them in and kept them calmed down.[6]

Clyde realized he could not be a full time preacher and support a family. There just wasn't enough interest in full gospel churches at that time, not even with the popularity of Aimee Semple McPherson. So he closed the church and continued working at the Home Café.

"I'll always be a preacher," he said. "My ordination papers are for life. When the opportunity arises for me to preach again, I will," he said. "I'll even start another little mission whenever God directs me to."

Crystal remembered the church at San Geronimo and the one in Las Vegas. She recalled that in one service at San Geronimo, there were only about six or seven people in the congregation. She remembered Clyde's preaching and then passing the offering plate. She thought to herself, *I wish this whole room were full of people and they would all give money so the church could stay open*. Crystal remembered that there were only about four people in attendance in the church in Las Vegas. She thought the same thing there and hoped more people would start coming to church.[7] Clyde was respected around town, and so was Audrey. Sometimes people called Clyde "The Preacher" and Audrey was known as "The Preacher's Wife," especially by the folks in San Geronimo and Mineral Hill, even many years later.

Audrey did not try to influence Clyde's decision to close the mission. It had to be his decision. Few people ever knew that from the time she accepted Jesus Christ as her personal savior, Audrey had wanted to be a missionary. She was pleased to be the wife of a preacher and to help build the first Full Gospel Church in the Mineral Hill area. However, Audrey and Clyde were practical enough to know that a family has to be provided for, and if a church cannot provide for the preacher and his family, it cannot thrive. She wrote:

> He [Clyde] asked me to marry him for two years and I finally did July 16, 1934. (That's another story.) Glen, his brother, told me he bet Clyde would have me down in the big woods of south east Texas working with the dirt poor while he preached to them. (And we would be dirt poor.) That hit me wrong and I vowed to myself never to go to Texas. After we were married he [Clyde] was working hours at the café so he couldn't go to church. Sometimes we went to Church of Christ started by Carringtons, meeting on Railroad. In 1935 or 1936 Ann and "Nick" Nickleson came to try to "start a work" in Las Vegas. I can't remember their affiliation but it was Pentecostal. They had three little kids, two girls and a baby boy. They rented the building west of the Optic office for a while and also had services at their house and around at other's homes.
>
> After Miss Kelton and Clyde's Mission, the Assembly of God had the little church a while. And then the Church of Christ rented it. I also went to services (maybe Foursquare) in a house located at University where they built Dr. Dillenger's office. I went to church twice on Sunday and Sunday School and once in midweek, usually Wednesday night.

When Crystal was born Clyde wanted to take her to Los Angeles to the Foursquare Temple and have her "dedicated to the Lord." Of course we were poor as church mice and couldn't do it.[8]

The Simpsons went to Sister Kelton's church services often, as long as it was there. "But they didn't have the $10 per month rent for the building so had to give it up."[9]

After the summer at the ranch when I was a baby, the only place available to rent in town was at El Moro Apartments where the Las Vegas Hospital had been when Milly was born—until a place at the Carringtons' apartments became available. (The site of those apartments is now the site of Arrott House, Highlands University housing.)

The family often stayed at Forest Springs Ranch in the Fifteen Dollar House on vacations. Audrey wrote:

> About the time Dorothy was born in 1944 we had Ramón Abeyta come up from San Geronimo to build another cabin for a bed room. Clyde was working in town and commuting back and forth to his work as a fireman at Camp Maximiliano Luna—24 hours on and 24 off. This log room was built about 20 feet back of the Fifteen Dollar House. It was 12 x 14 feet with a small window in the east side and a piece of broken windshield in the gable end for light. The east window was a pane of glass 12 x 36 inches held in place by lath nailed around the edges. The door was again plain lumber nailed together with a six inch board just below the top of the boards and the bottom another board catty-cornered from top to bottom and gave the door added strength.[10]

That cabin later served as an extra bedroom/store room when we moved to the ranch in 1949. Additionally, a small cabin was built a few yards across from it and it served as a chicken house when we lived there from 1949 to 1951. The three little log cabins served the Simpson family very well until the 1971 forest fire.

The year 1944 was good in many ways. There was hope that the tide was turning and that World War II would soon be over. Little did anyone know that not far away from quiet little Las Vegas, scientists were busy working on a weapon that would end the war.

Audrey continued to write, even after she had two children to keep up with. She wrote a poem, "Free Lance—Unemployed—Housewife," published by *Kansas City Poetry Magazine*.

And now what are you writing, they all say.
Well, come take a look at my busy day.
Children to care for and garden to weed,
Washing to work on and chickens to feed,
With home cares piled round me and just like a wall
They better ask, are you writing at all?[11]

Audrey wrote often, even with all the other work she had to do. Clyde was gone much of the time, working. Audrey was busy caring for their two daughters. She had always wanted children. Now she had two. There would be more hardships and sorrows ahead—and another daughter in her future. Children gave her and Clyde a goal to work for. Audrey thought life would continue to get better and better. But as 1944 progressed, news from overseas was not good.

2

Their Son's Brave Hearts

ecember, 1941 was an especially dark time for Addie Simpson and her family. Not only did the news of the Pearl Harbor attack in December cause them alarm and sorrow but it was in that month that William Ernest Simpson died. He had been the victim of a stroke while he was in Las Vegas. Then he went back to the farm in Oklahoma and finally moved back to Texas. In December, 1941 he died at the age of 66 and was buried in Clovis, New Mexico.

Then Addie Bain Simpson lived in Albuquerque. The Simpsons were among the early pioneer Clovis families who had established numerous businesses and homes there, but after her husband's death Addie chose to live in the Duke City. Mary Simpson, Addie's daughter, lived with her mother and cared for her in her last years.

After Ernest Simpson died, Crystal missed her Grandpa. She remembered:

He showed me how to put on my coat over a long-sleeved sweater. You hold the edge of the sweater sleeve in your hand while you pull the long coat sleeve down over it. That way, the sweater sleeve is all smooth and not wrinkled up under the coat![1]

Audrey was glad Grandpa Simpson had been able to enrich his granddaughter's life. He would be greatly missed.

Many of the local men had been sent overseas to fight the war. Some volunteered while others were drafted. Clyde was not called up for several reasons. He was married with a family, he was around 30 years of age—too old to be among the younger soldiers sent into combat—and he was an ordained Minister of the Gospel. Clyde worked as a fireman at Camp Luna, the Army camp just outside of Las Vegas where soldiers were stationed for training during the war. Audrey, like many housewives, grew a Victory Garden.

One of the Shearers' neighbors near the Old Homestead Ranch was a young man named Ray McCarty. He left for training in the Army. Mr. R. A. Shearer and his son Charles Vivian Shearer wrote letters to their friend Ray.

In a letter to Ray dated June 2, 1942, "Ranch" from "The Shearer Family," Charles Vivian Shearer wrote that they were in the process of moving to the ranch but were in need of having the road fixed and the big adobe house finished. Apparently Ray had a cabin near the Falls Creek crossing, as Vivian talked about doing road work near there. Vivian was struggling with his health. He had hired Hilario Abeyta to make adobes, with Manuel helping him for several weeks. Vivian said he hoped to get started on the sawmill work soon. Vivian went on to write about how Audrey and Clyde "have their cabin about done" and were doing a "pretty good job for a couple of kids" that had never done anything like that. He said Clyde was going to help him with the house and the road work.[2]

Soon Ray was fighting overseas. He sent letters—called V Mail—and they had a censor's stamp on them. In a letter dated March 19 [no year given] Ray wrote:

Hello Mr. Shearer:

Received a letter from you last night. Enjoyed it very much. There isn't much news to write, but thought I would draft you a few lines to let you know I am still in the fight. I am bunking in a German school house tonight. Have electric lights and a stove. If it wasn't for guard, think I could get a good night's sleep. We have a radio too.

Wish you could hear the news the Germans give us in English. They try to fool us by trying to make us think it is coming from the

States. They have a woman that does most of the talking. She can speak good English and must know the ways of the U.S. pretty well. But somebody ought to tell her she is just wasting her breath. Their [sic] is a big American flag waving in the town I am in. It sure looks good to.[sic]
Your friend,
Ray[3]

Another letter in its original envelope was preserved. The envelope was stamped U. S. Army Postal Service, 255, May 22, 1945, A. P. O. and also had a stamp on the lower right hand side of the envelope: "Army Examined" Lt. Wm. H. Phelps. It was to R. A. Shearer, Box 7, Las Vegas, New Mexico. The letter was from P. F. C. Ray McCarty, 38102776, Co-A. 15. Arm. Inf. Bn., A. P. O. 255, c/o P. M. N. Y. N. Y. It was written on American Red Cross stationery:

Germany
Sat. May 19

Dear Mr. Shearer,
 Well, I am back in Garison [sic] again. I am telling you it is hard to get use [sic] to, after being a fighting soldier for ten months.
 We are having dry runs, I guess. You know what they are in the Army. Have to learn how to shoot a riffle [sic] and so on.
 Some times I wonder who won this war. The Germans are walking around here as free and happy as can be.
 I don't have enough points to get out on. So guess I will have to stay in until I am 42. That is if I can live that long in the Army. But think I will get a furlough in the States before to [sic] long.
 I only have three battle stars for extra points which make 68. From what I heard today I might get two extra ones for the battle from the Roar River to the Elbe. But still I won't have enough as that would only be ten more points. I never was wounded like most of them in the company, so I can't get no points thir. [sic] It is just tough luck for me. Well I am use [sic] to it so can take it. Can't kick for their [sic] are plenty of friends of mine that will never come home.
 Seen [sic] my brother a few days ago. I have seen him three times since January. We were both in the ninth army. And was [sic] both in the first army together. He is in the second armored division. He is a mechanic in a Mt Co. I am in the infantry in the fifth division.
 Think my brother is on his way home. He has been over seas 32 months.

Guess you are having a good spring back home now. Sure wish I was their.[sic]

I have got to go for chow so will close. Write and tell me all the news you know.

Your friend,

Ray[4]

Most of the able bodied young men had gone to fight the Axis powers overseas, including Clyde's youngest brother, Donald Clifford Simpson. Donald, affectionately called "Donnie," was the seventh and youngest son of William Ernest Simpson and Addie Bain Simpson. Born January 3, 1925, Donald was only nineteen years old when he was sent overseas. Clyde worried about his youngest brother. Donald was a favorite, the darling of the family. When Donnie was little, Clyde would cook up a batch of candy for him. Then he and Clyde would eat the whole thing, never offering any of it to the other children, despite their sisters' protests.[5]

On June 27, 1944, Donald had received the Air Metal award. A copy of the citation reads:

> For exceptionally meritorious achievement, while participating in heavy bombardment missions over enemy occupied Continental Europe. The courage, coolness, and skill displayed by this enlisted man upon these occasions reflects great credit upon himself and the Armed Forces of the United States.
>
> Air Medal General Orders, No. 240, Hq, 3d Bombardment Division, A P O 559, 27 June 1944 for Donald C. Simpson 38412844 Sergeant, 570th Bombardment Squadron, 390th Bombardment Group (H) by command of Major General Partridge: Official: O. T. Draewell, Major, Air Corps, Adjutant General and A. W. Kissner, Brigadier General,
>
> U. S. A., Chief of Staff."[6]

Donald was engaged to a girl before he was sent overseas. She wrote to him often, as did Addie, Rhea, Audrey and Clyde, and other family members.

In one of her letters, Audrey wrote about the arrival of the new Simpson baby, Dorothy. Donald wrote back that he hoped to return home soon to see the new arrival. Donald's last letter was to his mother, written on July 31, 1944. He wrote to "Dearest Mother" and talked about various members of the family. He said he had received a letter from Bob and was sorry to hear that Opal had an operation but hoped she was well. He wasn't clear about whether she had a baby or not. (The reference was to the fact that the doctor had misdiagnosed Opal, thinking she had a tumor and then discovered she was pregnant. The baby, Donna, was not born until October, 1944.) Donald also said he owed letters to several of his brothers and sisters and would try to find time to write.

Unfortunately, Donald never had the time. On August 7, 1944, Clyde's youngest brother was killed in a plane over Poland. He was a tail gunner on a B-17 "Flying Fortress." Clyde had hoped Donald would soon see the newest addition to the family, Donald's six-month-old niece, Dorothy. But Donald would not see his twentieth birthday.

A newspaper article reported the story with a picture of Sgt. Donald C. Simpson.

> An Eighth Air Force Bomber Station, England—One of the first Americans to lose his life in combat on the eastern front has been buried by the Russian army with full military honors.
>
> On August 6, Sgt. Donald C. Simpson, 20, of 3307 Magnolia Avenue, Beaumont, Texas, ball turret gunner on a B-17 Flying Fortress, had flown with the Eighth air force from England to attack an aircraft factory near Gdynia, Poland, and land in Russia. The next day they took off from Russian bases to attack a Nazi oil refinery in Poland and return to Russia. It was during this attack that Simpson was hit by anti aircraft flak.
>
> He was given emergency first aid treatment by the plane's navigator, Second Lieut. Mario J. Valente, 23, of 79 Belden Street, New Britain, Conn., and respiration was administered by the bombardier, Second Lieut. Saul P. Zieff, 26, of 3230 Cruger Avenue, Bronx, N.Y., as the wounded man began to lose consciousness from loss of blood.
>
> The pilot, First Lieut. Burao [Bruno] N. Latici, 23, of Putnam, Conn., opened the throttles wide in a race to try to save his wounded gunner. He landed on the first airfield sighted behind the Russian lines, but the sergeant died just before the Fort's wheels touched the ground.
>
> Lieutenant Latici and the rest of his crew had to continue with the rest of their bomber group on August 8 when the Fortresses went on from Russia to strike a German airfield in Rumania and land in Italy.
>
> They were not present when the sergeant was given a ceremonial military burial, but other members of Simpson's group were, and they returned to England to tell of the tribute paid by the Russians to the Texas sergeant who gave his life in his flight from Russian soil.

Sergeant Simpson's mother, recently of Beaumont, now [August, 1944] is making her home in Orange.[7]

The caption under the photograph in the newspaper says:

Sgt. Donald C. Simpson of Beaumont was buried with full military honors in Russia. The ball turret gunner was killed by flak when his Eighth air force B-17 Flying Fortress attacked a Nazi oil refinery in Poland from a Russian base. This picture was taken while he was in training in the United States, as a private first-class, before going overseas.[8]

Below is The Citation of Honor from the United States Army Air Forces for Sergeant Donald C. Simpson "Who gave his life in the performance of his duty August 7, 1944."[9]

He lived to bear his country's arms. He died to save its honor. He was a soldier . . . and he knew a soldier's duty. His sacrifice will help to keep aglow the flaming torch that lights our lives . . . that millions yet unborn may know the priceless joy of liberty. And we who pay him homage, and revere his memory, in solemn pride rededicate ourselves to a complete fulfillment of the task for which he so gallantly has placed his life upon the altar of man's freedom.
Signed by H. H Arnold, General. U.S. Army.[10]

A letter was written to Donald's mother on September 6, 1944 by one of Donald's friends, the pilot of the plane in which he was shot, First Lieut. Bruno N. Latici, 23, of Putnam, Conn., who was reported to have "opened the throttles wide in a race to try to save his wounded gunner." He wrote:

Dear Mrs. Simpson,
    First of all I want to send my deepest regrets and sympathies. It was a great shock to us who knew and worked with Donald, but it must be more of a blow to you at home.
    I'm so terribly sorry that I won't be able to give you all the information you would like to have, due to strict censoring it's impossible on my part.
    I will give your letter to our intelligence officer and he will submit it to higher headquarters and they, I'm sure, will help you out.
    I can only say that Donald was in no pain when he left us, he

just closed his eyes as if going to sleep. He did not leave a message for his family.

I know how you feel about the impersonal telegram with no information. I have just gotten word that my brother has died in action in France and I cannot get any more information.

The war department will send you a letter with all the details but I can't promise when you will get this letter. Meanwhile I hope I can get some action through the intelligence officer.

I will write again.
Sincerely,
Bruno Latici[11]

Unfortunately, the pilot who took time to write to the mother of his tail gunner and friend, even while grieving for his own brother, could not keep his promise to write again. On September 9, 1944, the entire crew was shot down and the men became prisoners of war.[12] On the back of a photograph of the plane Donald and his crew were flying was a note stating that the crew had all been lost. The photo showed the plane, a B-17 F, the Flying Fortress. The handwritten note on the back of the photo said:

This is a picture of Donnie's plane. We found it interesting and a nice addition to our research. We also found that the crew (Donnie's) was shot down and became POW's on Sept. 9, 1944 (Donald Simpson's crew)[13]

The Simpson family never knew the fate of Donnie's crew. At least they knew what had happened to Donald.

After the war Donald's body was taken to Belgium for re-burial in the cemetery Neville en Condroz, one of the big cemeteries for Americans and others killed in World War II.

A letter to Donald's mother told of the service:

This morning I had the sad privilege of presiding over the religious service on the occasion of the burial of your son, Sgt. Donald C. Simpson, at the American cemetery of la Neuville en Condroz.

During this moving ceremony, I read the Biblical passage from Jeremiah's Lamentations, Chapter 3, verses 19-33 and 55-57. We prayed that God bestow his divine consolation upon you. We also prayed for the peace of the world.

May Christ, our Hope and our Peace, remain in your heart.

Please accept my deepest sympathies through Jesus Christ our Savior.[14]

A ship was dedicated to the memory of Donald Simpson. (MV Whale Knot, MSCM Hull 2205, PSY Hull 328, 11-30-44) It was christened, and his mother was given a big bouquet of flowers, with family members standing by.[15]

Donald had taken out insurance so his mother received a monthly payment for the rest of her life. She was able to live more comfortably because of his foresight.

In later years, Audrey would learn stories of hardships suffered by others during World War II. Millicent's third husband, Dr. Gordon E. Wickman, was one of those. According to the Obituary in the *Las Vegas Daily Optic*, during World War II, Gordon Wickman lived five years on the sea, one year on a freighter, three years in the Coast Guard on the Great Lakes, and one year on an aircraft carrier.[16] It was then that he learned that his little boy had been killed in a tragic street accident. But the War was at its most crucial point and not a man could be spared, so he was not allowed to go home to attend the funeral of his son. Gordon Wickman graduated from the University of Minnesota in 1937 with his D. D. S. After the war, he practiced dentistry, first in Waupaca, Wisconsin and then in Las Vegas, New Mexico. Gordon and his wife Arlene had two other children, Dale and Sally Wickman.[17] After Arlene died, Gordon married Milly Dixon.

Other family members and friends served in World War II. The aftermath of the war left many households empty. Fortunately, Betty's husband Stanley Hardin returned unharmed. But Stanley's sister June waited to hear news of her husband, Ed Lenden, who was missing in action. She never knew what happened to him. After several years, June finally remarried.

When 1944 ended, Audrey, like everyone, was relieved. She believed things had to get better. Audrey wrote a verse for New Year's for 1945. It was entitled, "The Two Gun Years." She later commented on the margin of the typed manuscript, "Punk verse but you get the idea." It is unknown whether it was published.

> We're tradin' in that '44
>   Won't worry with it any more.
> Trials an' troubles, blood an' tears—
>   '44 served the fightin' years.
> Our new '45 can bring peace fer a spell.
>   If we pull an' work an' shoot like hell!![18]

Stanley A. Hardin, born October 19, 1916, was living in Pajarito, New

Mexico, when he met Betty Clements and they married. Stanley then joined the Army Air Corps and was sent with the Thirty-Fifth Photographic Reconnaissance Squadron to Kunming Air Base in China. On his journey to his assignment, Stanley wrote a letter to his daughter Tana who had been born in September of the previous year. The letter was dated, "India, June 12, 1944." It was later printed in the *Raton News*:

> Miss Tana Marie Hardin,
> Raton, New Mexico.
>
> Dearest Tana:
> Today you are nine months old, and although you can't read this yet maybe Mother will save it till you get old enough to understand it.
> This is the first letter I have ever written you; but it probably won't be the last. I hope that before long I will be able to take you on my knee and talk to you and be a real dad instead of just a letter or a picture on the mantle. But until this war is over, I have a job to do that is even more important than being the dad of a sweet little girl like you.
> I am writing this letter from an army tent "somewhere in India." There isn't any floor in the tent, not any chairs or table. It is so hot that the sweat is dripping from my nose and chin and I have to wrap a towel around my arm to keep the sweat on my arm from soaking up this sheet of stationery.
> You are a very lucky little girl, Tana, to have been born in a country like America. You will never realize just how wonderful a place it is unless you ever have to leave it.
> In America health and cleanliness are more or less the rule; here, filth and disease are prevalent. It seems impossible that human beings can exist in such filth. The water here is not fit to drink unless it has been boiled or otherwise purified. Vegetables are not fit to be eaten because the ground in which they are grown has been fertilized with human waste. Women follow the cattle around and pick up the manure which they pat into thin cakes to use for fuel.
> There are beggars here literally by the thousands, ranging in age from children not much older than yourself, Tana, to the gray haired and toothless.
> Quite a few of the beggars are blind, lame, or have some affliction; but most of them are just plain beggars. None of them ever do anything to earn their alms, like singing or selling trinkets, or anything like that.

They just hold out their hands and cry, "Buckshush, sahib, buckshush."

Under normal conditions, Tana, you can expect to live to be about 60 or 70 years old; here the normal life span is around 26 years.

As I said before, you were very lucky to be born in America, living the American way of life. And remember this, Tana, it's worth any sacrifice to keep that way of life and all it stands for free and unchallenged.

Your loving dad,

Lt. Stanley A. Hardin[19]

Sometime later, Stanley had just completed a mission and was returning to his base at Nanning when he was forced down. He had become lost in a thunder storm and his radio failed. He was running out of gasoline from a defective fuel line. Later a mechanic told him that with a ruptured gas line like that he was lucky the plane did not blow up.[20]

Stanley knew he had to bail out and ditch the plane or else try to land and save the plane as well as himself. He saw an open field where he could try to land. The problem was that it was full of holes. Miraculously, he landed his P-38 safely and was unharmed, avoiding all the holes. Later Stanley learned that the holes in the field, which had been a rice paddy, had been dug to keep the enemy from landing there.

Stanley was relieved when his plane came to a stop and he was not seriously injured. But he saw Oriental soldiers approaching his plane, their guns pointing at him. He did not know if he was in enemy territory or not! It was a relief to see the white sixteen-point star on their caps instead of the red rising sun of the Imperial Japanese Army—which it could have been. Stanley opened his flight jacket and showed the soldiers the American flag that was sewn on his flight jacket. They then put down their weapons and began to welcome him. Stanley learned that two pilots had tried to land there and had been killed due to the holes in the field. He also found out that the enemy was only a few miles away and advancing. Stanley was cared for until he was able to return to his base after about a month. During that time the courageous Chinese people treated him as an honored guest. They camouflaged his plane, carried gasoline up the river, and filled in the holes in the field so that he could take off as soon as the gasoline line was repaired.[21]

Since he had no radio, and communication was very slow, Stanley was listed as missing in action. Betty received the dreaded telegram and spent one or two days of agonizing worry before word arrived that Stanley was alive and well but unable to return to his base until the plane could be repaired. (A mechanic was sent from Stanley's base to repair the fuel line and the radio.)

Stanley learned a great respect and affection for the Chinese people who carried on as well as they could despite hardships. He learned much about their culture. Lt. Stanley Hardin flew fifty combat missions in the China-Burma-Indian theatre. Of the seventeen pilots in the Squadron, only nine returned home.[22]

After the war, Stanley attended the Palmer Chiropractic School in Davenport, Iowa and had a successful career as a Doctor of Chiropractic Medicine. He was a favorite uncle; all my cousins enjoyed his company. At family reunions, the children would always gather around him as he had many funny stories to tell, puzzles to solve or magic tricks to show. He had a tremendous vocabulary and played word games with us. He learned to ride a unicycle and sometimes rode it to his office. The first time I climbed Starvation Peak near Bernal was with my Uncle Stanley and Aunt Betty, along with my cousins Tana and Janie. Betty and Stanley made old fashioned ice cream, pop corn balls, and taffy. Stanley enjoyed making sour dough bread. Betty had a lovely voice and sang solos at church and for weddings. She also made beautiful wedding cakes. She made the cake for Crystal's wedding and for my wedding, among many others.

In spite of his dangerous missions during the war, Stanley did live to see Tana grow up, as well as his two other daughters Janie and Twila. Betty and Stanley lived in Portales where he had a thriving chiropractic practice. Betty died in 1975. Stanley then married Wynona Taylor in the spring of 1976 and spent his last years with her. After the war, Stanley had joined the Air Corps Reserve and was a Lieutenant Colonel at the time of his death in April of 1982. Tana kept a few souvenirs of her father's military service, including his flight jacket.

Stanley wrote up his experiences soon after returning. Years passed. He asked me if I would type his manuscript, and I did. But he did not find a publisher for his memoirs. After his death, I submitted his manuscript to a publisher, Heritage Books, and the book was finally published: *From Pajarito to Lungchow: Memories of Photographic Reconnaissance Pilot* by Stanley A. Hardin as told to D. A. Simpson.[23]

Many husbands, brothers, uncles, or cousins never came home from the war. Some of the boys Audrey went to school with went overseas and never returned. Audrey wrote a poem entitled "High Country Lament" which was published in *The Denver Post*. I read it on April 28, 2000 at a special Veteran's Day program held at Ilfeld Auditorium on the campus of New Mexico Highlands University when I was Chair of the Department of Communication and Fine Arts. The program, called "America the Beautiful" featured special music and speeches, as well as Audrey's poem.[24] It was received very well. Although the names in the poem were pseudonyms, the men were real—young men Audrey had known, some most of her life. They were New Mexicans who took up the call to fight for their country's freedom. Now they were gone and Audrey missed them. She wrote this tribute to them:

> The peaks whisper from snow to snow.
> They ask—Where did our young men go?
> Where is José? And where is Juan?
> Now what of Mike and tow-head Lon?
>
> We fed them well and watched them grow.
> Forever ours—they drank our snow!
> Those riding, whistling, stalwart men
> They've gone—when will they come again?
>
> José fought Japs—an old owl hoots.
> His Pinto feels another's boots.
> And Mike—starved in enemy camp—
> Left none to light his cabin lamp.
>
> Young Juan died over German land.
> His creek roars WHERE? through red rock sand.
> Lon went to sleep breathing green sea.
> Old Baldy sighs—he belonged to me.
>
> The peaks salute their sons' brave hearts
> Nobly dead on earth's far parts.
> But wind sobs on the fir-tipped pass
> While aspens weep in mountain grass.[25]

3

Troubles

Fire! Someone called the Las Vegas Volunteer Fire Department one night to report the store at 420 Tenth Street was on fire

The Carringtons' grocery store had patrons from all over town. During the war, supplies were often meager and rations were common place. Ruth Carrington made every effort to help her customers. She liked running the store, as well as the apartments. W. I. Carrington spent much of his time keeping the house and apartments in good repair.

It was determined that the fire had been deliberately set. A teen-ager named Rusty (a pseudonym) had been seen hanging around the store quite frequently. The eighteen-year-old was the main suspect, but there was no evidence against him. Rusty was a known troublemaker. The Las Vegas High School had been set on fire, and he had been the main suspect, although there was no proof.

The Simpson family lived at the Carrington place. Audrey was preparing a meal and asked Crystal to go next door to the Carringtons' store to get something she needed. Rusty was there, but no one else was around at the moment. Rusty exposed himself to Crystal, saying some obscene things. Crystal immediately ran out of the store and back to Audrey; she told her mother what Rusty had said and done.

Audrey immediately told Ruth Carrington who then confronted Rusty and his parents, describing Rusty's behavior and what Crystal had told Audrey.

Rusty's parents decided to send him away to another state, presumably where he could get help. Unfortunately, the store burned down the night before Rusty left town. The Fire Department quickly put out the fire, but the store was ruined.

Ruth Carrington did not have the heart to start over with the grocery store. All her stock was gone. The house was repaired and rented out once again as an apartment house.

In about 1946, Clyde and Audrey had an opportunity to buy property on Eighth Street Extension, about two miles from downtown Las Vegas. They acquired the land from a man referred to here as Lonnie Benson. (a pseudonym) Lonnie had been found guilty of drunk driving and leaving the scene of an accident. He had hit a prominent citizen's car and left the scene. But the police found evidence linking Lonnie to the accident. He confessed to the hit and run incident, admitting he had been intoxicated at the time. Lonnie was sued. The only way Lonnie could get out of the mess was to sell his house and property. He needed $500.00 to stay out of jail.[1]

Clyde and Audrey had about $500.00 in the bank, money they had saved since they had bought the ranch property in 1942. They needed a place in town so they could work and keep the girls in school—and owning a place was more desirable than renting. With his job at Camp Luna, Clyde was making more money than he ever had made. He always put away about $25.00 a month. They gave Lonnie $500 as a down payment on his place—several acres and a house on Eighth Street Extension. After Lonnie got out of his legal entanglements, he moved his family to Albuquerque.

The house was better than any Audrey had lived in before. It had an indoor bathroom, hot and cold running water, and a furnace. Audrey wrote later:

> We bought a house on 8th St. extension. The place needed remodeling, which took us some time. Clyde dug out the basement and enlarged it. We painted and improved the house. I planted 100 strawberry plants in the back yard. While unloading fertilizer on them, Clyde swung an arm through the back window of our Model A and had to have stitches on his arm. While it was crippled, a 26 inch snow fell the last of April. I heard the flat roof on our house creaking and creaking under the weight of the snow. While listening to the roof creak, I considered the alternatives—stay in a nice warm bed and maybe have the roof cave in on me and a resultant mess to clean up, or get up and do my duty by shoveling the snow off. I remembered snow caving in the roof of the kitchen in a place when we lived in Lagunita. It was a flat roof covered with about a foot of dirt as the old houses used to be built. I will never forget the big mess of shattered lumber and piles of dirt all over the table and stove. So duty won. At 2 a.m. I got up and climbed up on the roof. Snow was falling and the quiet of the town was notable. Carefully so as to not fall through or off the roof, I shoveled snow, tons and tons of snow. As I pushed or lifted that heavy collection of snowflakes, I felt sorry for myself and resolved to never again live in a flat roofed house[2]

She never did. As Audrey and Clyde improved this place on Eighth Street (now on Erb Drive) Clyde built a small, one-room log cabin on the lower side of the lot, intending to use it as a chicken house. Audrey was glad to have the chicken house, but it was built right in the middle of her strawberry bed.

"The war was over by that time and the Government was selling the old barracks at Camp Luna. Clyde bought $90 worth of them [two barracks] and other things from the Camp from Bob Wester."[3] Houses all over Las Vegas sprang up from barracks. Gallinas Street School and one or two buildings at Highlands University were from barracks. A church or two used them. And some people, including Clyde, bought them to build homes. Clyde made several purchases. There were some big, famed oil paintings that had apparently been abandoned by the soldier artists. Clyde brought several home and repaired the broken frames. There were three oil paintings by the same artist, Danny Abbott. One was of a cougar or mountain lion, standing majestically on a cliff. One depicted three horses at play—a black horse, a bay, and a Palomino. And one was a portrait of a Native American in full headdress and body paint sitting on a black and white horse. We always wondered what became of the artist named Danny Abbott. The picture of the cougar was so realistic that when Audrey hung it up in the cabin at the ranch, two dogs came in, looked up at the picture, and began to bark! Those pictures graced the walls of the Simpson's home for many years—until the fatal fire consumed them in 1971.

Soon after Clyde finished the chicken house and had started to build a big house out of barracks—next to the main house—Bill and Helen Reid came to Las Vegas and needed a place to live. They had been living in a little trailer house in Santa Fe. Clyde and Audrey sold the house that had been Lonnie's along with some of the property and moved into the little log cabin until Clyde could finish the bigger house he was building out of barracks.

When Clyde, Audrey, Crystal and I moved into the one-room "chicken house," there were no more luxuries. Audrey didn't like going back to the primitive way of living but she was well adapted to it; and it was only temporary. Soon Clyde finished the new "Army barracks" house. The walls were intact, so all he had to do was set them up, put a roof on them, and do any remodeling he wanted. Audrey described the building process:

> Using the old barracks sections, each 4 x 8 feet, Clyde began building us another house. He mixed cement by hand in a wheelbarrow and built the foundation, inserting bolts every 2 feet that would extend from the cement into the bottom of the 2 x 4 of the barracks' sections. After the foundation was finished, I helped hold the sections in position while he fastened them down. I also helped hold them as he nailed 2 x 6's along the tops of the walls to hold them together upright. Sometimes he propped them up with 2 x 4's, one inside and one outside while we prayed the wind

wouldn't blow and tear our barracks house up. Once the walls were in place he struggled with putting the roof sections up. We used ropes and pulleys, with me holding rope on the groundside, holding things in place while he nailed them as he balanced in thin air. It was still a shell divided into rooms, but it had real windows and doors since they were already in the sections. We moved into it and began to finish it. Then Clyde sold it [the first barracks house] and it was back to the little log cabin.[4]

They sold that first barracks house to Lelama Henry, the Carringtons' daughter. Then Clyde began to build the second barracks house, next door to the first one, and again we lived in the one room log cabin temporarily. As soon as the walls and floors were in place in the second barracks house, we moved into it. Lelama kept the first barracks house a short while and then sold it to a couple named Meyers.

Audrey had a piano that had belonged to Mabel's Uncle Frank Waddell in Illinois. When Uncle Frank died, Mabel traveled by train and bought back some of the furniture she had inherited, including the piano. There were, in fact, two pianos, and Audrey ended up with one of them.

At the time Clyde was building the second barracks house, Audrey's piano was sitting at the Carringtons' house. When we moved to Eighth Street Extension, Clyde promised to move the piano as soon as he could. Audrey explained:

> Clyde started another foundation for another barracks section house west of the first. Our piano had been shoved from pillar to post—that is from one place to another, and was [partially] blocking Mrs. Carrington's hallway so as soon as the foundation was in Clyde put in a floor in one front corner and we moved the piano onto that floor and covered it with a canvas cover. Then we built the house around it.[5]

Like many family heirlooms, the Tryber & Sweetland piano, which was made in Chicago over 100 years ago, had been in the family for five generations and had traveled several hundred miles in its time. It was moved over the worst possible roads and barely escaped destruction. It was the main musical attraction for various church services and it skirted a devastating fire. It escaped abandonment. And it had a house built around it. My story published in *Antique Almanac* described the piano. I wrote, "It has been cursed for its enormous weight and blessed for its rare tone and beauty."[6]

The piano had an interesting history. In the 1880's Beulah Lea Waddell was born to Charles E. and Cora Waddell who lived on a farm in Gilmer Township near Columbus, Illinois. Charles was Mabel Waddell's uncle (her father's brother.) Charles and Cora had two children, Elliot and Beulah. Beulah developed tuberculosis, so outdoor activities were curtailed. The Waddells bought the piano for her entertainment. Beulah was very close to her aunt, Laura Waddell, so when Laura married Thomas Polk Pierce and moved to Canon City, Colorado, Beulah went with her. Beulah died in 1914. When her father Charles died, the piano was given to his brother, Obadiah Franklin Waddell, who lived at Quincy, Illinois. When he died, his only surviving heir was his niece—the daughter of his deceased brother Edward Albert Waddell—Mabel Waddell Shearer. Mabel had the piano moved to her home in New Mexico. But since her husband's job required frequent moves, Mabel left the piano in Santa Fe with her daughter Opal. When Opal and Bob decided to move, they were going to leave the piano behind, as it was too heavy to move. Audrey learned that the piano was to be abandoned, so she paid $25.00 to have the piano moved to Las Vegas—about 65 miles from Santa Fe.

The piano served as the music for many church services in our home, first on Eighth Street and later on Seventh Street. In the mean time, the piano was moved to the ranch when we lived there for two years and then moved back. When the house on Seventh Street was sold, the piano went back to Mabel Shearer's house where she was living on Montezuma Road. (Fortunately, the piano was sitting at Grandma Shearer's house when the 1971 fire took our houses at the ranch.) When my Grandma Shearer gave it to me, it was moved several times and finally was moved to my home at Forest Springs Ranch.

I enjoyed hearing my Grandma Shearer playing that old piano. Two of her favorite songs were "The Little Brown Church in the Wildwood" and "Battle Hymn of the Republic." When I was six, I began playing that old piano and composed a song called "How Jesus Loves." It was sold to a children's magazine.[7] Later I took piano lessons from Mrs. B. B. Barilla in Las Vegas. At the age of sixteen I was elected church pianist for Emmanuel Baptist Church. I played for many church services from that time on.

In the article "Traveling Piano," I included a photograph of Crystal standing by the piano singing as I accompanied her, as well as a later picture of my one-year-old daughter, Laura Lea Beimer, sitting at the piano in 1974. Later my second daughter, Rose, enjoyed the piano. I concluded the article by stating that my granddaughter was now learning to play.

A piano that was purchased to give a frail consumptive girl a pleasant diversion has given many others pleasure throughout the years. The child born in the 1880's had no idea that the piano she loved so well would be played and enjoyed in the 1990's, having survived over a hundred years of traveling. Today my four year old granddaughter Caitlin [Nelson] sat at the piano and tried to pick out a tune. I hope the piano stays in the family a long time. But I hope it doesn't have to travel too many more rough roads.[8]

Since that article was written, my grandson Wade James Nelson and my granddaughter Jessica Mitchell have also enjoyed the piano. The Tryber & Sweetland piano, purchased for Beulah Lea, has been enjoyed by my daughter Laura Lea, my daughter Rose, and my three grandchildren throughout the years. It has provided pleasure for six generations from the late nineteenth century into the twenty-first century.

As Audrey and Clyde were working on the second barracks house on Eighth Street Extension, they finally had some help. Audrey had befriended some new-comers in town, John and Dorothy Roelfs. The Foursquare Gospel Church decided to start a church in Las Vegas, New Mexico. I recall seeing a man, a woman, and a little girl get out of their car which was parked in front of the J.C. Penney store on Douglas Avenue—now Bealls. The little girl was wearing a beautiful scarlet colored winter coat. I noticed she was about my age. Little did I know that we were to become good friends.

After meeting the Roelfs, Audrey learned that they needed an inexpensive place to stay. Audrey and Clyde, having ties with the Foursquare Church themselves, invited the Roelfs, with their four-year-old daughter Joyce, to put their little trailer house on the Eighth Street property where they would live until they could build a church and a parsonage. There was plenty of room for the trailer on the property. Audrey and Clyde wanted to help them and to help establish the new church.

The Roelfs used the large living room of our home for church services until a church building could be put up. Audrey and Clyde helped finance and helped in the actual construction of the Foursquare Gospel Church building on Seventh Street. Audrey provided meals much of the time. Clyde encouraged John to purchase barracks for building the church, as they were inexpensive and durable. As John Roelfs helped Clyde with the Simpson's second barracks house, he was convinced that barracks would work for a church building. Audrey wrote:

> We had a little help in setting up these walls as the John Roelfs were camped in our yard in their little trailer home. He was a pretty good

> carpenter, so it was not long until this house was in place—walls and roof and floor. It was still one large room, with the piano in one corner, when a group of Foursquare preachers came from around the state and Colorado to put up a Foursquare church from more barracks sections they had acquired from Camp Luna. We set up long tables in our one big room and served meals there for all of them while they put up the church building at 1620 Seventh Street.[9]

In Audrey's "Notes on my Life," she continued: "They [the preachers] stayed at our place—ate there—people brought in food, and we had a fine time. The men worked with John Rolfs, and Dorothy Rolfs helped get meals."[10]

Audrey wrote a story, "Just a Little Thing," describing the building of the church and some of the church services. She observed several healing miracles.

> After much hunting and dealing they [the Foursquare Church] bought the lot on Seventh Street Extension. John liked the ease with which Clyde, working alone, made the barracks sections form into a house. So Clyde helped them make arrangements to obtain more old barracks sections from Camp Luna.
>
> Somehow they got all of the building material for a 28 by 60 foot building to put on their lot. It was to contain a large auditorium in the front and a four room apartment for living quarters in the back. When the time came for raising [putting up] the buildings pastors and workers came from churches in Trinidad, Colorado, Raton, Albuquerque, and several other places in New Mexico. Our big bare room that would eventually be a house was used as a meeting place and headquarters for the group. Saw horses with boards laid over them made long tables for serving meals. Make shift benches served as chairs. Local people brought in bowls and kettles of food. Joyce and my 3 1/2 year old Dorothy rushed around the tables, putting out flatware and napkins.[11]

About twenty-five people gathered around the make-shift table at meal times. Folding chairs were brought in to accommodate everyone for the church services in our home.

Audrey wrote that several people noticed that I had a very large wart on the back of my hand between the thumb and finger. It stuck up more than a quarter of an inch above the surrounding skin. Audrey had asked Dr. Mortimer about it. He said it was just a common wart, nothing to worry about. At one of the meetings, we all stood and John Roelfs suggested that we each pray silently for a special need. I was standing beside my mother with my hand stretched out on a chair in front of me. Audrey wrote about a miracle she observed: "As I looked down at it [hand with the wart] I thought, 'I should pray for that wart to go away.'"[12]

> They [the Roelfs] always prayed and they often asked for silent requests. Dorothy's hand was beside me and the ugly big wart stuck up by her thumb. I saw it and thought I should pray it be taken away, and then thought that was not important enough. I should make a big request. Suddenly I noticed it was gone.[13]

At the same time my mother was praying, I was also praying for my wart to go away, believing that God would immediately make it disappear. I was looking at the wart as I prayed. I watched my wart begin to grow smaller and smaller as we prayed. By the end of the prayer time, about 3 or 4 minutes, the wart was completely gone.

Mother was amazed and she told the congregation what she had observed—that as everyone was praying, my wart disappeared. Everyone looked and began praising God.

"It was just a little thing to pray for," Audrey said. "I could have prayed for something bigger."

"There are no little things," John Roelfs replied. "To God, all things are important. And Jesus said that little children are always special." There were several healing miracles that took place about that time. The faith of many people was rewarded. Audrey's faith was renewed as she saw one miracle after another.

The Roelfs moved over to the Seventh Street property (1620 Seventh Street) as soon as it was acquired and began holding services in the big auditorium as soon as the building was finished. In the back of the house there were three rooms, a kitchen-dining room, bathroom, and two small bedrooms. The Roelfs moved into the back parsonage.

In the meantime, Clyde and Audrey were still working on the interior of the Eighth Street house. The big room was divided into several rooms. There was a big oil heater. There was a faucet outside the house, so water could be carried in. But there was no hot water. And the "bathroom" was an outhouse. Although it was still "unfinished," Audrey and Clyde soon had a big new house to live in, located in what is now Erb Drive. In those days it was out in the country. Bill and Helen Reid were living in the Benson house they had bought, close to Eighth Street. The Meyers lived in the first barracks house between the Reid house and the Simpson house, the one Lelama had sold. The

Simpsons lived in the third barracks house—where the piano "gave the new living room a touch of class," Audrey said. She was glad to be living in a large house again, and she was delighted with the huge back yard where she worked to coax the earth to bloom with all kinds of flowers, as well as a very large vegetable garden.

When I was four years old, I spent most of my time playing with our nearest neighbors, Bill and Helen Reid's kids. Billy was the oldest, several years older than Crystal. Stella was next, just older than Crystal, who was ten. Thelma Jean was just younger than Crystal. Then there was Johnny, just about a year older than I. Joanie was just my age. Next was Pearl, a year or two younger than I, and then the youngest ones: Mary, Violet, Margaret Alta, and the baby, Pat. Audrey was kind to the Reids, always helping in any way she could. She always shared her garden produce with them. Some of the Reid children said Audrey seemed like a second mother.

Audrey, always very protective of her younger brothers and sisters, was perturbed when she heard that her sister Milly was having some trouble in New York.

Millicent Shearer had sung for the U. S. O. at Camp Luna (just outside of Las Vegas, New Mexico) when soldiers were stationed there during World War II. There she had met a soldier from New York, Morton S. Alpren. His mother was no longer living, but his father was well known, wealthy, and was Jewish. Morton and Milly soon became engaged. But Vivian did not like the idea of his daughter marrying a New Yorker and leaving New Mexico. When Morton's father came to visit and meet his future daughter-in-law and her family, Vivian became very irate. He told the elder Mr. Alpern to leave his home, adding a few insults. Undoubtedly, as a doting father, no man would have been "good enough" to marry his young daughter, regardless of the suitor's race or religion—especially one who would take her far away across the county.

Vivian's opposition caused a slight delay in the marriage and, needless to say, put a damper on it. But Milly was over eighteen, so Morton and Milly were married in June of 1944 and moved to New York City soon thereafter. At first she sent home letters telling of the exciting life in New York. She sent business cards such as one from Samuel Alpren & Son Fabrics Corp., 1457 Broadway, New York 18, N. Y. and another from Hotel Alamac, Broadway at 71st Street, New York 23, New York. Before long, Milly was homesick and unhappy most of the time, even though she never had a dull moment in New York. She was shown much of New York and met some celebrities—actors, movie stars and singers. One person she met was Stan Lee, the great writer and creator of Captain America, Spiderman, Batman and other such characters. He became editor-in-chief of Marvel Comics, of which "Millie the Model" was the longest running humor comic.

Morton Alpern's family was a part of the New York social set. Milly was beautiful and was a wonderful singer. She could have had a career as a singer. She was at least as beautiful— even without wearing make-up and her having her hair done—as most of the movie stars and singers of her time. Her voice was far better than some of her famous contemporaries. However, Milly was unhappy and decided to file for a separation or divorce.

Mabel and Vivian saw a New York newspaper clipping from August 21, 1946 which gave scandalous details about Milly's pending divorce. The head line said: "Hubby Rations Love, Wife Hits the Ceiling." Mabel and Vivian were mortified that the papers would print such personal details and exploit someone's pain in that way. The paper, *Daily Mirror,* printed a full-body picture of Millicent Alpern. The caption said: "War Romance Sours: Mrs. Millicent Alpren sues over lack of attention while hubby argues she was 'too demanding.'"[14] Milly was described as a girl who grew up on a ranch, while her husband Morton was a rayon executive who was too busy to give her the attention she craved. Milly was quoted as saying that Morton made love as if it were an obligation and Morton was quoted as saying that he simply did not have the stamina to keep up with his wife's desires. Morton also accused Milly of sleeping with a friend. The article stated that Millicent was "asking for $75.00 temporary weekly alimony with $2000 for legal fees."[15]

Audrey remembered that Milly was born September 3 and her twenty-first birthday was coming up. She wrote the following birthday greeting and letter to Milly on August 25, 1946:

> Dear Milly,
>
> Happy Birthday! I don't owe you a letter but maybe by the time you get this I will have one from you and will answer it ahead of time. Mother showed me the clippings you sent her. My word!! Or something less mild. I thought them cleverly written—but what a subject. I had been expecting something like this but it sure was a shock to the folks. I knew you were too cute to pass unnoticed even in a N. Y. court room. But it would be nice if it hadn't had to be a slight scandal to make them thar yeller sheets.
>
> I have still been having my name in the paper or on the radio nearly every week for months. But it has been respectable so far—and nothing very exciting either—and I hope it stays that way. [reference to her circulating a petition regarding Camp Luna's future.]
>
> After C. C. [Crystal Clydine's] birthday it was in both places—

Lelama flew over and dropped long streamers of hair ribbons to her for a birthday gift—and that was news—probably the first time a gift was personally delivered by plane here.

Last week—or the one before—I won the second price in the Swift & Co. nationwide letter contest on ways to improve the marketing of their products. The first was won by a New Jersey man—$75.00. Mine was $50.00 and it comes in handy for unexpected luxuries. So that was news too.

Any way more power to you—but remember you are just a little country girl in a city full of criminals dressed in respectable folks' clothing. So for pity sakes don't get taken for a ride. In any respect, I suppose since mother says you have a guardian that he thot [thought] you should have some alimony. But if it was me I would say good riddance and let the diamond chips fall where they may. And I wouldn't want a cent of his dough. That was the only thing that struck me wrong in the write up. That angle might make it look like you were just another little gold miner from them thar hills. And you know you aren't. For out here the men are men and the women like them that way—and money don't count. Nor even enter into the picture with any importance. So if you have any choice in the matter and if it isn't all over with I'd just let the money part go by and I think you will find that you will be making plenty of big green stuff in your own right before many moons pass. And if you aren't—what the heck! There's life in the old gal yet—and tomorrow is another day. And that book of yours may get you more publicity than "Forever Amber" got its author.

Crystal can't start to school when it starts as the Dr. says it might endanger her heart. I have to make her rest for hours in bed every day. She hasn't rheumatic fever but her nervous trouble could run into heart complications so I am not looking forward with pleasure to teaching her when school starts. I might as well be at the ranch. Best laid plans of mice and men—dontcha know.

But we are fixing this up pretty comfortable. I bought an electric heater for my study—for early morning when winter comes. That is the only time I have for good writing and so I'll need heat. My calm collected words won't keep me warm.

I'd better close and quit burning the midnight juice. Please do take good care of your pretty little self—looking as big as life out of a New York paper. And remember that some of these new found friends may just be sticking around for the cut they hope to get if things break like they want them to and like they plan for them to. In other words don't be surprised if the worst comes out in your fellow men—just see that it doesn't come out in you. Stick to the honest, straight and narrow road to fame. And you will be away ahead in the long run. I'm not preaching—but I do know a thing or three that other people think is hid under a bushel. I can sometimes see clearly in the dark—so watch out for my sweet little sister—and bring her safely home to see us one of these days.

Lots of Love from

Audrey and family

P.S. Those reporters liked you so they went easy on you. See that they keep thinking that you are sweet and simple. If they don't think this, they can tear you to such little shreds that there won't be any pieces left to reach the heights with.[16]

The birthday party Audrey referred to in her birthday letter to Milly was a wonderful event. Crystal had her eighth birthday on July 30, 1946. Lelama, daughter of W. I. and Ruth Carrington, had a learner's permit to fly. There were wide open spaces between the houses in the sparsely populated Eighth Street Extension. So Lelama flew over and dropped birthday gifts, mostly colored papers tied up with long, colored ribbons. All the children at Crystal's birthday party were excited. When they heard the plane, they ran to pick up the beautifully colored ribbons and color books she'd tied and dropped. Lelama was a good "bomber" pilot. She dropped the gifts only a few yards from the house. The children ran behind the house to the very back of the property and picked up the gifts. We thought it was the most spectacular birthday party ever—for a plane to fly over and drop gifts! There were quite a few children at the party, including Eleanor Spiess, daughter of Waldo Spiess—a lawyer who later became a judge—and the Reid children. I remember racing with the other children—and lagging behind—a few yards down the back of the place to an empty field below our house where we picked up all the brightly colored gifts that had been dropped from the plane.

An item in the *Las Vegas Optic* reported the party under the Miscellaneous Section in early August of 1946. The article, "Plane Drops Birthday Gift to Miss Simpson," included:

> Crystal Clydine Simpson entertained sixteen young friends with a birthday party at her home on Eighth Street Extension, July 30th.
> While the party was in progress, Mrs. Lelamae [sic] Henry,

Secretary of the Las Vegas Airmans' Club, flew a Watson Training plane over the party. Mrs. Henry dropped Crystal Clydine a gift of many colored hair ribbons. The ribbons streamed prettily through the air to the waiting children.[17]

Lelama was married to Herby Henry. But Lelama could not tolerate his drinking. Lelama and Herby Henry lived for a short time next door to Audrey and Clyde in the house Clyde had built on Eighth Street. Lelama divorced Herby in 1948 and sold the property. Lelama also owned a large piece of mountain property which had been purchased by Ruth Carrington, neighboring the Simpson ranch in the Mineral Hill area.

Lelama married E. E. "Pete" Gardner. The Carringtons and the Gardners were like family to the Simpsons throughout the years. In 1998, I spoke with Lelama and mentioned what a wonderful birthday party Crystal had in 1946, thanks to her wonderful idea of flying over and dropping the gifts. Lelama said she had to get special permission from the F. A. A. to fly that low and to go on this special "mission." I told her it was the most unique and wonderful birthday party any child could have and that all of the kids would remember it for a life time. She smiled and said she had wanted to do something the children would all enjoy, something different, something extra special for Crystal.[18] It certainly was something special!

Audrey's letter encouraged her sister. Milly left New York and returned to New Mexico to stay with her parents for a while. She got a divorce and did not ask for alimony. Milly's son Roger Lee Alpern was born on August 14, 1947 in Pecos, New Mexico where Mabel and Vivian were living. Roger's grandparents kept him for quite a while because Milly was away, traveling with friends, perhaps job hunting. Roger had an opportunity to learn a great deal from Mabel and Vivian. He would "help" his grandpa "fix" a vehicle or build something. By the time he was three or four years old, Roger could see any car on the highway and call out what it was: "1940 Ford!" he'd sing out, or "1939 Chevy!" he'd point with delight. His grandparents taught him as much as they could, realizing that a young child can absorb a great deal of knowledge. Roger grew up to earn a Ph.D. and he became a nuclear physicist.

Some of Vivian's letters indicate how worried he was about Milly and how protective he felt about Roger. While keeping Roger in their care, Mabel and Vivian worried about Milly and wondered when she would settle down. Then Milly married Orval Dixon. Vivian also opposed that marriage. Few men were good enough for his daughter, and he did not think Orval would be a good father for Roger. Milly ignored her father's advice, as she had before. Vivian wrote in a letter: "Milly came and got Roger a couple weeks or so ago. Brought Orval along and everybody seems to accept him but me. I just couldn't make the grade and disappeared when they came."[19]

It was difficult for Mable and Vivian to part with their grandson after having cared for him full time for quite a while. When Milly and Orval showed up to take Roger away, there was a tearful parting.

Audrey, always concerned for her sisters and brothers, hoped Milly would find happiness. Some years later, there was a divorce. Milly got a job and moved with the children to Breckenridge, Colorado. She liked her work there and the children learned to ski. However, Roger broke his leg when he was skiing. Mabel Shearer went to stay with her grandson and help as he made his recovery. Since Milly was working full time, Mabel's help was invaluable. After a few years, Milly bought her family back to New Mexico.

Audrey wrote about many unusual events in her life. She wrote about an incident when Clyde was working at Camp Luna in the Fire Department. On one occasion they were planning to go to the ranch on Cyde's time off, but Crystal was sick so Audrey stayed home with her. Clyde went to the ranch by himself in the tan, 1937 Ford sedan. He stayed all night. The next day on the way back to town the car broke down. Clyde walked until he was able to catch a ride into town. He knew what was wrong, so he immediately went to buy the part he needed to fix the car. Then Audrey and Clyde asked their neighbors, the Myers, to take them out to the car which was stalled in Santillanes Canyon, just about a mile from Forest Springs Ranch. While Crystal and I stayed with another neighbor, Audrey went with Clyde to put in the car part. The Meyers did not wait to follow the Simpsons into town. As soon as they saw that Clyde had the car started, they went on home. Audrey prayed that the car would make it out of the mountains so they could get home that day.

When they were about three miles from Las Vegas, the Ford, which had been going about thirty miles an hour, suddenly just stopped. Puzzled, Clyde got out, looked under the hood, and did various things but could not get it started again. Finally he walked to the nearest telephone in town and called a garage to send out a tow truck to pull the car into town. Audrey wrote:

> The mechanic that drove the tow truck climbed down and lifted the hood of the car.
> Clyde said, "I just put in a new part and it ran just fine until now."
> "Hells bells!" The mechanic said. "You put the part in backwards. A car couldn't possibly run with that part stuck in there that way. I don't know how you got here."

"Well, we came right along," Clyde said.

The mechanic put the part in correctly and we drove on home OK with no more trouble.[20]

When Vivian and Mabel were living near Bernal (about sixteen miles southwest of Las Vegas) we had a wonderful Thanksgiving at their home. Their house was near the railroad tracks, and I remember watching the new trains with diesel engines go by. There were still some trains with the old steam engines, and some of them went chugging by too, belching black smoke. While the women cooked the dinner, Crystal and I entertained ourselves looking at tall stacks of comic books Frank Shearer had collected. That was the era of Dick Tracy, Superman, Little Lulu, Donald Duck, Mickey Mouse, Mighty Mouse, Andy Panda, and Woody Woodpecker, to mention a few. We thought our Uncle Frankie was so smart to be able to read all those comics!

When it was time to eat, the family sat around the big dining room table. The adults talked and we children listened. Uncle Stanley told about his experiences in China when his plane went down in 1944. Audrey's step-father, Vivian, talked about some of his travels and experiences. Vivian's mother put in a few words of wisdom here and there. Edward Clements joked and talked about his work in the mountains. Frankie made lots of funny comments to keep us entertained. Sometimes he put on a magic show for us. Stanley had helped him learn some magic tricks and encouraged him, so Frank had learned quite a few tricks. The other family members all had their share of stories and jokes.

While Audrey's family moved around, she and Clyde stayed in Las Vegas. Their friends the Carringtons, too, stayed in their big brick home at 921 Lincoln Avenue. Lelama and Pete Gardner, with their children Bill, Jack, Ruth and Mike, also lived in Las Vegas, often visiting their mountain ranch. Ruth Carrington loved the ranch where there was a big log cabin on a hillside above Santillanes Creek. "If earth is this beautiful, we cannot begin to imagine how beautiful heaven must be," she said.

The Carrington home in Las Vegas was often a hub of activity in the neighborhood. At Halloween, nearly every kid in town knew where to find a warm welcome and a treat—at the Carrington house at the corner of Lincoln and Tenth Street. The treats—candied applies, popcorn balls, fudge, and other home-made delights—were always prepared in abundance so no little ghost or goblin was turned away empty handed.

Lelama was a striking, attractive woman. She worked at Los Alamos labs before the atomic bomb was developed. Lelama dressed in good taste and was a dignified, Christian lady. In later years I told Lelama that her name had become associated in our household with being well groomed and looking nice. She beamed and said, "Part of the secret of looking nice is to have self-confidence. My mother always told me to hold my head up high, walk tall, and be confident."[21]

Lelama was a lifelong member of the Church of Christ. In later life, she was a charter member of Las Vegas Crime Stoppers. She was active in the New Mexico Court Update program for many years. She was even deputized by the San Miguel County Sheriff for a time. She was a home maker and a mother, and like her parents, she was also a good neighbor and friend. She always stood up for what was right.

Audrey, like Lelama, fought for what she thought was right. After Camp Luna closed at the end of World War II, Audrey began to circulate a petition. Audrey's birthday letter to Milly referred to the fact that her name had appeared "in the paper or on the radio nearly every week for months."[22] That reference was about a controversial issue that occurred after the soldiers left Camp Luna. The U. S. Government wanted to make a huge training camp there. The proposal split the town. Some citizens wanted it because it would bring business into Las Vegas. Others did not want it because Las Vegas would become a "military" town and lose its small town atmosphere. Some people did not want a bunch of soldiers in the town. They felt it would not be a safe place for their children. Others didn't think the area could support so many people due to lack of water and so on. Ernest "Ernie" Thwaites of KFUN Radio was against bringing in all those soldiers because he believed the area could not support so many people. There simply wasn't enough water. And Las Vegas certainly would no longer be a quiet, small town. On the other hand, Walter Vivian of the Las Vegas Daily Optic, supported the idea, saying that the town needed more industry to thrive. Thwaites and Vivian had kept up a continual feud for years, as competitors for advertising and as political opponents as well; but this disagreement was one of the most intense. Audrey, Lelama, the Carringtons, and many others sided with Ernest Thwaites against bringing in the military camp.

Audrey had a different reason for opposing the camp. She feared that the Government wanted to buy up the whole mountain range behind Las Vegas for military training. Audrey did not want to have to sell "her" mountains! She knew they would offer a "fair price" for the ranch property and she would have no choice but to sell. As she took petitions around town and wrote numerous Letters to the Editor, she was fighting to save her mountains from becoming a shooting range, a fenced off military field for artillery training. "I was not against bringing in soldiers. I was against losing my mountains to the government!" she explained.

Ernie Thwaites was not one to give up a fight when he thought he was right. In 1941 Ernest N. "Ernie" Thwaites and his wife Dorothy had come to Las Vegas to establish the first radio station there. Ernie Thwaites built and operated KFUN, along with Dorothy. They lived in a house next door to the station. KFUN had a 250 watt transmitter, 1230 on the radio dial. In 1943, the station was broadcasting the Office of War information bulletins, with 15 minutes of a Spanish version of "Uncle Sam Speaks." There were eleven hours of Spanish programs, accounting for about twenty percent of the station's revenue. Many of the listeners were Spanish speakers. Spanish, along with English, was an official language of the State under the Treaty of Guadalupe Hidalgo, an agreement between the United States and Mexico at the time New Mexico became part of the United States of America. So when the Office of Censorship told KFUN to observe its code to halt foreign-language broadcasting unless it was strictly scripted and monitored, Thwaites refused. He was a loyal, solid American citizen, but he thought the Government was wrong on this issue.

The Office of Censorship did not like the fact that KFUN's Spanish announcers did not follow a script, took music requests, and made *ad lib* comments in Spanish. Thwaites stood alone in his refusal to comply. The National Association of Broadcasters, to which he belonged, as well as his personal lawyers, refused to back him up. They urged him to comply with the code of the Office of Censorship. But Thwaites would not give in. It was the first time any publisher or broadcaster had refused to do what the Office of Censorship had requested. Thwaites said that his station, at 1230 kilohertz, could be no threat to national security. It was 275 miles from Mexico and three times that distance to the Pacific Ocean. The transmitter signal disappeared within about 300 miles; certainly it could not reach across the ocean. Thwaites said the agency was "hampering, heckling and hamstringing" the station and that it would be utterly preposterous for him to prepare scripts and monitor all the Spanish broadcasts.[23] In a letter in August of 1943 Thwaites accused the agency of being "judge-jury-and-executioner" and stated that "your threatened action is an unwarranted infringement upon freedom of speech and therefore a threat to our whole Democratic structure."[24]

Thwaites' loyalty to his Spanish listeners, to honoring the Treaty of Guadalupe Hidalgo, and to his belief in his Constitutional rights as a broadcaster with freedom of speech were commendable. He stood alone, but when his cause was right, he was adamant. He finally complied just long enough to "get them off his back" and then went right back to this regular Spanish programming. They left him alone after that. When it came to other controversial issues, such as the proposed military camp, Thwaites took an equally strong stand.

Walter Vivian wrote many editorials and Ernie Thwaites delivered many radio commentaries regarding the proposed camp. In addition to circulating a petition against bringing in the soldiers, Audrey also wrote editorials that were printed in the *Optic*. She made a few enemies. One day she was shopping in Newberry's, a store on Douglas and Sixth Street. She started to go across the street to Funks', another five and ten cent store. As she crossed the street, Audrey saw a woman point to her and say to her companion: "See that women over there? She's against the Army Camp! I'm going to shoot her the first chance I get!"

Even Clyde was unhappy. Audrey wrote:

> Camp Luna closed. Clyde was out of a job. He was mad at me for helping get one thousand names on a petition to keep Camp Luna from becoming an Army camp for 20,000 . . . soldiers. The town was divided on the issues—business men wanting it and most local people protesting it. Dick Whorton was putting in the Skyline Night Club.[25]

Finally, the military authorities decided to build the camp elsewhere, so peaceful Las Vegas remained the same. People soon forgot about the issue. Audrey's mountains were safe.

Dick Whorton wanted Clyde to be the chef at the new Skyline, a restaurant and night club north of downtown Las Vegas. He said he would have it built to Clyde's specifications if Clyde would agree to be the chef. He knew Clyde was a good cook with experience at the Home Café. With Camp Luna closed, Clyde needed a job, so even though he didn't like the idea of working at a night club, he agreed. Audrey didn't like the fact that liquor was served there and tried to talk Clyde out of accepting the job. Her fears were not unfounded. Before very long, Clyde started drinking.

When Audrey married Clyde, he did drink once in a while. Then he started preaching, and he didn't drink at all. Even though his church closed and he no longer preached, he was still an ordained minister and wouldn't drink. But when Clyde started working where liquor was served, it was too much of a temptation. Some people thought it was funny to lead the "preacher" astray and would tempt him to smoke and drink. He gave in to temptation and started down a long road of misery.

Clyde starting seeing another woman, referred to here as Anita (a pseudonym). Anita worked with him, first at Camp Luna and then at the Skyline. They spent many hours on the job together. Clyde worked until ten p.m. but often he stayed much later.

Audrey did not know about Anita, although others in town knew she was seeing Clyde. They had seen Clyde's car parked at her house. Finally Mabel

Shearer told Audrey that everyone knew Clyde was seeing this woman Anita. Audrey didn't believe her mother.

Audrey wrote: "He [Clyde] was carrying on with a bar maid, which I did not know for a couple of years as CC [Crystal Clydine] was so sick; and he had started drinking again."[26]

Audrey did not drive. She had never had occasion to learn or to get a license. Clyde did all the driving and did not encourage Audrey to learn. One night when Clyde was supposedly working overtime, Audrey got a taxi cab and took it to the street in old town where she was told Anita lived. Sure enough, Clyde's car was parked in front of the woman's house. Audrey asked the taxi driver to wait. As Audrey approached the front door of the house, her blood was pounding in her temples.

Audrey knocked on the door. An elderly woman slowly opened it. Audrey assumed the woman was Anita's mother. Audrey asked for Clyde. The older woman said something in Spanish. Then in English she said, "He's busy." Audrey pushed her way in and noticed an elderly man sitting on the couch, probably Anita's father.

Audrey could see from where she was standing that Clyde was sitting on a bed in the bedroom by Anita. Audrey was furious. She pushed her way past the elderly woman and stalked into the bedroom.[27] Clyde was astonished to see his wife. He had been sitting on the bed, drinking and laughing with Anita. When they saw Audrey, they froze.

"Clyde, get in the car!" Audrey demanded. "We're going home!"

Clyde got up without a word and left with Audrey.

Later Audrey admitted she was so furious that if she'd had a gun, she would have shot them both.

"I understand what a crime of passion is. It's a good thing I didn't have a gun. I was white with rage," she said.

Later Audrey said, "Everyone in town knew about Clyde and his girl friend—except me. Not even my mama would tell me, and she knew. When she finally told me, I found it hard to believe."[28]

Audrey could never talk about "that woman" without getting angry. Apparently Anita had married a Camp Luna Soldier, had a baby, and then had been divorced. Sometimes we would see her on the street and Crystal would whisper to me, "Don't look now but that woman over there is Daddy's girl friend." I only caught one or two quick glances at her. She had black hair and brown eyes, was slim, and wore tight clothes.

Clyde admitted he had been seeing Anita for quite a while. He asked for a divorce, but Audrey wouldn't agree to give him one. After Audrey found out about the girl friend, she refused to give Clyde a divorce for a year "so he wouldn't marry his bar maid."[29] Anita called Audrey on the telephone several times and threatened her, even threatened us children. She wrote threatening letters as well.

Finally, Clyde decided he didn't want a divorce after all. But he was still seeing Anita. It was then that Audrey divorced him. She later admitted she wouldn't give him a divorce when he wanted it, but when he didn't want it, she divorced him. The main reason was that she'd had all she could take of his running around with the other woman and of his drinking. He was well on his way to becoming an alcoholic.

Clyde left town with Anita, taking the family car. Audrey got a divorce in 1947. Left with no transportation, we had to walk to town, about two and a half miles one way, to get groceries and carry them back. It was very seldom that someone offered a ride.

I remember those long, hot walks to town and back. I was four years old and Crystal was ten. One day Mama and I were walking down Douglas Avenue from the corner where the Bank of Las Vegas is located toward the next corner of the block where Murphey's Drug Store is located. Mother always had errands to do such as going to the bank. That day I was especially tired. The next thing I knew, my mama was carrying me. I had fallen asleep! The Carringtons' house was our place of refuge more than once. When Audrey had done her errands, we would often stop at the Carringtons' home just a couple of blocks from Douglas Avenue, the main street down town. Ruth Carrington always offered us something to eat or drink. She had no car, or didn't drive, so she couldn't give us a ride home with our sacks of groceries.

The Carrington house was a beautiful two-story, brick house with a wonderful lawn and yard. There was usually a little garden in the backyard and there were always flowers, including lovely lilacs all along the sidewalk leading to the front door. The lawn was green and carefully manicured. The neighborhood children always asked to play on the lawn and were respectful of the property. There was a front porch with a white railing all the way around it. The main front door led into a hallway. To the right was a door that led into the first apartment. The other apartments were up the very steep stairway to the left. Half way up the stairs on the wall to the left was a beautiful window with colored glass. There were three or four apartments upstairs. In the main part of the house where the Carringtons lived, there was a big living room, a big bedroom, a good-sized kitchen with a walk in-pantry, and a bathroom. The kitchen door opened into the backyard. The ceilings were very high. There was an ivy plant in the kitchen that ran all the way around the kitchen ceiling. There was an old "grandfather" clock in the living room that gave the date as well as the time. The windows were large and let in plenty of sunshine. The main door had a transom above it which could be kept opened for air circulation. The house had beautiful hardwood floors, although there was a carpet in the living room. There was a little child's chair that every child loved to sit in. Mr. Carrington made much of the furniture himself. He was a very good carpenter. He ran a repair shop and specialized in sharpening tools, especially saws and lawn mowers.

To the west of the back door, on the Tenth Street side, Ruth Carrington had a large flower garden. There were roses, hollyhocks, black-eyed Susans, daisies, larkspurs, snapdragons, morning glories, sunflowers and irises. There was a yellow rose bush to the west of the house, between the main house and the little house that was the store. There were red, pink and white roses as well. Ruth Carrington recalled that couples used to plan their weddings for the time when her rose bush bloomed so they could have some of her special roses for their weddings.

Audrey loved the special white roses that grew in the Carringtons' garden at their home at 921 Lincoln. She wrote an item for the *Las Vegas Daily Optic* about those roses:

> Countless brides in early day Las Vegas carried a bridal bouquet of white roses from the bushes in the yard of the old Wells [Carringtons'] home at the corner of what is now Lincoln and Tenth St. And those bushes, or their descendants, still bloom today, with early June roses of pure white.
>
> Flowers were often scarce before the advent of a florist and a green house in the wild "cow town" of Las Vegas. When better homes were established in the new section of town, near the new Santa Fe Railroad, roses, lilacs, and other shrubs and flowers came in on the rails winding from the north and east. And cuttings were provided for their new neighbors from the gardens of the well established homes in the old town near the plaza of Las Vegas.
>
> Housewives with green thumbs nursed the new plants around the new homes until thriving trees, shrubs, bushes and flowers brightened the meadows on the east side of the Gallinas where tall meadow grass had recently fattened the valley herds.
>
> Today, many of the original bushes and trees have grown sturdy and old, weathering countless storms, and bringing cool greenery to the valley. The original rose bushes at 921 Lincoln, continue to produce white roses blooming again this year, in early June.[30]

The lilacs in the front yard and to the side of the house gave their sweet scent to the yard every spring. There were two apple trees in the yard. In late summer, Ruth always made apple sauce, apple butter, canned apples and apple pies. On the east side of the house was a pear tree. Ruth made deserts and canned many pears.

Across the street on the west side of Tenth Street were black walnut trees. W. I. Carrington showed his grandchildren how to peel the outer layer covering the rock hard nut. Their fingers would be dyed black from the hulls. Once they had cleaned a batch, he would crack the nut with a hammer so they could share the meat of the nut. Later, nearly all the black walnut trees were cut down because people didn't like the "mess" the nuts made on the sidewalk. Audrey deplored all the "slaughtering of trees" around the town and wrote editorials about it.

Crystal and I thought of the Carringtons as our "other" grandparents; we spent many happy hours at their place. Our own barracks house on Eighth Street was simple in comparison. Crystal rode her bicycle about two and a half miles to Douglas School every day. She tried riding the bus, but the other children were so unruly and mean that Audrey decided Crystal did not need to go through dealing with vicious kids on a bus in addition to all her other problems. Riding the bicycle was not without its own problems, however. Crystal was chased by mean dogs, for one thing. She wished we lived closer to town.

When Clyde left, Audrey was heartbroken. Crystal and I suffered the heart break only the children of divorce know. Sometimes when Crystal was away at school, Audrey found time to sit down. She would find herself weeping, tears rolling silently down her cheeks. Then I would climb up on Mama's lap and pat her cheek or trace the tears down her cheeks with my small finger.

"Why are you crying, Mama?" I would ask.

Audrey would reply, "I just feel like it." Or "Oh, sometimes I just feel sad."

I wanted to comfort her and would pat her shoulder. Mama's cheeks were so wet I looked for a dry spot to kiss. I would kiss my mother in front of her ear or behind her ear because I couldn't find a dry spot on her face. Later, Audrey wrote a poem entitled "Kisses:"

> The old ladies' kiss is damp and cold.
> The old man's kiss shows he is old.
> The Lover's kiss is sweet and warm,
> Like hot sunshine on a summer morn.

But the kiss I find very dear,
Is that five year old kiss beside my ear.[31]

Crystal became nervous and did poor work at school. Her teachers were not very understanding and were extremely demanding. Audrey worked with Crystal to help her improve her grades. Reading disorders such as Dyslexia were not well known, so Crystal was never diagnosed. It took hours for Audrey to help Crystal learn her lessons due to Crystal's trouble with reading and spelling.

The doctor said he feared Crystal might be getting "rheumatic fever" and her heart might be affected, so he ordered bed rest. Then Audrey took Crystal to Socorro where her sister Betty and her husband Stanley Hardin were living. Stanley had opened his chiropractic practice there. They invited Crystal to stay so that Stanley could give her daily treatments.

While Crystal was in Socorro, I had to play alone. I missed my big sister. I remembered that on my fourth birthday, she woke me up that morning and said in an excited voice, "Today's your birthday!" I didn't see what was so exciting about it. "You're four years old today! And it's your first *real* birthday because you were born on leap year!"

I didn't say much in response.

"Aren't you excited? It's your birthday!" Crystal grinned at me. "You're having a party and you'll get presents!" she exclaimed.

I did have a great party—all the Reid kids and a few other friends were there. My mother always made my leap year birthdays special.

When I was sixteen, my mother's friend and colleague at the Las Vegas Daily Optic, Jean Whiting, wrote a feature story on leap year birthdays, including an interview with me and a boy who had also been born on February 29, 1944 in Las Vegas. His name was Mark Anthony "Mickey" Montoya, the son of Mr. and Mrs. Abelino Montoya. The headline of the story was "Short On Birthdays Maybe, But They'll Only Be 20 When Their Friends Are 80." Jean took a photograph of each of us, his at work at Columbia Supermarket and mine sitting at a desk at the Optic across from my mother's desk.[32]

While Crystal was in Socorro, her best friend, Eleanor Spiess, missed her also. Eleanor Spiess lived just down the road from us. Her grandmother, Mrs. Randall, sometimes walked over to our house to visit with Audrey. Mrs. Randall had grown up in Taos. She knew many stories about New Mexico's history. One story she told Audrey was about the infamous Billy the Kid. She said that everyone thought that Billy's girl friend near Fort Sumner was the daughter of a wealthy rancher, Mr. Maxwell, a girl named Paulita Maxwell. But Mrs. Randall said the girl friend was not the rancher's daughter. Billy was, instead, in love with one of the servant girls. Some said the girl was a full-blood Navajo adopted by the rancher. Others said she was a Spanish-American señorita who worked at the ranch. Mrs. Randall insisted that she knew the story from a reliable source and that her version was the accurate one.

Eleanor had a brother—Randall—and two older sisters, Jeannette and Anne. The sisters were both getting married, having a double wedding. Mama and I went to the Funks' store to find some dishes. They had to be green or yellow because those were the colors they had chosen. Mama found some that we thought were just right. The beautiful wedding was held in the garden at the Spiess' place. I wished Crystal had not had to miss it. However, after Crystal returned home following her visit with Aunt Betty and Uncle Stanley, she seemed much better.

If the divorce and Crystal's illness were not enough to cause Audrey trouble, the nearby neighbors got very angry at Audrey. She never knew why. She didn't know if there was some gossip about her divorce or if there was some business transaction they were unhappy about. They wouldn't speak to us or, if they did, they said angry things. One day I was in the back yard playing when the man shouted at me, using obscenities. I went into the house and told my mother what he had said, asking her what the words meant.

My mother was furious. She immediately went out and yelled at the neighbor who was still in his yard. She bawled him out soundly. She said something like: "You can be mad at me if you like, but don't you ever speak to my little girl that way again!"

Whether it was due to Audrey's wrath or not, the neighbors moved away soon after that.

Mother and I went on the bus to Socorro to bring Crystal back home with us. We stayed overnight. It was very hot that summer. There was no air conditioning and there were very few fans. I remember that we had a wonderful Chinese dinner that Betty and Stanley prepared for us the next day. Stanley had been given gifts by his Chinese friends when he was overseas during World War II. Among the items he brought home were some chop sticks. He had learned to use an acabus when he was in China. He had one and showed us how to use it. He was very fast with it but considered himself slow. He said his Chinese friends were much faster.

Betty and Stanley were in Socorro for a while. Then they moved to Las Vegas where they lived in a house on Fourth Street. Then they decided to move to Portales where Stanley had a good opportunity to set up his chiropractic practice in a larger office.

Whenever Audrey thought of the people who caused her grief, she remembered she could count on her good friends and her family. Although she did not tolerate wrong doing, Audrey tried to give people the benefit of the doubt when she could. If someone said something critical about a person, Audrey would often come to that person's defense. "Most people try to do the best they can," she often said.

The family had been through many hardships. After World War II ended, it seemed that life would be good. But there was even more grief ahead.

4

An Empty Saddle

Audrey, Crystal and I attended Jessica Shearer's wedding at the Methodist Church in Las Vegas in 1947. Jessica had met George F. Hays in high school and they decided to get married soon after they graduated. It was a beautiful wedding. Afterwards there was a big reception at the hall on what is now the Highlands University golf course. I remember all the people dancing and enjoying the party. Then Jessica and her husband—everyone called him Tetter—went out the door while the crowd cheered and threw rice as they drove away on their honeymoon.

Jessica had spent some time as my babysitter. She had held me and rocked me to sleep, singing the song made popular by Judy Canova, "Go to Sleep my Little Baby." She was very talented. She made matching western style shirts for her husband and herself. They wore them one spring day when they came to visit Audrey in the house on Eighth Street Extension. I remember Audrey took a picture of them, using colored film, something new that she had not used before. She wanted to show the beautiful colors of their shirts. The snapshot today is faded, but it shows the happy, attractive couple wearing their matching western shirts, blue jeans, brown belts and brown boots. Tetter was wearing a cowboy hat. His tall, slim figure and Jessica's shorter, slim figure stood out against a blue sky.

In August, Tetter wanted to compete in the Teddy Roosevelt Cowboys' Reunion rodeo, hoping to win a prize. Jessica didn't want him to, nor did his parents. Bull riding was too dangerous. But he persuaded Jessica that he'd had lots of practice and he would be OK.

Audrey, Crystal and I attended the rodeo on Sunday, August 7, 1949. Grandma Mabel Shearer was sitting close to the arena with Jessica. Audrey, Crystal and I sat to the far left of them, a few bleachers up higher. Crystal sat next to Audrey so she could ask questions about the events.

The rodeo was a big event in those days, part of the annual Cowboys' Reunion weekend, so the stadium was full. Part of the celebration was a rodeo in which competitors came from all over the nation. The bull riding event was the most exciting of the entire afternoon.

"The next contestant is Tetter," I heard Crystal exclaim. She was sitting on my right. "Watch!"

Tetter came out on the furiously bucking bull and was thrown off; but before he could get up, the bull jumped on him. I did not understand what had happened.

Audrey fell sideways across our laps.

I asked Crystal, "Why is Mama sleeping?"

"I think she fainted," Crystal said. "Something bad happened."

Several other women sitting around us passed out as well.

In a moment Audrey regained consciousness. She explained what had happened to Tetter. Then the ambulance came in and took him away. Jessica and her mother went with him to the hospital.

During that afternoon, one other cowboy had been injured, and an ambulance had come into the arena and taken him away. Later, after Tetter was hurt, the ambulance brought the first cowboy back. He stood in the center of the arena, held up his arms to show that he was OK, and the crowd cheered to see that he was all right. Mother, Crystal, and I waited a while to see if the ambulance would bring Tetter back, like the other cowboy, but it did not.

After a while, Audrey joined Mabel and Jessica at the Las Vegas Hospital. There was much worry and waiting. Crystal and I sat in the car each time Mama visited the hospital, as children were not allowed in.

Rev. John Roelfs and his wife Dorothy were holding church services in the newly built Foursquare Gospel Church at what is now 1620 Seventh Street. In the big auditorium, Dorothy would play her accordion, we would sing hymns, and then John would preach. They also had Sunday School and many of the neighborhood children heard the gospel message for the first time. There were many games and activities. They also held many prayer meetings. Audrey was a firm believer in divine intervention and in personal prayer for healing.

When Tetter was in the hospital, critically injured, Audrey sat with Jessica and Mabel at the hospital, offering all the love and support she could. Someone took Crystal and me to the Foursquare Church where services were being held. Crystal and I missed Mother; she usually sat between us. When John Roelfs asked for prayer requests, we knew that Audrey would ask for healing for Tetter. Crystal was very shy but she gathered up her courage and raised her hand. She asked for prayer for our Uncle Hayes. Everyone knew why Audrey was absent and hoped her brother-in-law would soon recover. John asked the congregation to pray with him for the young cowboy's full recovery. We believed Tetter would be healed. Healing miracles had been happening, not only in our little church, but all over the nation.

It was about that time when America was touched by the great healing ministries of some of the great evangelists such as Oral Roberts. He never claimed any credit for himself. He could not heal anyone. God worked through him; he gave all the credit to God. But he could not explain why some people were healed and others were not. In his autobiography, Oral Roberts wrote that he was surprised that not everyone he prayed for was healed. He would feel the presence of God in his right hand and usually the person he was praying for would feel it also. Many were healed at that moment or started to mend just then. But for some healing did not come, although they would be drawn closer to God even if healing did not come. In later years, he and his wife Evelyn faced personal tragedy in the sudden death of their daughter Rebecca and her husband Marshall Nash in a plane crash over Kansas on their way to Tulsa. They left three children behind. As Oral and Evelyn Roberts prayed in their grief, an insight came to the preacher. He told his wife that he had realized that "God knows something about this that we don't know."[1] Someday they would understand. Until then, they trusted God's will.

Audrey, too, prayed for understanding and trusted God's will.

Tetter had critical internal injuries. He died on Tuesday, August 9, 1949. Funeral services were held on Thursday, August 11, 1949. *The Las Vegas Daily Optic* related the following:

> Funeral services for George "Teet" Hayes, Jr., 19, who died yesterday afternoon as the result of injuries incurred in the Cowboys' Reunion arena Sunday when he was thrown from a Brahma bull, will be held Thursday at 2:30 from the Rogers Funeral chapel.
>
> Hayes incurred fatal chest injuries when the bull stepped on him after he had been thrown just after leaving the chute.
>
> Rev. Fulton Moore, pastor of the First Methodist church, will officiate at the services. Interment will be in the family plot in Masonic cemetery.
>
> Members of the Mounted Patrol will serve as casket bearers. The

body will lie in state at the funeral chapel this evening from 7:30 until nine o'clock.

Hayes was born at Littlefield, Tex., the son of Mr. and Mrs. George Hays, Sr., who now reside at Serafinea. [Serafina] Besides his parents, he is survived by his widow, Mrs. Jessica Shearer Hayes, 520 Washington, three sisters, Barbara, Ardath and Genevieve, two brothers, Howard and Gordon, all of Serafinea,[Serafina] and a half-brother, Earl Manlove, who is now in Mexico City.

He was a grandson of Mr. and Mrs. Joe T. Morrow of Albuquerque, formerly of Las Vegas.

"Teet" attended Las Vegas high school and recently had been employed by the REA [Rural Electric Association] in construction work.[2]

After the funeral, another article appeared in the *Las Vegas Daily Optic* which provided more details. It stated that the funeral for the "well known young Las Vegas man" who died from "injuries he sustained Sunday at American Legion Park" was attended "by a multitude of the young man's friends and realtives."

Karl Molton accompanied by Mrs. L. C. Elliott on the chapel pipe organ sang two solos, "Empty Saddles in the Old Corral" and "Home on the Range." Many beautiful floral tributes sent by his friends, covered the chapel altar and reception rooms. Interment was made in the family plot in Masonic cemetery with the following members of the State Mounted Patrol serving as casket bearers and honorary escort: Jas. A. Whitmore, Julius Romero, Floyd Post, Jack Hermes, Gus Voss, Leo Teague, John Day, and Rudolph Laumbach.[3]

Audrey wept when "Empty Saddles in the Old Corral" filled the chapel with the words that were so true. In a letter dated August 12, 1949, Charles Vivian Shearer, Jessica's father, wrote in a letter to his sister Arolvi who lived in California:

Our teachings of composure, acceptance, and "God Speed" in the face of death have been tried to the limit. Jessica proved to be a better disciple than I. I was much more emotionally affected—or rather seemed to have less control than she. It seemed so hard to realize that it had to happen to her. All her plans and hopes for the future so tragically shattered.

She hardly shed a tear. At times I know it was hard for her to hold in. I hope that she did not overdo it. It seems that some release of tension should be good. Her Mother-in-law was also the most composed woman I ever saw. It was her composure that helped Jessica through it.

She [Vivian's mother] wanted to go in yesterday to see the casket and flowers and a last look at Teeter. She stayed in Jessica's room with Milly during the funeral. Betty and Milly and Jessica were all here last night.

Jessica is the best there is and it has shocked me to see her world shattered so suddenly. And the way she accepted it would put any [one] to shame. Mabel stood up under it very well also, but Jessica showed us how to do it.

Down the river this morning I passed the pole where Teeter was when I took a picture of him a week or so before you came. It is not yet developed. Further on I passed his REA [Rural Electric Association] truck with the crew stringing wire. I have not yet been sufficiently conditioned to utter an emotionally heartfelt prayer of joy because he has gone on to something better. I still have feet of clay and it brought a catch to my throat as I passed. I still think Jessica should be encouraged to let down and have a good cry.[4]

Tetter's little brother, Gordon Hayes, was about my age. Eventually, we were in school together. We both graduated from Robertson High School.

Crystal had taken great courage to ask for prayers for Tetter, believing that he would be healed. When God did not answer in the way Crystal expected, she was disappointed. But Audrey's wise words gave us great comfort. "When we can't understand, we just cling to faith."

We attended many rodeos after that one, but Audrey would never stay for the bull riding event. It was always the last event on the program. "We have to go now. It's almost time for them to start the bull riding event," she would tells us. We didn't protest. We didn't especially want to stay for it, either. And we knew it would upset Mother. So we always made our way down through the crowded bleachers to the car before the dreaded event began.

When Audrey was 29 years old, in 1941, she wrote a poem which was published, entitled, "Departure."

Why weep ye that this body passed away?
'Twas but a soul's abode for one short day.

Canst thou not see?

'Tis my old home—not me.

I soar aloft to hunt a castle new.
Ye must not mind. Anon thou wilt soar too.[5]

Jessica, the young widow, grieved for her husband. But life had to go on. She married David "Red" Braziel, a man she had met at work at the telephone company. Her father Vivian wrote a letter to his sister Arolvi and her husband Paul on January 21, 1950, commenting on her re-marriage:

> Don't know if we told you that Jessica was married again on December 7th. Did not tell us for a long time. He is working for telephone company. Ambitious and hard working makes about $500 per month. They live in midget apartment.[6]

Jessica's husband "Red" did very well in his work and was transferred with the telephone company to Santa Rosa. Later they moved to Tucumcari where they brought up their five children.

Mabel and Vivian were looking forward to retirement and hoped to live at the Old Homestead Ranch. Vivian wrote:

> And when I retire, where else can we land? It does give a person a pause to consider that at the end of the productive portion of life, you find nothing accumulated, and entering the non-productive period plus a physical disability, it becomes necessary to try to earn and provide the security that it was impossible to provide in the productive period. Perhaps we would not even have the ranch if it had not been given to us. I do appreciate the gift and the giver. [R. A. Shearer][7]

Vivian and Mabel were taking care of Vivian's parents. Vivian's mother, Ollie Shearer, was living with them and Vivian's father, R. A. "Grandfather" Shearer was living at the ranch some of the time.

The family went through much trouble in the 1949-1950 period of time. Audrey wrote about the time she and Clyde separated:

> Like many couples while we were as poor as church mice, we lived happily in a struggle to survive. But when we began to make more money than we had ever had before in our entire lives, Clyde went wandering, to put that very tragic time briefly. I got a divorce.[8]

Audrey now had to face life as a single mother. She had no job, no car, and Crystal was not well. With a sorrowful heart, Audrey began to plan how she could bring up the girls on a very limited income.

Since Forest Springs Ranch was in Clyde's name, due to Edith Shutt's having made the deed out to him, part of Audrey's divorce agreement requested that the ranch be signed over to her as her exclusive property. Clyde signed the property over to Audrey on February 10, 1948, Warranty Deed #2398, Box 161, Page 183, according to Audrey's notes.[9]

When school started in the fall of 1949, we moved into town from our Eighth Street Property. Mother rented the Carrington's little Tenth Street house. Audrey worked part time and Crystal was in school. I started Kindergarten. Since we had no car, we walked to and from school, several long blocks.

Audrey realized that we needed to heal from the trauma of the divorce and from the troubles the family had gone through, the losses we had experienced. She thought of Donald whose life had been sacrificed for freedom. She thought of Clyde and his decision to leave the family. She thought of Tetter whose empty saddle would remind the family of the tragic rodeo. And she was concerned about Crystal's health.

Audrey determined to move to the ranch. She stated that there was no way to live in town, financially, so moving to the ranch was the best option. With the help of friends, we were able to move all our belongings in one day except the piano. Audrey had a professional mover bring the piano out in his big truck later on. It went into the cabin behind the Fifteen Dollar House, the one we used as an extra bedroom in the summer. The Fifteen Dollar House was much smaller than the house we had been living in on Eighth Street. And we would be very isolated. However, the solitude of the country beckoned us.

It seemed to Audrey that she was closer to God in the quiet seclusion of the forest. As always when she was in need of inspiration, Audrey looked to the mountains.

5

Thanksgiving under the Pines

"Won't you miss school?" Joyce asked.

"No. I hate school. I have a mean teacher and she gives me F's," Crystal replied.

"I'll miss kindergarten," I chimed in. "I have nice teachers and I learn things."

Joyce Roelfs was my age and would be living in town and going to kindergarten. She looked at me with sympathy.

"Well, at least you have lots of room to play here," she said.

On Thanksgiving Day, 1949, Audrey, Crystal and I, along with Bonnie, the collie, and the cat Spot, moved from Las Vegas to our Forest Springs Ranch, all our possessions piled up in a school bus.

How did Audrey arrive in that point in her life? After Clyde left, taking the car, life became very difficult. One of the houses that had been sold provided a thousand dollars, and Audrey used that to live on after Clyde left—for the first year. She worried about how she could pay taxes and upkeep on the house, utilities, and other monthly expenses. Audrey applied for several jobs and worked for a while. She worried about Crystal's health. Crystal seemed better after the chiropractic treatements Stanley gave her but only stayed at the Hardins a month, as she was homesick.

In early fall of 1949, Audrey enrolled Crystal in the fifth grade. I started going to a kindergarten conducted by Louise Harris and Thelma Frank at a house on Eighth Street. We lived in Carringtons' little rent house on Tenth Street so Audrey could walk to work at the telephone company where she was conducting surveys. Crystal walked with me to the kindergarten, then went back to Douglas School. I walked home by myself after school, about seven blocks. Crystal was not doing well in school. Audrey knew she needed to stay home with Crystal. She also knew that we could live at the ranch on very little income.

It was in November that Audrey decided to sell the last of the Eighth Street property and move to the ranch. How sick Crystal was—or if she was sick at all—is uncertain. She had trouble with her school work due to reading difficulty. Audrey noticed she "read backwards." Today she might have been diagnosed with a reading or visual difficulty. She was nervous and anxious, but children of divorced parents often are. Crystal never developed any kind of heart trouble. At the time, however, Dr. Mortimer said Crystal should be taken out of school, so Crystal was only in the fifth grade a short time. Audrey wrote in an story published in I*mpact*:

> Back in the late 1940s, my eldest daughter, Crystal, suddenly came down with a severe illness. "Can't say it's rheumatic fever," our doctor said. "Can't say it isn't either."
>
> Crystal was 10 years old at the time, and we were living in Las Vegas, N.M. Though the doctor did not know exactly what was ailing Crystal, he did know she needed complete rest, solitude even, to get well.
>
> As fond as we were of Las Vegas, I knew Crystal would have a hard time finding peace and quiet in the city. That's when I thought of the cabin.
>
> If Crystal couldn't find solitude there, if she couldn't get better there, she couldn't get better anywhere.[1]

Audrey knew she could make it financially, just barely, by living on the ranch property. Her income would consist of monthly payments from the sale of the houses and Clyde's child support. Audrey hoped to be successful in her freelance writing. She also hoped to grow a big garden and get some chickens.

It was on that warm, sunny Thanksgiving Day in 1949 that we found ourselves moving to our home in the high country. Our friends, Rev. and Mrs. John Roelfs, helped us move, using the school bus John had acquired. Bonnie sat in her own seat with her face to the window, excited to be going to the mountains.

The road was narrow, with deep ruts in places and pot holes in others. There were many curves and steep, winding hills. There were streams to ford. I do not know how John got that wide, long school bus over the narrow road through the village of San Geronimo and on for another three and a half miles up the mountain. But I always thought that "our preacher" John Roelfs had extra help from above. One time I had heard him remark that he had never seen hail; he was from California. "I wish it would hail so I could see what it looks like," he said in a casual manner. Were we surprised the next day when we got the biggest hail storm of the decade! He regretted his wish. However coincidental it may have been, I realized even then that one should be careful what one wishes for!

The trip took nearly two hours as the heavy bus labored over the unpaved, washed out roads leading to the foot of Barillas Peak where our ranch bordered the Santa Fe National Forest. After arriving at the site, everyone began unloading the bus and setting things in the yard. Audrey wanted to clean the Fifteen Dollar Cabin out before moving everything in. Fortunately, the two smaller log cabins that had been built in back of the main one could be used for storage or extra bedrooms.

For Thanksgiving Dinner, Audrey opened a twelve-ounce can of luncheon meat. She pulled the key from the bottom of the can and expertly separated the top of the can from the bottom to let the pink-colored meat slide onto a white platter. Then she sliced the meat. White bread, meat, lettuce, along with mustard, mayonnaise and dill pickles, were passed around. Mother helped us girls to make our sandwiches. We were seated on long wooden benches that Clyde had made in a little opening in the oak grove in front of the house. In front of the benches, there were big, round, flat tree stumps that Clyde had placed there as "tables."

John led a prayer of Thanksgiving, remembering to thank God for America and the blessings of freedom. The war was over and the soldiers had returned home. America was the strongest nation in the world. It was a good time to be alive. We ate our Thanksgiving dinner under the oak trees in the golden autumn sun. The pine-scented air and clear, blue sky made the picnic delightful.

John and his wife Dorothy said they would miss us at church services. Audrey had no telephone and no transportation. They wondered about her supplies and said they would check on us as often as they could. They expressed their appreciation for the many meals Audrey had shared with them—including this one. We did not miss turkey and all the trimmings. Others may have been enjoying turkey, dressing, pumpkin pie and other pastries, but we felt no lack. We enjoyed our picnic type lunch and laughed and talked, enjoying each other's company.

Crystal, Joyce, and I talked about how nice it would be for us to live in the woods with blue jays, woodpeckers, robins, meadow larks and other birds waking us every morning. The fresh mountain air, our healthy appetites, the warmth of our friendship, and the genuine thankfulness we all felt made up for any lack in the cuisine.

The six of us sat under the sheltering oak trees near the little log cabin we were to call home. Under the warm golden autumn sun, we enjoyed a friendship with our companions in the solitude of a wilderness beauty that few Americans could boast they had done. There is truth in the scripture from *The Holy Bible,* "Proverbs," Chapter 17, Verse 1: "Better is a dry morsel, with quietness therewith, than a house full of . . . strife."

There was no strife in our lives that day. There was the joy of friendship and the solitude of the majestic mountains in their autumn attire. There was the quietness of understanding and thankful hearts. There were many other memorable Thanksgiving Days in my childhood—glorious feasts of turkey and all the trimmings with rich deserts following. There were wonderful family reunions on Thanksgiving at Grandma Shearer's place or at Grandpa Clements' place or at Granny Simpson's place. But the Thanksgiving of 1949 where we enjoyed a friendship with our companions in the pine-scented solitude of the Sandre de Cristo Mountain range was one of the most memorable. Never before or since has there been such a Thanksgiving Day! Audrey wrote years later:

> They [the Roelfs] were at our house one Thanksgiving [1948] after Clyde left and we only had a can of Spam to share with them, probably potatoes too. It was the next Thanksgiving Day in 1949 that they moved us to the ranch in the school bus he drove. By that time I had moved to Mrs. Carrington's little house at 420 10th street. So they came there and loaded up and we came to the ranch. I hadn't been up here for a couple of years. The Fifteen Dollar House—14 foot by 16 foot log cabin—was full of mice and rat tracks. They [John and Dorothy Roelfs] helped take everything out of it so I could clean and mop. Then they helped put the double bed back in and the rest of the stuff had to be stacked in the front yard. They hated to go off and leave us. We must have looked very pitiful, but I got a fire started in the little cook stove Clyde bought for $40 from Ilfelds just before you couldn't find one to buy. And I fixed supper and we were home.[2]

The log cabin had a window on each side of the house, one facing east and one facing west. The northern wall had only one or two tiny windows near the top of the wall—"peek holes" Audrey called them. The door faced south where a little clearing in the trees gave a view of the babbling brook. From there we could get water as long as the creek was running. When it dried up later, we had to walk to the spring for water. There was no electricity, no running water in the house, no telephone and no transportation. A path behind the house led through the oak bush to the outhouse which sat high above the edge of Roaring Canyon.

As the sun began to go over the mountains, Dorothy Roelfs asked Audrey, "Are you sure you'll be all right here alone?"

"Oh, yes," Audrey assured her friends.

The bed had been made up with clean sheets. Tomorrow Audrey would clean the cabin and move everything inside either the main cabin or one of the storage cabins. She had plenty of coal oil for the kerosene lamp. There was water from the spring. We had coal, groceries, and the basic necessities.

"I only wish you had a telephone," Dorothy added. "John and I will worry about you and have no way to contact you."

"I'll write," Audrey promised. "The mail carrier comes around twice a week, so I can post the mail and pick up mail then."

"But that is a long walk to the mail boxes," Dorothy said.

"It's about three and a half miles by the road but I can cut across country, so it will be about five and a half miles round trip."

Mother had assured John and Dorothy that we would be fine. But in spite of her assurances, they lingered. Could there be wild animals about? Mother affirmed that there were but assured them that our collie Bonnie would protect us and that they could not break into the sturdy log cabin.

"Don't worry. God will take care of us. He always has," Audrey declared.

There was a tearful parting. John, Dorothy and Joyce crossed the bridge over the creek and John turned the school bus around. They waved their final good-byes and headed for Las Vegas before dark.

Indeed, 1949 was a good time to be alive. On Thanksgiving Day in that year, 148,527,000 Americans enjoyed a prosperous post-War economy under Harry Truman's Fair Deal. Most Americans were employed, although taxpayers complained that the federal payroll, including armed services, was ten billion dollars a year. The Government payroll alone cost each federal taxpayer $227.00 a year. Additionally, there were 8,000,000 families and individuals with incomes of less than $1000 a year and almost a third of the nation had less than $2000 a year to live on. But for the most part, Americans had much to be thankful for.

Russia had developed an atomic bomb—thanks to espionage—but in 1949 America was still the strongest nation in the world. That year Secretary of State Dean Acheson visited West Germany's President Theodore Heuss. And while Gene Autry had entertained audiences with his cowboy music, Bob Hope had covered 50,000 air miles and visited 65 cities. John L. Lewis was king of the coal miners. Joe DiMaggio homered four times in his first three games after weeks of inactivity nursing a heel injury—to help sweep the Red Sox to victory. J. Edgar Hoover's FBI had 4,100 agents. In March of 1947, President Truman had given the FBI the assignment of checking into the loyalty of 2,500,000 federal employees.

In 1949 George Bernard Shaw was ninety-three years old. Prince Charles celebrated his first birthday. Shirley Temple was twenty-one years of age. *Cheaper by the Dozen* was at the top of the U.S. best seller lists. Writers William Faulkner, Ernest Hemingway and Robert Frost continued to head the writers' popularity list. Polio was still not conquered, but progress was being made to develop better drugs for fighting tuberculosis. The sanatoria regimen was working and soon a pill would make TB a scourge of the past. All in all it was a good year.

In the middle of that first night, Audrey heard a noise and turned on the flashlight. A big pack rat sat on the top of the cupboard, wiggling his whiskers and tapping his tail. He was annoyed that intruders had taken over his home. The next morning Audrey mixed mud and stopped up all the holes the rats had dug between the logs. After that there were no more rats or mice, especially when several cats got busy hunting around the place. In an article, "Homestead in Happy Canyon," which was published in *New Mexico Magazine*, Audrey wrote:

> In late November with all our household goods, my girls and I came home.
>
> Friends and relatives said in horror, "You can't live up there on that isolated mountain ranch! It's unthinkable for a woman alone with two small daughters and no means of transportation to live 18 miles from Las Vegas and three-and-a-half miles from the mail box."
>
> To me it wasn't nearly as unthinkable as watching Crystal, my oldest, fade away under the stress of city living. She had spent a year in bed and several sickly years trying everything the doctors ordered. Now I was determined to try my own remedy, *mountain medicine*.[3]

In the article, Audrey described our arrival, stating that the long bus was too heavy to risk going over the little bridge Clyde had built, so everything was unloaded on the lower side of the bridge and carried a few yards to the front of the Fifteen Dollar House.

> With the sun sinking behind the purpling mountains, they hated to leave us with our things out in the yard. But I cheerfully waved them on. The fresh pine smell was invigorating. Red bronze oak leaves rustled in the evening breeze, whispering "Welcome!" And old Barillas Peak looked down benevolently. The girls and I were home again![4]

Thanksgiving Day, 1949, found Audrey, Crystal and me alone in the mountains, the mountains Audrey had grown to love and that we girls would learn to love. If Mother was afraid, she didn't show it. She kept her a couple of rifles, one under the bed and one in the closet, "in case of emergency."

We went to bed that Thanksgiving night content to be in our mountains, happy to count our blessings.

6

Christmas at Forest Springs

Our first Christmas at the ranch, 1949, was characterized by mild weather. Indian summer lingered while Audrey cleaned the cabin and moved things into place. Audrey wrote:

During the day the golden sun was lavish with wonderful warmth. But the nights were cold, promising snow at any time. I contracted for some wood hauling and cutting and began the happy task of living in the mountains with Dorothy, age five, and Crystal, eleven.[1]

The creek, singing in Happy Canyon in front of the cabin, dried up shortly after we arrived. So we carried every drop of water we used from the nearest spring up the canyon. The spring flowed directly from the mountain side and did not freeze over, even at eighteen degrees below zero.

Audrey walked to the mail box twice a week to get the mail. She would get a ride to town with the mail carrier sometimes. Once in a while friends brave enough to travel the bad road got Audrey's list of groceries in the mail and brought them out. Sometimes Mabel and Vivian came out and brought supplies in the little 1946 "Willy" jeep.

As Christmas approached, several relatives and friends sent us Christmas packages, including Audrey's friend in California, Mrs. Knox. Eleanor Spiess always remembered Crystal. Someone sent us a nativity scene with figures made of a white chalk-like material, along with the paints to color them. We enjoyed painting the figures, giving Mary a blue and white garment, brown clothes for the shepherds, and colorful garb for the wise men—purple, blue, and orange. There were cattle and sheep, too.

The nativity scene was carefully set on a little bench near the tree. Throughout the next ten years, at least, the figures that had been given to us were always put out before Christmas. After a few years, the figure of Mary was chipped, but Crystal and I used water colors to cover the bare spots. A shepherd's head that had broken off was carefully glued back on. Joseph was missing an arm but Crystal and I made a little cloak out of scrap material to cover him so the missing arm would not be noticed. The figure representing the infant Jesus in His manger remained intact at the center of the scene, with Mary and Joseph looking over him, surrounded by shepherds and cattle and sheep. That first Christmas I took the toy hen that laid marble "eggs" and added it to the nativity scene. Crystal argued that a hen didn't belong in the nativity scene.

"Why not?" I retorted. "A stable is a barn, isn't it? So it must be on a farm or ranch. So they must have chickens." The hen stayed along with the cattle and sheep. If I could take liberties with the traditional nativity scene, Crystal could too. She added a rubber cow that did not match the other cattle. Audrey admired our additions.

One day before Christmas we went out at mid-day to our "Christmas Tree Hill," an enormous hillside consisting of fir trees of various sizes and kinds, including very old, large ones. Audrey took an ax and cut down a Blue Spurce, one that came up nearly to the ceiling of our cabin. We put it in a bucket of sand. Mother told us how lucky we were to own a ranch with our very own Christmas trees "in our back yard."

"All we have to do is walk out and pick one, cut it and bring it in. Some people pay a lot of money to go into a forest and find a tree to buy and bring it home," Audrey said.

We had some decorations in a box from past Christmases and we made many of them ourselves. We wanted snow for Christmas, but there was no snow.

Audrey told us that when she and Clyde were first married, he had said that celebrating Christmas was unBiblical, that it was a foolish tradition, and no true Christians would celebrate it with presents, a tree, and so on. Audrey remembered her Christmas in Taos which had nearly been a disaster—with no tree, no gifts, no Santa—until her grandmother's package had arrived from Nebraska, delivered by a dedicated postmaster. She knew that the "tradition" was important to children and could help them appreciate the spirit of giving and the true meaning of Christmas. She agreed with Clyde that it should not be turned into a commercialized frenzy but that the true meaning should be honored. She told him it was not wrong to have a tree or a few gifts. Audrey had convinced Clyde. They always had a tree and celebrated Christmas within the family in a quiet, joyful way. Ironically, our daddy seemed to enjoy Christmas more than anyone. He delighted in wrapping up gifts for us. And he enjoyed trying to guess what each package under the tree contained. Clyde always read "the Christmas story" from the Gospel of Luke every Christmas before we opened our presents so that we would remember the true reason for giving, that it was the birthday of the King. He or Mother explained the meaning of Christmas, the coming of the Christ Child to redeem the world from sin. We knew Jesus was born of a virgin and was the Savior of the world. We knew Christmas was a time to thank God for sending His Son to the world to save us from sin. It was a time to give, just as the wise men had brought gifts to celebrate the birth of the infant Jesus.

Crystal and I made most of our gifts that year. We made mother some "decorated" stationery. Santa left nuts and hard "ribbon" candy in our stockings. Our gifts included paper dolls, color books and a few clothes. To this day the scent of fir tree needles brings back the memories of that happy Christmas when I was five years old, going on six.

Christmas Day, 1949, was a warm, sunny day. The morning was crisp and cool, but by afternoon the sun was out. Crystal and I played with our simple gifts, happy that Santa Claus had found us at the ranch.

The piano was in the back "bedroom" cabin. I enjoyed playing it. Audrey wrote:

> I got Ramón Santillanes to finish it. [the back bedroom cabin] Then I had Leroy Wicks of Wicks Transfer Company bring my piano out. Dorothy had a natural talent for music so we needed it here. [at the ranch] We managed to get it into the cabin. There was room for it and my desk, a chair, and a bed.[2]

Audrey also put up one of the Danny Abbott oil paintings, a large framed picture of a mountain lion. We had been given two Cocker Spaniels shortly after we moved to the ranch. As mentioned before, when the dogs saw the picture for the first time, they began to bark at it. Audrey speculated that they must have seen a cougar before and thought this one was coming in the "window" of the framed picture!

We went out nearly every day to pick up sticks and pieces of wood to burn in the stove. Every day we walked to the spring—usually twice a day—to carry buckets of water back to the house—for drinking water, cooking water, and water for washing dishes and washing ourselves. We took baths in a big, round tub. Mother heated the water on the wood stove. We also washed our hair at the same time, with mother assisting in the process. Audrey wrote in her notes, "A Walk for Water:"

> The big spring was about 1,000 steps from our log cabin and back. When we went after water three times a day that was 3 times 1000 steps. [to and from the spring] But usually we cut it down to two trips a day carrying a five gallon bucket in each hand. Once at the spring, set the bucket down and lean over the water with a sauce pan with a handle, gently dip into the

water—don't stir up sand. The life blood of the mountain and moisture that eased our parched throats drained out of the side of the creek bank. After we had our cabin built, Clyde took an ax and pounded a pipe into the hill side so that the water drained through the pipe. Then it was easy to fill the bucket under the flowing water at the end of the pipe. If you don't bang the buckets and walk with a silent Indian step you may hear turkey talk as a mama coaches her brood. Once when they were startled I counted 43 young turkeys taking to the trees—flying in an explosion of feathered wings.[3]

Audrey and Crystal carried the larger buckets. I carried a small lard bucket. Whenever we went looking for wood or carrying water, Audrey would point out the various plants, trees, and so on. Mother would call our attention to the breeze that caressed the tops of the pine trees and made them sway gently in a gay dance.

"Listen, girls! The trees are talking to us!"

"What are they saying, Mama?" We'd ask in unison.

"They are saying, 'Hello, Crystal. Hello, Dorothy. Hello Audrey! We're glad to see you today! We're glad you're here,'" Audrey replied.

"Oh, Mama, do the trees really talk to us?" I asked.

"Certainly they do," Audrey replied.

Audrey sold numerous stories and won several contests with her writing. In 1949 she published a verse entitled, "He Passed Here":

God, Worker of Miracles, passed this way,
For here we can see His Works today.
See that mountain high and fair.
See that child with golden hair.
See that smile of milky sheen.
See that forest brightly green.

Yes, God with Miracles passed this way!
For here we can see His Works today.[4]

7

Cabin for Three

The one-room log cabin that housed us for two years had a veritable life and death of its own. The Fifteen Dollar House was born in the frigid, drenching paroxysms of spring storms during the wet season of 1943 and died in the searing flames of a fire, cremated one dry summer twenty-seven years later. It was reduced to ashes in the prime of its life. But while it lasted its log arms protected its family well.

The cabin sheltered our three lives from November, 1949 to August, 1951, that crucial period of time when its protection was vital to our survival, especially when winter temperatures dropped to as low as 34 degrees below zero or when we were stalked by starving wildlife.

I would lie in bed in the evening and look at the logs across the ceiling, thinking of how my parents had peeled the bark off each of them and laid them up there. The strong, solid pine pillar they had placed in the center of the room under the two ridge poles stood in the center of the room like a solitary soldier holding up our roof, a sentry guarding the house from disaster. After a few years, little horizontal ink marks, an inch or so apart, appeared to decorate the pole on two sides with the record of growth, each mark appropriately dated, of course—mine on one side, Crystal's on the other. Every so often Mama would have me stand up against the pole, put a ruler against the top of my head, and mark the spot with a pen or pencil and write in the date. Then we could see how much I'd grown since the last mark was made. Crystal went through the same routine.

The kerosene lamp we used for light at night, before we got electricity, cast shadows about the room to transform the interior of the cabin from its day light character to an entirely different night time decor. Crystal showed me how to use my hands to make shadow pictures on the wall.

We felt safe in our cabin, secluded behind a solid front door. Daddy had made the front door by nailing together boards and putting roofing material on the outside. A board on the inside, running across the horizontal boards, added reinforcement. A large hook on the inside was our secure "lock." But the pins of the door hinges were upside down, and they gradually yielded to the law of gravity and worked their way out, the heavy head of each pin slowly easing down. Having the door come off its hinges might have been no problem except that it happened at very inconvenient moment.

One evening just before dusk, Audrey, Crystal and I were sitting on the bench in front of the house. We knew the wildlife rightfully claimed these mountains. We were the intruders but were tolerated because we were harmless—unlike hunters who came from town carrying the long sticks that could reach out with noise and fire and bring sudden death to a deer or a turkey. The only thing we carried were buckets to get water from the spring. We never ventured out of the yard when sun-down approached. We were about ready to go into our cozy cabin for the night when suddenly we heard a low-pitched sort of grunting approaching us from a ridge above the creek. There was no mistaking that sound. It was a bear. We knew that bears were more afraid of us than we were of them. But Audrey always said bears could be dangerous, especially a mama bear with cubs when she thought they needed protecting.

"Quick! Get inside!" Mother whispered. "That's a bear and it's coming this way!"

Crystal and I stepped lightly inside the cabin door while mother, just behind us, swung the door shut to close us safely in. At that moment the door fell off its hinges and slid to the ground with a thud.

Audrey quickly found a hammer. Her hands trembled as she sat the door back in place and began to pound the pins back into their proper position. With the first stroke of the hammer on metal, the loud complaining of the bear ceased and we heard no more sounds. Still, we knew the creature was out there, probably watching us. Audrey got the pins into place within a couple of minutes or so and we closed the door, hooking the lock security. We all sighed with relief. It took Mama's hands a few seconds to stop shaking.

The two small cabins behind the Fifteen Dollar House gave us extra space. We used the east cabin as a summer bedroom and storage room and the west cabin as a chicken house. But the east cabin needed a stove. There was a stove in the cabin but it had never had the chimney put in, so it was useless. Audrey wrote:

> The two 12 foot by 12 foot cabins behind the Fifteen Dollar House served as bedrooms or storage rooms. When it got cold I knew I needed a stove in the bedroom cabin. There was no roof jack in the roof. I climbed up on the roof with a saw and wire cutters and cut out a large square of the asphalt roofing. Then I struggled with the saw to cut through several one inch boards that formed the roof. I cut a good big area and placed the roof jack—a piece of tin with a chimney about six inches long on it—over the hole. After nailing the edges of the jack in place I put two lengths of

stovepipe over the top on the outside of the roof jack. Later when I sat up a little tin heater the chimney from it went from the stove up into the lower side of the roof jack where it fit tightly. As most home fires in our mountain west are caused from faulty chimneys, I always tried to see that ours were made with plenty of air space around the chimney, with no wooden areas within 18 inches or 2 feet.[1]

I remember seeing my mama up on the roof struggling with a saw and putting in the chimney. I was impressed by a woman's doing what I believed to be a man's job! She was strong enough to saw through the wood and put in the chimney and stove.

Audrey would get up early each morning and write. On cold mornings, she would get warm by the wood-stove as she heated water for tea or made oatmeal or corn meal mush for our breakfast. After we got chickens, we always had eggs for breakfast. In fact, eggs were the staple for each meal. We had them boiled, fried, and in many foods such as omelets, custards, and cakes. Mama made "hash," which consisted of onions, potatoes and eggs—sometimes a little canned meat—and other such meals. She made desserts which required beating egg whites for a long time, as we had no electric mixer.

Undoubtedly each morning Audrey would look out to see what kind of day it might be. We were in a canyon between two creeks, but the sunlight came through the trees and shone in our east window every morning. The door faced south, and often we propped it open to let in the fresh air and sunshine. Audrey's "Sunshine is an Elf" was published in *The Joy Bearer* in 1949:

> With most all of her quite hidden,
> In the dark shadow of the trees,
> I wouldn't know that she was there,
> But her locks shimmed in the breeze.
>
> 'Though all of her that I can see
> Is shiny waves of golden hair,
> I know that what Mom calls sunlight,
> Is really, true, an elflet fair![2]

Audrey's mail was her vital link to the outside world so she walked to the mail box near San Geronimo about twice a week. It was too far to take us girls. Crystal wasn't physically well enough for that much exercise, and my short legs tired out after two or three miles. Sometimes there would be a check in the mail.

Audrey depended on the mail carrier, and he was very reliable. Sometimes she composed poetry as she walked. A letter was found in her notes. It is not clear to whom the letter was written or when it was written:

> Here is some minute verse that you might care to glance upon. Did I tell you how pleased I was when I found I could make rhymes? I wrote this last walking in the rain a week or so ago. My meter is not much good but I enjoy trying—when the spirit moves me. Love from Audrey.
>
> LIFE COMES FROM ABOVE
> We lift our lips up to the breeze,
> The arid, dying, earth and I.
> New Essence fills the parched trees,
> As sweet rain falls from the sky.
> New life wells up within us now,
> While rain removes dry death's frown.
> Gladness lights our fevered brow,
> As the drops of life drip down. [3]

Audrey's parents had taught her how to "read" the sky. She knew when the clouds held hail, knew when a storm was imminent. She knew what the wind did to the clouds, how rain clouds looked, and when the clouds held the promise of snow. She knew the feel of the air, the change of the seasons as fall approached. She wrote:

> Somehow we know it.
> The little people of the forest and I.
> There is a change, unseen across the sky.
> There is a change.
> August sun scorches each pine.
> The wind moves with a sultry whine.
> Bees buzz frantically, while young birds flutter, trying their wings.
> This poem falls flat as a flitter, but the change is there.
> Anyone unfamiliar with nature's signs, whispered to those aware,
> Know it is there—
> Not an electric, frantic change
> Just a soft, first faint forecast of winter.[4]

Audrey wrote another poem, this one scribbled on the back of an envelope, about the changes of seasons. It is not known whether the poem was published.

> Freckle time is coming
> And barefoot!
> I can almost feel the ground
> Under my bare toes.
>
> Oh, I can smell the spring,
> See wild geese on the wing,
> Hear the snow begin to melt!
> Stop and look and listen!
>
> Can you feel the spring?
> Barefoot time is coming
> Crocus peek around
> Feel the earth awaken
> Smell the damp, warm ground.[5]

Audrey dreaded hunting season when irresponsible hunters sometimes invaded "her" mountains and killed "her" wildlife. She felt very possessive about nature's bounty that surrounded her. She did not want it trampled on, destroyed. In the fall of 1950 some hunters camped in a field just below our place. We did not discover they were there until we heard their vehicle as they were leaving. After they left, we walked down the canyon to see if all was well. They'd left their campfire smoldering! The red-hot embers could have started up and set the forest on fire. Of course, Audrey immediately put it out, with a loud tirade against reckless hunters. Such careless individuals often destroyed our fences, letting livestock in or out. Naturally, Audrey realized that not all hunters are irresponsible, and many do obey the law. She also understood the need for hunting game for food to feed a hungry family. However, many of the hunters she had encountered were not responsible. Some would even injure an animal and let it run off to suffer and die, leaving the meat to the coyotes. Once Audrey wrote:

> We hear the crack of the hunter's gun
> North, South, East and West
> And cower and hide and stay inside
> While white tails of the frightened deer
> Bounce from hill to clump of brush.
>
> One season of the year
> Scares us all to pieces,

> For North, South, East and West
> Each man thinks he knows
> What's best
>
> So North, South, East and West
> The hunters fire at running deer
> And I hide in my cabin
> Cold with gun-shy fears.[6]

With each season, change came and brought about yet another season to inspire Audrey. She wrote a poem, "Only the Wind and Rain:"

> Only the wind and rain dares
> Attack the tumbleweeds and nettles,
> Beating them to nothing.
> But they will be back again next spring
> And I can fight them once more.[7]

The first year when we had no electricity life was inconvenient, but we were used to it. We never had a refrigerator while living in the Fifteen Dollar House, but Mother made gelatin dessert when the weather was cold enough; she sat the bowl outside in a safe place. By morning the dessert was firm. The problem of water, however, was not easily solved, especially during the drought. Still, we were able to manage with walks to the spring—and later to Grandma's well a half mile over the hill.

Dorothy and Crystal Simpson with collie Bonnie at Forest Springs Ranch, 1950
Source: Simpson Archives, photo by Audrey Simpson

After a day of various chores to survive in the mountain wilderness—carrying water, gathering in wood, feeding the animals, caring for the garden, preparing meals—Audrey was glad to sit quietly in the evening twilight and listen to the night hawks soar and the sound of crickets chirping happily. When it was time to settle in for the night, she would close the door, hook it securely, and turn her attention to her girls, for it was story time and prayer time—time to thank God for another day beneath the Sangre de Cristos.

The Fifteen Dollar House, with its two back cabins, was a wonderful home for us for the two years we lived there. Then it was a wonderful vacation home for the entire family after Daddy returned. The cabin for three then became the cabin for five—but that's a story for later. While it was a cabin for three, it provided everything we needed in a home because of Audrey's faith, courage, and hard work to endure regardless of circumstances.

8

Reading and Writing Lessons—and Another Fire

Crystal and I had lots of time to study, to read, and to play indoor games when inclement weather prohibited outdoor activities. We had very few toys but we made up games.

Every day mother would teach me to read out of the Dick and Jane series she obtained from the school superintendent. That first year I went through twenty-one first grade readers and read other texts and story books as well. I wrote letters to friends and relatives. At Christmas time, I wrote to Santa Claus, and my letter was read along with many others on KFUN's letters to Santa program. Home-schooling is common place now, but in those days it was almost unheard of.

Crystal got much of her practice in writing and spelling by corresponding with pen pals from The Cheerful Greetings Club, known as the CGC Club, where people from all over the United States corresponded with one another—all invalids or "shuts-ins."

Audrey read to us. She read the Bible every evening. And she read us many other books as well. We usually went to bed soon after dark to save the kerosene. Even after we had electricity, we did not stay up late. Before going to bed, Mother would always read some Bible verses and we would pray. As we lay in the darkness, Mother would tell stories. Most of them were good vehicles for teaching us about life. She tried to tell true stories that would challenge us to think and develop our moral values. Mother talked about natural history, great men and women of the past and present, how to get along in all kinds of situations, and told us about the Bible, especially miracles of the Bible. She talked about science, literature, and her own experiences. She shared just about everything she had read about or learned or experienced. There were classics, such as Aesop's fables, fairy tales, historical and mythological tales, and stories Audrey made up. But our favorite type story was usually a "true" story about Audrey's childhood. We learned a great deal from our mother's experiences.

"Tell us a story about when you were a little girl," I would beg.

"Yes, one we haven't heard before!" Crystal would add.

And there was always a story, one we had heard before or, sometimes, one we had not heard before. We were fascinated by a story about how two-year-old Opal played with "a little man," like an elf or leprechaun. Audrey was jealous because she couldn't see the little man, nor did she have a miniature playmate of her own. So she told Opal she had a little playmate, too; but she didn't. We liked stories about Grandpa Clements, Mother's father, and about Grandma Shearer, her mother. We liked to hear about how Edward ran away from home and Audrey persuaded him to come back. We liked to hear about how Audrey and Opal baked a cake for their mother and hid it in a suitcase. We liked to hear about the wild horses, especially the ones she helped tame.

And always, there were the lessons Audrey taught in her stories. Then it would become question and answer time. Crystal and I would bring up questions about nature, about astrology, about mineralogy, about history, about literature, about science, about theology—anything and everything. And Mother would share her knowledge—knowledge that was vast because she had always been such an avid reader.

Audrey also read aloud to us. She had a 1912 *Book of Knowledge* set that the Waldo Spiess family had given her. That set of children's books contains fiction and non-fiction: history, science, literature, and many other areas of learning, along with pictures and drawings. I had several books of my own such as Little Golden Books, as well as my school books.

The books Audrey read to us were too difficult for us to read ourselves. She read *Five Little Peppers and How they Grew*, by Margaret Sidney; *The Bobbsey Twins at the Seashore* by Laura Lee Hope; *Dorothy and the Wizard in Oz* by L. Frank Baum; and the Howard R. Garis *Uncle Wiggily* stories about the rabbit gentleman's adventures. Audrey also read *Polly: A New Fashioned Girl* by Mrs. L.

T. Meade, a book that had belonged to her grandmother Alice Waddell.

In later years, she would read *The Secret Garden* by Frances Hodgson Burnett. By that time Crystal and I were reading books on our own more than ever. Some years later I read *Beautiful Joe: A Dog's Own Story* by Marshall Saunders. I so liked the character of Laura, the girl who was kind to animals, that when I had a daughter of my own, I named her Laura. I had a doll named Rose named after a Rose in one of the fairy tales I'd heard. I thought Rose was a beautiful name. So I named my second daughter Rose.

Audrey could never read the sad parts of a story without weeping. When she read Eric Knight's *Lassie Come Home,* the tears ran down her cheeks and her voice broke as she read about the death of the little dog, Toots, when the Peddler Rowlie was attacked by robbers and Toots faithfully fought to the death. She wept again when she came to the conclusion of the story where Lassie finally made it home, nearly dead, before her true owners nursed her back to health. She wept when Jo died in *Little Women* by Louisa May Alcott. She wept when she read about the fawn Bambi at the point where Bambi's mother was shot and killed by hunters. Crystal and I had seen the Walt Disney movie of Bambi, but to hear our mother read the book *Bambi* by Felix Salten was a truly unique experience. Audrey also cried when the mare Ginger died from years of overwork and abuse in Anna Sewell's *Black Beauty*. Mother would keep right on reading through her tears. She wept when she read *The Little Match Girl* by Hans Christian Andersen and *The Littlest Angel* by Charles Tazewell. She cried through much of the Johanna Spyri book, *Heidi*. Crystal and I both knew she wept through it because Mama loved the mountains as Heidi did; and she understood how home sick one could get upon having to leave them. We never asked Mama why she was crying. Often we were keeping back the tears ourselves.

Audrey was as free with her laughter as she was with her tears when she read aloud. She laughed when she read us comic books: Little Lulu or Donald Duck or Woody Woodpecker. But she laughed the most when she read some of my Little Golden Books to me such as *Bertram and the Ticklish Rhinoceros* by Paul Gilbert. She also enjoyed the original *Rudolph, The Red-Nosed Reindeer* by Robert L. May. It was distributed by Montgomery Ward, was written in verse form, colorfully illustrated, and was an over-night sensation. Later the song "Rudolph, The Red-Nosed Reindeer" was popular.

Sometimes I would notice Audrey reading a book or magazine and weeping. It would be an adult story that was too complex to read to us, but she would tell us about it. One such book was *The Snow Goose* by Paul Gallico. Another was a story in a magazine. It was about two little boys in heaven prior to their being born into this world. They hesitated to "take the plunge" into this earthly life. They didn't want to be separated, even for a little while. They didn't want to feel lonely. They vowed they would find each other and be friends throughout life. They planned their lives and their deaths. They knew they would return to the heavenly regions after their lives were over and be together always. They didn't want to go to earth but knew they needed to experience this life in order to learn and grow so that they would appreciate heaven—and God—more fully.

"Is it a true story, Mama?" I asked.

"No," she whispered through her tears. "Not exactly."

"Then why are you crying?" Crystal asked.

"Because I think it could be true," Mama replied through her tears. Then she sighed, "And because I know how the little boys must have felt."

Sometimes Audrey read us a story she had written. She wrote a children's story called "Little Cowboy." She sent it to a publisher or two but it was not accepted. She put it away in hopes of getting it published after re-working it later—but it was lost in the 1971 fire along with many of her other manuscripts—published and unpublished.

Since Audrey read a few verses from the Bible every evening, we went through the entire Bible in a few years. Then we would start over again. If we had questions, we would ask and she would explain. We learned King James English quite well in that manner. Every Sunday morning we held Sunday School and Church. Mama taught the lesson and then we sang and read the Bible and prayed. There was always a church program on the radio and we listened to it. One of my favorite religious programs was "Unshackled," sponsored by Pacific Garden Mission in Chicago. Little did I know that years later, touring Chicago as part of a book I would write, I would visit that very place and be given a tour of the old mission.

Before we went to sleep, we would always pray. I was first, then Crystal, and then Audrey. Mama's prayers were quite long because she mentioned each person in the family. I often wonder if the family members ever knew Audrey prayed for each of them every night. She told us many stories of how prayer had changed things. I think she kept a prayerful spirit most of the time. Sometimes she would be driving us somewhere and I would see her lips moving.

"What are you saying, Mama?" I'd ask.

"I was praying," she would reply after she'd finished.

In later years when she worked for the newspaper, Audrey said she always prayed before she went into the building for work—for everyone to work in harmony, for no major problems to arise, for everything to go well that day. And she said it always did! "But if I was in a hurry and forgot to pray, things usually didn't go so well," Audrey said.

There is a poem entitled "The Reading Mother" by Strickland Gillilan expressing appreciation for a mother who read to her children. I had such a mother. I was pleased that my mother was not ashamed to cry and to laugh over the great stories of literature. She was genuine. She didn't pretend to be someone she was not. When Audrey felt something, you knew it, whether it was anger, joy, or sorrow. Audrey's influence definitely taught us to love to read and to enjoy learning.

We all missed Clyde. Some of the music I heard on the radio reminded me of Daddy. He liked Country/Western and his favorite singers were Hank Williams, Eddie Arnold and others of that era. I felt sad and the songs on the radio made me feel worse. I knew Crystal and Mama were hurting too, but we hardly ever mentioned it because we didn't want to make each other feel worse. Crystal had been so upset that she developed her "illness" which may have been nothing more than "nerves" or "anxiety."

December 31, 1949—the last day of the year—was a cool, crisp, sunny morning. Audrey got up as usual to build a fire in the wood stove and feed the animals, then start clicking away on the typewriter. When she stepped outside she thought she caught a faint whiff of smoke on the distance mountain air. She wasn't sure. She decided that in a little while she would walk up to the Forest Springs Ranch Mesa and see if she could see any smoke anywhere. The old wagon road to the Mesa went up a hill to the west of our cabin, leveled out, then turned into another hill, and finally reached the top of the flat land. The people who lived up there in previous years had used that road, and we used it to walk to the Mesa nearly every day to look at the countryside. Before long, Audrey heard the sound of an approaching vehicle. She looked out and saw Vivian, Mabel and Jessica.

"Grandfather Shearer's house is on fire!" Mabel told us.

"Is it going to burn the whole forest, Grandma?" Crystal asked.

"I hope not," Mabel replied. "Right now it is only burning his house. They have it contained. Some men from San Geronimo are already up here helping to make sure the fire doesn't spread."

Grandfather Shearer took care of himself, got his own wood, cooked, worked outside, enjoyed his life in the mountains where he had homesteaded in 1906. He had accumulated a life time of books in his library, as well as many antiques. He enjoyed his music and played the organ beautifully.

Apparently Grandfather had started a fire in his wood stove as usual that morning when the roof caught on fire. He tried to put it out but couldn't. He used his telephone with the line to the Forest Service so they could send some men to fight the fire. They also notified men in the surrounding area, as well as Vivian, so they could come and help.

We went over to Grandfather Shearer's place. By the time got there, the fire was out. The house was smoldering. Later Audrey wrote:

Mother and Jessica drove up and said Grandfather's house had burned. He built a fire in the a.m. and sparks got under the shingles. CV [Charles Vivian] had been going to re-roof it but hadn't yet. Grandfather tried to get the organ out but couldn't; it got stuck in the door, and he burned his hands. Everything burned except the family Bible.[1]

After the beautiful antique organ was stuck in the doorway, Grandfather couldn't get anything else out of any size. He did throw small things out the windows, including some of his books. But before long, the smoke was too bad, and he could no longer rescue any of his things. He worked to contain the fire so it would not spread from the house to the nearby trees. Soon help arrived. Grandfather picked up the few things he had managed to salvage and Vivian helped him box them up. He would have to find a place in town to stay, Vivian said. Grandfather argued that he could stay in one of the little cabins. But Vivian and Mabel convinced him to go to town until he had a chance to recuperate. They didn't want to take any chances with his health, as he was eighty-nine years old. His hands were suffering from burns and he had inhaled smoke. They thought he should see a doctor. Besides it was winter time and he needed a good wood supply at hand. He didn't need to be carrying wood in and setting up house in another cabin, they argued. They'd take care of him in town.

That night Crystal and I stayed in Vivian's little one-room cabin near the adobe house on the Old Homestead Ranch. Grandma Shearer put us to bed. Apparently Audrey had stayed in town to help Grandfather get settled. As Grandma was staying good night to us, she saw a straight pin on the floor, bent over and picked it up and said, "If you find a straight pin on the floor and pick it up, it means good luck. We surely could use some good luck after this terrible day."

Vivian and Mabel got Grandfather settled in an apartment in town. He should be fine, they thought. But two and a half months later, March 15, 1950, he died.

Audrey explained to us that in his old age, all Grandfather Shearer had left in life were "his pretty things—his books, his music, his view from the window of the mountains. When he lost those things, he had nothing left to live for." He'd lost a life time collection of keep sakes and mementos—photographs and other things he couldn't replace. Audrey had an understanding of how difficult it is to start over with nothing. Even when people donate things to start over, it is not the same as having your own. Some things are simply irreplaceable.

"How could he start over at his age? He no longer wanted to live," Audrey said.

Audrey had seen the destruction of fire too many times in her life. She knew how it took the spirit out of a person, how it wounded the spirit so deeply that recovery was difficult if not impossible. For an elderly person, it could be impossible.

Someone heard about the tragedy and asked Audrey, "Did Mr. Shearer die in the fire?"

"No," Audrey replied. "But the fire killed him. He died of a broken heart."

I realized later what an amazing man R. A. Shearer was. I thought, *I knew a man who remembered when the Civil War ended!*

Years later Audrey wrote about Grandfather Shearer's highly treasured organ that had been stuck in the doorway. The 1958 *Las Vegas Daily Optic, Rodeo Edition* story was entitled: "Organ At Shearer's Pioneer Attraction:"

> At the turn of the century music was as popular as it is now and much harder to obtain.
>
> One widely known musical instrument of the Las Vegas area was a little organ that arrived in Las Vegas in 1905 by way of Wyoming, when the R. A. Shearer family shipped all of their household goods here.
>
> It livened up the air where the Shearer's had the Savings Bank Store at what is now 518 Sixth. When they moved to their homestead ranch in the Mineral Hill district, the little upright organ went along. When area ranchers held a dance at the Ferndele store and post office at the Shearer ranch, the little organ made sweet music for the couples whirling over the rough board floor.
>
> If the dance was not at the Shearer's, 18 miles west of Las Vegas, the family loaded the little organ into a spring wagon and transported it in style across the miles of mountainside to the neighbor's community dances.
>
> Dr. Ollie Shearer made the organ sing with her nimble fingers. Its music was loved and known all over the pine and aspen country of the Mineral Hill district. Its tone remained round and sweet, through the depression of the 1930's and after World War II.
>
> Then fire struck the Shearer ranch home in 1949. R. A. Shearer, 89 years old and alone at the ranch, tired to save the melody-maker. With fire flaming all around him he tugged at the little organ. Fire fell from

the living room ceiling and caught in the cloth behind the open work in the front of the organ. He had to let it burn along with the rest of the ranch home and its contents.

Today, some of the forest dwellers, passing old houses where the little organ once sang, claim they hear its music swelling over the mountainside. And if the moon is full above the Sangre de Cristos, they say that if you sit quietly in the shadow of a pine tree for an hour you are sure to hear the little organ singing a lullaby to the stars.[2]

As soon as frost left the ground that first spring, Audrey had the garden plowed and planted peas, corn, beans, radishes, lettuce, onions, beets, turnips, three kinds of squash, pumpkins, cucumbers, spinach and carrots. They came up beautifully from the damp soil, promising a bumper crop—if it rained enough.

But the summer of 1950 was dry. One day on the road to town in Vivian's little 1946 "Willy" Jeep, we saw some neighboring ranchers, Warren Walker and his family. There was no traffic, so we stopped to visit briefly.

"It looks like the country is just gonna dry up and blow away," Mrs. Walker said, while her husband nodded his head.

"It's drier than I've ever seen it," Audrey agreed.

Audrey wrote a wonderful short story based on the true events she had witnessed as a child growing up in the villages of northern New Mexico. Although the characters were fictitious, the story included the tradition of taking San Isidro, the little hand-painted wooden saint of the farmers—brought from Spain by the early settlers—and showing him the dry fields. A procession would carry him up to a hill top and let him see the country side. He and his pair of oxen that pulled his little wooden plow would be shown the need for rain. Then they would return him to the church and rain would always come afterwards.[3]

I seemed to gain a desire to write from watching my mother work and seeing her successes. I liked listening to radio dramas. At age six, I wrote a story of my own about a bad man's greed for gold and how he learned that the gold he had stolen did not bring him happiness. He reformed. "The Bad Man and the Gold" was written in pencil on a school tablet with many misspelled words, but my mother told me it was an excellent story and encouraged me in my creative writing.

As previously mentioned, I composed a song. I sang it to Mother. I had made up a little tune to go with the words. Audrey was impressed and sent my verse to a publisher of children's religious works, a Sunday School magazine. They used the verse. It was about how Jesus loves everyone. I received $1.00 for the verse. Mother took me to the bank to cash my check—my first ever. The clerk asked me if I wanted a paper dollar or a silver dollar. I asked for the silver dollar. I still have that dollar, as well as the check stub. My mother boasted for years that I became a professional writer at the age of six. I still have the first dollar I ever made. My mother took a photograph of me with my letter of acceptance and check when I was standing in front of the lilac bushes at the Carringtons' house.

Audrey worked on her writing early every morning before we girls were up. She sold quite a few short items, some articles, and won some writing contests during that time. After breakfast we usually walked to the spring. Audrey carried two large buckets; Crystal carried one or two large ones, and I carried a small lard bucket or two. In the winter we melted snow—if there was any—to use for washing.

Crystal and I used our imaginations and made up stories or games to play. When we played in "Happy Meadow" across the creek below our house, we enjoyed the wild flowers and shade of the trees. We called the special oak grove there "The Fairy Trees" where we believed the forest fairies danced and played.

With laughter and tears—the happy events and the sad events—coloring our days, ours was a simple life but would be remembered as the best time of our lives for growing closer to nature and to one another.

9

Stranger by the Roadside

In the summer time Crystal and I slept in the back cabin so Mother could get up early and write without waking us with the tapping of her Royal Typewriter. However, the typing didn't disturb us even when we were in the main cabin. We were used to it.

Audrey won several writing contests. Once she won about $150.00, a considerable sum in 1951. It was a radio contest. The company that sponsored it was asking for true animal stories. Audrey wrote up a true story about our Cocker Spaniels, Pete and Swifty. She won second place in the nation-wide contest.

A friend from Las Vegas, Mrs. Leatherman, gave Audrey two black Cocker Spaniels. She said they should never be separated because they were so close. She jokingly told Audrey that sometimes she thought they believed themselves to be human.

"They've got class," she declared.

We had several cats and Crystal's collie, Bonnie. We did not need any more pets. But Mrs. Leatherman was moving and could not take her dogs. Audrey said we would give them a good home in the mountains. The only request Mrs. Leatherman made was that the pair never be separated. "They are like a couple," she said. "They have been together all their lives. I don't think either one would survive long without the other."

Pete and Lelama Gardner brought the dogs to us in their car one morning. Crystal teased me. She said, "The dogs names are Pete and Lelama."

"They can't be!" I exclaimed.

Finally she laughed, "No, but the male's name is Pete. The female is Swifty."

The dogs adapted to their new ranch home very well. They were always together, almost in an intimate way like the proverbial "old married couple." If one dog was distressed, the other was too. If one lay down for a nap, the other did too.

Every morning when we walked to the spring to carry home our daily drinking water, the dogs went with us on the trail which was lined with ponderosa pines, spruce, fir and aspen trees. But when Swifty had new puppies, she had to forgo the walk. Pete always stayed at the cabin with her then.

Swifty had mothered several litters, always taking excellent care of her offspring until Audrey found a home for them. Soon after the birth of a new litter, one of the pups died. Audrey placed the dead puppy on a high table at the front of the house while we went to the spring for water. Mother told us that as soon as we returned we would find a good spot to bury the puppy. Audrey had always taught us to revere life. When any of our animals died, we provided a proper burial.

When we returned from the spring, Audrey suddenly stopped before we reached the cabin. "Stop!" she ordered in a loud whisper. "Look over there!"

Swifty had jumped up on the high table and had retrieved her dead pup as Pete looked on. Something compelled us to silence. We froze in our places and watched. Swifty and Pete turned from the house and began a slow, dignified procession. Swifty walked slowly down the road, carrying the pup in her mouth. Pete, about three feet across from her, stepped in perfect time. We followed quietly, keeping a distance so our presence would not disturb the dogs. They crossed the bridge, Swifty on one side, Pete just across from her on the other side.

Not far below the house, across the creek, the dogs came to a clearing in the oak brush just a few feet beyond the road. We watched Swifty sit down under a tall pine tree and gently lay—not drop—the puppy on the ground. Then Pete began to dig and scratch until he had dug a hole in the soft black soil. When he finished, he sat down beside the hole and waited. Swifty again picked the puppy up in her mouth and placed the little body into the hole. Then she sat while Pete got up and scratched the dirt back into the hole until the hole was completely covered up with the soft earth.

After Pete had thoroughly covered the little grave, the two dogs turned slowly and again marched in measured, stately steps back up the road to the house and their remaining pups. Pete never missed a beat. He stayed exactly the same distance across from Swifty and stepped in perfect time with her dignified walk. There was no eulogy and no dirge of organ music that day. But we had no doubt that we had just observed a funeral. And watching from our secluded position, we hoped we had not intruded upon the sacred ceremony of the bereaved parents. Audrey later submitted the story for the contest. She cited a passage from an anonymous ancient Greek poet:

> Stranger by the roadside, do not smile
> When you see this grave, though it is only a dog's.
> My master wept when I died, and his own hand
> Laid me in earth and wrote these lines on my tomb.[1]

Many times in her life Audrey had buried a deceased pet. She knew how sorrowful it was to put one's loving pet into the ground. But she had never observed dogs burying their own. Crystal and I saw it and knew it to be true. Although I was only about six years of age, I remember the incident clearly. I remember how astonished we were. It was for that story that Audrey won the contest for true animal stories. I was glad she had shared it.

I remember Mama's surprise and awe—and her eyes misted with tears—when said, "Mrs. Leatherman was right. Those dogs have class."

10

Little Joys

Audrey was writing every day, and much of her work was being published. One story she published under the name A. C. Clements in *Western Sportsman* in August of 1950. It was called "Bear On A Grey Hackle." She described a fishing trip in which she and some friends camped high above the old Terrero mines. After catching fish, they decided to explore a cave only to discover it was occupied by a bear. In the ensuing excitement, the bear, trying to get away from the people, brushed across the author (Audrey) who was lying in the cave. The bear stepped on a hat that had a fishing hackle in it, catching the hackle in his paw. The story concluded:

> When my guides and I finally rounded up the frightened horses, we followed the bear's trail for a short distance. I dismounted and got a good look at its tracks. They were much wider and longer than my own. In the soft earth, where that bear's track showed like a pattern in clay, I plainly saw the print of my grey hackle on its barbed back! The bear had it on his heel.
>
> It's the first time I ever had a bear "take" grey hackle. I wonder what happened to it.
>
> Next day I lost a prize fly to an old grandpa so big I couldn't even show him. The day after that I caught a twenty-five-inch speckled beauty in swift water. This one nearly gave me heart failure.
>
> But neither trill compared to the jolt that big black gave me when he trampled me in the cave and ran away with my grey hackle.[1]

Audrey also had an article published in the December of 1950 *New Mexico Magazine*, "The Fort that Won the West." She used several black and white photographs she had taken of the ruins at Fort Union. This was before Fort Union was designated as a national monument. She pointed out that it was the fort that protected the Santa Fe Trail. Also, Fort Union was one fort that did not fall to the Confederate Army and so perhaps saved the whole west from the Confederates and "perhaps even changed the course of the Civil War."[2] She outlined the history of the fort, citing Brigadier General Stephen Watts Kearney who marched into Santa Fe on August 18, 1846 and announced that the people were now American citizens; to provide protection, he directed that a fort be established overlooking Santa Fe. During the 1849-1850 period, five raiding tribes—the Utah's, Kiowa's, Navajos, Apaches, and Comanche's—caused property loss that was estimated in official records at $114,500. "The Indians swooped down upon settlements, wagon trains and ranches at will, killing and plundering, kidnapping and driving off stock."[3] Fort Marcy was unable to protect the traders' slow freight wagons over the long miles from St. Louis."[4]

Colonel Edwin Vose Sumner was assigned the command of the 9th military district and he began a series of forts, "with the master fort, Union, built in the Mora river country."[5] In the fall of 1851 the first house on the Fort Union site was built by Capt. W. R. Shoemaker, ordnance officer. In the spring of 1852, the first fort was constructed of pine logs covered with earth and lumber. "The place was not fortified, but had an arsenal."[6] Later, during the Civil War, General Canby moved the fort a mile north. It was enlarged and improved.

> The map of Fort Union as of 1866 shows the fort in the new location. A tunnel had been dug from the arsenal about a mile up the canyon to a spring so that men could get water in case of Indian attack and siege. Another tunnel also led from the arsenal to the new fort. By 1875 the arsenal was supplied with water from a well and from two cisterns holding 18,000 gallons each. The main portion of the fort was apparently also supplied with water from two cisterns holding 24,000 each. The cisterns may still be seen at the ruins.[7]

The article continued to state that at one time the fort housed one thousand and more troops and had stable facilities with a capacity of a thousand head of stock. The Sutler's store did a daily average of $3,000 business. The corn cribs and hay barns were large enough to store two million bushels of grain and two thousand tons of hay. After the coming of the telegraph and the railroad, Fort Union was abandoned as an economy measure by the U.S. Army on February 21, 1891.

> Gradually the buildings have melted down. Neighboring ranchers and townspeople have helped themselves to timbers, bricks, and anything else of value that they could carry off.
>
> "And why not?" they say. "Nobody cares about the old fort. If we use some of it we are preserving it. We aren't vandals. We are relic hunters. We love the old things of the fort, where others who had charge of them once cared nothing for them and left them to ruin."

But there are only memories left today—a few gaunt walls and chimneys and memories of war-whoops and high-wheeled wagons and hard-riding, fast shooting men in blue who fanned out from Fort Union to help make New Mexico a peaceful place to live.[8]

It is amazing that such detailed research—with five photographs and a map—was done by a woman on a manual typewriter living in a one-room log cabin with no electricity, no running water, no transportation, and no telephone. Computers and the internet had not even been dreamed of. But she had photographs from previous visits to Fort Union, taken with her little box camera. Little did she know the impact of her story. Her article, one of the few about the fort at that time, may have been one of the influential elements that led to public demand that Fort Union be preserved—and finally led to its becoming the national monument that it is today.

Audrey, with her manual typewriter and box camera, may have had more influence than she realized. The last three paragraphs of her story, above, carried a powerful dictum: *Preserve it or lose it forever*. A story in the *Las Vegas Optic*, using the title of Audrey's story, later reported:

> Fort Union National Monument, about 26 miles north of Las Vegas, is a spot of great historical interest and truly deserves the name of "The Fort That Won the West."
>
> In 1955 Ft. union became a National Monument. Now thousands of visitors can reach this important shrine of history and recall heroism of the men in blue as they defended the Santa Fe trail travelers and created for the U. S. A. a glorious past and future.[9]

As a free lance writer, Audrey had sporadic income of varying amounts from stories she sold, along with writing contests she won. Clyde sent child support of eighty dollars a month. Audrey got fifty dollars a month from the Reids for the sale of the house on the corner on Eighth Street; later when Audrey sold the house we had been living in Audrey got another thirty-five dollars a month. So she had a total of about one-hundred and sixty-five dollars a month to live on. But often the house payments were late. Sometimes the buyers skipped a month. So there was no sure or steady income. After Audrey rented the cabin on the south end of the place to writers John and Dorothy Heller, she got a little more, something like thirty dollars for a six-month period. After she raised chickens, she could have sold eggs, but there was seldom anyone around to buy them. She did sell the Cocker Spaniel puppies from time to time.

Audrey knew we could not have lived in town on that meager income. Mother was able to stretch the grocery bill by baking bread and making simple but nutritious meals. Our grocery bill was supplemented by our garden vegetables and, later, by the chickens and turkeys which provided eggs and, sometimes, meat. We lived comfortably without running water, electricity, central heat, telephone, refrigerator or transportation. Before very long we obtained a radio that ran on batteries, so we could listen to a few programs in the evening. We were so happy we did not think about what we didn't have. We thought about what we did have that so many in the world were deprived of—fresh mountain air, sunshine through the tall pine trees, flowers in the meadows, babbling brooks when the rains came, white snow to play in (sometimes), a warm stove with wood and coal to keep it going, fresh spring water, fresh baked bread to eat, good books to read, a kerosene lamp and flashlights to get through the night, a radio to keep us in touch with the world, wonderful dogs, cats, and, best of all, the company of one another.

But Audrey did not anticipate the drought. So the anticipated garden vegetables did not always materialize. Nor did she anticipate that the money she counted on would not always come in. When the anticipated payments did not arrive, Audrey would write and ask when she could expect a payment. The answer, if there was one, would be "soon." People didn't seem to realize how much Audrey depended on those monthly payments to buy food and necessities for herself and her girls. At least Clyde's child support was nearly always on time.

Audrey found out later that Bill Reid was getting deep into debt. He had ten children to feed and was unable to pay his enormous grocery bill. The Reids did finally pay off the house—only to lose it. They lost the property for the grocery bill. The Reids—all twelve of them—-moved back into their little trailer house until they could afford a house in Santa Fe.

One morning while we girls were still asleep, Audrey got up early and walked up the hill above the house. She had been worried about money. Where was the income she was counting on? She had been depending on other people—Clyde's child support and the monthly income from the houses she'd sold. Now she knew she needed to depend solely on God, the Source of all things. She prayed, she sobbed, she cried. When she finished pouring out her heart to God, she had a sense of peace and confidence. She had turned her money problems over to God.

"I didn't worry about money after that," Audrey said. "I made up my mind to let God handle it. And the money did come in, sometimes in little trickles, but we had enough. I knew I could depend on God." If the payments were late, she still had her writing income, small as it was.

While they were still living on Eighth Street, Clyde and Audrey had rented their Ten Dollar House to the Hellers, a New York couple—writers. (Opal and Bob had deserted the cabin they had moved into in March of 1942.) The writers had left after a year, but after Audrey moved back to the ranch, the Hellers wrote that they wanted to return to the mountains. However, they felt they needed more room. So Audrey hired Ramón Santillanes to build a log cabin on the Forest Springs Ranch property, just a few yards below the fence line of the Shearer property—not far from where the Ten Dollar House sat. Audrey helped with the building, although Ramón and his boys did most of the heavy work. Audrey told the couple, John and Dorothy Heller, that they could live in the new cabin and use the old Ten Dollar House for storage (with the Shearers' permission) so they could have both houses. Ramón's labor and material for the roof and glass for the windows made the total cost about one-hundred dollars. In the gable ends were large panes of glass, thirty-six inches by thirty-six inches, so there was good light in the room. This new cabin, which we always called "Hellers' Cabin," was the sixth cabin Audrey had helped to build.

Hellers' Cabin was near the big spring we referred to as "the lower spring." Happy Creek ran down the hill just below the cabin and flowed into the big water hole where the spring was located. There was an open space for a garden below the house. In fact, Audrey had used that space for a garden before. The writers from New York were looking for just such an isolated place where they could do their work in solitude. John and Dorothy Heller happily moved into the new cabin. They had no car, no telephone, and no luxuries. They carried water from the creek or the spring just a few yards below the house. Every so often they would walk up the canyon to visit with us or we would occasionally walk to their cabin to visit them. Audrey didn't feel quite so isolated when there were people living just down the canyon. Since they were writers too, Audrey enjoyed visiting with them. The Hellers stayed for about a year.

When we weren't outside doing chores, we sometimes listened to the radio. We heard the news, various types of music, and enjoyed comedy shows such as Jack Benny. Sometimes we listed to "soap operas" such as Stella Dallas and to dramas such as Sky King, The Lone Ranger, Dr. Christian, and many others. Radio Station KFUN in Las Vegas gave us daily news. Audrey remembered the first KFUN broadcast on December 25, 1941. The sound was intermittent, as Ernie Thwaites was working out the "bugs" to get the station on the air. Every morning there was local news and weather. I remember waking up to the theme song, "Top of the Morning" which I liked. My favorite program was Bobby Benson, the little boss of the B-Bar-B Ranch. Of course we had our favorite westerns such as Roy Rogers or Sergeant Preston of the Yukon with his lead dog, Yukon King. Listening to the radio was one of the joys of life, something we considered a luxury. Electricity was, too.

Sometime in late 1950 the REA came through. They asked Audrey if she wanted electricity. Of course she did. We thought we were rich after that. Audrey bought a little electric radio, so we didn't have to worry about running down a battery. With light, we could read after dark. Audrey bought a little hot plate so we could cook or heat water without having to "fire up" the big kitchen range with wood and coal—unless the oven was needed. Audrey made several loaves of bread every week, mixing up the batter, letting it sit so the yeast could rise, and then baking the loaves when she had the kitchen stove just the right temperature. The smell of bread cooking in that little log cabin was nothing short of divine, to say nothing of the taste. As winter approached, Audrey bought an electric space heater to help heat the one-room cabin. It warmed up the cold mornings and evenings when a fire in the stove would have used too much wood. It was a life saver when the outside temperatures dropped and even the wood stove could not warm the cabin.

Audrey allowed Crystal to do some school work. Also, Crystal helped tutor me, and that helped her own reading skills. Audrey spent most mornings "home schooling" us. Later, Audrey wrote:

> "What do you do with your spare time?" I am often asked. What spare time? The days rush by. The weeks and months are jet-propelled. The time from butterflies to snowflakes is all too short.
> As we are four-and-a-half miles from the nearest school and have no school bus route nearer than the school house, I got books from the County School Superintendent and I teach the girls myself. With daily lessons, ordinary house work, carrying water when the creek is dry, and walking the long rough miles up and down the canyon after the mail, I have little spare time.[10]

Crystal and I adjusted quite well. At first I missed Kindergarten. I missed my friends like Alice Winston and Bert Forbes and Jay Harris. I missed the teachers, Mrs. Harris and Mrs. Frank. I also missed some of the things we had in town such as fresh milk or hot and cold water from a faucet. But we had lived in fairly primitive conditions before and we were comfortable in our log cabin.

We acquired a cat that we had for many years. She was all black, so we named her Inky. Lelama Gardner spent the summer at her ranch. Her cat had several kittens. At the end of the summer when Lelama went back to town, she could not catch all of the kittens, as they were quite wild. Audrey, Crystal and I carried milk to them every day, walking from our place down Santillanes creek to the Gardner place. Gradually, they became tamer and we were able to catch them all except one. The solid black kitten was too wild. After we took the other kittens home with us, Inky was alone. So she wandered down the canyon to the Ranney place. Mrs. Ranney let us know she had the kitten and wanted us to come and get it. Mother tried many times but could not catch Inky. Finally, Mrs. Ranney fed the kitten on her enclosed porch and closed the door. Then Mr. Clark Ranney was able to get the kitten into a gunny sack. He rode his horse to our place, carefully bringing his "passenger," the black kitten. We kept her in the cabin a few days but were never very successful in taming her. However, she knew she had a home with us, and when we moved back to town, she moved with us, first to the Carrington place and then to our house on Seventh Street.

As November approached, we knew it was going to be Mama's birthday. We asked Audrey what she needed so we could buy her a gift the next time we went to town. She told us she could use some under wear; she needed panties.

Soon we went to town and stayed at the Carringtons all day. While Mother did her errands, Crystal and I were allowed to shop at the two dime stores on Douglas Avenue. We checked both stores before deciding on a purchase. The best prices that day were at Newberrys.

At the store, a lady asked the usual, "May I help you?"

Crystal, in her most grown up twelve-year-old voice, said, "We are looking for panties."

"The panties are over here," the lady indicated. "What size do you want?"

Crystal and I looked at each other in surprise. We had both forgotten to ask Mama what size she wore. We had a hasty, whispered conference.

"She's pretty big," I said.

"And she's pretty old," Crystal said. "So she can't wear a small size."

"I think the size has something to do with the age," I agreed. "How old is Mama?"

"I don't know," Crystal said.

"I think about fifty," I said. "Size fifty sounds about right."

Crystal hesitated a moment. She wasn't sure Mama was as old as fifty—or that age and size were connected. But she turned to the clerk and said, "Size fifty."

The clerk's eyes got big and she said, "I'd have to send in a special order for that size."

"Well, what big sizes do you have?" Crystal asked.

The lady showed her some big sizes. We found some we thought looked like they'd fit. We bought them.

Later we told Audrey about the entire incident, leaving out no details. Mother laughed until she almost cried. She told us she wore a large size, but not anything as large as size fifty. "I don't think they even make any that big," she said.

"Well, how old are you?" I asked.

She told us she was thirty-seven. That sounded pretty old, but not as old as fifty.

Mama explained that the clothing size didn't necessarily coincide with a person's age.

She laughed about our shopping trip for a long time, and so did we. Mama would often joke, "If I gain much more weight, I'll be ready for those size fifty panties you were going to buy me for my birthday!"

Once or twice Clyde came to visit us. He'd just show up. One time Crystal heard the special hand whistle he had taught her where he'd cup his hands together and blow through his fingers a certain way. I never mastered it but Crystal did. She heard that sound down the canyon when we were playing outside in the yard one day.

"It's Daddy!" Crystal exclaimed.

I was afraid to hope it was true. "Are you sure?" I asked.

"I'll show you." She proceeded to whistle back. There was an immediate return whistle. Crystal whistled again. Again there was a return whistle, a little closer.

"It's Daddy for sure!" Crystal said, and in a few minutes we saw him walking up Happy Creek. Someone had given him a ride to San Geronimo and he had walked from there. Each time he showed up we would hope he'd stay, but he never stayed more than a day or two. He would usually show up unexpectedly.

One morning Crystal and I were sleeping in the big double bed in the Fifteen Dollar House when we heard voices: Daddy and Mama talking quietly. It was a familiar sound. But we both knew Daddy was gone so we thought we were dreaming. Then we woke up to realize it was true. Daddy was there and it was just like old times again, hearing our parents talking quietly in the morning.

"Daddy! When did you get here!" Crystal exclaimed, sitting up in bed.

"Early this morning," he replied happily.

We both got up and hugged him. Mama got breakfast for all of us, cooking on the kitchen range. The wood-stove helped heat the cabin as the oven baked bread; the stove top heated water for tea and cooked pan cakes all at the same time. Daddy didn't stay long, but we always hoped there would be another morning that we'd wake up to those voices: Daddy and Mama talking quietly. Everyone once in a while our wish would come true. We hoped someday he'd come back to stay.

11

No Rain and No Rain

The kitchen stove had to be fed continuously in order to cook or to keep the house warm. It was also used to heat water for washing and baths. We were kept busy gathering twigs, small branches, bark chips, pine cones and pine needles. We had a small wood pile and a sack of coal. Audrey knew that a cold spell would deplete it quickly. She was grateful that the first winter was mild, although she was not happy about the lack of moisture.

On February 28, 1950 I awoke to my "birthday," the day we would celebrate since there was no 29th that year. I went outside in my nightgown to greet the day. It was warm and sunny. I was six years old, thrilled at how big I was, almost grown up, I thought. I opened my gifts after a week of anticipation, trying to guess what was in the packages. Mother and Crystal had gone shopping when were in town a week before, riding in with the mail carrier, Mr. Trujillo. We stayed overnight at the home of the Carringtons and went back with the mail carrier the next day. A big red package I'd poked and pinched would not yield a clue to its contents. But when I opened it, it was a pair of denim jeans. I hated pants, especially denim and corduroy. I wanted to wear pretty dresses all the time. Of course dresses were not practical in the mountains, and more than one hem was ripped as I ran through the woods. But the birthday cake and "party" Mama and Crystal gave me made up for any disappointment in the gift. Besides, Mama had bought me a gift I wanted about that time when we went shopping at the J. C. Penney store for shoes. Audrey bought me a pair of shoes for my birthday. I wanted red ones but all they had were brown or black leather. However, while at the store I saw some little brightly painted wooden ducks—a mother with three little ducklings behind her, all attached. One would pull a string attached to the mother duck and the ducklings would follow, as they were all on little wheels. A metal "clicker" on the bottom "clicked" every time it revolved so it sounded like ducks "quacking." I often wondered what my mama gave up to buy me that toy.

I wanted ice cream for my birthday. Of course there was no refrigerator and no way to bring some from town. Audrey baked a birthday cake. In past years there had been fresh snow on the ground and we had gone out and gathered some clean snow. Then Mama mixed it up with milk, (usually canned milk), vanilla, and sugar. We had "snow ice cream." It was almost as good as "store bought" ice cream." But this dry year there could be no ice cream.

In April or May of the first year we were at the ranch, we planted a garden half way between the spring and the house in a spot that had been cleared a few years earlier for a garden spot. It was near the creek for easy access to water. We planted onions, radishes, lettuce, carrots, peas, corn, and several others things such as pumpkins. But the second year was very dry.

There had been very little snow that winter and almost no run-off from the mountains to feed the life-giving streams. Our little creek beds were dry. The summers of 1950 and of 1951 there was almost no rain. The ground cracked, groaning under parched, straw-like grass. Finally most of the grass died. The clover had not survived the dry month of June. The pines lifted their branches helplessly pleading for rain. The Tecolote River was reduced to a trickle of its normal flowing stream, and Falls Creek was dried up in places. Our own faithful spring continued to provide our drinking water but was shared with nearly every animal in the area, as it was one of the only watering places in the area, besides the spring at the lower end of the place near Hellers' Cabin. Wildlife seemed to abandon the area for more desirable habitats. A few birds remained, complaining under the hot July sun.

Vivian had retired from the Soil Conservation Service at the age of sixty. Mabel and Vivian had moved to their big adobe house over the crest of the hill across the way. Also, John and Dorothy Heller were settled into their cabin down the canyon. Fortunately, they had "the lower spring" just a few yards from their cabin. The two biggest springs, the Upper Spring and the Lower Spring, never completely dried up.

Sometimes we would go to town with Grandma and Vivian in their jeep to purchase supplies. Except for what we grew or were able to bring from the store occasionally, we had few fresh vegetables or fruits. But Audrey kept canned food, rice, flour, and other basics on hand. She baked bread in the oven of the kitchen wood stove. There was no fresh milk, and we missed that. Whenever we went to town we bought some and drank it right away. Of course, we had canned milk and Mother made cocoa quite often.

One day we returned from town with a quart container of fresh milk. Crystal's hand shook as she poured the milk into two tall glasses, one for me and one for herself. In her excitement, Crystal accidentally knocked over her own big glass, and the milk ran down the table onto the hard cement floor. She began to sob inconsolably.

"Don't cry," I said. "I'll give you mine." I pushed my glass toward her.

"No. I don't deserve it after I spilled mine," Crystal said.

"You didn't mean to," I said.

"I should have been more careful," Crystal admonished herself through her sobs.

"There's still some left in the carton," I said. "You can have all the rest."

"No," Crystal said with a wail.

About that time Audrey came in from outside and surveyed the scene, a glass shattered into several pieces on the floor surrounded by the ruined milk now making a puddle on the linoleum under the kitchen table.

"Don't cry over spilt milk," Audrey said, using the oft quoted cliché. "It's only milk. Be glad you didn't get cut." Audrey quickly cleaned up the mess. But there would be no more fresh milk until the next time we went to town, maybe a couple of months later. Audrey said we would make a cake, hoping we would forget about the milk incident.

With no snow that winter, Audrey hoped for spring rains. Even though they did not come, the three of us hoed the garden. We carried some water from the spring for the little corn plants, onions, radishes, and other green leaves that pushed through the rich black soil. We succeeded in growing the small garden with almost no rain. It was in the garden that spring that we saw the biggest horned toad we had ever seen. Mother always had her little Brownie box camera handy. She took a picture of it with us sitting in the garden soil beside it. We held a 12-inch ruler near it to show how big it was. Then we turned the little creature loose. From head to tail, it measured about nine inches long on the ruler.

Spring ushered in a warm summer. Where Happy Creek usually babbled beyond the front hillside of our cabin and Roaring Creek dashed over big rocks in Roaring Canyon behind our cabin, now the creek beds were rock and dry sand. Crystal and I had always enjoyed wading in those creeks. Now we got our exercise carrying water from the spring.

In those days planes went over to "seed" the clouds. Usually there would be a big rain storm in eastern New Mexico or Texas, but where they had "seeded" the clouds above northern New Mexico the wind came up and blew them away. Of course the officials tried to explain why their project did not work, as in the newspaper report of the *Las Vegas Daily Optic* which said that following a conference of directors of the southeastern New Mexico Precipitation Research Corp., the president of that group announced that cloud-seeding operations "have been suspended for the rest of the season; due to general movement of moist air streams further west than normal, there have been few opportunities for cloud-seeding. This has resulted in erratic, widely scattered showers over the area."[1]

Audrey wrote a poem, "Weather Man's Blues." She may have been thinking of the popular policy of "seeding the clouds," but in spite of the planes overhead, the dry country got no rain, while there were floods following the "seeding" in other places, such as neighboring Texas. The poem was published in the *Rodeo Edition* of *the Las Vegas Daily Optic* in 1952.

> The Weatherman was never always right.
> And now his is a much worse plight.
> His Weather Forecast suffers an even worse Hex
> Unless notified daily by rainmaker X.[2]

A poison called Compound 1080 was used to kill off the prairie dogs and coyotes. The Nelson place, about three miles from our ranch where an old tuberculosis home had been in the late 1800's, was filled with prairie dogs. There was an huge field which we called "Prairie Dog Town." All the prairie dogs were poisoned through the place we called "Nelson's Prairie." When they died, the coyotes died, and so did the rabbits, mice, birds, insects, and other life forms. Various predators and scavengers that ate the toxic bodies of those killed by the poison also died. Some of the poison washed into waterways; some adhered to vegetation and was eaten by livestock. Additionally, the death of rodents caused many larger predators to prey on livestock—so the entire project backfired.

The coyotes were also the target of the poison. Audrey heard that one coyote died in a creek in the area and that a man had taken a drink from the creek just downstream and was poisoned. A newspaper article in the *Las Vegas Daily Optic* warned of the danger of "1080:"

> A widespread search was underway in Greater Las Vegas today for a quantity of deadly poison and parents were particularly warned to caution their children against handling any boxes they might find.
>
> The poison was stolen from a car on the Plaza last night by someone who broke into the vehicle.
>
> It was contained in a tool box about 10 x 24 inches.
>
> The poison is "1080" and is used to exterminate rodents and at one time was widely used in coyote-poisoning drives but was found to destroy other animals and birds.
>
> The box was taken from a car owned by Pat Harris, Albuquerque, a representative of the Orin Exterminating Co.

Police warned that even handling the poison could be harmful because it will burn human skin.

"Children must be protected from handling the poison," Chief Matt E. O'Brien of the city police warned.

If anyone finds a suspicious looking box, which may have been abandoned by the thief, it should be left alone and police called.

Police believe the person taking the box was not aware of its deadly contents.[3]

DDT was also popular after World War II. Audrey had fought bed bugs and other insects all her life and thought she would try it. One could buy it in a liquid, put it in a round glass canister, and pump it with a metal pump that shot it out from the pointed front end of the "gun." Audrey went all over the house spraying corners and floor boards. She noticed, however, that I would always get sick the next day. She decided that I was "allergic" to DDT and didn't use it after that.

The summer of 1950 Audrey ordered 50 baby chickens. The mail carrier brought them. Audrey had turned one of the back cabins into a nice chicken house. Later, she also ordered six little turkeys. All of them lived.

Our diets improved. Where before we subsisted on the vegetables from our garden and canned goods or dried foods, we could now have fresh eggs. Once the hens began to lay, we found at least a dozen eggs a day in their nests. Audrey made omelets, deviled eggs, and custards. We had hard boiled eggs, fried eggs, and eggs in almost every recipe. We never tired of them. Once in a while Audrey killed and prepared a chicken for a rare feast.

Mother allowed one or two of the hens to "set" and we waited eagerly for the new chicks to peck through their shells and pop out. Sure enough they did—all but one. We watched the little chickens thrive under the hen's protective care.

Audrey raised Cocker Spaniel puppies and then sold them or gave them away when they were old enough. There were several litters of puppies, most of them black, but sometimes there was a red-colored one or a blond one—and once a pure white one! The white one was so rare Mother would not sell it. She gave it to her sister Jessica.

The only task Audrey dreaded was that the tails had to be "docked" if they were to be sold. Everyone expected Cocker Spaniels to have docked tails. So as soon as the puppies were old enough, Audrey took the ax and held the puppy down on a wooden bench with one hand and with the other hand made a quick downward "chop," removing the end of the puppy's tail in one fell swoop.

Swifty, the mother of the pups, was always nervous when this ritual took place and spent considerable time comforting her offspring afterwards. Audrey always apologized before and after the act, but she knew it had to be done if the puppies were to find good homes.

Forest Springs Ranch was so isolated we sometimes felt we were the only people in the world. Our place was the last private property on the road, with the National Forest behind us. Unless they knew the road, most people got lost when they were looking for our place. Audrey wrote that when the Rural Electric Association (REA) came through, they put in the lines to the Shearer place, but the contractor said he couldn't find the Simpson place.

> They hadn't asked anyone how to get here. So they skipped my place. I was here all the time, so had to fuss at the REA to get them to come back and run the half mile line over the hill to my place as originally promised.[4]

The cost of electricity was a little more than $6.00 a month for several years, until the installation costs were met. Then it was less. We felt really modern.[5]

Most of the time life was routine. But sometime in 1950 Audrey had abdominal pains. Dr. Mortimer was out of town, so Audrey went to see the colleague who was covering his cases. That doctor told her she should go to the hospital and have her gall bladder out. Crystal and I stayed with the Carringtons while Audrey was in Saint Anthony's Hospital. We slept in the Carringtons' basement room that had been fixed up as a guest bedroom as well as a storage room. Mother told Crystal and me that if anything went wrong and she couldn't take care of us anymore, we should ask to live with our Grandpa Clements and Mabel who lived in Albuquerque. We were afraid Mama would die. Ruth Carrington was very reassuring. She had been a practical nurse during World War I and knew a great deal about illness and surgery.

However, Audrey did not have the surgery. Before it was scheduled, her physician returned. Dr. Mortimer disagreed with his colleague. He said the tests did not show that the gall bladder needed to come out. Audrey recovered from whatever was bothering her. She had pains in that area off and on, but they always went away so she never went in for surgery. Years later it was discovered that she had "silent" gall stones.

When Grandma and Vivian had to go to town, we were often invited to go along to get groceries. Sometimes Audrey took a load of clothes into one of the "help yourself" laundries to wash. Vivian's 1946 "Willy" jeep didn't carry many passengers. But Audrey, Crystal and I sat on the little narrow back seat while our grandmother sat in the front passenger seat and Vivian drove. We piled our sacks of groceries and laundry around us when we made the return trip. Sometimes Mama bought us a rare treat in town such as a soft drink or a candy bar. We made a large sized chocolate bar last nearly a week by eating only one of its small squares a day.

Ramón would sometimes ride his horse up the canyon from San Geronimo, usually accompanied by "Pres" or Jerry or Manuel. Once in a while Anadina would come along. She was a little older than Crystal. We were always glad when she came. Sometimes we played "baseball" with a ball and any big stick we could find to hit it with. Our "baseball park" was beyond our cabin, just across the creek to the west in a big, grassy open area surrounded by big pine trees.

Ramón did not speak English very well, and Audrey did not speak Spanish, although she understood it fairly well. Still, they managed to communicate. He talked about various events. Once he told Audrey that one of his cows had been hit by lightning. They talked about the drought. His cows were not doing well. There was hardly any grass.

"No rain and no rain," he lamented, shaking his head slowly.

"No rain," my mama agreed, shaking her head. "It's very bad."

"Very bad," Ramón nodded.

Audrey would always ask them to stay for a meal. They liked Audrey's "Midwest" style of cooking which was different from the Southwestern style they had nearly every day. After lunch, Ramón would sit in our one rocking chair while Mama sat on the big kitchen stool and the boys would stand around or sit on one of the other little benches. Ramón was about eight or ten years older than Mama, and he would often talk about the old days and how the grass and the crops grew so well. Sometimes Ramón would bring us goat's milk. Sometimes he and the boys cut up wood for our stove. Years later, "Pres" told us that their father worried about the woman living alone with two little girls and tried to check on us as often as he could. For the most part, we were safe. The greatest threat was fire.

In an article in *New Mexico Magazine,* Audrey wrote:

> June came. The dry month. The danger month in the mountain forests. For it is then that timber becomes so dry that one tiny spark may cause a roaring inferno. Every mountain dweller, human or animal, cringes at the sight of wild smoke, and shudders at the thought of forest

fire. And yet unthinking people, out to enjoy the beauty of the forests, daily drop careless matches and cigarettes that can turn wonderland into charred desolation in a few hours.

In the middle of June I stepped out of the cabin one noon and smelled smoke. I raced through the trees up the hill to my look out [the Mesa] to see where the smoke was coming from. A thin white column rose to the southwest. The wind was blowing directly from it towards us. From my low forest encircled hill I could not tell whether or not the fire was in the next canyon. I rushed back to the cabin and took my girls and their two little cousins who were visiting to the big open field below the cabins, telling them to stay there.[6]

Tana and Janie Hardin were spending a few days with us. It was a wonderful treat for us to have our cousins to play with. Sometimes Mother invited one of the Reid children to come out. Sometimes she invited one of our other friends—or a relative. While Audrey investigated the smoke, we sat in the flat, open field that years later would be the site of the new, big ranch house. We sat on Audrey's suitcase of valuable papers and photographs. Audrey wrote:

> I grabbed the hoe and rake and was going to see if I could do any good in stopping the fire. If it was close I would go to it and start raking a fire line and try to hold it until help came from miles below. For with fire, time is everything. Getting on one fast may mean the difference in the burning of an acre and the burning of a thousand acres.
>
> It was hard for me to leave the girls sitting forlornly on our suitcase of pictures in the clearing. But that was the safest place for them, away from the cabins built in the heavy brush and timber. I assured them that if the fire was close and coming toward us I would be back at once and we would walk out of the forest. But if it was not too bad and I could reach it, it might be controlled quickly. However, one thin little smoke, left alone a few hours can damage much of a forest.
>
> As soon as I topped the south ridge out of Happy Canyon, I saw that the fire was probably three miles over the ridges from my place. The wind was fanning the fire and it was growing in wild haste. Seeing that it was too far away for me to do any good, I hurried back to the girls who were greatly relieved to have their mother at home instead of out fighting forest fires.
>
> I kept an uneasy watch on the smoke which often turned to nasty black puffs as the fire topped out into an inferno in the tree tops. I

have seen a forest fire jump a full half-mile at a time. So although it was not close, as long as there was a fire in the mountains I watched it. By next morning the whole mountain side was covered with a thick pall of smoke, cutting visibility and making breathing difficult. This fire burned hundreds of acres of fine timber before it was controlled.[7]

Near the end of summer the springs were nearly dried up. There was just enough water trickling out of the hillside to fill up the hole of the upper spring every day. Every animal in the country was drinking from it. Audrey decided it wasn't running enough for us to drink out of it. She was very health conscious and didn't want to take a risk. She even took us to Dr. Mortimer every year for a typhoid shot so we wouldn't get typhoid fever! There was no one up above us—just the National Forest—so there wasn't much danger. But she wouldn't take any chances with our health, especially when we were isolated in the mountains with no transportation if we got sick. We walked across the top of the big hill between our house and the Old Homestead Ranch—about half a mile—to get drinking water from the Shearers' well there.

As mentioned before, Crystal belonged to The Cheerful Greetings Club (CGC) so she had lots of pen pals to correspond with. Crystal soon developed quite a long list of correspondents. Crystal discovered there were many people, some younger than herself, who had to remain bed ridden due to various conditions. Some were recovering from polio. Others had been born with birth defects. There were many reasons why they were "shut-ins." Usually they didn't write about their ailments. After all it was supposed to be club to help one another cheer up. Sometimes they sent little gifts such as handkerchiefs they had decorated or other arts and crafts items. Crystal usually received at least five letters every time Mother got the mail. Crystal Simpson became so well known to the post office officials that sometimes she got mail which had been incorrectly addressed. Once she even got a letter that was addressed to "Crystal Simpson—New Mexico."

Audrey walked to the mail box near San Geronimo every other day—a seven mile round trip—because she didn't want to leave the mail in the box. In those days there were no locks on the boxes.

The Hellers decided to leave, perhaps because the spring was drying up. Audrey wrote:

> After they [John and Dorothy Heller] left we had a drought. Our springs and gardens dried up and there was no rain. We carried water from a well more than 1/2 mile over the hill, or rather a young mountain. The drought got worse and worse.[8]

When we went into town, which we did about every month, Vivian, Mabel and Mother would do their errands. We would usually rendezvous at the Carrington's house. While we were waiting for Vivian to return with the jeep to pick us up, Mother would visit with the Carringtons while Crystal and I played out in the big yard. Crystal met the boy across the street. His name was David. She had a crush on him. At the ranch she would talk about "next time we go to town" and how she wanted to get to know David better. She asked me to help her. She was going to wait until he was outside and then walk along the side walk in front of his house. I was supposed to walk a short distance behind her. She was going to drop a handkerchief. If David didn't immediately pick it up and give it to her, I was supposed to go up to David and say, "My sister dropped her handkerchief." Then he surely would notice and pick it up and give it to her.

"What then?" I'd ask.

"Then we'll talk and he'll invite me to go out with him for an ice cream soda at Murphey's Drug Store," Crystal replied.

I told Crystal I thought I was too shy to play that role, but she convinced me it was her only hope for happiness, so I finally agreed to do it.

However, opportunities were few and far between. The next time or two we were at the Carringtons we did not see David outside.

We did see Ramón and his family several times that summer.

"Maybe the rains will come and at least save your corn," Mama said.

Ramón shook his head slowly. He knew it was too late this year to save his crops. He could only hope to save his cattle.

But, as Ramón had said, there was "no rain and no rain."

Audrey wrote a poem about rain, a sort of prayer. In fact, she said often after she read the poem some rain would fall within a day or two. She called it her "rain poem." She believed the rain was an answer to the prayer.

The rain poem was published first in *New Mexico Magazine* and later in a little hardback, *Fiesta: An Anthology of Southwestern Poets*. It was entitled, "Prayer for Rain:"

> WHATEVER the RAIN MAKERS name and crown
> If it is not GOD who sends the rain down,
> We now pray to THEE in desperate pain.
> SEND THE RAIN! SEND THE RAIN! SEND THE RAIN!
>
> SAN ISIDRO from farmers turns his head,
> Our springs all are dying, the crops are dead.

Oh, SAN ISIDRO, have we made it plain?
SEND THE RAIN! SEND THE RAIN! SEND THE RAIN!

INDIAN RAIN GOD who answers their prayer,
Can YOU ease this white one's drouth-ridden care?
Tall trees are withered, the cows are insane,
SEND THE RAIN! SEND THE RAIN! SEND THE RAIN!

ONCE MORE white man's GOD, to you I'm turning,
For the sun is red, the earth is burning.
We pray for black clouds with lightning chain.
SEND THE RAIN! SEND THE RAIN! SEND THE RAIN!

GOD OVER ALL, can YOU hear my wild cry?
See our earth is cracked and my spring is dry.
GOD UP ABOVE, feel our dusty land's pain.
SEND THE RAIN! SEND THE RAIN! SEND THE RAIN![9]

12

Crystal's Courage

It was twilight in the summer mountains. The drought had left the air still. Only an occasional listless cricket could be heard—or a night hawk diving for a tidbit here and there. We bathed in the luxury of electricity now, listening to the radio, cooking on a hot plate.

Crystal, twelve years old, helped with everything: chopped wood, carried it in, washed dishes (with my help) carried water, hoed the garden, and fed the chickens, right along with Audrey. I often thought of Crystal as my brave sister. She would be scared to death but she'd go ahead and do what needed to be done any way. She would tackle anything. She did much of the housework when Mother would let her. When she was an "invalid," Mother wouldn't let her do anything. But as soon as Dr. Mortimer declared that Crystal was apparently well, she began to do as much as she could to help. (He never made a diagnosis, so we never knew why Crystal was supposed to stay out of school and rest. Audrey thought Crystal was sick; but both Crystal and I later decided she was only nervous and anxious due to circumstances such as her daddy's leaving, her frustration at being unable to read, her teacher's failure to understand, etc.)

One day I did not feel well. Mother checked my temperature periodically and seemed worried. That evening my temperature shot up to about 104 degrees F. Mother probably thought of all sorts of possibilities, including Rocky Mountain Spotted fever which one can get from mountain ticks. She was concerned about ticks and checked our ears often to be sure we hadn't acquired any.

About 9:00 p.m. Audrey decided she had to get me to town to the doctor. With no telephone and no car, Mother knew she would have to walk to the Shearers to get help. She didn't want to leave me, so she decided to send Crystal the half mile over the top of the hill and into the next canyon to Grandma Shearer's house. My uncle Frank could then drive the jeep over and take us to town.

There was no moon that night. Crystal had never gone over to Grandma's house alone, certainly not in the dark. Mother armed her with a good flashlight and told her the dogs would keep any wild animals away. Crystal knew the path well, but her imagination was sufficiently active to conjure up unthinkable creatures lurking behind every tree.

"Bonnie will protect you," Mother assured her. "And take Pete and Swifty on their leashes so they'll be right beside you."

I knew Crystal was scared but she didn't protest. "I'll go as fast as I can," she said. "Don't worry."

Crystal sat out armed with her flashlight and the three dogs. Mother worried until she heard the sound of the jeep approaching some forty-five minutes or so later.

Crystal later admitted to me that she had been very scared, but she knew I was sick and she had to do what needed to be done.

I was apprehensive about going to the doctor, especially at night. I was hoping and praying I would get well in a hurry so we wouldn't have to make the long trip into town at night.

Frank brought the jeep up to the door, stopped, got out, and came in. He asked if Audrey needed him to help with anything. She didn't. We got in and Mother settled me down on her lap, wrapped in a blanket. Crystal sat in the back of the jeep, glad her nightly walk was over.

Frank got behind the wheel. Then the jeep wouldn't start. Frank tried over and over again, but he could not start it. Audrey noticed my fever had broken and told Frank to forget it.

"Dorothy's better now. We'll see what we need to do in the morning,"

Audrey said. She made up a cot where Frank could sleep. In the morning Frank went out to see if he could figure out what was wrong with the jeep. He got in to try to start it. It started right up.

Mother took me to the doctor as I still had a low fever. Dr. Mortimer's office was at 720 University on the corner of University and Eighth Street. It was a modern, comfortable office with an intercom system to call patients in. The doctor gave me penicillin shots—the panacea of the day. We stayed at the Carrington house and went to the doctor every afternoon for a few days. Then one day mother took me to the dentist and the trouble was found. The last time he had worked on my teeth, he had not completed the job. The dentist had left a wad of cotton in a tooth and it had collected bacteria and was full of decay. As soon as the cotton was removed, I was well—no more fever. His mistake caused a lot of misery.

The only time I saw Crystal really scared was one day when she and Bonnie had been walking to take some eggs to the Gardner place. Lelama Gardner spent part of her summer at her cabin just south of ours, about a mile away. Crystal had done this errand numerous times before. She took Bonnie with her. But this time, Crystal came back to the cabin, out of breath from running and crying.

"There was a flying saucer and it landed right over there in the trees. And I'm afraid the little men took Bonnie!" Crystal sobbed. "We have to go and rescue Bonnie!"

Mother grabbed her rifle and immediately decided to investigate.

"I'm going to go and find out what happened," Audrey said. "Dorothy, you stay here in the cabin with the door locked. Don't go outside until we get back."

"We won't be back until we find Bonnie," Crystal added.

I thought, *What if they don't come back? What if the little men from outer space should take Mama and Crystal away? What will I do?* I always minded my mama so I knew I was supposed to stay in the cabin. But what would I do if they didn't come back? I decided I'd have to walk down the road to San Geronimo to get help if they didn't return. I would rather have gone with them and faced the aliens than to stay by myself, wondering if they would ever return. I was six years old and I knew I could walk down the road to San Geronimo if I had to. I decided to wait until I ran out of food. If they weren't home by then, I'd go find help. I knew I should obey Mother and stay in the cabin. But I was sure she didn't mean I had to stay there until I starved to death.

After about half an hour they returned, Bonnie with them. She had just run off into the trees chasing a rabbit. We later learned that Crystal had seen a meteorite. The radio news that evening confirmed that a huge meteorite had fallen and landed about 100 miles away from our ranch. Crystal had seen "a flaming arrow." She had heard radio programs about flying saucers, so when she saw something streak through the sky, she concluded it was a UFO. The eggs were all broken along the road but there was no harm done. Crystal and I were glad that there were no little men from outer space coming to kidnap Bonnie. Audrey later wrote a poem after Crystal's "flying saucer" experience:

> Flying saucers? They are not new.
> Nor objects up around the moon.
> Old Mother Goose had soaring cows
> And saucers flying with a spoon.[1]

Crystal had faced the pitch darkness of the forest to walk for help when I might have had a serious illness. She did it to save her little sister. And she had been willing to face aliens from outer space to demand the return of her Bonnie.

Crystal Simpson with collie Bonnie, 1951. *Source:* Simpson Archives, photo by Audrey Simpson

I thought my sister was the bravest young girl ever to walk through a dark forest at night. Audrey's courage had been passed along to her daughter Crystal.

13

The Barbed Wire Phone Line

Audrey wrote in later years about our isolation. The electricity and telephone gave us such a feeling of luxury and security. In 1983 Audrey wrote an article, "My Lifeline in the Mountains," published in *Impact* of the *Albuquerque Journal*. She described how she got an idea for better communication at very little cost.

> The cabin was isolated. Our mailbox was a four-mile walk down a rocky canyon trail. Crystal, Dorothy and I got along well up there, remote as the place was. Only one thing bothered me: What if an emergency should occur? How would I call for help? We had no telephone.
>
> The only phone line in the area belonged to the Forest Service. Though the line ran right near our home, it was used solely to alert rangers in case of fire. There was no way I could hook up to it.
>
> The lack of a telephone worried me. I was out walking one afternoon, fretting about it, when I remembered something from my childhood in the tall corn country of Nebraska. All the farms in my town, I recalled, were tied together with a telephone line that hung on fence posts. The line was not your usual line. This one was made of barbed wire.
>
> My mother lived a mile away. She was the one I would call first should trouble arise. If I could run a barbed wire line from my cabin to hers, it might keep me from worrying. But how could I do it alone?[1]

Audrey decided to ask her little brother Frank and Ramón's oldest boy, Presillano Santillanes, to string up the barbed wire line for her. At nineteen years of age, "Pres" was a year older than Frank, and they got along well. Audrey paid them a good wage for their hours of work. The two young men worked to wind the line through the timber and over the hill from Audrey's cabin to the adobe house where Mabel, Vivian, and Frank lived. Audrey wrote:

> While living in my isolated Forest Springs Ranch, in the mountains 18 miles west of Las Vegas, N.M., I wanted a telephone. I

had moved back to the ranch in 1949 to help my ten year old daughter recuperate from an illness.

The nearest neighbor lived four miles away near my mail box. For years I walked the four miles down the canyons and four back up that rocky [road] to get my mail. It arrived every day in summer and Tuesday, Thursday and Saturday during wintertime. Usually I went alone, for it was too far for Miss Ten [Crystal] and Miss Five [Dorothy] to walk.

Although we were getting along fine, I worried that in case of an emergency it would be a long time before we could get help. The Forest Service old phone line ran within a city block of my tiny cabin. I recalled using that line as a teen-ager, but in 1950 I could see no way that I could hook on to that line.

I also recalled that back in the tall corn country in Nebraska, when I was a child, all of the farms were tied together with a telephone line hung on fence posts. I wanted one of Mr. Alex G. Bell's gee-gaw's.

My mother and step-father, Mr. and Mrs. C. V. Shearer, and a son Frank moved back to their Old Homestead Ranch in 1950. From their home to my cabin it was one mile by the road. I immediately thought of bringing them even closer by phone line.

I persuaded Frank and another teen-ager, Presillano Santillanes (more recently San Miguel County Sheriff) to string barbed wire for a telephone line for me. It would wind through the timber and over a young mountain to the Shearer's from my primitive little cabin.

I bought four rolls of barbed wire, each a quarter of a mile long. They hung it with insulators on pine trees until they reached the fence between Shearer's place and mine.

The wire was strung through insulators at each post so it wouldn't touch something or ground out. At the Shearer's adobe house and at my cabin the wire was connected to old fashioned box wall phones, each holding two batteries made for this type phone. They had hand cranks to turn so that the phones would ring. After the barbed wire was in place we heard good strong rings. But with my private line there was no "rubbering" such as in Nebraska. Back there, short or long rings in various combinations, called each farm. However, whether it was their ring or not, every phone receiver came off the hook in the whole area. They called it "rubbering" meaning "listening in" to keep up with their neighbors' business.

The Shearers were re-connected to that Forest Service line as my step-grandfather, R. A. Shearer, had been a fire guard for years. If someone had weak batteries on the old Forest Line or were clear over at the far end in Sapello Canyon at the Barker's (Charles and S. Omar's folks) the ringy ding ding might be shaky. But we could tell what ring it was. And sometimes we would "rubber" to find out whether or not there was a forest fire in the area.

That thin silver wire ran from the Sapello, paused on top of Hermit's Peak lookout station, visited the Gallinas Ranger station, zigzagged to the Tecolote canyon, visited several ranches and San Geronimo before climbing Barillas Peak to the look-out tower. Then it glittered along the west side of the mountains to Pecos town. There one long ring would alert the Forest Service Ranger Station. When anything went wrong with that line, such as a tree falling on it, the Ranger or the nearest rancher, took an axe and pair of pliers and repaired it.[2]

In the Shearer home and the Simpson home, the "telephone men" fed the barbed wire through the kitchen windows to old-fashioned, box wall telephones, each holding two batteries. To ring the phones, one would crank them by hand.

Audrey and her mother didn't have a problem with eavesdropping since they were the only persons on the line. And the reception was excellent. Now Crystal and I could talk to our Grandma Shearer any time we wanted! Mother and Grandma usually talked a couple of times a day. If Vivian happened to be going into town, it was a great convenience to ask him to pick up the items we needed such as butter or flour. Fortunately, there was never a medical emergency, but the telephone did help in many ways. There was one emergency for which it did come in handy:

> My homemade telephone did prevent one potential disaster, however. It was in the 1950's, and I happened to look out my cabin window one morning to spot a forest fire on the southwest side of Barillas Peak. Picking up the old crank, I rang my parents. They in turn called the Forest Service. Just In the nick of time, the fire was stopped.[3]

Audrey concluded her story with the lines, "When you have your own barbed wire phone line, there's no such thing as a bill."[4] In another story Audrey wrote about the wonderful telephone:

> In August Mr. Bell's invention became a reality to us again. I bought barbed wire and my young brother and another teen-ager strung several rolls of the wire on the fence posts and pine trees from their house to

mine. We had old-style hand-ringing box phones fastened to our wall at each end of the line.

The service is wonderful on this barbed wire phone line. For the line is never busy when we want to use it. We can talk for hours without bothering anyone, for there is no one else on this private line. No one rings in our ear. And there is far less static than on most other lines. Knowing that help is within phoning distance gives us a wonderful sense of security, making my barbed wire phone line worth many times its cost.[5]

Audrey submitted an article for publication entitled "Dear Ma Bell." The story was accompanied by photographs along with typewritten photograph identifications. The article included details similar to those above, with one or two differences.

Dear Ma, you keep turning up in the news, with a lot of problems. I have had a long acquaintance with Mr. Alex G. Bell's brain child and I had my own private telephone line once. My little line never gave me any trouble. So, in case you have forgotten, let me remind you of basic service in the old days.

I remember when Mr. Bell's contraption was a novelty in the tall corn country of Nebraska. Then we were tied to all of our neighbors by a telephone line hung on fence posts. Then everyone had a big box-like phone nailed to the farm house wall. When someone turned the handle of the phone in their home, every other phone in the neighborhood rang. At once each phone came off the hook as neighbors "listened in." They called [it] rubbering. That is when I learned never to say a derogatory thing about anyone.

"Be careful what you say. The receiver might be down," Grandpa warned us.

In recent years I found Mr. Bell's gadget is still very accurate in picking up conversations when the receiver is off the hook. Then I was on an eight party line. Somebody left the receiver out of place. For hours no one else could call in or out on that line. While people wanting to use the line yelled and whistled into their 'phones, trying to get the attention of the guilty party, the rest of us on that line could hear every word spoken in that home. Yes, Ma [Bell], Grandpa was right.[6]

Audrey then told about how the barbed wire telephone to her mother's house worked so well. She said, "We never got a wrong number and it was never busy unless we used it."⁷ Audrey wondered why the telephone company, in the 1980s, charged so much and yet provided such poor service. The telephone was out of order quite frequently. Since Audrey was isolated and alone much of the time in those days, she complained about the poor service. In her article, "Dear Ma Bell," she concluded with the following:

> There was no more expense after that private barbed wire line of mine was in place. Ma, it lasted 30 years, with the same batteries and no line trouble. Then, in 1971, a forest fire came five miles over the mountain. It destroyed my cabins, the Shearers' house, our wall phones and trees and fence posts that held my private line.
>
> Now that your lines and telephones are established, Ma, how come this talk of raising phone rates? Do you think Alex G. Bell would approve of all the electronic gadgets that seem to cost a fortune to install? Aren't you afraid your customers will be priced right off your lines? If they are, somebody is going to be selling a lot of barbed wire, as many of us switch back to basics.⁸

Audrey submitted her story to *Empire Magazine* of *The Denver Post*. She wrote in a letter dated August 4, 1985 to the editor of that publication:

Dear Editor:

When I talked to someone there on the phone last week, they suggested a cover letter. Here it is, although I think this article is self-explanatory ("Dear Ma Bell")

I have had a long acquaintance with the *Denver Post*, selling them several articles from the age of 16—as Audrey Clements. I continued to free-lance after I married Clyde Simpson in 1934. We had three daughters, Crystal, Dorothy and Holly.

I continued free-lancing, selling to a number of markets, until going to work for the Las Vegas Daily Optic in 1953. As society editor, church page editor and general reporter, I worked for the Optic about 15 years, resigning after Clyde died in 1965.

In August, 1966, I resigned to return to my Forest Springs Ranch and free lance writing. I sold *Empire Magazine* a story in 1967, according to a friend. All my records and MMS were burned in the 1971 forest fire, along with my cabins, main house and all contents.

I had to return to Las Vegas until I could get another cabin built by my sons-in-law. The trauma of the fire and getting all three girls through college delayed my writing.

Now, past 70, I still sell some short items.[9]

A rejection letter dated August 10, 1983 from the editor of *Empire Magazine* was filed with this story. Audrey never let rejections discourage her. She said placing a manuscript was like finding the right home for a pet. There has to be a good match between the person and the pet. Not finding a good match doesn't mean there is anything wrong with the pet. So one continues to hunt until a good match is found—and the story is published.

I remember that with my grandmother and Vivian Shearer just half a mile away over the ridge between our places (a mile away by the road) we did not feel so isolated. After we had a telephone we didn't think we were isolated at all! Not only did we have a telephone, but Vivian Shearer had an amateur radio license. After he sat up a radio stack in his little cabin near the big adobe house on the Old Homestead Ranch, he took a test which allowed him to speak over the waves, as well as using code. Before long, Jessica Braziel also took the test and became a "ham." Later, Vivian's other daughter Milly became a "ham." Vivian not only reported news to us from all over the world, but he helped us keep up with the family gossip. He could talk to just about any one. We thought it was a marvel! Radio and telephone (of sorts) had come to our ranch. We were part of the civilized world now!

Crystal and I always thought the telephone was a modern day miracle. Our favorite telephone was the one that kept us from total isolation, the private line we always called "the barbed wire phone."

14

Phone Call from Santa Claus

Following the drought of the summer of 1950, there was another dry winter. Christmas, 1950 was mild and there was little snow. Again, Audrey took Crystal and me to get a Christmas tree from Christmas Tree Hill. We decorated it with the old Christmas balls we had used for years, plus home-made paper chains. We also had tinsel left over from past years. It was made of lead, so each individual "icicle" that was put on the tree could be saved for the next year.

Thanks to Audrey's successful writing, we had a little more money than we'd had the Christmas before. Mother made a trip into town with her mother and Vivian to get us some gifts. We sat up the old nativity scene once again. The Virgin Mary's blue robe and hood was still the most beautiful color of the entire scene, I thought. We did not forget the true meaning of Christmas—the coming of the Christ Child to redeem the world from sin. We enjoyed wrapping presents because it was a time to give, just as the wise men had brought gifts to the infant Jesus.

Santa Claus was the saintly old man who lived at the North Pole and kept the spirit of the first Christmas alive by giving gifts and encouraging others to give gifts. Of course, children's parents had to cooperate with Santa. We knew that. Santa had to have lots of helpers. But we knew there was a "real" Santa, and he would find our little cabin in the mountains.

One afternoon I was looking out the window watching the snowflakes fall, hoping for a white Christmas. There was barely enough snow to cover the ground. Audrey was peeling potatoes to make some of her wonderful potato soup which consisted of potatoes and onions cooked with canned milk, butter, salt and some other seasonings.

"Mama, what kind of houses do the starving people live in?" I asked.

"You mean the people in India or China?" Audrey questioned.

I nodded.

"I guess they live in houses about the size of our closet," Audrey replied. "Maybe a little bigger than that."

I looked around the room. There was a double bed in the corner and a small cot under the window where I was sitting. There was a kitchen table under the opposite window. The cook stove stood in the back of the cabin. A tall wooden stool held our drinking-water bucket, covered with a dish towel. A little cupboard for dishes on the wall at the left and above the stove was just the right size. On the right of the stove was another cupboard. In the corner of the room near the front door was a big white refrigerator crate that Daddy had turned into a closet. He had put hinges on the door and a hook to shut it. Inside, a broom handle had been nailed in place for the clothes to hang on. I tried to imagine anyone living in a house that small.

"What about the poor people in this country?" I asked.

"There are people in the village who don't have much, but they have adobe houses and wood heat. They have some cattle or sheep or goats. They sometimes have a milk cow or chickens. They grow corn and beans in the summer. But they have very little," Audrey said.

"Well, who are the poorest people in the village?" I asked.

"There's a family with five children and only the father to take care of them," Audrey replied.

My heart went out to the five motherless children. That must be the most terrible kind of poverty, to have no mother to teach you things, to cook, to tuck you in at night, to tell you stories, to smooth over your hurts and your worries. It was bad enough to be missing a father. But it was hard to imagine life without a mother.

"The children don't have good clothes or shoes to wear. They have to help with the farm work, so they can't go to school. They can't read, so they have no books. They don't have a good car. They can't afford electricity. They don't have much food. But they manage somehow. They live near the river, so they have lots of water nearby," Audrey continued.

I felt very fortunate. There was a fire in the stove, we had plenty of blankets and clothing, food in the cupboard, books to read, a radio to listen to, and now, this year, electricity! Most of all, there was my big sister and my mama. I looked at Audrey as she was making us a good supper. Even at that young age, I knew I had an amazing mother.

"Mama, we should get a box of gifts together for the poor people around here, like the five children in the village," I said.

"Yes, we should," Audrey agreed. "You can go through the closet and find some clothes you don't wear any more that are still good. And we can make oatmeal cookies. And you can make some nice colored paper chains like you made for the Christmas tree," Mama suggested. "Yes, we can get something together."

"How will we get it to them?" Crystal—more practical minded than I—asked.

"We can walk," I replied. "Next time Mama goes for the mail we can go and take the presents on down to the village."

"That's a long ways," Crystal reminded me.

"We can do it, can't we Mama?" I asked.

"Well, maybe, if the weather warms up." Audrey replied."If it's too cold for you girls to walk that far, I'll take the package myself next time I go for the mail."

"But it may snow and we won't be able to go anywhere until after Christmas," Crystal added.

"Well, we have got to give something to the *poor* people," I exclaimed.

Audrey nodded in agreement, sighed, and put another stick of wood on the fire.

"I don't think it's going to snow," Audrey said, wishing the country would get at least a little more moisture.

The weather did warm up and one day we walked to the village and went to the home of the five motherless children. The oldest girl was holding a little lamb by the stove, feeding it from a bottle. Like the girl herself, the little creature had no mother. We sat and visited for a while, and in return for our little box of gifts, we were given tortillas and cheese to take home with us. There was a little snow on the ground. By the time we reached Happy Meadow on the way home, my feet were so cold they were hurting even though I was wearing over boots. When we reached our cabin, we were very cold but happy that we had shared what we had with the family in the village, and they had shared with us.

One evening shortly before Christmas the telephone rang. Grandma Shearer and Mama talked on the telephone quite a bit, so that was not unusual. However, this time Audrey said, "It's Santa Claus. He wants to talk to you girls to ask what you want for Christmas."

There was a long moment of surprised silence. Crystal and I looked at each other in amazement. Then there were excited whispers as Crystal and I conferred. Who could be on the telephone besides Grandma or Vivian? Maybe it was Frank playing one of his jokes. He was always playing jokes and doing magic tricks. He could probably change his voice to sound like Santa Claus. But Frank was in California with his aunt—at least we thought he was.

"It's really Frank, isn't it?" Crystal asked.

"This is Santa Claus. He wants to talk to you girls. Who wants to be first?" Mama asked.

"You go first," Crystal said to me.

"No, you go first," I said.

"You're the little one. You should talk first," Crystal urged.

"But you're the oldest. You should talk first," I argued.

"You go first. He wants to talk to the youngest first," Crystal replied.

"I'm too shy," I argued.

"I'm too old," Crystal insisted. I knew she was shy and embarrassed, just as I was.

"I'm too little and shy," I persisted.

"Someone has to go first! Mama's holding out the phone!" Crystal exclaimed in desperation.

I could tell Crystal would not give in. So I went with great trepidation to take the receiver from Mama and stepped up to the speaker part of the telephone.

"Hello," I said into the speaker which protruded from the front of the wall telephone. I spoke in a very small, shaky voice. I held the receiver to my ear and heard a man's voice I didn't recognize. Santa's cheerful voice at the other end asked me how I was doing. The unknown voice carried on a pleasant conversation with me and asked what I wanted for Christmas. I managed to reply to his questions and mention one or two things I wanted. Then, with great relief, I gave the telephone receiver to Crystal. She talked more eloquently than I had and told him several things she wanted. Then she gave the telephone back to Mama. Audrey said good-bye to Santa and began to talk to Grandma again.

Crystal and I had long discussions about who the Santa Claus could have been. How could the real Santa Claus be on a line that only extended to Grandma's adobe house? Was Santa at their home? There was an animated discussion about how Santa Claus could have called on that private line from the North Pole. Mother didn't seem to know either. Crystal thought it was our uncle Frank. It didn't sound like Frank, but Frank could have changed his voice. However, we were not sure Frank was even at the ranch. He came and went quite a bit. He had been going to school in California, living with his father's sister and her husband, Arolvi and Paul Dale. So if Frank wasn't there, who was on the telephone as Santa?

In the end, Crystal and I decided it was the real Santa Claus and that somehow he had hooked into our telephone line. We didn't think he had been at Grandma's house. We figured he was at the North Pole and had found a way to get onto our private line between our house and Grandma's.

"There's no other way to explain it," Crystal said. "It was the real Santa Claus."

Then she told me the story she'd told me many times, at my request, about how she had seen the real Santa Claus one Christmas Eve when she and I were sleeping at Grandma's big adobe house on the couch in front of the huge fireplace.

"I heard him come down the chimney and opened my eyes just enough to see him. I saw him fill our stockings that were hanging in front of the fireplace." She was convinced it was true, and so was I. I envied her for being able to wake up and see the real Santa. Every Christmas I hoped to do the same, but I never did.

However, I always remembered that I did have a conversation with the real Santa the Christmas of 1950 as he magically called us over our one-party, barbed wire telephone line!

15

Thirty-two Below in Sunny New Mexico

Santa was true to his word. He visited us on Christmas Eve and left even more gifts than he had the year before. Our stockings were filled with nuts, candy and an orange or two. I received the doll and a doctor's kit I wanted. We also received books, color books, and paper dolls. Mother bought us a little red wagon. She also gave us a rope which we were supposed to use to practice rope tricks. She must have been remembering how her father taught her rope tricks when she was a kid. Since Christmas Day was warm and sunny, we were able to go outside and practice.

We received several packages in the mail from friends in Las Vegas and elsewhere. In addition to presents from our Grandma Mabel Shearer and Vivian, there was a package from our father's mother, "Granny" Simpson, and from our great grandmother, Alice Applegarth Caldwell who lived in Portland, Oregon. Grandpa and Mable Clements sent a package. Of course Daddy sent gifts. Other gifts came from friends such as the Carringtons and the Gardners in Las Vegas, Mrs. Knox in California, and our summer neighbors, Mr. and Mrs. Clark Ranney who owned a place just below Gardners. They lived in their country home in the summer and moved back to Texas for the winter. I received a little China tea set from the Ranneys. We also received some paper dolls, a bride and groom set we enjoyed. Crystal received a wonderful fold-out, three room cardboard doll house from Eleanor Spies. We probably played with that doll house more than anything else. We had some doll house furniture and a few dolls made for a doll house, including a little rubber man and a rubber woman and several rubber babies. We also had a little rubber cow and I had a little chicken that laid a marble "egg" when her feet were pressed down on a surface. (We had used the cow and chicken in the nativity scene. But after Christmas, we added them to our doll house.) Audrey wrote later:

> For Christmas I gave the girls a large red wagon. It proved a wonderful help in carting things about the place. And because we never could seem to get enough wood on hand to be really safe during a prolonged snowstorm, we spent an hour or two every afternoon picking up small

dead wood and pitch pine knots from the surrounding forest. This gave Crystal something really useful to do. She began to improve rapidly. Roses bloomed in both girls' cheeks and the warm winter sun tanned them nicely. Crystal gained twenty pounds in a few months.[1]

There were other friends that I never met, including Mrs. Radant who lived some place back east. Many of the people Audrey corresponded with were "met" when they wrote to tell her they liked one of her poems or stories. Audrey never met Mrs. Radant in person, a friend who wrote to her for years after she read one of Audrey's articles. When Mrs. Radant died many years later, she left Audrey in her will. Audrey was able to purchase an upright freezer with the money her thoughtful friend had left her.

Another faithful correspondent was Fred A. Stone from Los Angeles, California. He began to write when he saw Audrey's article on the lynx cat, described later. He sent us gifts and wrote to us often. He became a good family friend and even came to visit us. He said he was an actor and knew many of the movie stars personally. (This man was *not* the Fred Andrew Stone who was born in August of 1873 and died in March of 1959, the American actor who began his career as a performer in circuses and minstrel shows, then went on to act on vaudeville and become a star on Broadway.) The Fred A. Stone we knew had apparently played quite a few small parts, both as a stage actor and later in some movies and television programs. However, he did not talk much about his work, so we never got any details about what plays or movies he had been in. If he wrote about these in letters to Audrey, I was not aware of it.

The day after Christmas Bill Reid brought his entire family to visit. Some of the kids took the little red wagon up the nearest hill and rode down in it, tipped it over, and bent up the handle. It was still usable, but was no longer in "new" condition. That wagon was not just a toy. As mentioned above, it helped us survive, as we used it to collect wood for our fire. Audrey wrote in "Homestead in Happy Canyon:"

> So you think it is cold? Try 34 below zero in a one room 14 x 16 log cabin heated by a small cook stove [and small electric space heater.]
> I never did get my feet warm that bitter winter unless I stuck them in the oven of the little cook stove that heated our 14 by 16 log cabin. That was the second winter after my divorce. I had moved back to this primitive cabin with my two daughters after my divorce was final. I could not live in town on the $80 a month their father contributed to their support; and with the 11 year old ill and needing constant attention,

I could not leave her and go to work. The only alternative was to come to the ranch in the Sangre de Cristos where we could exist.

When the thermometer plays hide and seek in the bottom of the glass our New Mexico Sangre de Cristo mountains are cold! And if there is much snow on the ground the mercury seeks solace in the bottom of the glass every night. During the fall my 11 year old and 5 year old daughters and I had hunted the timber around the cabin for wood. Daily we took the girls' red wagon and picked up chips and small limbs and broken branches to keep the cook stove fired up. It took what we could haul in an afternoon to last that evening and the next day. We struggled to get a wood supply ahead for when the snows came. Finally I hired a neighbor to cut a cord of wood for us. I knew it wouldn't last the winter so continued to go out and hunt wood when the snow wasn't too deep.

It was an interesting cortege. CC or DA took turns pulling the wagon followed by 2 black cocker spaniels, a collie, a huge Tom Cat, Mr. Cat, Mrs. Cat and five kittens.[2]

New Year's Day in 1951 promised no break in the drought. There were a few snow flurries once in a while, but no accumulation. Toward the end of January a cold snap hit like a knife's razor edge. The thermometer dropped so low one evening that Audrey let all the dogs and cats into the house. Bonnie gratefully accepted the invitation, along with Pete and Swifty and their new litter of puppies. There were one or two cats, one with some new kittens. So in all there were 19 dogs and cats in the house. Audrey was clearly worried. She knew the little log cabin had no insulation—just mud between the logs and a roll of roofing material over the top poles that made up the roof. She hoped the wood for the fire in the stove would hold out. She kept the fire up all night with wood and coal. She also kept the little electric space heater going. That heater was a life saving addition to our cottage.

That night the temperature dropped to 34 degrees below zero. Audrey knew her thermometer was accurate. She had never seen it drop so low! At Blue Haven Camp about fifteen miles across the hill, the same temperature was reported. The temperature reported from the Las Vegas airport was 30 degrees below zero. Audrey wrote later:

During one cold spell when the thermometer hit 34 [degrees] below zero, I had put the kids' goldfish bowl on the back of the small kitchen range and kept a fire in the stove all night and the water in the bowl froze solid—as did the fish. During those real cold times I kept the girls in bed to keep them from freezing their feet on the icy floor, and I wore overshoes at all times, but still couldn't get my feet warm unless I stuck them in the oven of the kitchen stove.[3]

Our little log cabin with the cement floor and mud chinking between the logs somehow provided enough shelter. Mother was afraid to let the fire in the stove burn down, so she got up often during the night to feed it more wood and coal. We had no electric blankets in those days, but we wore warm clothes and piled on all our blankets. We all slept in a big double bed, so our body heat, combined with the body heat of all the animals in the house, helped. Sometimes Mama heated an iron, wrapped it in a towel, and put it at our feet in bed. The cement floor was always icy. The animals had various old blankets or rags to sleep on.

As mentioned, the water in the gold fish bowl froze solid. Audrey had put the little gold fish bowl on the back of the warming shelf above the wood stove to keep the water in the bowl from freezing. The shelf was part of the kitchen range itself. It sat directly over the iron surface of the stove where the four lids with handles could be opened to insert wood. But in spite of all her efforts, the water in the gold fish bowl froze solid. In the morning, "Goldie," our pet fish, was encased in ice and could not move.

"Goldie froze to death!" Crystal wailed.

"Oh, no! Goldie!" I shrieked.

"We'll see." Mama replied. "Maybe not. We'll let the water thaw out gradually and maybe the fish will be OK."

Sure enough, after the water thawed out, Goldie began to swim around normally again. The fish lived a long time after that.

The morning after the frigid night, Audrey told me and Crystal that it was too cold for us to get up. Mama made hot cocoa for us to drink. She cooked a pan of corn meal mush for our breakfast—with canned milk and sugar on it. We listened to KFUN and heard how cold it was in Las Vegas—almost but not quite as cold as our mountain. We were to stay in the bed all day, bundled up in blankets. We played with paper dolls and some of our toys, read books, colored in color books, and listened to radio programs. Audrey got up and prepared meals and did a few things. Every once in a while she would open up the oven door, sit near it, and put her feet up on the door to get them warm. Audrey kept a tea kettle on the top of the stove.

Fortunately, the electricity stayed on. There was very seldom a power failure in those days. Since the little electric heater helped us survive, we were grateful for the electricity. While Crystal colored and Audrey kept her feet up on the oven door, I surrounded myself with my dolls.

Crystal and I also spent hours playing with the card board doll house she had received from Eleanor. Opened up, it had three open front rooms and no roof. We made up stories about children who found an abandoned house out in the forest. They had no parents, and they were lost. So they moved in. They had chickens (I had my hen that laid a marble egg) and a cow (Crystal's little rubber cow.) We imagined that we grew a garden and gathered wild berries. We thought our story was quite original. We had never heard of the *Boxcar Children* series. But in the fourth grade I discovered the Boxcar children with delight.

We could also play with paper dolls while we were in bed to keep warm. We had a set of bride and groom dolls, complete with brides' maids and maids of honor. We pretended to have a double wedding, dressing the dolls up for the special events of their lives.

Sometimes in the evening while we warmed our feet on an iron foot warmer, we would think about our wonderful Christmas. We had good friends and relatives. They had remembered us for Christmas. We had good neighbors. They had shared what they had with us. We had helped some of the "poor people" who lived nearby. And the real Santa Claus had called us on our grandma's telephone.

We listened to the radio and our favorite programs, sometimes while we were in bed keeping warm. Naturally, we listened to the local news, read by Ernie or his wife Dorothy Thwaites. Then there was the national news carried through the network which at that time was NBC. (Later they changed to ABC.) About that time we began to listen to Paul Harvey every day. We listened to mysteries, dramas, music programs, religious programs, children's programs, anything Audrey would allow. We enjoyed Dragnet, Meet Corliss Archer, Fibber McGee and Molly, and Art Linkletter's "People Are Funny." We also liked "Queen for a Day" with Jack Bailey. We enjoyed the Hallmark Hall of Fame. We also listened to comedians such as Jack Benny, Dennis Day, "Red" Skelton, and Bob Hope. We heard Grocho Marx. We enjoyed "Father Knows Best." I fell in love with Bobby Benson of the B Bar B Ranch and greatly admired his horse Amigo.

Audrey still wrote, sometimes wrapped up in a coat and wool scarf. There was a radio contest for writers to submit a script for the weekly Dr. Christian show. The role of Dr. Mark Christian was played by Jean Hersholt. (Later, when many radio shows converted to television programs, the role went to MacDonald Carey.) Dr. Christian was one of the first of the "doctor" shows that later became popular. Audrey submitted a story about a mother and a little girl living in the isolated mountains. The little girl got sick and the mother found a way to call for help—and the doctor managed to get across the flooded river. Mother read us the story and we thought it was excellent. When we listened to the winning script on a special program, we thought our mama's story was better. Hers had a happy ending. The winner's did not. It was a tear jerker. Naturally, we thought Audrey should have won.

Audrey was always the winning story teller with us girls. She told stories she made up and true stories, stories about her childhood and about her family—like the story of living in Taos when Opal almost died of diphtheria but was given a chance to get good medical care by a stranger who showed up unexpectantly at the door. "He was an angel sent by God at just the right moment," Audrey said. "Maybe he was just an ordinary man. But to us he was a guardian angel."

Audrey knew how to make Christmas fun for her girls, even in the isolation of the winter mountains. The winter of 1950-51, with the phone call from Santa and the frigid temperatures in January, was memorable. After that cold spell, the weather returned to "normal," although it was still very dry. Audrey worried about our water situation. But she knew she would handle it. Audrey was, by now, an old hand at survival. Audrey had handled wild horses, avoided cougar and bear attacks, and killed rattlesnakes. She kept a loaded firearm within easy reach. But when a wild animal threatened her home—and refused to leave when she shot to scare it away—she faced a new challenge.

16

Valiant Bonnie

Since our grandma now lived just over the hill, about half a mile's walk, we would often go to visit her, especially when we had to carry buckets of water over the top of the hill from the well which was about a quarter of a mile from her adobe house. After a visit with Grandma, we would walk up to her garden area, pump water into our buckets, and carry them home. Once in a while Vivian or Frank would drive the little jeep over with some water for us. We sometimes had enough to wash a load of clothes in an old-fashioned tub with a scrub board. More often, Vivian took us to the "help-yourself" laundry in town and we carried back bags of wet clothes to hang up on the clothesline when we got home. There were no plastic bags in those days; the laundry bags were made of strong cotton. Nor were there any plastic water jugs. How much easier it would have been to carry a plastic jug with a lid and a handle than to try to keep water from spilling out of the top of a metal bucket!

My grandma Mabel Shearer had a wonderful old-fashioned sewing machine, and she often made us clothes. For my birthdays she nearly always made me a dress. Usually she used flour sacks for material. In those days the big flour sacks were made of brightly colored cotton. There was enough material for a dress for a little girl. When I got bigger, Grandma made pinafores because they required less material. Many of the little girls I knew wore dresses made of flour sack material.

Grandma had a nice collection of antiques, some of which she inherited from her uncle Frank. She had two pianos, several rocking chairs, lamps, and other antiques. She had a "horse-hair" chair which was made of many horse hairs put together across the seat. Grandma Shearer had some old paper dolls that had been Milly's and Jessica's. Sometimes I was allowed to play with them, very carefully. She had an oil-cloth table cloth, popular at that time. She baked bread and often made a cake or cinnamon rolls. We were often invited to eat with her, Vivian, and Vivan's mother, "Great Grandma," who moved to the ranch to stay after Grandfather Shearer died. In the summertime, we had watermelon.

Grandma showed me a little about playing the piano. I was able to "play by ear," and could play anything I heard after a few practice tries. I also made up songs, including, "How Jesus Loves" which Audrey typed and sent to a publisher, as mentioned before. Audrey had no way to send in the melody, but the verse was accepted for publication. I was pleased when I received the dollar in pay. At age six, I decided I wanted to be a writer like my Mama, and I had a good start.

We had not seen anyone for a long time, so we were surprised when a man in a grey business suit came walking up to our house. He had left his car on the other side of the bridge. He announced that he was the U.S. Census Taker and had heard that someone was living in these isolated woods. He had come to count us! We were impressed with his assiduity. He dutifully asked Audrey the questions on the form and expressed amazement that we lived so independently in such an isolated area.

Audrey briefly explained the origins of the little cabin that became our cherished home. She told him that in 1942 she and Clyde had purchased 160 acres and later another 80, a total of 240 acres situated at the foot of Barillas Peak. Some of this land, a mile long and a quarter of a mile wide, had been part of a homestead belonging to the Santillanes family, homesteaded in the late nineteenth century. The other part had been homesteaded by the Shearers. The 160 acres were purchased for $1.56 an acre, a total of $250.00. The adjoining 80 acres were purchased for $4.37 an acre, or $350 total. The total $600 she and Clyde paid for the 240 acre place was named Forest Springs Ranch. Since 1942 was a wet year, little springs could be seen throughout the "ranch" where little green meadows, deep canyons, and high mesas added variety to the densely forested land. Here and there an outcropping of huge rocks on a hillside provided still another change of scenery. In 1942 she and Clyde had built a twelve by twelve foot log cabin on the Shearer place called the "Ten Dollar House." That first structure served as a crude shelter until the more sturdy and slightly more costly Fifteen Dollar House could be built on their own property in early 1943.

"This cabin was fourteen feet by sixteen feet and cost $15.50. Altogether the cabin consists of two-hundred and thirteen trees: four of them for the foundation logs, fifty-six for the walls, two ridge poles, one center pillar, and the one hundred and fifty roof poles," Audrey explained.

"You really know a lot about your little house," the man exclaimed.

"I should, since it took my blood, sweat, and tears to help build it," Audrey replied.

Later we heard that on his way back to town, the census taker damaged the oil pan on his car when it hit bottom and scraped one of the many protruding rocks on the road through Santillanes Canyon. He had to walk to San Geronimo to get help. He certainly earned his pay that day.

Crystal's most constant companion was the collie, Bonnie. Clyde had bought the puppy when Crystal was two years old. Bonnie was smart, loyal and courageous, very protective of her home and her family. She had been hit by a car when she was a puppy; one back leg was a little shorter than the other because her broken leg had not healed properly. But she ran nearly as fast as any other dog. She had also been poisoned by someone in town. She had almost died. She had been very sick for several days. She learned two lessons in town—not to chase cars and not to eat anything unless it was given to her by a family member.

The Cocker Spaniels had "class" and so did Bonnie. Additionally, Bonnie had a certain courage, a tenacity of purpose in her valor that can only be called "heart."

Bonnie was very protective, especially of Crystal. Wherever Crystal went, Bonnie was not far away. Bonnie never barked unless something was very near the house. The other dogs barked at anything, but if Bonnie barked, we knew something Bonnie considered threatening was nearby. Bonnie also knew the word "Sic-um." It was a word used to mean, "Go get him," or "Attack." Mother only used it when she wanted Bonnie to chase something out of the yard. In town she used it to tell Bonnie to chase away a wild dog or to scare away an intruder. It was a word that wasn't used very often, but Bonnie knew that word meant business and was only used in an urgent situation.

In the spring of 1951 we began to notice that a chicken disappeared every few days. Audrey knew there were wild animals around. One time Bonnie barked so furiously that Audrey got up and opened the door enough to let her in. Bonnie had jumped in as though she barely had time to save herself. The next morning there were huge tracks of a mountain lion in the layer of soft snow outside the door.

Although Audrey knew predators were nearby, she felt secure with the 22 caliber rifle she had been given by Clyde. As a girl, Audrey was taught to shoot. And she never stopped practicing. She often went out to target practice, setting up a cardboard target against a hillside. Sometimes she put a tin can up on a tree limb. She hardly ever missed her traget. Audrey always kept her gun loaded in case of an emergency.

One day we went to the spring for water. We had Bonnie, Pete and Swifty, and a half-grown puppy we had kept, a blond female I named Corliss after the "Meet Corliss Archer" radio series. When we returned, a rooster was lying dead in the front yard. He was still warm. The dogs had evidently scared away the animal that killed it, as they had returned from the spring just ahead of us. Audrey wondered what would be bold enough to invade the yard in broad daylight, especially with the noises of dogs and human voices so near.

That evening we were listening to Clyde Beatty's "Circus and Wild Animal Show" on the radio. Just then we had our own wild animal show!

We heard the chickens making a terrible racket in front of the chicken house behind our main cabin. Audrey rushed out and around the corner of the house. As she stepped out where she could see past the end of the main cabin, she saw a big lynx cat killing a hen. Audrey was about twenty-five feet away from the cat. The animal must have seen her and surely picked up the human scent, but he paid no attention to her.

Audrey ran back into the cabin, grabbed the 22 caliber rifle, and hurried back out. She knew the slug from that rifle would only wound the cat, and a wounded animal is dangerous. She didn't want to actually shoot the cat; she just wanted to scare the animal away. So she fired shots near the lynx to frighten him. But he did not budge. He kept chewing on the hen.

Then Audrey realized he must not be a normal cat. Perhaps he was starved, old, sick, or used to human scent. In an article published in 1953, "A Lynx Raided my Home," published by *Western Sportsman*, Audrey wrote:

> I was standing at the corner of the cabin, ready to dash around it and back into the front door if the cat came toward me. I kept firing

away as fast as I could when I finally noticed dust and leaves jumping around the cat. I was shooting wild. I steadied myself, took careful aim, and fired. There was only a click—the gun was empty.

I hurried back into the house, dumped a box of shells on the bed so I could grab some quick, and reloaded the rifle.[1]

Crystal and I had just stepped out on the front step when Audrey came rushing back in to load the gun. "You girls stay in the cabin!" she ordered. "There's a lion out there!" We watched her hands shaking as she loaded the gun. I wondered how she could manage to load it with her hands shaking like that. When she said there was a lion out there, I began to imagine something like the Metro-Golden Meyer lion, a big African lion.

After mother went back outside, Crystal went out on the step again to peek around the corner. However, I stayed in the doorway, afraid to go any further.

I wrote an article which was published by *Cappers* in 1998. I wrote about my recollections of that day. I recalled:

It was early spring, and the lynx was hungry. Too old to hunt, he found our chickens easy prey. I was only 5 or 6 at the time. Mother thought that if the cat was bold enough to catch chickens just a few yards from our house, he might be bold enough to attack us girls.

Mother ran into the house to load her 22 caliber rifle. With trembling hands, she put in the shells. She went out and shot off a few rounds to frighten the cat away, but he just sat there looking at her, with feathers in his mouth.

Bonnie had been out in the woods but came rushing in when she heard the gun shots. Pete and Swifty and their pup were there barking furiously.[2]

When Audrey came back out of the cabin with her gun fully loaded, she saw the lynx getting up and walking along the little path behind the chicken house.

Just then Bonnie came racing out of the woods. She circled the lynx cat once. Audrey thought maybe if Bonnie would bark and chase the cat, it would go off somewhere and never return.

"Bonnie! Sic-um!" Audrey commanded.

Bonnie looked up at her as if to say, "Do you really mean it?" And then without another second's hesitation, she charged. Audrey later wrote:

The lynx grabbed her by the throat and clawed with all four feet. Bonnie yipped in pain but got a grip on the cat. The two snarled and chewed and struggled.

The cocker spaniels came in then. These little fellows have got sand in their craws—they piled into the fight without hesitation. They got well clawed for their trouble.[3]

Audrey was chagrined that she had said, "Sic-um." She hadn't meant for Bonnie to actually attack the lynx. She only wanted Bonnie to bark and chase it away. After the Cocker Spaniels each a received heavy blow, they ran into the bedroom cabin to hide under the bed. They were not cowards but they knew when to retreat from a lost cause. They knew they couldn't kill that big cat.

But Bonnie would not give up, even though she was experiencing the worst pain of her life and was losing the fight. Audrey wanted to get a shot in to save Bonnie, but she was afraid she'd hit the dog. Audrey wrote:

Bonnie and the vicious lynx fought furiously. I moved up as close as I dared, trying to get an opening so I could shoot again. Things cleared up some when the cocker spaniels finally decided they'd had enough and moved away. But I still had trouble getting a clear shot.

I finally spotted a brief opening and fired. That time I sent a bullet crashing through the cat's spine. It went limp.

Bonnie shook it savagely, to be sure it was dead, then dropped it. She was bleeding.[4]

I wrote in later years that it was certainly not my mother's ambition to become a big game hunter. Indeed, we felt sorry for the old lynx. He had been through a severe winter. He was so old his teeth were worn down. He had been trying to survive. But Audrey feared he might kill all of our chickens, leaving us without our main food supply. And when the cat and Bonnie fought, Mother had no choice. She had to keep him from killing Bonnie. It was amazing that she killed the cat with one shot, especially when the cat and dog were tumbling over and over in their fierce battle. I wrote that it was Daddy who provided the bacon, but it was Mama who saved the eggs.[5]

I was somewhat dismayed to see the lynx cat after Audrey had killed it and held it up for a photograph. It was about as tall, in length, as I was, but it was no African lion. It was skinny and didn't look too much different from an overgrown alley cat. However, I had heard the fight and seen the dogs afterwards.

I knew it was a dangerous animal. Audrey wrote in her article:

> I am not a hunter. I am the mother of two daughters who live with me in a little cabin in the Sangre de Cristo Mountains, eighteen miles west of Las Vegas, New Mexico. Not once did I ever dream that I would face a raiding Lynx right there beside our home—a big cat that had come up to the cabin in broad daylight, was terrorizing our dogs, killing our chickens, and threatening to take over.[6]

Audrey was every bit a mother, protecting her children. And Bonnie was all that a protective, loyal dog could be.

Mother came in and told us what had happened. Bonnie limped into the cabin door and lay down, exhausted and wounded.

"Bonnie! Bonnie!" Crystal cried out. "Bonnie's going to die!"

"No. She's wounded, but she'll live," Mother assured her. "We won't let her die. She was fighting to save us from that big cat. She was saving her family."

"She's our hero," Crystal said."

"Yes, she's a heroine, all right," Mother agreed.

We gave Bonnie every bit of nursing care we could. We all gathered around her and told her how good she'd been, that she had saved our lives. She knew she'd done well. She wasn't about to give up and die, not after living through the fight of her life.

We bathed Bonnie's wounds in ST-37, the antiseptic mother used for all our scratches and scrapes. We put water and food where Bonnie could get it. She got extra food whenever she wanted it, including canned milk with eggs whipped up in it.

We did not ignore the other dogs. They had tried their best. We praised them and fed them extra food as well. The injuries Pete and Swifty received were deep and painful, but one strike from the big cat did not inflict the harm Bonnie had received from dozens of bites and scratches.

"I'm sorry I told Bonnie 'sic-um'," Mother said. "I didn't think she'd be brazen enough to actually attack. But she thought she was saving us," Mother told us. "She was in a fight to the death. She wasn't going to give up. She would have died to defend us. She almost did."

"You must be a really good shot to be able to kill the lynx and not hit Bonnie," Crystal said.

Audrey replied, "My daddy and mama taught me to shoot. They said you can't make mistakes when you've got to use the gun. I've practiced a lot. But still, it was a lucky shot."

The dogs made a full recovery. Bonnie had deep scratches and bites in her flesh, but she still had her heavy winter coat, and Audrey thought that helped a little. After a couple of weeks, Bonnie was out running around the forest again.

Audrey Simpson with lynx cat she shot. *Source*: Simpson Archives, photo by Clyde J. Simpson

Audrey put a chain around the big cat's neck and had Crystal hold it up so she could take a picture of it with her box camera. The next day Clyde showed up unexpectedly, as he did sometimes. He took a picture of Audrey holding the big cat up. He didn't stay long, but we had a good visit. Later Audrey wrote several stories about her adventure with the lynx cat. Some of them were published, including the story in *Western Sportsman*. She had quite a number of letters in response to that story, which included some of the photographs of Audrey and the lynx cat. She had a couple of marriage proposals! One of the letters she received was from actor Fred A. Stone from Los Angeles, California. She wrote back and he became a faithful pen pal and friend. He must have felt sorry for a woman alone in the mountains with two girls to support. He always sent gifts at Christmas, Easter, for our birthdays, and any time at all. He also wrote letters to us girls. Apparently he had no family and he "adopted us." We appreciated his kindness and his friendship, and his gifts made a big different to us. It was a friendship that lasted many, many years, and it all started with a letter resulting from the story Audrey published about the lynx cat and our brave dog Bonnie.

"Bonnie is the bravest dog ever," Crystal said. "She was fighting for us. She didn't care if she was getting killed by that cat. She wouldn't have given up."

"You're right. She has the loyal heart of a champion. She is our valiant collie," Mama said.

"What does *valiant* mean?" we asked in unison.

"Brave or courageous," Audrey replied. Then she quoted William Shakespeare, from *Julius Caesar,* Act II, Scene II:

Cowards die many times before their deaths;
The valiant never taste of death but once.

Bonnie Snow-white Lassie was, indeed, a valiant collie. She was the smartest, bravest dog I ever knew. Shakespeare was not thinking of a dog when he wrote those lines. But Shakespeare did not know our Bonnie.

"Bonnie, our valiant collie," Audrey said, gently patting the triumphant pet.

We thought our mother was pretty valiant herself.

17

Mountain Top Farewell

"To be a successful writer, there is one main thing you have to do," Audrey once advised some aspiring authors. "Write!" Audrey explained that writing must be a priority that one consistently practices in order to attain success.

In the mountains, Audrey continued to write. She had disciplined herself to write at least two hours every day, inspired by every day observations and occurrences. She decided she wanted to climb to the top of Barillas Peak, no easy feat, but she didn't want to go alone. Pete and Lelama Gardner were on vacation at the Gardner place down the canyon, so Audrey asked Pete if he wanted to climb the peak. He did, so he, Audrey, and Crystal made the climb, going up the Big Cross Trail. I stayed at the Gardner cabin with Lelama, as Audrey thought the climb would be too much for a six year old, and Lelama did not want to go. The Big Cross was still there at the time. After that climb, Audrey wrote an article, with photographs, entitled, "The Big Cross Trail" which was published in *New Mexico Magazine* in March of 1951.

Audrey wrote that one of the main arteries of travel from the east side of the Sangre de Cristo mountain range to the west side a hundred years ago or earlier was the Big Cross Trail. It was one of the earliest routes for foot and horseback travel, connecting the settlements of Las Vegas, Gallinas, and San Geronimo on the east side with San Luis, Las Colonias, and Pecos on the west side of the range. It crosses the divide just north of Barillas Peak. She wrote directions on how to get to the Trail:

> The road goes through the old village of San Geronimo and into the mountain forest road to the San Geronimo Ranger Station. There, about 18 miles from Las Vegas, the forest markers point out the Big Cross Trail.[1]

Audrey speculated that the Trail had been used by Native Americans even before Spanish settlements were established.

> There is a deep indentation of the Santillanes canyon on the east, with a comparatively short but abrupt lift over the divide and then it drops down into the Sebadilla Canyon on the west side of the mountains. From the Sebadilla the trail follows across lesser divides through the Hartman and La Cueva canyons and down into Las Colonias on Cow Creek.[2]

She pointed out that the Trail was well established by the 1850s and was a well-known short cut. Using it saved two day's traveling time between Las Vegas and Santa Fe.

> When this section of the mountains was taken into the National Forest in 1910, the big cross on top of the divide which gives the trail its name, was already weathered and old. A native born in San Geronimo seventy-six years ago says the original big cross on the divide burned when fire swept the top of the mountain. The people replaced the original cross in 1884 with the cross that stands there today.[3]

Audrey explained that every passer-by on the old Trail adds a rock or two to the large pile at the foot of the cross, although no one seems to know why such a tradition was started. Audrey wrote:

> We climbed the Big Cross trail to the top of the divide, starting from San Geronimo Ranger Station. The snug cabin is now unoccupied. [Since then the cabin was burned in the 1971 fire, so it no longer exists.] The forest sign says three miles to Sebadilla Canyon, which heads just over the divide from the Big Cross. Following the beautiful Santillanes Canyon we climbed steadily upward, following a fair road. A car could follow this road for at least a mile beyond the Ranger Station. And a jeep could easily travel another half mile up the canyon road. When we left the road and reached the steeper part of the trail, we were on the "new" trail built in the spring of 1911. This trail, built while Assistant Ranger A. J. C. Wells was stationed at the San Geronimo station, was constructed by a crew of men under the supervision of Robert Palmer. C. V. Shearer was fire guard at the time and was given the task of laying out the trail.[4]

C. V. Shearer laid out the Trail. Then a crew of about ten men was employed for about two weeks to build the Trail up the east side. The Trail to the west, as well as the north and south Trail on top of the ridge, was constructed later.

> We followed hair-pin curves and climbed the switchback. From open spots in the timber we could look for many miles out across the eastern part of New Mexico. San Geronimo was at our feet. To the north is the Elk Mountain or High Line Trail—laid out as a fire trail in the days when a fire guard had to cover a specific route of travel each day.
> From the Big Cross it is a two-mile hike on up to Barillas Peak to the 100-foot lookout tower on top of the peak. From this tower on a clear day one can see out into Texas, Kansas and Oklahoma—north into Colorado and south to El Paso—panoramas that few people get to see these days when the new trails of concrete and asphalt follow the low valley routes.[5]

Audrey described the Big Cross as she saw it on that day in March of 1951. Her story had photographs in it, and she had several more that weren't used in the story, including one of the Big Cross. One of her photographs of the Big Cross was later used in an item in the *Las Vegas Daily Optic*. She also wrote several items for the *Optic* regarding the Trail, including, "Early Main Route To Ancient City North of Barillas:"

> A short cut to Santa Fe crosses the Sangre de Cristo mountain range just north of Barillas Peak. It was one of the early main routes used

to save two days of time between Santa Fe and Las Vegas.

For more years than living men can remember it has been called The Big Cross Trail. It gets its name from a huge cross sitting on top of the saddle in the range north of Barillas peak.

The present cross was raised in 1884 after a former cross burned in a forest fire. Travelers on the trail each place a rock or two at the foot of the cross. A custom of the country, there are two versions of the reason for this.

One story says that the travelers are placing their burdens at the foot of the cross. The other story says that if one places a rock there and makes a wish it is sure to come true.

The natives of the mountains used to make a pilgrimage up the steep mountain side to the big cross. They carried the image of San Isidro, patron saint of the farmers, in order that he might see the condition of the land in drought time.

There is no better place for a "view" than this high point. You can see for miles, with ruts of the trails cut by ox wagons standing out against the land to the east. San Geronimo plaza is a dot far down in broken canyon country.

The trail winds through heavy forest where deer, bear, lynx cats and mountain lions are common. Four trails meet at the cross. One goes down the east side of the range to San Geronimo and Las Vegas. The other drops into the Sebadilla canyon on the west side and over the mountains to Las Colonias and Pecos. To the south the trail climbs out of the saddle up Barillas where a Forest Service lookout tower stands.

Northward there is a trail following the top of the Sangre de Cristo Mountains called the High Line Trail. Travel on those trails has to be on foot or on horseback. Even a jeep can't reach their higher stretches.

Visitors planning to travel to the big cross should leave Las Vegas on highway 85 [State Highway 283 today]. Travel south about two miles to the Mineral Hill road. Turn west through Kearney's Gap and head for the mountains. Your car might take you a mile beyond the San Geronimo ranger station where forest markers point the way to the big cross trail. After that you hike if you want to see the big cross that marked the short cut to Santa Fe.[6]

Penitentes used that trail on Holy Thursday as they conducted their religious ceremonies.

In the late summer of 1951, Mother, Crystal and I climbed up the little mountain between our place and The Old Homestead Ranch. We had made this hike many times before as we went over the hill to Grandma and Vivian's house. Now we were going to get a ride with Vivian into Las Vegas. But this was no ordinary trip for supplies. On this day we were leaving our mountain cabin to move to town. School would be starting soon.

We topped the big hill just at sunrise and sat in our usual resting place on the big rocks. Daylight's first orange and pink rays touched the top of the mountains, turning them from night's black shadows to a deep purple hue. Even as we watched, the orange turned to rose, the rose to pink, the pink to gold above the mountains—the sharp Sangre de Cristo range turning from purple to deep blue.

I noticed that the warmth of the first morning rays fell on Crystal's face. A little breeze blew through the top of the pines.

"Listen to the pines," Audrey said.

"What are they saying, Mama?" I asked.

"They're saying good-bye Audrey, good-bye Crystal, good-bye Dorothy. Come back again soon."

There was a sort of strain in my mother's voice. She was trying not to cry.

This August of 1951, we were looking down the hillside to our own Happy Meadow. We were walking over the hill where the little grey jeep belonging to the Shearers would take us into town, to school, to a new kind of life. That jeep had made many trips to town and only got stuck in the mud once, as far as I knew. That was when Frank, my fourteen-year-old uncle, was driving it and tried to go around a lumber truck that was stuck in the middle of the road.

Audrey had known for a while that it would be time to move to town just before school started. She wrote that the drought got worse. The little spring had almost dried up. We carried all our water from the Shearer place. "In order to survive we had to move back to town. Briefly we moved a few things, leaving most at Forest Springs."[7] Audrey wrote:

> There was a drought. The girls and I had to carry water 3/4 mile in buckets from mother's well over a little mountain. I wrote a prayer verse for rain—published later in *New Mexico Magazine* and in an anthology. I remember reading it at a meeting [probably the Pen's Women's Club] and while at the meeting it thundered and rained.[8]

Audrey sold something to *Saturday Evening Post*. That helped provide the money to move to town so we could go to school.

I would be going to school for the first time. Now, sitting at the top of the hill between our ranch and the Old Homestead ranch, we were filled with a sense of sadness felt by those who say good-bye to one place and walk into another.

I was sure Mother had mastered the language of the trees. She always told us what she thought the trees were saying.

"What else are they saying, Mama?" I asked.

"They are saying, 'We don't want to you leave, but we know you have to go to town to learn and to do things. But we will always be here waiting for you to welcome you.'"

"How did you learn to understand the trees?" Crystal asked.

"You learn the ways of nature," Mother replied.

Now, standing on the hilltop, thinking of the life we were leaving behind—just the three of us in a one-room log cabin nestled among the pines—I thought my mother was very wise. We had learned a great deal from her in the two years we had lived in our little cabin.

I had mixed feelings about leaving. I had been happy in the mountains but I did want to go to school and experience life "in town." We had talked about what we wanted to study and do in the future. Crystal, age thirteen, said she'd like to be a teacher. I wasn't sure yet. I knew I wanted to write.

At age seven, I was acutely aware of the change. I wondered about the future. I felt a sense of sadness that things would never be quite the same. Leaving the mountains for town was a little frightening. I looked around at the sunrise, at my mother and sister, and thought how nothing ever stayed the same.

Maybe it was then that Audrey thought of this poem, "Record Run," that was published in *The Joy Bearer:*

> How many days has this play run?
> The World's the stage billing the sun.
> He plays his role, warm right straight through,
> With shinning brilliance, not missing a cue.
> At last he bows behind the peaks.
> Night drops purple with golden streaks.
> He never heeds the encore calls.
> Work is done when the curtain falls.[9]

I wished that the few minutes we spent watching the sunrise on that hill top could have lasted much longer. I didn't want it to end. But I knew there were many good things ahead of us, and I was ready to travel down the road to town, to a new life, to new learning.

I wonder if Audrey was remembering that moment when she wrote the poem, "Mountain Daybreak" which was published in the *Las Vegas Daily Optic* several years later:

> Tall pines are black lace,
> Outlined on moon's gold.
> Deep spring is pale ice,
> A deep silver cold.
>
> Young fawn, dappled shadow,
> Is asleep in wild fern.
> Red raspberries glisten
> Across the big burn.
>
> Bright stars blink farewell,
> All night light is gone.
> Pink waves of morning
> Announce mountain dawn.[10]

The day when we were to move to town, Audrey, Crystal and I walked across the path to Mabel and Vivian's place, leaving our cabin silent in early morning solitude. It was just after the sun came up, about six in the morning. As we rested from our climb on the big rocks at the top of the hill where we'd stopped so many times before, sometimes with heavy buckets of water from the Shearer's well, we listened to the pines telling us farewell. Our lives were changing forever. Never again would the three of us live in the little one-room log cabin. We would stay overnight whenever we came out on a weekend or vacation. We hoped to live there again someday, but we knew that wouldn't happen for a long time.

Audrey's heart must have been heavy with the thought of leaving her beloved mountains, even though she wanted her children to have a chance for a good education. The three of us would never be as close as we had been during that time when the little log house was truly a cabin just for three.

Part 111
Back to Her Mountains

1

A Bride Again!

As a writer, Audrey was not always paid by check. Sometimes she was paid with copies of the publication. Sometimes she was paid with a prize, as when she won a contest through a radio program sponsored by a big paint company. She won about forty gallons of paint. Since we were moving to town, Audrey traded the paint to the Carringtons for rent, as they needed paint to keep up the apartments. Audrey again rented the Carringtons' little house at 420 Tenth Street. Audrey's *Saturday Evening Post* item, for which she received cash, also helped.

When we moved from Forest Springs Ranch to Las Vegas in August of 1951, Audrey planned to work while Crystal and I were in school. She had no job prospects but hoped to get a job as a journalist. Audrey realized that she needed to take a class or two. She had taken a few classes at New Mexico Highlands University in the past. In the fall of 1951, Audrey enrolled in an evening class at Highlands University and studied under the very capable journalism professor, Mr. Harry Lancaster.

I was five when we moved into the Fifteen Dollar House and seven when we moved back to town in 1951. I was enrolled at Gallinas Street School, just a couple of blocks down the street from our house. The principal and second grade teacher was Margaret Goddard (Mrs. Charles Goddard.) She was skeptical as to how well I would do in second grade since I had never been to school before, and she wanted me to go into first grade. Mother explained that she had home schooled me and talked her into letting me try second grade. I found the work very easy, stayed in the second grade, and enjoyed school.

Crystal went to Douglas School, just a few block or two from the Carringtons' place. She went into the sixth grade with Mrs. Watson. She was behind in school due to the years she had missed. She felt self-conscious because she was older than the other students in her grade. However, an understanding principal, Paul Smith, moved Crystal up to the Seventh Grade. She was still behind two years, but she didn't feel so out of place. She continued to struggle with her reading, but she managed to make passing grades through very hard work and with tutoring from Audrey.

Jessica had a Chevrolet that had belonged to her late husband, Tetter

Hayes. Jessica had re-married and did not need the old Chevy, so she agreed to sell it to Audrey. With a learner's permit, a few lessons from one or two people, and a lot practicing, Audrey got her license. She learned to park, using two trees in the Carringtons' yard near the street where there was a parking place. It was wonderful to have transportation. When the weather was good we could go to the ranch and enjoy a day or two "at home" in our mountains.

We liked living in town as far as having access to the grocery stores, making friends, and having fresh milk delivered to our door by the local dairyman. We liked having hot and cold running water. There was a flush toilet. There was a gas heater and a kitchen range. Crystal and I were allowed to walk to the post office, just a block away, to buy candy. In the lobby, there was a counter with candy and school items such as pencils and Big Chief tablets. The visually challenged man behind the counter, possibly a War veteran, sold candy and school items to the children from Douglas School and the surrounding neighborhood for many years. We also were allowed to go to a grocery store just a block down the street. Once when Crystal was away, Audrey mentioned she needed a couple of items. I was feeling quite grown up and begged her to let me go to the store for her alone. It was the same store where Audrey had been embarrassed when she had tried to sell her chickens and that had refused Clyde credit. Audrey let me go there to buy some bread and milk. I was so short I could not reach the taller shelves or the counter. I said something that they thought was funny, so I, too, was laughed at. I didn't ask to go to that store by myself for a long time after that. However, as soon as Audrey got her driver's license and we had a car, we shopped at the Safeway store on Douglas Avenue. Later, when Donald and Rachel Whorton put in a grocery store on Seventh Street across from the Optic, we shopped there. Audrey always gave rides to friends she ran across when they needed transportation. One such friend was Jo Raymond, who worked at the J. C. Penney store on Douglas Avenue for many years. She did not have a car, so whenever Audrey saw her at the Safeway store, she would offer a ride. Jo would gratefully load up her groceries and Audrey would drive her home. She lived just a few blocks away from the store but too far to carry very many sacks of groceries.

We soon discovered there were disadvantages to living in town. Keeping four big dogs in a little apartment house was not very practical, especially when we were gone most of the day. So Audrey advertised to give Pete and Swifty away. A nice couple came to see them. The man picked Swifty up and held her in his lap. She looked embarrassed. They agreed to take Swifty—but not Pete. Someone else took Pete a day or two later. I was very sad. I suppose Mother and Crystal were too. For one thing, Audrey had promised Mrs. Leatherman never to separate Pete and Swifty. I believe it was one of the few promises Audrey ever broke. She did it out of necessity because circumstances had changed. She assured us that both dogs would have a good home. We kept Bonnie and my young dog, Corliss.

Bonnie was twelve years old and missed the ranch. She liked running free in the mountains. One day Crystal and I went to the Surf Theatre to see a Lassie movie. We came home looking forward to seeing Bonnie. She was just as great, if not greater, than Lassie, we thought— just as smart and courageous. In her own way she was famous. Her picture had been in several photographs with us in stories Audrey had published. Yes, we agreed, Bonnie was the best dog in the world.

When we got home Bonnie was gone! We discovered that Audrey had taken Bonnie to the veterinarian to have her euthanized. Audrey explained that Bonnie was old and sick; she couldn't let the dog suffer. Crystal was heart-broken. She had not had a chance to say good-by. Audrey thought she was doing the best thing. She, too, was grieving over Bonnie.

Audrey drove the old Chevy out toward to the ranch to bury Bonnie in the country. Rain clouds were threatening and Mother was afraid to drive all the way out, as she did not want to chance getting stuck in the mud. So Bonnie ended up in an unmarked grave along the country roadside.

As Audrey dug a grave and placed Bonnie in it, Crystal and I looked on in sorrow.

"Bonnie won't have a grave stone with her name on it," Crystal protested through her tears.

"No, but she still has a permanent monument," Mother explained, wiping her own tears away. "It's in our hearts."

Bonnie had belonged to Crystal since she was two years of age. And I had never known a day without Bonnie in my life. Now we had to realize that life is filled with changes—including disappointment and sorrow. But there were joys, as well.

Crystal finally had an opportunity to get to know David, the boy she liked. He now lived just across the street from us! What good fortune for Crystal, I thought happily. It was good fortune for me, too. Now Crystal could get to know David without going through the "dropped handkerchief" routine.

David invited Crystal to go with him to a Boy Scout function at Douglas School. I will never forget how pretty she looked for her first date! She dressed up in her best dress, one Mrs. Knox had sent from Orange, California. Mrs. Knox had a girl just older than Crystal. She and Audrey had met at the Carringtons' place where they both had rented apartments. When she moved, Mrs. Knox told

Audrey she would send her daughter's clothes when she outgrew them if Mother would just pay the postage on the packages. Crystal was happy to have the clothes, as most of them were fairly expensive and were in nearly new condition when they arrived. The dress she wore for the big event was silk, with a colorful floral pattern against a turquoise blue background. It had a brown velvet bodice. When David came to the door to call for her, Audrey greeted him and said she hoped they'd have a good time. Apparently they did. I thought it was a dream come true for Crystal—to finally get a date with David! They were both about thirteen years of age, but I thought of them as nearly grown up. We were disappointed when David and his family moved out of town soon after that.

We made new friends in the neighborhood and at school. Crystal liked Betty Sue Turner, who lived a couple of blocks down the street on Lincoln Avenue. There were other kids in the neighborhood such as Kenneth and Richard "Dickie" Tuttle. They were enrolled at Gallinas Street School, so I got to know them, as well as others my age such as Bobby Korte, Jerry Fredericks, William "Butch" Rhodes, and Velva Sue Cooper (later Velva Sue Axtell after her mother re-married.) I had made friends in kindergarten. Now I had a chance to see them again and to make new friends, including a girl whose parents had moved to Las Vegas from New Orleans, Louisiana. Her name was Judith F. Beil. Judy's father, Wallace C. Beil, was an ophthalmologist. (The previous ophthalmologist in Las Vegas, Dr. Butterfield, had died suddenly, leaving a widow and children.) Judy was to become my lifelong friend.

Dr. Wallace Beil opened an office in Las Vegas. He and his family lived at Montezuma. They raised Tennessee Walking Horses. Judy and I became best friends. Sometimes she came home with me to the apartment to eat lunch. Other times we ate at the school cafeteria—which was in the old Armory building on Douglas Avenue. We competed in our school work. We both usually made A's.

July sometimes invited me to go horseback riding at her place, and I learned to ride, with the help of Judy and her father. Dr. Beil and July also taught me to ice skate at the Montezuma ponds near her home. Mother bought skates for me and for Crystal and took us skating several times. As always, Audrey was interested in places of local interest, in history, and she was fascinated with nature. She loved the Montezuma ponds which had been used to obtain ice in the early days and then, after refrigeration, the ponds were used for recreation. Audrey wrote a story for the *Las Vegas Daily Optic:* "Gallinas Ponds Used for Storage and Ice-Skating:"

> Most visitors and all residents of Las Vegas are familiar with the ice skating ponds in the Gallinas canyon near Montezuma.

Summer and winter the canyon with its scenic drive and free facilities is a playground for all comers.

For an unusual thrill try this in Gallinas canyon when the ice has stilled the singing water. Stop beside the pond across from the abrupt cliffs. Get out of your car and talk to the mountain. Each word will be repeated clearly by the echo of the vertical rocks.

If you should be lucky enough to try this at night when the moon is full, the eerie beauty of the sharp cliff with its crown of tall pine will more than repay one for the time it takes to drive the six miles from Las Vegas.

The echo may be heard in the summer time, too. But the sound does not have the bell tones of winter for there is the song of the waters that the echo must compete with.

Next time you are in Gallinas Canyon, summer or winter, speak to the cliff. You will be pleasantly surprised.[1]

After the second and third grades, Judy Beil and I were not always in the same class or the same school. However, we saw each other often. We played board games such as Sorry, played with dolls, played Jacks, hop scotch, or jump rope, and shared our favorite books. One Christmas my best friend Judy gave me a most wonderful gift. I had admired her Little Lulu doll. I was surprised and delighted when she gave it to me, as it was one of her favorites. I learned the meaning of true giving from people like Judy who gave from the heart.

On Saturdays Crystal and I would walk about three blocks to the downtown movie theatre, the Surf. We also sometimes went to the theatre in "old town," the Kiva. There had been one other theatre—the Coronado—but it was sold and became part of Gambles Store. When I was about five years old, I went to see "The Red Shoes" at the Coronado with Mother and Crystal. Soon after that it went out of business. The "movies" were always a great thrill for me. The first one I remember was Walt Disney's "Song of the South" shown at the Surf Theatre when I went with Mama, Daddy, and Crystal. I was about three.

Our move to town was a big change. It provided opportunities for Audrey to develop her career. Mabel, too, was dealing with changes. Frank, after graduating from high school and then staying for a while in California with Arolvi and Paul, joined the Air Force in 1953. Mabel and Vivian were alone except when some of the family visited them, bringing along grandchildren. Frank was the last of Mabel's seven children to leave home. Mabel wrote a verse at Christmas time:

Christmas doesn't mean a thing
With loved ones far away
I weep and wish that I could skip
That sad (one-happy) day.

My children all have gone away
My heart is cold as stone
My sins lie heavy on my head
And, thus, I must atone.

Oh, that I might ascend tonight
On Bethlehem's star's bright beam
I would pass on to other scenes,
To sing a happier theme.
Adieu[2]

Mabel, pondering the birth of the Christ child, must have thought about how Mary held her newborn Infant, just as Mabel had held seven of her own. Mabel missed her children. Fortunately, there were many grandchildren to care for, and Mabel always seemed to be taking care of one or another of them, so she didn't have much time to be lonesome.

One day Audrey saw an ad in the paper for a reporter. When she went in for an interview, she got the job at the Las Vegas Optic, owned at that time by Lincoln O'Brien. Walter Vivian was the editor and his wife Delma worked for the Optic as well. Walter knew how well Audrey could write because he'd seen her work for quite some time. He knew she'd had items published off and on in the *New Mexico Magazine* and other such places. She had also written "Letters to the Editor" from time to time. Audrey was hired to go to work immediately as reporter and as Society Editor. She had to "beat the bushes" and work hard to get local news to make the Society Page (later the Women's Page) interesting and informative for the Las Vegas subscribers. She had always wanted to work at the Optic, although the wages were very moderate. Five years before that she had seen an ad but hadn't applied. She knew she probably could have had a job before, but at that time she didn't have the nerve to go and apply. With some course work from the Journalism Department at Highlands University, her confidence was boosted.

When Audrey was hired, a news item came out in the New Mexico Highlands University newspaper, *The Candle*:

New "Optic" reporter is Mrs. Audrey Simpson, former Highlands student who studied English with Dr. Burris and journalism with Harry Lancaster.

Although born in Lincoln, Neb., reporter Simpson, a friendly brunette with a sympathetic manner, claims Las Vegas as her home town. She has lived in the windy meadows city since childhood.

Now that her daughters are eight and fifteen respectively, she has more leisure for writing, an avocation she has carried on as a free lance for many years. A frequent contributor to the *New Mexico magazine, Denver Post,* and several poetry magazines, she said her most remunerative writing was the "Perfect Squelch" published in the *Saturday Evening Post* last summer to the tune of a hundred bucks. "I wouldn't mind doing one of those every day or one month per year," she said with a meaningful wink in the direction of her new boss, Editor Walter Vivian of the Optic.

In the magazine, "*Profitable Hobbies*" Mrs. Simpson described the construction of a mountain log cabin which she and her husband built nine years ago. Asked if it was livable, she assured us it was still standing "and what's more it hasn't leaked yet."

Mrs. Simpson is president of the Las Vegas branch of the National League of American Pen Women.[3]

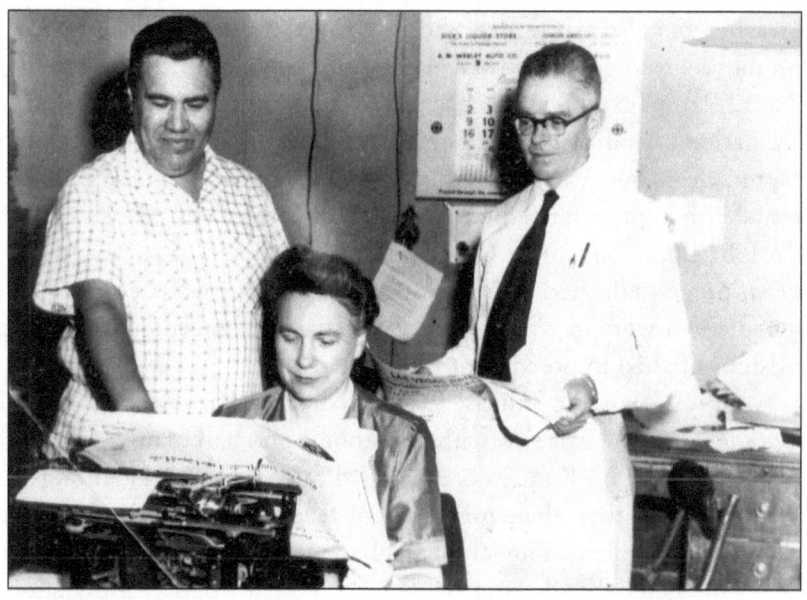

Dan Martinez, Audrey Simpson (seated) and Walter Vivian, Optic Editor, 1953
Source: Simpson Archives, photo by *Las Vegas Daily Optic* photographer

Audrey helped establish a Las Vegas chapter of the International Pen Women's Club and was soon elected President of the local organization where women encouraged each other to write and publish their best. Some of the members were Mrs. B. B. (Glydia K.) Barila (my piano teacher); Lois Roquemore (the school teacher); and Clare Turlay Newberry, a professional artist and writer.

Clare Turlay Newberry was a tall, striking, attractive woman. She had grey hair, kind eyes, and a beautiful smile. She had married Henry V. Trujillo and moved to Las Vegas. They had a daughter, Felicia Noelle Trujillo, about my age. Clare had an older son from a previous marriage. She wrote children's books about cats and illustrated them. At her home near the Plaza in old town, she had numerous cats, all of them serving as models for her books. Felicia also served as a model, as had the older child. Felicia and I often played while our mothers visited. After Clare and her family moved to Santa Fe, Audrey and Holly went to visit them in their new home. We had many first edition, autographed copies of Clare's books. They included first editions of *April's Kittens*; *Babette*; *Ice Cream for Two*; *T-Bone, the Babysitter*; *Marshmellow*; *Mittens*; *Pandora*; *Percy, Polly and Pete*; *Smudge*; and *Herbert the Lion*. Most of these books were signed: "To Audrey." They all burned in the tragic 1971 fire, along with letters and photographs Audrey treasured.

Another of Audrey's friends, Lois Roquemore, wrote poetry. Audrey encouraged her to write. She was a very talented woman, not only as an elementary school teacher, but also as a writer. She also played the organ for church. She was a loving mother and grandmother. After Lois' husband died, Lois retired and moved to El Paso, Texas. She was brutally attacked one night when some vicious Mexican nationals came over the border and broke into her house. She fought and resisted them but was badly injured in the process. After she made a full recovery, she met and married Leo F. Carden with whom she shared her last years. In 1984 Lois Roquemore Carden published a book of poetry entitled, *The Heart That Sings*, dedicated to her husband Leo. Her love poems are exquisite and a tribute to a woman whose heart was capable of enormous love in spite of the hardships life had imposed upon her.

Audrey's keepsake suitcase held a scrapbook Crystal was given in the second grade when she was sick with pneumonia and had to miss some weeks of school. Her teacher, Lois Roquemore, was dedicated and understanding—unlike one or two of the other elementary school teachers who did not understand Crystal's reading problem. The scrapbook had pictures from magazines pasted in it and was supposed to be all about Crystal. Each picture had a little caption. Each classmate had helped make the book for Crystal. Such an outstanding teacher inspired Crystal and she later became an excellent teacher.

Sometimes the Pen Women met at various homes, including Audrey's. The women would encourage one another in their writing and would report on their most recent publications. One of Audrey's successes was reported in the *Las Vegas Daily Optic* on April 27, 1953:

> Another Las Vegan will be represented in the National League of American Pen Women southwest regional contest to be held in Salt Lake City in June.
>
> Mrs. Audrey Simpson received word from Dr. Lena Creswell, state president of the organization, that her juvenile story, "The Green Cake" had been picked from New Mexico Pen Women entries to compete in the regional contest for juvenile stories.
>
> Mrs. Simpson is president of the Las Vegas branch of the Pen Women. Mrs. C. F. Shupp, vice president, had her poem, "Flight" chosen last week for entry in the regional contest.[4]

One of the most interesting meetings of the Pen Woman was when Betty's husband, Stanley Hardin, spoke to the group. The *Las Vegas Daily Optic* printed a story that was undoubtedly written by Audrey:

> Dr. Stanley Hardin, who served in the U. S. Air force from 1942 to 1945, described his first combat mission in southern China to the Las Vegas branch of the National League of American Pen Women meeting Tuesday night at the home of Mrs. L. T. Smith.
>
> Dr. Hardin, who served as a Captain flying a P38 photo reconnaissance plane, was forced down by a leak in a gas tank on his first assignment. He landed in a rice paddy near enemy territory. His plane was undamaged, Dr. Hardin reported.
>
> Dr. Hardin described the walled city where the "Chamber of Commerce" presented him with gifts and a "key" to the city, honoring him as an American officer who was assisting in protecting their land from the Japanese invasion.
>
> Gifts presented to him the first day of his arrival consisted of food, their most valuable possession, Dr. Hardin said. This included a soft shelled turtle, ducks, and chickens in bamboo baskets, eggs, a freshly scrubbed live pink pig and six cans of baby food.
>
> During his 30 day stay in the area while waiting for gas to be floated to him on the river, Dr. Hardin learned to use an abacus, the Chinese adding machine, which he demonstrated to the Pen Women.

Dr. Hardin described an 18 course banquet given in his honor by customs officials. This consisted of roast duck, fish, beef, bird nest soup, lotus-seed soup, fried chicken and walnuts, aged salt eggs, turtle soup and turtle steak, and many other things, each served as a separate course during the lengthy banquet.

Dr. Hardin displayed pictures of the area, chop sticks, rice straw saddles, Chinese money and many other items he brought home from China. Guests of the Pen Women were Dr. and Mrs. Hardin, Mrs. L. T. Bogmenko and Mrs. Gerald Thomson.[5]

In May of 1953, Betty Hardin was hostess to the group. The *Optic* reported:

Several markets were discussed during the meeting of the Las Vegas Branch of the National League of Pen Women meeting Thursday night at the home of Mrs. Stanley Hardin.

Several women read their work. Markets to submit this work to were then picked by Mrs. Audrey Simpson, president of the group, from a national list of writer's markets. Poetry and juvenile stories were stressed during the evening.

Ms. Jessie Ticer and Mrs. Gerald Thomson were guests of the Pen Women. Mrs. Hardin served refreshments.

At the close of the meeting the sudden death of Bernard Barilla [Barila] was announced. As a group the Pen Women extended member Mrs. B. B. Barila, his mother, their deepest sympathy.[6]

A short time after moving into the apartment house on Tenth Street, Audrey, Crystal and I moved from that little house into an upstairs apartment at Carringtons, perhaps because the rent was cheaper. It was an apartment with a large living room and a large room which served as a bedroom with a kitchen. There was a large pantry, closet, and door which opened onto a little balcony facing the Carringtons' backyard. There were big windows in each room. We shared the bathroom down the hall with residents in the other two or three upstairs apartments. There was also a little refrigerator in the hall that we were all allowed to share.

We were saddened when Corliss was hit by a car. Mother had let Corliss out early one morning and the young dog ran into the street. We buried her in the country near the place where we had buried Bonnie.

The traffic on those narrow streets was dangerous. Sometimes Audrey went to meet me after school. Once I was walking on the sidewalk across the street from the school. Audrey was walking on the other side, going toward the school. I was so surprised and happy to see my mother coming down the street that I dashed across toward her just as Groth's Grocery truck was speeding down the hill. The driver was looking down at a list of things to see where his next delivery was. I ran across the street without looking, although I knew better. Audrey later said she was petrified. The driver slammed on his brakes just in time. Mother told me in a shaking voice never to cross the street without looking both ways. After that I was more careful.

Apparently the McCarthy Era had an impact, even in quiet little Las Vegas and its surrounding mountain communities. J. Edgar Hoover left no stone unturned. Soon after we had moved into Las Vegas, Audrey got a telephone call from an agent of the Federal Bureau of Investigation who said he was investigating reports that some neighbors in the area were Communist spies. He knew that Audrey was familiar with the persons in question. He wanted to visit with her and obtain more information about those former neighbors who had suddenly moved into the area and then, just as suddenly, moved away. The agent came to Las Vegas and talked to Audrey. She said she had wondered why the neighbors had abandoned their home overnight and were never seen again. Audrey told the agent what she knew, and he continued his investigation but found no evidence that the people in question were Communists or that they were spies. That was one of two times Audrey was asked for assistance by an agent of the F.B.I. The other time was when Clyde's sister, Mary Simpson, was applying for a job with one of the military bases in Albuquerque and she needed a high security clearance. Audrey gave Mary a good recommendation, answering the agent's questions about Mary's loyalty to the United States and so on. As the agent was about to leave, he commented that he was surprised that Audrey had given Mary an outstanding recommendation.

"Why would that surprise you?" Audrey asked.

"Well, you divorced her brother, so sometimes there is bitterness toward an ex-spouse's family," he replied. "Yet you said nothing negative about your ex-husband's sister."

"There was nothing negative to say," Audrey said. "I have no bitterness. I simply told you the truth."

Mary got the job and kept it until she retired.

Audrey was active in the Parent Teacher's Association (PTA) and attended nearly every meeting at Crystal's school and at mine. She participated in fund raising events and got to know all the teachers.

When I went into the third grade at Gallinas Street School, my teacher was Mary Solomon. She had been my mother's teacher! Audrey had told me about watching Mary Grobarth as a bride, seeing her from the window of the house the Clements were living in. She was a wonderful teacher, a widow with many years of teaching experience. Judy Beil, my best friend, was also in her class. We both agreed that Mrs. Solomon was a great teacher.

A popular project took place at Christmas time. It was called "Operation Christmas," a post-War effort to make Christmas cheerful for deprived children. A *Las Vegas Daily Optic* article, "Jaycees Campaign for Discarded Toys," stated that members of the Greater Las Vegas Junior Chamber of Commerce, who were sponsoring "Operation Christmas" for underprivileged children in the area "will make a house to house canvass tonight to collect toys and clothing for the project."[7] Those donating toys were asked to place them in boxes on their front porches and turn on porch lights.

Another article in the *Optic* stated that the goal for Operation Christmas was set between 3,000 and 5,000 gifts—toys and clothing.

> All toys are acceptable by the Jaycees. Toys that seem broken beyond repair will be used for parts to repair other toys. Four collection boxes have been placed about the town for those wishing to drop toys into them. Anyone who is missed in the toy drive may call "Operation Christmas" and a collector for the Jaycees will pick up the toys or clothing.[8]

An item in a 1952 *Las Vegas Daily Optic* indicated that the schools were involved in the project.

> School children are taking discarded toys to school to be donated to the "Operation Christmas" sponsored by the Junior Chamber of Commerce this year. The teachers are collecting the toys to be repaired and distributed by the Jaycees.
>
> "Operation Christmas" reports that they not only need more toys and clothing, they also need help in repairing both toys and clothing. Organizations or individuals who can help in repairing will be welcomed at "Operation Christmas" 528 6th St.
>
> "Operation Christmas" now has a telephone installed at the headquarters on Sixth Street. The phone is answered until 4 p.m. each day. Anyone wishing to donate toys or clothing may pick up their telephone and ask for "Operation Christmas," and someone will call for their donations.[9]

This unique kind of re-cycling of used toys and clothing has gone the way of the telephone system where one would pick up the black phone receiver and hear "Operator," or "Number Please." Then the caller would give a number such as 656 or simply ask for the company or party by name, such as "Operation Christmas." Nowadays donations that are collected are expected to be new, unopened toys or clothes—or better yet, monetary donations. Not many organizations exist that repair and re-cycle. Yet that project, along with food drives, was very helpful in providing for the underprivileged in the community. Audrey was very supportive of the project. We always donated something, and I remember seeing the hard working volunteers in our local "Santa's workshop" getting toys ready for Christmas. The drive was very successful for a small town of about 15,000. *The Las Vegas Daily Optic* reported:

> More than 1,000 toys were collected during the Wednesday night drive conducted in Las Vegas by the Jaycees, according to James Elliott, chairman for Operation Christmas.
> Many of the toys had already been repaired and a number of new toys were contributed in the porch light collecting. Toys that needed repair will be repaired by the Jaycees.
> Anyone who wishes to contribute toys may call "Operation Christmas" and the toys will be picked up. The Operation Christmas headquarters at 528 6th St. will be open daily from 9 to 12 a.m. and 1 to 4 p.m.[10]

Every year the children would participate in special holiday events. Naturally, Christmas and Easter were big events. But there was a day that was celebrated in Las Vegas much more enthusiastically than it sometimes is today: May Day. A big celebration with a May pole dance took place, with much rehearsing by the children in order to impress the parents in attendance at the special event. An *Optic* story reported:

> A May Day festival is planned for May First at the Gallinas street school as the final celebration of the school year. The affair will be held at the school grounds beginning at 6 p.m. unless it rains. In that event it will be held in the Armory. The Las Vegas high school band will be present to play during the festival.
> The affair, which is open to the public with no charge, will consist of a program of folk dances. The first grade, under the direction of Miss Virginia Mainz, will present rhythm dances.
> Folk dances, "Chimes of Dunkirk" and "Hansel and Gretel" will

be presented by the second grade under the direction of Mrs. Margaret Goddard. Mrs. Mary Soloman, teacher of the third grade, has a program of "Heel and Toe" and "The Rye Waltz."

The fifth grade, under the direction of Benny Padilla, will present "The Spanish Circle Waltz" and "The Guitar Polka." All but the first grade will dance "La Raspa" and "Varsoviana."

All of the grades will join in dancing around the Maypole. Romain Mender will act as Queen of the May Festival, due to the fact her birthday falls on May First.

Gallinas PTA members will serve refreshments during the festival.[11]

We learned to go in and out and around the Maypole, holding colored ribbons. All of the teachers were very active in the events, such as carnivals and parties, as were many of the parents. Audrey always helped with the event.

Polio was rampant in those days. Audrey was afraid we would get polio, and we tried to avoid crowds. All the children had little cardboard envelopes with slots in them for dimes, and we participated in the "March of Dimes" collection for finding a cure for polio. When the vaccine was finally discovered, it was a wonderful victory.

Tuberculosis was also still a problem. The school physician, Dr. Volney Cheney, came around to examine the school children. He put down the names of those to go for a chest X-ray. A mobile unit came and some children were taken into the big truck for a chest X-ray. I was very thin and I was among those selected to get a chest X-ray.

So many children were malnourished in those days that the school milk program was started. Audrey was very supportive of that program, as she knew many children went to school hungry. Every morning and afternoon the milk cart came around. We could buy a small carton of milk for two cents or chocolate milk for three cents. Audrey hardly had two cents to spare, but she always made sure we had lunch money and milk money. (There were no free lunches in those days. Children who couldn't pay could work in the cafeteria for their lunches.)

The school nurse checked the children's hair every year for lice—*piojos,* the children called them. One little girl had them every year. She would be given a shampoo to take home to use. But every year she had them when the nurse came around again.

Audrey was not only reporter and Society Editor, but she was made Church Page Editor. When the *Rodeo Edition* was put out each year, she worked over time, writing extra stories. One year, July 31, 1952, Audrey wrote some verses that were included in the *Rodeo Edition* of the *Las Vegas Daily Optic*. One was a poem, "Cowboy's Questionnaire":

> Where was I born? Is that what you said?
> On the Mountains Back-bone, in a tarpaulin bed.
> How old I am now? I don't rightly know,
> It's been so long since I started to grow,
> Now what kind of schools did I attend?
> Why the school of hard knocks that's got no end.
> Where have I been workin'? On my own spread.
> Herdin' my cattle and buildin' a shed.
> Yep, I'm married. To a red-headed gal,
> At home or on horseback, perfect pal.
> Kids? Sure, I'm proud to say that I got two.
> One is a yearlin', the other's brand new.
> My religion? Well—it's my own pet brand,
> All learned from God's Work in my mountain land.
> If that's all yer questions I'll hit the trail
> 'Cause Pintos tired standin' hitched to a rail.[12]

Audrey took us to the ranch on many weekends and holidays. Mother always said she felt "revived" and "refreshed" after even an afternoon of breathing the sweet-scented mountain air. She often gave us a history lesson along the way as we passed by various places. She pointed out where the ruts of the Santa Fe Trail could still be seen through the well-known Kearney's Gap southwest of Las Vegas on the San Geronimo-Mineral Hill Road. A sawmill is located in part of that area now. Just beyond that there were places where the wagons would stop for a night where there was a creek and a spring for watering the livestock, as well as refreshing the weary travelers. There was a little hill Audrey always called "the Torreón" or fort just past Kearney's gap, next to where the Las Vegas City wells are located now. The travelers built this fort as a lookout point to watch for hostile natives. Today the hill with its rocks along the top can still be seen, but few people would know that the remains of the Terreón are there. Audrey wrote a story, "Torreón Guarded Kearney's Gap In Days Of Long Ago," for the *Las Vegas Daily Optic*:

> Old timers say that a Torreón, pronounced toe-ray-own, rose from the hillside at Kearney's Gap, southwest of Las Vegas. These watchtower forts were once common in many villages of New Mexico.

The Torreón, a round tower-like fort of native stone and adobe, was placed on the old Santa Fe Trail at the gap as a fort and outpost for the Plaza in the meadows. Here too, according to an old timer, the Pony Express [riders] changed horses. This gave the riders a fresh mount for the final spectacular dash into Las Vegas from Santa Fe.

There are ruins of many old houses just through the gap as one leaves Las Vegas on the Mineral Hill road. Perhaps some old timer knows the exact location of the old Torreón, supposedly on the hill on the right side of the road as the traveler passes through the gap.

The Santa Fe Trail followed along the line of hills from Las Vegas and crossed through the gap from east to west on the route to Santa Fe, we have been told, heading for the next water holes, or springs.[13]

In a similar article, Audrey elaborated in the *Rodeo Edition* of the *Las Vegas Daily Optic,* celebrating the Fourteenth Annual Teddy Roosevelt's Cowboys' Reunion which was held the first Friday, Saturday and Sunday each August.

Kearney's Gap, to the right of Highway 85 [now State Highway 283 off of Interstate 25] as you travel south of Las Vegas, is about two miles from town. This historic spot where a dry arroyo cuts through the steep rocky hills is mentioned in New Mexico history as a place named after Gen. Stephen Watts Kearney, after taking the territory by proclamation in a speech at Las Vegas on Aug. 15, 1884. Gen. Kearney expected to meet a large force of Mexicans defending the land at the Gap.

As Kearney marched on to Santa Fe on August 17, 1846, the battle did not materialize. The history books do not mention the reason. Kearney expected the Mexicans to make a stand at the Gap. But if the old timer was right about the Torreón defending the spot it was no doubt a well known fort on the trail to Santa Fe.

Karney's Gap, a place where the General did not have to fight, has been known as a picnic spot for Las Vegans for many years.[14]

Audrey talked about the Santa Fe Trail and the Pony Express. She proudly explained that her mother's great uncle was one of the three men who started the Pony Express. Mabel Waddell Shearer often told the story of her father's uncle, William Bradford Waddell. He, along with William H. Russell and Alexander Majors, were in the freighting business and decided to start the Pony Express. It was a success while it lasted.

As we passed through the village of Agua Zarca, Audrey would talk about the history she knew of the village which no longer exists except for a stone building and stone ruins. The ruins are four miles southwest of Las Vegas on what is now State Highway 283. She talked about the story of raiding Native Americans causing the Spanish villagers to flee to the safety of Las Vegas. The old priest stayed behind to hide the money, jewels and valuables of the villagers before escaping to Las Vegas himself. However, he was overtaken and killed, and the villagers never found where he hid the valuables. Audrey said she read in an old *Optic* from the 1880s that some soldiers from Fort Union had been camped in the area of Agua Zarca and had found a cache of great value. However, the article did not say what became of the treasure. With such stories to entertain us on our way, the trip over the rough road went quickly. Audrey would naturally inform us of the history of Las Vegas, which she was very familiar with. Audrey wrote "Las Vegas Founded In 1835 Is Home of Rodeo, Rough Riders," for the July 30, 1958 *Rodeo Edition, Las Vegas Daily Optic:*

> Las Vegas, steeped in history of the Southwest, was a lively place by the time Teddy Roosevelt and his Rough Riders decided to hold their reunion and meeting in Las Vegas in what is now Lincoln Park, in 1899.
>
> In 1835 Las Vegas was founded, marking an important milestone in Southwestern history. Beginning as a small settlement it grew in importance as the Santa Fe trail freight wagons groaned to a stop in the lush meadows and tired oxen watered in the cool waters of the deep Gallinas river.[15]

Audrey said she had "printers-ink" in her blood, and perhaps she did since her father got his first job in a newspaper print shop. Whenever the *Rodeo Edition* of the *Optic* came out, she often added "fillers" and other items but was not always given a byline. Here is an example from the 1952 *Optic Rodeo Edition*:

> About 1840 one tenth of the inhabitants of New Mexico were killed by small pox. An old graveyard, used by Las Vegas at the time of that epidemic, was on the hill at the end of Columbia Ave. where the Highlands Arts and Crafts building now stands.[16]

Audrey ran across many interesting items such as the fact that one man in the 1840's by the name of Aubrey, a trapper and guide and expert horseman, had won a $10,000 bet that he could ride on horseback from Santa Fe to the Missouri River in six days. In her research for the *Las Vegas Daily Optic*, Audrey also read and noted that *El Crepuculo,* the first newspaper published in New Mexico, was founded in Taos and published for a month in 1835 by Padre Martinez.[17] Audrey also wrote short items for the *Optic* such as the following:

> Tecolote, 10 miles south of Las Vegas on Highway 85, is said to be older than Las Vegas. It was supposed to have been settled in 1824 by Salvador Montoya while Las Vegas was being established in 1833.
> During the time the U. S. Army was campaigning against the Indians there was an army post at Tecolote. The ruins of the headquarters buildings and the large stables are still visible there.
> Down the Tecolote River from the village are the remains of a rather large Indian village.[18]

Audrey also wrote two stories about Watrous for the same *Rodeo Edition* of the *Las Vegas Daily Optic* in 1952. One was entitled: "Watrous Built in Beautiful Valley North of Vegas." The other one was entitled: "Barclay Fort at Watrous Once Protected Section." Both gave a wonderful history of the people and the historical events of that area.

Audrey also included poetry she wrote for the *Las Vegas Daily Optic Rodeo Edition*, such as "Mountain Sunset:"

> Pink tipped mountains
>   Wind blows cold,
> Sky all snow mist
>   Turned to gold.[19]

We missed Clyde. We had not seen him in quite a while. Daddy sent letters and, on special occasions, sent gifts. Mother was trying to move on with her life after nearly four years of separation.

On Sundays Audrey drove us out to the Foursquare Gospel Church on Seventh Street Extension. Today Seventh Street is a hub of activity in Las Vegas. In those days, there were only one or two homes in the area. Most of the land was vacant. The church at 1620 Seventh Street was one of the few buildings out that far on Seventh. The Roelfs had moved away from Las Vegas. We had attended the last church service they held, and there was a tearful parting.

"If we don't see you again on this earth, we will see you in heaven," John said.

After the Roelfs left, a new minister for the Foursquare Gospel Church came to take over, a woman who had a daughter about Crystal's age. Mother always referred to the preacher as "Sister Estelle." (Spelling is uncertain.) She was a wonderful preacher, a kind and compassionate woman.

Clyde Simpson, photo sent to Crystal and Dorothy Simpson, about 1951. *Source*: Simpson Archives

One weekend Audrey took Sister Estelle and her daughter to the ranch with us. Mabel and Vivian were still living in the big adobe house. We stopped there before going over to our own cabin. Grandma had baked a cake and welcomed all of us in her usual friendly manner.

Our guests thoroughly enjoyed the mountains. As Audrey drove back to town, she and Sister Estelle visited. Audrey told her about the two years we had lived in the little log cabin after Clyde had left. She talked about the divorce.

After listening a while, Sister Estelle exclaimed, "Why, Audrey, I believe you're still in love with Clyde."

"I never stopped loving him," Audrey conceded.

Then Sister Estelle said the words I will never forget: "Then I'm going to pray for Clyde to come back and for you to get married again. You two should be together."

About a month later, with no notice, Clyde showed up at our apartment. Crystal and I were always surprised and happy to see our daddy.

In her notes Audrey recalled how powerful Sister Estelle's prayers were:

> We started to church at the Foursquare where Sister Estelle was

minister. I needed a job. We didn't have enough to live on in town unless I could find a job. Sister Estelle prayed I would get one and the next day there was an ad in the Optic. It was for a newspaper job. I went in and saw Mr. Vivian and got a job as Society Editor and general reporter. I started to work for $35.00 a week on March 15, 1952. Every day before I entered the plant's door I prayed to keep my job and for help in doing everything in the best and most expedient manner.

Sister Estelle decided I still loved Clyde so she prayed we would be re-united. We were.[20]

Clyde told Audrey he was coming back to stay in Las Vegas. He had left his girl friend in Colorado. He could get his old job back at the Home Café or else at one of the other restaurants in town, as he was an excellent fry cook. He asked Audrey to marry him again. He had been staying with his mother in Albuquerque and she talked to him about getting back to Las Vegas to take care of his family.

Naturally, Crystal and I were delighted that our daddy had come back. We knew he was courting Mama and hoped she'd agree to marry him again. Clyde told Audrey he had repented and that God had forgiven him. He asked Audrey to forgive him, and she did. She agreed to marry him again. On June 8, 1953 Clyde and Audrey were married at the home of Betty and Stanley Hardin at 1036 Fourth Street. Crystal and I spent the night at the Hardins while Clyde and Audrey went on a short "Honeymoon."

That evening Stanley walked with us a few blocks to a new place that had opened called "The Dairy Queen" and bought ice cream cones for Tana, Janie, Crystal and me. That act of kindness has stayed with me all these years. Every time I go into that Dairy Queen in Las Vegas, I remember how much it meant to me and to Crystal for Stanley to take the time to take us there. Betty, too, was a wonderful role model for children. She was strict and never let them get away with wrong doing, but she also was very understanding. We thought she was a wonderful aunt.

Mother took time off from work and we all spent a vacation at the ranch. We girls slept in the main Fifteen Dollar Cabin and Clyde and Audrey slept in the back "bedroom" cabin. The creek was running again, and we had a wonderful time. An article in the *Las Vegas Daily Optic*, written by Audrey, appeared the next week:

An archway in the Dr. Stanley Hardin home served as the setting for a simple Monday noon wedding when Mrs. Audrey Simpson and

Clyde Joseph Simpson exchanged vows. The Rev. J. D. Pontius performed the single ring ceremony.

The couple, who were originally married in 1934 and separated in 1948, were attended by Dr. and Mrs. Stanley Hardin and the couple's daughters, Crystal and Dorothy Simpson who served as maid of honor and flower girl, respectively.

Mrs. Simpson wore a printed nylon afternoon dress and a white straw hat trimmed with pearls. Her corsage was of Pina roses.

Matron of honor, Mrs. Hardin, Mrs. Simpson's sister, wore a printed silk dress with white accessories and a rose corsage. Maid of honor, Crystal Simpson, wore a blue dress with red accessories and a red corsage. As flower girl, Dorothy Simpson wore all white including a white ribbon headdress with white flowers in her hair. Preceding the ceremony Mrs. Hardin sang "I Love You Truly."

Following the wedding a family dinner was held at the Hardin home, highlighted by a wedding cake baked and decorated by Crystal and Dorothy Simpson. The cake baked in the shape of a large heart was topped by frosted rose buds of pink and yellow and a blue ribbon decoration to represent a wedding knot.

Mrs. Simpson, President of the Las Vegas branch of the National League of American Pen Women, has been society editor for the Optic since March, 1952. She is presently on two weeks' vacation from her duties with the Optic.

Mr. Simpson, formerly a long time resident of Las Vegas, has been serving as a chef in Albuquerque for the past year. Following a two week's vacation spent with their daughters visiting various points in Northern New Mexico, Mr. and Mrs. Simpson will be at home in Las Vegas.[21]

I was glad that Sister Estelle's prayer for Clyde to return and marry Audrey again had been answered. But the preacher had left, as the church was not doing well in Las Vegas. In fact, Audrey found out that the Foursquare Gospel Church people were going to sell the property and house on Seventh Street. The Church was pulling out of Las Vegas due to lack of support. The people at the Foursquare Headquarters had written to Audrey to ask if she or anyone she knew might be interested in buying the property. (One of the preachers who had been in Las Vegas probably told them she was a supporter and might be interested in buying the property.) Audrey and Clyde had helped them build that place. They had given the preacher and his family a place to stay, had given as much financial help as they could, and had attended services there. The Foursquare Gospel Church offered the property and house to Audrey for four-thousand dollars. They let her buy it with nothing down and about forty-five dollars a month. Audrey's support of the Church was rewarded many times over by the good offer they made her for the property. Within the first year of her agreeing to buy the Seventh Street property, as Audrey was sending in monthly payments, the Church authorities sent her all the papers on it and said it was all hers. She just had to continue to make payments until it was paid off. They got out of having to pay taxes and other things that were a nuisance to them, so they turned it over to Audrey. She paid it off before very long. Although Audrey had started the negotiations before she and Clyde were married, eventually the house was placed in both names. Audrey wrote:

> I was dealing for the church building on Seventh Street. We had to cut our way through the heavy growth of weeds to get to the back door. A couple of months after we re-married in June, 1953, we moved into that house. It had a three room apartment at the back with a large auditorium in the front. Gradually we remodeled it. There was no opening from the auditorium to the back apartment, so one of the first things was cutting a door. We removed the closet between the two bedrooms, so that we had a narrow hallway, then cut out the door into the auditorium. We just cut out the entire wall the same side as the little hallway so that we could get into the front without going around outside to the front door. This gave us a large "front" room which had been the church auditorium. Clyde was working nine hours a day, 12:00 noon to 9:00 p.m. at the Home Café with one day a week, Monday, as his day off. So he had to do all of his house building in his spare time. As he was still not well, he always took a nap for an hour or so before he went to work at noon.[22]

In the 1940's, little did Audrey and Clyde realize that the building at 1620 Seventh Street which they had helped to build for a Foursquare Church would someday belong to them as a home—a house which was twenty-eight feet by sixty feet in size. Audrey wrote: "The Foursquare people decided to give up the church in Vegas so Clyde and I bought the building in August of 1953 and moved in. Clyde began remodeling. I worked day and night and the girls grew up."[23]

When Clyde and Audrey married in June, there was no job available at the Home Café, so Clyde worked for the 85 Restaurant on Grand Avenue for a while. Soon, however, there was a job at the Home Café for more pay, so Clyde resigned from the 85 Café and went back to his old stomping grounds at the

Home Café. He made about thirty dollars a week. Between Audrey and Clyde, they were able to buy necessities and have a little left over to improve the house.

Crystal, Clyde, Audrey, Dorothy Simpson, June 8, 1953 wedding dinner
Source: **Simpson Archives, photo by Betty Hardin**

In our spare time, we worked on improving the yard and the house. There were some perennial flowers planted at the side of the house and some other plants and shrubs as well. Crystal and I grew flowers. Once or twice we took second and third prizes at a local flower show. The arrangements were judged not only by the beauty and quality of the flowers but on how well they were arranged. We were competing with wealthy home owners, women who stayed home every day to keep house and tend their gardens. We were busy school girls and our parents worked full time. Consequently, we were proud of those prizes.

Little did Audrey realize when she moved to the ranch in 1949 with her daughters that within four years she would be re-married to Clyde, would be buying a large house in Las Vegas, and would have a job as a journalist—a career she'd always wanted. The only thing better would be to live at the ranch in a big ranch house—the dream Audrey and Clyde worked for. But they knew it would happen someday. In the meantime, they enjoyed the ranch on holidays and worked to make their house in Las Vegas the very best and happiest home possible.

As mentioned previously, Audrey loved wildlife and did not like irresponsible hunting. If a man hunted to feed a hungry family, that was different. There were times she had wished she and her family had been able to have meat when her mother could only manage meager meals of pinto beans with bread. But Audrey did not like the idea of killing game for no reason, as some hunters would shoot an animal and then leave the carcass to rot. Her poem "Game-Keeper" in the *Las Vegas Daily Optic's Rodeo Edition*, reflected that attitude:

> Deep in forest where the lights are dim,
> High on the mountain by black rock rim,
> Come the city men in caps of red.
> They ask me to show where the wild deer bed.
> Seen any tracks? And Where? they say.
> My eyes blink dull in the bright of day,
> For I play dumb, and I will not tell,
> But I know where. I know very well.
> I know steep trails where the wild deer lurks.
> I know which pine holds the rooting turks.
> I know deep caves where the black bears dwell.
> Hunters for fun cannot make me tell!
> While they are hunted, my good friends cower,
> In an aspen grove or rocky tower,
> Watching for barrels that gleam and glow,
> Watching of hunters through veils of snow.
> Look to your lives, my beautiful friends!
> I hope you hide till the season ends.
> I love you wild and I want you free.
> And you shall die not because of me.[24]

Whenever Audrey saw a deer, she would remember her poem and hope the animal would live through another hunting season.

"You shall die not because of me," she'd say under her breath.

The Church, The House, The Home

When we moved into the house at 1620 Seventh Street in the summer of 1953, there was a great deal to be done. There was cold running water in the house but no hot water heater. There was a bathtub and toilet but they were not hooked up. The bathtub could be used, as it drained outside, so Mama heated water on the kitchen stove in big pans and gave us enough water, added with the cold, for a bath. There was an outhouse at the back of the property. The city sewer line and city gas line had not yet come through. Only a few people lived in this "country" area outside of town known as Seventh Street Extension. The water was hooked up to city water and we had electricity, but there were no other city services. However, that part of the area was building up fast, so in a short time city gas and sewer lines became available; and as soon as possible we got hooked up to them.

One of the first things we did was water the dying lawn and fir trees in front of the house. Those trees had come from Forest Springs Ranch! The Roelfs had come up and picked them out with us and had transplanted them to the front of the church. They were very small, but they had thrived. We also watered the flowers that were planted along the side of the building. The back yard consisted of a tire swing, a playhouse that John had built for Joyce, the outhouse, a storage shed, and weeds. But soon Audrey and Clyde turned the back yard into a vegetable garden. We enjoyed the play house, and it also served as a tool shed for Clyde's various implements.

We enjoyed seeing all the green things come alive. The lawn was amazing. Almost overnight it turned from yellow-brown stubble to green grass again. We had feared it was hopelessly dead. Also, the flowers along the house began to bloom.

There was no electric stove in the kitchen—just a hot plate. One of the first purchases for the house was a hot water heater. There was an old coal furnace in the basement, but Audrey was afraid if it got too hot the house would burn down. So we used it in the most bitter winter days for a short time only. There was an old oil heater that we used for a while, but as soon as city gas lines came in, Clyde purchased a gas heater and a kitchen range—after digging the line. We also had an indoor bathroom at last, after the city sewer line came through, so

Daddy did away with the outhouse. He dug the ditch from the house to the city line, nearly to the back of the property, to put in the pipes.

Then a refrigerator was purchased. It was the first time I could remember ever having a refrigerator! With a car, hot and cold running water, a heater, a gas cook stove, and a refrigerator, Crystal and I thought we were rich. But best of all we now had both parents again, and it was a happy family. Each Christmas we would all go to Christmas Tree Hill at Forest Springs Ranch and pick out a tree. The house in town had high ceilings, so we would get one that came up to the ceiling.

Our neighbors, the Maloofs, had been in their house next door for several years and had all the modern conveniences. George Maloof managed a store in old town that his mother had established. He had married Cora McGrath, daughter of Tom McGrath, one of the old-timers in Las Vegas. At that time they had two children: Wardie Jo and Georgie. Later they had Zian. They were very good neighbors and welcomed us enthusiastically.

On his days off, Clyde did a tremendous amount of work on the house. He put a door way between the parsonage and the auditorium to open up the house. The former auditorium made a nice living room. Clyde petitioned off about half of it. One half made a big living room and the other half made two bedrooms, one of each side of a hallway leading into the doorway he had cut between the auditorium and parsonage. The only problem was that the auditorium part of the house was lower than the parsonage part, so he had to put a step in the doorway. Later, after Holly was born, he made a ramp so she would not fall and could go down the ramp in her walker. Audrey recalled:

> Eventually we tiled the floor of the combination dining room and kitchen. The two small bedrooms were left without closet space so we knew one of the first items of change was to build closets. Clyde bought sheet rock and 2 x 4's and began making bedrooms and closets. The auditorium was divided so that we had a 16 x 20 foot living room across the front of the building with two bedrooms. When the bedrooms were partitioned off we left a four foot hall between them as access from the front of the building to the back. Clyde built closets along the east wall of the north bedroom and along the west wall of the south bedroom. After the partitions were in came the taping of the cracks between the sheetrock and painting the entire walls. One bedroom was colored pink, the other blue. We found colors really make a difference in the warmth of a room. The blue room always felt gloomy and cold. The kitchen had been a ghastly green, so we repainted it to a light cream. It took us years to remodel to 28 by 60 foot building.[1]

Clyde put cement sidewalks around the house and finished the basement. Clyde enlarged the basement and put in some good solid steps. Audrey wrote, "Clyde hauled more than 100 wheelbarrows full of dirt from the basement and remodeled it into a storage and work shop."[2]

After several years of drought, finally rain came. Sometimes it came all at once. One summer it rained so hard water came up over the door of the basement (which was just a few inches off the ground) and flooded the basement. After that, Clyde built up the cement around the door so that it would not flood so easily again. He made the basement room that housed the furnace quite large. It was the Cold War era, and everyone was supposed to have a fall-out shelter. That basement was ours.

The House on Seventh Street, left to right: Bob Simpson, Opal Simpson, Dorothy Simpson, Crystal Simpson and Betty Hardin, 1954. *Source:* Simpson Archives, photo by Charles Vivian Shearer

When I was nine years old, my mother wanted me to have piano lessons. The old piano had been moved from the ranch and sat in our big living room, the room that had once been the church auditorium. I began lessons with Glydia K. Barila. Crystal wanted to take lessons too, but Mother could only afford to pay for one of us. Mrs. Barila was kind enough to invite Crystal to sit in on the lessons, saying she could learn as I learned. Crystal sat in on one or two lessons but she felt that it didn't seem right somehow, so after that I went for lessons alone. We had recitals once or twice and year, and since Crystal had a beautiful voice and sang in church, Mrs. Barila asked her to sing at the recitals. Accompanied by Mrs. Barila, Crystal sang beautiful songs Mrs. Barila had composed. She sang "Señorita," "I Wake Up Smiling," and "Merry-Go-Round." Then several children and I participated, playing memorized pieces. Usually more than a dozen parents and friends attended, including Audrey. Glydia Barila had a music club for the children where we learned about composers and such. Jimmy Leger was the reporter of the group, and items about our meetings appeared in the *Optic*. Jimmy later majored in music and became a music professor at New Mexico Highlands University. Audrey and my piano teacher—who was also an aspiring writer and artist—were good friends.

My parents sacrificed for me to have piano lessons. I began to play the piano in church when I was fifteen and became the church pianist at Emmanuel Baptist Church when I was sixteen. I was church pianist wherever I went for years, including a little Spanish mission in Salt Lake City when I was a student at the University of Utah. Crystal and I participated in many music performances of one kind or another—at church, at recitals, at school events. Sometimes Crystal sang for various programs and I accompanied her. At home we enjoyed our piano and often entertained for family gatherings. Crystal was encouraged in her singing and that led to a music scholarship to Highlands University. Had she not received that scholarship, she would not have attended college. And had she not attended college, I probably would not have either. She encouraged me.

One day Audrey was out in the garden early in the morning, just after sunrise. She and Clyde grew peas, green beans, onions, pumpkins, squash, radishes, and other vegetables. One year Clyde grew green chile. On this particular morning, Audrey looked up and saw a cigar shaped "plane" flying low over the area. But it made no sound. She saw what looked like windows all along it. Then, suddenly, it took off at an incredible speed and was gone. Audrey was not so skeptical about UFO's after that.

Since we had a big house in a fairly central location, we began to hold family reunions there. Most years all seven of Mabel's children came. They always visited with Mabel and Vivian. Through the years, Bob and Opal brought Bobby, Jackie, and Donna from Silver City. Edward and Volene with Shirley and Eddie came from Grand Junction, Colorado. Betty and Stanley came from Portales with their children, Tana, Janie and Twila. Milly and Orval came from Pot Creek, bringing Roger, Sam, and Dianna. Jessica and her husband "Red" Braziel came from Santa Rosa with their children: Dwight, Russell, Yvonne, Yvette, and Paul. Frank and his wife, Margaret, traveled from Texas with Frankie Allen, Carol Ann, and Carl.

Sometimes members of Clyde's family would also visit. After Donald's death Clyde only had five siblings: Glen, Ouida, Clyde, Robert (Bob), Rhea, and Mary Valina Simpson. Rhea and her husband, Clint Oglesbee, had one daughter, Adele. Tommy and Ouida Sheffield had several children, including a daughter about my age, Jewel. Glen and his wife Clarabelle also lived in Albuquerque with their children, Marilyn and Jerry. We saw Bob and Opal fairly often, especially after they moved from Reserve, New Mexico to Las Vegas in 1961.

Jessica's children had red hair, like their father. Sometime after one of Jessica's children was born, Audrey wrote a poem, "Relative-ly Speaking."

> Auntie says, "Oh!
> How cute!
> But boy! That red hair!
> I wonder where
> It came from?"
> And you know
> She doesn't care.
>
> Grandma looks at baby.
> She comments on his eyes.
> "Just like his grandpa's—
> Let me rock him if
> He cries."
>
> Daddy says, "Hi,
> Bouncer!"
> While kissing a pink cheek,
> He thinks how long
> the time
> 'Till they can fish
> the creek.[3]

There were other reunions that we attended. We sometimes went to Albuquerque to have Thanksgiving or Christmas dinner at the home of Clyde's mother Addie Simpson (our granny) or at the home of Audrey's father, "Jack" Clements (our grandpa.)

Our grandpa and his wife Mabel had bought a house on South Broadway. Crystal and I, as well as Bobby, Jackie, Donna, Shirley, Eddie, Tana, Janie and other relatives always enjoyed visiting Grandpa Clements and Mable. They had several dogs and cats, including Grandpa's Teddy, a collie. Grandpa Clements had rescued several animals, including a cat that had been hit by a car and had lost an eye. He loved animals and had great empathy for them. Once he saw a man beating his dog. He grabbed the man and took away the stick he was using. He threw the stick away in disgust and told the man he'd beat him within an inch of his life if he ever saw him hurting an animal again. The surprised man didn't offer to fight.

"Since you don't want this dog, I'm taking him," Grandpa said.

"Go ahead. You'll see he's no good," the man retorted.

The dog turned out to be a loyal pet, one of the best Grandpa had ever had.

Donna and I were almost the same age, and as double cousins, we were like sisters. We enjoyed running through the sand hills in Grandpa's big yard on South Broadway, a place that was almost out in the country in those days. I was sad when Grandpa and Mable sold that place. But the wind blew the sand around unmercifully. Grandpa and Mabel both had asthma. So when Grandpa Clements became ill, they moved to another house near a beautiful green park.

We had not had any pets since Corliss was hit by a car. But now we had a big place on Seventh Street, so of course, we had pets. We had kept our cat, Inky, and she presented us with kittens every so often. Some we placed in homes and some we kept. We also were able to have a dog. Clyde acquired a medium sized, black and white dog he named Duke. Daddy brought him home to me. I spent a great deal of time playing in the backyard with Duke after school and on weekends. I was ready to start the sixth grade when Duke got very sick. Mother called Dr. C. E. Miller, the veterinarian, and he came to the house. He said there was no hope for Duke; he had hepatitis. Duke was euthanized. I was grief stricken, even though Mother tried to explain it was the only kind thing to do. School started the next day or two, so I had my work to keep me busy. And then Clyde brought home another black and white dog he named Laddy. (Daddy always named the dogs; that was his job.) Little did we know that Laddy would get hepatitis, too, as the organisms stayed in the soil. So he, too, had to be put down. After that we always got immunizations for our dogs.

Dr. Miller was a tall, elderly gentleman with grey hair. He wore a big hat and cowboy boots. I remember hearing the local news read by Ernie Thwaites on KFUN one evening when he announced the sudden death of Dr. Miller and hailed him as a hero. The doctor had been riding in the backseat of a car and apparently had seen a crash coming. A little girl, a relative, was sitting beside him. It was said that Dr. Miller wrapped his big body around the little girl in order to spare her from the impact and saved her life, but his own body was crushed in the wreck.

Only a few years later, in 1963, Ernie Thwaites himself died a sudden death when his private plane, which he flew all over the state to cover news, was caught in a thunder storm and he was killed. There was a great void in the town after Ernie Thwaites was gone. He had been a kind of spokesman for Las Vegas, even though not everyone agreed with his conservative Republican views. After some time the station was managed by Dennis Mitchell, who eventually bought KFUN and ran it for many years until he retired and sold it to Mr. and Mrs. Joseph Baca.

Audrey's career was thriving. She not only wrote as a reporter for every day news at the *Optic,* but she also interviewed people, attended meetings, wrote feature stories, and wrote items of historical interest. She searched old papers and wrote about long forgotten legends, facts, and stories of local interest. For instance, she wrote a brief history of Las Vegas, giving a description of the area. She wrote for the *Optic*:

> The first people in the valley named it Las Vegas, the meadows. And the river was called Gallinas, for the wild turkeys that nested the length of the stream.
>
> But the land is still the same. The sun shines brightly over the meadows. The same incredible blue looks down on the adobe homes. And even as in 1821 when the first settlers are said to have petitioned the Mexican government for a grant of land here in the big meadows, today the people look upon their rio Gallinas and Las Vegas and know that they have a fine place in which to live.[4]

Although *Gallinas* means chicken, it is interesting to know that it was actually named for turkeys!

Many people did not know about the successful businesses and industry of early Las Vegas. Audrey wrote another *Optic* item, "Sugar Cane Once Grown in Las Vegas Section:"

> Everyone is familiar with the corn, chile, and frijoles, or pinto beans, grown in every cleared strip of land around Las Vegas.
>
> A less publicized crop that was once widely grown in the warm cedar country in San Miguel county is sugar cane.
>
> Many of the little fields, cleared of small branched cactus, piñon and cedar trees, were used to raise sugar cane. And today some of them still grow sugar cane.
>
> There are still a number of sugar cane mills in the country. These mills are fashioned so that the green cane is crushed between rollers. The rollers are powered with a horse walking in a circle rotating the mill.
>
> Juice squeezed from the cane by the mill drips into a trough

which leads into a kettle. The kettles of syrup are then boiled, often over an outdoor fire, until the syrup reaches the right consistency.

There used to be a sugar cane mill at Chapelle. There are still mills in working order at Trujillo and Delia. The one at Delia is sitting right next to the highway on the road to Santa Rosa.

C. A. Sullivan at Delia reports that in recent years he has processed as much as 1,000 gallons of sugar cane syrup. This syrup was jugged and sold in Mora, Ocate and other northern communities. Little money is handled in such transactions. The syrup is traded for chickens, peas, beans or other ranch produce.

A stalk of sugar cane, cut from the field, is used by country children in place of lollipops.

O. F. Baca, San Miguel county agriculture agent, reports that the sugar cane grown around Las Vegas makes an unusually excellent quality of molasses. It is mostly grown by the people in small quantities for home use. The quality is outstanding due to our climate and growing conditions, Baca says.[5]

Another, much larger, industry was sawmilling. In a story, "Lesperance Sawmill One Of Pioneer Industries," *Las Vegas Daily Optic*, Audrey wrote that pioneer residents recall that large sawmill operations were once conducted on Falls Creek, west of Las Vegas. An old history book points out that in the 1890's the Pedro Lesperance sawmill was sixteen miles west of Las Vegas.[6]
Audrey's *Optic* article stated:

> A pioneer resident was Pedro Lesperance who had a sawmill in the 1890's in the Mineral Hill area, 16 miles west of Las Vegas. Pedro Lesperance was born in Sorel, Quebec, Canada in 1839, came to New Mexico in 1857 to stay with an uncle who had been in New Mexico since 1822. Pedro inherited his uncle's property in 1879 after working with him through the years. The sawmill, built shortly after he arrived in New Mexico, was said to be powered by water and had a capacity for cutting 8,000 feet of lumber every day. Pedro married Miss Sabastina Benavides in 1863. They had seven children living in the 1890's. In more recent years there has been a Lesperance sawmill, moved about the Mineral Hill district by descendents of Pedro Lesperance. Lumber cut on the Lesperance mill is to be found in the construction of many homes around Las Vegas. Another early day saw mill furnished lumber for Ft. Union. It was located above Las Vegas Hot Springs. It was owned by Whitlock and Lease. It was a

water mill with the old fashioned upright saw, said to have a capacity for cutting 1,000 feet a day.[7]

In another article for the *Las Vegas Daily Optic*, Audrey wrote:

> Sawmill operations in the Las Vegas area have been an important part of the economy of the area since the old fashioned water mills were placed along numerous streams to operate on water power with their whirling saws tearing big pines into rough lumber for many of the buildings in Las Vegas.[8]

Audrey's little Brownie box camera not only came in handy for family events, but she also used it for photographs to accompany articles she sold. Additionally, she found it came in handy for the *Optic* stories. In the *Rodeo Edition* of the *Las Vegas Daily Optic*, July 31, 1952, she had a picture of the Big Cross from "The Big Cross Trail."[9] She also had a picture of a snow scene, "Mountain Winter."[10] And Audrey included a picture of our Fifteen Dollar House which had the caption:

> Mountain cabins like this are common around Las Vegas. They are used as year-around homes by many people. An axe, a saw and a hammer are all the tools required to build this type of cabin. Even the inexperienced ax man can build one of these cabins within ten days for small cost.[11]

Audrey enjoyed sharing her knowledge and her experiences, one reason she enjoyed writing. She always extended kindness to everyone. If she baked several loaves of bread, she would take a loaf to someone—to her mother or a friend. Audrey explained that she didn't give things away because she expected something but rather for the joy of giving. "A writer can give something to the world no one else can give if the words are right," she said.

3

A Notebook in her Hand:
Newspaper Reporter, Journalist, Author

As a journalist, Audrey always said she had a "nose for news." She was Society Page Editor, Church Page Editor, and general reporter for the Las Vegas Daily Optic. She attending meetings, reported on social events, wrote feature stories, and conducted interviews.

There was an organization of some of the ministers called "The Ministerial Alliance." The ministers often brought news to her. After Audrey retired, someone once commented that Audrey was the most "ecumenical" reporter they knew; she didn't show any bias for one religion over the other. She gave equal space to all of them and treated everyone fairly and impartially. She didn't impose her own views on others but was ready to listen to their concepts.

"Why should I show favoritism of one religion over the other?" she said. "I believed in giving all of them fair and equal coverage."

Audrey had been saved in the Church of the Nazarene, baptized in The Church of Christ, and attended several churches. As a minister's wife, she had helped found the "Full Gospel Mission" in San Geronimo and the Las Vegas church where Clyde preached. She had attended the Baptist church. She had helped build the Foursquare Gospel Church in Las Vegas. As far as she could tell, God was to be found in any place where true believers come to worship. She didn't believe that "anything goes." She believed Bible principles should be followed. But she didn't believe in splitting hairs over irrelevant matters, either.

Audrey's job was not easy. She would walk around town every afternoon talking to people and asking if they had any news such as upcoming weddings, family reunions and other social events for the Society Page. Some people didn't want their names mentioned in the paper. One lady called her up and bawled her out for using her name in a society page item, probably as having been in attendance at some social event or a member of a club that had met.

"Never use my name without my express permission!" the woman ordered her. Audrey always believed that a soft answer turns away wrath, so she was polite. But later she thought of a "perfect squelch" that she published in

The Saturday Evening's Post "Perfect Squelch" feature. Writing under her middle name, Shirley, she told of a newspaper reporter's being told by an irate lady never to use her name without her calling and giving permission. The reporter answered, "Does that include your obituary notice?" The *Post* cartoonist showed an editor sitting behind his desk with a typewriter in front of him and a visor over his eyes, telephone to his ear, and the telephone line coming from the place the woman was calling from—a place filled with smoke, fire, and pitch forks.

Audrey was paid a hundred dollars for that story. She had also had another "Perfect Squelch" published in which she told about tourists who visit New Mexico curio shops with the idea of seeing everything and buying little or nothing, giving the clerks a difficult time.[1] That "Perfect Squelch" also brought Audrey a hundred dollar check.[2]

Many of the stories which appeared in the *Optic* were written by Audrey with no bi-line. The only way someone would know now that those stories were hers is that she had saved a few papers and marked the stories she wrote with her initials or had written the comment, "My Story, by Audrey" in her handwriting. There are very few newspapers left in the Simpson Archives due to the fire of 1971. However, Mabel Shearer had a few Optics she had saved because Audrey's stories were in them—some marked with Audrey's initials—and several editions of the Optic were saved when Audrey evacuated the house prior to the fire.

One such story which Audrey indicated she had written was entitled, "Visit of Teddy Roosevelt Is Recalled by Vegas Pioneer." It appeared in the August 1, 1957 *Optic*. Audrey thought she was very fortunate to get to meet some of the "old-timers" such as some of the rough riders or prize winning cowboys.

One story that did have a bi-line was, "Indians Captured Boy, Adopted Him; Made Subject of History." It was in the *Rodeo Edition, Las Vegas Daily Optic*, August 1, 1957 and told a fascinating, true story. Audrey interviewed people and referred to a book, *Andele or the Mexican-Kiowa Captive*. It was written by the Rev. J. J. Methvin, Superintendent of Methvin Institute, Andarko, Oklahoma Territory. The book was copyrighted in 1899. It told the details of the capture of fourteen-year-old Andres Martinez on October 6, 1866. Apparently in 1872 when soldiers from Ft. Sill attempted to take a census of Indians, they found fourteen white captives.[3]

Audrey often commented that she wrote a large portion of some of the *Las Vegas Daily Optic Rodeo Editions*. Indeed, her marked copies show that she wrote many of the items which appeared in those editions. However, some newspapers in the family files were not marked. Undoubtedly some of the stories with no bi-line were written by Audrey. Stories with no bi-lines include the following headlines from the July 30, 1958 *Las Vegas Daily Optic*: "Early Cowpunchers

Rugged Individuals"(story and photograph of S. Omar Barker); "Bulldogging Champ Recalls Rodeoing," (interview and photograph of Dee Bibb); "The 'Cowboy' Is A Working Hand As Well As Rodeo Hand;" "Pickup Men Look Out for Horse Too;" "Long Journey from Germany To Vegas" (interview and photograph of Ludwig Ilfeld); "Las Vegas Founded In 1835 Is Home of Rodeo, Rough Riders;" "Rodeo Scoring Makes Every Rodeo A 'Must';"and "Bulldogging Got Name From Lip Biting Cowboy."

That last story said that cowboys call the event *bulldogging* because Bill Pickett, the cowboy who invented it, used to bite the lip of the steer, bulldog fashion, to encourage it to fall down. But in the rule book it's called *steer wrestling*, a title that is a more accurate description of the skill. The story said that Pickett had pounced on his first steer from horseback in a rage after the intractable critter refused to be driven into a corral. The promoters of the wild west show he was working for in 1902 thought it was a good stunt and Pickett performed it as an exhibition for several seasons. "Years before it evolved into a contest event, the cowboys quit biting the steer. But the name stuck."[4]

One story with no bi-line in that 1958 *Rodeo Edition* of the *Optic* which was marked as Audrey's was an interview with Charles O'Malley, a long-time Las Vegan who had served as parade marshal "in all the 43 years since the first cowpoke tasted the dust in the local Cowboys' Rodeo and Reunion."[5] Audrey quoted O'Malley as stating that he had lived in Las Vegas since 1899 and never regretted a minute of it. O'Malley started his career in the telephone and electrical business in San Francisco when he worked for the Edison Company. Then he worked in Colorado for the telephone companies. Audrey quoted O'Malley: "Those were still the days in Colorado when you could see gold bars piled in stacks with United States soldiers around to see that nobody got too grabby."[6] Then the Las Vegas Independent Telephone Company brought O'Malley to the Meadow City to take part in a battle with the Colorado Bell Company. O'Malley was a part-owner of the Las Vegas Independent Telephone Company and said that their rates were lower than the Colorado company. He got out of the telephone business in Las Vegas in 1907 and went into general electrical contracting business. He had a little electrical shop in Las Vegas.

Audrey must have been impressed about O'Malley's telephone company stories. She wrote in the margin of the front page of that paper: "My story on O'Malley tells of 2 phone companies." Audrey enjoyed writing up her interviews and often talked of interviewing some of the "old-timers." She interviewed, among others, some of the original Rough Riders; Dee Bibb; Tom McGrath; and other prominent citizens. I believe she also interviewed actor Cliff Robertson when he came to the rodeo one year but I have no papers on that interview.

Audrey would sometimes mention how much she had enjoyed an interview and some of the things she had learned. One day I mentioned that S. Omar Barker had spoken to one of my classes at Highlands University about poetry. Audrey asked if he told the story about his brand. When I said he had not, she proceeded to tell the story. Mr. Barker wanted to apply for a brand. He wanted to use his initials, and to make it unique, he wanted one of the letters to be lying sideways, instead of vertical, or what is called "lazy." He said he was refused for that request when he put in his application because "Some other 'lazy-S O B' had already applied for the brand and beat me to it."

Among the many stories that did not list Audrey's name as the author (but were marked by her) was one called "Cowgal's Dream Broken by Horse Bear Spooked" which appeared in the July, 1952 *Rodeo Edition* of the *Optic*. It was based on Audrey's own experience.

>Did you ever wonder what a cow gal dreamed about as she loped along the trail?
>
>You're right! And here is the true story of the way one cow gal's dream went. Her hair was flying in loose curls below her gray Stetson. She was wearing a loose leather thong under her chin to hold the hat in place as she cut the breeze down the canyon. There was a light rain falling so she had on a loose unbuttoned slicker.
>
>The gal had already ridden 20 miles that day so she figured her bronc was pretty well wore down and wouldn't spook easy. She sat easily in the saddle, her movements one with the bay horse. She held the bridle reins lightly, not thinking of riding, the horse, or the trail.
>
>The gal was dreaming. Dreaming of a wedding. Her own. And that tall wide shouldered cow puncher from Blue Canyon was beside her.
>
>Oh it wasn't an ordinary wedding. This wedding she was dreaming of was being held in front of a packed grandstand at the Cowboy's Reunion. She was wearing a fringed doeskin skirt and blouse, white boots, and hat—and riding a white horse. Her bridegroom was riding a Palomino.
>
>The band would strike up the wedding march and she would ride slowly across the arena to the preacher on an iron gray horse. The cow puncher would be waiting there with his hat pushed back and his blue eyes shining.
>
>No, maybe he better not have a hat on. Let the ring bearer on the Shetland pony carry his hat until after the ceremony.

As soon as the preacher finished reading from the Book the bride and groom, amid the cheers of a thousand leather lunged friends, would swing their horses and dash full tilt out of the arena.

While the gal was dreaming of racing with the puncher on the Palomino a big black bear paused in the timber beside the trail. He sensed the intruder and turned to crash through the brush.

The bay horse, who had no part in the dream, smelled the bear and heard the crashing. He stood straight up on his hind feet in the trail, whirled, and ran back the way he had come.

The gal's hat few over her face with the sharp turn. The Slicker flipped up and tangled over her head. She had been sitting relaxed as she dreamed, her hand holding the reins loosely.

In a flash at the horse's first movement her knees gripped the animal like a burr and her fingers grasped the reins tightly, trying to control the runaway horse.

With the other hand she worked at untangling the slicker from around her head and getting the hat, still held by the chin strap, from in front of her face. At the same time she was riding. Riding the runaway bay like the born horsewoman she was.

Since she could not see she had to give the horse his head. And yet pull up some without turning him with the pressure of the reins on his neck.

By the time she got untangled she was a mile along the trail from where the bear spooked the bay.

She finally controlled the frightened horse, turned him around and headed back along the trail, easing him around the spooky spot.

The bear and the dream have vanished. The Gal and the rider on the Palomino? Their little cow gals and cow punchers are expert riders.[7]

Anyone knowing Audrey would know this story was autobiographical. Audrey, "a born horsewoman," had ridden her horse in similar circumstances, encountered bears and mountain lions, handled run-away horses and tamed wild colts. And all the time she had dreamed of living in her mountains with the man of her dreams, having a big ranch house of her own, bringing up their children under the sheltering arms of the friendly Sangre de Cristos. She dreamed of having a college degree and being a successful writer. Some of her dreams came true. Many felt short of her expectations. But whatever happened, the mountains were always there, sometimes brutal, always beautiful, forever solid and secure.

A Pencil Over her Ear: Writer, Editor, Career Woman

Audrey's "trademark" was a pencil over her ear. Audrey was ambidextrous, so when one hand got tired of writing, she switched to the other. She took many notes, as part of her job was attending meetings and reporting on them. She always needed her pencil handy, whether she was typing on her manual typewriter at work or doing some free lance writing on her old manual Royal typewriter at home. So she would "park" her pencil behind one ear or the other. She wore her hair pulled back in a pun or, more often, in two braids that were then twisted up around her head with some curls puffed up in front of the braids. In any case, her ears were exposed, so putting a pencil behind one of them was handy when she wanted to reach up and grab it to write a hasty note. No rummaging through a purse or pocket book for her. And many dresses had no pockets. So the pencil went behind an ear.

Audrey Simpson at her desk at the Optic, 1957
Source: **Simpson Archives, photo by** *Las Vegas Daily Optic* **Photographer**

Audrey was elected "reporter" for nearly every organization to which she belonged, including Business and Professional Women, Rebekahs, Does, and the Pen Women's Club. Everyone depended on her to "get the story right." She covered weddings and other social events as Society Editor at the Optic. Many times I saw her multi-tasking: typing or writing notes while talking on the telephone while reading what was coming over the teletype, for instance.

The *Rodeo Edition* of the *Optic* was a tremendous amount of work but it was different from the daily routine and allowed Audrey to do some creative writing rather than the straight reporting she usually did. A typical Society page of the *Las Vegas Daily Optic* in the 1960s was entitled "*Patios, Places and People: For and About Women*, Audrey Simpson, Editor, Woman's Page." It would have items about weddings, engagements, bridal showers, and would often have pictures of such events. It had "Hospital Notes" which gave patients admitted and dismissed from St. Anthony's Hospital and the Las Vegas Hospital "in the past 24 hours." It gave "New Arrivals" for the births of babies at the two local hospitals, giving names of parents and sometimes grandparents. It also had the "Calendar" which gave upcoming social events. It featured Audrey's "*Por Aqui En Las Vegas*" which gave news items about social events. She mentioned individuals returning from vacation, visitors to families in Las Vegas, family reunions, and so on.

A typical Church Page in the 1960s, "Strong Churches Make Strong Communities," would feature "Minute Meditation," an article written by one of the local ministers; news about church events; stories about churches; and news about special services or ministers

As mentioned before, Audrey wrote a large part of every special *Rodeo Edition* of the *Las Vegas Daily Optic*. In the July 30, 1958 edition, she wrote about the traditional rooster pull in "Rooster Pull Is Sport of Riders In Area Villages."

> This combined horse race and display of acrobatic skill brings out every girl in the village dressed in her best; and the middle-aged and old men and women who watch recall that many a young man has won his wife at a rooster pull.[1]

In the 1960's the *Optic* put out their special "Rodeo and Fiesta" edition. Audrey wrote many stories for those special papers. She was given a bi-line for some of them such as "Fiesta Traditional Good Time in Vegas:"

> Fiesta! In this land of legends the very word makes the heart beat faster and feet tingle in anticipation of music, dancing and frolicking fun of all types.

> In the early days many Saint's Days were observed with Fiesta, some lasting nearly a week. The old time Spanish families often set aside certain days each year for feasting and entertainment at the scattered ranches in the vast valleys and mesas of New Mexico.[2]

The story went on to describe celebrations such as horse races, dancing in the plazas and "merry making lasting for long hours." She described one of the most common events, "the rooster pull," previously described. Then the article went on to describe the music, "ranging from old traditional Spanish dances, popular with Dons of Coronado's time, to that of the present." Audrey mentioned that the music was provided by a couple of guitarists and a violinist, "playing fast numbers in order that gay caballeros might swing brightly dressed señoritas or señoras to the type of music that fires the blood and adds to the festive mood."[3]

Indeed, those rodeo/fiesta days were spectacular. A big parade preceded the events. Our neighbor, George Maloof, was the Parade Marshal. An ad in the *Optic* showed him with "Greets and Welcome" and mentioned the "Payless Grocery" owned by Mrs. O. Maloof. The Mounted Patrol always played a big role in the activities. The Thursday, July 1, 1965 *Las Vegas Optic* had a picture on the front page of W. R. "Shy" Scheihagen, the man who directed arrangements for the Cowboy's Reunion Rodeo for Mounted Patrol Troop 3 which sponsored it. Many well known Las Vegans took part in the annual event. The July 6, 1965 *Rodeo Edition* of the *Optic* had a picture of the famous Dee Bill with a caption: "Half a Century in rodeo, Dee Bibb, Las Vegas rancher, served as field judge in timed events in the 27th annual Cowboy's Reunion Rodeo here July 2-5. Bibb, former World Champion bulldogger appeared in his first rodeo in 1915." The photo of Bibb was taken by a colleague of Audrey's at the Optic, Mr. Bill Magill.[4] Audrey knew Dee and his wife Mable for many years. After Dee passed away, Mable lived many years and was one of Audrey's good friends.

The well known writer and poet, S. Omar Barker, also contributed some items to the *Rodeo Edition, Las Vegas Daily Optic*. In the July 30, 1958 edition, his photograph appeared along with an interview. The story said that he had served as rodeo publicity director on several occasions during the early 1920's and at the time, 1958, he was President of Western Writers of America. He was quoted:

> "The men who served as directors of the early Reunion did much to channel my writing efforts toward the depicting of the West as those men and others like them actually lived it," he explains. "The tough fiber of their minds and bodies, their sense of fairness, their broad vision, and their grass-roots humor, all taken together in many combinations

represents the best that the West had to offer."⁵

The Cowboy's Reunion Rodeo usually had three performances, Friday, Saturday, and Sunday. Even after "the last man" of the rough riders was gone, the festivities continued. The June 11, 1964 *Las Vegas Daily Optic* had a banner headline, "Welcome Rough Riders, Rodeo Visitors." A picture featured Ozella Todhunter (widow of one of the rough riders) and Secretary of the Rough Riders Association, shown with Texas Judge Frank Roberts who was President of the Rough Riders Association, and with his nurse Marie Oates. Dick Sanafelt and Charles Hopping were also shown in uniform. The article below the picture was written by Audrey Simpson. She told about Mrs. Ozella Todhunter, widow of Rough Rider Ed Todhunter, sometimes known in Las Vegas as "Mrs. Rough Rider" due to her work with the Rough Riders Association and interest in obtaining a memorial for Theodore Roosevelt's men who stormed San Juan Hill in Cuba during the Spanish American War. The article told about her, her husband, and the Rough Riders. Audrey wrote:

> She (Mrs. Todhunter) talked to everyone she met about a memorial for the Rough Riders here in Las Vegas, and in 1954 the famous band decided to meet here annually "to the last man."
>
> The men wanted a place to collect and store their relics, rather than a monument, so the idea of a museum developed, she explained when interviewed. It was officially decided that a museum would be established in Las Vegas as half of the regiment were New Mexico men and they had no memorial at all. The Rough Riders had begun to send Mrs. Todhunter relics in 1953, continually adding to the collection until she had to rent a house to house it. Dr. George P. Hammer sent a machete he picked up on San Juan Hill, and a screw from the Battleship Vizzcaya, among other things.⁶

Audrey would often come home and talk about the interesting people she had interviewed. She spoke about interviewing some of the rough riders and others who made the parade and rodeo so interesting.

Every day Audrey met deadlines. She took telephone calls any time of the day or night at home, as people often called her to give her news items. The heading of the *Optic's* Society Page, "Patios, Places and People: For and About Women," had a line beneath it: "Audrey Simpson, Editor, Woman's Page - Phone 425-6796 or Home 425-7477." That was an invitation for readers to call her at home. And many people did. Audrey put in more than eight hours a day, especially when she had to attend meetings, weddings, etc. in order to write up a report. In a feature about Audrey for the *Optic*, Reporter Millicent L. Gensemer wrote:

> She [Audrey] has been society editor for the Optic since 1952 with the exception of one period of ten months when she was hospitalized for a serious illness. Especially interested in the civil improvement of Las Vegas, she is diligent in the public services she can render through the calendar notices and stories of the activities of the various organizations of the community. While she might be swamped with items to be written before her deadline, those who call additional news will only hear her courteous and pleasant voice giving sole attention to their needs. Nor does she confine her work to office hours but like a true reporter is always on the lookout for news and is never too busy to accept calls at her home day or night.[7]

Audrey was the charter president for the Las Vegas Branch of the National League of American Pen Women. As mentioned before, Audrey often invited the women to meet in her home to share their ideas, their manuscripts and their successes as writers. Audrey also belonged to several other organizations, including the Order of Eastern Star, the BPO Does Drove No. 136, and the Naomi Rebekah Lodge No. 1. The Las Vegas Branch of the Business and Professional Women's Club, in which Audrey served in several official capcities, provided a scholarship to help me to attend Highlands University.

Audrey knew how to keep secrets. She knew many, for people would confide in her and then ask her not to tell. When she interviewed people for feature stories, they would often tell her an interesting story and then say, "Don't print that. In fact, don't ever tell anyone." When she said she wouldn't tell, she had to be true to her word.

Once Audrey was asked to write a wedding story where the "sister" of the bride was actually the mother of the bride, and the "mother" of the bride was actually the grandmother of the bride. The situation had resulted when a teenager had become pregnant out of wedlock. So the young woman's mother assumed the role of mother of the new baby. Everyone just assumed she'd had another baby late in life. The actual mother of the baby, the teenager, was assumed to be the baby's sister. So the child was brought up thinking her grandmother was her mother; and her actual mother was, she thought, her sister. Finally, the baby daughter grew up and became engaged. By then she knew the truth and wanted a big wedding but didn't want small town scandal. Somehow Audrey managed to write the story without mentioning any of the relationships, just describing the bride and groom, members of the wedding party, family, etc., using names but not disclosing relationships.[8]

Sometimes Audrey overheard things she wished she hadn't. One time before she worked for the Optic, Audrey was at a meeting and was sitting behind a university president. He was boasting to a friend that he had acquired some property he had wanted to obtain for the university. Two elderly women—sisters—had a house next to the university property and had resisted selling to the university for years. Their house had burned down one night. The women had escaped in their night gowns, but their pets—all their cats—burned. Audrey remembered that night—seeing the two ladies standing on the side walk, crying, as their house burned. She was shocked to hear the president say that he was glad the situation had been "taken care of" and that the two women finally sold the property to the school after their house had burned to the ground. Audrey thought he implied that the fire had been intentionally set. He was gloating. Audrey wondered if he even had any sympathy for the poor sisters and their cats. That president did not stay at the university very long. He moved on and died in another state.[9]

Although her righteous anger flared up when she knew someone was wrong, Audrey was always pleasant to everyone whenever possible. Most of the time she was congenial, optimistic, and gave everyone the benefit of the doubt. Mrs. Gensemer concluded her story in *The Optic*:

> At home, at work or club meetings, she shows a keen interest and sympathetic understanding of people, an understanding which last year enabled her to turn the simple facts of the family's expedition to find a Christmas tree into a delightful children's tale. It is this understanding and kindness that has endeared her to the many who dial the Optic number and ask for "Audrey, please."[10]

Audrey was well acquainted with most of the writers—and aspiring writers—in the area. In addition to S. Omar Barker and his wife Elsa, Audrey worked with various writers, editors, and journalists. As mentioned before, she knew Milton Callon and Clare Turlay Newberry. She also knew professors such as Lynn I. Perrigo whose historical writing was well-known. Harold F. Thatcher also liked history and wrote articles about local history, some of which were used in the *Las Vegas Daily Optic*. He admired Audrey's writing and sometimes discussed local history with her.

Audrey bought the set of classical books called *The Great Books of the*

Western World. It was a sacrifice, but she wanted her family to have them for the benefit of our educations and for reference. She paid something like six dollars a month for a year or two. (They were among the few books that were saved from the 1971 fire.)

Crystal and I adapted to Mom's work schedule, as well as to our dad's. He worked from 12:00 noon to 9:00 p.m. He was usually off on Monday. He was still drinking. Audrey didn't mention it much, but we knew he was an alcoholic. He would drink at home some nights but he never missed a day of work. Crystal and I worried about him. I became very nervous. Mother took me to Portales to stay for a couple of weeks with Betty and Stanley. Stanley gave me chiropractic treatments and Betty's sensible approach soon set me right. I enjoyed my stay with them, even though I was homesick. Apparently Betty and Stanley's "therapy" worked. I was fine after I returned home.

Whenever weather permitted and Clyde wasn't working on a project to improve the Seventh Street house, he would work at the ranch. Audrey and Clyde enjoyed their lives in town but they still dreamed of living at the ranch. They had picked out a spot in an open field just below the site of the Fifteen Dollar House. Although Clyde had once strayed away, he was making an effort to set things right. He was a faithful husband and devoted father. He was still addicted to alcohol, but in time he was able to overcome that.

Audrey was a Society Editor who attended a variety of social events and rubbed shoulders with the rich and famous at times. But Clyde called her his mountain gal. She was still Audrey of the Mountains and dreamed of the day the family could live at their Forest Springs Ranch beneath the beautiful Sangre de Cristos.

5

Holly: Heavenly Blessing

ne day in August, 1954, Audrey was working in her garden when she injured her leg slightly. A few days later Audrey developed pain and swelling in the leg. The doctor said she had phlebitis thrombosis, a deep blood clot in the leg. She had to go to the hospital and get hooked up to an I.V. for blood thinner. Audrey probably had a condition known as Factor V Leiden—which can now be detected in a blood test, but was unknown at that time—a condition where the blood clots too readily. Audrey probably inherited it from Mabel, as Mabel also had blood clots in her legs from time to time, especially after childbirth.

I remember the evening the ambulance came to our house to take Mother to the Las Vegas Hospital, which was on Eighth Street. Nothing like that had ever happened before. Crystal and I were terrified. We were afraid Mother would never come home. Our neighbor, Cora Maloof, saw the ambulance leave and came right over to ask what was wrong. She saw two tearful girls trying to explain that their mother had become ill and the doctor had called an ambulance. She was sympathetic and said to let her know if she could be of any help.

I was in the fourth grade at Mora Avenue School. Mrs. Brown was my teacher. I remember some of my classmates: Jimmy Sampson, Billy Dixon, Roberta Belcher, and Bobby Jones. My best friend Judy Beil was attending a different school, and I missed her in my class, although we still visited when we had an opportunity.

I was enjoying the school year until Audrey got sick. I went by the hospital every day on my way home from school. But there was a rule that anyone under fourteen could not go in. I would go into the lobby and into the next room where there was a big window and one could view all the newborn babies—but children weren't allowed beyond that point where there was a nurses' station. I wished I could disguise myself as a fourteen-year-old so I could get by them. My mothers' room was just around the corner from the nurses' station—only a few feet.

Had I been braver, I might have watched until there were no nurses around and hurried into her room. My father had done that when I had my tonsils out at the age of four. That had been at the old Las Vegas Hospital on Sixth Street. Only a mother could stay with or even visit a young patient. Not even fathers were allowed in. I was glad Mother was there when the ether wore off. She told me Daddy would have been there but wasn't allowed. Sometime in the afternoon after I was awake, Daddy showed up. "I was able to sneak past the nurse," he said. He brought me a gift and then quietly left. I don't think anyone knew he had paid an unauthorized visit! But, unlike my father who could be bold, I was too timid to try to get past the nurse.

The hospital was built around a patio which was not off limits. On three sides, hospital rooms lined the patio and each room had a window. I found my mother's window, and every day I would go to the window of her room through the back of the patio. Standing on my tiptoes, I could see her through the screen of her window, which she kept open.

Crystal was old enough to be admitted. I envied her. She could go right into Audrey's room while I had to stay with my nose pressed against the window screen to try to hear what was being said and manage a few words to my mother.

It seemed Audrey would be in that hospital bed for months. Indeed, it was over a month before she was to be allowed to go home. The doctor wanted to make sure the blood clot was dissolved.

One day I was at the patio window with my nose pressed against the screen when Dr. H. M. Mortimer came into my mother's room. He was talking to my mother when he saw my face against the screen. He must have been a little surprised. Audrey told him I came every day to see her through the screened window and was unhappy because I wasn't allowed in.

There was a hallway just around the corner of my mother's room, straight down from the nurses' station. At the side of that hallway was a door which opened into the patio—just a few yards from my mother's room. Dr. Mortimer left my mother's room and came through that doorway into the patio.

"Come in," the doctor said. "You can come and see your mother."

Surprised, I followed the doctor into my mother's room. None of the nurses dared to say a word. Dr. Mortimer was lord of that hospital, along with only one or two other powerful doctors in town. If he said the hospital rules could be broken, no one questioned him.

As Dr. Mortimer left, he told me I could stay until visiting hours were over. In later years, I wondered if Dr. Mortimer ever knew what that small kindness meant to me. Crystal and I were both terrified that Audrey would not recover. To be barred from my mother when she was ill was torment. To be able to kiss her and sit next to her gave me indescribable joy. The next day I had to return to my patio window to see Mama, but I'd had a few minutes to sit by her and see her face without the screen between us. Because Dr. Mortimer took time out of his busy schedule to notice a timid child, I'd had a "real" visit with my mother.

While Audrey was in the hospital, she told Dr. Mortimer she thought she might be pregnant. Audrey wrote in her notes entitled, "Holly:"

> When you are 42, been in the hospital weeks and weeks fighting for your life against blood clots—seeming to float up against the ceiling in a struggle to breathe—or keep the silver cord—and then suddenly you find out you are pregnant—the shock is bound to kill or cure.
>
> The nurse had finally unpinned me from the bottle containing a few drops of powerful anti-coagulant. (I was still very weak but could move around some in the bed.) I had lain perfectly still in the same position with one arm strapped down so the needle with the drip giving drops could enter one of my collapsed veins. When several nurses and the

Doc often what seemed like hours of effort bending over me struggling to finally get that needle in the vein inside my right wrist I was extremely careful to see that I did not wiggle it out. I didn't move except my hips off and on the bed pan for about 2 weeks. When the myriad of blood tests showed I might not kick off from a clot, they unpinned me from the bottle. I moved very little and then very gently. Later, I concluded this minor moving when the fetus was in a critical preliminary stage might have bad results for the child.

When Dr. Mortimer came one morning I said that I had been getting thinner every day—except in the middle. "Do you suppose I'm pregnant?"

"We'll see," says he.

After examining me, he announced, "You're pregnant, about 3 months along." He turned away and walked to the window. "I don't know what to do about it!" he said, in a soft, almost under his breath voice.

"Well," I said, pretty stunned, "I'm depending on you to pull me through as you have before!"

He turned and smiled and said, "I'll try."

That night I told Clyde. "So there we are again—at least 6 months to go. First time I ever had a lengthy stay in the hospital I come out pregnant!" We laughed. But it was no joke.

The next a.m. Deborah S. came in to bathe me and I told her while dripping a few tears into the wash cloth. She was thrilled and said how thankful she and her husband would be if only she might be pregnant. That cheered me up some—but I was still so weak from the long bout with phlebitis thrombosis that I could not see how I could stand any more physical torture the hospital nurses and doctors could dream up. Only a day or two before I had nearly had hysterics when approached with the umpteenth needle. There wasn't a place in me that hadn't had a needle hole repeatedly. I was getting about 27 injections or punctures per day when the nurse approached with that everlasting needle. I began to sob. The Doc took me off the needles and they began to give me the same medicine by mouth.

Then discovering I was pregnant, the Doc changed his procedures completely. Suddenly I was to sit up, move some. Finally drop my feet off the edge of the bed. Oh, how that pained. Each time my legs howled and screamed at me. I could only stand to put them down a minute or so. I kept thinking of the baby and gritted my teeth and kept working my toes and putting my legs up and down. I wanted my baby to have a chance at a good life and having a mother that could walk would be one important criteria. Finally I was released from the hospital into a hospital bed at home.[1]

Later, Audrey wrote: "Holly! How we love her—little Hollywood—Hollyberry—Geronimo! Pet names except the last. That was a visitor's designation for the little wild one."[2] Audrey and Clyde prayed for Holly as soon as they knew she was on the way. Audrey believed it was a miracle that Holly survived.

We were relieved and ecstatic when Audrey came home from the hospital. We waited on her as well as we could, and Grandma Shearer came and stayed for a while to help. After Audrey had been released from the hospital following a blood clot in her leg, she was still very ill.

Audrey once told of an experience she had as she lay so ill at home. She saw a dark shadow of a figure in the corner and she knew it was the Death Angel. She mentally sent a message: "No! I won't go! I have children to raise! I'm not ready to go and I refuse to go!" Then the figure disappeared.[3]

Apparently at some point Audrey had a blood clot in a lung. One night Audrey had a terrible pain in her chest. She asked Clyde to call the doctor. Clyde couldn't find the telephone number. So Audrey said, "Just pray for me. Wake up the girls and all of you pray for me." So Daddy, Crystal, and I stood around Audrey's bed, ours hands placed on her, and prayed. Then she felt better and was able to sleep normally. The next day the blood clot that had been in one lung was in the other one. She was told the only way it could have done that was to have traveled through her heart—and that should have killed her. But she continued to rest and blood thinners were taken until she was soon well enough to get up and around again. Everyone said it was a miracle. We believed our faith and the gift of healing made a difference in Mother's miracle healing and recovery. "The Great Physician gave me a special touch," Audrey said.

Without Audrey's paycheck, our cupboards were literally almost bare. Crystal and I never complained. We had been used to living on very little. A can of tomato soup and a few soda crackers often made a meal, and we did not expect more. One day after Audrey was able to be up again, she brought us home from school and we saw a box on the step of the side door that we used most of the time. It was a box of groceries with a tag that said "Anonymous." I thought my mother was going to cry. She was very touched. We never found out who sent the groceries, but we were very grateful. We realized whoever brought the box to our house knew that we used the side door instead of the front door most of the time—and knew we needed groceries!

Several people helped us a great deal, including our good neighbors, the Maloofs, and the Moores. John Moore, and his wife Edith, a nurse, had a girl just younger than I, Sarah. Crystal sometimes baby sat for them at their home across the street and down a few houses on Myrtle Avenue. Edith Moore went to the Emmanuel Baptist Church where we went, just on the other side of the Maloof home. She often stopped by to check on us and sometimes brought us clothes that we could wear. Grandma Shearer and Granny Simpson helped, too. Granny and her daughter Mary Simpson always gave us their old car whenever they bought a new one.

Clyde was drinking and Audrey kept hoping and praying that he would quit. His mother knew nothing about his drinking and would have been mortified. She sent a small check each week to help the family out, as she knew we often were short on money. Mother could have used the money for groceries or other necessities. But Clyde's drinking used up most of that money. It was frustrating for Audrey. Still, there was a new baby on the way—and new hope. Clyde and Audrey prayed the child would be healthy. Audrey later wrote in her notes, "Holly," written in 1981 to be part of an autobiography:

> If I can't remember every detail just right, please remember a lot of things have happened every day the last 26 years. Holly was born the morning of March 5, 1955 about 7:00 o'clock at Las Vegas hospital on 8th street in Las Vegas, New Mexico. I had been very ill since August 1, 1954 with phlebitis thrombosis and spent 6 weeks in hospital at that time. Mrs. Vivian came to see me and said I could claim unemployment insurance but I said no, I would quit, for doctor said I couldn't work anymore and I knew they needed someone to do my work. By using Heprin [or Heparin] and much prayer I lived through (more in religious section of book). I had been in bed much of the time at home and was not in good condition at age 43 to have a baby.[4]

Crystal and I anticipated the arrival of the new baby in our home, little understanding what a mother has to go through to bring that child into the world. Audrey wrote a lengthy manuscript to Holly about her birth:

> I woke up about 2 a.m. and told Clyde I needed to go to the hospital. He had drunk his usual 5th of whiskey the night before and didn't go to sleep until after midnight so was not able to do much but he said he was able to take me in the car. He was mighty shaky but we made it and I got to bed there. He stayed. Dr. M. had said to let him know the

minute I went to the hospital. I told the nurses but they never called him. When I was taken to the delivery room I told Clyde to call him himself. Which he did. Mortimer came at once and was angry because they had used the stirrups on me—he made them take them off and saw Clyde looking in the window and told the nurse to tell him to go wait in the lobby. They gave me a spinal so I knew all that went on.

I got to work and remember crying, "Oh, God, help me!" and then the doc tried to take the baby. He swore once and I thought he said "breach" but later he said it was not a breach birth. He used forceps to get hold of the baby. But when he pulled her out and they laid her on a table next to the delivery table and he said in a disappointed voice, "It's a girl" and I looked at you and you looked at me with all the knowledge of the world in your eyes and you really smiled. Then the nurse put drops in your eyes and I think hurt your lid. It made a big red place on your eyelid that stayed for a long time. I think she poked it with the dropper."[5]

Audrey, in writing her notes to Holly, recalled later:

The way you thrilled me when you looked into my eyes was wonderful. I was put back in my room where I was in with a Spanish woman. Her husband was there and said, "You sure did yell." I didn't know that I had. Clyde went home and teased the big girls. "We have the cutest little—-" and left the gender blank for a good while. Dorothy was jumping up and down yelling, "Tell us what it is!" She wanted a girl.

I knew that something was not normal about Holly and was heartbroken and blamed myself and Clyde for whatever her trouble—at the same time I knew she wouldn't be here without a purpose—a learning experience for her or for some of the rest of us. All I could do was pray her problems could be solved, more or less.

I had to stay there 5 days. There was a terrible dust storm when we went home in the car. The air was pure dust. Coming out of the sterile hospital I worried about Holly getting too much dust. We put her in the north bedroom at 1620 7th street and I kept as much dust out as possible. I nursed her so didn't have to worry about dusty milk or water. Before we left the hospital, they said we had to name you. We suggested many names and looked them all over. I wanted to call your middle name Alice for my grandmother as no one else in the family had her name. We wanted a good short name.

Holly was in the booklet they gave us. I had only heard it from a couple of people. So we chose Holly as short and not common name—standing for *holy*."[6]

Ruth Carrington came to the hospital to visit Audrey and Holly. She noticed that Holly had exceptionally good hearing. Audrey wrote that Mrs. Carrington thought "there was something wrong the way you waved one hand all the time—had no control of it as I held you over my shoulder."[7]

Audrey typed up an original "birth announcement" to send out. One of two groups had given her a baby shower, and now it was time for everyone to celebrate.[8] It looked like this:

EXTRA!
NEW EDITION!
YOUNG STRANGER SERIES
Latest of the Simpson Publications Title:
HOLLY ALICE
Editor.................Clyde Simpson
Publisher...............Audrey Simpson
This direct descendant of William the Conqueror, Revolutionary and Civil War Veterans, was previewed at Las Vegas Hospital, March 5, 7:58 a.m., 1955, weighing 6 lbs., 5 ½ oz. Former Simpson Editions also published in Las Vegas;
Crystal Clydine, July 30, 1938
Dorothy Audrey, Feb. 29, 1944

Family and friends appreciated the unique, clever announcement.

Betty and Stanley Hardin soon had an announcement of their own to make. Twila Dee Hardin was born November 30, 1955 in Portales. Attendance at the family reunions was growing!

After Holly was born, Audrey was sick with another blood clot in the leg. She was in and out of the hospital a couple of times with blood clots. But she had been given a miracle and she was steadfast in her faith. Although Holly would be diagnosed with mild cerebral palsy, she was a healthy baby for the most part. Audrey and Clyde were grateful for their answered prayers.

Clyde also needed a miracle. Audrey wrote that when she re-married Clyde, he was an alcoholic. He had been drinking heavily since before their divorce, as well as all the time he had lived with his girl friend out of state. Of course, he had promised to stop drinking, but he didn't. "He got dead drunk every other night until after Holly was born in March, 1955," Audrey wrote.[9]

She also recalled:

> Clyde kept getting drunk every other night after we got home from the hospital. After a few days (about 2 weeks) I pushed your [Holly's] bed into the girls' room. "I will not have her hearing your drunken babble half the night or have her smell that awful liquor." As far as I knew he didn't drink any more after that, at least not anything that smelled.[10]

Clyde was not well and the doctor told him he had kidney stones which should be removed. Clyde went on the bus to Albuquerque to have surgery to remove kidney stones. Mother, Holly and I went in the car the next day to be with him. I sat in the front seat of the car and held Holly much of the time while Mother drove.

Little did we know that the previous night things had changed. Clyde was in his hospital room, feeling frightened and claustrophobic. He believed God would heal him. Clyde prayed that night and asked God to heal him. He promised God he would never take another drink. He was healed and left the hospital in the middle of the night without telling anyone. In the morning the doctors and nurses were frantic, trying to find him.

"A patient scheduled for surgery doesn't just disappear!" one of the doctors fumed.

"We never saw him leave," a nurse explained.

"Mr. Simpson must be in this hospital some where!" another nurse exclaimed.

"Well, his clothes are gone, so he must have dressed and walked out," a nurse's aide declared.

Finally someone thought of calling to find out if he had left the hospital and gone home. They called his mother's home and Addie Simpson said, "Oh, yes, Clyde is sitting right here. He's fine. He doesn't need the surgery. God healed him."

When we arrived at Granny Simpson's home early in the morning, we were surprised that Daddy was there and wasn't in the hospital having the surgery!

Clyde never had any more kidney stone problems—and he kept his word. He never took another drink.

Life was good for the Simpson family after Audrey recovered and went back to work at the Optic. They had not replaced her. Crystal and I arranged our schedules so we could babysit most of the rest of the time. When we were both in school and Clyde and Audrey were at work, Grandma Shearer babysat. She and

Vivian had moved into town from the ranch. For a while they were in Santa Rosa and Mabel stayed at our home some of the time.

Then the Shearers had an apartment on Columbia, across the street from Carnegie Library. First they rented an apartment in the big house on the corner of Columbia and Sixth. Later they moved to an apartment in the house on the corner of Columbia and Fifth.

I walked from Paul Henry School, where I attended fifth and sixth grades, to Grandma's apartment after school. I thought it was wonderful that she lived just across the street from Carnegie Library; she could borrow books often. Mother would stop by for me and Holly after she got off work at five o'clock. Crystal either joined us there or walked home. Sometimes I went to the Optic after school to wait for my mother. I would sit in the back of the office and read the bound copies of the old *Optics*. I enjoyed Will Rogers' daily column in the 1930s editions.

In the summer time, Crystal and I did all of the babysitting. Audrey wrote:

> Mother [Shearer] took care of you [Holly] much of the time. I paid her $40 a month—enough for her to rent a place after she stopped staying at our house. She kept you at 2 different houses on Columbia—the end house at each end of the block opposite of Carnegie Library.[11]

When Holly was born, I was in the fifth grade at Paul D. Henry School. Mrs. Amy Lyster was my teacher, and I admired her very much. In the sixth grade, Mrs. Mildred Pierce was my teacher. She was a wonderful, compassion teacher. After school, Grandma would say, "You worked hard all day in school. You need some cocoa and some cinnamon rolls." She always had a treat for me while we waited for Audrey to come to get me and Holly. When I was in the fifth grade, my friend Judy Beil also attended Paul D. Henry School, so we spent many lunch periods after eating in the cafeteria walking to near-by stores or to the Dairy Queen. She spent some time at my house and I would sometimes go to her place at El Porvenir where we would ride horses.

Grandma always enjoyed her grandchildren and tried to teach them as much as she could. She had helped raise Roger, and then she discovered her work was not done when she was needed to help with Holly. She had an opportunity to help even more when Frank needed her. Frank was in the Air Force, stationed in Texas. Frank and his wife Dorothy Shearer had a little girl, Carol Ann, born June 12, 1954. Then their son Frankie Allen was born on June 7, 1956. Dorothy was ill with headaches. Then she died suddenly of a brain tumor. Mabel and Vivian said they'd take the children as long as necessary. The two children, Carol, about three years of age, and Frankie, about one, were with their grandparents about a year at the house on Columbia. Frank provided the finances and his parents provided the care in their home in Las Vegas. Then Frank married Margaret and the children were able to be with their father and step-mother. Another child, Carl Wayne Shearer, was born to Frank and Margaret on July 24, 1961.

When Holly was four years old, I was in the ninth grade at Robertson High School. I was taking a class in Home Economics and we had to do a project. My teacher, Mrs. Wells, suggested several things. The idea of giving a party appealed to me. With Holly's birthday coming up, my project was to plan and give her a party. I had to prepare all the refreshments myself, in addition to all the other chores. We invited, among others, Zian Maloof, the Gardners, the Pinkstons, the Suliers, and the Krauses. The party was a great success. I had spent a lot of time cleaning house. I expected Mrs. Wells to show up. The party was on a Saturday. But my teacher did not come. I still got an A, and best of all, Holly had a wonderful party.

Holly's best friends included Zian Maloof—the youngest daughter of George and Cora Maloof next door—and the two Sulier children, Linda Lou and Darrell. Jim and Macky Jo Sulier had built a home just across the fence from our backyard. Often when Crystal or I would hang up clothes in the backyard, we would see Mrs. Sulier hanging up her clothes in her back yard, so we would visit with her. She had a cheerful disposition and was a pleasure to know. I thought her two children were adorable. Holly's three closest neighbors—Zian, Linda Lou and Darrell—came to the birthday party, along with other friends such as Mike Gardner, the grandson of the Carringtons. Holly thought Linda and Darrell would always be her very best friends. Darrell even proposed a future marriage! But Macky Jo died suddenly when Darrell and Linda Lou were still in high school. Both Linda and Darrell died in their early twenties. Linda drowned and Darrell died a few years later in a private plane crash.

As a baby, Holly was slow to develop, but she was able to do just about everything everyone else did. Her left eye was weak and turned in toward her nose. Holly was supposed to wear a patch over the good eye to make the "lazy" eye work, but Holly refused to wear it. Mother took Holly to Dr. Beil, the ophthalmologist. He recommended surgery to correct the eye. But Audrey was afraid; she thought surgery might make the eye worse. Audrey wrote:

> Judy Beil Vaughan's father, Dr. Wallace C. Beil, the ophthalmologist in town, wanted you [Holly] to have eye surgery at 7 months. I couldn't see it—if anything went wrong and your eye went out instead of in they

would repeat and repeat surgery and still not get it right. When you were about 5 or 6 I took you to eye specialists. You started school with Dr. Vandermeer's bifocals. You wouldn't keep them on. You wouldn't keep a patch on your good eye to make the other one work. I took you to eye specialists in Santa Fe recommended by Dr. Dr. Carol Smith and to her.[12]

Holly did not have surgery and did have poor vision in one eye but was fitted with glasses and was able, when she was old enough, to see well enough to get a driver's license.

Holly spent a lot of time with her Daddy. He was almost always with her every morning before he went to work. He had a nickname for nearly everyone, and he called Holly "Little Toe." That started when she was a baby and he was marveling at how tiny she was. He said, "Look how tiny her toes are. They are so little! She's got such little toes!"

On his days off Clyde would take Holly with him to various stores in Las Vegas. They would play games and "try out" or "test" the toys. Sometimes he would buy her a toy or a book. Once when Holly was four years old they went to the Montgomery Ward Store on Douglas Avenue, next to the Bank of Las Vegas and across the street from Ilfeld Hardware. Clyde was looking at something and Holly was on the other side of the counter. When he looked up, he couldn't see her. He began to call her name and looked all over the store. She was nowhere to be found. Then he began to panic. They had no loud speakers to call her and no security guards to ask for help. He thought of the only person he knew to help—Audrey. He quickly crossed Douglas Avenue and walked down Seventh Street a block, turned the corner and went into the Optic building at 614 Lincoln Avenue. Clyde raced up the steep stairs and saw Audrey in her usual place at her typewriter behind her big desk facing the stairs.

"I can't find Holly!" Clyde gasped. "We were in Wards! She was right there at the counter and then she was gone! I checked all over the store!"

Audrey felt her stomach cave in. Her heart began to pound. Her thinking suddenly switched from the reporter concentrating on her writing to the astute mind of a mother whose baby is lost. She was the wife of a panic-stricken husband; she felt the panic rise in her own throat but she tried to remain outwardly calm.

"I have to go out for a few minutes," she told her a co-worker. And without another word she hurried down the stairs and out the front door with Clyde in the lead.

"Where could she be?" Clyde gasped as they walked with top speed back to Montgomery Wards.

"Let's have one more look through the store," Audrey said. "Did you ask the clerks if they'd seen her?"

"I asked a few people. I looked everywhere and then came to get you," Clyde admitted.

"Let's ask everyone in the store again if they saw a little girl wandering around," Audrey said. "Most of them know you and her so they'll know who to look for."

"She could have been kidnapped." Clyde said the words they were both thinking as their steps took them across the Douglas Avenue and back to the store. In those days kidnapped children were so rare that when such a crime occurred, the story made the national news. So it wasn't very likely. But it was possible.

"She might have been," Audrey agreed. "But I don't think it's too likely in the middle of the day in a store."

After a quick search of the store, with the help of the clerks, Audrey told the manager, "We're going to look outside for a while. We'll be back."

The manager knew Audrey and Clyde well. They had an account at Wards. They came in faithfully each month to pay on the bill.

When they were back outside the store, Audrey asked, "Where would you go if you were Holly and you couldn't see your Daddy in the store?"

"Back to the car," Clyde exclaimed. "I always told her if she got lost to go back to the car. It's in Safeway's parking lot."

Safeway was just across the street from the Bank of Las Vegas on Douglas Avenue and Seventh Street, across from the Surf Theatre. It was less than a full block from Montgomery Ward. Holly would have had to cross one street, Seventh Street, to get to the parking lot at the side of Safeway that faced Seventh Street. She had been taught to cross the street on the green light.

Audrey and Clyde hurried to the car. Sure enough, there was Holly sitting inside the car. No one locked their cars in Las Vegas then.

There were relieved words and a happy reunion. Audrey and Clyde praised Holly for doing the right thing when she got lost: going back to the car.

"What took you so long?" Holly wailed. "I was waiting here for hours!"

Holly was satisfied with the explanation.

"I'll hurry back to Wards to let them know we found her," Clyde said and took off in a rush to inform the employees of the store. Audrey stayed with Holly until Clyde came back.

"I need to get back to work," Audrey said when Clyde returned. "Thank God everything turned out all right."

Clyde was feeling guilty. "I don't know how I lost sight of Holly," he said.

"I looked up from the other side of the counter and didn't see you," Holly said. "I knew I was lost so I came back here to the car."

"You did the right thing," Clyde reassured her.

"Well, it all worked out so there's nothing to worry about," Audrey said.

There were many "expeditions" to the stores after that but Holly never again became "lost."

Often on Clyde's day off he would take Holly and go to the ranch. Usually Monday was his day off and Audrey had to work. Sometimes they both had the same day off—a rare holiday—and then the whole family could go to the ranch. Clyde began to work on building a big ranch house. Audrey and the girls helped when they could, and after Crystal married Wesley Lovett, he also helped.

In Millicent Gensemer's *Optic* story previously cited, a description of Audrey's busy life was given.

> On her days "off" her special pleasure is to go with her family to their mountain retreat where she steps from her role as society editor to "sling mud" as she terms the chinking of the log cabins, to throw a rock at a mountain lion that threatened once to jump on her from an overhanging ledge, and to turn calmly from such a task to cook her favorite meal—a hunter's stew.[13]

Mrs. Gensemer did not fail to mention Audrey's perpetual "copy pencil perched on her ear."

> Unable to find the time to enjoy housekeeping and cooking as she would like, she has developed two excellent cooks in her daughters, Crystal, a sophomore at Highlands, and Dorothy, a sophomore at Robertson High School and even little Holly, aged four, is learning to help in the culinary chores.[14]

Before we knew it Holly was old enough for kindergarten. Audrey wrote:

> When you got big enough to go to Kindergarten, Clyde or I would take you in the a.m. and I would go pick you up in the p.m. about the time Crystal or Dorothy would get home from school. When Mother wasn't around one of them always arranged to get out of school in time to look after you. I ran back and forth chauffeuring kids one place to another early or late. I went after you one time and saw you standing with your hat and coat on looking out at the backyard. Your whole body

was dejected, slumped and sad. You were all alone in the school room. When I called "Holly," you turned and came to life. Your whole being changed from deep dread to happy gladness. I decided then that place wasn't for you and that is when we began to arrange for one or the other of the girls to get home and look after you. You were so pitiful with your handicap and we each loved you the more for your helplessness. No one ever thought of you as the nuisance you have called yourself in recent years. You fought and yelled and screamed and we loved you even more for I knew if you hadn't had such a drive, you would have died before you were born.[15]

Holly went to first grade at Douglas School. Mary Covington was her teacher. A year or so later Mary Covington died in a tragic shooting incident.

When Holly was in second grade, she got very sick. The doctor said she had measles and chicken pox at the same time!

It was October or November. Clyde bought a little table organ for Holly. It was to be her Christmas present. But Holly was so sick that Clyde decided to give it to her early. He feared she might not live until Christmas. Clyde surprised her with it one day. Holly spent many happy hours playing simple songs on that organ. She still has it today, as it was one of the items saved from the 1971 fire. Audrey wrote about that time:

You [Holly] started school at Douglas School in 1961. Mrs. Covington was your teacher. You got real sick in Nov. and didn't go back to school until 1962. The teacher came to see you. You had measles and chicken pox at the same time. You were so sick we were afraid you wouldn't live until Christmas. Clyde bought you the little organ for about $35.00 which we didn't have—he charged it at Ward's. Then he gave it to you more than a month before Christmas to try to pull you out of it. Dr. Mortimer came by to see you several times. Lots of times you were too sick to go to the office. Clyde took care of you in the mornings and one or the other of the girls looked after you in the p.m., probably Crystal had the best hours but I don't remember.[16]

We all prayed for Holly to recover. Clyde prayed that if someone had to die that God would take him instead. Everyone felt helpless.

Audrey recalled that one of the women who worked at the Optic—Bobbie Akin—mentioned that her husband liked to play Santa Claus and asked if Audrey would like him to drop by the house to surprise Holly. Audrey wrote:

Just before Christmas—Christmas Eve, I think—Eugene Akin came dressed in a Santa Claus suit. I had you in the tub of warm water trying to make you break out. I covered you with a towel and persuaded him to come into the bathroom to see you. It really tickled you. He went around to all the little kids he knew.

It was either a few days after Christmas, or before that, you had a very high fever for days. We couldn't get it down. I went after Clyde after work at 9 p.m. and we talked as to whether we should call the doctor again or a preacher. I told him the Hackers were newlyweds and new in town and seemed dedicated Christians. So he said let's get them. They came at once and even while they prayed for you, your very high fever broke. You were asleep the whole time and you didn't know they were there. After that Harold Hacker walked [from their place downtown] out every afternoon to pray for you. She [Mrs. Hacker] said once "He really loved that little girl." We gave them coffee and crackers or cookies if we had some. Later she told me for days that was all they had to eat. So they fasted.[17]

Audrey said later that if she had known the Hackers were so hungry, she would have offered them more to eat, but she didn't realize they were going without food much of the time because they had no money. The Hackers remained in Las Vegas several years and sometimes held church services in our home, although no one attended except our family. Clyde and Audrey continued to pray for Holly, as did the rest of the family, and life returned to normal.

Holly and Clyde were inseparable. She was truly "the apple of his eye." Holly and her daddy played a lot of games. They watched cartoons together and a favorite one was "Top Cat." Clyde would be Officer Diddle and Holly would be Top Cat. A typical conversation would run something like:

"Officer Diddle, let's go to Gambles and look at the toys."

"OK, Top Cat. Let me see if I have any money." Here Clyde would pull all the change out of his trouser pocket.

"I've got eight-five cents, Top Cat. We can buy something to play with," Clyde would declare.

"I won't get lost this time, Officer Diddle," Holly would promise.

"If you do get lost, you know what to do," Daddy would coach.

"Yes. Tell a clerk to find you or go get into the car like I did before," Holly would reply.

"That's right, Top Cat," Clyde would smile.

Audrey wrote about the fun Holly and her daddy had when he was in charge of her care—usually every morning before he had to go to work. She also wrote in some notes about the comment a nurse had made when Audrey was in the hospital: "Holly and Clyde looking in the hospital window at me in April when I had an embolism. The nurse noted how much they looked alike. Remarkable a pretty girl even looks so much like her father."[18]

Audrey wrote:

> Sometime after the chickenpox and measles, you [Holly] began to have convulsions every so often. It was usually about 4 a.m. Dr. Mortimer suggested I take you to Dr. Carol Smith in Santa Fe, which I did—I don't remember when. She had a psychologist test you to see whether or not you were normal. Later Dr. Smith said there was good news and bad. You were normal but had cerebral palsy. Dorothy went with us so maybe it was before you went to school.
>
> The years of your convulsions were pure hell in some respects. I got so little sleep and was worried about you all the time at work. Sometimes you had one just about the time I had to go to work and would have to stick you in a tub of warm water to bring you out of it. You were never unconscious long but it always seemed like hours even if it was only a couple of minutes. Usually you would stiffen out and pass out and we would put you in the tub of water. Dr. Smith prescribed Dilantin for you and Benzedrine—I didn't want you becoming addicted to Bennies so I didn't give it to you much. You stopped the Dilantin yourself when you went to Santa Rosa [for the eighth grade] and you seemed better off without it. Whenever you came home and I made you take it you would get real sick and run a fever so it wasn't long until I realized it was too much for you. I took you back to Dr. Smith when you were about 15. I think she said how she was glad to see you doing so well.[19]

Dr. Smith said that Holly was fortunate that she had only mild cerebral palsy. The pediatrician said Holly could live a normal life. She predicted Holly would outgrow her medication, and she did, with no more convulsions.

Audrey told Holly she could do anything she set her mind to, that her handicaps were minor; and Holly grew up knowing it was true.

Finally the family enjoyed good health once again. Audrey wrote:

> After you [Holly] got well you went back to school and passed that grade. And I attended PTA meetings at Douglas once more. In the 3rd grade

you had Mae Hart [?] Dixon who had known us before she married, and I think Clyde took her out a few times. You did fine there with her. Maybe she taught 4th also. Then to the 4th grade and 5th with Cipriano Aguilar as teacher, I think. I would go to pick you up after school and either take you home if one of the girls was there—or to my office.[20]

Audrey and Clyde continued to work hard to make ends meet. The Optic had new owners and management. Mr. Larry Finch and Mr. Tom Wright were running the paper. They started putting out a Sunday edition, which meant working Saturday night until midnight or so. Holly always stayed up to wait for Clyde to get home from work after nine p.m. Audrey's late hours upset Holly as well.

Audrey Simpson at her desk at the Optic, May, 1961
Source: **Simpson Archives,** photo by *Las Vegas Daily Optic* **photographer**

"Somehow we got through one day at a time. We couldn't plan ahead 'tho we tried. When we could, we would come to the ranch," Audrey wrote.[21]

Clyde brought home a little black and white puppy for Holly. He named the dog Twinkles. She lived to be a very old dog and was a good companion for Holly. Twinkles had puppies, and we kept two of them, Smoky and Rocky. But not everyone in the neighborhood liked animals. Sometimes our pets were poisoned. Sometimes they were shot. Smoky was shot when he was in our backyard. The bullet went through his shoulder. He survived, with much nursing care from the family.

In August of 1959 we had a special visitor, Fred A. Stone, from Los Angeles, California. As mentioned before, he had written to Audrey since he read her lynx cat story in a magazine. He had sent us gifts and written to us. He had promised to pay us a visit someday, and he did, right after Crystal's twenty-first birthday. He was going to stay a few days, so we planned for him to have my bedroom and I would sleep in Crystal's bedroom with her.

I remember when he first arrived and we welcomed him into the house. He was wearing a light colored Western type suit, cowboy boots and a light colored cowboy hat. He handed me a jacket which he had been carrying over his arm and he took off his hat. He handed me his hat.

"Put these somewhere, Pigtails," he smiled. He had always called me Pigtails since I had sent him pictures of myself throughout the years. I always wore two long braids.

I went into my bedroom and put his jacket and hat on my bed. He saw where I put them and a look of horror crossed his face.

"Not on the *bed*!" he exclaimed, turning to Audrey. "She put my hat on the *bed*!"

Audrey quickly retrieved the hat and put it up on the shelf in the closet.

"What's wrong?" I asked.

"Putting a hat on the bed is bad luck," Mother explained.

"I never heard that one," I said. Later Audrey told me it was a well-known actor's superstition.

"Never mind," the actor said. "I want Angel to show me around." His nickname for Crystal was Angel.

Apparently Fred Stone had no close ties with any family members. He told us, "You can't pick your family, but you can choose your friends. I've chosen you as my family." Indeed, he never forgot to send us gifts on holidays and he wrote letters every few days for years. As mentioned before, he was not the Fred A. Stone of vaudeville fame who was born in 1873. This Fred A. Stone was younger but may have had roles in silent films when he was young. He never told us how old he was.

Four-year-old Holly disturbed him with her constant demanding. She frequently had temper tantrums and threw a few of them while he was there. He nicknamed her "Geronimo" because, he said, she couldn't be "tamed."

Fred wanted us to call him "Rocky." He took Crystal and me to Funk's dime store and told us we could buy whatever we wanted. We had been in that store many times, wishing we had money to buy a few things. But after being told we could buy anything, we actually couldn't find anything we wanted! I finally picked out a little iron horse for my horse collection. I'd been collecting little horses and had quite a herd of "wild horses."

Fred Stone wanted Crystal to return to California with him, but that was out of the question. After our family reunion, which had been scheduled prior to Fred Stone's visit, the actor left, with many pleas for us to come and visit him. We enjoyed his visit, as he told us about Hollywood, roles he had played—including some Shakespeare—actors he knew, and the early days of movie making. He was a handsome man, a little over six feet tall, had blue eyes and silver hair. He continued to correspond with us for many years. Audrey wrote in her notes, "Holly:"

> Mr. Fred A. Stone came to see us when you [Holly] were 4 or 5. When we were taking him to the ranch in the old Chevy and he said he would get married to make a home for the big girls if I would let him take them to Hollywood, I was so surprised I jerked the car wheel and fell off in the ditch. He and the girls walked on to the ranch and you [Holly] stayed with me and howled and howled. It was very hot and we were thankful when Vivian and Frank came to pull us out with the little jeep.[22]

Fred Stone talked about his days as an actor and the many celebrities he knew personally. He especially wanted Crystal to go to California with him. He said she could become a "star." However, Crystal declined the offer. He was present for one of our family reunions, so he got to meet everyone. He thought Milly's daughter Dianna was beautiful. He told Dianna, "I'm going to buy you a doll and send it to you, a doll as big as you are." And as soon as he got back to California, he did.

When Clyde and Holly went to the ranch, he would let her "drive," sitting on his lap and steering. He began to teach her how to drive and told her as soon as she was tall enough he would let her really drive. He wanted to teach her everything he could so she would have survival skills when she grew up. Both Clyde and Audrey always tried to be prepared for any possible emergencies. Clyde knew Holly needed to be prepared for life and for any crisis that might arise. Audrey wrote:

> As you [Holly] were 8 or 9 you would come to the ranch with Clyde and help him make cement for the floor of the other house. Sometimes he let you drive although you couldn't work the pedals. I wanted to fuss about it but decided Clyde felt so bad at times I figured he may have thought that if he couldn't drive, you could for him.[23]

Audrey thought perhaps Clyde wanted Holly to know how to drive the truck in case he collapsed and she had to drive to town. He sensed that his health was failing. He seemed to know his time was short.

6

Fire at the Office

At the Optic Audrey met the famous cowboy actor, singer, and narrator, Rex Allen. He was well known for his western movies as a singing cowboy. He narrated some of Walt Disney's movies and later starred in a television series. One day the celebrity stopped in Las Vegas on his way west. Audrey had an opportunity to interview him. She kept a photograph which had been taken of him, his wife, and herself standing by her desk at the Optic. She had the photo framed and put it on the wall behind her desk at work. She was very impressed with him and when he starred in the TV series, "Frontier Doctor," Audrey enjoyed watching the programs.

Audrey had only a few personal items at work. One of them was a Bible. She used it for reference and inspiration. One day Audrey left work as usual. She had put everything off her desk as she always did before she went home, except for one or two items, including the Bible. That evening she learned that the Optic building was on fire. The Fire Department put out the fire, but everything was smoke or water damaged. Audrey was surprised to see one thing that had not been damaged by water, smoke or fire—the Bible on top of her desk. In fact, nothing on the top of the desk was touched. It wasn't even water soaked. She remembered that one item from Grandfather Shearer's house which did not burn was the family Bible.

The next day the Optic put out a little two page paper that they printed at Highlands University. Audrey wrote a little verse which Walter Vivian put on the front page of the *Optic*: "Every Day Since 1879."

>Flames in the night,
>Scaring and tearing,
>Flicking and swearing,
>Crumbling and burning,

> Whipping and turning,
> Blacking years work away.
> Tradition is stronger
> Flames just make work longer
> Historic old Optic
> Is still printed today.
> —Audrey Simpson.[1]

Editor Walter Vivian wrote in his daily column for the *Optic*, "Along the Banks of the Gallinas:"

> Now we know how a displaced person feels.
> Here we are in Highlands University news room which has been converted into the Optic editorial office. Maybe we will be able to get a few hours college credit toward a degree in journalism.
> It was a hectic night, starting when the city police phoned with a curt message, "The Optic is on fire!"
> Firemen put forth a great effort but the blaze got too much of a head start and the damage was done.
> We can't begin to thank all the people who deserve a thanks for their efforts and for their expressions. So, a blanket thanks to all.[2]

Under one picture on the front page was the caption: "A historic landmark of Las Vegas was badly damaged Friday night when a fire of undetermined origin spread through the front of the Las Vegas Daily Optic."[3]

The main story described the event. The article appeared to the left of the "Picture Story of The Las Vegas Optic Fire" which featured photos of the ruins. The *Optic* story said, in part:

> Starting in an alcove dark room, fire last night [Friday, August 9, 1957] gutted the Las Vegas Optic plant.
> The fire was reported to desk sergeant Arthur Esquibel by Marilyn Wynn at 7:51. She reported smoke coming from the building. Police arrived at the scene at 7:52 and firemen seconds later.
> Inside the building was a roaring mass of flame and dense smoke. The blaze had such a start that firemen could only direct their efforts to controlling it from spreading to the rear and right sides of the building.
> Thick walls protected adjacent buildings, the T. J. Maloof and Kenneth Gifford establishments.

The center part of the old building was severely damaged. Editorial and business offices, a conference room housing the United Press teletype and reperferator [reperforator] and a Fairchild scan-o-graver were charred. The equipment was badly damaged.

Fire crept along the main ceiling and walls onto the back shop.

Linotypes were damaged by fire, heat and water. Other valuable printing equipment was also damaged. The press, recently installed, escaped with minor damage.

Firemen had difficulty extinguishing smoldering tight-wound paper.

Volumes of the *New Mexico Stockman*, printed in the last century and regarded as a collector's item, were burned. Optic files, however, had recently been stored in Wick's storage space.

Typewriters and other office equipment also were destroyed but records were intact in fire-resistant files.

Tom Wright, co-publisher of the paper, and members of the staff assisted in cleaning operations last night and continued in the operation today. Larry Finch, the other co-publisher, was attending the Indian Ceremonial in Gallup at the time.

Monetary loss was not immediately determined pending a complete inventory.

Today's issue of the *Daily Optic*, one of the oldest continuous daily publications in the Southwest, was printed in the Highlands University print shop and with the cooperation with the Smith-Hursh Printing firm.[4]

The staff moved around to where White's Auto was on Sixth Street to work until the building could be restored. Neighboring communities offered assistance. Emergency telephone facilities were installed in the rear of the plant. Gas and electric facilities were installed.

The Optic was printed off on the New Mexican presses in Santa Fe every day for a while. Everything in the building was ruined and water logged. Some files such as old copies of the Optic were ruined. On the back of the wall over Audrey's desk there was the picture of Audrey with Rex Allen. She noticed after the fire that they were taking everything down off the walls, so she took that picture off and saved it, as it was not damaged. (It later burned in the 1971 house fire.)

News of tragedy and loss were nothing new at the newspaper office— but this personal loss to the Optic was one that everyone hoped would not be repeated. Before long the newspaper was once again put out daily in a renovated building.

Audrey was grateful that her copy of *The Holy Bible* had not been damaged.

7

The House on Seventh Street

Many wonderful things happened at the house that had once been a church at 1620 Seventh Street in Las Vegas. Christmas was always special, with a big tree from Forest Springs Ranch. Each year brought its joys and sorrows, its family reunions, and special times. Usually Thanksgiving would be spent with Vivian and Grandma Shearer. Christmas would mean a trip to Albuquerque if the weather was good—to visit Grandpa Clements and Mable on South Broadway and to visit Granny Simpson and Mary Simpson on Tenth Street. Granny's house was surrounded with fragrant roses of all colors in the summer time. She had a big front yard with a weeping willow tree and a big back yard where she kept a few chickens. Mary did most of the yard work. But Granny took care of her chickens—and her cat Honey.

Crystal was chosen to sing in the high school operetta. She was an active member of the Concert Choir at Las Vegas Robertson High School. She tried out for a play and was chosen for the soprano lead in the high school operetta—based on *Die Fledermaus* composed by Johann Strauss, Jr. The popular Viennese operetta, called "The Bat," written in 1874, was a masterpiece. At the center of the story was the glamorous couple, Gabriel and Rosalinde von Eisenstein. Crystal played the beautiful Rosalinde—in the version adapted from the original and called "Operetta in Vienna." Rosalinde and her husband were the lead roles. Many of Crystal's friends had roles in the play. Anna Maria Montoya played the part of Crystal's maid. Other members of the high school choir had minor roles, including the very handsome, bright, popular Erik J. Mason.

Crystal's high school music teacher, Mr. Earl Haines, encouraged her. He was just out of college himself. He knew she needed financial help to go to college, and he urged her to apply for a scholarship. Crystal was known for her beautiful soprano voice and was awarded a music scholarship to New Mexico Highlands University.

At New Mexico Highlands University, Crystal enjoyed her classes, although she struggled with some of them due to her slow reading, the disability she'd had as a child. Still, with tutoring from Audrey—there were no university tutors or support services in those days—Crystal made good grades. Crystal sang at Emmanual Baptist Church and later at the First Baptist Church. She sang in the choir and sang solos for special music quite often. I did the same thing at Emmanuel Baptist Church—and played the piano. Crystal had belonged to Emmanuel Baptist but changed to the church downtown because her college friends went there. I often accompanied Crystal at various singing events.

When I was ready to think about college, Crystal encouraged me to apply for a scholarship. It was due to that encouragement that I applied for and received an academic scholarship to New Mexico Highlands University. Crystal had a job at the switchboard as an operator, and I also got a position there as a switchboard operator. Our supervisor, Ula Cumiford, gave us good advice and was very supportive. We were able to pay for our tuition and books through our scholarships and our work. The Business and Professional Women's Club also helped me with scholarships. Crystal and I shared several classes and helped each other with work. I often played the piano for Crystal as she prepared for various performances she was in. She took a part in numerous musicals at Highlands University, including *Brigadoon*. She did not have a major role but her friend Kathy Magill, the daughter of Bill Magill who worked at the Optic with Audrey, played the lead role of Fiona. At that time the Theatre Department was headed by Richard O'Connell; and excellent plays, including many of Shakespeare's plays as well as modern plays, were produced. He worked with the Music Department to produce popular musicals.

The entire family helped around the house, as well as the yard. Clyde enjoyed watering the grass and trees. The fir trees in the front yard, transplanted from our ranch, were very special. They grew and thrived. (After Audrey sold the place in 1966, they were taller than the house itself. They remained the beauty of the place until someone who bought the place cut them down in the 1990s.) Audrey loved the "wild" yellow Spanish roses in our yard. Indeed, they looked like wild rose bushes. The wild pink roses are more common. But the yellow roses have a wonderful, fragrant smell and are a brilliant yellow. Mother called them "Spanish Roses," and said they were brought from Spain. The plant was covered with little stickers or thorns and it spread like a weed. Our neighbor kept cutting them out, but Audrey refused to kill any that were in our yard. She let them grow because she loved the sight and smell of them. She wrote a poem about them:

The leaves were green and thick and wide.
"We have to cut them," Holly cried.
"Leave them, let them grow!
"Go around them when you mow!"

Then children came with summer
"Mom, we'll cut the weeds," they said.

"No, let them grow—already gold begins to glow
Beside the house, around the lawn
and in the corner near the lilac bush."

"They are weeds!" they wailed.
I fight back.
I like that type weed.[1]

    The Simpsons' back yard had a big vegetable garden. The surrounding homes did not have such gardens. They had manicured lawns. The neighborhood children seemed to congregate at our home, playing with Holly. Audrey asked one of the little girls why she liked playing in Holly's backyard. Audrey was thinking that the little girl's home had a much lovelier back yard. The little girl replied, "Because this yard has *dirt*!" The mystery was revealed. The children loved to dig in the dirt. Naturally, one cannot have a vegetable garden without "dirt," so the soil was plowed up and tiled every year. There was no well groomed lawn in our back yard. Those children knew that "dirt" was sometimes more fun to play in than grass.
    The house on Seventh Street was so large it made a good place to entertain friends and to hold meetings. Audrey's women's clubs often met there. Crystal's college friends often congregated there. Birthday parties and family reunions were held there. Church services were held there at times. It was a very happy home. We had a television set, so we kept up with the latest news and popular entertainers such as Elvis Presley and Pat Boone. We watched The Mickey Mouse club after school and enjoyed all the popular Westerns.
    Since my birthday was on February 29, Audrey always tried to give me a special party on that day every four years, although we always celebrated my birthday on February 28th when there was no leap year. In the second grade, she had conferred with Mrs. Margaret Goddard and given me a surprise party at school. In the sixth grade she had consulted with Mrs. Mildred Pierce at Paul D. Henry School, and I was given another surprise party. My classmates, such as

Ronne Wester, always enjoyed those parties. I enjoyed high school and was active in several clubs, along with classmates such as Marjorie Smith, Charlotte Bible, Diana Lucero, Dana Marvin, Alice Winston, Jay Harris, Bert Forbes, Alberta Gonzales, and Mac Bell. When I was sixteen Audrey invited some of my friends, mostly from Emmanuel Baptist Church, to a party at our house. My friends there included Tommy Gazaway, Jimmy Sampson, and Sarah Moore. When I was twenty and involved in speech and debate at Highlands University, Audrey gave me another surprise party, inviting my classmates from my debate club such as Dan Sanchez and Juanita Huie, my debate partner. Those were special days in my life, thanks to my mother's efforts to make my leap year birthday special. Audrey said, "As a child, having a birthday only every four years isn't much fun, maybe. But when you have your sixteenth real birthday, you'll be glad you only have a birthday every four years." She was right.

With her box camera nearby, Audrey would ask everyone at family events to line up for a picture. (Sometimes someone would volunteer to take a picture so Audrey could be in one.) Nearly every time someone would protest. Mabel would often say, "I don't look good enough for a picture." Audrey later wrote: "People who think they look terrible in today's pictures—Keep the picture and look at it ten years from now and you will see that you look pretty good."[2]

Later, pictures of the family lined up at a family reunion were highly cherished. Those not attending were greatly missed. For instance, Bobby Simpson missed a few get-togethers after he joined the Navy. He then married Erma Jean and they lived in the southern part of the State. Everyone who attended was grateful for the photographs later. When Wesley Lovett joined the family, he began taking many family pictures.

Once the ranch house was begun, most days off were spent there. Sometimes we would go to visit friends along the way. Audrey wrote a poem once when she stopped to visit and found no one at home. "Nobody Home" was published in the *Denver Post*:

> There's no smoke from the chimney,
> The gates are closed tight,
> Red hogs root slowly
> From morning 'til night.
>
> The white horses stand idle
> Beneath the tall trees,
> The ground's black with crows
> Blown in on the breeze.

The gray cat says I'm lonesome
Atop the hay stack.
The windmill groans loudly
With a crick in its back.

Far down in the field
Twenty cows eat hay.
But the place looks deserted
For the master's away.[3]

Three sisters: Dorothy, Holly and Crystal Simpson, 1962
Source: Simpson Archives, photo by Wesley Lovett

Audrey was well known, not only because she had lived in Las Vegas so long, but because she was always getting news from people. She was very pleasant to everyone and was well-liked. However, Audrey had her father's temper, and once she was angry, she could be a formidable opponent. Nothing made her more furious than when she felt her children's well being was threatened. It was then that the "mother bear" in her came out. If Audrey was angry with you, she could very skillfully, without using any obscenities, "chew you up and spit you out in little pieces"—to cite an expression we sometimes used. I heard her do that on the telephone when she was angry with one of my teachers.

When I was in the seventh grade, I had a teacher who left the room for quite a while. When he returned he was angry because the students weren't working. My friend Janie Power and I were doing our work. We were quiet and studious all the time, and the teacher knew we would not disobey his orders to work while he was gone. However, our classmates were all chattering away, not doing their reading. The teacher told us that as punishment we all had to write, "I will not talk while the teacher is out of the room." We had to write it ten thousand times.

Audrey knew I always had loads of homework. But this was a senseless assignment. She called the teacher at home that evening and told him it was totally unreasonable, and besides, I would not have been talking. He agreed that he knew Janie and I always obeyed and did our work but pointed out that he had to punish the whole class. My mother said ten thousand words—almost a novel—was ridiculous, a total waste of time. She angrily demanded that he change the assignment. She said, "My daughter will NOT do that assignment."

The next day the Castle Junior High School teacher, looking rather sheepish, reduced the assignment to writing the statement only a couple of hundred times.

When she attended PTA meetings, Audrey showed support for the teachers. However, when the teacher or school policy was clearly wrong, Audrey would voice her opinion vociferously. When Crystal was a senior in high school, the parents and teachers were meeting to discuss senior activities, advocating an all night party. Audrey argued against it. The other parents looked at her like she was being old-fashioned and overly strict. She said, "The others can do what they want, but my daughter is NOT going to an all night party."

The party was held and, of course, Crystal did not go. Some of the girls turned up pregnant after that night. Audrey could have said "I told you so" but she had the grace to keep it to herself.

Audrey told us that we had come from a long line of "fighters for the right, survivors in spite of hardships." She told us of ancestors who fought in the Revolutionary War. Audrey was proud that she was eligible to join the "Daughters of the American Revolution" although she never did. There was no chapter in Las Vegas. She told us the story of the only surviving family of the wagon train. Also, we were direct descendants of William the Conqueror through the Ogle/Waddell side of the family. Someone had also traced an ancestor to a passenger on the Mayflower, John Allerton, traced from William Harper Clements, Audrey's grandfather. Audrey emphasized that, like our tough ancestors, we must never give up but stay in the fight of life to survive no matter what. That did not mean that she did not get discouraged at times.

Once, in a moment of fatigue and despair, Audrey wrote a note in pencil on the last blank page of a book. Perhaps she and Clyde were having problems. Perhaps she was just tired and discouraged, realizing many of her goals in life had not been met. Most likely one of the short stories in the book made her sad, made her think of her own life and its difficulties. She wrote:

> I can't look back. If I do I want to cry and there is no time to cry. I am too busy fighting today's battles—and tomorrow's. Too soon it will be yesterday too, and I will still want to cry over it—over the bitterness, the frustrations and the things I wasn't able to do—not a bright prospect so I'll just keep fighting to give my kids a better chance—for my family were workers and didn't know there was a word like *quit*—came from a long line of women who picked and were picked by the wrong husbands.
> —A.C.S. [Audrey Clements Simpson][4]

Audrey hoped life would get easier, that she and Clyde could retire at the ranch, that she could be a great writer, that her children would be happy and successful. She had many dreams. But life in 1958 was as good as it was going to get in many ways.

Crystal and Wesley graduated from Robertson High School in 1958. Their classmate Eric J. Mason gave the student commencement address: "The Tall Men." Crystal sang the song, "Then You'll Remember Me." I thought her beautiful song was the best part of the entire program.

Our Grandpa Vern "Jack" Clements had been ill for some time. He and Mable had moved from their place in the "country" on South Broadway because of all the blowing dust. They lived at 504 Sycamore Southwest in Albuquerque, just across from a beautiful little park. Mable and "Jack" joined the Methodist church and were active members. They both had asthma, and Grandpa had some heart trouble as well. Mother always said he had weak lungs due to having barely survived double pneumonia when he had influenza in 1918. Also, he had suffered lead poisoning from his painting jobs.

On May 8, 1960 Mable called to say that "Jack" had died. We were all heartbroken. Audrey sat at the telephone with tears streaming down her cheeks. Her father had lived from December 19, 1891 to May 8, 1960—just sixty-eight years. We went to the funeral and tried to comfort Mable. She wept inconsolably even though she said she knew he was in heaven. She said she did not see how she could live without her "Jack." But she had to go on without him. She lived until

February 6, 1987 and died at the age of ninety-two.

When our Grandpa Clements died, Crystal was a student at Highlands University and I was a junior in high school. Crystal had been given an award for "perfect attendance" for four years of high school. I hoped to do the same but would not miss Grandpa's funeral. We had all loved him beyond words and we wanted to comfort Mable, for whom we had a great love also. At the funeral, Mother saw many friends and relatives she had not seen in years. There was a tall, dark woman who was in the line at the end of the service to pass by the casket. We were shocked to see her bend and kiss the body on the lips. Mother wondered if she was one of Vern's old girl friends.

When Audrey told her mother about Vern's death, Mabel Shearer, too, found tears in her eyes. Audrey often said her father was a man everyone loved. His grandchildren adored him. It was hard to imagine life in this world without him. Audrey, his oldest, felt very close to her father all her life. He had rescued her more than once from various situations. Once when she was very ill in the hospital and in the depths of despair, her father showed up unexpectedly and gave her the hope to fight on.

Audrey and Mable Day Clements spent time together after his death, and Audrey tried to encourage Mable. When Mable wanted to marry a man she had dated years before she met "Jack," Audrey encouraged her to do what she felt was right. Mabel married Russell Cowan and moved back to Missouri, her childhood home. Mother and Holly and I went with Betty Hardin to visit her there once. Mabel and Russell had a lovely house and yard and seemed quite happy. After Russell died, Mable moved to Colorado and lived in Grand Junction where she lived near Edward and his family.

On January 5, 1962, Addie Simpson died. It was bad weather, so Clyde went on the bus by himself to his mother's funeral. Even though we were sad about Grandpa's death—and two years later about our Granny's death—we had to continue with our daily lives. The sad times still gave way to happy times when we had family reunions at our house and most of the family came.

We were able to enjoy a few "luxuries." In 1957 Daddy had bought a reel-to-reel tape recorder. Crystal and I recorded music. Daddy recorded his violin playing and his singing. Crystal and I even made up our own "radio" dramas. Then when we were able to get a television set, we watched programs together. Clyde's favorite program was "Rawhide." Mother liked "Wagon Train." We all liked "Frontier Doctor" with Rex Allen as the star. We three sisters were very close and spent time playing various games and going places together.

Audrey Simpson, 1963. *Source*: Simpson Archives, photo by Wesley Lovett

After I received a scholarship to attend New Mexico Highlands University, Crystal and I had some classes together, including Chorus. Due to an overly demanding music instructor, I dropped Chorus and Crystal changed her major to Education. After receiving her degree, Crystal turned out to be one of the best elementary teachers in the area. She enjoyed teaching second graders. She probably would not have had such a satisfying career had she remained a music major. She did teach music for a year or two, but she ended up teaching second grade, as she was well qualified by the time she graduated with her B. A. in Elementary Education.

Crystal and Wesley L. Lovett had been dating since high school. Crystal was in the high school choir and then Wesley joined. Wesley took Crystal to the Sadie Hawkin's Day party where they won first prize for the best dressed couple. Sometimes they went to a movie. Audrey often invited Wesley to lunch or dinner at our house. He worked at Black's Grocery Store on Seventh Street early in the mornings, went to classes at the high school and worked for his lunch in the high school cafeteria. Then he worked after school. He worked at Highlands University in the Biology Department with Dr. Lora Shields. He was good with snakes, as he had played with them in the Chama area where he grew up. So he helped with the laboratory snakes.

Then Wesley and Crystal both went to college. Wesley went to Socorro to New Mexico Institute of Mining and Technology. He also went to New Mexico State University. Then he joined the Air Force. When Wesley's grandmother died, he was given leave to return to New Mexico. He came to visit Crystal, and their romance developed.

Wesley enjoyed spending time with our family and going to the ranch with us. He always brought his camera along. He took pictures of us along the way.

Dorothy, Holly, (in front) Crystal, and Audrey Simpson, Hermit's Peak in background, 1963
Source: Simpson Archives, photo by Wesley Lovett

Audrey, Holly, Crystal and Dorothy Simpson in front of the Fifteen Dollar House, 1963
Source: Simpson Archives, photo by Wesley Lovett

One evening we prepared a special dinner. I was in on a secret. Wesley was going to ask Crystal's parents for her hand in marriage. He had proposed and Crystal had said "Yes." It was on a Monday, Daddy's day off. Wesley and Crystal were excited and nervous.

As we sat around the dinner table, Crystal said, "We have something to ask you."

There was a pause. Then Wesley spoke up:"We'd like to get married."

Audrey and Clyde were very pleased and gave the couple their blessing.

Then there were wedding plans. Wesley and Crystal were married at the First Baptist Church in down-town Las Vegas. I was a bride's maid, along with our double cousin Donna Simpson and friend Jean Whiting who worked at the Optic. Holly was the flower girl. We went to a rehearsal ahead of time. Rev. John Ransdall, affectionately known as "Brother Johnny," was to perform the ceremony. He had been pastor at the First Baptist Church for many years.

When Wesley and Crystal were married October 27, 1962, Clyde was very proud as he walked his daughter down the aisle. When John Ransdall asked, "Who gives this woman away to be married?" Clyde spoke up proudly, "I do."

Audrey was as excited as any mother of the bride could be. She wrote up a wonderful wedding story for the Optic. It turned out to be a wonderful ceremony, with many friends and relatives in attendance. Betty Hardin made a wonderful wedding cake. There was a reception in the church basement.

Audrey and Clyde had given Wesley and Crystal their 1957 Chevy as a wedding gift so they would have transportation. It was one of the cars our granny had given Clyde and Audrey a few years before. Crystal and Wesley hid the car in the Carringtons' garage, thinking no one would find it there to "decorate it." But one of the relatives asked seven-year-old Holly where the car was. She didn't know better than to tell. So the car got well-decorated after all, with "Just Married" all over it.

Wesley was a year older than Crystal—born November 6, 1937. They had a lot in common and were destined to spend their lives together. Wesley had been stationed in New York. However, he was transferred to Denver where they headed after the wedding, grateful for the Chevrolet. We missed Crystal terribly but were glad to have Wesley in the family; and they always visited on holidays.

Wesley grew up in the Canjilon area on a ranch his grandparents had homesteaded after coming from Oklahoma. George Levi "Lee" Brand and Georgia Ann Brand brought Wesley up with a strong sense of moral values and a work ethic that helped him become independent. He was home schooled most of the time until he was invited to move into Las Vegas to stay with his sister Ruth and her husband Witt Harwell to attend high school. Wesley was close to his family in Las Vegas where another sister, Evelyn Wootton, and her husband, Dick Wootton, also lived.

Crystal and Wesley came home for Thanksgiving and Christmas after they were married. Then Wesley was transferred to Great Falls, Montana. When he was out of the service, he went to New Mexico State University and completed his degree. (Later, Crystal completed her degree at New Mexico Highlands University.) Wesley earned money as college photographer.

Thanksgiving at 1620 Seventh Street, left to right: Clyde Simpson, Audrey Simpson, Crystal Simpson, Mabel Shearer, Dorothy Simpson and Holly Simpson
Source: Simpson Archives, photo by Wesley Lovett

Audrey and Clyde were pleased that Crystal had married a good man. Holly seemed healthy and seemed to be thriving. Daddy went around singing his favorite songs, like "Jambalaya (on the Bayou)" made popular by Hank Williams or "Cattle Call" by Eddie Arnold. I didn't dislike Country Western music any more now that Daddy was home.

When I graduated from high school a year early and entered New Mexico Highlands University as an "early admission" student, I liked my classes and made some friends, although I missed my friends from high school. I was active at the Emmanuel Baptist Church and had some good church friends, including Tommy Gazaway who was just younger than I.

All of us were working to build our house at the ranch. Clyde laid foundation and poured cement. When Wesley was around, he helped.

Wesley Lovett on roof of ranch house; Clyde Simpson, standing, 1963
Source: Simpson Archive, photo by Audrey Simpson

We thought those good times would last forever; but nothing lasts forever, not even a happy family living in the 1950s and 1960s in a wonderful home.

Building the Dream Home

New Year's Day, 1965, saw a happy family gathering at 1620 Seventh Street. Mabel Shearer, now 75 years of age, wrote in Audrey's book:

Dear Audrey,
    What a nice dinner and visit we have had at your house this pleasant day.
    Betty's, Milly's, Crystal and Wesley are all here—and may we all be together often.
    May this year and each year following be happy and healthful and prosperous for you.
Love,
Your Mom[1]

Audrey had high hopes for that year. A move to the ranch was becoming a real possibility.

Audrey picked Clyde up from work at the Home Café every evening at nine. He entertained Holly a few minutes before she went to bed. Then Clyde and Audrey would visit about the day's activities, mentioning people they worked with. Clyde would talk about his day and people he'd encountered, sometimes telling about funny little things that had happened. Audrey would refer to the people she enjoyed working with at the Optic such as owner Lincoln O'Brien and his Chief Editor Walter Vivian and Walter's wife, Delma Vivian, also an editor; or the later owners Larry Finch and Tom Wright. Audrey enjoyed people she saw every day at work such as Manuel "Milkey" Maes, the circulation manager; Millicent Gensemer, another reporter; Jean Whiting, a young editor; or Bill Magill, a reporter and photographer. Sometimes she would relate the day's activities, mentioning co-workers such as Bobby Aken (Mrs. Eugene Aken) who was receptionist and business manager in the front office or Art Trujillo, a young sports editor and photographer—"a kid, but very smart and learning fast." Audrey also spoke about Clarence Falvey who started at the Optic as a printer and worked his way up to mechanical superintendent, the top job in the backshop. But before long the conversation would turn to their work on their house at the ranch.

Audrey and Clyde enjoyed the few holidays they had from the daily grind of work. Clyde worked nine hours a day cooking in a hot kitchen and only had one day a week off. Audrey put in extra hours at home. They treasured the few days when both were off at the same time, days such as Christmas or Labor Day.

One day in early spring when Audrey and Clyde went to Forest Springs Ranch, they walked along the path from the Fifteen Dollar House, across the bridge and into the open field where they had started to build their big ranch house, their dream home, a house nearly as large as the house on Seventh Street. On his days off, Clyde would work at the ranch, hauling sand and rocks to prepare for the cement foundation. The whole family would go out on weekends and work.

"This is a good place for our house," Audrey said. "I'm glad we chose this spot."

"Yes. It's close to the county road and the electric line," Clyde agreed. "This house will be big, something like twenty-two feet by sixty feet—almost as big as our house on Seventh Street."

They sat on an old log on the hillside.

"We're getting old," Clyde said, settling himself on the log.

"Well, maybe we can retire soon," Audrey replied. "We've worked furiously for years just to make ends meet." Audrey declared. "We've done a good job with the girls. They'll be OK. And now that Crystal's married and Dorothy is graduating from the University in June, we can slow down some. I can always teach Holly at home since the school bus doesn't come out this way."

"If anything happens to me, you and the girls will be OK," Clyde said. "Most of the bills are paid. Just put me in a wooden box and bury me under a pine tree up here on this hillside."

"You're going to live a long time yet," Audrey said. "You haven't had a drink in ten years."

"When I walked out of that hospital in Albuquerque that night, I was completely healed. I made a bargain with God that if He would heal me I would never take another drink. A man shouldn't bargain with God unless he knows he can keep his end of the bargain. I've done it only with God's help. When God healed my kidneys, He took away the alcoholism, too. But all the years I drank have taken a toll." It was true. Clyde looked and felt ten years older than he was.

"Well, God forgave you and I did, too," Audrey said. "You've been a good husband and father."

"These last ten years have been the happiest of my life," Clyde said. "I'm living proof of what forgiveness can do for a man. I'd like to get back to preaching. We could live here in the mountains and I could try to start a mission in the village again."

"Yes," Audrey agreed. "Soon we'll retire and have our dream home and you can have the freedom to do whatever you please instead of being tied down to that job."

"And you'll have time to write like you've always wanted to—my Sweetheart of the Mountains," Clyde smiled.

They walked back to the Fifteen Dollar House, hand in hand, commenting on the beauty of the mountains behind the place.

Clyde J. Simpson, 1964. *Source*: Simpson Archives, photo by Wesley Lovett

Mabel and Vivian had sold the Old Homestead Ranch to Bob and Opal Simpson after the Shearers had moved to Montezuma Road north of Las Vegas. Bob and Opal, too, wanted to retire and live at the ranch. They had several enterprises in mind, including accommodations for a small guest ranch and raising chinchillas. They had been living in Reserve where Bob was a mortician. After moving to Las Vegas Opal worked at Hilton Motors as a bookkeeper and Bob was on call at Johnsen's Funeral Home.

Bobby and Jackie were married. Donna stayed with us at the house on

Seventh Street for a while so she could attend Robertson High School while her parents were moving and getting settled. At the Old Homestead Ranch, Donna had the little cabin that had been Vivian's as her own, and once or twice I went out and spent the weekend there. Bob and Opal rebuilt the old stone house that had been Grandfather Shearer's, the house that had burned, and they lived in it when they weren't in Las Vegas. Donna graduated from high school. Donna and I were like sisters. We were nearly the same age, and we shared the same grandparents since our mothers were sisters and our fathers were brothers. We dreamed of our futures. We would both become teachers, marry and have children. We both liked creative writing.

Audrey and Clyde worked on the house at every opportunity. Clyde plotted out the space that he and Audrey and selected for their ranch house, just a short way down the canyon from the Fifteen Dollar House in an open field. Audrey wrote:

> After we got it [the house on Seventh Street] more or less as we wanted it we began building at the ranch once more. We were again hauling sand and rock for a foundation, but this time we had an old jeep truck so it was easier than using the little red wagon—though the wagon was still around and we did haul things in it at times.
>
> We picked a site below the other cabins in what had once been a field. It was somewhat protected by the hillside at the north and a little raise of ground to the west. We could not see the little cabins from this site.
>
> Once again we cut trees, still by hand, although chain saws were more common by 1960 when we started this building. Once more we struggled to get the logs peeled. As a spare time project, it took us more than two years to get the logs ready and then laid up. Crystal and Wesley [Lovett] were engaged to be married so he [Wesley] helped some on the building while on a month's leave from the U. S. Air Force.
>
> We planned this to be a full size house, with 8 foot ceilings and a large picture window on the south. The first room was 20 x 22. Once more we heaved and sweat to get the logs in place. These were much larger logs than those in the Ten and Fifteen Dollar Houses.
>
> Climbing 8 foot walls for access to the embryo rooms was too much. So Wesley cut a front door space in the crude logs so we could enter and exit easier. He cut a 40 inch span for we'd had experience with narrow doors in town. We wanted our mountain doors high and wide, if not handsome. A 20-inch door is an aggravation. You can't carry an

armful of wood in or a dishpan out. Your elbows won't fit.[2]

Clyde and Holly would go and work on the house when he had time off. Sometimes the entire family would go. Audrey wrote:

> Each week Clyde and Holly came out [to the ranch] on his day off and mixed cement for a floor, after he hauled tons of dirt and rocks to fill inside the foundation to make a level floor. The drop in the land was so much greater than it looked. We thought we built on a level spot but the down side proved to be nearly 3 feet lower than the upper side in that 22 foot space. He mixed cement in the wheelbarrow, hauling water from the creek in plastic bottles and jars. He would set up a frame about 4 x 4 feet square, put a layer of sand on top of the packed dirt of the under floor and then mix cement, one heaping shovel of cement to four heaping shovels of sand. This was mixed thoroughly while dry and then the water was added until it was less than soupy. As someone said, when it was poured it was supposed to look about the thickness of a fresh cow "chip." On a good long day he could mix two squares and pour it. Holly would use a trowel and help smooth it down.
>
> After the floor was in Clyde nailed 2 by 6's on the south side of the house for a large window. He cut out three logs, leaving a log at the top and bottom for support and something to nail 2 x 8's for window frames. We used three windows, making a six foot "picture window" that really warmed the house in the winter when the sun shone in. We also had one full sized window in the front, or east side of the house that gave us early morning sun all summer.
>
> The roof was the next big job. Clyde bought 4 x 4's about 6 feet long, which were cut to the right lengths by hand saw. Measuring for the center of the front and back walls, they started the supports for the main roof pole. In the beginning of the roofing project Wesley sat on the top log of the wall and nailed a 4 foot length of 4 x 4 with long spikes to the top log. Then he nailed a slightly shorter piece of 4 x 4 to that 4 x 4, repeating this until he had about 18 inches of 4 x 4's in place. At that point he lifted the heavy 26 foot log that would support the roof to the top of the 4 x 4's. Then they braced the 4 x 4's with a 2 x 4 so that they could not sway forward with their own weight. From then on it was a matter of main strength to get the roof tree in place. Wesley would lift the log, Clyde would shove a 4 x 4, slightly shorter than the last one, under the log. Wesley would nail it in place and standing on nothing but the slick

top log, lift the roof tree another four inches. This process was repeated with 15 pieces of 4 x 4's until the end supports were five feet high from the wall's top log to the resting place for the roof tree.[3]

Audrey wrote that she and Clyde, now "experienced" house builders, enjoyed working on their dream house where they would live after they retired. Their son-in-law Wesley was a great help. Audrey wrote in "Building Notes:"

> We decided that there should be two logs placed across on top of the gable ends to nail the 2 x 4's to hold up the 1 x 6 boards that would be the roof. Wesley and Clyde managed to get the roof on before Wesley left. That was a big help for Wesley's sky hook was a lot more substantial than Clyde's. After the boards were in place, heavy rolled roofing was used as the final touch.
>
> Then came the chinking between the logs. We used the same process as for the 10 and 15 dollar houses, filling in with small trees and mud. However, this being a real house, we cemented between the logs on the outside. This gave it a more finished look. It was a very neat and cute cabin.
>
> Inside Clyde finished the walls with 4 x 8 plywood sheets. We set up the old chicken house brooder stove.[4]

Until the new ranch house was finished, it was good to have the shelter of the Fifteen Dollar Cabin when the weather was unpleasant. We stayed there overnight when we had vacations. Sometimes a friend like Jean Whiting would go out with us to enjoy the beauty of the country.

Mabel Shearer's good wishes on New Year's Day in 1965 may have been remembered when Audrey looked at the beginnings of her dream home and thanked God for bringing her to this point in her life. But 1965 was to become a journey through the valley of the shadow. The dream home was not yet finished, but its completion was very near, with Wesley helping Clyde as much as he could. It seemed certain that Audrey and Clyde would spend their golden years together enjoying their mountains. Audrey was sure that retirement at the ranch was soon going to become a reality. She just didn't know that she would be alone.

9

The Day After Easter

When Crystal and Wesley moved, first to Denver, Colorado and then to Great Falls, Montana where Wesley was stationed in the Air Force, I was finishing my B.A. degree at New Mexico Highlands University with a major in Speech. I was looking forward to finishing my student teaching, graduating, and then going on for graduate work at the University of Utah. Holly attended Douglas School.

We missed Crystal but knew she and Wesley were happy. She had occupied the bedroom opposite Mama and Daddy's bedroom in what had been the auditorium part of the house, next to the living room. One could walk from Audrey and Clyde's bed room up the ramp and continue down the hall past the other two bedrooms. In the part of the rectangular house that had been a parsonage were the two smaller bedrooms, one on each side of the hallway. Holly had the bedroom on the north side and I had the bedroom on the south side of the house. Holly's was next to the bathroom. Then the hall opened out into the dining room and kitchen. We kept busy keeping the house clean because Crystal had done most of the work before.

We continued to hold family reunions at our home at 1620 Seventh Street after Crystal and Wesley were married. Milly and her three children had moved from Colorado into the home on Montezuma Road with Mabel and Vivian. Milly got a job at the New Mexico State Hospital as a secretary/typist in 1964. There she met Dr. Gordon "Doc" Wickman, the dentist, and after a few years they married. He had two children, Sally and Dale. Roger, Sam and Dianna finished school at Robertson High. As mentioned before, Roger went on for his Ph.D. and became a nuclear physicist. Sam Dixon joined the Marines and rescued the wounded in Vietnam helicopter evacuations. Dianna Dixon married. Grandma Shearer always prayed for her family, and she especially prayed for her two grandsons to return from the war safely. Both Sam Dixon and Dwight Braziel were in Viet Nam. Both did return to marry and have families.

Audrey and Clyde were working hard to provide a good life for themselves and their daughters, hoping to retire at the ranch. Audrey was often at her old Royal manual typewriter in the evenings. She usually had stories for the newspaper she had to finish in order to meet deadlines, but sometimes she had time for a little free lance writing. They did not go to church often. Clyde worked on Sunday. Audrey was usually exhausted from her job and had to use any spare time she had to do household chores. But they always maintained their faith. When I was about eight years old, I asked my mother what her favorite hymn was. She replied that it was "Jesus, Savior Pilot Me." I realized in later years how much the words of that song meant to her as she depended on Him, her Pilot, to guide her through the stormy waters of life. She wrote:

> My favorite church song, "Jesus Savior Pilot Me"—from when I was very small. Mother sang it beautifully, "Over Life's Tempestuous Sea." My favorite Bible Verse (besides the Beatitudes and the 23rd Psalm) "and we know all things work together for good to them that love God" Romans 8: 28. I have lived by all of these—or tried to.[1]

Sometimes it was hard to see how things could work together for good, but Audrey never lost her faith. On November 22, 1963, Audrey was in her usual place at her desk at the Optic as the lunch hour was approaching. Bill Magill was standing at the teletype just across the room when she heard him exclaim something like, "Oh, God!" Then he said, "The President's been shot!"

Audrey got up and watched the type as it came over the wire. She read where it said "three shots were fired" in downtown Dallas. Soon other Optic employees gathered around. By lunch time when Mother went to pick me up at Highlands University where I worked in the Speech office, it was known that President Kennedy had been shot and taken to Dallas hospital. I had heard the news from a student who had a radio and came into the building with the announcement. Mother and I went home and turned on the radio. We heard the announcement that the President was dead. Everyone was frightened, bewildered, and stunned. Mother went back to work and I went to my classes, but nothing much was done in class. It was as if we were under attack. Perhaps the war we feared was about to start. America and Russia had been in a cold war for years. No one knew what to think until the news came out that a lone gunman had been accused of the crime. All were glued to their television sets for several days after that.

Audrey told us to maintain our faith and we did. But often that faith was tested. One of those times was when Clyde had a heart attack in April of 1965. Crystal and Wesley were in Las Cruces where Wesley was finishing his degree. I was in Albuquerque where I was completing my last semester at Highlands University, doing my student teaching. Audrey wrote in her notes, "Holly:"

> I don't know where you [Holly] were going to school when Clyde had

his heart attack. I think it was on a Thursday or a Friday before Easter. I took him and maybe you as I went to work. I noted Dr. Mortimer at St. Anthony's [hospital] so I suggested he go in and see him there. That was about 8 o'clock. He had to wait there until about 10 a.m. before the doctor came out. The nurse didn't call him and Clyde didn't ask them to. When the Doctor came and saw him in the waiting room, Clyde told him he needed an exam. Doc said it would be cheaper at the office, so Clyde said he would see him there. I guess he walked to the office—or else walked home [several long blocks, either way] and called me. Anyway, at the office, doctor said he might have had a heart attack and should go to the hospital—so he went back to St. A. and they got him a room and made tests.[2]

Naturally Audrey was worried. Her notes continued:

When I went in after work I saw Clyde and he didn't seem too bad off. I had to leave Holly in the car while I went in. He [the doctor] had told the nurses to send the heart test by me and they sent it by mail. He [the doctor] said they would take another in the a.m. He still wasn't sure Clyde had a heart attack. I tried to calm Clyde down. Clyde was amused because someone from Meadow's Home came in and started to take him away to Meadows. The nurse saw them as they were taking him out and made them put him back to bed. Clyde wanted to go home. Dorothy came in for Easter vacation from practice teaching in Albuquerque. I was going to call Crystal but her time was so close [to have her baby]—less than 3 weeks I was afraid she and Wesley would come up so I wrote them a letter that they would get too late. Clyde told Doc he had claustrophobia and had to get out. Later Dr. Mortimer said, "I wonder why I never knew he had claustrophobia." I just said, "I guess because there wasn't much to do for it in the early days."[3]

Clyde was relieved to be out of the hospital and home again. He began to talk about his plans for after his recovery. He mentioned other fellows he knew who had survived heart attacks and how life went on for them at a slower pace. He planned to retire from the Home Café and move to the ranch. He figured he and Audrey had done it before; they could do it again. He said he planned to start up his full gospel mission again. He always wanted to do mission work and preaching. He would become an evangelist. They could home school ten-year-old Holly at the ranch.

But Audrey was not so optimistic. She wrote:

> Dr. said Clyde could go home Saturday evening. I called an ambulance—Rogers because they were so close to the hospital. They didn't come for more than an hour. Clyde was fit to be tied—so was I. Finally we got home and put him to bed on the couch in the front room. The doc said he could get up to go to the bathroom. That evening Mortimer came by and visited a long while. I called the Home Café and said Clyde had to quit due to heart attack. I knew Clyde felt his job was gone and was discouraged. All day Easter Sunday you [Holly] and Clyde lay on the couch watching TV. You looked so peaked and scared. Later you said, "I knew he was going to die." Dorothy was there too.[4]

I was staying at Jacqueline Simpson Rice's home, which was only a few blocks away from Del Norte High School where I was doing my student teaching. Audrey paid her for my room and board. Jackie's husband, Frank Rice, was a New Mexico State Police Officer. They had two little boys, Matt and Brett. I went home for Easter on the bus. It was then I realized Daddy was really sick. I knew he had been having the "flu" but didn't know he was having heart problems. I went to church on Easter and then stayed at the house all day. Opal and Bob came to visit. I went to bed that night hoping for the best, not expecting anything bad to happen the next day. But the next day came early. It was April 19, 1965. I wore a blue blouse with a turquoise blue skirt. I thought at first it would be like any other day, but I was wrong. Audrey wrote in her notes, "Holly:"

> After a restless night I got up early. I got a clean undershirt for Clyde and gave it to him to put on. He wasn't pleased and jerked the dirty one off and jammed his arms into the clean one holding it above his head. I don't know whether or not he had already gone to the bathroom. He began to feel bad and took a pill. I had bought $30.00 worth of medicine for him Saturday and never even opened or used most of it. He asked, "Would you rather I would go back to the hospital?" I said, "Whatever you want," and he said he didn't want to go back to the hospital. So I said, as I went down the hall, "I would rather have you at home for then I can look after you and Holly at the same time."
>
> He began to have real bad pain.
> "Do you want me to call the doc or a preacher?"
> "A preacher," he said.
> "Do you want me to call the old Baptist preacher that lived 3

doors down the street." [Rev. Noel Moore, Emmanuel Baptist Church.]

"No, I don't want him."

"I met the young new Assembly of God preacher," I said. "He seemed OK."

"Call him," Clyde said.

I did but it took a long while for him to get there. He read a psalm and prayed for him. It was a bad psalm choice.[5]

Audrey felt that everything was going wrong. She wrote:

> He [the young preacher] came in nicely dressed and devout. He prayed for Clyde and never asked the Lord to heal him. I felt Clyde get that—the lack of a prayer that he would get well—recover. I felt him give up with that prayer. Then I couldn't get the preacher to leave so I could be with Clyde. He hung on talking and talking. I finally got rid of him and went back to Clyde.
>
> He immediately said, "Call Holly."
>
> "She is still asleep," I said,
>
> "Call her. I want to see her." So I woke her up and she went into the bedroom.
>
> Opal came about that time and I called Dr. Mortimer. I called 2 or 3 times. His wife answered each time I think. He had to shave and eat, etc.[6]

Holly went in to the bedroom and talked to her daddy. Then she thought he was going to take a nap and left his room. But we kept checking to see how Daddy was doing, and he wasn't sleeping, so we'd both asked, "How are you feeling?"

Each time he would say, "A little better."

Finally Holly and I went into his room to again ask how he was feeling. This time he did not say he was feeling better.

He said the words to Holly he had said so often in their play, "Take care of yourself Top Cat."

Holly replied, "I will, Officer Diddle."

We left the room so he could rest.

Minutes later, Daddy began to cry out in extreme pain: "Jesus, help me!" Those were his last words. He passed out after that. Audrey wrote:

> Clyde was gasping and I knew he needed oxygen. So I couldn't

think how to get it except calling Johnson's ambulance, as they carried oxygen. I tried to put another glycerin in his mouth. Opal kept patting him and saying "Just rest." I felt his feet and they were still warm.

The doctor came and said, "How long has he been like this?"

"About 10 minutes," I said.

Dr. Mortimer listened to Clyde's heart and said in a very shocked voice, "Why, he's gone."[7]

Audrey wrote:

> The ambulance came right then and took him away. I wanted to get to talk to him but there were too many around and I never even got to say good bye. After they took him away Dr. asked if I was OK. "You have had other blows, haven't you?" I could only nod. "You might give me something for Holly," I said. He gave me some pills or capsules—three, I think.[8]

Holly and I had gone into the kitchen to get out of the way while the doctor was there.

It was twelve or thirteen steps from Audrey and Clyde's bedroom to the kitchen—into the hall from the bedroom, up the ramp, and down the hall between the two smaller bedrooms, past the bathroom, through the dining room and into the kitchen. I heard Dr. Mortimer's steps as he came up the ramp and down the hall toward us. A terrible feeling of fear gripped me. Then the doctor's tall, lanky figure, looming in the hallway, entered the kitchen. His face was solemn. Holly and I were scared of what he was going to say. Somehow I knew Daddy was gone even before the doctor spoke.

The doctor said sadly, "Your daddy is going to sleep for a long, long time."

I felt a terrible sinking feeling. I knew what he meant but I couldn't believe it. I felt the blood drain from my face.

For Holly it took longer to sink in. I think she asked the doctor what he meant and he told her plainly that her daddy had died. Holly started screaming and sobbing. The doctor left without another word.

Audrey had to deal with everything at once. She knew she had to get Holly to calm down. She wrote:

> I went in and called Mrs. Carrington. She was shocked. I asked her to talk to Holly. Which she did, explaining death is a part of life and to

be expected. Anyway, after she talked to Mrs. Carrington Holly was OK. Then I called Evelyn [Wootton] and asked her to get in touch with Wesley and ask him to tell Crystal and be sure she wasn't alone when he told her.[9]

Ruth Carrington had helped more than one person deal with death. She helped Holly calm down and realize that life must go on, that her daddy had gone on to heaven and would be in a happy place, that he would not want her to be unhappy. So Holly pulled herself together as well as she could. In later years, Holly showed her gratitude to Ruth Carrington. Holly stayed with her at her home after the elderly lady developed health problems and was diagnosed with Alzheimer's disease. Holly helped her with her meals and kept her company. When Ruth Carrington died, Holly attended the graveside services. She had brought a pine branch, with pine cones attached, from the ranch. She asked to lay it on the casket. Holly's simple gift showed she understood how much Ruth Carrington had loved the beautiful mountains and trees, how much she had loved nature, how much she had cherished her ranch.

Opal's presence was calm and reassuring. She helped Audrey think of the practical things that had to be done. Audrey wrote:

> Then I told Opal I had to get the life insurance paper out of the bank. I had kept that $1,000 Insurance Policy up for 20 years. It was 20 pay life and had to have a death reported within 24 hours. Opal and I went to the bank and got it out of the locked box. As we left Opal told Oliva Dychman that Clyde had died. I told her I only needed the insurance to give to the Mortuary. Opal took me to the Mortuary to pick out a casket. It wasn't that I didn't want him to have the best but I knew Clyde would think we got one too high priced, $700 and some dollars. The Mortuary guy was nice—Opal insisted we had to have a more expensive one as we had a social standing that had to be lived up to. There was just enough insurance, $1000 to pay the mortuary and pay the note he had at the bank. I still had to pay off the truck.[10]

Many people were surprised when a photograph of Clyde and a death announcement appeared on the front page of the *Las Vegas Daily Optic* the next day. Usually, only nationally known people or celebrities made the front page of the local newspaper at their deaths. But Audrey had worked for the Optic for over ten years, so it was a kind gesture on the part of the people at the Optic to put the notice and photo on the front page. It read, in part:

The funeral was held Wednesday, April 21. Honorary pallbearers were: Frank Shearer of Hamlin, Texas; Edward Clements, Grand Junction, Colorado; David Braziel, Santa Rosa; Dr. Stanley Hardin, Portales; and Martin Rapp from the Home Café; Dr. H. M. Mortimer; Fred Gerk; George Maloof; and E. E. [Pete] Gardner of Las Vegas.[11]

The *Optic* reported that relatives from out of town were: Mr. and Mrs. Thomas Sheffield and Jewel of Port Neches, Texas; [Thomas and Ouida Sheffield] Mrs. Clint Oglesby [Rhea] of Orange, Texas; Miss Mary Simpson; Glen Simpson; Mrs. Frank Rice and Matt and Brett; Mrs. Mable Clements, all of Albuquerque; Dr. and Mrs. Stanley Hardin of Portales; and Mr. and Mrs. David Braziel of Santa Rosa.[12]

Audrey wrote about the events that followed that dark morning, the day after Easter—April 19, 1965.

> Crystal and Wesley came from Las Cruces. Dorothy stayed over. Mary and Rhea and Glen and Mabel [Clements] came.
>
> The Home Café brought in a huge platter of fancy food. The Rebekahs brought one meal and many people brought many things. Betty and family and Jessica and family came. I don't remember if Frank and Edward came. I laid off work several days. I took Holly to the Mortuary to say good bye to Clyde and asked if she wanted to touch his hand. You [Holly] didn't. I still didn't get to talk to him as I would have liked to.
>
> The afternoon of the funeral Mrs. Carrington stayed at the house, 1620 Seventh Street. Rev. Moore gave the sermon and someone sang, not as good as our girls could sing. She [Mrs. Carrington] stayed with Crystal too while we went to the ranch where we had decided to have our cemetery. Bob had gotten some fellow to dig the grave. He also said the funeral was private so no one tried to come out but the family. Wesley drove me out in the truck. I forgot the ranch [house] keys. After the ceremony we women all walked up towards the house and they, Wesley and someone else, began to throw dirt into the grave on to the coffin. Those clods hitting the box rang in my ears and still do. I could hardly stand it. They pounded on the lid and I could hear the sound clear to the house and beyond. I guess you were there Holly but I cannot remember much after those clods hitting the casket of the one I loved so long. After a day or so everyone was gone. Rhea wanted to take you Holly to Houston. I told her I needed you worse than ever now.[13]

Audrey was grateful that Clyde's three sisters, Ouida, Rhea and Mary and his brothers, Glen and Robert, were all there. She was also grateful that her own brothers and sisters, their children, and other relatives and friends were nearby to offer comfort. Her step-mother Mabel Clements came from Albuquerque. And of course her own mother, Mabel Shearer, and step-father, Vivian Shearer, were there as well. Audrey continued her "Holly" notes:

> Somehow we got through the 6 weeks until school was out. You [Holly] would come down to the Optic to wait for 5 [five o'clock]. Once you were in such a hurry for us to leave that as I put my stuff away—cleaning off my desk—you grabbed my typewriter table and slammed it into the wall and my typewriter bounced off and broke something. I was terribly embarrassed and offered to pay to have it fixed. When Karen [Lovett] was born [May 5, 1965] we went to Las Cruces and helped Crystal out a few days. When Dorothy graduated from HU and was home for the summer I could rest easy during the day while I worked. [14]

Karen Clydine Lovett, Audrey's first granddaughter, was born May 5, 1965 in Las Cruces. We all regretted that Clyde never got to see Karen.

Audrey tried to carry on as usual at 1620 Seventh Street. She even held a family reunion there. We had lots of people at our house. The kids enjoyed playing on the front lawn. Clyde was so proud of that yard with the fir trees and the lawn. He had spent hours watering them and caring for them, so the front yard, while small, was very nice. Clyde had put in a front door with glass panes. Some of the kids were chasing ten-year-old Holly, playing tag. She ran up to the front door, stumbled, and pushed her hand through a pane of glass. Audrey rushed Holly to the emergency room. Dr. Mortimer removed glass fragments and stitched up her arm and wrist.

At age 21, I graduated from Highlands University in May, 1965 and enrolled at the University of Utah in Salt Lake City, as I had received a Graduate Assistantship. My Speech professor at New Mexico Highlands University, Walter F. Brunet, had encouraged me to apply for one and I had received several offers. I chose Salt Lake City because it was nearest home. Betty Hardin and Mother loaded up my belongings in Betty's car and she drove us to Salt Lake City. I had a very small dorm room, a single room. Audrey hated to drive away and leave me there, looking out from the second story window of my room. She said she would never forget getting into the car in the parking lot and seeing me at the window of the two-story building, waving, looking so alone in my pink dress. It was hard for her to realize her children were growing up. She wrote:

> Dorothy got a teaching fellowship to U of Utah at Salt Lake City. She had to be there a week early. Betty took Holly and Dorothy and me in September, 1965. We drove up over the Million Dollar Highway that scared me to Grand Junction and Edward's where we stayed all night. Then to Salt Lake and got Dorothy settled in her little room. Betty wanted to leave at once—it was raining—so we did—leave fail little Dorothy standing in that upstairs window in the dorm. We drove a hundred miles or so and headed for the Grand Canyon. Betty decided not to go to Grand Canyon so we headed back to the main highway towards Colorado and New Mexico. It snowed heavily. We almost wrecked once when Betty tried to pass something and there was a vehicle in the way. Later the windshield iced up and she got out her side to clean it off. So I got out my side to do the same and the door buttons were frozen shut. We couldn't open the car doors. Holly being inside opened them for us. It was snowing hard and if she hadn't been there we might have frozen. We drove straight through to Albuquerque and to some place. We got in there about 9 p.m.—a mighty lot of miles in 1 day. On our own with Dorothy gone! You [Holly] were 10 and could stay alone legally but I had to go to Legion Park School and pick you up after school each day. Sometimes you went to the Optic and sometimes stayed home alone. It was a very hard year. Once you [Holly] came out and started hitting some girl teasing you.[15]

It was a hard year for Audrey, alone in the house on Seventh Street, with Holly not well much of the time. Audrey wasn't well either. She wanted to retire.

Wesley and some of the local men helped finish the ranch house for Audrey. She sold the house on Seventh Street and moved to the ranch in 1966 after she decided to retire from the Optic. It was shocking to realize that she received more from Clyde's Social Security than she made working! She and Holly moved into the new house at Forest Springs Ranch. I returned from Salt Lake City, as I had a job teaching at West Las Vegas High School. Audrey recalled:

> When Dorothy was ready to come home from Salt Lake City, she got a school [teaching position] at West Las Vegas.
> Anyway, Dorothy was with you [Holly] the summer of 1966. I quit August 15 (I think) and began moving stuff to the ranch and had

Ramón and Jerry to help build the back rooms. I sold the 7th Street house to Cora Maloof.

Dorothy got an apartment on 6th Street that Mother used to have in the Coble House on the corner across from the Library. I helped her buy the little Buick, gave her the $600 down payment and she paid me back.

Crystal and Wesley and Karen came up at Thanksgiving and helped us with the final move. You were running a high fever so you stayed at Dorothy's a few days and [Dr.] Zold came to see you there—said you had "a little pneumonia." I took you out of Legion Park School and got books for you from the city school and had to order some. I finished teaching you the 6th grade and all of the Seventh. We had school in the mornings and I would assign you some home work. In Seventh they had the new math, and the teachers' booklet said to make the student do it the book way, not the older way. I gave up on it and taught you practical math that you would need later—like keeping check books, etc.[16]

Audrey saved one of Holly's Mother's Day cards she had made. The card is as follows:

> To a nice wonderful sweet loveable understanding mother
> May your day be as any other which will be filled with the happiness that you have enjoyed every since 3 daughters came rolling into your life.
> Happy Mothers Day
> Love,
> Holly[17]

Audrey, of course, wrote verses about her children, including the following for Holly:

> Here's to my Holly
> Alone on the ranch
> And not so jolly
> But you will see
> Queen of the mountain gals
> You will be[18]

I got a job teaching at West Las Vegas High School. At the end of the school year I returned to Salt Lake City to finish my Master's degree. I had bought a car while in Las Vegas, so I drove. Ruth Gardner traveled with me.

Since Audrey and Holly were living in the house Clyde had started—and Wesley had finished—Audrey determined to home school Holly. She wrote:

> I have Holly's school books now so we have started the school routine again. We have school all morning each day. She is in the 7th grade now. I had to order a teacher's book to go with her new Math book, for I am far from expert on that type of math.
>
> Dorothy had a nice trip to Salt Lake City, with Ruth—Lelama's daughter, who came home on the bus.[19]

I finished up my degree, working several part-time jobs, and graduated in June, 1968. I had taught Beginning Speech and had studied under some wonderful professors during the two years it took me to get my M.S. degree. The Chair of my Graduate Committee, Dr. E. J. Kerikas, helped me enormously, as did my Speech Communication professor, Dr. Royal L. Garff, who also served on my Graduate Committee.

None of the family was able to attend my graduation in June, 1968. I then had to decide whether to take a job offer in Utah or one in New Mexico. I took a job that had been offered at Santa Rosa High School. Holly could live with me and go to school there in the eighth grade. I rented an apartment in Santa Rosa and Mother helped me and Holly get moved in. We went to the ranch most weekends to spend time with Audrey in the big, new log cabin. Audrey wrote:

> Dorothy came back from Utah to get a school. She got a school at Santa Rosa teaching in high school. You [Holly] were ready for 8th grade. You went with her to the 8th grade. (The school burned in Santa Rosa, 8th grade in 1968. You graduated from the 8th grade in 1969.) You had trouble with your math but got through OK. You stayed at Santa Rosa through the 8th, 9th and 10th grades, coming home when you could, and I went down a time or two. I took Mable Bibb once.[20]

Audrey began to do more free lance writing, inspired by living under the gentle slopes of the mountains she loved. She was alone. But in another sense, she was not alone. She always said that God was her constant guide, so whenever she felt lonely, she called upon Him and He comforted her.

She would plant flowers in the mountain cemetery at their Forest Springs Ranch and remember Clyde. As she was planting some perennial sweet peas along the fence one day, Audrey remembered what Clyde had once said: "When I die, just take me and bury me in a wooden coffin under a pine tree at the ranch."

Audrey had made sure that his request was granted. The little land that had been set aside for the family cemetery was surrounded by pine trees, and Clyde's grave was under a big pine tree on the little slope. Every Easter we remembered that Clyde's death had occurred the day after Easter. Clyde had placed his trust in the One who made Easter possible with the joy and hope of the Resurrection.

In later years, when I put flowers on my parents' graves, I thought of S. Omar Barker's poem, "Mountain Cemetery." Used here with permission, it expresses the lovely solitude of the mountains that Audrey and Clyde loved.

> Pine trees grow there, God's own planting,
> On a hillside gently slanting
> To a little bench well hidden
> From the gaze of eyes unbidden.
>
> There the deer's step, light and quick,
> Treads the green kinnikinnick
> That comes leniently creeping
> Where beloved dead lie sleeping.
>
> There the bluejay's azure wing
> Is a wild, familiar thing.
> And green hills they loved the best
> Guard good mountain-folk at rest.[21]

10

Free-Lance

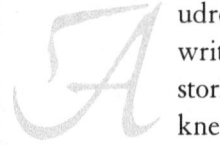udrey planned to live in her mountains and work as a free-lance writer. She hoped to write fiction and non-fiction—inspirational stories, historical pieces, poetry, and an autobiography. Those who knew her as a journalist missed her at the Optic. One lady told me:

"No one can write our stories up the way Audrey did! We miss her newspaper work!"

"Well, she's doing her creative writing now," I replied.

"I know she's good at it!" the lady said. "But no one can take her place as a Society Editor!"

Audrey continued to have trouble with her legs, spots that broke open and refused to heal. She'd had varicose veins when she was in her 30's. The doctor had "stripped" some of the veins. Then after the phlebitis thrombosis before and after Holly was born, her legs were weakened. She wore elastic stockings for years to help the circulation. I remember every day after work she would come home, pull off her stockings, and put her legs up. The doctor told her to keep her legs up as much as she could, but her job and her home responsibilities didn't provide much time for that. Finally, after Clyde's death and her move to the ranch, she had such bad leg ulcers that even driving the International Scout with standard transmission was difficult. Clyde had bought that Scout just before he died. His insurance helped pay it off. After the 1971 fire, Audrey bought a new International Scout.

Dr. Mortimer retired and Audrey went to Dr. L. Zold. In 1967, he recommended a specialist in Albuquerque. I took her to Presbyterian Hospital and stayed with my aunt, Mary Simpson, during that time. (About that time Glen Simpson, whose wife Clarabelle had died some time ago, re-married. He married Mildred in the Methodist Church.) The hospital stay was a disaster. Not only was the skin graft unsuccessful but Audrey developed phlebitis while she was there. And the skin graft left Audrey's bad leg worse than ever.

I was at the hospital with my mother the morning she realized she had phlebitis. One leg was swollen up twice the size of the other. She'd had the condition numerous times before, so she knew what it was. She told the young doctor when he came in that morning that she had phlebitis. He said, "It can't be phlebitis. You've had it before and you can't get phlebitis more than once." I wondered, *Where did he go to medical school?* My grandmother, my mother, and some of my aunts all had phlebitis more than once. Audrey finally convinced the doctor, and she was treated for phlebitis.

In later years Audrey sometimes developed blood clots in her legs—phlebitis or phlebitis thrombosis. Audrey suffered constantly with her leg problems, which grew worse with time. Nothing she tried would heal up the ulcers. Her legs continued to have open sores most of the time due to poor circulation. She finally had to quit driving because her weak legs could not handle the pressure of stepping on the break and the clutch of her standard-transmission, four-wheel drive pickup.

In spite of health problems, Audrey was very prolific. She compiled a partial list of her publications. Incomplete as it was, it mentioned some places where her work had been published:

> *N.Mex. Mag.* many times, verse and articles; *Empire* many times; *Denver Post; Southwestern Sportsman*; many small poetry and verse magazines; *True Treasure; Treasure World; American Baby; PTA Magazine; Profitable Hobbies; Saturday Evening Post*, twice; *Dog Fancy; Cat Fancy,* 1980; *Impact, Albuquerque Journal.*[1]

Audrey wrote a letter, perhaps one she hoped to send out to several publishers. It said:

> I have been a free lance writer since I sold my first article to the *Denver Post* for $5.00 at age 16.
>
> I worked from March, 1952 until August, 1966 for *Las Vegas Daily Optic*, with 10 months out to have a baby in 1954-55.
>
> Before and after the Optic, where I was Woman's Page Ed., general reporter, editorial writer and Church Page Editor, mostly at the same time, I wrote.
>
> I have had more than 100 articles and poems or verse published in little magazines, *New Mexico Magazine, PTA Magazine, Empire Magazine, Southwestern Sportsman, True Treasure, Treasure World, American Baby, Profitable Hobbies,* etc. and a couple of $100 Perfect Squelch items for the old *Saturday Evening Post*. All of my work, except verse in the little magazines and *N.M. Mag.* verses, was paid for in cash. I think I am ready to get to work again and wish to talk about a possible book.[2]

It is impossible to know how many of Audrey's stories and articles were published because the 1971 fire destroyed so many documents. The few things saved from the fire compose only a fraction of her work.

Audrey shared some of the tips of getting published with me, some "dos" and "don'ts" in dealing with editors and publishers. She also encouraged other writers, including myself, with the joys of writing and being published. She wrote:

> Maybe as a part time writer there are compensations you never thought of. For me these included a proposal of marriage, gifts of books, cash and being remembered in a will.

Of course there is always the joy of seeing your name or non-de-plume in print.

And nothing equals the delight of cashing your first check—mine was for $5.00 from the *Denver Post* when I was 16. To immortalize that memorable occasion, I bought hats for my 14 year old sister and my 7 year old sister and for myself. We had never owned real [store] bought hats and Miss 14 sure looked cute in her snug fitting Impress Eugenia hat.

"She writes," whispered by my friends and relations, was an ego booster that managed to counter rejection slips. So I kept on buying stamps and mm size envelopes and stamps and sending them hither and yon.

When divorce reduced the family size by one [Clyde] I persuaded my two little daughters that "Mom has to write for two hours every morning." When I did, a large percentage of my brain children began to find permanent homes.

I never wrote the great American novel or world shaking poetry. But what I did write was often printed. The added bonus for these scattered publications included a marriage proposal. I had written a hair-raising story telling about the time I had shot a lynx cat in my yard of my mountain cabin. It was printed in a magazine published in Texas. A very unflattering picture of me holding the lynx accompanied the article. It won the heart of a northwestern lumber jack. He wrote complimenting me on the wonderful fete of shooting that big cat and asking for my ringless hand in marriage. I answered every bit of "fan mail." But it took a good many diplomatic words to refuse his kind offer. He answered this by saying if I ever changed my mind, he would be waiting. Not that it makes much difference but his profession of undying love went up in smoke, along with anything else I had in the 1971 forest fire—losing his name and address. Another who introduced himself by wanting to come hunting in my mountains became a long time pen pal.

I never made a million writing but that first $5 check from the *Denver Post* back during the height of the depression.[3]

Audrey was apparently interrupted at that point and never finished that handwritten manuscript.

As soon as Audrey was settled into the ranch house, she began to write, using her old manual Royal Typewriter, pounding out her stories. If she received a rejection for a story, she would look for another market and send it out again, trying to find "the right home" for it—and more often than not she did. Sometimes she had only a very short item published but she was no less pleased than when a lengthy item was published. One such item was entitled, "Mail Order Plan." Audrey wrote: "If people ever tell you, 'Nothing is impossible,' ask them if they ever tried to get their names off a mailing list!"[4]

Audrey was delighted when she had a story accepted. An example of an acceptance was found in a card which said:

> *Capper's Weekly* is glad to send you payment for your contribution, and to thank you for your friendly interest in its behalf.
>
> Our friends and contributors do much to help us "make" the paper.
>
> From so many, the distinction of having a contribution chosen is rather more to be valued than the payment. We hope you will find both the distinction and payment acceptable and welcome.
>
> Payment for your story, Cake Finds Its Way Back Home, Feb. 5, 1980, Heart of the Home.
> Sincerely yours,
> Editorial Department
> Capper's Weekly[5]

Audrey was now living in a big, comfortable ranch home with a kitchen, dining room, three bedrooms, a big living room, and an indoor bathroom with hot and cold running water. She began making notes for more than one book. She had several in mind. One was to be an autobiography. Some of her notes reflect her thoughts:

> We welcomed everyone at our home—outlawed Texans, in Sacramento Mountains, blanketed Indians that came and watched Mama work in a two room house in Taos; Spanish American sawmill workers; all the people at Chapelle and Bernal, etc. and church people were welcomed and modern day wanderers called Hippies.[6]

Audrey was kind to new-comers in town who needed help. Rev. Harold Hacker and his wife, already mentioned, were looking for a building to start a church. They would leave for a while and then return to Las Vegas—off and on for several years. They usually had no money. After Clyde died Audrey was a widow with very little income, but she helped as much as she could. Sometimes the Hackers would come to visit and would even hold services at the ranch. Often they would spend days fasting and praying and loved the opportunity to be in the mountains. Audrey even allowed them to store their things in the bedroom cabin behind the Fifteen Dollar House until they could find a house of their own.

Once when the Hackers were visiting, Mr. Hacker said that during his time of fasting and praying, he had a vision. He said that Forest Springs Ranch was divinely protected. Audrey always felt that it was, in spite of the 1971 fire. After the fire, Hackers didn't come around much again, but they continued to write to Audrey and encourage her, especially to keep up her writing.

One story Audrey wrote was based on a true story. Since it was for a "confessions" type magazine, she did not get a by-line. It was about the life and death of Johnny, Bill and Helen Reid's son. Audrey had watched him grow up, along with the other nine Reid children. Audrey told about how Johnny loved the huge caterpillar tractors that his father so expertly used in his work. As a child, he had also loved the American flag. When Johnny, in his twenties, died tragically of a gunshot wound, Audrey attended the funeral at Glorieta Baptist Church.

> The huge caterpillar tractors, shoving tons of dirt and rock in a road construction job, snorted and growled in the mid-afternoon heat. A pall of dust hung over the New Mexico canyon country where the giant "cats" worked.
>
> I sat quietly and listened to the big "cat's" song, as it nearly drowned out the choir singing from the small church a few hundred yards from the heavy machinery. Ironic, I thought, that the big cats were background music now, for those giant caterpillar tractors were Johnny's first love.[7]

After the funeral, there were graveside services in the family cemetery. Johnny had served his country in the military. Audrey described how the big flag was removed from the casket, folded, and handed to Johnny's father. Bill was overcome with grief as he took the flag carefully and held it tightly against his chest and then stumbled blindly away from the graveside towards the music of the big "cats."[8] Audrey concluded: "And the big 'cats,' still building a road for tomorrow, roared farewell."[9]

Audrey recalled that she had always felt deep sympathy for her friends Bill and Helen Reid and their ten children. Audrey had loved each of the children as she watched them grow up.

In some handwritten notes, Audrey wrote about her experience at the graveside service for Johnny Reid:

I said softly, "Bill," and I reached for his hand and held it gently. I could feel some pressure, not much, but he never looked at me or let on that I was there. His head was turned away and he was apparently completely absorbed in conversation with the preacher and two of the pall bearers.

I stood there a second and then moved away to say all the pat sayings to the girls: "I'm so sorry." "You have my deepest sympathy." "We all loved him." "If I can do anything let me know!" And all the time I wondered was he really so involved with that man talk or was he trying to avoid looking at me for fear of breaking down and making a fool of himself.[10]

Audrey published numerous articles in *New Mexico Magazine*, including one about the Montezuma ice ponds. In the article entitled, "Winter Playground," she wrote a history of the Montezuma Hot springs, where a 300-room hotel was built in 1885. Several dams in the Gallinas were built. In the winter, huge ice houses were filled with ice from the ponds to help supply the AT & SF railroad system before dry ice came into common use. In 1903 the hotel closed and re-opened in 1922 as a Baptist College. After the depression of 1929, the college closed and the place was sold to the Committee of Bishops of the Catholic Hierarchy of the United States. The Montezuma Seminary was a place where young men from Old Mexico came to study for the priesthood and then returned to Mexico. Audrey wrote about how each winter the 20-30 Club of Las Vegas sponsored the ice skating at the ponds, and many people from Las Vegas enjoyed ice skating there.[11]

Sometimes Audrey wrote short pieces and submitted them to magazines. She wrote about an unusual experience she had when she turned on the radio to KFUN and heard their "Trading Post" where people can offer items for sale or trade. Audrey wrote:

> Someone broke into a couple of upstairs apartments owned by a friend of mine. Wooden door panels were shattered and the apartments burglarized. With inflationary costs of everything, she didn't see how she could buy new doors.
>
> When my husband and I were building a house her family had given us a door. Now she needed two of them. I felt bad, wanting to help, but had been ill and confined to the house. I had her need on my mind all day. She left town the next day and I put her need away in the back of my mind.

When I was getting lunch I had a funny feeling, a sudden urge to turn on the radio. I never listen to the radio at busy times for fear I will become interested in it and neglect my work. However, this 10th day of July, 1981, I had a strong urge, so I turned the radio on.

Immediately I heard, "For sale, two doors, one with windows, $35.00, the other $60.00."

"My friend can't afford to pay so much," I said aloud, while writing down a phone number.

Then another ad came on. "Two inside doors, $5.00 each." I wrote that down quickly. When my friend returned home, I told her about the ad and gave her addresses. Someone was remodeling a house. Luckily the doors were exactly what she needed.

Luck? I wonder. Something urged me to listen to the radio in time to hear of a place doors could be bought cheaply. I can't believe it was coincidence. It was a way I could repay my friend double for a past favor.[12]

Audrey worked on stories that were based on true experiences. One story, "Rio Grande Treasure" was published in *Treasure Trails* in 1973 and a similar story was published in *Treasure World*.[13] It was a true account of Clyde's childhood experience when he and his brother Bob were living in San Marcial, New Mexico. Their father, Ernest Simpson, worked for the railroad there. They were chasing a rabbit and found the ruins of an old village. They began to dig around the old church ruins, looking for the rabbit. They found gold and silver candlesticks, crosses, a golden chalice and blocks of gold and silver nestled in the remains of church vestments. They replaced the rotting viga over the cache and went home, planning to return later. However, they were afraid because of stories of the ghost of the priest who haunted the church. He supposedly had been killed by Native Americans who raided the village after he had hidden the valuables. So the two boys told no one of their find. They were busy with school and they never went back to claim the treasure they had found. In 1929 the Rio Grande flooded the village. What the river hadn't washed away, the Conservation District leveled and ditched with big machinery. There was no sign of the old village site. The town of San Marcial no longer exists. Audrey concluded her story:

Between Socorro and Cabello, along the Rio Grande River in New Mexico, lies a buried village with its buried church. And within the village—more secure than ever in its tomb of mud and silt—lies the hidden treasure of the old church.[14]

One story Audrey wrote but never finished or had published was a story she entitled, "The Guy in the Cowboy Hat." She wrote:

> "Hey kids! You want to go to the mountains today?" I called to my niece and nephew as I stopped in front of their house.
> "Sure!" they answered.
> "Ask your mom," I said. "And be sure to take sweaters along in case it rains."
> When the rains whip the mountains the mud gets so soggy it nearly pulls your boots off. I was used to driving a 4-wheel drive (International Scout) pick up around the mountains so even when the heavy thunderheads threatened above the Sangre de Cristo mountain range, I was not afraid. I had invited my niece and nephew to spend a few days at our cabin. My teen-age daughter and I picked up my niece and my 10-year-old nephew.
> We could see the frowning clouds sweeping closer as we topped the divide between the foothills and "our" mountains. I stepped on the gas to try to beat the rain. As the pickup bumped over the rough road, I said a prayer that I would beat the rain to the cabin. Then I saw it was too late. Already sheets of rain were pouring down, hiding the mountains.
> As the dirt road became rain slick, I fought the steering wheel to keep from slipping off the road into a ditch.[15]

Audrey wrote about how they made it through the gate and then the truck fish-tailed and slid. The back tires were in the side ditch. At least they were in their own yard and could walk to the house, although it was about a city block away. They had groceries in the back of the truck, so they would have to carry everything in. The rain had let up a little, but the road was about as muddy as it could get. They all took something to carry to the house and walked through the deep mud to the house. Audrey's story included the following:

> "How can we get the truck up here?" Holly said as we entered the house and set down the supplies.
> "It may rain every day so we may be stuck for a while," I said. "Unless we get shovels and dig out those back wheels so we can drive out of the ditch."
> Nobody wanted to go back out in the mud and dig. But Holly didn't like having the truck stuck in the road. She had helped shovel the truck out before and she knew it could be done.

"I'm going to try it and see if I can get the wheels out," Holly said.

I didn't want to leave my niece and nephew alone at the house so I said, "I'll watch from the window and if it looks like you can dig one wheel out, I'll go down and start up the truck and see if I can get out."

My niece wasn't feeling quite well after the "wild" ride, so she went to a bedroom to lie down. My nephew watched out the window as Holly began to dig a wheel out. Only one wheel was really deep, so if she could get the mud away from that one wheel, it would be possible to drive the truck out.

I turned away to put some of the groceries up when I heard the ten-year-old boy exclaim, "Who is that man? He's helping Holly dig!"

"What?" I knew it wasn't likely that a man had come along to help Holly.

"Yeah! There's a guy in a cowboy hat and he's helping Holly dig," the boy said, looking out the window.

I went to the window again and looked out. I saw only Holly. There was no man there. But Holly had dug a tremendous amount of mud away from the tire in just a few minutes.

"I'm going to go see if I can drive the truck out," I said.

"I'll come with you," my nephew replied.

There was no man there. But there was a big pile of mud where Holly had shoved out around the wheel.

Sure enough, the back wheel that had been impacted with mud was free. Audrey thought she might be able to get the truck out. She started it, got it out of the ditch, and drove the truck back up the muddy road to its place beside the house. Audrey's story concluded:

"Holly, you must be tired. I don't see how you dug that much mud away so quickly," I declared. "That was a tremendous job!"

"It was easy!" Holly exclaimed. "I hardly tried!"

"The guy in the cowboy hat was helping her," my nephew insisted. "I saw him."

I wondered. Little kids sometimes "see things" that adults can't see. Then I thought, *Clyde always wore a cowboy hat when he was "dressed up."*[16]

Audrey didn't understand, but she whispered a prayer of thanks to God for the help.

Audrey never finished that story because of the fire that occurred soon thereafter. But she attempted to write it up afterwards and the notes were found years later.

Audrey not only wrote fiction and non-fiction, but she also voiced her opinions in editorials quite often. She believed in the power of the pen. She thought a good letter could have a tremendous impact. She wrote complaining to "Dear Post Office" about the rising cost of postage stamps. In a letter she wrote:

> It seems that two dimes for a first class stamp is too much to send a skimpy letter from here to yonder. But maybe you all have the attitude held by an isolated country Postmaster back in the late 1920's or early 1930's. My mother took an envelope addressed to the East Coast, with proper 6 cent airmail postage on it.
>
> "You don't think that letter is goin' very far in an airy plane for 6 cents do you?"
>
> "They always have!" she answered
>
> "But no more!" he replied.[17]

In a letter to *Capper's Magazine*, Audrey wrote:

> In the Nov. 24 *Capper's* a lady mentioned the fact that the Post Office can't make up its mind on stamp prices. Most of us have stopped most correspondence, due to eating being more important than letters. It seems such a short time since stamps went from 10 cents to 13, 15, 18 and now 20 cents.
>
> I seldom get even one personal letter a month. But my mailbox is stuffed with junk mail. If the P. O. could charge more for junk mail, I might have to buy more fire starters but surely they could hold first class postage DOWN.[18]

Audrey was deluged with "junk mail." She thought the post office should do something about it and should bring down their costs for postage. She had an article published in the *Albuquerque Journal Magazine* in 1982. Wesley Lovett took a picture of a stack of mail which was used in the article. It included about 733 envelopes collected over about eighteen months. She pointed out that since she was only one of millions, the post office must be handling a tremendous amount of mail, most of it unsolicited advertisements such as those shown in the photograph. Apparently the Post Office had just announced that they were in the black for the first time since World War II (when letters went for three cents) so postage rates would not have to be raised until 1984. Audrey described the various ads she received. "If they didn't spend so much on advertising and postage, their products would be cheaper." Audrey said most of the ads ended up as "fuel for my wood stove."[19] Audrey gave a short history in her article, "Stamping Out Junk Mail":

> In case you have forgotten, Dear Post Office, first class mail went for 2 cents an ounce from 1919 to the summer of 1932. On July 6 of that year, first class postage rose to 3 cents, in spite of the Depression. I suppose that was due to the National Recovery Act which required that people work fewer days a week so that more might have jobs. Could that have been the P O excuse?
>
> For 26 years, from 1932 until Aug. 1, 1958, postage remained at 3 cents an ounce when it rose to 4 cents. Then it jumped to a nickel in 1963, and to six cents in 1968. From then on, it was 2 cents added every so often.
>
> It was while the 3 cent stamps were in use in the early 1950s that we found that the P O was exceptionally efficient. At that time my daughter, Crystal, corresponded with countless shut-ins around the nation. Every rural route mail day, I would walk four miles down the canyon and four miles back up the mountain, loaded down with her mail.
>
> Several times Crystal received letters addressed Crystal Simpson, Las Vegas, with no state mentioned. Now they would be returned to sender or sent to that gambling town in Nevada. Often there was no rural route or box number, but her letters still arrived. Postal workers, no doubt, became familiar with her name and address, a thing no machine could do.
>
> Postal workers' extreme efficiency was proved when she received several letters, at various times, with only her first name, *Crystal,* and nothing else but a stamp on the envelope! No doubt the senders meant to look up her last name, town, route and state but mailed the letters without that information. However, they came directly to our isolated southwestern area with no trouble at all.[20]

Audrey went on to say she wondered why postage is so high.

> First class stamps jumped to 8 cents in 1971, to 10 cents in 1974 and 13 cents in 1975. By 1978, we paid 15 cents to send a letter. In March, 1981, you raised the cost of a stamp to 18 cents and promptly followed that last November [1981] with the 20 cent stamp.[21]

Audrey's letter ended with an appeal to stop raising the cost of postage. Audrey also wrote letters complaining about the telephone service, as she often had to deal with her telephone going out, usually during storms and sometimes for as long as two weeks:

> In the old days my folks, the Shearers, were on the old Forest Service telephone line that ran from Pecos to the lookout tower on Barillas Peak and then along the eastern side of the Sangre de Cristo Mountain Range north to the Omar Barker place above Rociada. These old wall phones operated on six or eight inch batteries. I never knew of anyone having to put in new batteries more than once in three years. If a tree fell on the line we went out on horseback, cut the tree, tied the line back together again and it was never out more than a day and a half.
>
> Therefore, with all the expensive, modern equipment (which I help pay for at the rate of $30.00 per month to just have it available) it seems to me there is no excuse for the line to go dead and stay that way for a week (or more.)[22]

Audrey said she voted for the person, not the party. For the most part, she was conservative. She wrote a letter, probably to send to a newspaper, with the following opinion:

> Nothing but selfishness, hate or fear of the unborn is behind the cry for easily acquired abortion. The young wonder, "Would I be here if abortion had been easier?"
>
> They see a deplorable modern world—old men sending young men to kill and be killed in winless wars, and mothers, or potential mothers, speaking of killing, as in an abortion, as though it were a good and proper thing.
>
> Then while the world is swiftly sinking into deeper and deeper moral decay, the young turn to wild music or smoking pot, to try to ignore the impossible situations.
>
> State legislature after state legislature is bombarded with requests for legalizing or liberalizing abortion laws. If you have children, look at them. Which ones would you have done without? Which would you have eliminated if possible? If your answer is "none," there is still hope for a better world.[23]

Audrey ended by stating that she was glad she could look each daughter in the eye and say, "*I wanted you!*"[24]

Audrey wrote a letter against gun control. According to notes, Audrey had an editorial printed on April 15, 1981. The letter was sent on April 6, as follows:

> Dear Editor:
>
> The majority of the common people are against any more gun controls. Under present regulations all purchasers of ammunition are required to sign for it. Therefore, with modern computers every gun owner is easily identified without the added red tape and expense of more laws.
>
> No matter what proposed gun controls required, outlaws would retain their guns. This would leave the law-abiding *gunless* citizens helpless against the guns of criminals.
>
> As shown so tragically March 30, on TV, the LAW cannot protect us, any more than it could save President Regan and the other three, when the bullets began to fly.
>
> We know that so long as we all have guns, most of us law-abiding citizens can and will protect our families, our friends and ourselves.
>
> It is time for the Congress to change the laws so that criminals will no longer be coddled and be freed to strike again. And Congress should quit threatening to take away our Constitutional rights with threats of gun controls.[25]

Audrey's letters to friends reveal much of what was happening. In 1967 a letter to Mrs. Clark Ranney, the neighbor who lived down the canyon in the summer time, stated:

> Crystal and Wesley and Karen left yesterday after being here more than a week. I sure enjoyed having them. Crystal is such a wonderful help around the house and Wesley is a hard worker. He finished cementing the outside of the house between the logs, and installed a 220 electrical outlet so I can get an electric range—next spring, I hope. I plan to get an electric and coal and wood combination range. He also cut more than a cord of wood for my big box heater, which I heat and cook with now when it is cool enough. I use an electric hot plate for cooking when it is warm now.[26]

Audrey was still recovering from the surgery on her worst leg, a skin graft that failed to heal the leg ulcer. The surgery was in May, 1967. She wrote:

> My leg has been getting better, though it still drains—sometimes a heavy stream. I plan to go to town about the 20th to see Dr. Mortimer and then on to Albuquerque Sept. 21, as Dr. Brown wanted me to come back then for another check up. I don't get around much—keep my leg elevated most of the time as it swells badly if I don't keep it elevated. I am sure tired of this inactivity. I want to get outside and walk up and down these beautiful canyons again.[27]

Unfortunately, Audrey's legs were never completely well after that. The leg she'd had the skin graft on was the worst. The graft didn't "take" and the circulation was bad. Both legs had ulcers off and on that refused to heal. So she was unable to do much more than walk around the yard. She did continue to work in the garden as much as her legs would allow.

I had taught English at West Las Vegas High School during the 1966-67 school year. I was offered a contract to continue but I needed to return to the University of Utah to complete my degree. So in the fall of 1967 I returned to Salt Lake City. After I graduated in 1968, I returned to New Mexico. I taught high school English in Santa Rosa for three years, and Holly stayed with me to go to school. Then I married Gary Beimer. Soon after that I began my career at New Mexico Highlands University.

Vivian Shearer wrote many articles and was working on a book. Mabel corresponded with the children and grandchildren. She wrote of various events:

> Jan.1964—Milly's came from Breckenridge to stay—stayed until June, 1965—moved to house by Hosp.—stayed till June, 1967—moved to Johnsen apt.—stayed 'til June, 1968—Married Dr. Wickman June 8, 1968. Roger and Gail married June 19, 1968, kept Johnsen apt. Jan 15, 1969—CV has made 5 trips to Albuquerque to a heart specialist and seems to be better. Milly has been taking him down—next app't. March 6 to see doctor.[28]

Vivian never made the scheduled appointment. Holly was staying overnight at her Grandma Shearer's house when Vivian died suddenly, just collapsed as he was getting ready to take a bath. It was a great shock. He had lived from September 19, 1890 to March 3, 1969. Mabel wrote, "My Vivian passed away Mar. 3rd, 1969, here at home of a heart attack. I live here alone now and hope to be able to take care of myself and live here until year 2000. I'll be 110 years old."[29]

Mabel did take care of herself until her death, although Milly and "Doc" Wickman bought the property and lived next door so Milly could help care for her mother. Mabel always said she hoped she would not lose her memory or her mind as so many old people did. She did crossword puzzles and tried to keep her mind active. As a result, she did not lose her memory. Her mind remained sharp. She and Audrey conversed on the phone every day, and Audrey would often get her advice on everything, including her writing.

Audrey wrote an article which was published in *Capper's Weekly*, November 7, 1967:

> When I told my friends my new home was an isolated 20 miles away from town they were shocked.
>
> "Aren't you afraid for your mother to be so far up the mountain? some asked my daughter.
>
> "No," she answered. "I know Mother can take care of herself. She has a telephone and it is only a mile to the nearest neighbor."
>
> My husband and I had worked 30 years trying to retire to our mountains. After his death and after the girls were through college and on their own, I sold our house in town and I finished the big log house we had started years ago.
>
> Maybe it is for sentimental reasons (happy young days here) that I chose to live where only 4-wheel drive vehicles with low gears can lick the cow trails called roads. But I think it is more than that.
>
> I look out the windows of this snug house at "my" high mountain. It was "my" mountain when I was a child and it has not changed. It is still covered with a green velvet forest and each fall is sprinkled with the golden jewels of aspens. I am filled with joy and comfort as "I lift up mine eyes to the hills."
>
> I walk out into early morning stillness as each new sun shows above the big pines, and see gray shadows—"my" herd of deer—slipping silently thru the pines. Close at hand is the little meadow in the valley where countless birds enjoy tall grass as they migrate every fall and spring. I hear wild turkeys gobble along the creek and sometimes thrill to seeing a dozen in Indian file coming down for a sparkling drink.
>
> Behind the creek, a young mountain rises abruptly. This blend of stately Douglas fir and spruce was christened "Christmas Tree Hill" by our girls more than 25 years ago. Tall post oaks along the creek spread new green each spring.

They whisper all summer, then wave their yellow, bronze and red-gold leaves in the fall breeze, bidding me goodbye a thousand times before the snow drifts across the mountains.

When snow comes the identity of unseen forest animals is revealed to me as they leave tracks in the unbroken snow. When winter storms swoop down the ridges, howling winds highlight the snug warmth of my log house. I remember the many years I braved such storms on icy streets going to work while putting "the kids" through school. I throw another chunk of sweet smelling pine into my big box heater and I am content.

Every day I thank the good Lord for permitting me to live once again in my beautiful mountains. By being here I hope my grandchildren will have the chance to enjoy the fresh fragrance of these mountain meadows of God's wonderful creation, even as the rest of my family has enjoyed it.

So, trying to figure out why I selected this place for my home, I say for its closeness to nature, peaceful perfection, and for the scenery.[30]

Audrey was always kind to strangers and those in need. But she had no sympathy for the likes of the drunken hunters who showed up at her ranch house one night. They had ignored the "No Hunting" and "No Trespassing" signs and had no business on her place. Audrey respected hunters who obeyed the law, but too often they did not. These three men were very intoxicated when they started pounding on Audrey's screen door one night about midnight. Holly remembers the event very clearly. She and Audrey were sound asleep when the intruders awakened them.

Audrey grabbed her nearby gun and held it behind her back as she opened the front door just slightly, keeping the locked screen door between herself and the unruly men. The hunters said they were stuck in the mud and rudely demanded to use the telephone. Audrey was not going to let the inebriated men into her home where she and Holly were alone. She told them the telephone was out of order.

"Is your husband home? Maybe he can help us get our truck out of the mud," one man spoke up.

"My husband is sleeping," Audrey said curtly.

"Well, wake him up! We need his help!" another man insisted.

According to Holly, the men argued loudly for about ten minutes, trying to get Audrey to get her husband to come and help them.

Audrey was armed, but so were the men. They had their hunting rifles with them. As they continued to insist that she get her husband to help them,

Audrey decided she was tired of arguing with the drunken men.

"I told you, my husband is *asleep*—right over there in the *cemetery*!" She pointed to the cemetery on the hill across from her house. Immediately the men apologized and took off. She saw and smelled the fire they built to keep warm that night—even burning their spare tires. In the morning Audrey called a neighbor who came and pulled them out of the mud.[31]

Little did they know Audrey had been holding a gun in her hand, hidden behind the door. Clyde had been a gun collector and had left many firearms to choose from, including a pearl-handled revolver he had been proud of. Audrey was perfectly capable of defending herself and Holly.

Audrey had survived many hardships and endured countless blows. She'd had knives and rocks thrown at her. She had survived teasing, taunting and threatening as a young girl. She remembered a verse she had written when she was a kid. She called it "Code of the Clements' Kids" and recited it with her brothers and sisters:

> Give better than you get.
> And if you are kicked around just see that you
> Keep on kicking back.
> Never say down and never stay down.
> Laugh when you want to cry.
> If you have your back to the wall
> Fight—and get back up front.[32]

Yes, when life kicked you down, you just had to pull yourself up by your own boot straps and keep on surviving. No one, certainly not drunken hunters, could intimidate Audrey.

Audrey missed Clyde, but for the most part she was happy in the shadow of the lovely mountains. Little did she guess that her happiness would be dashed away in a single event that would turn her lovely velvet forest into charcoal, her beautiful mountain into a scarred, barren ruin. Only a forest fire could do that—a fire that was allowed to burn because the authorities who should have immediately put it out let it burn until it was too late.

11

All Day the Ashes Fell: Most Destructive Forest Fire

The tragedy of fire was nothing new to Audrey. She had been through several, including the one at Cuervo and the one that had made her run for her life with Crystal in her arms at the ranch. Even her place of work, the Optic, had been devastated by fire. Audrey had seen Grandfather Shearer's house burn. Little did Audrey guess at that time that she, too, would experience the same loss of everything that Grandfather experienced. The loss would deal her a crushing blow, but would not destroy her spirit.

Audrey worried about fire, especially during dry seasons, while she continued to write. Whenever she went to town in her International Scout, Audrey would scan the mountains on the way home, hoping she would not see the dreaded column of smoke on any of her beloved peaks, and praying for God's blessings on them.

Audrey wrote an article about her retirement, a story about a "visitor" coming to see her after she had moved to her mountain home. Undoubtedly, one of her friends from town such as Jean Whiting, did pay her a visit. Audrey, in the story below, imagined what her friend must have experienced.

> Where go newspaper women go when they retire? I bumped over unimproved mountain roads to the "retirement haven" of one Audrey Simpson (Mrs. Clyde J. Simpson) to find one unusual answer to my question.
>
> Audrey Simpson (Mrs. Clyde J. Simpson) had been very well known, a hard working, highly respected society editor, reporter—woman thought of when working on the daily newspaper for nearly 15 years in Las Vegas, New Mexico.
>
> Audrey, as she is called by most of the 15,000 people of the area in and around Las Vegas, New Mexico, where she served as reporter, Society Editor, Women's Page Editor and Church Page Editor simultaneously, retired to an isolated ranch in the Sangre de Cristo mountains in November, 1966.
>
> I could see the outstanding beauty of the mountains but the primitive log cabin nestled in a valley between the pine clad hills seemed

an odd place for a very active women to "retire" while in her mid 50's. She had been President of the Las Vegas Business and Professional Women's Club, two terms, was Charter President of the Las Vegas Pen Women's Club, a member of the Rebecca's Lodge #1 and of the Does 136—as well as taking an active part in many other civil affairs and attending many meetings in her capacity as Optic reporter.

Three big dogs raced to loudly greet my car as I pulled up the canyon in front of the log cabin. Audrey and her teenage daughter Holly stepped out the door and called the dogs. The barking stopped and friendly wags accompanied me into the house.

Audrey bustled about making coffee behind the book-case counter that divides her living room area from the kitchen. The room, 20 x 22 feet, held several [shelves of] over 200 books and stacks of countless magazines.

"You must read a lot," I said.

"That's a joke," Audrey answered. "These are things I planned to read when I retired but I haven't read them yet. There are 40 different publications there on that coffee table, with a year's copies of some of them. I scan them when they come in but mostly the newer ones go to town to my daughter Dorothy who teaches. If she didn't [take them] I would be buried under magazines. I just keep the ones I want to read further or use for reference, but they really stack up."

"These mountains are very beautiful, but so isolated," I began.

Anticipating my question, Audrey answered, "I know everyone wonders why I chose such isolation. The main answer is that Clyde and I worked for more than 24 years after we bought this place, hoping to spend our retirement years here. We spent every vacation up here working. We started this cabin in 1960 after using our Ten Dollar House and the Fifteen Dolalr Cabin we built for camping quarters throughout those years. After Clyde suffered a heart attack and died in 1965, I continued to work a year, while helping Dorothy attend the University of Utah at Salt Lake City, working on her Master's degree. However, I needed [leg] surgery and was so tired of the rat race and meeting a deadline every hectic morning that this mountain ranch beckoned more and more."

She paused and then continued, "I knew I couldn't live in town without working—too many expenses. If I sold our house in town on contract I could move up here into this unfinished cabin and with the social security received due to Clyde's death, Holly and I could manage to live here. I resigned from the Optic in August, 1966. I hired one of the neighbors and his sons to finish our cabin. Day after day I struggled to move stuff from our seven room house in town to this mountain cabin. Holly was in the 7th grade and I would leave town after taking her to school and get back to Vegas just as school was out for her. We moved here in November of 1966 and I started teaching her each day. We had school for three hours each a.m."

Mrs. Simpson had been a free lance writer prior to working at the Optic so had thought to get back to free lancing once free of deadlines.[1]

June was usually a dry month. On June 29, 1971, the most terrible fire of Audrey's life struck. The fire started in the Santa Fe National Forest. It was started by lightning. At that time the U. S. Forest Service's policy was not to fight fires that were started "naturally" by lightning. But after a few days they decided to fight it. It had already come over Barillas Peak and surrounding mountains; it was threatening the Las Vegas water supply area, among other things.

Audrey wrote about the storm that preceded the fire:

> On a Saturday night in late June Holly and my granddaughter Karen and I watched the black clouds roll along the top of the Sangre de Cristo Mountain Range. Our ranch is at the south end of those rock mountains, squeezed up during one of Mother Earth's travails—years ago.
>
> About one o'clock I woke to the crash of thunder. A violent storm was whipping the giant pines on the other side of the mountain. As lightning flashed again and again, the reverberations seemed to shake the very backbone of the divide between us and Sebadilla Canyon.[2]

Apparently that was when the devastating lightening hit the mountain. Karen Lovett was staying with her grandma for a few weeks, enjoying the summer. Wesley and Crystal were in Houston where Wesley worked for the public service company there. They were there several years until Wesley was able to get a job in Albuquerque with the Public Service Company of New Mexico. I was in Salt Lake City that summer. Had any of us guessed that such a catastrophic event was to occur that summer of 1971, we would have been sure to have been close at hand to help get things out of the fire's path. We would have helped Mother save all her photographs, manuscripts, books, antiques, and other irreplaceable valuables. But, of course, no one suspected such a thing would happen.

Audrey hesitated to evacuate. She prayed that the fire would not come across the mountain and the ranch would be spared. Her numerous telephone calls to the Forest Service gave her a false sense of security as she thought the fire fighters would surely put the fire out before it reached private land. But the Forest Service let the fire go until it was too late. By the time they started to fight it, the fire had reached private property.

As fire and smoke approached, Audrey knew she had to get out; but she had waited too long to save many valuables. Audrey evacuated, taking a truck load of things to her mother's house on Montezuma Road. Gordon "Doc" Wickman came and got several things, and a few other people helped. But there wasn't much time. Audrey, Holly and Karen loaded up Karen's dog Pinto, Pinto's puppies, and a few items. Some of the dogs and cats were nowhere to be found when they left. Audrey took her truck load to Mabel Shearer's house and left Holly and Karen with Mabel while she went back to try to get another load of valuables. Audrey also hoped to find the family pets and bring them to town. But Audrey was unable to get another truck load; the smoke was too bad. (As it turned out, she did not find the dogs and cats until after the fire had burned the place, but they had found safety; Audrey and Holly took them into town after the fire.) Audrey said she prayed that the fire would be put out, that it would not take any private property; but if it had to be, she prayed that Opal's house, at least, would be spared.

On June 29, 1971 the fire swept down the mountain. Opal and Bob Simpson were living at the Old Homestead ranch in Grandfather Shearer's renovated stone house—the one that had burned in 1949. Bob Simpson had refused to leave until the last minute when smoke drove him out. He watered down the stone house and got out as many things as he could. The big adobe house burned because Bob could not water it down, but the stone house where Bob and Opal were living did not burn. That part of Audrey's prayer was answered.

Audrey's new big house burned to the ground. So did the Fifteen Dollar House, the two cabins behind it, the Ten Dollar House, and "Heller's Cabin."

Then, after the day of the inferno, the countryside was blessed with rain. "The Forest Service didn't put the fire out; God did," Audrey said. Audrey and Holly returned to the site of their home after rain had put the fire out. Audrey wrote in her notes, "Notes about the 1971 Forest Fire:"

> The fellow in the truck ordered to keep everyone out of the fire area didn't lift a hand. He could tell by the set of my chin and the way I was barreling over the road that he had better not try to stop me. Maybe he knew I was heading for my burned home—the place the forest service people had promised to try to save if the fire came over the mountain and got close to it. And then no one turned a hand to try to save it.

The radio had quoted some Forest Service big shot as saying there were only a few deserted houses in the area. Of course they were deserted—The Forest Service men ran us all out, saying, and I quote, "We will try to save your house if the fire gets down here. We have planes with slurry. You don't have to worry." And then they let my home and those of other mountain dwellers burn to the ground and never turned a hand. My brother-in-law [Bob Simpson] refused to leave and they sent a state cop to take him out.

It was the most unbelievably mismanaged forest fire! I could not believe that any Forest Service people could know so little about fire fighting. I could not believe that they could have 1300 men on the fire and still let it burn nearly 13,000 acres. Of course many of the men were transported to town by bus for lunch and dinner—and their nincompoop bosses never did get down to the business of controlling the fire. Then after 2400 acres of private land had burned and 24 buildings, including my home and the irreplaceable collection of valuables gathered in the past 75 years by my family alone, the rains came and put the fire out.

One of those in charge [was] described by a local recipient of his neglect as "a green horn from the northwest, not yet dry behind the ears, didn't give a hot in hell whether or not we burned out." He [the green horn] had the nerve to tell my sister, [Opal Simpson] "You don't own this land. Nobody can own private land inside the National Forest." He didn't read the right books. Our lands were homesteaded here long before the U.S. Forest Service was ever established and before they arbitrarily set their lines across ranches and homesteads scattered all over the Sangre de Cristo Mountains in northern New Mexico. (The patent on my place was dated 1894.)[3]

Audrey wrote in her "Holly" notes about the 1971 fire that had been dubbed "The Cat fire":

In 1971 the fire came, June 26, 1971, and took our house and cabins, not to mention thousands of dollars worth of timber. You [Holly] went to Houston with CC. (Crystal Clydine.) There was nothing to do but go to Mother's—your Grandma Shearer. As soon as I could I got a trailer house from Delma (Vivian) Laude. We put it in Mother's yard and moved in. You cried every night—went to sleep crying. I tried to comfort you but wasn't very successful at it. Every day you said "I don't want to go to school," and every day I had to persuade you to go. Then came the cleaning up. So many of the Hippies [from a nearby commune] rallied around to help clean up and try to get logs ready to build with again. It was a long, hot summer. I don't remember how long you were gone to Houston. I know you found a scrap of unburned paper in the ashes that seemed to be a message of hope. Dorothy and Gary got married on May 13, 1972 at Crystal's in Albuquerque. The shock of the fire and loss of everything—house and 4 cabins and contents was a trauma I could scarcely stand. I tried to hide it and carry on but the hurt was terribly deep. I had been doing a lot of writing and some selling but I lost all interest when all mms. [manuscripts] burned and I haven't been able to get back. I guess you can't ever go back.[4]

Audrey did get back to her writing, but she didn't write much until she was able to move back to the ranch. Audrey and Holly lived several months in the little trailer next door to the Shearer house on Montezuma Road. Mabel was a great comfort to Audrey, as she had suffered many tragedies herself. Undoubtedly, being near her mother was a great help for Audrey.

Audrey and other homeowners whose places were burned were angry, not only because the Forest Service delayed fighting the fire until it was too late, but because when they did start to fight it, they did not save our homes. Some of the firefighters were accused of looting.

One of the neighbors stayed behind after evacuation orders were given, trying to get things loaded up to take into town. As the smoke finally drove him away from his house and he was leaving for town, he saw fire fighters carrying away some of his belongings and confronted the men. He was told, "It's going to burn anyway, so we might as well take it." Needless to say, he was furious but there was nothing he could do. At that point he was fleeing for his life.

We wondered if any of our five houses had been raided before they were burned. Audrey commented, "We heard that some of the fire fighters had been looting from the houses and cabins. ——— [a neighbor] caught them red-handed."[5]

A neighbor speculated (but could not prove) that some of the fire fighters may have even burned some of the houses to the ground after taking whatever they wanted out of them—houses that the fire would have missed—but their destruction would have been blamed on the forest fire.

Audrey had to deal with numerous problems. She wrote in her "Holly" notes:

I got the tin house to store at mother's the great deal of stuff given to us after the fire. I fell into the edge of the door and hurt my head and from then on my memory hasn't been so good. You can see the crease in my left forehead up to my hair line. Friend, the dog, got run over when I sent you [Holly] after the mail [from the box in the front yard] as you and Mother were fussing and I couldn't stand it. Two or 3 fellows materialized from nowhere and comforted you.[6]

The U. S. Forest Service never offered any kind of compensation to the homeowners who lost their property due to their failure to fight the fire until it was too late. They did not even offer an apology. In fact, they had the nerve to write to Audrey offering to sell her trees, seedlings or seeds, to help replace the trees that had burned on her place. They didn't even offer to give them to her.

Audrey wrote many letters after the fire, trying to make the U.S. Forest Service aware of their incompetence and trying to make the public aware of the need to protest against such policies as letting a fire burn if it resulted from natural causes or the policy of "prescribed burning." Audrey was right about such prescribed burns getting out of hand. Years later Yellow Stone National Park and then Los Alamos were only two examples of vast destruction of property due to the authorities losing control of "prescribed burns." In one letter, Audrey wrote:

For countless years the Santa Fe National Forest was laughingly called the "asbestos" forest because of the lack of fires. This was due to the prompt action of mountain dwellers who did not wait [to fight the fires.] The tragic Cat-Dog fire that destroyed more than 12,000 acres and now the disgraceful La Mesa Fire, part of which was also in the Santa Fe National Forest! I grew up on stories of "get to that smoke and put the fire out quick." All forest dwellers know the shudder of fear caused by a wisp of smoke from the smallest fire. And they also know that unless the small fire is hit in the beginning as hard as possible it will become a holocaust. Too often "experienced fire fighters" are brought in from the northwest where fire fighting is vastly different from New Mexico due to differences in climate and rainfall. Too many of these outsiders simply look on fire control as a money making job. They do not care about our timber losses, the death of irreplaceable wild life and the complete change in our ecology due to a fire that could have been prevented in the first place if a full scale [effort had been made.][7]

Audrey wrote to the U.S. Forest Service:

Newspaper articles have reported that the U.S. Forest Service has been asking for public comment. I think that we already have enough areas designated as Wilderness areas and that those now under evaluation should remain as multiple use areas. I also think that all areas should be accessible by roads or trails of some kind because multiple use is impossible without roads. Roads as access into Forest areas are also important in case of fire.

I hereby state that I am against the practice of clear cutting and the very damaging idea of letting forest fires burn themselves out, resulting not only in loss of timber but of also in loss of wildlife and possibly more important of all the depletion of our oxygen supply. These fires burn up oxygen at a terrible rate and then the fire blackened forest cannot give off oxygen as it did before. I am for multiple use of U. S. Forest lands, with access roads.[8]

Audrey was so adamantly against the policy of the prescribed burn that she wrote several letters such as the one below to the *Albuquerque Journal*:

Dear Editor:

A hard cover book, "The Use of the National Forest" was put out by the U. S. Dept. of Agriculture and the Forest Service, with Gifford Pinchot, Forester, in 1907. It lists long forgotten regulations for the Forest Service.

"The first thing that is made sure is that the timber is not burned up," they state on page 17. Later under the FIRE heading the department noted: "Look out for small fires; they start big ones. As soon as a fire is discovered, put it out."

In the old days a lightning strike was usually a small fire at first. The Ranger, or anyone who saw it, rushed to put it out before it became a wild fire. The Santa Fe National Forest used to be called the "Asbestos Forest" until recent years when the policy changed to the stupid "Let it burn if it is caused by lightning."

I do not think that the majority of the U. S. population knows that this unforgiveable policy has been in effect for far too many years or that every destroyed tree no longer removes carbon dioxide from the air, therefore adding to the "Green House" effect.

The tragedy of the loss of millions of acres of forests, including those in Yellowstone National Park, is a sad learning experience for all. The Public should demand that the policies of the early day Forest

Service be revived. With air power and modern equipment it is much easier to reach and put out forest fires now than in horse and buggy days. It is up to the public to demand that no matter what the cause, "As soon as a fire is discovered put it out."[9]

Audrey wrote a Letter to the Editor of the *Las Vegas Daily Optic* on October 8, 1988:

> Dear Editor:
>
> We keep hearing the same lame excuse for the disastrous fires in Yellowstone Park. "Fire in nature is a means of rebuilding and renewal," quoted from the *Las Vegas Optic*, Wed. Sept. 21, 1988, editorial page. "Lightning is a natural thing and the forest has to renew itself."
>
> Anyone with an iota of forest land experience knows that a forest is renewing and rebuilding itself every day without fires that completely destroy the ecological chain. The ill advised policy of letting lightning caused fires burn themselves out was established by people completely ignorant of the danger of fire—those who have never seen, smelled or been surrounded by Forest Fire.
>
> If officials had any first-hand knowledge of wild fire they would realize that in most small fires, birds and mammals are destroyed, while the fire also contributes to the feared "Green House" effect.
>
> Fuel buildup on the ground is deplored. However, that very decaying vegetation protects the forest floor, provides shelter for small animals, and most important, prevents erosion, holding water on the water shed. While decaying it naturally disappears, while making new soil. A fire may leave a nutrient residue, as claimed by some "school book" foresters; those nutrients wash away with the next rain and are forever lost to the forest.
>
> The 1971 fire in Santa Fe National Forest, in San Miguel County, near Barillas Peak, sprinkled Las Vegas with ashes and soot, and burned about 13,000 acres. In the last 17 years oak brush has filled in some scarred areas, while others haven't enough soil left to grow a sprig of grass.
>
> Immediately after that fire my daughter and I planted 400 pine trees and 25 fir trees. The firs were placed on northern exposure where once we had hundreds of Christmas trees [before they were burned in the 1971 fire.]
>
> The 25 all died. Along the edge of my garden we planted 40 pine trees. Only one survived there and now after a number of wet years it is

only about 10 feet high. Of the 400 we set out, only a handful survived.

A thousand years from now Yellowstone National Park will still be wearing the scars of the 1988 forest fires, for it takes hundreds of years for timber to grow into the giants that once graced Yellowstone Park.

Let us not white wash the government officials responsible for untold loss of beauty, not to mention financial loss. But let us insist that if a fire starts, from any cause, PUT IT OUT IMMEDIATELY.
Sincerely,
Audrey Simpson[10]

Audrey scribbled a verse the back of an envelope:

All day the ashes fell
Coming from that fiery hell
The mountains black
The sky is gray
With smoke that doesn't
Blow away.[11]

As Audrey and Holly hunted through the rubble of twisted metal and ashes, all that was left of forty years of hard work, Holly found a scrap of paper that had been under the bath tub, somewhat protected. It came from Oral Roberts' *Abundant Life* magazine. There was a picture of Oral Roberts with a statement. All that could be seen were part of the words:

Amen. In the name of Jesus of Nazareth . . . in His name be healed. Be healed . . . free by the power of God. God strengthen you. God strengthen your inner man, in your . . . God heal your body. God give you a whole new lease on life. I pray and I believe in the name of Jesus. Amen and Amen.[12]

Audrey sent a copy of the piece of paper and a letter to Oral Roberts. She wanted him to know that this piece of scripture is all that survived the fire of 1971. She wanted the evangelist to know how she had been inspired by his prayer. She wrote:

Dear Oral Roberts:

This is a reproduction of a page from some *Abundant Life Magazine*. Our house burned June 29, 1972, in a terrible forest fire that destroyed miles of our beautiful mountains. Later, as we hunted through the rubble of twisted metal and ashes, (all that was left of 40 years of hard work) my 16 year old daughter, Holly Alice Simpson, found this scrap of paper—burned all but this much. All our magazines and books were completely burned to ashes with not another legible word left—except this.

This message has a special meaning for us—a widow and her daughter. Although we are burned out completely, these words, literally from the ashes, helped keep our hope and faith alive. We re-read them and especially note, "God give you a whole new lease on life—."

I thought you might like to see this. May the Lord continue to bless you.

Sincerely,

Audrey Simpson[13]

Audrey could have given up as others have after such a disaster. But she did not. She believed God would truly give her a "whole new lease on life."

12

By Your Bootstraps

The defining moment in Audrey's life became June of 1971—before The Fire and After the Fire. It became a part of everyday conversation, a way of thinking.

Audrey sometimes said, "You have to pull yourself up by your own bootstraps." She undoubtedly had heard her parents say that more once. The idea that no one is going to help you, that you have to survive through your own struggling efforts, was true in many lives; and Audrey's was no exception. Audrey knew a fire in which everything is lost can be totally devastating. It had destroyed Grandfather Shearer's will to live. But at 58 years of age, Audrey did not give up. She was heartbroken, but she was determined to survive and to rebuild. She was not one to quit under any circumstances.

After the fire, Audrey received a little help, but for the most part, she had to start over on her own efforts. The small amount of insurance she had purchased on the house in the early 1940s could not begin to replace everything, could not replace such things as unique antiques, photographs, journals, rare books, and keepsakes.

"Never give up," was another motto she had heard often. She had learned to take one day at a time, praying for God's help as she pulled herself back up from the devastating blows that she received in life, blows that often bowled her over. Audrey kept the little scrap of paper from the Oral Roberts magazine as a reminder.

Sometime later, another scrap of paper was found. Audrey wrote:

> Scrap of paper that could still be read found in January, 1972 on floor of house under ashes:
> For there's nothing to fear
> You're as good as the best
> Strong as the mightiest too
> You can win in every battle and test
> For there's no one just like you.
> There's only one you in
> the world today.
>   — from *Dynamic Maturity.*

The other side of page said:

> There's nothing too good for you
> Nor heights where you cannot go
> It's something you have to know!
> There's nothing to fear
> You can and you will
> For you're the invincible you.
> So set your foot on the highest hill
> There's nothing
> You cannot do![1]

The verse inspired Audrey. Additionally, Audrey had many friends and relatives who helped as much as they could after the fire. Most of them had very little money to spare, but each one gave what they could to help—and Audrey deeply appreciated it. She had been active in several organizations, and now they pitched in to help. One of them was the Rebekahs. Audrey wrote a rough draft of a letter she sent to them, as follows:

Letter to the Rebekahs #1
Read at 1st Fall Meeting, 1971
Dear Sister Rebekahs,

    Thank you all for the morale building shower. Holly and I enjoy using the lovely things you all so thoughtfully gave me. Wonderful friends like you and all of your wonderful help make the world a brighter and happier place.

    May the Lord bless each and every one of you.

    Thank you all very much.[2]

In her notebook Audrey had a list of all the people who had given her gifts. She kept lists in order to send thank you notes. She also listed those who had given her monetary gifts. If Audrey's friends were not rich in finances, they were rich in their love, generosity and kindness. The total amount of money was less than $350.00, but Audrey felt that it was the thought, and not the amount she received, that was important. People like her friend, Mrs. Ranney, who lived in Texas, sent money. Among the gifts Audrey received were: silverware; glasses; cups; an iron skillet; cooking pans; dishes; baking dishes; towels; wash cloths; blankets; sheets; pillow cases; cookie sheet; mixing bowls; electric iron; toaster; clothes; and a washing machine. Audrey was grateful for every item she was given. There was a note on the first page: "Shower for Audrey Simpson, Hostesses—Annie B. Brown, Oleta Sterling, July 13, 1971, (after fire)"[3]

Audrey was grateful for the help, but every day was a new challenge after the fire. Audrey wrote later in her "Holly" notes:

> I just lived from day to day and so did you [Holly]. We came to the ranch whenever possible. I traded the old Scout for a new one in 1972. You drove it when I would let you as you got your drivers' beginner license the day after you were 15—at Santa Rosa where you took Driver's Training in school.[4]

While living in town, Audrey wrote a story published in September, 1980 *Cat Fancy*. Audrey told about how a neighbor was looking for his cat and discovered it was at the very top of a big tree, clinging to a limb, afraid to move. Audrey gave details about how Holly talked the cat out of the tree, giving it step by step directions as to how to move—and the cat followed her directions to get down. "Somehow it did understand each of Holly's explicit directions and it followed them."[5]

Holly graduated from Las Vegas Robertson High School. Wesley started to build a little log cabin immediately so that Audrey would have a place to move back into. It was a good, solid one-room log cabin with a cement floor, but it didn't have a bathroom or running water; so again, Audrey had an outhouse until the main ranch house was re-built, complete with indoor plumbing as the original one had been. Audrey and Holly moved into the little house, even before it was finished, while the big ranch house was being re-built on the original foundation.

In the fall, Holly enrolled at New Mexico Highlands University and lived on campus. All her expenses were paid through government grants. Audrey was alone when Holly was in school, but she was used to being alone. She wrote:

> Here I sit in my own home—it consists of bedrooms for two, linen storage area, clothes closet, family room with TV, radio and telephone, dining room with china closet and silver storage area, library, office, furnace room, laundry room and bathroom. No, mine isn't a camper or modern mobile home. Mine is a mountain log cabin, size 14 by 20 feet. Everything for my daughter and me are in this one room—except our refrigerator, which is outside. There just isn't any room for it in here. The bedroom bunk and a 3/4 bed that doubles for a couch is used by grandkids when they come home. We sit to watch the TV which sits on the chest of drawers across the room. A table holds plastic jars that double for silverware holders. There is a steel wall cabinet, shelves for a pantry and food storage—and in this energy saving area—only a cold water faucet in the sink. It is better than a cold-water flat in the city. And the biggest energy saver of all is an old box heater that serves as heating unit as well as cook stove. There is a small desk and there are shelves along the log walls for books.
>
> [There is] a row of clothes on hangers stuck on nails in the viga in front of the space. Yes, it's all here. Crowded? Yes, but so is a mobile home. If I want more, I just step outside. I have a view of the mountain range, the Sangre de Cristos and enjoy the fresh air and spring water. Oh, this is so called disadvantaged, rural scum type living, but I'm not a hippie. I've lived this way for more than 40 years here on the home place whenever I could escape the city rat race and find the mountain peace.[6]

At the end of the summer of 1971, Wesley and Crystal moved to Albuquerque from Houston and came to the ranch on weekends to work on the house. As soon as possible, Wesley, friends, and relatives began to build the big house back on the foundation Clyde and Wesley had built. It was finished in 1973 and Audrey moved into it.

Four generations: left to right, Audrey Simpson, Crystal Simpson Lovett, Karen Lovett, and Mabel Shearer, about 1971. *Source*: Simpson Archives, photo by Wesley Lovett

After Gary Beimer and I married, we moved to the Red River Hatchery where he had a job with the Game and Fish Department. Gary also helped with Audrey's house when he had time off. Before long we moved to Las Vegas. He also started to build our own house.

I was pleased that my best friend Judy had also moved back to Las Vegas. Judy Beil Vaughan graduated from the University of New Mexico with her M.D. She became a neurologist. She lived in Las Vegas for a few years with her husband, James Vaughan, a lawyer—and daughters Ellen and Betsy and son Lyman—before moving to Colorado and later to California. My mother's favorite childhood doll had been named Dorothy. My favorite had been named Rose. One of Judy's favorite dolls had been named Betsy. We each selected names for our daughters from those favorites names.

When Audrey moved into the big ranch house that had been built on the foundation of the original one, it was the last time she would move, after moving so many times in her life. She was thankful for everything that had been saved from the fire. Audrey had saved her suitcase of photographs and valuables from the fire. Several of her photographs, taken with her "Brownie" box camera, were published as part of stories she sold. Some were used in the *Las Vegas Daily Optic* when she worked there. Audrey's black and white photo of the Montezuma ice pond was used in *New Mexico Magazine* with the caption, "The finest natural skating pond in the State."[7]

Since Wesley had a better camera and did professional work, Audrey sometimes asked him to take photographs to go with her stories. Audrey wrote several articles about the forest fire, and she had Wesley's photos to show the devastation. She wrote in a Letter to the Editor, *Albuquerque Journal*:

> Burned timber leaves no place to hide for mountain lions, deer or turkey if any survived the flames. This picture [reference to a photograph to go with the story] taken following the 1971 Forest Fire west of Las Vegas, NM. at the foot of Barillas Peak shows only a very small portion of the 12,920 acres burned in the Santa Fe National Forest and on private lands, according to Forest Service estimation. Since the fire most of these trees have fallen in criss-cross patterns, making hazardous travel for everything except mountain lions. Our place, homesteaded by the Santillaneses in 1894, is high on the west side of the Sangre de Cristo mountains, about 18 miles from Las Vegas; after several years, oak brush and ground cover began to come back; until now there are plenty of places where mountain lions can slink about unobserved. Forest Springs Ranch rebuilt: This photo [reference to a photograph] taken in 1980 shows my cabin, which took more than a year of weekends to build, while the larger building took 4 years after the 1971 Forest Fire west of Las Vegas New Mexico destroyed my original home. I was standing inside my back door in the larger cabin when I saw a big mountain lion go around the northeast corner of the small cabin. Grass and oak brush is all that provides cover for wild animals today.[8]

Audrey sold a few stories after the fire. She made many notes, so there are lots of unpublished stories and verses such as one about the trees destroyed by the forest fire. The example below shows her work as she was putting together the rough draft for a poem:

> Robbed last year of their green robes by a raging blaze,
> Stark, blackened pines stand with upheld limbs,
> Waiting, waiting, waiting,
> Waiting to topple back to mother earth.

The wind—the wind that wildly whipped the blistering flames,
Destroying every living thing for miles along the mountain,
Returns growling, howling, with wild roar, tearing across steep slopes,
Blasting, torturing the bare branches that still reach upward.
The dead trees creak and moan beneath the beating air.
A rotted pine that once bent gracefully before the wind, whines, gives up.
Here for 500 years green tipped limber fingers
Reached in supplication to a turquoise sky
Waved to moon and stars or turquoise sky.
Wild turkey nested in their shade or roosted high at night.
Bird's nests graced the swaying limbs.
Blue Jays danced among the boughs.
Tassel eared squirrels found refuge from hungry coyote.
Gone, ALL GONE, burned by howling, fanning flames.
A tree, long standing, fights the wind,
A crack, a snap,
The once mighty pine shivers, gives up
Thrown downward dead arms and finger limbs break or probe stiffly
Into Mother earth.
Here on the Mountain even as men down below,
The eons come and ages go.
As from dust they grow in pleasant living years
And now by wind and fire to dust return.[9]

The fire caused more grief and distress in Audrey's life than one can imagine unless one has experienced the heartbreak suffered by losing a lifetime of irreplaceable treasures such as photographs, diaries, manuscripts, and other material goods. Audrey wrote:

Today I looked and looked
For one thin book.
Not very many shelves to hunt through,
Not like the hundreds once I had
Before the '71 forest fire.
I could not find the book
For which I looked.
It is one that held a prayer for rain.
It is so dry

And there are clouds
Across the sky.
So I look for the prayer
That brings the rain
Written in a thin book
That I cannot find.
That brings the rain
Written in a thin book
That I cannot find.
Oh, where is the rain
And that book of mine?[10]

Audrey did eventually find that book which contained her "Prayer for Rain" poem. It had been saved in the last minute rush to evacuate. Audrey had other rough drafts of poetry:

The roaring flames
Ate all the trees,
Killed the squirrels and birds and bees,
The wind was hot—the ashes dry
Rolling smoke and fire clouds filled the sky.
Ashes and charcoal bleak and dead,
The beaten mountain bowed its head.
Then the thundering rains came battering down,
Washing the top soil from mountain crown,
Taking the life blood from the mountain's side,
No green is left, no hope left—
The mountain died.[11]

Another verse was written on the back of a big envelope:

20 Miles of mountains
Standing green and grand
20 Miles of mountains
Fairest in the land.

Thunder roared and lightening hit
And man his duty did not do
and so the

20 miles of mountains
All gone up in smoke
20 miles of mountains
A sick and tragic joke.[12]

When Audrey was alone, she had time to write and to contemplate. But she often had unexpected visitors. There was a "commune" in the area in the 1960's and 1970's, and Audrey was often visited and asked for her advice on such things as planting and farming. She called it a "hippie" colony. Sometimes a couple came to visit her to ask advice, as they were attempting to live off the land. For instance, a hawk had killed a chicken and they didn't want to lose the meat. The couple asked Audrey how to get the feathers off the chicken. Of course, Audrey knew what to do and gave them good instructions.

Audrey also helped a group of Mexican nationals who were working near Santillanes Canyon. They were cutting trees that had been fire damaged. Sometimes they came over to use the telephone. Audrey wrote in an unpublished manuscript, "The Mexican Nationals and Me:"

> My kids and some of the neighbors took a year to build a small log cabin back on my mountain. The original house or cabin had been turned to ashes when the big 13,000 acres forest fire in June of 1971 south west of Las Vegas, New Mexico [burned the house.]
>
> Before it was clinked between the logs my teenage daughter and I moved in. We had been homeless for a year and it was good to get back home again even if we could look out between the log walls in every direction while the spring winds whistled through the cabin. Right after the fire the REA restored electric service and soon Mountain Bell kindly restored my telephone service—interrupted by the forest fire. When they installed a telephone in the unfinished cabin, I shut the telephone in a suitcase so that varmints such as rats or squirrels couldn't come in and chew the wires.
>
> While we finished the interior, our furniture consisted of a burned and warped bedstead and springs that had gone through the fire; somebody's old wooden bench; several sawed off chunks of logs served as chairs; some cardboard boxes stacked into shelf space held our dishes and kitchen equipment, all donated by various friends following the fire. A card table proudly held our [dinner].
>
> That telephone was the bait that drew the Mexican nationals. We could hear chain saws working so we knew a large number of men were

south of our place in Santillanes Canyon trying to harvest the burned timber for area sawmills. We were too busy trying to finish our cabin to check them out.

One morning a beat up old truck drove up to the cabin. I stepped out of my blue door, a gift from a friend in town. *"Buenos Dias,"* a handsome young man said as he got out of his truck. "Good morning," I answered. It is usual for New Mexicans to intermix English and Spanish languages.

"Yo quiero teléfono," he said, and went into a long story of broken machinery and no groceries "no *tengo* gas" for the saws. He wanted to call his boss in Las Vegas.

I invited him in and opened the suitcase to let him use the phone. He had the telephone number written on the inside of a paper match package.

I heard him rapidly repeat in Spanish all he had told me before. My Spanish was rusty from lack of use, but like swimming or riding a bike, you never forget it. One of the main improvements in communication in the past 50 years in New Mexico was the way the Spanish Americans now speak English. I have had little occasion to speak Spanish. Also the Old Mexican version is not quite the same as in New Mexico.

When he finished his phone conversation I asked, *"Café?"* [coffee]

When he said, *"Si, por favor,"* [yes, please] I started the hot plate and made coffee. Since I heard him say he was hungry I offered him crackers along with the coffee. He [Orlando] was really hungry.

I asked him where he was from and he gave me the name of a town I had never heard of in Chihuahua, Mexico. Over in Santillanes canyon, my telephone was evidently a conversation piece. Once or twice a week various workers would come over to use it, mostly to call the boss and ask for supplies.

For a while the first one that came over would accompany others to our cabin to show them the way. As summer wore on many different men and boys would come over and use the telephone. Always they offered to pay but I never would take money for it since it was not long distance calls. Usually they would drink coffee. After they were gone I would sterilize their cups by turning them upside down on the hot plate after rinsing them off. [Audrey was afraid they might have something contagious such as tuberculosis.] Following Orlando's visit, there was a steady stream of woodcutters, chainsaw men and timber workers from Santillanes Canyon, coming to see the burned out old lady with the telephone. A friend in Las Vegas loaned me a Spanish-English dictionary. My understanding and conversational ability improved. There was a nice 19-year-old, just out of high school, who had traveled extensively. He had been in 48 of the United States and Alaska. He was considering working his way to Hawaii next winter.

I soon learned to spot the better educated, higher class workers. Their clothing might be tattered and torn from working in the blackened timber. But the more affluent always wore real good, expensive looking boots and shoes.

When several came at once one would want to talk on the phone and the others would sit around the yard where we [Holly and Audrey] served them coffee *"con azúcar y leche."* [with sugar and cream.] I only had canned milk to go with sugar in their coffee if they wanted it. Mostly they were very polite, offering to pay for the phone and coffee and profusely thanking me before they left. When Jack Frost painted the oaks in bronze tones many hunted warmer climes. But Orlando and José and Jorge stayed on in a tiny trailer house in Santillanes Canyon.

When winter froze the land, Orlando brought an older man over to talk to the boss. I could tell he was very ill, probably had pneumonia. I could tell he wanted to go to town to a doctor and also to go home. The boss put him off until Orlando got on the phone and in no uncertain terms persuaded him to come get him. He was a rough looking character and if he hadn't been so sick I might have considered him dangerous. He had a sneer that boded ill for ignorant old ladies that couldn't even speak decent Spanish.

With New Years came Orlando tramping through deep snow and called the boss frantically. The ice was forming all over the inside of the little trailer house. They couldn't get warm though they had a tiny tin wood heater in it with a chimney going out a window. They were completely out of food. The roads were deep drifts, impassable even if they still had gas. The three were literally starving. I gave them several cans of food, some potatoes and some flour. My supplies were meager. I never found out who the boss was.

Somehow the men survived until they could go to town.[13]

The men had a little black and white dog. He usually accompanied the men to visit Audrey. When the men left, they abandoned the pet. One day the dog showed up at Audrey's house, starving. Like his Mexican owners, he knew the lady in the log cabin had food. Audrey fed him and he stayed. She named him "Taco." He understood commands in Spanish much better than English. He turned out to be a wonderful, protective watch dog. In fact, he died protecting his home when he was wounded by a predator. After some furious barking, the injured dog crawled up to Audrey's back cement step and lost consciousness. The loyal pet died defending the home that had taken him in.

Audrey noticed the beauty around her, even though the mountains were scarred and the trees that still stood were blackened, with the exception of a few that escaped the flames. The rain that put out the fire flooded through the canyon, moving sand and debris in its fury. The place where the Fifteen Dollar Cabin and the two back cabins had stood was nothing but ashes and twisted metal—and what was left of the iron kitchen range. The place where the Ten Dollar House had stood and where Hellers' Cabin had been were no better. The site of the new ranch house was a pile of rubble on the cement floor. However, after a few weeks life began to thrive again. Audrey noticed some Russian thistles in full bloom. She wrote:

> Just a Russian thistle
> No class or style at all
> A lavender buttonaire
> Too sticky to wear.[14]

She wrote, "Spring Gold," a poem which she apparently sent in for publication some place; but whether it was published is unknown.

> Who called them weeds?
> Who named them such?
> These lovely flowers
> We love so much.[15]

Audrey began to write more after she got settled into her new house. She recalled the many houses she had helped to build. Audrey made a list of the various building projects she had helped with. In part, it reads:

> $10 [cabin]; $15 [cabin]; cabin by Ramon [Hellers' Cabin]; the one in 1960 [ranch house]; 2 after fire— Re-finished [built] after fire. [small cabin and big ranch house] I am resigning from the house building. I have had a hand in building or remodeling 13 houses—homes for me and my family during the past 35 years. They ranged from a meager log cabin costing us $9.42, known forever after as the Ten Dollar House, to a remodeled

church and my present completely modern $1,800 log cabin. [cost of rebuilding the ranch house after the fire.] Our financial status always put us in the class with the *do-it-yourself-or-do-without* pioneer type. Back in 1941 my late husband, Clyde Simpson, was too ill to continue working in town. War time rationing was a threat so he sold our 4 new tires off the old 1929 Model A for 40 bucks. This, along with $10 we had after we paid our monthly grocery bill, gave us enough to build our Ten Dollar House and live 3 months in the mountains.

Here I sit in the nearly finished #13, comfortable and unharried and unhurried. Yes, I think I'll retire from house building. Except for finishing this one and building a chicken house. Oh, yes, Wes says we need a bedroom added to this house so when he and CC and K [Crystal and Karen] come home for weekends and vacations we won't be so crowed. Here we go again! I put my 2 cents worth in on each of them and hard work on a lot of them. And that doesn't include the leaning tower.[outhouse] List:

$10
$15
1 store house
2 store houses
1 Heller's cabin
1 8th Street house
1 "chicken house" on 8th street
1 Lelama's [8th street house sold to Lelama]
1 8th street house built around the piano
1 7th street house that was first a church
1 big house, first big ranch house
1, 2 and 3 and 4th cabins
1 better cabin
1 new big house
tin [storage] house[16]

If the loss of her houses at the ranch—and all her possessions—created disappointment and grief in Audrey's life in 1971, there was still more grief to come. Some people bought an adjoining piece of land and decided to quiet title. Since Audrey's place had never had a quiet title, there was a dispute over the boundary line. Audrey went to court and presented evidence in the way of old property descriptions, maps, and so on. But Audrey lost about five acres and other neighbors lost some land as well.

Audrey was just recovering from the loss and grief of the devastating fire when her mother became ill. Mabel was 83 years old. Milly and her husband, Gordon Wickman, had moved next door to help take care of her. But she was failing. Betty came from Portales to help care for her mother. Audrey went into town and helped as much as she could. But she wasn't well herself. She was still having trouble with the leg where she'd had a skin draft. It was worse than ever. She had to keep her legs bandaged most of the time due to the draining ulcers. She'd had bad legs since before she retired from the Optic, and they had been getting worse. She could hardly drive because using the brake and clutch caused stress on her weak legs.

Gary Beimer and I were living near Questa when our daughter Laura Lea was born January 8, 1974. When Laura was six months old, I took her to visit my Grandma Shearer—Laura's great grandma. When we went to visit Grandma, I was pleased that she held my baby and had a happy smile on her face. Her arms were weak, but they did not waver as she held Laura up and looked into her face. Laura began to make a sound like a crow—"Ca, Ca, Ca!" Grandma laughed. Laura shrieked happily. Of the dozens of babies Grandma had held and loved, Laura was the last.

One day Grandma Shearer had severe stomach pains and was taken to the hospital. A month after she had held her great granddaughter Laura, Mabel Shearer died—July 20, 1974.

As mentioned before, Mabel's mind was sharp until the day she died. Mabel had brought up seven children and helped with most of her grandchildren when they were small, including Roger, Holly, Frankie and Carol Ann. She went to Breckenridge to help care for Roger when he broke his leg. She and Vivian took in Milly and the three children after Milly lost her job in Breckenridge and needed a place to stay. She helped Audrey and Holly through the terrible time after the fire as they stayed in the little trailer next to her house on Montezuma Road. They had no place to go, but Mabel was there to help and encourage them. She always helped her family as much as she could. She had taught many children in her lifetime as a teacher.

When Mabel died the family missed her terribly. Audrey had talked to her mother on the telephone nearly every day and had seen her often. Audrey remarked that she and her mother were especially close because their ages were separated by only 21 years. Mabel had lived from October 26, 1890 to July 20, 1974.

Nearly every family member attended the funeral. All seven of Mabel's adult children were there. I remember standing at the edge of the cemetery after everything was over and everyone was leaving. Watching at the edge of the crowd, I saw my mother. Audrey stood at the grave of her mother and then slowly turned and walked away. It struck me suddenly that Audrey was totally alone. The others walked away from their mother's grave accompanied by somebody: Opal had Bob; Edward had Volene; Betty had Stanley; Milly had Gordon; Jessica had Red; and Frank had Margaret. But Audrey, a widow, walked away in solitary grief. Yes, we girls were there for her. But it wasn't the same as having a spouse to lean on.

Watching Audrey walk slowly away from her mother's grave, I thought, *"There is nothing so lonely in this world as walking away from a grave, alone."*

Then another blow came the next year. Betty had not been feeling well for a long time. She came to the ranch and stayed for a couple of weeks early in 1975. Audrey wondered what was wrong. Betty didn't volunteer to talk about what was bothering her. But before long she was in the hospital in Albuquerque. She was diagnosed with a liver disease. Audrey called and urged Betty to fight, to hang on. "Don't give up," she told her. But Betty was too weak to even hold the telephone very long.

Each night before bed we would always have our prayer time and Audrey would mention each family member by name, including nieces and nephews. But when someone needed help, she spent time alone praying for that person. Sometimes I would see Audrey down on her knees at her bedside, praying. I knew someone was in trouble because she prayed those intense prayers when she was asking for a miracle. As she worried about Betty, Audrey wrote this poem:

> He passed a miracle for me
> Not only once but 3 times 3
> I never knew the cost
> And now when all seems lost
> I'm full of dread.
> Oh, God! A miracle! Or she is dead.
> She never smoked.
> She never drank.
> Blessed! she always seemed to me
> And now, Oh Lord, she is dying,
> Dying and not yet fifty-three.[17]

Betty died on October 15, 1975. She would have been 53 on October 24. It was a blow to the family. Stanley, Tana, Janie and Twila had their faith to cling to. But life without Betty was going to be difficult.

Notes of a rough draft of an obituary for Betty were found years later in

Audrey's files; undoubtedly it was used in the local newspapers.

> Funeral Services for former Las Vegan, Elizabeth (Betty) Hope Hardin, 52, were held Friday at South Side Church of Christ in Portales, N.M.
>
> Born in Las Vegas, October 24, 1922, the daughter of Mr. and Mrs. L. C. Clements, she died in an Albuquerque hospital October 15, 1975. A graduate of Albuquerque High School, she was married to Stanley Hardin June 14, 1941 in Albuquerque.
>
> She is survived by her husband, Dr. Stanley Hardin of the family home in Portales; three daughters, Tana, Mrs. Bulen Barnes of Medford, Oregon; Janie Hardin of Albuquerque; and Twila, Mrs. Ron Harrington of Friona, Texas; and four grandchildren. Also surviving are two brothers, Edward Clements of Grand Junction, Colorado and Frank Shearer of Hamlin, Texas; and five sisters, Audrey Simpson; Opal, Mrs. Robert Simpson; and Millicent, Mrs. Gordon Wickman, all of Las Vegas, Jessica, Mrs. David Braziel of Tucumcari; and Ellen Grace, Mrs. Sam Williams of Albuquerque.
>
> She was preceded in death by her mother, Mabel, Mrs. C. V. Shearer of Las Vegas in July, 1974.
>
> Church of Christ ministers, Grover C. Ross, Jack Self and Steve Eclestein officiated the services. Church choirs from the New Mexico Christian Children's Home in Portales sang several numbers.
>
> The Hardins moved from Las Vegas to Portales in 1954. Mrs. Hardin was a member of the Church of Christ and Business and Professional Women of Portales.
>
> Mrs. Hardin served as secretary and bookkeeper at the Children's Home for the past 15 years. Honorary pall bearers were the staff and children from the Christian Children's Home. Burial was in Portales cemetery, Wheeler mortuary in charge of arrangements.[18]

Audrey had a deep love for each of her sisters and brothers. She had helped raise all them to some extent, some more than others. She had stayed home from school to take care of Betty, her baby sister. Betty, like Mabel and Audrey, had suffered from phlebitis. Apparently what is now known as Factor V Leiden, an inherited tendency for blood to clot too readily, was a problem for some family members, including Audrey. They were able to overcome it. But Betty could not survive the destructive liver disease that took her at a young age.

Audrey found it hard to believe that Betty would be the one of Mabel's seven children to die first. Audrey wrote a poem, "She Was Always Ready to Go."

> Among the stodgy people
> She was the brave and adventurous.
> She was always ready to go—
> Go in a plane, fly to Canada, drive to Mexico!
> Oh yes, she was always ready to go!
>
> Then phlebitis laid her low
> Her head said YES, but her lips said NO,
> No more wandering,
> No more get up and go.
>
> So still the one to try the new,
> She closed her eyes
> And away she flew.
>
> She'll bring laughter and joy
> To heaven on high
> Her love for all
> Will fill the sky.
>
> But to leave here so soon
> Oh why, Betty, Why?[19]

13

Another Wedding

Audrey had been alone a long time. She had resigned from the Optic in 1966. She loved living in her mountains, but without Clyde, it was lonely. Holly was there until she graduated from high school and then lived in the dormitory at Highlands University as a student. The new house was coming along nicely and Audrey had a place to live at the ranch again. She wrote:

> In 1973 I think Crystal came and went to HU and Holly looked after Karen until Crystal graduated. Holly rode the bus to Robertson HS until graduation in 1973. Laura was born in Albuquerque in 1974. We went to Crystal's for Xmas and I took care of Laura when D & G [Dorothy and Gary] went to Arizona when his mother died (Feb., 1974).[1]

Audrey discovered that her old friend William Albert Reid (Bill Reid) was also alone. Helen, his wife of many years and mother of their ten children, had died a few years before. Bill began to come to visit Audrey. Undoubtedly, she had many old feelings of the days when she was a teenager and Bill came to visit the family. Audrey recalled:

> Back in the early 1920's William Miles Reid and his son, W. A. "Bill" Reid, ran a sawmill in La Cueva, north of Sebedilla Canyon and the old village site of San Luis.
>
> The set up included a mill bought from Gross Kelly and Co. Reid got the contract to run the mill for a month—and put out 30,000 a week. Workers were people from upper and lower Colonias, one or two from Manzaneros and Pecos towns. The mill turned out about 10,000 feet of lumber a day, and later 3 times as much each day.[2]

Audrey recalled how Bill Reid had heard Edward singing "When It's Springtime in the Rockies," and knew Audrey liked that song. Bill often called Audrey "Sweetheart of the Mountains" and teased her about her bonny blue, eyes. They were eyes that twinkled when she was amused—Irish eyes, Clyde always said.

Audrey had always been very fond of Bill and had even had hopes they would marry someday. But Bill only had eyes for Opal and Opal wasn't interested in him. So when Opal and Bob married, Bill married Helen. Then Audrey had married Clyde. Now that both Audrey and Bill were alone, Bill realized he loved Audrey and proposed to her. They were married in a private ceremony at the ranch on October 17, 1976.

Audrey wrote: "My handsome cowboy got away—for 44 years—but he finally lassoed me. Well, it all started out with me looking on while my favorite cowboy wooed my younger sister."[3]

Bill had been a handsome cowboy but when he and Audrey married he was not well. Still he kept Audrey entertained with his many stores of "the old days." She wrote many of them down and hoped to publish some of them. Audrey found a little time to write when she wasn't cooking for Bill, cleaning house, canning fruit, making her bread-and-butter pickles, or doing one of dozens of other chores.

Bill's children had always been very dear to Audrey and she had always been like a second mother to them. Then she had actually become their stepmother. But all too soon Bill died, leaving Audrey alone once again.

Audrey summarized several events in a manuscript she wrote for Holly:

> You [Holly] graduated from high school in the Highlands University Gym. You started at HU and since I was at the ranch you stayed in Mrs. Carrington's front room downstairs and were supposed to keep her [house] clean. Grandma and Betty each died [Mabel died in 1974 and Betty died in 1975].
>
> Dorothy got a job teaching at Highlands University and moved from Questa. Gary quit the Fish and Wildlife Department and moved down in a week or two.
>
> I brought you home on most weekends when the weather was fit. After you got in the Drama Dept. you were happier going to school. You lived for Drama. The 2nd year you were in that Drama group I decided you would have to live in the dorm so you wouldn't have to walk home so far as late at night. [to the Carrington house.]
>
> You cut the apron strings and were trying to be independent.
>
> I never got to see you in any plays. You thought I didn't care but my leg was so bad so much of the time and I was struggling to stay out of the hospital—year after year.

You graduated from HU in 1980.[4]

Audrey's manuscript to Holly about her life concluded as follows:

> When you first went to Gallup Cathedral to teach I hoped you could get along OK with the sisters. It was good experience for you even if it didn't last. And it gave you a toe-hold even if you came home at Christmas. You were so discouraged when you didn't get a school in the Fall of 1981. I kept telling you [that] you would and if not you could do something else. Finally one came through and away you left again. This has been an isolated, hard year for you and me while you taught at Navajo kindergarten. But you are learning what it means to be on your own. A thing you will probably have to be for many years in the future.
> So good luck to you, Dearest Holly![5]

Bill died in his sleep on October 11, 1979. He had gone to visit his son, "little Bill" in California and stopped at the home of one of his daughters in Albuquerque to visit for a few days. He was 71 years of age.

Bill's funeral was October 15, 1979 at Glorieta, New Mexico and he was buried in the family plot. His father, his son Johnny, his first wife Helen, and his Uncle Tom Greer and wife Stella were buried there, along with other family members.

Somehow Audrey got through the funeral and said good-by to Bill's kids after they took whatever property of his they wanted. She had cared for each of them as she watched them grow up and begin to live their own lives.

Audrey's second marriage was short. She had loved Bill and would miss him. She wrote: "The last words I said to him were, 'I love you!' I couldn't have said that 50 years ago when I first fell in love with him. I was too shy then. And so was he."[6]

I once asked my mother how she managed when she was alone so much of the time. Audrey told me she depended on God and that He helped her through. She admitted, "I'm a scardy cat. I always have been scared—and still am."[7]

Yet Audrey showed great courage throughout her life as she tackled one challenge after another, in spite of any fears she may have had. As always, she depended on God to lead her through the dark paths of life. Sometimes when she was alone and the electric power was out, she felt especially lonely. Even then, she was inspired to write:

The electricity is out

And so is the phone
No T.V. or talking
'Cause I'm all alone.

I can sing me a song
Or play in the yard
But guess I'll stay in
And write you a card.

When the lights are all out
And so is the phone
I really feel lonesome
'Cause I'm all alone.[8]

After Bill's death, Audrey spent much of her time writing. An example of a rough draft, written as though by Bill Reid, follows:

From the halls of Audrey's cabin
To the Sebedilla Creek
I'll saddle up my pony
And ride up to Barillis Peak.
I'll climb up on the tower
And take a look around
To see what's happening above
As well as on the ground.
I'll take a squint at Hermit's
To see if there is smoke
And if there's nothing
It will build up all my hopes.
I will look up at the mountains
And also at the ground.
I'll mount up on my pony
And head for Hermit's Peak
And on to Elk Mountain
Onward I will go.
I will spend the night
At a town called Terrero.
Now my day is ended
Now my day is done.

> I know Audrey don't like beer
> So I am on the run.[9]

Audrey was constantly writing notes, notes for stories she hoped to finish and publish, notes for poems, notes for later. She wrote:

> "Aren't you sad, Grandma, to be so old?" my granddaughter asks.
> My goodness, no! I have been tested by life, gone through hellfire and storms—marriage, births and divorce and re-marriage. Life has kicked me around—-but whoever promised me a bed of roses—Anyway I am triumphant—I finally got to be a senior citizen![10]

In some of her notes, she scribbled, "Don't cry yet. You're only 80 years old." She wrote:

> I don't know what it all means. These years I have fooled around on this whirling earth. I have appreciated it and sometimes wondered which one was actually whirling the hardest.
> When I was nearly two I rode my first bucking horse on the prairies of Nebraska near Shelton, after Mother fought off an attempted rape down in Avis area in Southern New Mexico when I was just past one.[11]

Apparently this note (above) was to be a beginning of an autobiography. She had notes in various places such as: "I have licked all sorts of disasters, near starvation, blood clots, hospital stays, pneumonia, floods and drought, chicken-stealing Bob cats, run away broncs, loco cattle— and I raised three kids."[12]

In another place she wrote:

> A person is made up of many facets—many experiences, each contributing to the whole. And when is that end result reached? After eons . . . goes through each phase they are all thrown together and called LIFE. The difficulty is sorting out each section or part that makes that whole. Many things are interwoven to the point that they cannot be individually separated into their own little compartments. Even so, I will take some of these separate events that are woven into my existence. For instance, there are the reading, writing, and arithmetic classes called schools. I drifted through 13 of them before I finally graduated from high school,

class of 1934. I could make a statement that I got my 3 R's in 13 different schools before I finally got married. You could call that 14 by including hit or miss classes at Highlands University that resulted in credits that added up to what a freshman might accumulate before becoming a sophomore.[13]

Audrey had made an outline of her planned autobiography: "Book Chapters or Articles: Schools; Lovers; 3 girls; husbands, buried 2; married 3 times; fears; health; religion; friends; career; home; character; parents; fading out; animals and me."[14]

Audrey's handwritten notes also include the following:

Lives of frustration; good lives, useful lives; sad lives; Do the best you can lives; kicked by fate, ruined by flames, handicapped, deprived, but not depraved. No welfare clients; Poor as church mice, Needing so much and having so little; Grandfather's house burning or he still would be living; sad lives—dying by inches—trying—struggling, making like all is well—*"I'm happy, see I'm smiling"* and the tears drip down inside in a broken heart. Fifty good years. What was good about them? Learning from Grandfather and Vivian, wishing to learn from Great Grandma and prevented by many things! Miserable lives, living day-to-day lives; Struggle, Struggle, toil and trouble: *Lord help us to have better lives, easier times, happier times, a good house, health to clean up things.*[15]

In another place, Audrey wrote:

> I weep for Mama
> I weep for me
> I weep for people
> Where ever they be.
> What can I do?
> It's too late now,
> Or is it?[16]

In some of her notes Audrey wrote a rough draft of a poem:

> Watch the night come down
> From exciting mid-day—birds flying,
> Bees humming—

> High noon, full of life and vigor.
> Then slowly the sun lowers.
> Vigor recedes.
> Life slows down,
> Down to night,
> Black, lonely night.[17]

Audrey wrote a note about death. Perhaps she was remembering how she felt when Clyde was buried in the mountain cemetery, how the men threw in the dirt to fill in the grave, when she wrote:

> People claim the land but the land claims the people. Struggle and do without for 40 years. Built up the land and then it claims you and covers you over.
> The clods resound on the wooden box and shovel after shovel flings the land atop you. Oh yes, you claimed the land and now it has you.[18]

Audrey may have been thinking, too, about greedy people who take from others instead of placing value on the everlasting riches of heaven. What good does it do for them to accumulate riches and land? Audrey referred to Matthew 6:19-21 where Jesus said to lay up treasures in heaven rather than treasures on earth. She said:

"We never had much money, but Clyde always paid his bills on time. He was honest. He might have been weak and given in to temptation at times when he started drinking but he knew Jesus was the Way, the Truth and the Life."

Once Audrey recalled:

Clyde once he gave a sermon on the parable of the rich fool in Luke 12, verses 16 through 21. After he went through the story of the rich man who planned to build more store houses for all his riches—only to find that his soul was required of him that night—Clyde emphasized the point: "So is he that layeth up treasure for himself, and is not rich toward God." [verse 21] There is nothing wrong with having money and riches and land. God wants us to prosper. But taking it at the expense of someone else is wrong. Clyde made some bad mistakes, but he repented and God forgave him. After we re-married, Clyde had a new lease on life. He promised God that he would never take another drink that night in the hospital, and he was healed and forgiven. He never took another drink. He did his best to make up for the lost years when he wandered. He was a faithful husband and devoted father. He understood the Bible and learned what it meant to be "rich toward God."[19]

Audrey valued kind, fair, loving and generous characteristics and modeled them herself. She never discriminated against anyone because of race, religion, or color. Audrey wrote about death as the great leveler: "Through the ages people—bodies of all colors—melt back into the earth—one color once more."[20]

Audrey wrote a segment of her thoughts on her life:

Caramba! The years are getting away! When I come to the last judgment what can I say? I birthed 3 girls after I cried when the doc told me I would never have any children. I helped build 13 houses—and buried 2 husbands, spent 14 years meeting newspaper deadlines to put my kids through school, lost everything to fire. Oh! I have had a heck of an existence. But there's life in the old gal yet. I review my story so I will have it fresh in my mind when that final day whips across the horizon.[21]

Audrey might have added a few more items to her summary of accomplishments. She fought to keep the U.S. Government from confiscating her mountain to use as a military camp, using the power of the pen. She used her persuasive writing to convince the public that Fort Union should not be lost, and it was subsequently made into a national monument. She wrote editorials and letters to protest incompetence in the government and to deplore the rising costs of goods and services. Her writing and petitions helped get the San Geronimo-Mineral Hill Road improved and partially paved. Her writing supported American freedom, such as the right to bear arms, and decried policies she thought morally wrong. She was a journalist, always looking for news, hoping to preserve history, wanting to write to inform, to encourage, or to entertain.

She was a wonderful mother, not only to her three daughters, but to her sons-in-law Wesley Lovett and Gary Beimer. When she had an opportunity she was "mother" to the ten Reid kids and to the Santillanes Children.

The vigor of high noon was gradually becoming the darkness of the night she would have to face, "the inevitable darkness all must face alone—yet not alone—when the Light of Jesus is our Guide," she said. "He promised never to leave us or forsake us."

14

Generations

After Bill died, Audrey adapted to being alone once again. She wrote verses and stories, often based on her great empathy for people. Often when she drove by the State Hospital to visit her half-sister Milly on Montezuma Road, she noticed a woman sitting under a tree at the northern most edge of the hospital. She always felt sympathy for that woman. "She must want to get close to nature, and that's as far as she's allowed to go, so she sits under a tree and finds solace there," Audrey said.

Audrey wrote a poem about a woman she saw standing in the rain:

A little old lady
Under an umbrella
Dripping rain
Risks pneumonia
Escaping for the moment
Yet still chilled

She hunts warmth
Hastily looking up and down
In and out
Round and about
Little old lady
Envies the kids
Yodeling in the rain.[1]

As mentioned before, Audrey's health was not very good after her surgery in 1967. Her legs continued to have open sores most of the time due to poor circulation.

Audrey believed that hospitals could be dangerous places. She'd observed when she was in the Las Vegas Hospital before Holly was born that sometimes things did not go as well as they should. Her room was right off the main nurses' station, and with her exceptional hearing she overheard more than she wanted to at times.

When she was in Albuquerque for the skin graft on her leg, Audrey was careful to question her treatment to be sure mistakes weren't being made. Sure enough, one night a male nurse came in and started to put an ice pack on her neck. She said, "What's that for? I'm in here because of my bad leg."

He looked at the charts and then realized the ice pack was for another patient. Had she not questioned it, she'd have had an ice pack on her neck for no reason!

In 1979 Audrey had a transient ischemic attack, a TIA, but she made a quick recovery. In her later years she had several small strokes but recovered from each one quickly.

In the spring of 1981 Audrey became very ill. Her doctor sent her to a specialist in Albuquerque and he diagnosed pernicious anemia. He had her admitted to Presbyterian Hospital. She went through a frightening ordeal before the doctors decided all she needed was vitamin B-12. She had to get a B-12 shot every month for the rest of her life. When Audrey was in the hospital in Albuquerque, she was very watchful. Audrey wrote in her little notebook: "The crotchety old woman from Vegas—we could like her if they paid us."[2] This was a statement she'd overheard from one of the nurses, apparently complaining about the nurses' salaries.

Sometimes the nurses neglected the patients. Audrey's roommate was left on a bedpan for a long time while her buzzer for the nurse was ignored. Finally, Audrey was so upset about her roommate's plight that she began to yell, "Help! Help!" Finally someone in the hall came in and Audrey told them that her roommate had been sitting on the bedpan for hours while her buzzer for assistance had been ignored. At Audrey's insistence, her roommate finally got some help.

Audrey later wrote that unnecessary tests were done at the hospital—all under the guise of being "thorough." They did tests to diagnose the pernicious anemia, including a bone marrow test which was very painful. Audrey wrote in her notebook on May 29, 1981: "Down in the bowels of the building under tons of brick they wheeled me at such a rapid rate that I was addled, swerving in a wheel chair as though they were playing hospital."[3]

Later Audrey explained that the nurses' aides—or orderlies—who wheeled her for the bone marrow test took her too fast and she was frightened.

After Audrey was home again, she wrote a letter to Blanche Huddleston. Blanche and her husband Perry had been good friends of Mabel Shearer and remained life-long friends of the family. Audrey wrote in June of 1981:

Dear Blanche:

I was glad to get your letter, while being entertained in the Presbyterian Hospital in Albuquerque. I am now home and feeling better.

They gave me every sort of test you can imagine. They found that I had pernicious anemia. In spite of my six days at Las Vegas Hospital, they didn't find it. And I nearly conked out before I got to the Albuquerque Hospital. Anyhow they did find it.

The fates have been kicking us right and left. Milly's husband Doc [Wickman] tried to miss some cows and hit a stone wall three weeks ago last Sunday. Then the next week a 20-year-old rammed into Opal's daughter Donna's car and busted her right leg. She was in the same hospital I was and when I was. And I visited her a time or two. She is still there, but they did operate on her leg this week.

Doc [Wickman] is still in Saint Vincent's in Santa Fe, getting his broken jaws wired up. Milly has been staying with him. I tried to stay at their house to look after Arolvi and the house after this happened. But I got sicker and sicker till I didn't have the strength to continue. Now for the last of the bad news: Stanley Hardin's mother died a couple of weeks ago. Betty really loved her mother-in-law and they got along real well. [Betty had died in 1975.]

Clyde and Bob's oldest brother's funeral was Saturday June the 6th. Opal and Bob were not able to go [to Glen Simpson's funeral]. And I came home that day. I got to see Betty and Stanley's girls as they came to see me at the hospital before and after the funeral (Mrs. Hardin's.)

I suppose it is as hot over there as it is over here. It has been in the 80's for several days. We did have several rains. So Dorothy plowed mud as we came home about 9:30 p.m. from Albuquerque.

Crystal and Wesley and Karen left this a.m. to go to Roswell, T or C, Las Cruces and Carlsbad. A mighty long trip. He is on 2 week's vacation. They plan to come back here next week for a couple of days. I tried to get them to leave their 2 adult fox terriers and 5 puppies with their eyes barely open—but they thought it would be too much for me. I think they will be too much for them.

I am still quite weak and my hands and feet are numb—otherwise I would be O.K. I mailed that last letter without re-reading it so if there were more mistakes than usual that is one reason.[4]

The letter ends there. The letter was probably re-typed since it seems to have been a rough draft.

Audrey made a good recovery after her hospital stay in Albuquerque. Since she had to get a Vitamin B-12 shot every month, Audrey discovered another good doctor—Dr. Carl H. Gellenthien who had a clinic at Valmora. Valmora had been a tuberculosis sanatorium until the cure for TB had been found and the sanatorium was no longer needed. Then Dr. Gellenthien, who had been the Director of the TB Sanatorium, stayed on. He had a private practice, with patients coming from all over the country to see him. He took time with his patients and he was careful to make a good diagnosis before starting any treatment. He always said, "I listen to the patient. He's telling me what is wrong." He also was hesitant to do a lot of unnecessary testing. He said that doctors nowadays do too much testing. He believed the doctor should make the diagnosis first and the test should only be used to confirm it. Instead, too many doctors depend on tests to make a diagnosis and end up doing unnecessary testing.

I was writing the biography of Dr. Gellenthien after discovering the vast history available at Valmora.[5] So when I mentioned that my mother needed a doctor, Dr. Gellenthien said he'd be happy to see her. After over 50 years of practice, he was still taking new patients. Audrey had some good visits with Dr. Gellenthien each time she saw him.

When Dr. Gellethien died at the age of 89, he was greatly missed. Audrey scribbled a poem on the back of an envelope:

> All hail to the Doc,
> The best that we know!
> For 50 odd years!
> How we hate to see him go.
>
> Through thick and thin,
> 40 years in a row!
> Through pain and joy ,
> In sunshine and snow!
>
> All hail to our Doc!
> The best we all know!
> Through good times and bad
> How we weep that you go![6]

Unfortunately, Audrey never found another doctor that could begin to match Dr. Gellenthien's skill and care. She tried different ones in Las Vegas but none took the time with her that "Dr. G." had taken. When Audrey had a stroke one morning, we took her to the local hospital and a doctor she had been seeing in Las Vegas was called. We knew Audrey must have had a stroke because she was unable to talk. The doctor never showed up. Finally in the afternoon we gave up and took Mother home. We took her to another doctor the next day and he confirmed that she'd had a small stroke. After a few days Audrey regained her speech. Audrey continued to struggle day by day to overcome her health problems.

As the years went by, many friends and family members died. Audrey realized that life is very uncertain, can never be taken for granted. When Mrs. Tom Hardin died, Audrey recalled that Betty had said that her mother-in-law had requested that Betty sing a particular song at her funeral. As it turned out, Betty died before her mother-in-law did. If 1981 was a difficult year, so was 1982. Stanley Hardin died April 4, 1982 and Bob Simpson died on April 5, 1982. Both had become ill and were hospitalized in Albuquerque but doctors were unable to help them.

Opal continued to live for a time at the ranch, then sold it and moved to a little house on the corner of 5th and Washington. The Old Homestead Ranch was divided up and sold to different people, with the largest part sold to Elizabeth Orem who built a lovely house on top of the hill above where the old barn had been. Donna Dear and her husband John retained a small portion of the ranch. Donna had graduated from New Mexico Highlands University and taught school at Santa Rosa High School the same time I was there. Donna and John Dear divorced, and Donna retained the property where she and her two daughters, Denise and Becky, spent time on vacations in the mountains.

Another good neighbor throughout the years was Rex Hardaway. He and his wife Winny bought the old Pittman place, about two and one-half miles from Forest Springs Ranch. Rex and Winny were very helpful neighbors. Rex helped me get my vehicle out of the mud or snow more than once when I was stuck on the county road—including one time when I was stuck in a truck that had four-wheel drive and chains. I had to drive in everyday to teach classes at Highlands University and sometimes the road was impassable, especially the last four miles to the ranch.

In spite of hardships, Audrey never lost her sense of humor. After the fire when she moved back to the ranch to live in the one-room cabin Wesley had built for her, she did not complain about the lack of some of the conveniences most of us take for granted. For one thing, she had an outhouse which was used until the big ranch house was rebuilt and plumbing was put in. (The old outhouse, which had not been used for years, had survived the fire.) Instead of complaining about having to use an old-fashioned outhouse, Audrey wrote about it in a humorous way. Her article, accompanied by photographs, was published in the *Albuquerque Journal Magazine, Impact*, in May of 1980. The title was "Dear Census-Taker: Do I still call it a privy?" She explained the origins of that outhouse. Soon after Audrey moved to the ranch from town, before she had indoor plumbing, her nephew and a school friend offered to build her an outhouse. When Audrey moved into the little cabin after the fire, the old outhouse was again put into service. Audrey wrote:

> I showed them the site northwest of the cabin on the hillside in the Gambel oaks.
>
> "Gee!" my nephew said. "It is on a slant."
>
> "Everything is on a slant in these here hills," I replied, and left them.
>
> Later when I went out to check on them they were busy with pencil and paper."Oh, you draw up preliminary plans like real professionals," I said. They nodded.
>
> After lunch, I left them alone for an hour or so. When I went back and looked at their efforts, I saw the paper work showing up in the building. It was slanted to fit the angle of the hillside. They had used all of their high school math knowledge to figure the hill's slant, and then cut the boards on an angle to make the building fit the hillside.
>
> "Oh, dear!" I said. "All that extra brain work! What you have to do is build a straight box-like structure. Then put a couple of logs under the front of it to level it up."
>
> The next time I checked, they had the foundation for the seat in place. Being an ordinary, medium tall woman, I would have to climb up to reach the seat.
>
> Due to the high school manual training expertise, it looked like it was leaning backwards. The poor thing sat there, leaning backwards, half hidden in the oaks. We christened this vital piece of equipment "The Leaning Tower."[7]

Wesley remodeled it a little afterwards. He put in a commercial type seat with a lid on the high box and also a block to step up on to reach the seat. "The block was also a place to rest the feet so they would not dangle in thin air."[8]

Things went along as usual for the Leaning Tower, until 1971, Mr. Census.

Then, on a beautiful Sunday morning, June 27, a thin wisp of smoke rose behind the mountains. I called one of your fellow government agencies, the U.S. Forest Service.

"We had a little fire last night in the la Cueva, on the Pecos side of the range. It is controlled. Nothing to worry about," the man that answered the phone told me. It was about 10 a.m. and the fire was four or five miles away from my place. By 2 p.m. they were sending out men to order everyone out of the mountains.

"Get out! Get out right now!' they said.

Into my little Scout pickup I loaded my teen-age daughter, 6-year-old granddaughter, visiting from Texas, and her dog, Pinto, that had four pups against my explicit instructions in my favorite overstuffed chair, two days before.

With smoke billowing behind us, we headed out in a wild wind. We looked back. The entire mountain was afire. Evidently the people on the Pecos side thought they had the fire under control, but it got away. The wind came up and whipped it into an inferno.

That fire burned my home and my 40 years of hard work and irreplaceable mementos. They had 1,300 men fighting that fire, but it burned 13,000 acres of heavy timber before the good Lord sent the rain and put it out.

Mr. Census, your fellow agency never made a dent in controlling that fire. They had promised, but no one tried to save my house. They had bombers dropping slurry, but they never put a drop on my place. You can tell by looking at the poor scarred, ruined mountain, where they dropped slurry. Where it hit there are strips of living timber. The rest is burned.

You can tell the U.S. government, Mr. Census, that many think they [the U. S. Forest Service] are to blame for the loss of a number of homes, as well as 2,400 acres of private timber. They never reimbursed any of us as much as one cent for our losses.

Anyway, your last census paper went up in smoke in that terrible fire. There was nothing left of my place but twisted metal, melted glass and "The Leaning Tower." Somehow, unbelievably, my outdoor plumbing at the end of the path to the oaks survived. It was the only structure on the place to escape.

Heartsick and homeless, my daughter and I had to go live with my mother in Las Vegas. We returned every few days to scratch through the ashes, looking for scraps of our former lives. The Leaning Tower was the only shelter when a violent shower came down the mountain range.

By November, we had the ashes shifted and most of the mess removed. The Leaning Tower did double duty, also serving as tool shed for hoes, rakes and shovels. And it still does.

My question, Mr. Census, is whether I list the Leaning Tower as a privy or as a tool shed. Or do I mark down that I have indoor plumbing in my new house and completely ignore that faithful old Leaning Tower? Or do I mark down that I now have both indoor facilities and the Leaning Tower?

Please tell me soon before your census taker comes to take my census.
Sincerely,
The owner of the only Leaning Tower this side of Pisa.[9]

In a more serious vein, Audrey also wrote about the "hermit" of the nearby "Hermit's Peak." She had done some research in the past. She wrote for the *Las Vegas Daily Optic:*

One of the most impressive views of the Sangre de Cristo mountain range available to a traveler in an automobile, may be had on the Mineral Hill road eight or nine miles west of Las Vegas.

On top of the divide between the Tecolote and Gallinas watersheds, a superb view of the mountains extends from Colorado on the north to Carrizozo on the south. To the west the largest round maintain hump at the south end of the higher elevations is Barillas peak. The twin peaks in the center of the panorama are at the head of Falls Creek canyon.

Farther north Hermits Peak, once the home of a real hermit, raises its granite face more than 10,000 feet above sea level, against a backdrop of more mountains. At the foot of the divide is the Tecolote River with its fertile narrow valley lined with small settlements, Mineral Hill, San Geronimo, San Pueblo and on Highway 85 [now I-25] Tecolote town.[10]

Audrey decided to expand her findings into a lengthy article. She had written "Hermit Lived on Peak" for the *Las Vegas Daily Optic*, August 1, 1957. She cited information from the May 13, 1908 *Optic* story about the man who lived on "Old Baldy," the mountain near Las Vegas. The mountain was called "Hermit's Peak" after the Italian man who lived there. A society called Brotherhood of Hermits, which held services at El Porvenir, was organized to perpetuate his teachings. He had come from a rich family in Italy, lived in caves in Italy for a while, wandered all over the world, was a missionary to Indians in South America, came to America, and finally settled in New Mexico. He lived in caves—including the one at Kearney's Gap just southwest of Las Vegas—and subsisted on very little. It was believed he was a miracle worker. Visitors would find their way up the mountain where he lived, and he formed them into a society which he named "The Brotherhood of the Holy Cross." Audrey wrote in her *Optic* story that he placed fourteen crosses on the mountain.[11] He then went to the Organ Mountains near Las Cruces, intending to work his way to Mexico to work among the Indians in Mexico. Before he died, the holy man stated, "I am not a prophet nor a son of a prophet but I would not be surprised if some day you should see something miraculous on this spot."[12]

Later Audrey wrote the full length article that was published in *Old West* in its Spring, 1988 issue, "Hermit's Peak Legend." At one time the mountain was called "Old Baldy" but then it became known as "Hermit's Peak" after it was known that the "hermit" lived there. The mountain can be seen in many places in the Las Vegas area. A good view of it can be seen on the road from Las Vegas to San Geronimo. Many were inspired by the man from Italy, Giovanni Marie Augustino, who had a vision of the west and felt called to go to the Sangre de Cristo mountains of northern New Mexico. He stayed in various caves in the area, wanting solitude.

> [He wore] his leather shirt, which had sharp tacks driven through it from the outside. Since self-flagellation for religious reasons had come from Spain four hundred years earlier and had lasted through the years in New Mexico, the local people considered the Hermit an especially holy man.[13]

It was said that when "the hermit" first climbed to the top of the mountain, then called Old Baldy, he was almost dying of thirst. So he struck a rock and water poured forth. The spring on top of the giant rock mountain is still there. Such acts led people to believe he was a holy man, although he always told people he was not a prophet. He was revered, nevertheless. People attested to miracles he had performed. In 1867 Augustino left the mountain and went to the Organ Mountains near Las Cruces. He was murdered there April 17, 1869 and buried in Mesilla. The people of Las Vegas still honor the memory of the "Italian Holy Man" and so call the huge mountain that over towers the area "Hermit's Peak."[14]

Audrey also wrote about caves in the area. Her son-in-law Wesley liked to explore caves and often talked about the caves he'd been in. In the August 1, 1957 *Las Vegas Daily Optic, Rodeo Edition,* Audrey wrote a story entitled, "Two Caves In Area Offer Exploration." She described spelunking as one of the oldest sports—exploring caves. She described the San Geronimo Cave—located about a mile and a half above San Geronimo on the Tecolote River—and the cave just beyond the high point on the road up the Gallinas canyon. The article included black and white photographs and she gave detailed descriptions. The article had no credits or bi-line, but undoubtedly Audrey wrote the story using descriptions and photographs from Wesley Lovett.[15]

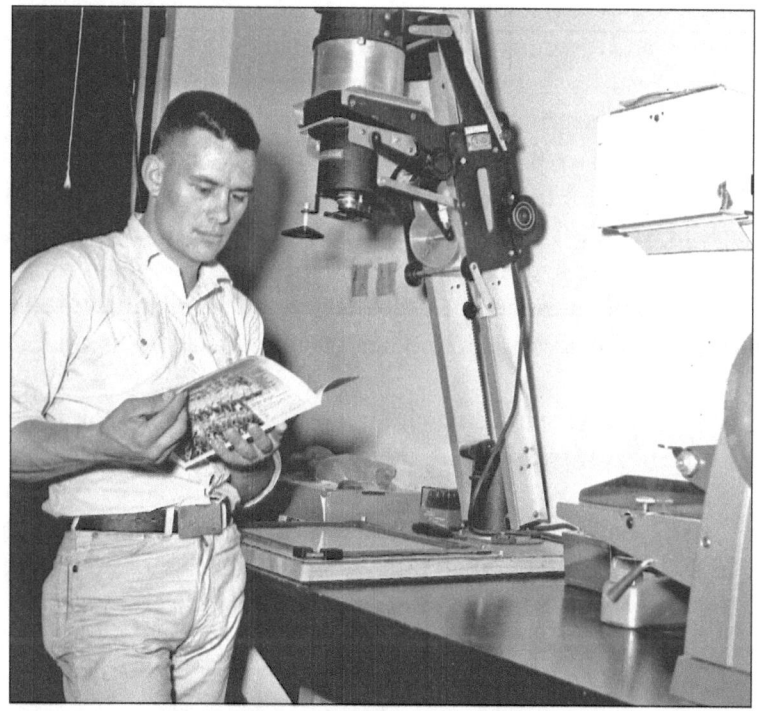

Wesley L. Lovett, 1960. *Source:* **Simpson Archives**

Audrey wrote an article which she submitted for publication, "Climbing the Organ Needle" which was stated as "by Wesley Lovett as told to Audrey Simpson." There were pictures Wesley had taken when he climbed the Organ Mountain near Las Cruces. It is unknown whether the article was published, but it probably was not. No acceptance or rejection letters were found with the story.

We headed for the Organ Needle in the mountain range raising more than 9,000 feet, overlooking the Rio Grande Valley. These peaks resemble organ pipes as they reach for the heavens under usually cloudless skies, 15 miles east of Las Cruces, and about 40 miles north of El Paso, Texas.[16]

In the autobiography Audrey was starting, she planned to have chapters about her childhood, with background on her ancestors. She planned to write something about her parents, step-parents, and her sisters and brothers. She planned to write about each daughter and about her grandchildren and great grandchildren. She might have called it "Generations" or she might have called it "Survival." Audrey was a survivor.

Audrey had struggled with finances all her life. After Clyde's death, she lived on Social Security that came for her and for Holly. When Holly's ran out, she wondered how they could live. She could apply for her own Social Security, which may have been a little more, but she wasn't old enough to get hers yet. It was a difficult period in her life, but she was able to get by. She also had a little income once in a while from the Oklahoma farm which Addie Simpson had left Clyde and he, in turn, had left to Audrey. There were some oil rights, among other things, so sometimes she received what she called "oil money." She also had a little income from her writing. And her "writing money" was what meant the most to her.

Audrey had watched own children—born in 1938, 1944 and 1955—as they grew up. She was pleased with their accomplishments. Wesley and Crystal lived in Albuquerque where Wesley, an electrical engineer, worked for Public Service Company of New Mexico and Crystal taught school. Later Wesley was transferred to Farmington with Public Service Company of New Mexico and Crystal taught second grade. She was a wonderful teacher, having struggled in school as a child herself. Her empathy and concern for the students made her a brilliant teacher.

Audrey was proud of her daughters. She wrote to a friend that Crystal had graduated with a B.A. degree from New Mexico Highlands University and had overcome a reading handicap and become an excellent elementary school teacher. Crystal worked with Navajo children at a school at Kirtland, New Mexico and did a wonderful job in teaching them English, reading and writing skills.

Holly met the challenges caused by cerebral palsy and graduated with a B.A. degree with an emphasis in Early Childhood Education from New Mexico Highlands University. Holly worked in several places, including Camp Monakiwa. She taught a year or two and worked with children in many different capacities. She was very good with children and animals. She helped with summer camps, taught children's theatre, and wrote some children's plays. She also worked some at a veterinary clinic, as she loved animals and was good with them. She always loved theatre and participated in many theatre events, doing everything from lights and sound effects to props to acting and directing. She served as an "extra" in numerous movies that were filmed in and around Las Vegas. She lived with Audrey and helped care for her mother in her last years.

Audrey helped bring up her grandchildren and enjoyed watching them grow. Wesley and Crystal's daughter, Karen Clydine Lovett, married Clifford Lester Graves II on December 27, 1985. They had two children, Clifford Aaron Graves, born June 8, 1988, and Amanda Elizabeth Graves, born June 15, 1990. After a divorce, Karen continued her education and became a nurse practitioner and midwife. She set up her own clinic in Edgewood and developed a successful career. She liked the photograph of her grandmother Audrey as a baby, held by her mother Mabel Clements in 1913. Karen used that photograph for her business cards and for the billbroad and sign at her office, New Mexico Primary Care & Midwifery Services, Inc., in Edgewood, New Mexico.

My husband Gary Beimer and I lived in Las Vegas for a while, but as soon as Gary finished building a house at the ranch, just down the road from Audrey's ranch house, we moved to the ranch with our daughter Laura Lea, who had been born January 8, 1974. Our second daughter Rose was born on May 9, 1985. Audrey's three grandchildren—Karen Lovett, Laura Lea Beimer and Rose Beimer—spent a great deal of time with their grandmother at the ranch. Since Laura and Rose lived just a few yards down the road, they saw their grandmother nearly every day.

Audrey struggled with her leg ulcers but otherwise was in fairly good health. She and Holly helped care for my little daughter Rose. I was a professor with full time responsibilities at New Mexico Highlands University. I was working on getting my doctorate, which was required for my position. I traveled to Albuquerque for classes while still teaching full time. My daughter Rose Beimer was born during that time. Then there was a divorce, and I was a single parent with two daughters to care for. If it had not been for Audrey and for Holly, I could not have managed. I graduated in 1989 from the University of New Mexico with an Ed.D. Nearly the whole family came to my graduation. Audrey wrote me a note on a card of congratulations:

>My Dear Little Girl
>All grown up—
>Congratulations on sticking
>to your goal until you finally

made it—Dear Doctor Dorothy
Love from
Mother.[17]

I later married Ian Croxton, a struggling British playwright, but the marriage only lasted a few months. With my mother's encouragement, I had received my B.A., M.S. and Ed.D. I followed after Audrey's love of creative writing. I had taught English and Speech at the high school several years and then taught English and Speech at New Mexico Highlands University. I became a tenured, full professor, a Department Chair, and an Associate Dean. I had numerous articles and a couple of books published. Audrey was always supportive. I married a third time but that marriage only last two years. After having three different last names, I took my maiden name back. Audrey taught me to love books, to have a passion for writing, and to desire to pass along knowledge and inspiration to others.

Laura Beimer married Randall W. Nelson in 1991. They had Caitlin Ruth Nelson, born April 26, 1992, and Wade James Nelson, born June 2, 1996. They both attended New Mexico Highlands University. Laura graduated in 1993 with a B.A. degree. At the same time, she graduated with her L. P. N. from Luna Community College. Then she began to work as a nurse and Randy worked as a livestock inspector. They divorced. Then Laura married Merle Mitchell on August 11, 2000. They had Jessica Noelle Mitchell, born December 16, 2002. Audrey did not live to see Jessica, but she did hold her great grandson Wade in 1996 when he was a baby. He was the last baby she ever held. After attending Highlands University with emphasis in art and in English, Rose married Mark E. Shore on October 30, 2006 and moved to Portland, Oregon—the very place Audrey had been tempted to go with her grandmother.

Audrey was pleased that she had accomplished her goal of putting her three daughters through school. She herself had not had the opportunity to finish college. She wanted her girls to have a better life. She helped bring up her grandchildren. She would have been pleased that her grandchildren and great grandchildren were able to obtain good educations.

Crystal, Dorothy and Holly gave Audrey a birthday party for her 75th birthday. Later, Audrey wrote a poem:

> Kids gifted me with many pens,
> Each holding brightly colored ink.
> I never know when I begin—
> Will this write red or green or pink?

I used to take a pen in hand,
No need to stop or think,
Or check the cap or colored band.
Pens *always* wrote with blue-black ink.

I really miss those good old days,
And often wish that they were back.
Then there was no rainbow craze
And all pens wrote in blue or black.[18]

Audrey wrote a birthday poem for Milly Wickman in 1992:

We greet your day
As it jets along
Salute! Salute!

Happy Birthday to youuuuu!
Happy Birthday to yuuuuuu!

How well I remember
Day 3 in September
When Millicent came
To light up the family game.
  —Audrey[19]

Audrey was proud of her grandchildren. She wrote down cute things they said. She wrote a poem one day when Laura saw a roadrunner. Although the roadrunner is New Mexico's state bird, there are very few in these northern mountains. They tend to live in the warmer, more desert-like areas. So it was very unusual to see one at the ranch. Audrey scribbled a rough draft of a poem:

Hurray!
Laura touched a roadrunner
Today.
A roadrunner has adopted our garden
Hurray!
Laura touched feathers soft and grey
Of a real live roadrunner
In the garden today!

> The bird has been making itself at home
> Hunting for food in the garden loam
> Laura moves quietly, a six year old can;
> The bird hid quickly beside a pan.[20]

Whether she wrote on the back of an envelope or sat at her typewriter, Audrey was always writing down her thoughts to share with others. She wanted her family and others to know that one can survive the most desperate circumstances if one has the will to do so. She planned her autobiography to describe how she had survived. She also planned to tell about her ancestors who had gone through even more difficult times—such as the soldiers who had fought in the great wars: William Thomson (an ancestor on the Waddell side of the family) who was a soldier in the American Revolutionary War; the two Applegarth ancestors who fought on the side of the north in the Civil War; Audrey's grandfather, William Harper Clements, who fought in the Civil War with the U. S. Volunteer Infantry and received a document signed by President A. Lincoln, October 1, 1864, commending him for his service. She could not forget about the great uncle (David Waddell) who was tomahawked and scalped and lived to be an old man; the uncle of William Harper Clements who had been the only survivor, with his wife and two children, to arrive in Oregon after traveling the Oregon Trail; the great uncle who had started the Pony Express, (William Waddell) whose company, Majors, Russell and Waddell lost about $200,000 but survived in spite of it; the courageous ancestor traced back from Audrey's grandfather, William Harper Clements, to John Allerton who came over on the Mayflower, having been born in Leydon, Holland (and died in Plymouth, Massachusetts); and the tough ancestor traced through Edward Albert Waddell's ancestor, Lucinda Ogle, to William the Conqueror. Of course, Audrey would mention the newest generation of heroes, including Clyde's brother, Donald Simpson, who fought the Nazi's on the Flying Fortress and was killed in air combat; Stanley A. Hardin, Betty's husband, one of the few pilots to return from World War II after flying many successful missions; and other heroes who lived quiet lives but showed their strength in surviving everyday problems.

Much of what Audrey wrote was lost in the fire. But many of her notes from after the fire, and some of her writings that were saved from the fire, reflect the wonderful book about her life she would have written had she been able to do so. Her failing health prevented her from finishing her autobiography. The writing she left was a great legacy to her family and to all who would take the time to read her story.

15

Leaving a Legacy

The years passed. Audrey was celebrating her 80th birthday. Her three daughters gave her a birthday party in Las Vegas, with numerous friends and relatives attending. A smiling picture of a very youthful looking Audrey—taken at the party— appeared in the *Optic*. The caption said, "Audrey Simpson remembers—Audrey Simpson reminisced Saturday on her fifteen years of service as Optic society editor and reporter. She was being honored by family and friends upon the occasion of her 80th birthday with a party at K-Bobs."[1] The photo was taken by Sharon Vander Meer of the *Las Vegas Daily Optic*.

The party was held on the Saturday before Audrey's November 11th birthday so more people could attend. Audrey's last name was now Reid but since most people knew her by her former name of Simpson, she continued to use it for her writing and for publicity.

Afterwards, Audrey wrote a thank you note, dated November 11, 1992, to Dorothy and Rose. She wrote similar notes to the other family members. The note to Dorothy and Rose said: "Thank you so much. I will always remember my 80th birthday party when you [and the others] made my day. Thanks again. Love from Mother and Grandma."[2]

Audrey expressed her gratitude in a recording on cassette tape. She said she'd seldom ever been given a birthday party. Her mother usually baked a cake and they had a family celebration. And when Audrey's daughters were old enough, they always baked a cake and had a "party" at home. "I remember for my 39th birthday, Crystal and Dorothy baked a cake and put all thirty-nine candles on it," Audrey said.

Audrey enjoyed her many friends even though she was fairly "housebound" due to her health in her last few years. Alta Beisman, Mable Bibb, Lelama Gardner, Edith Moore, Jean Whiting—the list goes on and on. She spent a great deal of time on the telephone with her relatives and friends even though she did not see them as often as she would have liked.

Opal attended Audrey's 80th birthday party in November of 1991. She was seventy-eight. But soon after that she became ill. She was diagnosed with lung cancer. She stayed at her home on the corner of Washington and Fifth Street as long as she could. Later Milly insisted that she live with her in the house on Montezuma Road. Milly took care of Opal, with the help of a home health care agency. Audrey herself was struggling with leg ulcers and other ailments and simply took one day at a time.

Since Mabel's death, Audrey and Milly talked on the telephone at least once a day. During Opal's illness, Audrey tried to keep up their spirits, talking to Milly and Opal on the telephone or, when she could get to town, going to see them.

The last time Audrey saw Opal was at Milly's house. Milly had sat up a hospital bed next to her own bed in her private bedroom. Audrey had come to town for a visit, but the black clouds were threatening a thunderstorm. Opal turned to Audrey and said, as she had so many times, "You better get home before it rains." Audrey nodded her agreement and, reluctantly, said good-by. Audrey must have been heart-broken when she realized that it was the final good-by. It was Opal who would first be going home.

Opal died on June 3, 1993. Audrey went to Opal's funeral. She saw relatives she had not seen in some time, including Bobby Simpson, Jacqueline Simpson Rice, Donna Simpson Dear and her family, and others. Undoubtedly Audrey thought about the people she had lost: Clyde in 1965 and Bill in 1979. She had lost her father in 1960, her mother in 1974, Betty in 1975, and Mabel Clements in 1987.

Opal's death must have been a very heavy blow. The two sisters had always been so close all their lives. Audrey had taken the role of "big sister" and been protective of Opal. They had gone to school together, depended on one another. With their mother gone, it seemed they had grown even closer. After Opal's death, Audrey's health gradually began to fail. Holly lived at home with her and was usually there to help, and I was living next door.

Milly called Audrey every evening and they talked. Milly began to record their conversations because Audrey would tell of their childhood days and talk about how things were in the early days in and around Las Vegas. Milly did not want the history to be lost. She and Audrey planned to put together Audrey's autobiography, and the tapes would help them write about Audrey's life. There were over thirty tapes, and they were very helpful in putting together this story.

Audrey knew how to age gracefully. She didn't believe in coloring her hair or using make-up to look younger. "A woman should look her age," Audrey said. Bill had tried to get her to use cosmetics, color her hair, try to look younger. But Audrey said she had earned every grey hair and wrinkle through honest hard work and worry. She wrote a rough draft of a poem:

> I looked at myself in the mirror,
> A long, not a hasty glance,
> And saw the turning of the years
> For all to see upon my face.
>
> They're etched upon my face, you know,
> Those days and years of long ago.
> Oh, that's a scratch the cat just clawed
> And there is where the baby kissed,
> And that's the place the big ball missed.[3]

Audrey could see the evidence of years of living. But she aged very well. Most people thought she was at least ten years younger than she was. She was pleased that she retained her excellent hearing and her eyesight was also good, although she finally needed glasses to read. At her eightieth birthday party, Audrey said, "I don't regret having another birthday—considering the alternative." She enjoyed a note written by Elsa Barker, the widow of S. Omar Barker, which came with a gift for Audrey's birthday. It said: "11-11, Many more birthdays! Birthdays, the only thing we can't live without. Love, me, Elsa Barker."[4]

Audrey wrote poems on her philosophy of life. Some of the best was written when she was very young. One such poem was published in *Today in Prose & Poetry* in 1941:

> Some part of me—the I—the soul—
> Cannot be free, untouched, and whole
> When I am in a crowd or mob.
> For every other I, or soul
> Bruises me with its silent sob
> And makes me a part of that mob.
>
> I must carry my soul away
> High in the mountains or to a bay
> Anywhere, that the skies are wide
> Giving my soul a place to pray—
> And silence—where my soul may hide
> In spaces flung both far and wide.[5]

Audrey wrote about death in lofty poems such as one called "All Advance" that was published in *The Friendly Journal* in 1941 when she was not quite 30 years old:

> Do not despair!
> We do not die!
> We travel on!
> Living through ages
> All progress onward.
> Every breathing soul
> Follows the pattern
> Of the Master Mind.
>
> It is intended,
> When the time is right,
> That all life step forth—
> Reach to better things.
> We do not die.
> We travel on.
>
> When the right time comes
> Nestlings leave their nest.
> As the old ties are severed
> They do not die.
> They travel on.[6]

Audrey sometimes worried about what would happen to her family after she was gone, especially Holly. But she should have known she had been a good role model, and the family would be fine. Mary Simpson put Holly in her will and left her the Simpson family farm in Oklahoma, as well as some other assets.

There is much more to say about Audrey's life. There are many more of her words to record even though many of her stories were lost in the fire and can never be recovered. But it is sufficient to say that she was a pioneer woman—an outdoors woman who knew how to camp and cook outdoors. She competed with the best of marksmen. She was one of the first female newspaper women in the State, a journalist and a free lance writer. She was a daughter, a sister, a wife, a mother, a grandmother, a great-grandmother. She was a Christian, a preacher's wife, a prayer warrior. She was all of those things and more, and her friends knew they were speaking to an extra ordinary woman when they called her on the phone and she said in her distinctive, melodious voice, "This is Audrey."

In January of 1997 Audrey became ill. She was diagnosed with a strangulated hernia. She told the doctor she didn't want to have any surgery. The surgeon told her it was a choice of having the surgery or a prolonged and painful death. "Well, I wasn't planning on living forever," she said. However, she reluctantly agreed to the surgery. She still protested, "I don't believe in this."

Audrey underwent surgery at the Northeastern Regional Hospital in Las Vegas. She was not responsive after surgery. I believe she could hear, however. Her niece Janie Hardin came by and in Janie's very kind and special manner, she said a few humorous things. I saw my mother smile. I knew she could hear Janie.

On January 27, 1997, Audrey's sister Jessica from Tucumcari sat up all night with her. Sitting by the hospital bed, Jessica stayed awake through the night to care for Audrey. Jessica had been the last sibling Audrey had charge of, as she was off on her own most of the time when Frank, the youngest Shearer child, came along. Audrey's decision to remain in New Mexico instead of moving to Oregon with her grandmother was largely because Jessica was on the way. Audrey could not leave her mother with a baby coming.

Audrey had stayed because of Jessica. Now, sixty-seven years later, Jessica stayed because of Audrey. She would not allow her sister to be alone her last night on earth.

In the morning Crystal came in and was there when Audrey's life was over about 8:30 a.m. on January 28, 1997.

After Audrey's death, Milly was heartbroken. They had been very close, especially in the last years. Milly died in March, just about two months after Audrey's life ended. Her husband, Gordon Wickman, died in June.

Audrey's final resting place in the Simpson cemetery at Forest Springs Ranch, next to Clyde's grave, is beneath the pine trees, surrounded by flowers—including the sweet peas Audrey planted years ago. Blue jays, robins, and other birds play in the branches of the trees under the circle of the blue sky. The mountains Audrey loved can be seen from the hillside where, at times, snow-kissed breezes carry clouds across the sky. There, as poet S. Omar Barker said, the gentle hills "they loved the best Guard good mountain-folk at rest."

When I was a little girl I asked about death. I wondered if we would be together in heaven. Audrey reassured me that for all believers, God would allow everyone's loved ones to be together in His House. She explained that our faith in Jesus would be rewarded. She made reference to a scripture that would later become one of my favorites—Chapter 11 of the gospel of John, verses 25 and 26 where Jesus spoke to Martha:

Jesus saith unto her, I am the resurrection, and the life: he that believeth in me, though he were dead, yet shall he live. And whosoever liveth and believeth in me shall never die. Believest thou this? She saith unto him, Yea, Lord, I believe that thou art the Christ, the Son of God . . . .

Audrey explained death to me in an analogy of a person taking off an old, worn out coat and tossing it away.

"The body wears out like an old coat. After it's no longer useful or needed, you just take it off and throw it away. It's not you. You go on and don't even miss it. That's how it is when you die. You just toss away your body like an old coat and go on."

After Audrey died I hung her grey coat in my closet where I could see it, as a reminder of what she'd said about how leaving this life is like taking off a coat and discarding something worn out to move on.

Audrey had lived 84 years. The "coat" was well-worn. She knew it was time to depart.

May we all move through this life—and beyond—as gracefully as she did.

NOTES

Part I
Mountain Girl

1

1. Audrey Simpson, "My Early Days," unpublished manuscript, n.d., Scrapbook 5, Simpson Archives, Las Vegas, New Mexico.
2. Ibid.
3. Ibid.
4. Ibid.
5. Desprez, Frank. "Lasca," in *The Best Loved Poems of the American People*, selected by Hazel Felleman, N.Y.: Doubleday & Company, Inc., 1936, pp. 257-259.
6. Audrey Simpson, "The Night I was Born," unpublished manuscript, n. d., Scrapbook 4, Simpson Archives, Las Vegas, New Mexico.
7. Audrey Simpson, "My First Days," unpublished manuscript, n.d., Scrapbook 7, Simpson Archives, Las Vegas, New Mexico.
8. Audrey Simpson, "My Early Days," op. cit.
9. Audrey Simpson, "My First Days," op. cit.
10. Millicent L. Gensemer, "Audrey Simpson: A Mother, Woman's Editor and Adventurer," *Las Vegas Daily Optic*, newspaper clipping, n.d., Scrapbook 2, Simpson Archives, Las Vegas, New Mexico.
11. Audrey Simpson, "My First Days," op. cit.
12. Ibid.
13. Audrey Reid, "Some Early Childhood Memories," unpublished notes, 1985, Scrapbook 7, Simpson Archives, Las Vegas, New Mexico.
14. Mabel Waddell, "Not for School but for Life We Learn," unpublished poem, *Pine Top School Souvenir*, 1911, p. 7. Scrapbook 1, Simpson Archives, Las Vegas, New Mexico.

2

1. Audrey Simpson, "My Early Days," op. cit.
2. Ibid.
3. Audrey Simpson, no bi-line, "Dog Was Horse Rider," *Las Vegas Daily Optic, Rodeo Edition*, Las Vegas, New Mexico, August 1, 1957, p. B10, marked copy indicating item was written by Audrey Simpson, Simpson Archives, Las Vegas, New Mexico.
4. Audrey Simpson, "Bronco Bustin' Dog," copy of original manuscript submitted to and published by *Dog Fancy*, Vol. 11, No. 7, December, 1980, p. 2, Scrapbook 3, Simpson Archives, Las Vegas, New Mexico.
5. Audrey Simpson, "Dog Was Horse Rider," op. cit.
6. Ibid.

3

1. Audrey Simpson, "My Early Days," op. cit.
2. Audrey Simpson, "My First Days," op. cit
3. Audrey Simpson, "My Early Days," op. cit.

4

1. Audrey Simpson, "My First Christmas," unpublished notes, n.d., Scrapbook 4, Simpson Archives, Las Vegas, New Mexico.
2. Audrey Simpson, "My First Days," op. cit.
3. Ibid.
4. Audrey Simpson, "My Early Days," op. cit.
5. Audrey Simpson, "My First Days" op. cit.
6. Gensemer, op. cit.
7. Audrey Simpson, "My Early Days," op. cit.
8. Audrey Simpson, "My First Days," op. cit.
9. Audrey Reid, interview by Millicent Wickman, Las Vegas, New Mexico, Tape 16, February 11, 1994, Simpson Archives, Las Vegas, New Mexico.
10. Audrey Simpson, "My First Days," op. cit.
11. Audrey Reid, interview by Millicent Wickman, Tape 16, op. cit.
12. Mabel Clements, "My Fingers Are So Small," unpublished poem, n.d., Scrapbook 1, Simpson Archives, Las Vegas, New Mexico.
13. Audrey Simpson, "The Night I was Born," op. cit.
14. Audrey Simpson, "My Early Days," op. cit.
15. Ibid.
16. Audrey Simpson, "Religious Experiences," unpublished notes, 1982, Scrapbook 6, Simpson Archives, Las Vegas, New Mexico.
17. Ibid.
18. Audrey Simpson, "Miscellaneous Notes," n.d., Scrapbook 6, Simpson Archives, Las Vegas, New Mexico.
19. Audrey Simpson, "Religious Experiences," op. cit.

5

1. Audrey Simpson, "Riding My First Bronc," unpublished notes, n.d., Scrapbook 4, Simpson Archives, Las Vegas, New Mexico, n.d.
2. Audrey Simpson, "My First Days," op. cit.
3. Gensemer, op. cit.
4. Mabel Clements, "Better'n Walkin'," unpublished poem, n.d., Scrapbook 3, Simpson Archives, Las Vegas, New Mexico, n.d.
5. Audrey Reid, "Recollections: Wagon Runs Over My Tummy When Car Scares Our Mules," copy of original manuscript submitted to and published by *Grit,* Wednesday, September 7, 1983, Scrapbook 2, Simpson Archives, Las Vegas, New Mexico.
6. Ibid.
7. Audrey Simpson, "My First Days," op. cit.
8. Audrey Simpson, "My Early Days," op. cit.
9. Ibid.

6

1. Audrey Simpson, "My Early Days," op. cit.
2. Audrey Reid, interview by Millicent Wickman, Las Vegas, New Mexico, Tape 8, May, 1987, Simpson Archives, Las Vegas, New Mexico.
3. Audrey Simpson, "My Early Days," op. cit.
4. Audrey Simpson, "Miscellaneous Notes," Scrapbook 6, op. cit.
5. Audrey Simpson, no bi-line, "Gold Tooth John Colorful Early Day Character," *Las Vegas Daily*

Optic, Rodeo Edition, Las Vegas, New Mexico, July 31, 1952, p. 5-B, marked copy indicating item was written by Audrey Simpson, Scrapbook 4, Simpson Archives, Las Vegas, New Mexico.
6. Audrey Reid, interview by Millicent Wickman, Tape 8, op. cit.
7. http:/home.earthlink.net/~case65/chapter5.htm, Chapter 5, "Descendants of Joseph Rhode."
8. Audrey Simpson, "Special Christmas," letter to the editor, for "Your Most Memorable Christmas" section, *Albuquerque Journal,* November, 1987, Scrapbook 7, Simpson Archives, Las Vegas, New Mexico.
9. Audrey Simpson, "Christmas in Taos," n.d., unpublished poem, Scrapbook 4, Simpson Archives, Las Vegas, New Mexico.

7

1. Audrey Simpson, "Riding My First Bronc," op. cit.
2. Audrey Reid, interview by Millicent Wickman, Las Vegas, New Mexico, Tape 31, May, 1994, Simpson Archives, Las Vegas, New Mexico.
3. Audrey Simpson, "Riding My First Bronc," op. cit.
4. Audrey Simpson, "Mom's Squeeze Play," copy of original manuscript submitted to and published by *The Denver Post Empire Magazine,* May 28, 1967, Scrapbook 8, Simpson Archives, Las Vegas, New Mexico.
5. Ibid.
6. Ibid.
7. Ibid.
8. Ibid.
9. Ibid.

8

1. Audrey Simpson, "Mom Saved the Bacon," copy of original manuscript submitted to and published by *Real West*, Vol. XII, Number 67, January, 1969, pp. 30-31, Scrapbook 4, Simpson Archives, Las Vegas, New Mexico.
2. Audrey Simpson, no bi-line, "Ma Saved the Bacon; Women Had Courage," *Las Vegas Daily Optic, Rodeo Edition,* Las Vegas, New Mexico, July 31, 1952, p. 3-B, marked copy indicating item was written by Audrey Simpson, Simpson Archives, Las Vegas, New Mexico.

9

1. Audrey Reid, interview by Millicent Wickman, Tape 8, op. cit.
2. Ibid.
3. Audrey Reid, interview by Holly Simpson, Las Vegas, New Mexico, Tape 1, August 21, 1992. Simpson Archives, Las Vegas, New Mexico.
4. Ibid

10

1. Audrey Reid, "Some Early Childhood Memories," op. cit.
2. Audrey Reid, interview by Millicent Wickman, Tape 33, Fall, 1994, Simpson Archives, Las Vegas, New Mexico.
3. Gordon Wickman, interview by Dorothy Simpson Beimer, Las Vegas, New Mexico, May, 1988.
4. http://virus.stanford.edu/uda/
5. Ibid.
6. Mabel Clements, "Notes on War," n.d., Scrapbook 1, Simpson Archives, Las Vegas, New Mexico.

7. Audrey Reid, interview by Holly Simpson, Las Vegas, New Mexico, Tape 1, August 21, 1992, op. cit.

11

1. T. F. Shirley, business card, Scrapbook 1, Simpson Archives, Las Vegas, New Mexico.
2. Audrey Reid, interview by Millicent Wickman, Tape 31, op. cit.
3. Audrey Reid, interview by Holly Simpson, Tape 1, op. cit.
4. Audrey Simpson, "Some Early Childhood Memories," op. cit.
5. Ibid.
6. Ibid.
7. Audrey Reid, interview by Millicent Wickman, Las Vegas, New Mexico, Tape 30, May, 1994 in Simpson Archives, Las Vegas, New Mexico.
8. Ibid.
9. Ibid.
10. J. B. Caldwell, "Officer of the Guard March," Waitsburg, Washington: Published by The Composer, Copyright MCMVII by J. B. Caldwell, Simpson Archives, Las Vegas, New Mexico.
11. Mabel Shearer, "Note," cover of sheet music, J. B. Caldwell, "Officer of the Guard March," Waitsburg, Washington: Published by The Composer, Copyright MCMVII by J. B. Caldwell, Simpson Archives, Las Vegas, New Mexico.

12

1. Audrey Simpson, "High-Wheelers of Santa Fe Trail May be Recalled," *Las Vegas Daily Optic, Rodeo Edition,* Las Vegas, New Mexico, July 31, 1952, p. 5-B.
2. Audrey Simpson, "Trail History is Reflected; Horse, Mule Caravans," *Las Vegas Daily Optic, Rodeo Edition,* Las Vegas, New Mexico, July 31, 1952, p. 6-B.
3. Milton W. Callon, *Las Vegas, New Mexico—The Town That Wouldn't Gamble,* Las Vegas, New Mexico: Las Vegas Daily Optic, The Las Vegas Publishing Co., Inc., 1962.
4. Milton Callon, interview by Audrey Simpson, Las Vegas, New Mexico, July, 1959.
5. Audrey Simpson, "Cowboy's Reunion Notes," unpublished notes, n.d., Scrapbook 5, Simpson Archives, Las Vegas, New Mexico.
6. Audrey Simpson, no bi-line, "Visit Of Teddy Roosevelt Is Recalled By Vegas Pioneer," *Las Vegas Daily Optic, Rodeo Edition,* Las Vegas, New Mexico, Thursday, August 1, 1957, p. 8, marked copy indicating item was written by Audrey Simpson, Simpson Archives, Las Vegas, New Mexico.
7. Ibid.
8. Audrey Reid, "Some Early Childhood Memories," op. cit.
9. Ibid.
10. Audrey Simpson, "Arriving in Las Vegas," Unpublished manuscript, n.d., Scrapbook 4, Simpson Archives, Las Vegas, New Mexico.
11. Audrey Reid, "Some Early Childhood Memories," op. cit.
12. Audrey Simpson, "Autobiography," unpublished notes, 1979, Scrapbook 9, Simpson Archives, Las Vegas, New Mexico.
13. "Sisters Celebrate 70th," *Vegas Victorian Gazette,* Las Vegas, New Mexico, Volume III, Issue 8, October, 1989, p. 5.
14. Audrey Simpson, no bi-line, "Road Runner is New Mexico Bird," *Las Vegas Daily Optic, Rodeo Edition,* Las Vegas, New Mexico, July 31, 1952, page. 7-B, marked copy indicating item was written by Audrey Simpson, Scrapbook 4, Simpson Archives, Las Vegas, New Mexico.
15. Audrey Reid, "Some Early Childhood Memories," op. cit.
16. Audrey Reid, interview by Holly Simpson, Tape 1, op. cit.

13

1. Audrey Reid, "Some Early Childhood Memories," op. cit.
2. Mabel Clements, letter from MacInerney Ranch to a friend, 1919, Scrapbook 3, Simpson Archives, Las Vegas, New Mexico.
3. http://www.aztlan.net/pena.htm
4. Audrey Reid, "Some Early Childhood Memories," op. cit.
5. Gensemer, op. cit.
6. Mabel Clements, "Notes of Wisdom," n.d., Scrapbook 1, Simpson Archives, Las Vegas, New Mexico.
7. Audrey Reid, interview by Millicent Wickman, Tape 30, op. cit.
8. Ibid.
9. Audrey Reid, "Some Early Childhood Memories," op. cit.
10. Ibid.
11. Ibid.

14

1. Mabel Clements, "Autumn Storm," unpublished poem, n.d., Scrapbook 3, Simpson Archives, Las Vegas, New Mexico.
2. Audrey Reid, interview by Holly Simpson, Tape 1, op. cit.
3. Audrey Reid, "Some Early Childhood Memories," op. cit.
4. Audrey Simpson, "Close Escapes," unpublished notes, n.d., Scrapbook 5, Simpson Archives, Las Vegas, New Mexico.
5. Ibid.
6. Mabel Clements, "Autumn Storm," op.cit.

15

1. Audrey Simpson, "Close Escapes," op. cit.
2. Audrey Reid, "Some Early Childhood Memories," op. cit.
3. Ibid.
4. Audrey Reid, interview by Holly Simpson, Tape 1, op. cit.
5. Audrey Reid, "Some Early Childhood Memories," op. cit.
6. Audrey Reid, interview by Millicent Wickman, Tape 8, op. cit.
7. Audrey Reid, "Some Early Childhood Memories," op. cit.
8. Audrey Simpson, "Pride Does It," copy of original manuscript submitted to and published by *New Verse Magazine*, May-June, 1951, p. 24.
9. Audrey Simpson, "Close Escapes," op. cit.
10. Audrey Reid, "Some Early Childhood Memories," op. cit.
11. Ibid.
12. Ibid.
13. Ibid.
14. Ibid.
15. Ibid.
16. Ibid.
17. Audrey Simpson, "Close Escapes," op. cit.
18. Mabel Clements, "Flowers," unpublished poem, n.d., Scrapbook 2, Simpson Archives, Las Vegas, New Mexico.

16

1. Audrey Reid, "Some Early Childhood Memories," op. cit.
2. Ibid.
3. Audrey Simpson, "Remembering Chapelle," n.d., unpublished notes, Scrapbook 4, Simpson Archives, Las Vegas, New Mexico.
4. Ibid.
5. Ibid.
6. Audrey Reid, "Some Early Childhood Memories," op. cit.
7. Ibid.
8. Ibid.
9. Audrey Reid, interview by Holly Simpson, Las Vegas, New Mexico, Tape 3, November 15, 1992, Simpson Archives, Las Vegas, New Mexico.
10. Audrey Reid, interview by Millicent Wickman, Las Vegas, New Mexico, Tape 25, March 16, 1994, Simpson Archives, Las Vegas, New Mexico.
11. Audrey Reid, "Some Early Childhood Memories," op. cit.
12. Ibid.
13. Audrey Reid, interview by Millicent Wickman, Las Vegas, New Mexico, Tape 29, April 18, 1994, Simpson Archives, Las Vegas, New Mexico.
14. Audrey Simpson, "Some Early Childhood Memories," op. cit.
15. Ibid.

17

1. Audrey Simpson, "Some Early Childhood Memories, op. cit.
2. Audrey Simpson, "Close Escapes," op. cit.
3. Audrey Reid, interview by Holly Simpson, Tape 1, op. cit.
4. Ibid.
5. Audrey Reid, "Some Early Childhood Memories," op. cit.
6. Audrey Simpson, "Betty," unpublished notes, n.d., Scrapbook 5, Simpson Archives,, Las Vegas, New Mexico.
7. Audrey Reid, "Some Early Childhood Memories," op. cit.
8. Audrey Simpson, "Betty," op. cit.
9. Audrey Reid, "Some Early Childhood Memories," op. cit.
10. Ibid.
11. Audrey Reid, interview by Holly Simpson, Tape 3, op. cit.
12. Ibid.

18

1. Audrey Simpson, "Betty," op. cit.
2. Audrey Reid, "Some Early Childhood Memories," op. cit.
3. Audrey Simpson, "Betty," op. cit.
4. Ibid.
5. Audrey Reid, "Some Early Childhood Memories," op. cit.

19

1. State Elementary Certificate, State of New Mexico: September 1, 1922, Scrapbook 2, Simpson Archives, Las Vegas, New Mexico.
2. Ibid.

3. Audrey Reid, "Some Early Childhood Memories," op. cit.
4. Ibid.
5. Ibid.
6. Ibid.
7. Audrey Simpson, no bi-line, "Rooster Pull Is Big Event Held by Top Horseman," *Las Vegas Daily Optic, Rodeo Edition*, Las Vegas, New Mexico, July 31, 1952, p. 7-B, marked copy indicating item was written by Audrey Simpson, Scrapbook 4, Simpson Archives, Las Vegas, New Mexico.
8. Audrey Simpson, "Betty," op. cit.
9. Ibid.
10. Ibid.
11. Audrey Reid, interview by Holly Simpson, Tape 1, op. cit.
12. Ibid.
13. Audrey Simpson, "Remembering Chapelle," op. cit.
14. Ibid.
15. Mabel Clements, "Christmas Note to Aunt Laura Waddell," n.d., Scrapbook 2, Simpson Archives, Las Vegas, New Mexico.
16. Audrey Simpson, "Betty," op. cit.
17. Audrey Reid, interview by Holly Simpson, Tape 1, op. cit.
18. Ibid.
19. Ibid.
20. Ibid.
21. Ibid.

20

1. Audrey Simpson, "Betty," op. cit.
2. Audrey Reid, interview by Millicent Wickman, Tape 29, op. cit.
3. Audrey Reid, interview by Millicent Wickman, Las Vegas, New Mexico, Tape 22, April 21, 1994. Simpson Archives, Las Vegas, New Mexico.
4. Audrey Simpson, no bi-line, "Bernal Recalled By Old-Timers," *Las Vegas Daily Optic, Rodeo Edition*, Las Vegas, New Mexico, July 31, 1952, p. 7B, marked copy indicating item was written by Audrey Simpson, Scrapbook 4, Simpson Archives, Las Vegas, New Mexico.
5. Audrey Reid, interview by Millicent Wickman, Tape 22, op. cit.
6. Audrey Simpson, "These Things Happened," unpublished manuscript, n.d., Scrapbook 5, Simpson Archives, Las Vegas, New Mexico.
7. Audrey Simpson, "Betty," op. cit.
8. Audrey Simpson, "These Things Happened," op. cit.
9. Audrey Reid, interview by Millicent Wickman, Las Vegas, New Mexico, Tape 6, April 23, 1987, Simpson Archives, Las Vegas, New Mexico
10. Ibid.
11. Audrey Simpson, "Betty," op. cit.
12. Audrey Reid, interview by Millicent Wickman, Las Vegas, New Mexico, Tape 1, August 21, 1992, Simpson Archives, Las Vegas, New Mexico
13. Mabel Clements, "Oh, God Give Me Courage," unpublished poem, n.d., Scrapbook 2, Simpson Archives, Las Vegas, New Mexico.
14. Mabel Clements, "Cramming," unpublished poem, n.d., Scrapbook 2, Simpson Archives, Las Vegas, New Mexico.
15. Audrey Reid, interview by Holly Simpson, Tape 3, op. cit.
16. Audrey Simpson, no bi-line, "Old-Timers Hand Down Chapelle Treasure Story," *Las Vegas Daily Optic, Rodeo Edition,* Las Vegas, New Mexico, July 31, 1952, p. 8-B, marked copy indicating item was written by Audrey Simpson, Scrapbook 4, Simpson Archives, Las Vegas, New Mexico.

17. Audrey Reid, "Recollections," letter submitted to the editor, *Grit*, February 12, 1986, Scrapbook 5, Simpson Archives, Las Vegas, New Mexico.

21

1. Audrey Simpson, "Salute Gregorio," unpublished manuscript, n.d., p. 6., Simpson Scrapbook 4, Simpson Archives.
2. Audrey Reid, interview by Holly Simpson, Tape 3, op. cit.
3. Ibid.
4. Audrey Simpson, no bi-line, "Bernal Historic Village 14 Miles South of Vegas," *Las Vegas Daily Optic*, *Rodeo Edition*, Las Vegas, New Mexico, July 31, 1952, p. 6B, marked copy indicating item was written by Audrey Simpson, Scrapbook 4, Simpson Archives, Las Vegas, New Mexico.
5. Audrey Simpson, "Fear—Our Deadly Enemy," copy of original manuscript submitted to and published by *The Joy Bearer*, Volume 14, Number 9, September, 1951, pp. 11-12.

22

1. Audrey Simpson, "Salute Gregorio," op. cit., pp. 1-2.
2. Ibid., p. 2
3. Ibid., p. 3
4. Ibid.
5. Ibid., p. 1.
6. Ibid., p 4.
7 Ibid., p. 2.
8. Ibid., pp. 4-5.
9. Ibid., p. 6.
10. Audrey Reid, interview by Holly Simpson, Tape 3, op. cit.
11. Audrey Simpson, "Salute Gregorio," op. cit.
12. Ibid, p. 7.
13. Ibid., p. 4.
14. Ibid., p. 9.

23

1. Audrey Simpson, "Betty," op. cit.
2. Ibid.
3. Ibid.
4. Ibid.
5. Audrey Reid, interview by Holly Simpson, Tape 3, op. cit.
6. Audrey Simpson, "Betty," op. cit.
7. Audrey Reid, Interview by Holly Simpson, Tape 3, op. cit.
8. Audrey Simpson, "Betty," op. cit.
9. Mabel Shearer, letter 1 to Charles Vivian Shearer, December, 1925, Jessica Braziel Archives, Tucumcari, New Mexico and CD numbers 093 and 094, Simpson Archives, Las Vegas, New Mexico.
10. Mabel Shearer, letter 2 to Charles Vivian Shearer, December, 1925, Jessica Braziel Archives, Tucumcari, New Mexico and CD numbers 093 and 094, Simpson Archives, Las Vegas, New Mexico.
11. Mabel Shearer, letter 3 to Charles Vivian Shearer, December, 1925, Jessica Braziel Archives, Tucumcari, New Mexico and CD numbers 093 and 094, Simpson Archives, Las Vegas, New Mexico.

12. Mabel Shearer, letter 4 to Charles Vivian Shearer, December, 1925, Jessica Braziel Archives, Tucumcari, New Mexico and CD number125, Simpson Archives, Las Vegas, New Mexico.
13. Mabel Shearer, letter 5 to Charles Vivian Shearer, December, 1925, Jessica Braziel Archives, Tucumcari, New Mexico and CD numbers 119 and 120, Simpson Archives, Las Vegas, New Mexico.
14. Mabel Shearer, letter 6 to Charles Vivian Shearer, December 15, 1925, Jessica Braziel Archives, Tucumcari, New Mexico and CD number 121, Simpson Archives, Las Vegas, New Mexico.
15. Mabel Shearer, letter 7 to Charles Vivian Shearer, December, 1925, Jessica Braziel Archives, Tucumcari, New Mexico and CD numbers 120 and 121, Simpson Archives, Las Vegas, New Mexico.
16. Mabel Shearer, letter 8 to Charles Vivian Shearer, December, 1925, Jessica Braziel Archives, Tucumcari, New Mexico and CD number 123, Simpson Archives, Las Vegas, New Mexico.
17. Audrey Simpson, "Betty," op. cit.
18. Audrey Reid, interview by Holly Simpson, Tape 1, op. cit.
19. Ibid.

24

1. Audrey Simpson, "My Early Days," op. cit.
2. Audrey Reid, interview by Holly Simpson, Tape 1, op. cit.
3. Ibid.
4. Audrey Simpson, "Betty," op. cit.
5. Audrey Reid, "Memoirs," Tape 3, November, 1992, Simpson Archives, Las Vegas, New Mexico.
6. Audrey Reid, interview by Holly Simpson, Tape 3, op. cit.
7. Audrey Reid, "Memoirs," Tape 3, op. cit.
8. Audrey Simpson, "Betty," op. cit.
9. Ibid.
10. *Madison, My Golden School Days: A Record Book of Happy Memories,* 1911, p. 13.
11. Ibid., p. 88.
12. Ibid., p. 25.
13. Audrey Simpson, "Betty," op. cit.
14. Audrey Reid, interview by Holly Simpson, Tape 1, op. cit.
15. Ibid.
16. Ibid.
17. Ibid.
18. Audrey Simpson, "These Things Happened," op. cit.
19. Ibid.
20. Ibid.
21. Ibid.
22. Ibid.
23. Ibid.
24. Ibid.
25. Audrey Simpson, "Betty," op. cit.
26. Audrey Simpson, "Desert Rain," copy of original manuscript submitted to and published by "Poems of New Mexico," *New Mexico Magazine,* Vol. 27, No. 6, June, 1949, p. 24.
27. Audrey Simpson, "Betty," op. cit.
28. Ibid.
29. Audrey Reid, "Memoirs," Tape 3, op. cit.

25

1. Audrey Reid, interview by Holly Simpson, Tape 1, op. cit.
2. Ibid.

26

1. Audrey Reid, "Miscellaneous and Various Notes," op. cit.
2. Ibid.
3. Mabel Clements, "Christmas List," n.d., Scrapbook 1, Simpson Archives, Las Vegas, New Mexico.
4. Mabel Clements, "Christmas Verses," unpublished Christmas poetry, n.d., Scrapbook 2, Simpson Archives, Las Vegas, New Mexico.

27

1. "Mineral City Boomed Before 1900s," *Las Vegas Daily Optic, Rodeo Edition,* Las Vegas, New Mexico, August 6, 1953, p. B1.
2. Ibid.
3. Ibid.
4. Audrey Simpson, "Mineral Hill Miner," *Las Vegas Daily Optic, Rodeo Edition,* August 1, 1957, Las Vegas, New Mexico, p. B4.
5. Audrey Simpson, "Riding my First Bronc," op. cit.
6. Audrey Simpson, "Everyone Has Choices," unpublished notes, n.d., Scrapbook 4, Simpson Archives, Las Vegas, New Mexico.
7. Ibid.
8. Audrey Simpson, "Day's Work," *Las Vegas Daily Optic, Rodeo Edition*, Las Vegas, New Mexico, August 1, 1957, p. B4.
9. Audrey Reid, interview by Holly Simpson, Tape 3, op. cit.
10. Ibid.
11. Audrey Simpson, "Everyone Has Choices," op. cit.
12. Ibid.

28

1. Audrey Simpson, "Riding My First Bronc," op. cit.
2. Audrey Reid, interview by Holly Simpson, Tape 3, op. cit.
3. Ibid.
4. Ibid.
5. State Elementary Certification, State of New Mexico: September 1, 1929 and expiring September 1, 1932, Simpson Scrapbook 2, Simpson Archives, Las Vegas, New Mexico.
6. Audrey Reid, interview by Holly Simpson, Tape 1, op. cit.
7. Audrey Reid, interview by Millicent Wickman, Tape 33, op. cit.
8. Ibid.
9. Audrey Simpson, "Grandpa and all," letter, December 19, 1919 in *Madison, My School Days: A Record Book for Happy Memories,* 1911.
10. *Madison, "My School Days: A Record Book for Happy Memories,"* op. cit. p. 89.
11. Audrey Reid, interview by Millicent Wickman, Las Vegas, New Mexico, Tape 24, March, 1994, Simpson Archives, Las Vegas, New Mexico.
12. Audrey Simpson, "Everyone Has Choices," op. cit.
13. Audrey Reid, "The Grocery Store," unpublished notes, n.d., Scrapbook 7, Simpson Archives, Las Vegas, New Mexico.

14. Audrey Simpson, "Jessica's Arrival," unpublished notes, n.d, Scrapbook 4, Simpson Archives, Las Vegas, New Mexico.
15. Audrey Reid, interview by Millicent Wickman, Tape 24, op. cit.
16. Audrey Simpson, "Jessica's Arrival," op. cit.
17. Audrey Reid, interview by Holly Simpson, Tape 3, op. cit.
18. Mabel Shearer, letter to Thelma Shirley, n.d., Scrapbook 1, Simpson Archives, Las Vegas, New Mexico.
19. Audrey Reid, interview by Millicent Wickman, Las Vegas, New Mexico, Tape 17, February 17, 1994, Simpson Archives, Las Vegas, New Mexico.
20. Mabel Shearer, letter to Mr. H, *The Denver Post*, n.d., Scrapbook 2, Simpson Archives, Las Vegas, New Mexico.

29

1. Audrey Simpson, "Betty," op. cit.
2. Audrey Reid, interview by Holly Simpson, Tape 1, op. cit.
3. Mabel Shearer, "Items Needed and Prices," Fall, 1930, Scrapbook 2, Simpson Archives, Las Vegas, New Mexico.
4. Audrey Simpson, "Mountain Living" notes, n.d., Scrapbook 6, Simpson Archives, Las Vegas, New Mexico.
5. Ibid.
6. Audrey Reid, interview by Holly Simpson, Tape 1, op. cit.
7. Ibid.
8. Mabel Shearer, "Sugar note," n.d., Scrapbook 2, Simpson Archives, Las Vegas, New Mexico.
9. Audrey Reid, interview with Holly Simpson, Tape 1, op. cit.
10. Ibid.
11. Ibid.
12. Mabel Shearer, letter to Frank Waddell, 1932, Scrapbook 2, Simpson Archives, Las Vegas, New Mexico.

30

1. Audrey Reid, interview by Millicent Wickman, Tape 31, op. cit.
2. Audrey Reid, interview by Holly Simpson, Tape 3, op. cit.
3. Shirley Giles, interview by Dorothy Simpson, Tucumcari, New Mexico, July 9, 2005.
4. Mabel Shearer, letter to Frank Waddell, op. cit.
5. Ibid.
6. Ibid.
7. Audrey Reid, interview by Millicent Wickman, Las Vegas, New Mexico, Tape 12, January 18, 1994, Simpson Archives, Las Vegas, New Mexico.
8. Audrey Reid, "Memoirs," Tape 3, op. cit.

31

1. Audrey Reid, interview by Holly Simpson, Tape 3, op. cit.
2. Ibid.
3. Audrey Reid, "Notes on Wild Horses," unpublished notes, n.d., Scrapbook 4, Simpson Archives, Las Vegas, New Mexico.
4. Audrey Simpson, no bi-line, "Wild Horse Herds Once Roamed Open Spots in Region," *Las Vegas Daily Optic,* Las Vegas, New Mexico, Thursday, July 31 1952, p. 5-A, marked copy indicating item was written by Audrey Simpson, Simpson Archives, Las Vegas New Mexico.

5. Audrey Reid, "Notes on Wild Horses," op. cit.
6. Audrey Simpson, "Religious Experiences," op. cit.
7. Audrey Simpson, "I'm Going Forward to Jesus," unpublished verse, n.d, Scrapbook 7, Simpson Archives, Las Vegas, New Mexico.
8. Audrey Reid, interview by Holly Simpson, Tape 1, op. cit.
9. Ibid.
10. Audrey Simpson, "Evening Rain," copy of original manuscript submitted to and published by *The Joy Bearer*, November, 1948, Vol. 11, No. 11, p. 11.

32

1. Audrey Reid, interview by Millicent Wickman, Las Vegas, New Mexico, Tape 11, January 15, 1994, Simpson Archives, Las Vegas, New Mexico.
2. Ibid.
3. Mabel Shearer, Christmas letter to a friend, n.d., Scrapbook 2, Simpson Archives, Las Vegas, New Mexico.
4. Audrey Reid, interview by Millicent Wickman, Las Vegas, New Mexico, Tape 34, Fall, 1994, Simpson Archives, Las Vegas, New Mexico.
5. Audrey Simpson, "Betty," op. cit.
6. Audrey Simpson, "Miscellaneous Notes," op. cit.
7. Audrey Simpson, "Maneuver for Victory," copy of original manuscript submitted to and published by *The Friendly Journal*, Vol. VIII, No. 3, (Oct.-Nov., 1942), p. 1.

33

1. Audrey Simpson, "Helping Mama," unpublished notes, n.d., Scrapbook 5, Simpson Archives, Las Vegas, New Mexico.
2. Audrey Simpson, "Miscellaneous Notes," op. cit.
3. Audrey Simpson, "I Hate Being Small," in "Mountain Living," notes, op. cit.
4. Mabel Shearer, "War Cake," notes, Scrapbook 2, Simpson Archives, Las Vegas, New Mexico, n.d.
5. Audrey Reid, interview by Millicent Wickman, Tape 22, op. cit.
6. Ibid.
7. Audrey Simpson, no bi-line, "Kearney's Gap Was Important Avenue For Early Travel," *Las Vegas Daily Optic, Rodeo Edition,* Thursday, August 1, 1957 p. B-4, marked copy indicating item was written by Audrey Simpson, Scrapbook 8, Simpson Archives, Las Vegas, New Mexico.

34

1. Audrey Reid, interview by Millicent Wickman, Las Vegas, New Mexico, Tape 2, December, 1986, Simpson Archives, Las Vegas, New Mexico.
2. Charles Vivian Shearer, letter about job interview, February 14, 1935, Scrapbook 2, Simpson Archives, Las Vegas, New Mexico.
3. Ibid.
4. Ibid.
5. Ibid.
6. Ibid.
7. Audrey Reid, interview with Millicent Wickman, Tape 2, op. cit.
8. Millicent Wickman, interview by Dorothy Simpson Beimer, Las Vegas, New Mexico, April, 1976.

35

1. Audrey Reid, interview by Millicent Wickman, Tape 24, op. cit.
2. Audrey Reid, interview by Millicent Wickman, Las Vegas, New Mexico, Tape 23, March 5, 1994, Simpson Archives, Las Vegas, New Mexico
3. Ibid.
4. Audrey Simpson, "Religious Experiences," op. cit.
5. Audrey Reid, interview by Millicent Wickman, Tape 22, op. cit.
6. Audrey Simpson, "Bonfire," copy of original manuscript submitted to and published by *New Mexico Magazine,* Vol. 22, No. 5, May, 1944, p. 20.
7. Mabel Shearer, "I Went to Buy a Hat Today," unpublished poem, n.d., Scrapbook 2, Simpson Archives, Las Vegas, New Mexico.
8. Audrey Reid, interview by Millicent Wickman, Tape 11, op. cit.
9. Audrey Reid, "Notes on the Carringtons," n.d., Scrapbook 4, Simpson Archives, Las Vegas, New Mexico.
10. Ibid.
11. Audrey Reid, "Memoirs," Tape 3, op. cit.
12. Ibid.
13. Ibid.

36

1. Audrey Reid, interview by Millicent Wickman, Tape 2, op. cit.
2. Gensemer, op. cit.
3. Audrey Reid, interview by Millicent Wickman, Tape 2, op. cit.
4. Audrey Reid, "The Grocery Store," op. cit.
5. Audrey Reid, "Crystal," unpublished notes, n.d., Scrapbook 5, Simpson Archives, Las Vegas, New Mexico.

37

1. Audrey Reid, interview by Millicent Wickman, Las Vegas, New Mexico, Tape 33, op. cit.
2. Ibid.
3. Dorothy Simpson Beimer, "Dr. Mortimer," in unpublished manuscript, "Early Doctors in Las Vegas," Las Vegas, New Mexico, Simpson Archives, November, 1980, p. 90.
4. Ibid.
5. Audrey Simpson, "Religious Experiences," op. cit.
6. Ibid.
7. Audrey Reid, "Crystal," op. cit.
8. Ibid.
9. Ibid.
10. Ibid.
11. Ibid.
12. Ibid.
13. Ibid.
14. Ibid.
15. Ibid.
16. Ibid.
17. Ibid.
18. Audrey Simpson, "Religious Experiences," op. cit.
19. Ibid.

1. Audrey Reid, interview by Holly Simpson, Tape 3, op. cit.
2. Ibid.
3. Charles Vivian Shearer, "Man's Stewardship of the Earth" and "The Conservation of Soil and Moisture," *New Mexico Highlands University Bulletin* 147, Las Vegas, New Mexico: New Mexico Highlands University, November, 1943, pp. 3-27.
4. Ibid.
5. Ibid.
6. Ibid.

1. Audrey Simpson, "My Book," op. cit.
2. Audrey Simpson, "Ten Dollar House," copy of original manuscript submitted to and published by *New Mexico Magazine*, February, 1943, pp. 11-12, 24, in Scrapbook 5, Simpson Archives, Las Vegas, New Mexico, 1942.
3. Audrey Simpson, "My Book," op. cit.
4. Ibid.
5. Ibid.
6. Ibid.
7. Audrey Simpson, "Ten Dollar House," op. cit.
8. Ibid.
9. Audrey Simpson, "My Book," op. cit.
10. Ibid.
11. Ibid.
12. Ibid.
13. Ibid.
14. Ibid.
15. Ibid.
16. Ibid.
17. Ibid.
18. Ibid.
19. Audrey Simpson, "Ten Dollar House," op. cit.
20. Ibid.
21. Ibid.
22. Audrey Simpson, "My Book," unpublished manuscript, n.d.,Scrapbook 5, Simpson Archives, Las Vegas, New Mexico, n.d.
23. Clive Arden, *The Enchanted Spring,* N.Y.: Grosset & Dunlap Publishers, 1935.
24. Audrey Simpson, "The Urge Behind the Ego," n.d., unpublished manuscript in Simpson Archives, Las Vegas, New Mexico.
25. Audrey Simpson, "My Book," op. cit.
26. Ibid.
27. Ibid.
28. Audrey Simpson, "Ten Dollar House," op. cit.
29. Ibid.
30. Audrey Simpson, "My Book," op. cit.
31. Ibid.
32. Ibid.
33. Ibid.
34. Ibid.
35. Ibid.

36. Ibid.
37. Audrey Simpson, "Ten Dollar House," op. cit.
38. Audrey Simpson, "My Book," op. cit.
39. Ibid.
40. Ibid.
41. Audrey Simpson, "Ten Dollar House," op. cit.
42. Ibid.
43. Ibid.
44. Audrey Simpson, "My Book," op. cit.
45. Ibid.
46. Ibid.

40

1. Audrey Simpson, "Next Door to Heaven," copy of original manuscript submitted to and published by *New Mexico Magazine*, Vol. 24, No. 2, February, 1946, pp. 19,39,41, Scrapbook 5, Simpson Archives, Las Vegas, New Mexico.
2. Ibid.
3. Audrey Simpson, no bi-line, "Mineral Belt was Boosted in 1907, *Las Vegas Daily Optic*, *Rodeo Edition*, Las Vegas, New Mexico, July 31, 1952, p. 3-B, marked copy indicating item was written by Audrey Simpson, Scrapbook 4, Simpson Archives, Las Vegas, New Mexico.
4. Audrey Simpson, no bi-line, "Coal Outcrops in Las Vegas Section," *Las Vegas Daily Optic*, *Rodeo Edition*, Las Vegas, New Mexico, July 31, 1952, p. 7-B, marked copy indicating article was written by Audrey Simpson, Scrapbook 4, Simpson Archives, Las Vegas, New Mexico.
5. Audrey Simpson, "The Mineral Hill-San Geronimo Road," in "Public Forum," *Las Vegas Daily Optic*, September 15, 1945, newspaper clipping, Scrapbook 4, Simpson Archives, Las Vegas, New Mexico.
6. Audrey Simpson, "Mineral Hill Road," n.d, Scrapbook 5, Simpson Archives, Las Vegas, New Mexico.
7. Audrey Simpson, "Several Camps for Young People," n.d., letter to the editor, *Las Vegas Daily Optic*, Las Vegas, New Mexico, manuscript in Scrapbook 5, Simpson Archives, Las Vegas, New Mexico.
8. Audrey Simpson, "History of the Mineral Hill Road," manuscript submitted to "Letters to the Editor," *The Las Vegas Daily Optic*, Las Vegas, New Mexico, n.d., Scrapbook 7, Simpson Archives, Las Vegas, New Mexico.
9. Ibid.
10. Ibid.
11. Ibid.
12. Audrey Simpson, "For About 70 Years," in "Letters to the Editor," *Las Vegas Daily Optic*, Las Vegas, New Mexico, n.d., newspaper clipping, Scrapbook 5, Simpson Archives, Las Vegas, New Mexico.
13. Audrey Simpson, letter to San Miguel County Commissioners, February 15, 1986, Scrapbook 5, Simpson Archives, Las Vegas, New Mexico.
14. Presillano Santillanes, interview by Dorothy Simpson Croxton, Forest Springs Ranch, January 30, 1997.
15. Ibid.
16. Audrey Simpson, "History of Forest Springs Ranch, Including Digressions About Area," notes, n.d., Scrapbook 3, Simpson Archives, Las Vegas, New Mexico.
17. Audrey Reid, "Forest Springs Ranch History," unpublished notes, n.d.,Scrapbook 3, Simpson Archives, Las Vegas, New Mexico.
18. Audrey Simpson, "History of Forest Springs Ranch, Including Digressions About Area," op. cit.
19. Audrey Reid, "Forest Springs Ranch History," op. cit.
20. Audrey Simpson, "History of Springs Ranch History," op. cit.

21. Ibid.
22. Audrey Reid, "Forest Springs Ranch History," op. cit.
23. Audrey Simpson, "History of Forest Springs Ranch including Digressions About Area," op. cit.
24. Audrey Reid, Notes in Memo Book, Simpson Archives, Las Vegas, New Mexico, n.d.
25. Audrey Reid, "Forest Springs Ranch History," op. cit.
26. Audrey Reid, "Miscellaneous Notes," op. cit.
27. Audrey Simpson, "My Book," op. cit.
28. Ibid.
29. Ibid.
30. "Obituary," Presillano Santillanes, *Las Vegas Daily Optic,* Las Vegas, New Mexico, August 18, 1997, p. 8.

41

1. Audrey Simpson, "My Book," op. cit.
2. Audrey Reid, "Forest Springs Ranch History," op. cit.
3. Ibid.
4. Audrey Simpson, "Next Door to Heaven," op. cit.
5. Audrey Simpson, "My Book," op. cit.
6. Ibid.
7. Ibid.
8. Ibid.
9. Ibid.
10. Ibid.
11. Ibid.
12. Ibid.
13. Ibid.
14. Audrey Simpson, "Next Door to Heaven," op. cit.
15. Audrey Simpson, "My Book," op. cit.
16. Ibid.
17. Ibid.
18. Ibid.
19. Ibid.
20. Ibid.
21. Audrey Simpson, "We Housed Ourselves For $15.50," copy of original manuscript submitted to and published by *Profitable Hobbies*, February, 1949, Scrapbook 5, Simpson Archives, Las Vegas, New Mexico, pp. p. 50.
22. Audrey Simpson, "My Book," op. cit.
23. Audrey Simpson, "Next Door to Heaven," op. cit.
24. Audrey Simpson, "My Book," op. cit.
25. Audrey Simpson, "Next Door to Heaven," op. cit.
26. Audrey Simpson, "The Big Cross Trail," *New Mexico Magazine*, Vol. 29, No. 3, March, 1951, pp. 46-47.
27. Audrey Simpson, "Hermit's Peak Legend," copy of original manuscript submitted to and published by *Old West*, Vol. 24, No. 3, Spring, 1988, pp. 49-51.
28. Audrey Simpson, "Next Door to Heaven," op. cit.
29. Gensemer, "Audrey Simpson," op. cit.

42

1. Audrey Simpson, "Next Door to Heaven," op. cit.

2. Ibid.
3. Ibid.
4. Ibid.
5. Audrey Reid, "Forest Springs Ranch History," op. cit.
6. Audrey Simpson, "Next Door to Heaven," op. cit.
7. Audrey Simpson, "We Housed Ourselves for $15.50," op. cit.
8. Audrey Simpson, "Mountain Dusk," *Las Vegas Daily Optic*, August 1, 1957, p. B1.
9. Audrey Reid, "History of Forest Springs Ranch," op. cit.

Part II
Cabin for Three

1

1. Audrey Simpson, "Anticipation," copy of original manuscript submitted to and published by *The American Baby: The National Magazine for Mothers of Infants*, July, 1944, p. 9, Scrapbook 5, Simpson Archives, Las Vegas, New Mexico.
2. Audrey Simpson, "Religions Experiences," op. cit.
3. Mabel Shearer, letter about Dorothy Simpson's birth, February 29, 1944, in Scrapbook 2, Simpson Archives, Las Vegas, New Mexico.
4. Audrey Simpson, "Religions Experiences," op. cit.
5. Ibid.
6. Ibid.
7. Crystal Simpson Lovett, interview by Dorothy Audrey Simpson, Las Vegas, New Mexico, October 5, 2006.
8. Audrey Simpson, "Religious Experiences," op. cit.
9. Ibid.
10. Audrey Simpson, "My Book," op. cit.
11. Audrey Simpson, "Free Lance—Unemployed—Housewife," copy of original manuscript submitted to and published by *Kansas City Poetry Magazine*, Vol. 10, September Issue, August, 1950, p. 14, Scrapbook 4, Simpson Archives, Las Vegas, New Mexico.

2

1. Crystal Simpson Lovett, interview by Dorothy Audrey Simpson, op. cit.
2. Charles Vivian Shearer, letter to Ray McCarty, June 2, 1942, Scrapbook 3, Simpson Archives, Las Vegas, New Mexico.
3. Ray McCarty, letter to Charles Vivian Shearer, March 19, Scrapbook 3, Simpson Archives, Las Vegas, New Mexico.
4. Ray McCarty, letter to R. A. Shearer, May19, 1945, Scrapbook 3, Simpson Archives, Las Vegas, New Mexico.
5. Rhea Oglesbee, interview by Dorothy Audrey Simpson, Forest Springs Ranch, Las Vegas, New Mexico, August 16, 2007.
6. Air Metal citation copy for Donald Simpson from Rhea Oglesbee Archives, Scrapbook 3, Simpson Archives, Las Vegas, New Mexico.
7. "Beaumont Flier Killed by Flak: Sgt. Donald Simpson Dies Of Wounds Received Over Poland," newspaper clipping from Rhea Oglesbee Archives, n.d. and CD numbers 4 and 084, Simpson Archives, Las Vegas, New Mexico.
8. Ibid.

9. Citation of Honor, copy of certificate, Rhea Oglesbee Archives, Scrapbook 3, Simpson Archives, Las Vegas, New Mexico.
10. Ibid.
11. Bruno Latici, letter to Addie Simpson, September 6, 1944, Rhea Oglesbee Archives, and CD numbers 4, 0167, and 0168, Simpson Archives, Las Vegas, New Mexico.
12. Donald Simpson and his crew, note on back of photograph, n.d., Rhea Oglesbee Archives, and CD numbers 3 and 079A, Simpson Archives, Las Vegas, New Mexico.
13. Donald Simpson's plane, "Flying Fortress," note on back of photograph, n.d., Rhea Oglesbee Archives and CD numbers 4 and 079A, Simpson Archives, Las Vegas, New Mexico.
14. R. Gilly, Pastor, letter to Mrs. [Addie] Simpson, Herstal, Belgium, March 28, 1951, Rhea Oglesbee Archives, and CD numbers 4 and 017, Simpson Archives, Las Vegas, New Mexico.
15. Note on photograph of MV Whale Knot, n.d., Rhea Oglesbee Archives and CD numbers 4 and 077, Simpson Archives, Las Vegas, New Mexico.
16. "Obituaries, Dr. Gordon Evert Wickman," *Las Vegas Daily Optic*, Las Vegas, New Mexico, June 20, 1997, p. 5.
17. Ibid.
18. Audrey Simpson, "The Two-Gun Years," December, 1944, Scrapbook 3, Simpson Archives, Las Vegas, New Mexico.
19. Lt. Stanley A. Hardin, Letter from India to Tana Marie Hardin, Raton, New Mexico, June 12, 1944, Tana Marie Hardin Archives, copy in Scrapbook 7, Simpson Archives, Las Vegas, New Mexico.
20. Stanley A. Hardin as told to D. A. Simpson, *From Pajarito to Lungchow: Memoirs of Photographic Reconnaissance Pilot Stanley A. Hardin, Lt. Col., U.S.A.F., Ret.,* Bowie, Maryland: Eagle Editions, An Imprint of Heritage Books, 2003.
21. Ibid.
22. Ibid.
23. Ibid.
24. "America the Beautiful," program, New Mexico Highlands University, Las Vegas, New Mexico, April 28, 2000.
25. Audrey Simpson, "High Country Lament," *The Denver Post,* newspaper clipping, Simpson Scrapbook 3, Simpson Archives, Las Vegas, New Mexico, n.d.

3

1. Audrey Reid, interview by Holly Simpson, Las Vegas, New Mexico, Tape 13, August 28, 1993, Simpson Archives, Las Vegas, New Mexico.
2. Audrey Simpson, "My Book," op. cit.
3. Ibid.
4. Ibid.
5. Ibid.
6. Dorothy Simpson Croxton, "Traveling Piano," copy of original manuscript submitted to and published by *Antique Almanac*, Vol. 3, Issue 8, October, 1996, p. 10.
7. Dorothy Simpson, "How Jesus Loves," copy of original manuscript submitted to and published by "Counsellor's Corner," *My Counsellor*, Chicago, Illinois, 1951.
8. Dorothy Simpson Croxton, "Traveling Piano," op.cit.
9. Audrey Simpson, "Notes on my Life," unpublished manuscript, Scrapbook 4, Simpson Archives, Las Vegas, New Mexico.
10. Ibid.
11. Audrey Simpson, "Just a Little Thing," n.d., unpublished manuscript, Scrapbook 7, Simpson Archives, Las Vegas, New Mexico.
12. Ibid.
13. Audrey Simpson, "Notes on My Life," op. cit.

14. "Hubby Rations Love Wife Hits the Ceiling," *Daily Mirror,* New York, New York, August 21, 1946, n.p., newspaper clipping, Scrapbook 34, Jessica Braziel Archives and copy in Scrapbook 3, Simpson Archives, Las Vegas, New Mexico.
15. Ibid.
16. Audrey Simpson, letter to Millicent Alpern, August 25, 1946, Scrapbook 3, Simpson Archives, Las Vegas, New Mexico.
17. "Plane Drops Birthday Gift to Miss Simpson," newspaper clipping from *Las Vegas Daily Optic*, Las Vegas, New Mexico, n.d., Scrapbook 2, Simpson Archives.
18. Lelama Gardner, interview by Dorothy Simpson Croxton, Las Vegas, New Mexico, August 25, 1998.
19. Charles Vivian Shearer, letter to Arolvi and Paul, January 21, 1950, Jessica Braziel Archives, and CD number 012 in Simpson Archives, Las Vegas, New Mexico.
20. Audrey Simpson, "These Things Happened," op. cit.
21. Lelama Gardner, interview by Dorothy Simpson Croxton, op. cit.
22. Audrey Simpson, letter to Millicent Alpern, op.cit.
23. Michael S. Sweeney, *Secrets of Victory: The Office of Censorship and the American Press and Radio in World War II,* University of North Carolina Press, 2001, p. 115.
24. Ibid.
25. Audrey Simpson, "These Things Happened," op. cit.
26. Ibid.
27. Ibid.
28. Ibid.
29. Audrey Simpson, "These Things Happened," op. cit.
30. Audrey Simpson, no bi-line, "Early Day Roses Still Bloom Here," *Las Vegas Daily Optic*, Las Vegas, New Mexico, July 3, 1954, p. A-4, marked copy indicating item was written by Audrey Simpson, Simpson Archives, Las Vegas, New Mexico.
31. Audrey Simpson, "Kisses," copy of original manuscript submitted to and published by *Kansas City Poetry Magazine,* Vol. 10, No. 8, p. 14, May, 1950, Scrapbook 7, Simpson Archives, Las Vegas, New Mexico.
32. Jean Whiting, "Short On Birthdays Maybe, But They'll Only Be 20 When Their Friends Are 80," *Las Vegas Daily Optic*, Las Vegas, New Mexico, n.p., newspaper clipping marked February 29, 1960, Scrapbook 5, Simpson Archives, Las Vegas, New Mexico.

4

1. Oral Roberts, *Expect a Miracle: My Life and Ministry, An Autobiography,* Nashville: Thomas Nelson Publishers, 1995.
2. "Funeral Services for Rodeo Victim Set for Thursday, *Las Vegas Daily Optic,* August 10, 1949, newspaper clipping, Scrapbook 8, Simpson Archives, Las Vegas, New Mexico.
3. "Final Rites Held George F. Hays, Victim of Rodeo," *Las Vegas Daily Optic*, August 11, 1949, newspaper clipping, Scrapbook 8, Simpson Archives, Las Vegas, New Mexico.
4. Charles Vivian Shearer, letter to Arolvi and Paul Dale, August 12, 1949, Jessica Braziel Archives and CD number 017, Simpson Archives, Las Vegas, New Mexico.
5. Audrey Simpson, "Departure," copy of original manuscript submitted to and published by *Today: In Prose & Poetry*, Vol. 1, No. 4, March-April, 1941, p. 17.
6. Charles Vivian Shearer, letter to Arolvi and Paul, January 21, 1950, op. cit.
7. Ibid.
8. Audrey Simpson, "My Book," op. cit.
9. Audrey Simpson, "Memo Book," op. cit.

5

1. Audrey Simpson, "My Lifeline in the Mountains," copy of original manuscript submitted to and published by *Impact, Albuquerque Journal Magazine*, Volume 6, Number 47, September 1983, in Scrapbook 7, Simpson Archives, Las Vegas, New Mexico.
2. Audrey Simpson, "My Book," op. cit.
3. Audrey Simpson, "Homestead in Happy Canyon," copy of original manuscript submitted to and published by *New Mexico Magazine,* Vol. 29, No. 12, December, 1952.
4. Ibid.

6

1. Audrey Simpson, "Homestead in Happy Canyon," op. cit.
2. Audrey Simpson, "My Book," op. cit.
3. Ibid.
4. Audrey Simpson, "He Passed Here," copy of original manuscript submitted to and published by *The Joy Bearer*, September, 1949, Vol. 12, No. 9, p. 16

7

1. Audrey Simpson, "My Book," op. cit.
2. Audrey Simpson, "Sunshine is an Elf," copy of original manuscript submitted to and published by *The Joy Bearer*, Vol. 12, No. 10, October, 1949, Scrapbook 7, Simpson Archives, Las Vegas, New Mexico.
3. Audrey Simpson, "Life Comes From Above," unpublished poems, Scrapbook 6, Simpson Archives, Las Vegas, New Mexico.
4. Audrey Simpson, "Forecast of Winter," unpublished poem , n.d.,Scrapbook 7, Simpson Archives, Las Vegas, New Mexico.
5. Audrey Simpson,"Freckle Time is Coming," unpublished poem , n.d., Scrapbook 7, Simpson Archives, Las Vegas, New Mexico.
6. Audrey Simpson, "We Hear the Crack of Hunter's Gun," unpublished poem, n.d., Scrapbook 7, Simpson Archives, Las Vegas, New Mexico.
7. Audrey Simpson, "Only the Wind and Rain," unpublished poem, n.d., Scrapbook 7, Simpson Archives, Las Vegas, New Mexico.

8

1. Audrey Simpson, "These Things Happened," op. cit.
2. Audrey Simpson, no bi-line, "Organ At Shearer's Pioneer Attraction," *Las Vegas Daily Optic Rodeo Edition,* July 30, 1958, p. A1, marked copy indicating item was written by Audrey Simpson, Simpson Archives, Las Vegas, New Mexico.
3. Audrey Simpson, "A Walk for Rain," unpublished manuscript, Scrapbook 7, Simpson Archives, Las Vegas, New Mexico, n.d.

9

1. Anonymous, *"Epitaph of a Dog,"* in *Poems from the Greek Anthology*, translated by Dudley Fitts, New York: A New Directions Paperbook, 1956, p. 114.

10

1. A. C. Clements, "Bear On A Grey Hackle," copy of original manuscript submitted to and published by *Western Sportsman*, Vol. 10, No. 5, July-August, 1950, p. 17, Simpson Scrapbook 8, Simpson Archives, Las Vegas, New Mexico.
2. Audrey Simpson, "The Fort that Won the West," copy of original manuscript submitted to and published by *New Mexico Magazine*, Vo. 28, N. 12, December, 1950, pp.14-15, Scrapbook 8, Simpson Archives, Las Vegas, New Mexico.
3. Ibid., p. 45.
4. Ibid.
5. Ibid.
6. Ibid.
7. Ibid., p. 47
8. Ibid, p. 49.
9. "Fort Union, Historic Outpost, Now is National Monument," *Las Vegas Daily Optic,* Wednesday, July 30, 1958, p. A1.
10. Audrey Simpson, "Homestead in Happy Canyon," op. cit.

11

1. "Cloud-Seeding Operation Halted For This Season," *Las Vegas Daily Optic*, Las Vegas, New Mexico, July 25, 1952, p. 1.
2. Audrey Simpson, "Weather Man's Blues," *Las Vegas Daily Optic*, *Rodeo Edition*, July 31, 1952, p. 2B, Scrapbook 2, Simpson Archives, Las Vegas, New Mexico.
3. "Poison Search Pressed Here," *Las Vegas Daily Optic*, Las Vegas, New Mexico, August 20, 1953, p. 1.
4. Audrey Simpson, "My Book," op. cit.
5. Ibid.
6. Audrey Simpson, "Homestead in Happy Canyon," op. cit.
7. Ibid.
8. Audrey Simpson, "My Book," op. cit.
9. Audrey Simpson, "Prayer for Rain," copy of original manuscript submitted to and published by "Poems of New Mexico," *New Mexico Magazine*, Vol. 29, No. 7, June, 1951, p. 26 and in *Fiesta: An Anthology of Southwestern Poets*, Albuquerque: Albuquerque Branch of the National League of American Pen Women, 1952, p. 24, Simpson Archives, Las Vegas, New Mexico.

12

1. Audrey Simpson, "Hey! Riddle, Riddle!" copy of original manuscript submitted to and published by *Scimitar and Song,* Vol. XIV, No. 1, July, 1951 in Scrapbook 7, Simpson Archives, Las Vegas, New Mexico.

13

1. Audrey Simpson, "My Lifeline in the Mountains," op. cit.
2. Audrey Simpson, "Barbed Wire Phone Line," unpublished manuscript in Scrapbook 7, Simpson Archives, Las Vegas, New Mexico, n.d.
3. Audrey Simpson, "My Lifeline in the Mountains," op. cit.
4. Ibid.
5. Audrey Simpson, "Homestead in Happy Canyon," op. cit.
6. Audrey Simpson, "Dear Ma Bell," manuscript, n.d., Scrapbook 7, Simpson Archives, Las Vegas, New Mexico.
7. Ibid.

8. Ibid.
9. Audrey Simpson, "Letter to the Editor," *Empire Magazine, The Denver Post,* August 4, 1985, Scrapbook 7, Simpson Archives, Las Vegas, New Mexico.

15

1. Audrey Simpson, "Homestead in Happy Canyon," op. cit.
2. Audrey Simpson, "Various Notes," n.d., Scrapbook 7, Simpson Archives, Las Vegas, New Mexico.
3. Audrey Simpson, "My Book," op. cit.

16

1. Audrey Simpson, "A Lynx Raided my Home," copy of original manuscript submitted to and published by *Western Sportsman*, March/April, 1953, p. 9, Scrapbook 7, Simpson Archives, Las Vegas, New Mexico.
2. Dorothy Simpson Croxton, "Mom Did What She Had to Do," copy of original manuscript submitted to and published by *Cappers,* May 5, 1998, p. 24, Simpson Archives, Las Vegas, New Mexico.
3. Audrey Simpson, "A Lynx Raided My Home," op. cit.
4. Ibid.
5. Dorothy Simpson Croxton, "I Remember the Day the Lynx Attacked," *Backwoods Home Magazine,* No. 44, March/April, 1997, pp. 53-54.
6. Audrey Simpson, "A Lynx Raided My Home," op. cit.

17

1. Audrey Simpson, "The Big Cross Trail," op.cit.
2. Ibid.
3. Ibid.
4. Ibid.
5. Ibid.
6. Audrey Simpson, no bi-line, "Early Main Route To Ancient City North of Barillas," *Las Vegas Daily Optic, Rodeo Edition,* Las Vegas, New Mexico, July 31, 1952, p. A5, marked copy indicating story was written by Audrey Simpson, Scrapbook 8, Simpson Archives, Las Vegas, New Mexico.
7. Audrey Simpson, "My Book," op. cit.
8. Ibid.
9. Audrey Simpson, "Record Run," copy of original manuscript submitted to and published by *The Joy Bearer*, August, 1951, Scrapbook 7, Simpson Archives, Las Vegas, New Mexico.
10. Audrey Simpson, "Mountain Daybreak," *Las Vegas Daily Optic,* August 1, 1957, p. B8.

Part III
Back to Her Mountains

1

1. Audrey Simpson, no bi-line, "Gallinas Ponds Used for Storage and Ice-Skating," *Las Vegas Daily Optic,* Las Vegas, New Mexico, Thursday July 31, 1952, p. 3-A, marked copy indicating item was written by Audrey Simpson, Scrapbook 8, Simpson Archives, Las Vegas, New Mexico.
2. Mabel Shearer, "Christmas Poem," unpublished poem, n.d.,Scrapbook 2, Simpson Archives, Las Vegas, New Mexico.

3. "Former Highlands Student at 'Optic'," newspaper clipping, *The Candle*, Las Vegas, New Mexico, Friday, March 21, 1952, Scrapbook 2, Simpson Archives, Las Vegas, New Mexico.
4. "Vegas Juvenile Story Chosen in PW Contest," *Las Vegas Daily Optic*, Las Vegas, New Mexico, Monday, April 27, 1952, p. 2.
5. "Pen Women Hear Dr. S. A. Hardin," *Las Vegas Daily Optic*, Las Vegas, New Mexico, Wednesday, March 11, 1953, p. 2.
6. "Mrs. Hardin Hostess as PW Pick Markets," newspaper clipping, *Las Vegas Daily Optic,* Las Vegas, New Mexico, marked copy indicating item was written by Audrey Simpson, with handwritten date "May 13, 1953," Simpson Archives, Scrapbook 8, Simpson Library, Las Vegas, New Mexico.
7. "Jaycees Campaign For Discard Toys," newspaper clipping, n.d., *Las Vegas Daily Optic*, Las Vegas, New Mexico, Scrapbook 8, Simpson Archives.
8. "Toy Drive Planned by Local Jaycees," newspaper clipping, n.d., *Las Vegas Daily Optic*, Las Vegas, New Mexico, Scrapbook 8, Simpson Archives.
9. "School Children Give Jaycees Toys," newspaper clipping, 1952, *Las Vegas Daily Optic*, Las Vegas, New Mexico, Scrapbook 8, Simpson Archives.
10. "Operation Christmas Collects 1000 Toys," newspaper clipping, n.d., *Las Vegas Daily Optic*, Las Vegas, New Mexico, Scrapbook 8, Simpson Archives.
11. "Gallinas School May Day Festival To Be Held Friday," newspaper clipping, *Las Vegas Daily Optic,* handwritten date, April 30, 1953, Simpson Archives, Las Vegas, New Mexico.
12. Audrey Simpson, "Cowboy Answers the Questionnaire," *Las Vegas Daily Optic*, *Rodeo Edition,* July 31, 1952, p. 2B, Scrapbook 2, Simpson Archives, Las Vegas, New Mexico.
13. Audrey Simpson, no bi-line, "Torreón Guarded Kearney's Gap In Days Of Long Ago," *Las Vegas Daily Optic, Rodeo Edition,* July 30, 1958, p. C4, marked copy indicating item was written by Audrey Simpson, Simpson Archives, Las Vegas, New Mexico.
14. Audrey Simpson, no bi-line, "Kearney's Gap Torreón Protected Travelers," *Las Vegas Daily Optic Rodeo Edition,* July 31, 1952, p. 5-A, marked copy indicating item was written by Audrey Simpson, Simpson Archives, Las Vegas, New Mexico.
15. "Las Vegas Founded In 1835 Is Home of Rodeo, Rough Riders," *Las Vegas Daily Optic Rodeo Edition*, July 30, 1958, p. B5, Simpson Archives, Las Vegas, New Mexico.
16. Audrey Simpson, no bi-line, "An Item From History," *Las Vegas Daily Optic, Rodeo Edition,* July 31, 1952, p. 4-B, marked copy indicating item was written by Audrey Simpson, Scrapbook 4, Simpson Archives, Las Vegas, New Mexico.
17. Audrey Simpson, no bi-line, "An Item From History," *Las Vegas Daily Optic*, *Rodeo Edition*, July 31, 1952, p.5-B, marked copy indicating item was written by Audrey Simpson, Scrapbook 4, Simpson Archives, Las Vegas, New Mexico.
18. Audrey Simpson, no bi-line, "Tecolote One of Oldest in State." *Las Vegas Daily Optic*, *Rodeo Edition*, July 31, 1952, p. 5-B, marked copy indicating item was written by Audrey Simpson, Scrapbook 4, Simpson Archives, Las Vegas, New Mexico.
19. Audrey Simpson, "Mountain Sunset," *Las Vegas Daily Optic*, *Rodeo Edition,* Las Vegas, New Mexico, July 31, 1952, p. 8-B.
20. Audrey Simpson, "These Things Happened," op. cit.
21. "Optic Society Editor Marries on Monday," *Las Vegas Daily Optic,* Las Vegas, New Mexico, June 9, 1953, p. 2.
22. Audrey Simpson, "My Book," op. cit.
23. Audrey Simpson, "These Things Happened," op. cit.
24. Audrey Simpson, "Game-Keeper," *Las Vegas Daily Optic, Rodeo Edition*, July 31, 1952, p. 2-B

2

1. Audrey Simpson, "My Book," op. cit.
2. Ibid.

3. Audrey Simpson, "Relative-ly Speaking," copy of original manuscript submitted to and published by *Caper's Weekly*, February 22, Scrapbook 1, Simpson Archives, Las Vegas, New Mexico, n.d.
4. Audrey Simpson, no bi-line, "Vegas, Then and Now; Time, People Changed," *Las Vegas Daily Optic*, Las Vegas, New Mexico, July 31, 1952, p. 8-A, marked copy indicating story was written by Audrey Simpson, Simpson Archives, Las Vegas, New Mexico.
5. Audrey Simpson, no bi-line, "Sugar Cane Once Grown in Las Vegas Section," *Las Vegas Daily Optic*, July 31, 1952, p. 5-A, marked copy indicating story was written by Audrey Simpson, Scrapbook 8, Simpson Archives, Las Vegas, New Mexico.
6. Audrey Simpson, no bi-line, "Lesperance Sawmill One Of Pioneer Industries," *Las Vegas Daily Optic*, Las Vegas, New Mexico, July 31, 1952, p. 4-B, marked copy indicating item was written by Audrey Simpson, Simpson Archives, Las Vegas, New Mexico.
7. Ibid.
8. Audrey Simpson, no bi-line, "Sawmills In Area Important Part of Las Vegas Economy," *Las Vegas Daily Optic*, July 30, 1958, p. A3, marked copying indicating story was written by Audrey Simpson, Simpson Archives, Las Vegas, New Mexico.
9. Audrey Simpson, no bi-line, "The Big Cross Trail" photograph, *Las Vegas Daily Optic Rodeo Edition*, July 31, 1952, p. 1C, marked copy indicating the photo and caption were written by Audrey Simpson, Simpson Archives, Las Vegas, New Mexico.
10. Audrey Simpson, no bi-line, "Mountain Winter" photograph, *Las Vegas Daily Optic Rodeo Edition*, July 31, 1952, p. 5C, marked copy indicating the photo and caption were written by Audrey Simpson, Simpson Archives, Las Vegas, New Mexico.
11. Audrey Simpson, no bi-line, "Mountain Cabins Like This," photograph, *Las Vegas Daily Optic Rodeo Edition*, July 31, 1952, p. 3C, marked copy indicating the photo and caption were written by Audrey Simpson, Simpson Archives, Las Vegas, New Mexico.

3

1. Shirley Simpson, "The Perfect Squelch," copy of original manuscript submitted to and published by *The Saturday Evening Post*, Vol. 223, No. 52, June 23, 1951, p. 109.
2. Shirley Simpson, "Some People You Meet," copy of original manuscript submitted to and published by *The Perfect Squelch, A Saturday Evening Post Feature Book*, edited by Ashley Halsey, Jr., N.Y.: A. S. Barnes and Company, 1952.
3. Audrey Simpson, "Indians Captured Boy, Adopted Him; Made Subject Of History," *Las Vegas Daily Optic Rodeo Edition*, Las Vegas, New Mexico, August 1, 1957, p. B-4.
4. "'Bulldogging' Got Name From Lip Biting Cowboy," *Las Vegas Daily Optic*, Las Vegas, New Mexico, July 30, 1958, p. B6.
5. Audrey Simpson, no bi-line, "O'Malley Is Parade Marshal 45 years," *Las Vegas Daily Optic*, Las Vegas, New Mexico, July 30, 1958, p. B7.
6. Ibid.
7. Audrey Simpson, no bi-line, "Cowgal's Dream Broken by Horse Bear Spooked," *Rodeo Edition, Las Vegas Daily Optic,* July, 1952, p. 5-B, marked copy indicating item was written by Audrey Simpson, Scrapbook 4, Simpson Archives, Las Vegas, New Mexico.

4

1. Audrey Simpson, no bi-line, "Rooster Pull Is Sport of Riders in Area Villages," *Las Vegas Daily Optic Rodeo Edition*, July 30, 1958, p. A1, marked copy indicating item was written by Audrey Simpson, Simpson Archives, Las Vegas, New Mexico.
2. Audrey Simpson, "Fiesta Traditional Good Time in Las Vegas," *Las Vegas Daily Optic, Rodeo and Fiesta Edition*, Las Vegas, New Mexico, 1965, p. 2, Scrapbook 7, Simpson Archives, Las Vegas, New Mexico.

3. Ibid.
4. "Half a Century in Rodeo," *Las Vegas Daily Optic,* Las Vegas, New Mexico, July 6, 1965.
5. "Early Cowpunchers Rugged Individuals," *Las Vegas Daily Optic*, July 30, 1958, p. B1.
6. Audrey Simpson, "Mrs. Rough Rider Busy During Reunion," *Las Vegas Daily Optic*, *Rodeo Edition,* June 11, 1964, p. 9.
7. Gensemer, op. cit.
8. Audrey Reid, interview by Millicent Wickman, Las Vegas, New Mexico, Tape 3, February, 1987, Las Vegas, New Mexico, Simpson Archives, Las Vegas, New Mexico.
9. Ibid.
10. Gensemer, op. cit.

5

1. Audrey Reid, "Holly," unpublished notes, Scrapbook 5, Simpson Archives, Las Vegas, New Mexico, no date.
2. Ibid.
3. Ibid.
4. Ibid.
5. Ibid.
6. Ibid.
7. Ibid.
8. Audrey Simpson, Holly's Birth Announcement Card, March, 1955, Scrapbook 5, Simpson Archives, Las Vegas, New Mexico.
9. Audrey Simpson, "These Things Happened," op. cit.
10. Audrey Reid, "Holly," op. cit.
11. Ibid.
12. Ibid.
13. Gensemer, op. cit.
14. Ibid.
15. Audrey Reid, "Holly," op. cit.
16. Ibid.
17. Ibid.
18. Ibid.
19. Ibid.
20. Ibid.
21. Ibid.
22. Ibid.
23. Ibid.

6

1. Audrey Simpson, "Every Day Since 1879," *Las Vegas Daily Optic*, Las Vegas, New Mexico, Saturday, August 10, 1957, p. 1.
2. Walter T. Vivian, "Along the Banks of the Gallinas," *Las Vegas Daily Optic*, Las Vegas, New Mexico, August 10, 1957, p. 1.
3. "Fire Gutts Daily Optic Plant: Equipment Badly Damaged by Blaze," caption under photograph," *Las Vegas Daily Optic*, Las Vegas, New Mexico, August 10, 1957, p. 1.
4. "Fire Gutts Daily Optic Plant: Equipment Badly Damaged by Blaze," *Las Vegas Daily Optic*, Las Vegas, New Mexico, Saturday, August 10, 1957, p. 1.

7

1. Audrey Simpson, "The Leaves Were Green," unpublished poem in Scrapbook 6, Simpson Archives, Las Vegas, New Mexico, n.d.
2. Audrey Simpson, "Various Notes," op. cit.
3. Audrey Simpson, "Nobody Home," manuscript for *The Denver Post*, n.d. in Simpson Archives, Las Vegas, New Mexico.
4. Audrey Simpson, Note, December 28, 1958, written in back of the book *Wild Streets: Tales of the Famous Frontier Towns,* edited by Don Ward, Doubleday & Co., Inc., Garden City, N.Y.: 1958, in Simpson Archives, Las Vegas, New Mexico.

8

1. Mabel Shearer, "Note to Audrey," *Madison, My Golden School Days: A Record Book of Happy Memories,* op. cit., p. 65.
2. Audrey Reid, "My Book," op. cit.
3. Ibid.
4. Audrey Simpson, "Building Notes," unpublished handwritten notes, n.d., Scrapbook 8, Simpson Archives, Las Vegas, New Mexico.

9

1. Audrey Simpson, "Religious Experiences," op. cit.
2. Audrey Reid, "Holly," op. cit.
3. Ibid.
4. Ibid.
5. Ibid.
6. Ibid.
7. Ibid.
8. Ibid.
9. Ibid.
10. Ibid.
11. "Obituary," Clyde Joseph Simpson, Tuesday, April 20, 1965, *Las Vegas Daily Optic,* newspaper clipping ,Scrapbook 7, Simpson Archives, Las Vegas, New Mexico.
12. "Obituary," Clyde J. Simpson," April 22, 1965. *Las Vegas Daily Optic,* newspaper clipping, Scrapbook 7, Simpson Archives, Las Vegas, New Mexico.
13. Audrey Simpson, "Holly," op. cit.
14. Ibid.
15. Ibid.
16. Ibid.
17. Holly A. Simpson, Mother's Day Card verse, 1966, in Scrapbook 5, Simpson Archives, Las Vegas, New Mexico.
18. Audrey Simpson, "Here's To My Holly," unpublished poem, n.d., Scrapbook 5, Simpson Archives, Las Vegas, New Mexico.
19. Audrey Simpson, Letter to Mrs. Clark Ranney, 1967, Scrapbook 8, Simpson Archives, Las Vegas, New Mexico.
20. Audrey Simpson, "Holly," op. cit.
21. S. Omar Barker, *Sunlight Through the Trees*, Las Vegas, New Mexico: Highlands University Press, 1954, p. 47.

1. Audrey Simpson, "Miscellaneous Notes," op. cit.
2. Audrey Simpson, letter to potential publishers, Forest Springs Ranch letter head, Scrapbook 5, Simpson Archives, Las Vegas, New Mexico, n.d.
3. Audrey Reid, "Notes About Writing," unpublished notes, Scrapbook 7, Simpson Archives, Las Vegas, New Mexico, n.d.
4. Audrey Simpson, "Mail Order Plan," copy of original manuscript submitted to and published by *True Romance,* "Pet Peeves," October, 1970, Scrapbook 8, Simpson Archives, Las Vegas, New Mexico.
5. Editorial Department, "Payment for your Story" card, *Capper's Weekly*, n.d., Scrapbook 7, Simpson Archives, Las Vegas, New Mexico.
6. Audrey Simpson, "Remember the Years," unpublished notes, Scrapbook 6, Simpson Archives, Las Vegas, New Mexico, no date.
7. Audrey Reid, no bi-line, "The Boy Who Lived Flags," copy of original manuscript submitted to and published by *True Romance: The All-Story Magazine,* Vol. 88, No. 5, July, 1969, 49, marked copy indicating item was written by Audrey Simpson, Simpson Archives, Las Vegas, New Mexico.
8. Ibid.
9. Ibid.
10. Audrey Reid, "Miscellaneous and Various Notes," op. cit.
11. Audrey Simpson, "Winter Playground," copy of original manuscript submitted to and published by *New Mexico Magazine*, Vol. 28, No. 1, January, 1950, pages 23, 44-45, Scrapbook 8, Simpson Archives, Las Vegas, New Mexico.
12. Audrey Reid, "Favor Doubly Repaid," unpublished manuscript, n.d., Scrapbook 7, Simpson Archives, Las Vegas, New Mexico.
13. Audrey Simpson, "Rio Grande Treasure," copy of original manuscript submitted to and published by *Treasure World*, Vol. 3, No. 3, August-September, 1969, pp. 20-22, Simpson Archives, Las Vegas, New Mexico.
14. Audrey Simpson, "Rio Grande Treasure," copy of original manuscript submitted to and published by *Treasure Trails, Old West,* Vol. 1, No. 4, Fall, 1973, p. 13, Simpson Archives, Las Vegas, New Mexico.
15. Audrey Simpson, "The Guy in the Cowboy Hat," unpublished notes, Simpson Archives, Las Vegas, New Mexico, n.d.
16. Ibid.
17. Audrey Simpson, "Dear Post Office," unpublished letter, n.d., Scrapbook 7, Simpson Archives, Las Vegas, New Mexico.
18. Audrey Simpson, "Dear Kate," unpublished Letter to the Editor, *Capper's Magazine*, n.d., Scrapbook 7, Simpson Archives, Las Vegas, New Mexico.
19. Audrey Simpson, "Stamping Out Junk Mail," copy of original manuscript submitted to and published by *Albuquerque Journal Magazine*, Vol. 5, No. 44, August 17, 1982, pp. 12-13, Simpson Archives, Las Vegas, New Mexico.
20. Ibid.
21. Ibid.
22. Audrey Simpson, letter to telephone company, Scrapbook 8, Simpson Archives, Las Vegas, New Mexico, March 18, 1985.
23. Audrey Simpson, "Young Resent," unpublished letter, Scrapbook 7, Simpson Archives, Las Vegas, New Mexico.
24. Ibid.
25. Mrs. W. A. Reid, Sr., "Letter to the Editor," *Albuquerque Journal*, Albuquerque, New Mexico, April 15, 1981.
26. Audrey Simpson, letter to Mrs. Clark Ranney, 1967, op. cit.

27. Ibid.
28. Mabel Shearer, "Notes, March, 1969 Scrapbook 8, Simpson Archives, Las Vegas, New Mexico.
29. Mabel Shearer, "Notes, June, 1969," Scrapbook 8, Simpson Archives, Las Vegas, New Mexico.
30. Audrey Simpson, no bi-line, "Log House Keeps Her Snug in Mountains," copy of original manuscript submitted to and published by *Capper's Weekly*, Volume 91, No. 40, November 7, 1967, p. 4, marked copy indicating item was written by Audrey Simpson, Simpson Archives, Las Vegas, New Mexico.
31. Holly Simpson, interview by Dorothy Simpson, Forest Springs Ranch, March, 2008.
32. Audrey Reid, "Miscellaneous and Various Notes," op. cit.

11

1. Audrey Simpson, "Where Do Newspaper Women Go?" unpublished manuscript, n.d., Scrapbook 6, Simpson Archives., Las Vegas, New Mexico.
2. Audrey Simpson, "Notes about the 1971 Forest Fire," unpublished notes, Scrapbook 8, Simpson Archives, Las Vegas, New Mexico, n.d.
3. Ibid.
4. Audrey Reid, "Holly," op. cit.
5. Ibid.
6. Ibid.
7. Audrey Simpson, letter on firefighting, n.d., Scrapbook 7, Simpson Archives, Las Vegas, New Mexico.
8. Audrey Simpson, letter to the U.S. Forest Service, n.d., Scrapbook 6, Simpson Archives, Las Vegas, New Mexico.
9. Audrey Simpson, Letter to the Editor, *Albuquerque Journal*, Albuquerque, New Mexico, n.d., Scrapbook 6, Simpson Archives, Las Vegas, New Mexico.
10. Audrey Simpson, Letter to the Editor, *Las Vegas Daily Optic*, October 8, 1988, Scrapbook 6, Simpson Archives.Las Vegas, New Mexico.
11. Audrey Simpson, "All Day the Ashes Fell," unpublished poem, n.d., Scrapbook 6, Simpson Archives, Las Vegas, New Mexico.
12. Oral Roberts, "New Lease on Life," partial paper from *Abundant Life Magazine,* n.d., Simpson Archives, Las Vegas, New Mexico.
13. Audrey Simpson, letter to Oral Roberts, n.d., Scrapbook 7, Simpson Archives, Las Vegas, New Mexico.

12

1. Audrey Simpson, "Memo Book," notes, op. cit.
2. Audrey Simpson, Letter to Rebekahs #1, Las Vegas, New Mexico, Fall meeting, 1971, Simpson Archives, Las Vegas, New Mexico.
3. Audrey Simpson, "Memo Book," op. cit.
4. Audrey Reid, "Holly," op. cit.
5. Audrey Simpson, "Manx ESP," copy of original manuscript submitted to and published by "Cat-ching Up," *Cat Fancy*, Vol. 23, Number 9, September, 1980, p. 2, Scrapbook 8, Simpson Archives, Las Vegas, New Mexico.
6. Audrey Simpson, "Miscellaneous Notes," op. cit.
7. Audrey Simpson, no bi-line, "Las Vegas Offers Winter Fun," caption under photograph in *New Mexico Magazine*, Vol. 28, No. 12, December, 1950, p. 40, marked copy indicating item was written by Audrey Simpson, Scrapbook 8, Simpson Archives, Las Vegas, New Mexico.

8. Audrey Simpson, "Notes About the 1971 Forest Fire," notes, Scrapbook 8, Simpson Archives, Las Vegas, New Mexico, n.d.
9. Audrey Simpson, "Burned Tree Poem," unpublished notes, n.d., Scrapbook 6, Simpson Archives, Las Vegas, New Mexico.
10 Audrey Simpson, "Today I Looked," unpublished poem, n.d., Scrapbook 7, Simpson Archives, Las Vegas, New Mexico.
11. Audrey Simpson, "The Roaring Flames," unpublished poem, n.d., Scrapbook 7, Simpson Archives, Las Vegas, New Mexico.
12. Audrey Simpson, "Twenty Miles of Mountains," unpublished poem, n.d., Scrapbook 7, Simpson Archives, Las Vegas, New Mexico.
13. Audrey Simpson, "The Mexican Nationals and Me," unpublished notes, n.d., Scrapbook 8, Simpson Archives, Las Vegas, New Mexico, n.d.
14. Audrey Simpson, "Russian Thistle," unpublished poem, n.d., Scrapbook 7, Simpson Archives, Las Vegas, New Mexico.
15. Audrey Reid, "Spring Gold," manuscript, April, 1986, Simpson Archives, Las Vegas, New Mexico.
16. Audrey Simpson, "Building Notes," op. cit.
17. Audrey Simpson, "He Passed a Miracle for Me," unpublished poem, 1975, Scrapbook 7, Simpson Archives, Las Vegas, New Mexico.
18. Audrey Simpson, "Obituary for Betty Hardin," notes, n.d., Scrapbook 8, Simpson Archives, Las Vegas, New Mexico.
19. Audrey Simpson, "She Was Always Ready to Go," 1975, unpublished poem, Simpson Scrapbook 7, Simpson Library, Las Vegas, New Mexico.

13

1. Audrey Simpson, "Holly," op. cit.
2. Audrey Reid, "Miscellaneous and Various Notes," op. cit.
3. Ibid.
4. Audrey Reid, "Holly," op. cit.
5. Ibid.
6. Ibid.
7. Ibid.
8. Audrey Reid, "The Electricity is Out," unpublished poem in Scrapbook 6, Simpson Archives, Las Vegas, New Mexico, n.d.
9. Audrey Simpson, "Bill's Excursion" in "Miscellaneous Notes," op. cit.
10. Audrey Simpson, "Miscellaneous Notes," op cit.
11. Audrey Simpson, "On This Whirling Earth," in "Miscellaneous Notes," op. cit.
12. Ibid.
13. Audrey Simpson, "Life," in "Miscellaneous Notes," op. cit.
14. Ibid.
15. Ibid.
16. Audrey Simpson, "I Weep," in "Miscellaneous Notes," op. cit.
17. Audrey Simpson, "Down to Night," unpublished poem in Scrapbook 6, Simpson Archives,, no date.
18. Audrey Simpson, "Remember the Years," op. cit.
19. Audrey Simpson, "Miscellaneous Notes," op. cit.
20. Ibid.
21. Audrey Simpson, "Can This Be Really I?" unpublished notes, Scrapbook 6, Simpson Archives, Las Vegas, New Mexico, n.d.

1. Audrey Simpson, "A Little Old Lady," unpublished handwritten poem, n.d., Scrapbook 7, Simpson Archives, Las Vegas, New Mexico.
2. Audrey Simpson, "Memo Book," op. cit.
3. Ibid.
4. Audrey Reid, letter to Blanche Huddleson, June, 1981, Scrapbook 7, Simpson Archives, Las Vegas, New Mexico.
5. Dorothy Simpson Beimer, *Hovels, Haciendas, and House Calls: The Life of Carl H. Gellenthien, M.D.*, Santa Fe: Sunstone Press, 1986.
6. Audrey Reid, "All Hail to our Doc!" unpublished poem, n.d., Scrapbook 7, Simpson Archives, Las Vegas, New Mexico.
7. Audrey Simpson, "Dear Census-taker: Do I still call it a privy?" copy of original manuscript submitted to and published by *Albuquerque Journal Magazine Impact*, Volume 3, Number 32, May 27, 1980, pp.12-13, Scrapbook 8, Simpson Archives, Las Vegas, New Mexico.
8. Ibid.
9. Ibid.
10. Audrey Simpson, "Impressive View of Mountain Range," *Las Vegas Daily Optic,* Las Vegas, New Mexico, August 1, 1957, p. B-1, Scrapbook 8, Simpson Archives, Las Vegas, New Mexico.
11. Audrey Simpson, no bi-line, "Hermit Lived on Peak," *Las Vegas Daily Optic,* August 1, 1957, p. B12-13, marked copy indicating item was written by Audrey Simpson, Scrapbook 4, Simpson Archives, Las Vegas, New Mexico.
12. Ibid., p. 13.
13. Audrey Simpson, "Hermits Peak Legend," copy of original manuscript submitted to and published by *Old West*, Vol. 24, No. 3, Spring, 1988, p. 50.
14. Ibid.
15. Audrey Simpson, no bi-line, "Two Caves In Area Offer Exploration," *Las Vegas Daily Optic, Rodeo Edition*, August 1, 1957, p. 13B, marked copy indicating item was written by Audrey Simpson, Simpson Archives, Las Vegas, New Mexico.
16. Wesley Lovett as told to Audrey Simpson, "Climbing the Organ Needle," unpublished manuscript, n.d., Scrapbook 8, Simpson Archives, Las Vegas, New Mexico.
17. Audrey Reid, Graduation Card of Congratulations to Dorothy Simpson, n.d., Simpson Archives, Las Vegas, New Mexico.
18. Audrey Reid, "Birthday Aftermath," unpublished poem, n.d., Scrapbook 7, Simpson Archives, Las Vegas, New Mexico.
19. Audrey Reid, "Happy Birthday poem to Milly," September 3, 1992, Scrapbook 7, Simpson Archives, Las Vegas, New Mexico.
20. Audrey Reid, "Laura Touched a Roadrunner," unpublished poem, n.d., Scrapbook 6, Simpson Archives, Las Vegas, New Mexico.

1. "Audrey Simpson Remembers," caption under photograph taken by Sharon Vander Meer, *Las Vegas Daily Optic, Monday*, November 9, 1992, p. 4, Simpson Archives, Las Vegas, New Mexico.
2. Audrey Reid, "Thank You" note to Dorothy and Rose, November 11, 1992, Scrapbook 8, Simpson Archives, Las Vegas, New Mexico.
3. Audrey Reid, "I Looked at Myself in the Mirror," unpublished note, n.d., Scrapbook 7, Simpson Archives, Las Vegas, New Mexico.
4. Elsa Barker, Birthday note to Audrey Simpson, November 11, no year, Scrapbook 7, Simpson Archives, Las Vegas, New Mexico.

5. Audrey Simpson, "Song of the Individualist," copy of original manuscript submitted to and published by *Today in Prose & Poetry*, Vol. 1, No. 3, January-February, 1941, Scrapbook 7, Simpson Archives, Las Vegas, New Mexico.

6. Audrey Simpson, "All Advance," copy of original manuscript submitted to and published by *The Friendly Journal*, Vol. II, No. 3, Issue 9, October-November, 1941, Waterbury, Conn., p. 5.

REFERENCES

Air Metal Citation, Donald Simpson. Copy from Rhea Oglesbee Archives, Scrapbook 3, Simpson Archives, Las Vegas, New Mexico.

"America the Beautiful." Program, New Mexico Highlands University, April 28, 2000, Las Vegas, New Mexico.

Arden, Clive. *The Enchanted Spring*. N.Y.: Grosset & Dunlap Publishers, 1935.

"Audrey Simpson Remembers." Caption under photograph by Sharon Vander Meer, *Las Vegas Daily Optic* (Las Vegas, New Mexico), Monday, November 9, 1992, p. 4, Simpson Archives, Las Vegas, New Mexico.

Barker, Elsa. Birthday note to Audrey Simpson, November 11, no year, Scrapbook 7, Simpson Archives, Las Vegas, New Mexico.

Barker, S. Omar. *Sunlight Through the Trees*. Las Vegas, New Mexico: Highlands University Press, 1954, p. 47.

"Beaumont Flier Killed by Flak: Sgt. Donald Simpson Dies Of Wounds Received Over Poland." Newspaper clipping from Rhea Oglesbee Archives, n.d., Scrapbook 3, Simpson Archives, Las Vegas, New Mexico and on CD numbers 4 and 084 in Simpson Archives, Las Vegas, New Mexico.

Beimer, Dorothy Simpson. "Dr. Mortimer." Chapter in unpublished manuscript, "Early Doctors in Las Vegas," Las Vegas, New Mexico, Simpson Archives, November, 1980, p. 90.

Beimer, Dorothy Simpson. *Hovels, Haciendas, and House Calls: The Life of Carl H. Gellenthien, M.D.* Santa Fe: Sunstone Press, 1986.

"'Bulldogging' Got Name From Lip Biting Cowboy," *Las Vegas Daily Optic* (Las Vegas, New Mexico), Wednesday, July 30, 1958, p. B6.

Caldwell, J. B. Caldwell. "Officer of the Guard March." Sheet music, Waitsburg, Washington: published by The Composer, MCMVII by J. B. Caldwell, Simpson Archives, Las Vegas, New Mexico.

Callon, Milton W. *Las Vegas, New Mexico—The Town That Wouldn't Gamble*. Las Vegas, New Mexico, Las Vegas Daily Optic, The Las Vegas Publishing Co., Inc., 1962.

Callon, Milton W. Interview by Audrey Simpson. Las Vegas, New Mexico, July, 1959.

Citation of Honor. Donald Simpson. Copy of certificate, n.d., from Rhea Oglesbee Archives, Scrapbook 3, Simpson Archives, Las Vegas, New Mexico.

Clements, A. C "Bear On A Grey Hackle." Copy of original manuscript submitted to and published by *Western Sportsman*, Vol. 10, No. 5 (July-August, 1950), p. 17, Scrapbook 8, Simpson Archives, Las Vegas, New Mexico.

Clements, Mabel. "A Thrilling Book." Unpublished poem, n.d., Scrapbook 2, Simpson Archives, Las Vegas, New Mexico.

Clements, Mabel. "Autumn Storm." Unpublished poem, n.d., Scrapbook 3, Simpson Archives, Las Vegas, New Mexico.

Clements, Mabel. "Better'n Walkin'." Unpublished poem, n.d., Scrapbook 3, in Simpson Archives, Las Vegas, New Mexico.

Clements, Mabel. "Christmas List." n.d., Scrapbook 1, Simpson Archives, Las Vegas, New Mexico.

Clements, Mabel. Christmas Note to Aunt Laura Waddell, n.d., Scrapbook 2, Simpson Archives, Las Vegas, New Mexico, n.d.

Clements, Mabel. "Christmas Verses." Unpublished Christmas poetry, n.d., Scrapbook 2, Simpson Archives, Las Vegas, New Mexico.

Clements, Mabel. "Cramming." Unpublished poem, n.d., Scrapbook 2, Simpson Archives, Las Vegas, New Mexico.

Clements, Mabel. "Flowers." Unpublished poem, n.d., Scrapbook 2, Simpson Archives, Las Vegas, New Mexico.

Clements, Mabel. Letter from MacInerney Ranch to a friend, Winter, 1919. Scrapbook 3, Simpson Archives, Las Vegas, New Mexico.

Clements, Mabel. "My Fingers Are So Small." Unpublished poem, n.d., Scrapbook 1, Simpson Archives, Las Vegas, New Mexico.

Clements, Mabel. "Not for School but for Life we Learn." Unpublished poem, *Pine top School Souvenir*, 1911, p. 7, Scrapbook 1, Simpson Archives, Las Vegas, New Mexico.

Clements, Mabel." Notes of Wisdom," n.d. Scrapbook 1, Simpson Archives, Las Vegas, New Mexico.

Clements, Mabel. "Notes on War," n.d., Scrapbook 1, Simpson Archives, Las Vegas, New Mexico.

Clements, Mabel. "Oh, God Give Me Courage." Unpublished poem, n.d., Scrapbook 2, Simpson Archives, Las Vegas, New Mexico.

"Cloud-Seeding Operation Halted For This Season." *Las Vegas Daily Optic*, (Las Vegas, New Mexico), July 25, 1952, p.1.

Croxton, Dorothy Simpson. "I Remember the Day the Lynx Attacked." *Backwoods Home Magazine*, No. 44 (March/April, 1997), pp. 53-54.

Croxton, Dorothy Simpson. "Mom Did What She Had to Do." Copy of original manuscript submitted to and published by *Cappers* (May 5, 1998), p. 24, Simpson Archives, Las Vegas, New Mexico.

Croxton, Dorothy Simpson. "Traveling Piano." Copy of original manuscript submitted to and published by *Antique Almanac*, Vol. 3, Issue 8 (October, 1996), p. 10, Simpson Archives, Las Vegas, New Mexico.

"Descendants of Joseph Rhode." Chapter 5, http:/home.earthlink.net/~case65/chapter5.htm.

Desprez, Frank. "Lasca," in *The Best Loved Poems of the American People*. Selected by Hazel Felleman, N.Y.: Doubleday & Company, Inc., 1936, pp. 257-259.

"Early Cowpunchers Rugged Individuals." *Las Vegas Daily Optic* (Las Vegas, New Mexico), July 30, 1958, p. B1.

Editorial Department, "Payment for your Story" card. *Capper's Weekly*, n.d., Scrapbook 7, Simpson Archives, Las Vegas, New Mexico.

"Epitaph of a Dog." *Poems from the Greek Anthology*. Translated by Dudley Fitts, New York: A New Directions Paperbook, 1956, p. 114.

"Final Rites Held George F. Hays, Victim of Rodeo." *Las Vegas Daily Optic* (Las Vegas, New Mexico), August 11, 1949, newspaper clipping, Scrapbook 8, Simpson Archives, Las Vegas, New Mexico.

"Fire Gutts Daily Optic Plant: Equipment Badly Damaged by Blaze." Caption under photograph, *Las Vegas Daily Optic* (Las Vegas, New Mexico), August 10, 1957, p. 1.

"Fire Gutts Daily Optic Plant: Equipment Badly Damaged by Blaze." *Las Vegas Daily Optic* (Las Vegas, New Mexico), August 10, 1957, p. 1.

"Former Highlands Student at 'Optic.'" *The Candle*, New Mexico Highlands University (Las Vegas, New Mexico), March 21, 1952, Scrapbook 2, Simpson Archives, Las Vegas, New Mexico.

"Fort Union, Historic Outpost, Now is National Monument." *Las Vegas Daily Optic* (Las Vegas, New Mexico), July 30, 1958, p. A1.

"Funeral Services for Rodeo Victim Set for Thursday." *Las Vegas Daily Optic* (Las Vegas, New Mexico), August 10, 1949, newspaper clipping, Scrapbook 8, Simpson Archives, Las Vegas, New Mexico.

"Gallinas School May Day Festival To Be Held Friday." Newspaper clipping from *Las Vegas Daily Optic,* (Las Vegas, New Mexico), handwritten date, April 30, 1953, in Simpson Archives, Las Vegas, New Mexico.

Gardner, Lelama. Interview by Dorothy Simpson Croxton, Las Vegas, New Mexico, August 25, 1998.

Gensemer, Millicent L. "Audrey Simpson: A Mother, Woman's Editor and Adventurer," *Las Vegas Daily Optic* (Las Vegas, New Mexico), n.d. newspaper clipping, Scrapbook 2, Simpson Archives, Las Vegas, New Mexico.

Giles, Shirley. Interview by Dorothy Simpson, Tucumcari, New Mexico, July 9, 2005.

Gilly, R., Pastor. Letter to Mrs. Addie Simpson, Herstal, Belgium, March 28, 1951, Rhea Oglesbee Archives and CD numbers 4 and 017, Simpson Archives, Las Vegas, New Mexico.

"Half a Century in Rodeo." *Las Vegas Daily Optic* (Las Vegas, New Mexico), July 6, 1965.

Hardin, Lt. Stanley A. Letter from India to Tana Marie Hardin, Raton, New Mexico, June 12, 1944, Tana Marie Hardin Archives, copy in Scrapbook 7, Simpson Archives, Las Vegas, New Mexico.

Hardin, Stanley A. as told to D. A. Simpson. *From Pajarito to Lungchow: Memoirs of Photographic Reconnaissance Pilot Stanley A. Hardin, Lt. Col., U.S.A.F., Ret.,* Bowie, Maryland: Eagle Editions, An Imprint of Heritage Books, 2003.

The Holy Bible, King James Version, N.Y.: Oxford University Press, 1967.

"Hubby Rations Love Wife Hits the Ceiling." *Daily* Mirror (New York, New York), August 21, 1946, n.d., newspaper clipping, Scrapbook 34 in Jessica Braziel Archives, copy in Scrapbook 3, Simpson Archives, Las Vegas, New Mexico.

"Jaycees Campaign For Discarded Toys." newspaper clipping from *Las Vegas Daily Optic* (Las Vegas, New Mexico), n.d., Scrapbook 8, Simpson Archives.

"Las Vegas Founded In 1835 Is Home of Rodeo, Rough Riders." *Las Vegas Daily Optic Rodeo Edition* (Las Vegas, New Mexico) July 30, 1958, p. B5, in Simpson Archives, Las Vegas, New Mexico.

Latici, Bruno. Letter to Addie Simpson, September 6, 1944, Rhea Oglesbee Archives, and CD numbers 4, 0167, and 0168, Simpson Archives, Las Vegas, New Mexico.

Lovett, Crystal Simpson. Interview by Dorothy Audrey Simpson, Las Vegas, New Mexico, October 5, 2006.

Lovett, Wesley, as told to Audrey Simpson. "Climbing the Organ Needle." Unpublished manuscript, n.d., Scrapbook 8, Simpson Archives, Las Vegas, New Mexico.

Madison. My Golden School Days: A Record Book for Happy Memories. n. p., 1911.

McCarty, Ray. Letter to Charles Vivian Shearer, March 19, 1944, Scrapbook 3, Simpson Archives, Las Vegas, New Mexico.

McCarty, Ray. Letter to R. A. Shearer, May 19, 1945, Scrapbook 3, Simpson Archives, Las Vegas, New Mexico.

"Mineral City Boomed Before 1900s." *Las Vegas Daily Optic Rodeo Edition*, (Las Vegas, New Mexico), August 6, 1953, p. B1.

"Mrs. Hardin Hostess as PW Pick Markets." Newspaper clipping, *Las Vegas Daily Optic* (Las Vegas, New Mexico), marked copy indicating item was written by Audrey Simpson, with handwritten date "May 13, 1953," Simpson Archives, Scrapbook 8, Simpson Library, Las Vegas, New Mexico.

Note on back of photograph of Donald Simpson and his crew, n.d., Rhea Oglesbee Archives, and CD numbers 3 and 079A, Simpson Archives, Las Vegas, New Mexico.

Note on back of photograph of Donald Simpson's "Flying Fortress" plane," n.d., Rhea Oglesbee Archives and CD numbers 4 and 079A, Simpson Archives, Las Vegas, New Mexico.

Note on photograph of MV Whale Knot, n.d., Rhea Oglesbee Archives and CD numbers 4 and 077, Simpson Archives, Las Vegas, New Mexico.

"Obituary, Clyde J. Simpson," *Las Vegas Daily Optic* (Las Vegas, New Mexico), April 22, 1965, newspaper clipping, Scrapbook 7, Simpson Archives, Las Vegas, New Mexico.

"Obituary, Clyde Joseph Simpson." *Las Vegas Daily Optic* (Las Vegas, New Mexico), April 20, 1965, newspaper clipping, Scrapbook 7, Simpson Archives, Las Vegas, New Mexico.

"Obituary, Dr. Gordon Evert Wickman." *Las Vegas Daily Optic*, (Las Vegas, New Mexico), June 20, 1997, p. 5.

"Obituary, Presillano Santillanes." *Las Vegas Daily Optic* (Las Vegas, New Mexico), August 18, 1997, p. 8.

Oglesbee, Rhea Simpson. Interview by Dorothy Audrey Simpson, Forest Springs Ranch, August 16, 2007.

"Operation Christmas Collects 1000 Toys." Newspaper clipping from *Las Vegas Daily Optic*, (Las Vegas, New Mexico), n.d., Scrapbook 8, Simpson Archives.

"Optic Society Editor Marries on Monday." *Las Vegas Daily Optic* (Las Vegas, New Mexico), June 9, 1953, p. 2.

"Pen Women Hear Dr. S. A. Hardin." *Las Vegas Daily Optic* (Las Vegas, New Mexico), Wedneday, March 11, 1953, p. 2.

"Plane Drops Birthday Gift to Miss Simpson." Newspaper clipping, n.d., *Las Vegas Daily Optic*, Las Vegas, New Mexico, Scrapbook 2, Simpson Archives.

"Poison Search Pressed Here." *Las Vegas Daily Optic* (Las Vegas, New Mexico), Thursday, August 20, 1953, p.1.

Reid, Audrey. "All Hail to our Doc!" Unpublished poem, n.d., Scrapbook 7, Simpson Archives, Las Vegas, New Mexico.

Reid, Audrey. "Bill's Excursion" in "Miscellaneous Notes." Unpublished notes, Scrapbook 4, Simpson Archives, Las Vegas, New Mexico, n.d.

Reid, Audrey. "Birthday Aftermath." Unpublished poem, n.d., Scrapbook 7, Simpson Archives, Las Vegas, New Mexico.

Reid, Audrey, "Birthday Poem to Milly." Unpublished poem, September 3, 1992, Scrapbook 7, Simpson Archives, Las Vegas, New Mexico.

Reid, Audrey (no bi-line). "The Boy Who Loved Flags." Copy of original manuscript submitted to and published by *True Romance: The All-Story Magazine,* Vol. 88, No. 5, July, 1969, p. 49, marked copy indicating item was written by Audrey Simpson, Simpson Archives, Las Vegas, New Mexico.

Reid, Audrey. "Crystal." Unpublished notes, n.d., Scrapbook 5, Simpson Archives, Las Vegas, New Mexico.

Reid, Audrey. "The Electricity is Out." Unpublished poem, n.d., Scrapbook 6, Simpson Archives, Las Vegas, New Mexico.

Reid, Audrey. "Favor Doubly Repaid." Unpublished manuscript, n.d., Scrapbook 7, Simpson Archives, Las Vegas, New Mexico.

Reid, Audrey. "Forest Springs Ranch History." Unpublished notes, n.d.,Scrapbook 3, Simpson Archives, Las Vegas, New Mexico.

Reid, Audrey. "The Grocery Store." Unpublished notes, n.d., in Scrapbook 7, Simpson Archives, Las Vegas, New Mexico.

Reid, Audrey. Graduation Card of Congratulations to Dorothy Simpson, n.d., Simpson Archives, Las Vegas, New Mexico.

Reid, Audrey. "Holly." Unpublished notes, n.d., Scrapbook 5, Simpson Archives, Las Vegas, New Mexico.

Reid, Audrey. "I Looked at Myself in the Mirror." Unpublished note, n.d., Scrapbook 7, Simpson Archives, Las Vegas, New Mexico.

Reid, Audrey. "I Weep," in "Miscellaneous Notes." Unpublished notes in Scrapbook 4, Simpson Archives, Las Vegas, New Mexico, n.d.

Reid, Audrey. Interview by Holly Simpson. Las Vegas, New Mexico, Tape 1, August 21, 1992, Simpson Archives, Las Vegas, New Mexico.

Reid, Audrey. Interview by Holly Simpson. Las Vegas, New Mexico, Tape 3, November 15, 1992, Simpson Archives, Las Vegas, New Mexico.

Reid, Audrey. Interview by Holly Simpson. Las Vegas, New Mexico, Tape 13, August 28, 1993, Simpson Archives, Las Vegas, New Mexico.

Reid, Audrey. Interview by Millicent Wickman. Las Vegas, New Mexico, Tape 1, August 21, 1992, Simpson Archives, Las Vegas, New Mexico.

Reid, Audrey. Interview by Millicent Wickman. Las Vegas, New Mexico, Tape 2, December, 1986, Simpson Archives, Las Vegas, New Mexico.

Reid, Audrey. Interview by Millicent Wickman. Las Vegas, New Mexico, Tape 3, February, 1987, Simpson Archives, Las Vegas, New Mexico.

Reid, Audrey. Interview by Millicent Wickman. Las Vegas, New Mexico, Tape 6, April 23, 1987, Simpson Archives, Las Vegas, New Mexico.

Reid, Audrey. Interview by Millicent Wickman. Las Vegas, New Mexico, Tape 8, May, 1987, Simpson Archives, Las Vegas, New Mexico.

Reid, Audrey. Interview by Millicent Wickman. Las Vegas, New Mexico, Tape 11, January 15, 1994, Simpson Archives, Las Vegas, New Mexico.

Reid, Audrey. Interview by Millicent Wickman. Las Vegas, New Mexico, Tape 12, January 18, 1994, Simpson Library, Las Vegas, New Mexico.

Reid, Audrey. Interview by Millicent Wickman. Las Vegas, New Mexico, Tape 16, February 11, 1994, Simpson Archives, Las Vegas, New Mexico.

Reid, Audrey. Interview by Millicent Wickman. Las Vegas, New Mexico, Tape 17, February 17, 1994, SimpsonArchives, Las Vegas, New Mexico.

Reid, Audrey. Interview by Millicent Wickman. Las Vegas, New Mexico, Tape 22, April 21, 1994, Simpson Archives, Las Vegas, New Mexico.

Reid, Audrey. Interview by Millicent Wickman. Las Vegas, New Mexico, Tape 23, March 5, 1994, Simpson Archives,Las Vegas, New Mexico.

Reid, Audrey. Interview by Millicent Wickman. Las Vegas, New Mexico, Tape 24, March, 1994, Simpson Archives, Las Vegas, New Mexico.

Reid, Audrey. Interview by Millicent Wickman. Las Vegas, New Mexico, Tape 25, March 16, 1994, Simpson Archives, Las Vegas, New Mexico

Reid, Audrey. Interview by Millicent Wickman. Las Vegas, New Mexico, Tape 28, April 1, 1994, Simpson Archives, Las Vegas, New Mexico.

Reid, Audrey. Interview by Millicent Wickman. Las Vegas, New Mexico, Tape 29, April 18, 1994, Simpson Archives, Las Vegas, New Mexico.

Reid, Audrey. Interview by Millicent Wickman. Las Vegas, New Mexico, Tape 30, May, 1994, Simpson Archives, Las Vegas, New Mexico.

Reid, Audrey. Interview by Millicent Wickman. Las Vegas, New Mexico, Tape 31, May, 1994, Simpson Archives, Las Vegas, New Mexico.

Reid, Audrey. Interview by Millicent Wickman. Las Vegas, New Mexico, Tape 33, Simpson Archives, Las Vegas, New Mexico, Fall, 1994.

Reid, Audrey. Interview by Millicent Wickman. Las Vegas, New Mexico, Tape 34, Fall, 1994, Simpson Archives, Las Vegas, New Mexico.

Reid, Audrey. "Laura Touched a Roadrunner." Unpublished poem, n.d., Scrapbook 6, Simpson Archives, Las Vegas, New Mexico.

Reid, Audrey. Letter to Blanche Huddleson, June, 1981, Scrapbook 7, Simpson Archives, Las Vegas, New Mexico.

Reid, Audrey. "Life," in "Miscellaneous Notes." Unpublished notes in Scrapbook 4, Simpson Archives, Las Vegas, New Mexico, n.d.

Reid, Audrey. "Memoirs." Las Vegas, New Mexico, Tape 3, November, 1988, Simpson Archives, Las Vegas, New Mexico.

Reid, Audrey. "Miscellaneous and Various Notes." Unpublished notes, n.d., Scrapbook 5, Simpson Archives, Las Vegas, New Mexico.

Reid, Audrey. "Miscellaneous Notes." Unpublished notes in Scrapbook 4, Simpson Archives, Las Vegas, New Mexico, n.d.

Reid, Audrey. "Notes About Writing." Unpublished notes, n.d., in Scrapbook 7, Simpson Archives, Las Vegas, New Mexico, n.d.

Reid, Audrey. Notes in Memo Book, n.d., Simpson Archives, Las Vegas, New Mexico.

Reid, Audrey. "Notes on the Carringtons." Notes, n.d., Scrapbook 4, Simpson Archives, Las Vegas, New Mexico.

Reid, Audrey. "Notes on Wild Horses." Unpublished notes, n.d., Scrapbook 4, Simpson Archives, Las Vegas, New Mexico.

Reid, Audrey. "On This Whirling Earth," in "Miscellaneous Notes." Unpublished notes in Scrapbook 4, Simpson Archives, Las Vegas, New Mexico, n.d.

Reid, Audrey. "Recollections." Letter to Editor, *Grit* (February 12, 1986), n.p., Scrapbook 5, Simpson Archives, Las Vegas, New Mexico.

Reid, Audrey. "Recollections: Wagon Runs Over My Tummy When Car Scares Our Mules." Copy of original manuscript submitted to and published by *Grit,* Wednesday, September 7, 1983, Scrapbook 2, Simpson Archives, Las Vegas, New Mexico.

Reid, Audrey. "Some Early Childhood Memories." Unpublished notes, 1985, Scrapbook 7, Simpson Archives, Las Vegas, New Mexico.

Reid, Audrey. "Spring Gold." Manuscript, April, 1986, Simpson Archives, Las Vegas, New Mexico.

Reid. Audrey. Thank You Note to Dorothy and Rose, November 11, 1991, Scrapbook 8, Simpson Archives, Las Vegas, New Mexico.

Reid, Mrs. W. A., Sr., "Letter to the Editor." *Albuquerque Journal* (Albuquerque, New Mexico) April 15, 1981, Scrapbook 6, Simpson Archives.

Roberts, Oral. *Expect a Miracle: My Life and Ministry, An Autobiography*. Nashville: Thomas Nelson Publishers, 1995.

Roberts, Oral. "New Lease on Life." Paper fragment from *Abundant Life Magazine,* n.d., Simpson Archives, Las Vegas, New Mexico.

Santillanes, Presillano. Interview by Dorothy Simpson Croxton, Forest Springs Ranch, January 30, 1997.

"School Children Give Jaycees Toys." Newspaper clipping from *Las Vegas Daily Optic* (Las Vegas, New Mexico), 1952, Scrapbook 8, Simpson Archives, Las Vegas, New Mexico.

Shearer, Charles Vivian. Letter about job interview, February 14, 1935, Scrapbook 2, Simpson Archives, Las Vegas, New Mexico.

Shearer, Charles Vivian. Letter to Arolvi and Paul Dale, August 12, 1949, Jessica Braziel's Archives and CD number 017 in Simpson Archives, Las Vegas, New Mexico.

Shearer, Charles Vivian. Letter to Arolvi and Paul, January 21, 1950, Jessica Braziel's Archives and CD number 012 in Simpson Archives, Las Vegas, New Mexico.

Shearer, Charles Vivian. Letter to Ray McCarty, June 2, 1942, Scrapbook 3, Simpson Archives, Las Vegas, New Mexico.

Shearer, Charles Vivian. "Man's Stewardship of the Earth" and "The Conservation of Soil and Moisture." *New Mexico Highlands University Bulletin.* 147, Las Vegas, New Mexico: New Mexico Highlands University, November, 1943, pp. 3-27.

Shearer, Mabel. Christmas letter to a friend, n.d., Scrapbook 2, Simpson Archives, Las Vegas, New Mexico.

Shearer, Mabel."Christmas Poem." Unpublished poem, n.d., Scrapbook 2, Simpson Archives, Las Vegas, New Mexico.

Shearer, Mabel. "Items needed and prices list." Fall, 1930, Scrapbook 2, Simpson Archives, Las Vegas, New Mexico.

Shearer, Mabel. "I Went to Buy a Hat Today." Unpublished poem, n.d., Scrapbook 2, Simpson Archives, Las Vegas, New Mexico.

Shearer, Mabel. Letter 1 to Charles Vivian Shearer, December, 1925, Jessica Braziel Archives, Tucumcari, New Mexico and CD numbers 093 and 094, Simpson Archives, Las Vegas, New Mexico.

Shearer, Mabel. Letter 2 to Charles Vivian Shearer, December, 1925, Jessica Braziel Archives, Tucumcari, New Mexico and CD numbers 093 and 094, Simpson Archives, Las Vegas, New Mexico.

Shearer, Mabel. Letter 3 to Charles Vivian Shearer, December, 1925, Jessica Braziel Archives, Tucumcari, New Mexico and CD number 125, Simpson Archives, Las Vegas, New Mexico.

Shearer, Mabel. Letter 4 to Charles Vivian Shearer, December, 1925, Jessica Braziel Archives, Tucumcari, New Mexico and CD numbers 119 and 120, Simpson Archives, Las Vegas, New Mexico.

Shearer, Mabel. Letter 5 to Charles Vivian Shearer, December 15, 1925, Jessica Braziel Archives, Tucumcari, New Mexico and CD number 121, Simpson Archives, Las Vegas, New Mexico.

Shearer Mabel. Letter 6 to Charles Vivian Shearer, December, 1925, Jessica Braziel Archives, Tucumcari, New Mexico and CD numbers 120 and 121, Simpson Archives, Las Vegas, New Mexico.

Shearer, Mabel. Letter 7 to Charles Vivian Shearer, December, 1925, Jessica Braziel Archives, Tucumcari, New Mexico and CD number 123, Simpson Archives, Las Vegas, New Mexico.

Shearer, Mabel. Letter about collecting money, n.d., Scrapbook 1, Simpson Archives, Las Vegas, New Mexico.

Shearer, Mabel. Letter about Dorothy, February 29, 1944, Scrapbook 2, Simpson Archives, Las Vegas, New Mexico.

Shearer, Mabel. Letter to Frank Waddell, 1932, Scrapbook 2, Simpson Archives, Las Vegas, New Mexico.

Shearer, Mabel. Letter to Mr. H. *The Denver Post*, n.d., Scrapbook 2, Simpson Archives, Las Vegas, New Mexico.

Shearer, Mabel. Letter to Thelma Shirley, n.d., Scrapbook 1, Simpson Archives, Las Vegas, New Mexico.

Shearer, Mabel. "My Pupils Dear." Unpublished poem, *Pine Top School Souvenir*, 1911, Scrapbook 1, Simpson Archives, Las Vegas, New Mexico, p. 7.

Shearer, Mabel. "Note." Cover of sheet music note, J. B. Caldwell, "Officer of the Guard March," Waitsburg, Washington: Published by The Composer, MCMVII, Simpson Archives, Las Vegas, New Mexico.

Shearer, Mabel. "Note to Audrey." Note in *Madison, My Golden School Days: A Record Book of Happy Memories,* n.p., 1911, p. 65.

Shearer, Mabel. "Notes, March, 1969." Simpson Scrapbook 8, Simpson Archives, Las Vegas, New Mexico.

Shearer, Mabel. "Notes, June, 1969." Scrapbook 8, Simpson Archives, Las Vegas, New Mexico.

Shearer, Mabel. "Sugar." Note, n.d., Scrapbook 2, Simpson Archives, Las Vegas, New Mexico.

Shearer, Mabel. "War Cake." Notes, Scrapbook 2, n.d., Simpson Archives, Las Vegas, New Mexico.

Shirley, T. F. Business card. Scrapbook 1, Simpson Archives, Las Vegas, New Mexico.

Simpson, Audrey. "A Little Old Lady." Unpublished poem, n.d., Scrapbook 7, Simpson Archives, Las Vegas, New Mexico.

Simpson, Audrey. "A Lynx Raided my Home." Copy of original manuscript submitted to and published by *Western Sportsman* (March/April, 1953), p. 9, Scrapbook 7, Simpson Archives, Las Vegas, New Mexico.

Simpson, Audrey. "Anticipation." Copy of original manuscript submitted to and published by *The American Baby: The National Magazine for Mothers of Infants*, July, 1944, p. 9, Scrapbook 5, Simpson Archives, Las Vegas, New Mexico.

Simpson, Audrey."A Walk for Rain." Unpublished manuscript, n.d., Scrapbook 7, Simpson Archives, Las Vegas, New Mexico.

Simpson, Audrey. "A Walk for Water." Unpublished notes, n.d., Scrapbook 7, Simpson Archives, Las Vegas, New Mexico.

Simpson, Audrey. "All Advance." Copy of original manuscript submitted to and published by *The Friendly Journal,* Vol. II, No. 3, Issue Nine (Oct.-Nov., 1941), p. 5, Scrapbook 7, Simpson Archives, Las Vegas, New Mexico.

Simpson, Simpson. "All Day the Ashes Fell." Unpublished poem, n.d., Scrapbook 6, Simpson Archives, Las Vegas, New Mexico.

Simpson, Audrey. (no bi-line) "An Item From History," *Las Vegas Daily Optic, Rodeo Edition,* (Las Vegas, New Mexico), July 31, 1952, p. 4-B, marked copy indicating item was written by Audrey Simpson, Scrapbook 4, Simpson Archives, Las Vegas, New Mexico.

Simpson, Audrey. (no bi-line) "An Item From History." *Las Vegas Daily Optic, Rodeo Edition,* July 31, 1952, p. 5-B, marked copy indicating item was written by Audrey Simpson, Scrapbook 4, Simpson Archives, Las Vegas, New Mexico.

Simpson, Audrey. "Arriving in Las Vegas." Unpublished manuscript, n.d., Scrapbook 4, Simpson Archives, Las Vegas, New Mexico.

Simpson, Audrey. "Autobiography." Unpublished notes, 1979, Scrapbook 9, Simpson Archives, Las Vegas, New Mexico.

Simpson, Audrey."Barbed Wire Phone Line. " Unpublished manuscript, n.d.,Scrapbook 7, Simpson Archives, Las Vegas, New Mexico.

Simpson, Audrey. (no bi-line) "Bernal Historic Village 14 Miles South of Vegas." *Las Vegas Daily Optic, Rodeo Edition* (Las Vegas, New Mexico), July 31, 1952, p. 6B, marked copy indicating item written by Audrey Simpson, Scrapbook 4, Simpson Archives, Las Vegas, New Mexico.

Simpson, Audrey. (no bi-line) "Bernal Recalled By Old-Timers." *Las Vegas Daily, Optic Rodeo Edition* (Las Vegas, New Mexico), July 31, 1952, p.7B, marked copy indicating item was written by Audrey Simpson, Scrapbook 4, Simpson Archives, Las Vegas, New Mexico.

Simpson, Audrey. "Betty." Unpublished notes, n.d., Scrapbook 5, Simpson Archives, Las Vegas, New Mexico.

Simpson, Audrey."The Big Cross Trail." Copy of original manuscript submitted to and published by *New Mexico Magazine,* Vol. 29, No. 3 (March, 1951), pp. 29, 46-47, Scrapbook 8,Simpson Archives, Las Vegas, New Mexico.

Simpson, Audrey. (no bi-line) "The Big Cross Trail." Photograph and caption, *Las Vegas Daily Optic Rodeo Edition,* (Las Vegas, New Mexico), July 31, 1952, p. 1C, marked copy indicating the photo and caption were by Audrey Simpson, Simpson Archives, Las Vegas, New Mexico.

Simpson, Audrey. "Bonfire." Copy of original manuscript submitted to and published by *New Mexico Magazine,* Vol. 22, No. 5 (May, 1944), p. 20, Scrapbook 6, Simpson Archives, Las Vegas, New Mexico.

Simpson, Audrey. (no bi-line) "The Boy Who Loved Flags." Copy of original manuscript submitted to and published by *True Romance: The All-Story Magazine,* Vol. 88, No. 5, July, 1969, p. 49, marked copy indicating item was written by Audrey Simpson, in Simpson Archives, Las Vegas, New Mexico.

Simpson, Audrey. "Bronco Bustin' Dog." Copy of original manuscript submitted to and published by *Dog Fancy.* Vol. 11, No. 7 (December, 1980), p.2, Scrapbook 3, Simpson Archives, Las Vegas, New Mexico.

Simpson, Audrey. "Building Notes." Unpublished handwritten notes, n.d., Scrapbook 8, Simpson Archives, Las Vegas, New Mexico.

Simpson, Audrey. "Burned Tree Poem." Unpublished poem, n.d., Scrapbook 6, Simpson Archives, Las Vegas, New Mexico.

Simpson, Audrey. "Can This Be Really I?" Unpublished notes, n.d., Scrapbook 6, Simpson Archives, Las Vegas, New Mexico.

Simpson, Audrey. "Chasing Wild Horses." Unpublished, handwritten notes, Simpson Archives, Las Vegas, New Mexico, n. d.

Simpson, Audrey. "Christmas in Taos." Unpublished poem, n.d., Scrapbook 4, Simpson Archives, Las Vegas, New Mexico.

Simpson, Audrey."Close Escapes. " Unpublished notes, n.d., Scrapbook 5, Simpson Archives, Las Vegas, New Mexico.

Simpson, Audrey. (no bi-line) "Coal Outcrops in Las Vegas Section," *Las Vegas Daily Optic Rodeo Edition*, (Las Vegas, New Mexico), July 31, 1952, p. 7-B, marked copy indicating item was written by Audrey Simpson, Scrapbook 4, Simpson Archives, Las Vegas, New Mexico.

Simpson, Audrey. "Cowboy Answers the Questionnaire." *Las Vegas Daily Optic, Rodeo Edition* (Las Vegas, New Mexico), July 31, 1952, p. 2B, Scrapbook 2, Simpson Archives, Las Vegas, New Mexico.

Simpson, Audrey. "Cowboy's Reunion Notes." Unpublished notes, n.d., Scrapbook 5, Simpson Archives, Las Vegas, New Mexico.

Simpson, Audrey. (no bi-line) "Cowgal's Dream Broken by Horse Bear Spooked." *Las Vegas Daily Optic, Rodeo Edition* (Las Vegas, New Mexico), July, 1952, p. 5-B, marked copy indicating item was written by Audrey Simpson, Scrapbook 4, Simpson Archives, Las Vegas, New Mexico.

Simpson, Audrey. "Day's Work." *Las Vegas Daily Optic, Rodeo Edition*, (Las Vegas, New Mexico,) August 1, 1957, p. B4.

Simpson, Audrey. "Dear Census-taker: Do I still call it a privy?" Copy of original manuscript submitted to and published by *Albuquerque Journal Magazine Impact*, Albuquerque, New Mexico, Volume 3, Number 32, (May 27, 1980), pp.12-13, Scrapbook 8, Simpson Archives, Las Vegas, New Mexico.

Simpson, Audrey."Dear Kate." Unpublished Letter to the Editor, *Capper's Magazine*, n.d., Scrapbook 7, Simpson Archives, Las Vegas, New Mexico.

Simpson, Audrey. "Dear Ma Bell." Letter to the Editor, *Empire Magazine, The Denver Post,* August 4, 1985, Scrapbook 7, Simpson Archives, Las Vegas, New Mexico.

Simpson, Audrey. "Dear Ma Bell." Unpublished manuscript, n.d., Scrapbook 7, Simpson Archives, Las Vegas, New Mexico.

Simpson, Audrey. "Dear Post Office." Unpublished letter, n.d., Scrapbook 7, Simpson Archives, Las Vegas, New Mexico.

Simpson, Audrey. "Departure." Copy of original manuscript submitted to and published by *Today: In Prose & Poetry*, Vol. 1, No. 4 (March-April, 1941), p. 17, Scrapbook 7, Simpson Archives, Las Vegas, New Mexico.

Simpson, Audrey. "Desert Rain." Copy of original manuscript submitted to and published "Poems of New Mexico," *New Mexico Magazine*, Vol. 27, No. 6, June, 1949, p. 24, Scrapbook 7, Simpson Archives, Las Vegas, New Mexico.

Simpson, Audrey.(no bi-line) "Dog was Horse Rider." *Las Vegas Daily Optic Rodeo Edition* (Las Vegas, New Mexico) August 1, 1957, p. B10, marked copy indicating item was written by Audrey Simpson, Simpson Archives, Las Vegas, New Mexico.

Simpson, Audrey. "Down to Night." Unpublished poem, n.d., Scrapbook 6, Simpson Archives.

Simpson. Audrey. (no bi-line) "Early Day Roses Still Bloom Here." *Las Vegas Daily Optic* (Las Vegas, New Mexico), July 3, 1954, p. A-4, marked copy indicating item was written by Audrey Simpson, Simpson Archives, Las Vegas, New Mexico.

Simpson, Audrey. (no bi-line). "Early Mail Route To Ancient City North of Barillas." *Las Vegas Daily Optic, Rodeo Edition* (Las Vegas, New Mexico), July 31, 1952, p. A5, marked copy indicating item was written by Audrey Simpson, Scrapbook 8, Simpson Archives, Las Vegas, New Mexico.

Simpson, Audrey. "Editor, Special Christmas." Letter to the Editor, *Albuquerque Journal*, for "Your Most Memorable Christmas" section, Scrapbook 7, Simpson Archives, Las Vegas, New Mexico, November, 1987.

Simpson, Audrey. "Evening Rain." Copy of original manuscript submitted to and published by *The Joy Bearer*, Vol. 11, No. 11, (November, 1948), p. 11, Scrapbook 8, Simpson Archives, Las Vegas, New Mexico.

Simpson, Audrey. "Every Day Since 1879." *Las Vegas Daily Optic* (Las Vegas, New Mexico), August 10, 1957, p.1.

Simpson, Audrey. "Everyone Has Choices." Unpublished notes, n.d., Scrapbook 4, Simpson Archives, Las Vegas, New Mexico.

Simpson, Audrey. "Fear—Our Deadly Enemy." Copy of original manuscript submitted to and published by *The Joy Bearer*, Volume 14, Number 9 (September, 1951), pp. 11-12, Scrapbook 6, Simpson Archives, Las Vegas, New Mexico.

Simpson, Audrey."Fiesta Traditional Good Time in Las Vegas." *Las Vegas Daily Optic, Rodeo and Fiesta Edition* (Las Vegas, New Mexico), 1965, p. 2, Scrapbook 7, Simpson Archives, Las Vegas, New Mexico.

Simpson, Audrey. "The Fire, 1971." Unpublished notes, n.d., Scrapbook 8, Simpson Archives, Las Vegas, New Mexico.

Simpson, Audrey."For About 70 Years." Letter to the Editor, *Las Vegas Daily Optic,* Las Vegas, New Mexico, n.d., newspaper clipping, Scrapbook 5, Simpson Archives, Las Vegas, New Mexico.

Simpson, Audrey. "Forecast of Winter." Unpublished poem, n.d., Scrapbook 7, Simpson Archives, Las Vegas, New Mexico.

Simpson, Audrey. "The Fort that Won the West." Copy of original manuscript submitted to and published by *New Mexico Magazine,* Vol. 28, No. 12 (December, 1950), pp.14-15, 44, 47 and 49, Scrapbook 8, Simpson Archives, Las Vegas, New Mexico.

Simpson, Audrey. "Freckle Time is Coming." Unpublished poem, n.d., Scrapbook 7, Simpson Archives, Las Vegas, New Mexico.

Simpson, Audrey. "Free Lance—Unemployed—Housewife." Copy of original manuscript submitted to and published by *Kansas City Poetry Magazine,* Vol. 10 (September Issue, August, 1950), p. 14, Scrapbook 4, Simpson Archives, Las Vegas, New Mexico.

Simpson, Audrey. (no bi-line) "Gallinas Ponds used for Storage and Ice-Skating." *Las Vegas Daily Optic,* (Las Vegas, New Mexico), Thursday, July 31, 1952, p. 3A, marked copy indicating item was written by Audrey Simpson, Scrapbook 8, Simpson Archives, Las Vegas, New Mexico.

Simpson, Audrey. "Game-Keeper." *Las Vegas Daily Optic, Rodeo Edition* (Las Vegas, New Mexico), July 31, 1952, p. 2-B.

Simpson, Audrey. (no bi-line given) "Gold Tooth John Colorful Early Day Character." *Las Vegas Daily Optic, Rodeo Edition,* (Las Vegas, New Mexico), July 31, 1952, p. 5-B, marked copy indicating item was written by Audrey Simpson, Scrapbook 4, Simpson Archives, Las Vegas, New Mexico.

Simpson, Audrey. "Grandpa and all." Letter, December 19, 1919, found in *Madison, My School Days: A Record Book for Happy Memories,* 1911.

Simpson, Audrey."The Guy in the Cowboy Hat." Unpublished notes, n.d., Scrapbook 6, Simpson Archives, Las Vegas, New Mexico.

Simpson, Audrey. (no bi-line) "Hail Tumbles Down on Country in Wild Spree." *Las Vegas Daily Optic,* Las Vegas, New Mexico, July 31, 1952, p. 1A, marked copy indicating item was written by Audrey Simpson, Scrapbook 4, Simpson Archives, Las Vegas, New Mexico.

Simpson, Audrey. "He Passed a Miracle for Me." Unpublished poem, 1975, Scrapbook 7, Simpson Archives, Las Vegas, New Mexico.

Simpson, Audrey."He Passed Here." Copy of original manuscript submitted to and published by *The Joy Bearer,* Vol. 12, No. 9 (September, 1949), p. 16, Scrapbook 6, Simpson Archives, Las Vegas, New Mexico.

Simpson, Audrey. "Helping Mama." Unpublished notes, n.d., Scrapbook 5, Simpson Archives, Las Vegas, New Mexico.

Simpson, Audrey. "Here's To My Holly." Unpublished poem, n.d., Scrapbook 5, Simpson Archives, Las Vegas, New Mexico.

Simpson, Audrey. (no bi-line) "Hermit Lived on Peak." *Las Vegas Daily Optic* (Las Vegas, New Mexico), August 1, 1957, pp. B12-B13, marked copy indicating item was written by Audrey Simpson, Scrapbook 4, Simpson Archives, Las Vegas, New Mexico.

Simpson, Audrey. "Hermits Peak Legend." Copy of original manuscript submitted to and published by *Old West,* Vol. 24, No. 3, (Spring, 1988), pp. 49-51, Scrapbook 7, Simpson Archives, Las Vegas, New Mexico.

Simpson, Audrey. "Hey! Riddle, Riddle!" Copy of original manuscript submitted to and published by *Scimitar and Song,* Vol. XIV, No. 1 (July, 1951), Scrapbook 7, Simpson Archives, Las Vegas, New Mexico.

Simpson, Audrey."High Country Lament." Copy of original manuscript submitted to and published by *The Denver Post,* Scrapbook 3, Simpson Archives, n.d.

Simpson, Audrey. "High-Wheelers of Santa Fe Trail May be Recalled." *Las Vegas Daily Optic, Rodeo Edition* (Las Vegas, New Mexico), July 31, 1952, p. 5-B.

Simpson, Audrey. "History of Forest Springs Ranch, Including Digressions about Area." Unpublished notes, n.d., Scrapbook 3, Simpson Archives, Las Vegas, New Mexico.

Simpson, Audrey. "History of the Mineral Hill Road." Letter to the Editor," *The Las Vegas Daily Optic* (Las Vegas, New Mexico), n.d., Scrapbook 7, Simpson Archives, Las Vegas, New Mexico.

Simpson, Audrey. Holly's Birth Announcement Card. March, 1955, Scrapbook 5, Simpson Archives, Las Vegas, New Mexico.

Simpson, Audrey. "Homestead in Happy Canyon." Copy of original manuscript submitted to and published by *New Mexico Magazine,* Vol. 29, No. 12 (December, 1951), Scrapbook 6, Simpson Archives, Las Vegas, New Mexico.

Simpson, Audrey. "I Hate Being Small," in "Mountain Living." Unpublished notes, n.d., Scrapbook 6, Simpson Archives, Las Vegas, New Mexico.

Simpson, Audrey. "I'm Going Forward to Jesus." Unpublished verse, n.d., Scrapbook 7, Simpson Archives, Las Vegas, New Mexico.

Simpson, Audrey. "Impressive View of Mountain Range." *Las Vegas Daily Optic,* (Las Vegas, New Mexico), August 1, 1957, B-1, marked copy indicating item was written by Audrey Simpson, Scrapbook 8, Simpson Archives, Las Vegas, New Mexico.

Simpson, Audrey. "Indians Captured Boy, Adopted Him; Made Subject Of History." *Las Vegas Daily Optic, Rodeo Edition,* (Las Vegas, New Mexico), August 1, 1957, p. B-4.

Simpson, Audrey. Interview with Milton Callon. Las Vegas, New Mexico, notes, Scrapbook 3, Simpson Archives, Las Vegas, New Mexico, July, 1959.

Simpson, Audrey. "Jessica's Arrival." Unpublished notes, n.d., Scrapbook 4, Simpson Archives, Las Vegas, New Mexico.

Simpson, Audrey. "Just a Little Thing." Unpublished manuscript, n.d., Scrapbook 7, Simpson Archives, Las Vegas, New Mexico.

Simpson, Audrey. (no bi-line) "Kearney's Gap Torreón Protected Travelers," *Las Vegas Daily Optic, Rodeo Edition* (Las Vegas, New Mexico), July 31, 1952, p.5-A, marked copy indicating item was written by Audrey Simpson, Scrapbook 8, Simpson Archives, Las Vegas, New Mexico.

Simpson, Audrey (no bi-line). "Kearney's Gap Was Important Avenue For Early Travel," *Las Vegas Daily Optic, Rodeo Edition*, August 1, 1957, p. B-4, marked copy indicating item was written by Audrey Simpson, Scrapbook 8, Simpson Archives, Las Vegas, New Mexico.

Simpson, Audrey. "Kisses." Copy of original manuscript submitted to and published by *Kansas City Poetry Magazine,* Vol. 10, No. 8 (May, 1950), p. 14, Scrapbook 7, Simpson Archives, Las Vegas, New Mexico.

Simpson, Audrey. (no bi-line) "Las Vegas Offers Winter Fun." Caption under photograph, *New Mexico Magazine*, Vol. 28, No. 12 (December, 1950), p. 40, marked copy indicating item was written by Audrey Simpson, Scrapbook 8, Simpson Archives, Las Vegas, New Mexico.

Simpson, Audrey (no bi-line). "Lesperance Sawmill Once Of Pioneer Industries." *Las Vegas Daily Optic*, (Las Vegas, New Mexico), July 31, 1952, p. 4-B, marked copy indicating story was written by Audrey Simpson, Simpson Archives, Las Vegas, New Mexico.

Simpson, Audrey. "The Leaves Were Green." Unpublished poem, n.d., Scrapbook 6, Simpson Archives, Las Vegas, New Mexico.

Simpson, Audrey. Letter on firefighting, n.d., Scrapbook 7, Simpson Archives, Las Vegas, New Mexico.

Simpson, Audrey. Letter to the Editor. *Albuquerque Journal* (Albuquerque, New Mexico), n.d., Scrapbook 6, Simpson Archives, Las Vegas, New Mexico.

Simpson, Audrey. Letter to Mrs. Clark Ranney, 1967, Scrapbook 8, Simpson Archives, Las Vegas, New Mexico.

Simpson, Audrey. Letter to Millicent Shearer Alpern, August 25, 1946, Scrapbook 3, Simpson Archives, Las Vegas, New Mexico.

Simpson, Audrey. Letter to the Editor. *Empire Magazine, The Denver Post,* August 4, 1985, Scrapbook 7, Simpson Archives, Las Vegas, New Mexico.

Simpson, Audrey. Letter to the Editor. *Las Vegas Daily Optic* (Las Vegas, New Mexico) October 8, 1988, Scrapbook 6, Simpson Archives, Las Vegas, New Mexico.

Simpson, Audrey. Letter to Oral Roberts, n.d., Scrapbook 7, Simpson Archives, Las Vegas, New Mexico.

Simpson, Audrey. Letter to potential publishers, n.d., Scrapbook 5, Simpson Archives, Las Vegas, New Mexico.

Simpson, Audrey. Letter to Rebekahs #1. Las Vegas, New Mexico, Fall, 1971, Scrapbook 8, Simpson Archives, Las Vegas, New Mexico.

Simpson, Audrey. Letter to San Miguel County Commissioners, February 15, 1986, Scrapbook 5, Simpson Archives, Las Vegas, New Mexico.

Simpson, Audrey. Letter to telephone company, March 18, 1985, Scrapbook 8, Simpson Archives, Las Vegas, New Mexico.

Simpson, Audrey. Letter to the U. S. Forest Service, n.d., Scrapbook 6, Simpson Archives, Las Vegas, New Mexico.

Simpson, Audrey. "Life Comes From Above." Unpublished poem, n.d., Scrapbook 6, Simpson Archives, Las Vegas, New Mexico.

Simpson, Audrey. (no bi-line) "Log House Keeps Her Snug in Mountains." Copy of original manuscript submitted to and published by *Capper's Weekly*, Volume 91 No. 40, (November 7, 1967), p.14, Scrapbook 8, Simpson Archives, Las Vegas, New Mexico.

Simpson, Audrey. (no bi-line) "Ma Saved the Bacon: Women Had Courage." *Las Vegas Daily Optic* (Las Vegas, New Mexico), July 31, 1952, p, 2-B, marked copy indicating item was written by Audrey Simpson, Scrapbook 4, Simpson Archives, Las Vegas, New Mexico.

Simpson, Audrey. (no bi-line) "Mail Order Plan." Copy of original manuscript submitted to and published by "Pet Peeves," *True Romance,* (October, 1970), Scrapbook 8, Simpson Archives, Las Vegas, New Mexico.

Simpson, Audrey, "Maneuver for Victory," copy of original manuscript submitted to and published by *The Friendly Journal*, Vol. VIII, No. 3 (Oct.-Nov., 1942), p. 1.

Simpson, Audrey. "Manx ESP." Copy of original manuscript submitted to and published by "Cat-ching Up," *Cat Fancy*, Vol. 23, Number 9 (September, 1980), p. 2, Scrapbook 8, Simpson Archives, Las Vegas, New Mexico.

Simpson, Audrey. "The Mexican Nationals and Me." Unpublished notes, n.d., Scrapbook 8, Simpson Archives, Las Vegas, New Mexico.

Simpson, Audrey. (no bi-line) "Mineral Belt was Boosted in 1907." *Las Vegas Daily Optic, Rodeo Edition* (Las Vegas, New Mexico), July 31, 1952, p. 3-B, marked copy indicating item was written by Audrey Simpson, Scrapbook 4, Simpson Archives, Las Vegas, New Mexico.

Simpson, Audrey. "Mineral Hill Miner." *Las Vegas Daily Optic, Rodeo Edition* (Las Vegas, New Mexico), August 1, 1957, Las Vegas, New Mexico, p. B4.

Simpson, Audrey. "Mineral Hill Road." Poem, n.d., Scrapbook 5, Simpson Archives, Las Vegas, New Mexico.

Simpson, Audrey. "The Mineral Hill-San Geronimo Road." *Public Forum Las Vegas Daily Optic* (Las Vegas, New Mexico), September 15, 1945, p. 4, Scrapbook 4, Simpson Archives, Las Vegas, New Mexico.

Simpson, Audrey. "Miscellaneous Notes." Unpublished notes, n.d., Scrapbook 6, Simpson Archives, Las Vegas, New Mexico.

Simpson, Audrey. "Mom Saved the Bacon," Copy of original manuscript submitted to and published by *Real West,* Vol. XII, Number 67 (January, 1969), pp. 30-31, Scrapbook 4, Simpson Archives, Las Vegas, New Mexico

Simpson, Audrey. "Mom's Squeeze Play." Copy of original manuscript submitted to and published by *The Denver Post Empire Magazine,* (May 28, 1967), Scrapbook 8, Simpson Archives, Las Vegas, New Mexico.

Simpson, Audrey. (no bi-line) "Mountain Cabins Like This." Photograph and caption, *Las Vegas Daily Optic, Rodeo Edition* (Las Vegas, New Mexico), July 31, 1952, p. 3C, marked copy indicating the photo and caption were by Audrey Simpson, Simpson Archives, Las Vegas, New Mexico.

Simpson, Audrey."Mountain Daybreak." *Las Vegas Daily Optic* (Las Vegas, New Mexico), August 1, 1957, p. B8.

Simpson, Audrey."Mountain Dusk.*" Las Vegas Daily Optic* (Las Vegas, New Mexico), August 1, 1957, p. B1.

Simpson, Audrey. "Mountain Living." Unpublished notes, n.d., Scrapbook 6, Simpson Archives, Las Vegas, New Mexico.

Simpson, Audrey (no bi-line). "Mountain Winter." Photograph with caption, *Las Vegas Daily Optic, Rodeo Edition* (Las Vegas, New Mexico), July 31, 1952, p. 5C, marked copy indicating the photo and caption were by Audrey Simpson, Simpson Archives, Las Vegas, New Mexico.

Simpson, Audrey. "Mrs. Rough Rider Busy During Reunion." *Las Vegas Daily Optic, Rodeo Edition* (Las Vegas, New Mexico), June 11, 1964, p. 9.

Simpson, Audrey. "My Book." Unpublished manuscript, n.d., Scrapbook 5, Simpson Archives, Las Vegas, New Mexico.

Simpson, Audrey. "My Early Days." Unpublished manuscript, n.d., Scrapbook 5, Simpson Archives, Las Vegas, New Mexico.

Simpson, Audrey. "My First Christmas." Unpublished notes, n.d.,Scrapbook 4, Simpson Archives, Las Vegas, New Mexico.

Simpson, Audrey. "My First Days." Unpublished manuscript, n.d., Scrapbook 7, Simpson Archives, Las Vegas, New Mexico.

Simpson, Audrey."My Lifeline in the Mountains." Copy of original manuscript submitted to and published by *Impact, Albuquerque Journal Magazine*, Albuquerque, New Mexico, Volume 6, Number 47 (September,1983), Scrapbook 7, Simpson Archives, Las Vegas, New Mexico.

Simpson, Audrey."Next Door to Heaven." Copy of original manuscript submitted to and published by *New Mexico Magazine*, Vol. 24, No. 2 (February, 1946), pp. 19,39,41, Scrapbook 5, Simpson Archives, Las Vegas, New Mexico.

Simpson, Audrey. "The Night I Was Born." Unpublished manscript, n.d., Scrapbook 4, Simpson Archives, Las Vegas, New Mexico.

Simpson, Audrey. "Nobody Home." Copy of original manuscript submitted to and published by *The Denver Post*, n.d., Simpson Archives, Las Vegas, New Mexico.

Simpson, Audrey. "Note." Note written in back of book, December 28, 1958, *Wild Streets: Tales of the Famous Frontier Towns,* edited by Don Ward, Doubleday & Co., Inc., Garden City, N.Y.: 1958, Simpson Archives, Las Vegas, New Mexico.

Simpson, Audrey."Notes About the 1971 Forest Fire." Unpublished notes, n.d., Scrapbook 8, Simpson Archives, Las Vegas, New Mexico.

Simpson, Audrey. "Notes on the Carringtons," n.d., Scrapbook 4, Simpson Archives, Las Vegas, New Mexico.

Simpson, Audrey. "Notes on my Life." Unpublished manuscript, n.d., Scrapbook 4, Simpson Archives, Las Vegas, New Mexico.

Simpson, Audrey. "Obituary for Betty Hardin." Notes, n.d., Scrapbook 8, Simpson Archives, Las Vegas, New Mexico.

Simpson, Audrey. (no bi-line) "Old-Timers Hand Down Chapelle Treasure Story." *Las Vegas Daily Optic*, (Las Vegas, New Mexico), July 31, 1952, p. 8-B, marked copy indicating item was written by Audrey Simpson, Scrapbook 4, Simpson Archives, Las Vegas, New Mexico.

Simpson, Audrey. (no bi-line) "O'Malley Is Parade Marshal 45 years," *Las Vegas Daily Optic*, (Las Vegas, New Mexico), July 30, 1958, p. B7, marked copy indicating item was written by Audrey Simpson, Scrapbook 4, Simpson Archives, Las Vegas, New Mexico.

Simpson, Audrey."Only the Wind and Rain." Unpublished poem, n.d., Scrapbook 7, Simpson Archives, Las Vegas, New Mexico.

Simpson, Audrey (no bi-line). "Organ At Shearer's Pioneer Attraction." *Las Vegas Daily Optic, Rodeo Edition,* (Las Vegas, New Mexico), July 30, 1958, A1, marked copy indicating item was written by Audrey Simpson, Simpson Archives, Las Vegas, New Mexico.

Simpson, Audrey. "Prayer for Rain." Copy of original manuscript submitted to and published by "Poems of New Mexico," *New Mexico Magazine*, Vol. 29, No. 7 (June, 1951), p. 26 and in *Fiesta: An Anthology of Southwestern Poets*, Albuquerque: Albuquerque Branch of the National League of American Pen Women, 1952, p. 24, Simpson Archives, Las Vegas, New Mexico.

Simpson, Audrey. "Pride Does It." Copy of original manuscript submitted to and published by *New Verse Magazine* (May-June, 1951), p. 24, Scrapbook 8, Simpson Archives, Las Vegas, New Mexico.

Simpson, Audrey."Record Run." Copy of original manuscript submitted to and published by *The Joy Bearer* (August, 1951), Scrapbook 7, Simpson Archives, Las Vegas, New Mexico.

Simpson, Audrey. "Relative-ly Speaking." Copy of original manuscript submitted to and published by *Capper's Weekly,* February 22, Scrapbook 1, Simpson Archives, Las Vegas, New Mexico.

Simpson, Audrey."Religious Experiences." Unpublished notes, 1982, Scrapbook 6, Simpson Archives, Las Vegas, New Mexico.

Simpson, Audrey. "Remember the Years." Unpublished notes, n.d., Scrapbook 6, Simpson Archives, Las Vegas, New Mexico.

Simpson, Audrey."Remembering Chapelle." Unpublished notes, n.d., Scrapbook 4, Simpson Archives, Las Vegas, New Mexico.

Simpson, Audrey. "Riding My First Bronc." Unpublished notes, n.d.,Scrapbook 4, Simpson Archives, Las Vegas, New Mexico.

Simpson, Audrey. "Rio Grande Treasure." Copy of original manuscript submitted to and published by manuscript prepared for *Treasure Trails, Old West,* Vol. 1, No. 4 (Fall, 1973) pp. 12-13, Simpson Archives, Las Vegas, New Mexico.

Simpson, Audrey. "Rio Grande Treasure." Copy of original manuscript submitted to and published by *Treasure World*, Vol. 3, No. 3, (August-September, 1969), pp. 20-22, Simpson Archives, Las Vegas, New Mexico.

Simpson, Audrey. (no bi-line) "Road Runner is New Mexico Bird." *Las Vegas Daily Optic*, *Rodeo Edition* (Las Vegas, New Mexico), July 31, 1952, page. 7-B, marked copy indicating item was written by Audrey Simpson, Scrapbook 4, Simpson Archives, Las Vegas, New Mexico.

Simpson, Audrey. "The Roaring Flames." Unpublished poem, n.d., Scrapbook 7, Simpson Archives, Las Vegas, New Mexico.

Simpson, Audrey.(no bi-line) "Rooster Pull Is Big Event Held by Top Horseman." *Las Vegas Daily Optic*, *Rodeo Edition* (Las Vegas, New Mexico), July 31, 1952, p. 7-B, marked copy indicating item was written by Audrey Simpson, Scrapbook 4, Simpson Archives, Las Vegas, New Mexico.

Simpson, Audrey. (no bi-line) "Rooster Pull Is Sport of Riders in Area Villages." *Las Vegas Daily Optic, Rodeo Edition* (Las Vegas, New Mexico), July 30, 1958, p. A1, marked copy indicating item was written by Audrey Simpson, Simpson Archives, Las Vegas, New Mexico.

Simpson, Audrey. "Russian Thistle." Unpublished poem, n.d., Scrapbook 7, Simpson Archives, Las Vegas, New Mexico.

Simpson, Audrey. "Salute Gregorio." Unpublished manuscript, n.d., Simpson Archives, Las Vegas, New Mexico.

Simpson, Audrey (no bi-line). "Sawmills In Area Important Part of Las Vegas Economy." *Las Vegas Daily Optic* (Las Vegas, New Mexico), July 30, 1958, p. A3, marked copy indicating item was written by Audrey Simpson, Simpson Archives, Las Vegas, New Mexico.

Simpson, Audrey. "Several Camps for Young People." Letter to the Editor, *Las Vegas Daily Optic* (Las Vegas, New Mexico), n.d., Scrapbook 5, Simpson Archives, Las Vegas, New Mexico.

Simpson, Audrey. "She Was Always Ready to Go." Unpublished poem, Simpson Scrapbook 7, Simpson Archives, Las Vegas, New Mexico, 1975.

Simpson, Audrey. "Song of the Individualist." Copy of original manuscript submitted to and published by *Today in Prose & Poetry*, Vol. 1, No. 3 (January-February, 1941), Scrapbook 7, Simpson Archives, Las Vegas, New Mexico.

Simpson, Audrey. "Special Christmas." Letter to the Editor, for "Your Most Memorable Christmas" section, *Albuquerque Journal,* November, 1987, Scrapbook 7, Simpson Archives, Las Vegas, New Mexico.

Simpson, Audrey. "Stamping Out Junk Mail." Copy of original manuscript submitted to and published by *Albuquerque Journal Magazine*, Vol. 5, No. 44, (August 17, 1982), pp. 12-13, Simpson Archives, Las Vegas, New Mexico.

Simpson, Audrey (no bi-line). "Sugar Cane Once Grown in Las Vegas Section." *Las Vegas Daily Optic* (July 31, 1952), p. 5-A, marked copy indicating item was written by Audrey Simpson, Scrapbook 8, Simpson Archives, Las Vegas, New Mexico.

Simpson, Audrey. "Sunshine is an Elf." Copy of original manuscript submitted to and published by *The Joy Bearer*, Vol. 12, No. 10 (October, 1949), Scrapbook 7, Simpson Archives, Las Vegas, New Mexico.

Simpson, Audrey. (no bi-line) "Tecolote One of Oldest in State." *Las Vegas Daily Optic, Rodeo Edition* (Las Vegas, New Mexico), July 31, 1952, p. 5-B, marked copy indicating item was written by Audrey Simpson, Scrapbook 4, Simpson Archives, Las Vegas, New Mexico.

Simpson, Audrey."Ten Dollar House." Copy of original manuscript submitted to and published by *New Mexico Magazine* (February, 1943), pp. 11-12, 24, Scrapbook 5, Simpson Archives, Las Vegas, New Mexico.

Simpson, Audrey. "These Things Happened." Unpublished manuscript, n.d., Scrapbook 5, Simpson Archives, Las Vegas, New Mexico.

Simpson, Audrey. (no bi-line.) "They're All Loaded, Remember." *Las Vegas Daily Optic, Rodeo* Edition (Las Vegas, New Mexico), Thursday, July 31, 1952, p. 1-B, marked copy indicating item was written by Audrey Simpson, Scrapbook 4, Simpson Archives, Las Vegas, New Mexico.

Simpson, Audrey. "Today I Looked." Unpublished poem, n.d., Scrapbook 7, Simpson Archives, Las Vegas, New Mexico.

Simpson, Audrey. (no bi-line) "Torreón Guarded Kearney's Gap In Days Of Long Ago." *Las Vegas Daily Optic, Rodeo Edition* (Wednesday, July 30, 1958), p. C4, marked copy indicating item was written by Audrey Simpson, Simpson Archives, Las Vegas, New Mexico.

Simpson, Audrey. "Trail History is Reflected; Horse, Mule Caravans." *Las Vegas Daily Optic, Rodeo Edition*, (Las Vegas, New Mexico), July 31, 1952, p. 6-B.

Simpson, Audrey. "Twenty Miles of Mountains." Unpublished poem, n.d., Scrapbook 7, Simpson Archives, Las Vegas, New Mexico.

Simpson, Audrey. (no bi-line) "Two Caves In Area Offer Exploration." *Las Vegas Daily Optic, Rodeo Edition* (Las Vegas, New Mexico), Thursday, August 1, 1957, p. 13B, marked copy indicating item was written by Audrey Simpson, Simpson Archives, Las Vegas, New Mexico.

Simpson, Audrey. "The Two-Gun Years." Unpublished poem, December, 1944, Scrapbook 3, Simpson Archives, Las Vegas, New Mexico.

Simpson, Audrey. "The Urge Behind the Ego." Unpublished manuscript, n.d., Simpson Archives, Las Vegas, New Mexico.

Simpson, Audrey. "Various Notes." Unpublished notes, n.d., Scrapbook 7, Simpson Archives, Las Vegas, New Mexico.

Simpson, Audrey. (no bi-line) "Vegas, Then and Now; Time, People Changed." *Las Vegas Daily Optic* (Las Vegas, New Mexico), Thursday, July 31, 1952, p. 8-A, marked copy indicating item was written by Audrey Simpson, Simpson Archives, Las Vegas, New Mexico.

Simpson, Audrey. (no bi-line) "Visit Of Teddy Roosevelt Is Recalled By Vegas Pioneer." *Las Vegas Daily Optic, Rodeo Edition* (Las Vegas, New Mexico), Thursday, August 1, 1957, p. 8, marked copy indicating item was written by Audrey Simpson, Simpson Archives, Las Vegas, New Mexico.

Simpson, Audrey."We Hear the Crack of Hunter's Gun." Unpublished poem, n.d., Scrapbook 7, Simpson Archives, Las Vegas, New Mexico.

Simpson, Audrey. "We Housed Ourselves For $15.50." Copy of original manuscript submitted to and published by *Profitable Hobbies*, February, 1949, Scrapbook 5, Simpson Archives, Las Vegas, New Mexico.

Simpson, Audrey. "Weather Man's Blues." *Las Vegas Daily Optic, Rodeo Edition* (Las Vegas, New Mexico), July 31, 1952, p. 2B , Scrapbook 2, Simpson Archives, Las Vegas, New Mexico.

Simpson, Audrey. "Where Do Newspaper Women Go?" Unpublished manuscript, n.d., Scrapbook 6, Simpson Archives, Las Vegas, New Mexico.

Simpson, Audrey. (no bi-line), "Wild Horse Herds One Roamed Open Spots in Region." *Las Vegas Daily Optic, Rodeo Edition* (Las Vegas, New Mexico), Thursday, July 31 1952, p. 5-A, marked copy indicating item was written by Audrey Simpson, Simpson Archives, Las Vegas New Mexico.

Simpson, Audrey. "Winter Playground." Copy of original manuscript submitted to and published by *New Mexico Magazine*, Vol. 28, No. 1(January, 1950), pp. 23,44-45, Scrapbook 8, Simpson Archives, Las Vegas, New Mexico.

Simpson, Audrey. "Young Resent." Unpublished letter, n.d., in Scrapbook 7, Simpson Archives, Las Vegas, New Mexico.

Simpson, Dorothy. "How Jesus Loves." Copy of original manuscript submitted to and published by "Counsellor's Corner," *My Counsellor,* Chicago, 1951.

Simpson, Crystal. Interview by Dorothy Simpson, July, 2006, Las Vegas, New Mexico.

Simpson, Holly A. "Mother's Day Card" verse, 1966, Scrapbook 5, Simpson Archives, Las Vegas, New Mexico.

Simpson, Shirley. "The Perfect Squelch." Copy of original manuscript submitted to and published by *The Saturday Evening Post,* Vol. 223, No. 52 (June 23, 1951), p. 109.

Simpson, Shirley. "Some People You Meet." Copy of original manuscript submitted to and published by *The Perfect Squelch, A Saturday Evening Post Feature Book*, Edited by Ashley Halsey, Jr., N.Y.: A. S. Barnes and Company, 1952, Scrapbook 8, Simpson Archives, Las Vegas, New Mexico.

"Sisters Celebrate 70th." *Vegas Victorian Gazette* (Las Vegas, New Mexico), Volume III, Issue 8, October, 1989, p. 5.

State Elementary Certificate, State of New Mexico: September 1, 1922, Scrapbook 2, Simpson Archives, Las Vegas, New Mexico.

State Elementary Certification, State of New Mexico: September 1, 1929 and expiring September 1, 1932, Scrapbook 2, Simpson Archives, Las Vegas, New Mexico.

Sweeney, Michael S. *Secrets of Victory: The Office of Censorship and the American Press and Radio in World War II*. Chapel Hill, North Carolina: University of North Carolina Press, 2001.

"Toy Drive Planned by Local Jaycees." Newspaper clipping from *Las Vegas Daily Optic* (Las Vegas, New Mexico), n.d., Scrapbook 8, Simpson Archives.

"Vegas Juvenile Story Chosen in PW Contest." *Las Vegas Daily Optic* (Las Vegas, New Mexico), April 27, 1952, p. 2.

Vivian, Walter T. "Along the Banks of the Gallinas." *Las Vegas Daily Optic*, (Las Vegas, New Mexico), August 10, 1957, p. 1.

Waddell, Mabel. "My Pupils Dear." *Pine Top School Souvenir*, n. p., 1911, Scrapbook 1, Simpson Archives, Las Vegas, New Mexico, p. 7.

Whiting, Jean. "Short On Birthdays Maybe, But They'll Only Be 20 When Their Friends Are 80." *Las Vegas Daily Optic* (Las Vegas, New Mexico), n.p., newspaper clipping marked February 29, 1960, Scrapbook 5, Simpson Archives, Las Vegas, New Mexico.

Wickman, Gordon. Interview by Dorothy Simpson Beimer. Las Vegas, New Mexico, May, 1988.

Wickman, Millicent. Interview by Dorothy Simpson Beimer. Las Vegas, New Mexico, April, 1976.

Wickman, Millicent. Interview by Dorothy Simpson Croxton about Audrey Simpson's Article, "Gateway to Conquest," *New Mexico Magazine*, Vol. 46, No.10 (October, 1968) pp. 18–19.

www.ingramcontent.com/pod-product-compliance
Lightning Source LLC
Chambersburg PA
CBHW020628230426
43665CB00008B/85